THE PELICAN HISTORY OF ART

EDITED BY NIKOLAUS PEVSNER

Z4

ART AND ARCHITECTURE IN FRANCE 1500 TO 1700
ANTHONY BLUNT

ANTHONY BLUNT

ART AND ARCHITECTURE
IN FRANCE
1500 TO 1700

PUBLISHED BY PENGUIN BOOKS

Penguin Books Ltd, Harmondsworth, Middlesex
Penguin Books Inc., Baltimore, Maryland, U.S.A.
Penguin Books Pty Ltd, Mitcham, Victoria, Australia
Penguin Books (Canada) Ltd, Toronto, Canada
Penguin Books (S.A.) Pty Ltd, Cape Town, South Africa

★

Text printed by Richard Clay & Company Ltd, Bungay, Suffolk
Plates printed by Hunt, Barnard & Company Ltd, Aylesbury
Made and printed in Great Britain

★

CONTENTS

Chapter 1

From the Invasion of Italy to the Battle of Pavia
1494–1525

Chapter 2

The Middle Years of Francis I
1525–1540

v

CONTENTS

Chapter 3

The Classical Period of the Sixteenth Century
1540–1565

Chapter 4

The Wars of Religion
1560–1598

Chapter 5

Henry IV and the Regency of Marie de' Medici
1598–1630

CONTENTS

vii

CONTENTS

The Plates

LIST OF FIGURES

LIST OF PLATES

65 Germain Pilon: Tomb of Valentine Balbiani. Before 1583. Louvre, Paris

66 Germain Pilon: The Virgin. c. 1580–5. Height 70 ins. Louvre, Paris

67 Germain Pilon: Head of Cardinal Birague. After 1583. Louvre, Paris

68 Germain Pilon: The Deposition. c. 1580–5. $18\frac{7}{8} \times 31\frac{7}{8}$ ins. Louvre, Paris

69 (A) Jean Cousin the Younger: The Last Judgement. $57\frac{1}{2} \times 55\frac{1}{8}$ ins. Louvre, Paris
   (B) François Quesnel: Mary Ann Waltham. 1572. Earl Spencer, Althorp, Northamptonshire

70 (A) Antoine Caron: Augustus and the Sibyl. $50 \times 66\frac{7}{8}$ ins. Louvre, Paris
   (B) Anonymous artist: Woman choosing between Youth and Age. Late 16th century. Earl of Elgin, Broomhall, Fife

71 (A) Place des Vosges (Place Royale). Begun 1605. Paris
   (B) Rémy Collin: Stables of the Château of Fontainebleau. 1609

72 (A) Place des Vosges (Place Royale). (From an engraving.) Begun 1605. Paris
   (B) Claude Chastillon and Jacques Alleaume: Place de France, Paris. 1610. Engraving by Chastillon

73 Chapel of the Château of Fontainebleau. c. 1615–25

74 (A) Salomon de Brosse: The Luxembourg Palace. Begun 1615. Paris
   (B) Jean du Cerceau: Hôtel de Sully. 1624–9. Paris

75 Pierre Le Muet: Hôtel Duret de Chevry. 1635. Now part of the Bibliothèque Nationale, Paris

76 (A) Pierre Le Muet: Hôtel d'Astry. c. 1645. Paris
   (B) Hôtel de Châlons-Luxembourg. 1623 (?). Paris

77 Château of Brissac, Maine-et-Loire. 1606

78 (A) Château of Rosny, Seine-et-Oise. c. 1600
   (B) Château of Grosbois, Seine-et-Marne. c. 1600

79 (A) Salomon de Brosse: Château of Blérancourt. 1614. Engraving by Silvestre
   (B) Salomon de Brosse: Palais de Justice. 1618. Rennes

80 (A) Derand: St Paul-St Louis. 1634. Paris
   (B) Salomon de Brosse: St Gervais. 1616. Paris

81 (A) Ambroise Dubois: Sacrifice at the tomb of Neoptolemus. Fontainebleau
   (B) Toussaint Dubreuil: A Sacrifice. 75×55 ins. Louvre, Paris

82 Jacques Bellange: The Annunciation. Badische Kunsthalle, Karlsruhe

83 (A) Jacques Bellange: The Annunciation. Etching. British Museum
   (B) Jacques Bellange: The Hurdy-Gurdy Player. Etching. Royal Library, Windsor

84 Jacques Bellange: The Three Marys. Etching. British Museum

85 (A) Callot: The Agony in the Garden. 1625. Wash drawing. Chatsworth, Derbyshire
   (B) Callot: Landscape. Pen drawing. Chatsworth, Derbyshire
   (C) Callot: Scene from the Grandes Misères de la Guerre. 1633. Etching. British Museum

86 Callot: Florentine Fête. 1619. Etching. British Museum

87 (A) Jacques Callot: The two Pantaloons. 1616. Etching. British Museum
   (B) Claude Deruet: Fire. $44\frac{1}{2} \times 102\frac{1}{4}$ ins. Museum, Orleans

88 Claude Vignon: The death of a Hermit. c. 1620. $65 \times 51\frac{1}{2}$ ins. Louvre, Paris

89 Frans Pourbus the Younger: The Duc de Chevreuse. 1612. Earl Spencer, Althorp, Northamptonshire

90 Lemercier: The Church of the Sorbonne. Begun 1635. Paris

91 François Mansart and Lemercier: The Val-de-Grâce. Begun 1645. Paris

92 (A) Lemercier: Château of Richelieu. Begun 1631. Engraving by Marot
   (B) Lemercier: Richelieu, Indre-et-Loire. Air view. Begun 1631

93 (A) and (B) François Mansart: Château of Berny, Seine. Begun before 1624
   (C) François Mansart: Hôtel de la Vrillière, Paris. Begun 1635. Engraving by Marot

94 François Mansart: Château of Balleroy, Calvados. c. 1626

95 François Mansart: Château of Blois. Orleans Wing. 1635–8. (Copyright Country Life)

96 (A) François Mansart: Château of Blois. Staircase (from a drawing by Sir Reginald Blomfield). 1635–8
   (B) François Mansart: The Visitation. Dome. Begun 1632. Paris

97 (A) François Mansart: Hôtel d'Aumont, Paris. Staircase. 1665
   (B) François Mansart: Château of Maisons, Seine-et-Oise. Balustrade of staircase. 1642–8

98 François Mansart: Château of Maisons. Vestibule. 1642–6

99 François Mansart: Château of Maisons. Frontispiece. 1642–6

PREFACE

THIS book is designed to cover French art during the sixteenth and seventeenth centuries. The main emphasis has been laid on the major arts, and certain subjects, particularly the applied arts, have of necessity been dealt with in a rather summary manner, or only where they are directly relevant to developments in other fields. But even within the major arts themselves the space allotted to different parts has varied according to the particular problems presented. So, for instance, the sixteenth century has been discussed in greater detail than, say, the art of Versailles, because, whereas in the case of the latter the main outlines are already well known, the earlier period still presents so many difficulties and obscurities that a summary would be impossible, and the evidence has to be set out in detail. In particular, the origins of French art in Italy and elsewhere have usually been studied in such general terms that it seemed essential to establish more precise points of contact and to define the exact sources on which French painters, sculptors, and architects drew when they visited Italy and other countries. Only in this way can the development of French art be seen as part of the general European tradition, and its peculiar qualities isolated.

I am keenly aware of the problems left unsolved in this book, but many of them, particularly those connected with art in the provinces, cannot be solved till much more work has been done on archives and on the smaller museums of France. It is therefore inevitable that many points should at present be put forward as tentative suggestions and should be subject to correction.

In the preparation of this volume I have received help of varied kinds from many different people both in this country and in France. It would be impossible to acknowledge every instance individually, but certain special debts must be mentioned. First I must thank those private owners and directors of museums who have generously allowed me to reproduce works in their possession. To my colleague, Professor Johannes Wilde, I owe the deepest gratitude for his constant help and inspiration during the whole period when I was working on the book, and for his kindly and constructive comments on it when it was in manuscript. Professor E. K. Waterhouse has over a long period of years continually supplied me with information about French painting from his unrivalled store of erudition, and, in addition, he and Dr Margaret Whinney read the proofs and made many useful suggestions and corrections. Mrs Peter Coope helped me in the troublesome pursuit of photographs in various parts of France. The assistance which I have received from many members of the staff of the Courtauld Institute, particularly from members of the Photographic Department, has been too constant to admit of acknowledgement in detail. The heaviest load, however, has fallen on Miss Elsa Scheerer, who has, with unfailing patience and kindness, prepared the final manuscript, read proofs, prepared the index, and carried out all those most difficult and unrewarding tasks which are involved in seeing a book such as this through the press.

CHAPTER I

FROM THE INVASION OF ITALY TO THE BATTLE OF PAVIA
1494–1525

HISTORICAL BACKGROUND

FROM the point of view of French art the most important historical events of the years 1494–1525 were the campaigns of Charles VIII (reigned 1483–98), Louis XII (1498–1515), and Francis I (1515–47) in Italy, which produced as a direct result a reverse invasion of France by Italian taste.

From a strictly historical point of view, however, other developments of greater significance were taking place; for these years mark an important stage in the evolution of France as a modern state. During the following period the French monarchy which had been no more than the nominal head of a feudal agglomeration of territories was to become the effective controller of a relatively centralized nation. Louis XI had done much to break down the strength of the feudal nobility and to concentrate the effective power of government in his own hands, and Louis XII and Francis I were to continue the process. At the same time they strove to break the spirit of the États and the Parlements, which were another source of resistance to complete centralization. Here their task was harder, because these bodies, representing the new aristocracy of the towns, had a solid basis of power in their wealth, and could always resist the collection of taxes. In the end, however, by an ingenious combination of compromise and economy under Louis XII and a skilful development by Francis I of the authority of the provincial governors appointed by the Crown, the Parlements found themselves unable seriously to resist the wishes of the central power and, except in the matter of taxation, usually in agreement with its policy. Finally the Concordat of 1515 had provided the King with an almost endless supply of rewards for his servants in the form of bishoprics and abbeys which not only depended on his personal gift but had the added advantage of not being hereditary, thus binding each recipient to him afresh. In this way Francis I, having reduced the independence of the feudal nobles and centralized a great part of the power and wealth of the kingdom in his own hands, had gone far towards the construction of that personal absolutism which was to be the characteristic of the French constitution for the next two hundred years.

In foreign policy a parallel change had taken place. At the beginning of the period with which we are here concerned, Charles VIII invaded Italy primarily with the intention of satisfying dynastic claims on the kingdom of Naples. But by the time of the disaster of Pavia, with which the period ends, the Italian campaigns had taken on an

I

entirely different character. They had developed into a struggle between the growing power of France, relatively small but united and organized on modern principles, and the vast agglomeration of the Habsburg territories, Spain, and the Empire, still broken up by feudal separatism and weakened by out-of-date administration.

As the Crown became the centre of French administration, the Court became the focal point of culture in the kingdom. Under Louis XII it was possible for a great minister like Cardinal Amboise to be the leader of taste, far in advance of the King. But in the following reign everything centred on the group round the King and his sister, Margaret of Navarre, and the most important works in the arts and in literature were executed under their direct patronage.

From the first years of his reign Francis I made it plain that he intended to form a court which could rival those of Italy in culture and would be a fair setting for a great king. For this reason he collected round him men of letters, thinkers, humanists, painters, and builders, each of whom had a part to play in building up the setting against which the King wished to be seen and the reputation of a great patron which he aimed at leaving to posterity. It was as a result of this policy that there arose the new wing of the château of Blois and the château of Chambord, the first of the royal buildings; and it was as part of the same plan that Francis tried to lure to France the greatest artists of Italy, failing in the case of Michelangelo but succeeding in that of Leonardo.

The great noble families were also active as patrons, particularly in architecture, but they were equalled in importance by the newly enriched *bourgeois* servants of the Crown. Whereas under Louis XI there had been but one Jacques Cœur, there was now a host of such patrons – Semblançay, Bohier, Briçonnet, to mention a few – who built town and country houses and encouraged all the arts.

Centralization was, however, far from complete. The Court was still mobile, and Paris had not yet attained its position as the political and cultural centre of the country. Before 1525 the region of the Loire valley was in advance of the capital in architecture and the allied arts. The Court spent much time there on account of the hunting; the aristocracy remodelled its castles in the district; the valley was rich in agriculture; and towns like Tours and Orleans were rapidly developing as centres of trade.

The direction taken by artistic life under Louis XII and Francis I was, as has already been said, fixed by the influence of Italian culture. Before the invasion of Charles VIII French writers and artists had, of course, already been conscious of what was happening on the other side of the Alps, and in the field of pure classical learning it can even be said that the Italian campaigns did not exercise a very serious influence, since humanist studies were well established in Paris before 1494. But in most other fields Italian taste began to flood into the country as Frenchmen came back from Naples or Milan. However, as has often been pointed out, their understanding of the Italian Renaissance was in many ways superficial. What attracted them above all was the luxurious manner of living displayed at the Italian courts. Italian gardens, Italian dress, Italian manners were for them the real discoveries. Platonic philosophy, Florentine painting, monumental architecture do not seem to have impressed them deeply; nor do they seem to have shown any great interest in the works of antiquity, which they must have seen in Italy.[1]

The character of the first invasion of Italian taste can be clearly seen in French literature of the early years of the reign of Francis I. The most successful poet of the time was Lemaire de Belges, who still belongs to the late medieval school of tortuous poetry practised by the Grands Rhétoriqueurs. If he occasionally turns to Petrarch for an idea, the influence of the great Italian poet never penetrated below the surface of his art. Even Clément Marot in his early works still writes in the same manner. He was better versed in Italian literature than Lemaire, but he only absorbed such elements as would not conflict with his playful and ingenious conception of poetry.

Parallel with this court-poetry and independent of it a tradition of learned humanism was being built up. The pioneer work of men like Robert Gaguin had prepared the way for the colossal learning of Guillaume Budé, but his scholarship was so academic that it never came into contact with the real literary movements of the time. Even with the more likable Lefèvre d'Étaples, whose humanist studies were for a moment flavoured with Platonism, the effect of his work was more apparent in the field of religion than of literature. It was, however, men like Budé and Lefèvre who founded in France those Greek studies which were to have such revolutionary effects in the next generation, when classical scholarship was to be fused with a great literary movement.

The period up to 1525 was one of transition. Francis I himself reflects both the past and the future. In one way he was the last product of chivalry; in another the first modern King of France. In culture Italy was the rage, but was understood only as a mode of manners or a source of conceits imposed on medieval traditions. We shall see that in the visual arts Italian forms were at first used in an equally superficial way.

ARCHITECTURE

The Introduction of Renaissance Motives from Northern Italy: The first Châteaux of Francis I

The earliest traces of Italian Renaissance influence on France appear several decades before the invasion of 1494, but they are spasmodic. The painter Jean Fouquet had visited Rome in the middle of the fifteenth century, and the miniatures of the Hours of Étienne Chevalier are full of fine and well-understood Italian decorative detail.[2] A little later René of Anjou had attracted many Italian craftsmen to his Court in Provence, and one of them, Francesco Laurana, had built what was probably the earliest purely Italian work on French soil, the chapel of St Lazare in the church of La Major at Marseilles (1475–81) (Plate 2A).[3] But this model was too far away from the main centres of artistic activity in France to bear any fruit.

More important was the arrival in France of Italian engravings and illustrated books towards the end of the fifteenth century. Through them French engravers and publishers became acquainted with Italian decoration and in due course came to imitate it. In the Terence printed in Lyons in 1493 we see a crude attempt to render the *putti*, the fruit-swags, and the shell-niches of the Quattrocento. But in the *Roman Hours* published in Paris in 1502 the detail is much finer and better understood, though still mixed with

Gothic elements. By the time of the Paris Origen of 1512 the transformation is complete, at any rate as far as the decorative parts of the wood-cuts are concerned.[4]

If the style of the Origen differs so much from that of the Terence, the change is no doubt due to the campaigns in Italy and the arrival in France of Italian craftsmen. Even Charles VIII, after the short and disastrous campaigns of 1494, brought back with him from Italy a band of artists who introduced the ideas and methods of their country to France. On the whole it was the architects among these foreigners who exerted the least permanent influence on France. The two most important – Fra Giocondo, who stayed from 1495 to 1505, and Giuliano da Sangallo, who came on a short visit in 1495 with Cardinal Giuliano della Rovere – left no traceable works. The third – Domenico da Cortona, a man of much more slender talent – only established himself as a recognized architect about 1519, that is to say twenty-four years after his arrival and at a time when the manner of the Italian Renaissance was well known through other channels. The sculptors were of greater importance, and some, such as Guido Mazzoni, exercised an influence on architectural decoration; but they will be considered in a later section.[5]

The effect of the campaigns of Louis XII and Francis I (1500–25) was naturally more profound. As a result of them Milan was a French dependency almost continuously for twenty-five years and Genoa for a shorter period. French soldiers and statesmen were constantly visiting these cities, sometimes accompanied by French artists. They commissioned works from local craftsmen, whom they sometimes brought back with them on their return to France so that they might continue to decorate their châteaux, an abbey in which they were interested, or the tomb which they were building for themselves.

Very soon French artists began to learn from the Italian visitors, and trained themselves to copy the new style. They rapidly became competent at this imitation, and generally speaking it is impossible to disentangle the exact shares of Italian and French craftsmen in the work before 1525. The documents are rarely explicit, and though they often mention a number of names, Italian and French, they hardly ever define the exact function of any one craftsman. Moreover, not only did the French imitate the Italians, but the latter also adapted themselves in certain respects to the demands of local traditions and materials, so that in the end there is no firm basis for distinguishing the shares of the two groups, and those who claim to do so are often actuated more by a spirit of national pride than by one of genuine criticism.

The fact that French contacts with Italy were with the northern provinces, above all with Milan, was perhaps lucky, because in Milan French patrons found the kind of architecture to appeal to them. The seigneur of the time of Louis XII and Francis I had been brought up surrounded by Flamboyant Gothic, a style notable for the ingenuity of its forms and the elaboration of its decoration. With this training they would hardly have taken to the cold intellectualism of Florentine Quattrocentro architecture, which in their eyes would have been merely bleak. Their taste is clearly shown by the few comments which Philippe de Commynes makes on the buildings which he saw. In Venice he was deeply impressed by all the palaces because of the richness of their materials on the outside and of their decoration within. In the Certosa of Pavia he becomes ecstatic and calls it 'the finest church I ever saw, and all of fine marble'. Now, on Florentine principles both the fifteenth-century palaces of Venice and the Certosa would have been almost barbarous in their profusion of ornament and marbles and in the survival of Gothic elements; but to Commynes and to his French companions these were precisely the objectives sought.

It was actually more from the Certosa than from any other building that French decoration of the early sixteenth century derived. Lying within easy reach of Milan, it provided an accessible model, and the façade of the church, of which the lower part was built between 1490 and 1498, is perhaps the most remarkable piece of fantasy in north Italian architecture of this period. With its profusion of coloured marbles, its surface fretted into reliefs, decorative or representational, and its every pilaster carved into a candelabrum, it presented a whole nearer in its lavishness to the spirit of Late Gothic than to that of Brunelleschi. In the cloisters the French would have found the same type of decoration executed in terra-cotta, a technique which was also to be imported to France. The style had, moreover, already been married with Gothic in Milan, and in buildings such as Filarete's Ospedale Maggiore the French could see pointed arches accompanied by classical ornament, precisely the combination which they were themselves to produce in their own châteaux.

The French seem actually to have turned their backs, as it were, on the examples of purer Renaissance style, even when these were presented to them. For in Milan itself the tradition of Florentine Quattrocento architecture was to be seen in Michelozzo's Portinari Chapel in the church of S. Eustorgio, a direct descendant of Brunelleschi's Pazzi Chapel; and, further, between 1482 and 1499 Bramante was building in Milan two works which laid the foundation of sixteenth-century classicism: the churches of S. Maria presso S. Satiro and S. Maria delle Grazie. But, for all the French cared, Bramante might almost not have existed.

Generally speaking, it was the decoration and not the forms of Milanese architecture that the French took home with them. And at first they applied this decoration almost without change to the forms traditional in their own country. This produced that strangely hybrid quality which characterizes the architecture of the period up to 1525. An Italianate door will be applied to the round tower of a château still wholly medieval in feeling; a low relief candelabrum will decorate the jamb of a Gothic door; the space between the ribs of Flamboyant vaulting will be covered with classical carving. On Italian standards the result is of course barbarous; and yet the style of these early years of Francis I has its own quality. The Gothic structural tradition was still vigorous enough to carry off the union with Milanese ornament.

During the greater part of the sixteenth century the Kings of France were the most important patrons of architecture; but they were far from being the only ones, and they were not always ahead of their subjects. The earliest example of architectural decoration in the Italian taste is probably the decoration of the pilasters of the Easter Sepulchre in the abbey church at Solesmes (1496),[6] and the form in which it appears is typical. The Entombment group itself is a piece of Late Gothic naturalistic sculpture, and its architectural setting is of Flamboyant design except for the two side pilasters, which are decorated with rich Italianate candelabra, imitated from the type to be found in the

Certosa. The sculptor of these pilasters was very probably one of the Italians brought back by Charles VIII, who is believed to have contributed to the payment for the work at Solesmes.[7]

No doubt Charles VIII's work at the château of Amboise was more substantial and important; but hardly anything of it survives.[8] It seems to have consisted of individual pieces of decoration and of separate works brought from Italy, and not to have included any general attempt to Italianize the château as a whole. Louis XII appears to have been even less advanced than his predecessor in the matter of architecture, and the wing which he added to Blois (c. 1498–1504) shows hardly a trace of Italian influence.[9] The case was, however, quite different with his minister, Cardinal Georges d'Amboise, who acquired a passion for all things Italian and made a real innovation by his introduction of Italian decoration on a large scale in his château of Gaillon (begun in 1501), which became a centre whence the style radiated all over Normandy. Moreover, one of his nephews, who was Bishop of Albi, commissioned the decoration of the vault of the cathedral by Italian painters in 1511;[10] another, Artus Gouffier (d. 1519), built the earliest wing of the great house of Oiron with fine Italian decorative detail;[11] and a third, Guillaume Bonnivet, began the château of the same name (between 1513 and 1516) completely in the new manner.[12]

Other less distinguished families also played their part in the diffusion of Italianism in France. A typical example is the Bohier family. One brother, Thomas, a rich financier, was the builder in 1515 of the earlier parts of Chenonceau. He was related through his wife, Catherine Briçonnet, to Duprat, the builder of Nantouillet, and Gilles Berthelot, who constructed Azay-le-Rideau. The other brother, Antoine Bohier, had visited Italy in 1507, brought back Italian sculptures, and later employed Italian craftsmen on the redecoration of the church at Fécamp, of which he was abbot.

Fécamp is the most important ensemble of ecclesiastical decoration carried out in the first decade of the sixteenth century. Antoine Bohier's first action was to commission from Girolamo Viscardi, whom he no doubt met on his visit to Genoa in 1507, the tabernacle, the sarcophagus, and the reliefs which are still to be seen above the high altar of the church. These, though strictly speaking works of sculpture, must have acted as useful models for local architects interested in the new style of decoration. Secondly he caused stone screens to be made to enclose all the chapels round the choir of the church (Plate 5). We do not know the exact date at which they were undertaken, but it must in any case have been well before the abbot's death in 1519. In their general conception the screens follow a Late Gothic type to be found, for instance, not far away at Eu, but the decoration is purely Italian.[13] It is generally believed that these screens were carved by Italian craftsmen working in Normandy, and this is highly probable. They must have been executed on the spot, but the detail is too accurate for a Frenchman at this date. The same sculptors no doubt also executed the door to the sacristy, but here the French influence is stronger, for though the pilasters are Italianate, the form of the arch is Late Gothic.

Gothic and Italian elements can be seen more sharply juxtaposed in the tomb of Raoul de Lannoy and his wife in the church of Folleville (Plate 1).[14] The tomb itself with the recumbent figures and the inscription supported by *putti* was not originally designed to stand in a niche, but was intended to be placed with one side along the wall of the chapel. It is of pure north Italian design, and is signed by Antonio della Porta, called Tamagnino, and his nephew Pace Gaggini, who worked on the Certosa of Pavia and later set up a studio in Genoa. Lannoy was governor of that town during the years 1507-8, and it was no doubt then that he ordered the tomb. At his death in 1513, however, it had not been set up, and it was his widow and his son who built the chapel and gave the tomb its present setting, probably before 1524.

The contrast between tomb and setting is remarkable. The former is purely classical; the latter consists of two rich Flamboyant ogee arches, above which the wall is carved in low relief with a pattern Italian in style, but entirely different from the work of the two Genoese sculptors. It was probably executed by a Frenchman trained in the workshop of Gaillon or Fécamp, the latter being perhaps the more likely origin, since Lannoy was a friend of Antoine Bohier and no doubt in contact with him in Genoa and when both men were back in France. In this monument all three components of the art of Louis XII can be seen: pure Italian classicism, Flamboyant Gothic, and a local imitation of motives imported from south of the Alps.

In contrast to this composite work there are examples of wholly Italian tombs, such as that of Bishop Thomas James in the cathedral of Dol (*c.* 1507)[15] by Antonio Giusti and that of Cardinal Briçonnet (d. 1514), father-in-law of Thomas Bohier, in Narbonne Cathedral, the author of which is not known, but was probably Italian.

Of later examples still mixed in style the most remarkable is to be found in the church of St Pierre at Caen, of which the east end was built by Hector Sohier between 1528 and 1545 (Plate 4A). Structurally it is a Late Gothic building, and internally the vaulting goes through every convolution known to Flamboyant builders, particularly in the lady-chapel, which rises to double the height of the ambulatory (Plate 4B). But from the ribs and bosses hang, as it were, stalactites of pierced Italianate decoration. On the outside the effect is more sober. The form of the chapels is still Gothic, and the windows, though round-headed, still have Gothic tracery. The pierced balustrade, however, is more fanciful, and the artist has given free rein to his imagination in the candelabra which replace the finials. The two elements, French medieval and north Italian Quattrocento, here stand clearly distinguishable, and yet the result is not discordant.[16]

In secular architecture the vital steps towards Italianism can be seen taking place at Gaillon. Cardinal Amboise began the rebuilding of the château in 1501, and it was nearly completed at the time of his death in 1510. The first wings, constructed between 1501 and 1508, were still in the Flamboyant style, without any trace of the new manner, but in the latter year foreign workmen began to arrive and a change of style becomes apparent. Among the first artists was a Genoese sculptor referred to as Bertrand de Meynal. In 1508 he brought to Gaillon the great fountain sent from Genoa and commissioned from Pace Gaggini and Antonio della Porta in 1506 (Plate 2B).[17] In the same year another Italian, called in the accounts Jérôme Pacherot (perhaps Girolamo Pacchiarotti),[18] carved the frame for Colombe's St George (Plate 16) which formed the altarpiece of the chapel, in which Andrea Solario was decorating the walls with frescoes, including portraits of the Cardinal and his family.[19] As at Fécamp, this first phase, the importation of Italian works, was the prelude to setting Italian sculptors to work on the building itself, and in those parts of the château erected from 1508 onwards Italian decoration can be seen. The most important is the entrance gate (Plate 3), the decoration of which probably dates from 1508. In structure this is still the fortified entrance to a medieval château, but the decorative elements are Italian, with Lombard pilasters, grotesque friezes, and shell-heads to the windows. But the disposition of this ornament is in accordance with Gothic methods. Notice, for instance, how the windows on the three floors are linked together by the flanking pilasters to form a vertical panel such as is found on a Flamboyant château like Josselin. The windows themselves are still mullioned; for it was not till many years later that the French abandoned this practice. The interior of Gaillon seems to have been decorated in the same style, as we can judge from the chapel stalls, now at St Denis, which are covered with fine low relief grotesques;[20] and the château was surrounded by gardens made probably by the Italian designers who worked at Amboise and Blois.[21]

Before discussing the first great royal building schemes of Francis I, Blois and Chambord, mention must be made of three smaller châteaux built for private patrons, independent of the royal models, and in one case at least begun before them. These are the châteaux of Bury (Plate 8A; 1511–24), Chenonceau (Plate 10; begun 1515), and Azay-le-Rideau (Plate 6; 1518–27), all three built for rich *bourgeois*. They have one feature in common, namely a new regularity in plan. Gaillon had been built on the site of an earlier castle, and the Cardinal had largely accepted the irregularities of the older foundations. But the three châteaux under consideration are all planned on a strictly rectangular system. The part of Chenonceau built at this period is the simplest, and consists of a square block with a turret at each corner and a corridor through the middle (Figure 8), a plan which repeats fifteenth-century models such as Martainville. An Italian feature is the straight staircase, doubling back on itself, which replaces the usual French spiral. Azay is more unusual in its L-shaped plan, but it presents symmetrical façades in almost every view. Bury, built for Florimond Robertet, is altogether more revolutionary, and indeed sets the type for French château design for more than a century. The buildings are grouped round a court, one end of which is occupied by the *corps-de-logis* containing the principal rooms, and rising in the middle to a higher pavilion. Along the two sides stretch wings, one consisting of lesser rooms and the other of a long gallery. The fourth side is filled by a lower range of buildings with an arcaded cloister, in the middle of which opens the main entrance to the château. In one respect Bury is more medieval than Chenonceau and Azay, for it retains its round towers at the corners, whereas in the two smaller châteaux these are reduced to turrets, which are more easily absorbed into the Renaissance character of the building.

The three châteaux are, however, similar in their treatment of the elevation. Each storey is ornamented with very flat pilasters, and is bounded by strong horizontal string-courses above and below it. The result is that the wall is divided up by a network of lines crossing at right angles, which pattern out the surface, but hardly disturb its flatness. It is, in fact, a completely non-plastic wall treatment. In all three buildings the dormers are a prominent feature, and are early examples of the type to be found in all

8

the Loire châteaux, still medieval in form but decorated with dolphins and candelabra in the new manner. At Azay a prominent feature is the main entrance to the *corps-de-logis* (Plate 6), a tall, narrow, four-storeyed pavilion in which the Orders are applied one above the other but are sometimes interrupted by the insertion of a niche in the middle of a pilaster. Once again the vertical emphasis is strong, not only in the entrance pavilion but also in the arrangement of the windows, which, as at Gaillon, are linked to form vertical strips.

When we come to the châteaux of Blois and Chambord the scale of work changes; we move from the country house to the palace. Blois was Francis I's earliest passion, and six months after his accession in 1515 we find him giving orders for extensive building operations there.[22] During the following nine years there rose the wing which bears his name and which stands to-day, slightly truncated on the court side and heavily restored, as the first great monument of the reign. In plan it has nothing novel to offer, for, in spite of the grandeur of his ideas, the King allowed himself to be tied by the remains of surviving medieval buildings. The court façade (Plate 7) and the flight of rooms behind, which were the first to be built, are constructed on old foundations, and even the great staircase replaces a tower of roughly the same shape. On the opposite front overlooking the town (Plate 8B) the new *loggie* and the rooms which they veil, probably built after 1520, are constructed between three medieval round towers, one of which is clearly visible at the extreme right, while the other two have their foundations incorporated in the new structure. This economical use of existing foundations accounts for certain irregularities in the design of the wing. Neither façade is symmetrical; on the court side the staircase was roughly central before the seventeenth-century reconstruction cut off the end bays, but the arrangement of windows was always irregular, as we can see from du Cerceau's engravings. On the outer front the aberrations are even more marked; some bays are separated by single pilasters, others by double, others by double pilasters enclosing a niche, all apparently without rhyme or reason.

This irregularity proves that although French builders had learnt the idiom of Italian decoration, they had not yet absorbed the basic principles of Renaissance architecture. It does not, however, alter the fact that the Francis I wing is an effective and original building. Of the two façades, that on the court is the less remarkable. Its general disposition is in line with what we have seen at Bury and Azay, and the only important element is the staircase. This is an admirable example of the attitude of French architects of this period towards tradition. In its general principle the staircase is only the last of a long line of spiral staircases to be found in France throughout the fifteenth century. Often, as at Châteaudun, it is incorporated in the main block of the building, but in many cases – for instance in the house of Jacques Cœur at Bourges – it stands out from the façade in a polygonal pavilion, and in some examples it is open. In many respects therefore the Blois staircase is traditional, but the old type is translated into a completely new idiom. Here it is no longer merely a question of the decorative detail, most of which incidentally dates from the nineteenth-century restoration. For the first time one can speak of a feeling of monumentality in French Renaissance architecture. Compared with the light surface patterning of Azay or of the façade itself at Blois, we have here the impression that the architect has thought in three dimensions. The ramp carves out a definable space, and both it and the piers create emphatically the impression of weight. The play is in depth, in a series of planes in the thickness of the polygonal drum of the tower. On the outer surface are the verticals of the piers, decorated with niches below and pilasters above. Across these run the three bands of open-work balustrade, sloping and set slightly back; and behind them again in the third plane are the lines of the ramp itself, sloping a little more steeply than the balustrade. Inside the staircase tradition reigns unchallenged except for decorative detail; for the structure and vaulting are purely Gothic.

The façade over the town is an altogether original conception. The sharp cliff on this side seems to have held an irresistible attraction for architects. The medieval castle had been built along the edge of the flat area at its top, with only the three round towers projecting and built up from the lower level. Francis I, however, boldly set the façade forward some twenty feet, to the outer points of the towers, and was therefore forced to build a vast substructure to support the *loggie* above. For the right-hand half the rock was still relatively near, but on the left it ran sharply back, so that a whole extra floor could be inserted between the substructure and the normal ground floor of the main building. As we shall see later, in the seventeenth century François Mansart was tempted to be even bolder, and his final design would have carried the front another thirty feet into space.[23]

The idea of an arcaded *loggia* on the outside of a château was not altogether new in France. It had already been used in Gothic form at Amboise and in the earlier wing at Gaillon, built between 1502 and 1506, but at Blois the scheme is grander in conception. There are two sets of *loggie* one above the other, and over them a third floor of flat-headed openings separated by free-standing columns. The source of this design is evidently the *Loggie* of the Vatican, in which two floors of round-headed and one of flat-headed *loggie* rest on a solid ground floor. We must suppose that the French builders were fairly well up to date in their information about building in Rome, for the *Loggie* were not finished till 1519. On the other hand, the drawings or description of the *Loggie* from which they worked cannot have been very accurate, for nothing could be less like them in feeling than the Blois façade. The irregularity in the elevation has already been pointed out, but there are other differences of importance. The arches are slightly flattened, instead of having the pure semicircle of Bramante, and, except on the top floor, the galleries at Blois are not properly speaking *loggie* at all, since they are merely very deep recesses closed by glazed windows. These differences effectively destroy the essential qualities of Bramante's design: regularity, mathematical perfection, and lightness.[24]

At Blois are summed up the strength and weakness of French architecture in the earlier years of Francis I. The strength consists of imaginative inventiveness and structural skill, both qualities resulting from the medieval tradition, and of a certain *finesse* in the adaptation of Italian ornament. The weakness lies in the naïve and often clumsy imitation of Italian design, imperfectly understood. The impression made by the château on a strictly classical mind is well conveyed by La Fontaine's description of it, though he must have been alone at his time in preferring the sixteenth-century wing to that of François Mansart: 'The part built by Francis I, seen from the outside, pleased me more than anything else. There are many little galleries, little windows, little balconies, little ornaments without regularity or order; these make up a whole which is big and rather pleasing.'[25]

Up to this stage in the development of French sixteenth-century architecture the buildings were to all intents and purposes anonymous. We often know the names of master masons involved, but in no case, except that of St Pierre at Caen, is there any reason to suppose that they were responsible for the design of the building. Further, the arguments about the shares of French and Italian craftsmen are, as has been said, futile.

Figure 1. Château of Chambord: Plan

The only clear fact is that in planning and structure the French mind dominates, and in decoration the Italian; the nationality of the actual executants is of purely academic interest.

But in the case of Chambord (Figure 1; Plate 9A) both these problems are posed in a new and more definite manner: there is every probability that the original designer was an Italian, Domenico da Cortona, but on the other hand his plans seem to have been modified in the course of execution by French masons.[26]

The known facts are as follows. Francis I, attracted by the site of Chambord as a hunting lodge, first caused plans to be drawn up for a château there in 1519. Work was probably begun soon afterwards, but was interrupted from 1524 to 1526 by the Italian campaign and the King's captivity. It was then actively continued, and the main keep was being roofed in 1537; the east wing was being constructed in 1539 and the west in 1550, that is to say, after the death of the King. As it stands to-day Chambord is essentially a French medieval château with square keep flanked by round towers from which run ranges of lower buildings, again with towers at the corners, the whole being surrounded by a moat.[27] In one respect, however, the planning is unusual, namely, in the keep itself, which is divided into four parts by a Greek cross, the arms of which lead from the entrances to the central staircase (Figure 1). This arrangement leaves in each corner a square space divided into a large room, two smaller ones, and a closet, that is to say, into the *appartement*, which was to be the regular unit of French domestic planning for the next two centuries. This seems to be its first appearance in France, and its origin is worth investigating. It appears in the original wooden model designed and executed almost certainly by Domenico da Cortona and known to us through the drawings made by Félibien in the seventeenth century.[28] According to tradition, Domenico da Cortona was a pupil of Giuliano da Sangallo, whom he accompanied to France on his visit in 1495, the master soon returning and the pupil remaining. Now we find an arrangement closely similar to the Chambord plan in the villa built by Giuliano for Lorenzo de' Medici at Poggio a Caiano.[29] Here are the four groups of rooms arranged in the corners of a square, and although the intervening spaces are filled in a slightly different way, they are occupied on two sides by vestibules, as at Chambord. In fact, it seems almost certain that Domenico borrowed this disposition from his master, and so set a fashion which was to become purely French; for in Italy this particular design was not followed up.

Apart from this important detail of planning, little of Domenico's original design survived in the executed building. Even the plan was altered in one respect, for Domenico had proposed a straight staircase doubling back on itself in one arm of the Greek cross, an arrangement reminiscent of Chenonceau. In the building itself this disposition was changed, and the famous spiral staircase was inserted at the central point of the Greek cross. This staircase is a purely French invention, similar in general design to that at Blois, and having precedents for the double ramp in medieval examples, of which the most famous was in the Bernardine College of Paris. In elevation the alterations made to the Italian model were much more drastic. Domenico's keep was to be surrounded on the ground floor by an open *loggia* of round-headed arches, and on the upper floors the windows, though themselves mostly square-headed, were to be enclosed in blind arcades. In the actual building these Italian elements have disappeared, and the elevation is treated in the manner which we have noticed at Azay and on the court façade at Blois, with string courses and flat pilasters.

In its general appearance Chambord is entirely French and still largely medieval. The massive round towers with their conical tops could be matched in any fifteenth-century château. What is original is the treatment of the roof (Plate 9B). Standing on the flat terrace of which it consists, the spectator has the impression of being surrounded by a forest of chimneys, turrets, and dormers, all different and all of the most complex form. The fantasy of the design brings this roof into line with the strangest inventions of Flamboyant Gothic. The detail, however, is not only Italian, but of purer Italian design than

had so far been seen in France. Some of the dormers are like those at Blois or Azay, except that they have panels of coloured marble let into their surface; but others are altogether new in their plastic conception. The niche decorating the chimney in the middle
of plate 9B, for instance, is hollowed almost into a half-cylinder, topped by a shell half-
dome and flanked not by pilasters but by free-standing columns. We have already
noticed this sense of spatial design in the staircase at Blois, though there it was expressed
in a more strictly French idiom. In both, however, it prepares the way for what was to
come in the next period.

We have already seen that the richer *bourgeois* played an important part in the evolution of the château, and naturally their share is even greater in town houses. In their
corporate activities they were responsible for the rebuilding of many town-halls in the
new manner, and the changes which they introduced can be seen by the comparison
of two almost contemporary examples, at Compiègne (1502–10) and Orleans (Plate
11B; 1503–13). The Compiègne Hôtel de Ville is still a Franco-Flemish Flamboyant
building with a belfry in the middle and, between the windows, niches with statues of
kings of France. At Orleans the fifteenth-century belfry was preserved and the new
town-hall built separately in front of it. The general design is like that of Compiègne,
and even incorporates the same niches and statues, but the decoration is Italian, with
pilasters partly fluted and partly decorated with candelabra and with a shell cornice of a
kind to be found later on the court façade at Blois. Below each window is a pair of *putti*
supporting the arms of the town, an unusually advanced conception for such an early
date.[30]

The same development can be seen in the private houses built by the wealthier financiers in the towns. The great model of these, and one which for long was not to be sur-
passed in splendour, was the house of Jacques Cœur at Bourges, built in the Late Gothic
style between 1445 and 1451. The arrangement round a partly arcaded court was generally followed in the sixteenth century, for instance in the transitional example of the
Hôtel d'Alluye at Blois, built before 1508 by Florimond Robertet, the creator of Bury.
Here we find the usual mixture of elements, Late Gothic arches with Italianate capitals
and a pierced balustrade of dolphins running above the upper arcade. The Hôtel Lallemant at Bourges, mainly completed by 1518, is still Gothic in its design, but has fine and
relatively pure Italianate detail.[31] Fully in the style of Francis I is the Hôtel Pincé at
Angers (Plate 11A), built on an L-shaped plan, of which the left-hand wing and the staircase tower date from 1523–33. Here are still the mullioned windows, the turrets, and the
high-pitched roofs of a medieval building, but dormers and windows are all ornamented
with rich decoration in the style of the Loire châteaux.[32]

The period of French architecture from 1494 to 1525 was a transitional phase in which
Italian ideas were grafted on a very lively medieval tradition, the two elements still remaining distinct. In the next period they become more closely fused, and architects,
while remaining distinctively French, show a greater understanding of Italian principles
and skill in adapting them to their needs, instead of copying blindly and often inappro-
priately.

SCULPTURE

Guido Mazzoni, the Giusti, Michel Colombe

In sculpture as in architecture a strong Gothic tradition still flourished at the end of the fifteenth century, and well into the sixteenth century we find works of high quality produced in this style all over France.[33] Examples of Italian work had begun to arrive in France long before the Italian campaigns, but, as in the case of architecture, without exercising any perceptible influence.[34]

At the turn of the century, however, a more consistent Italian influence begins to be felt. In 1502 Louis XII commissioned a tomb in honour of his ancestors, the Dukes of Orleans, which was originally set up in the church of the Célestins in Paris, but is now at St Denis (Plate 12A). The contract of 1502 mentions the Genoese sculptors, Michele d'Aria and Girolamo Viscardi, and the two Florentines, Donato di Battista Benti and Benedetto di Bartolommeo, who had settled in Genoa. This tomb shows a compromise scheme which was to become common in the next decades, consisting of a purely Italian sarcophagus supporting a recumbent figure, or *gisant*, in the traditional French manner. In this case the style of the drapery suggests that the *gisant* was actually executed by the Italian sculptors, probably on a French design; but we shall see later that sometimes the two parts were by artists of different nationalities. The novelty of this tomb, apart from the strictly classical arcade round the sarcophagus, lies in the introduction in this arcade of the figures of the twelve apostles, which replace the *pleurants* usual in French tombs.[35]

There is no reason to believe that any of the artists involved in the Orleans tomb actually came to France; and the first sculptor who can be traced there is Guido Mazzoni, who was brought back by Charles VIII from Naples in 1495. He was born in Modena and had worked for some years in his native district, but moved to Naples in 1489. His works in Italy consist mainly of terra-cotta groups, usually of the Entombment, marked by an extreme naturalism of style which derives largely from northern Gothic sources.[36]

Such groups were already popular in France in the late fifteenth century, and Mazzoni's skill in them would no doubt have been welcomed by his new patrons. We have no proof that he executed works of this type in France, but Vitry is probably right in attributing to him the 'Death of the Virgin' in painted stone at Fécamp.[37]

The only work by Mazzoni for which we have documentary evidence is the tomb of Charles VIII at St Denis, now destroyed, but known from engravings.[38] It consisted of a rectangular sarcophagus on which was the figure of the King kneeling at a prie-Dieu, surrounded by four angels. This arrangement was more French than Italian and was probably derived from the tomb of Louis XI at Cléry, but the figure had greater freedom of movement than would have been possible in a French tomb. The sarcophagus was decorated with roundels in which were half-figures of the Virtues, or possibly of *pleurants*, an arrangement new in France, and probably inspired by reliefs to be seen on the façades of certain north Italian buildings.[39] We know little more of Mazzoni's activities in France, beyond that he supplied medallions for Gaillon. In 1507 he went back to

Modena, returning to France for the years 1509–11, but without apparently undertaking any important work.

Mazzoni was soon followed by the Giusti brothers, who settled in Tours, changed their name to Juste, and formed a dynasty of sculptors lasting till after the middle of the century. The two of importance are Antonio (1479–1519) and Giovanni (1485–1549), who came to France together probably in 1504 or 1505. Antonio is known to have re-visited Italy between 1508 and 1516, during which period he owned a house in Carrara where Michelangelo sometimes stayed when supervising the quarrying of marble.[40] He may therefore have brought back to France information about artistic events in Italy which had taken place since the brothers had left the country, and it was probably he who introduced certain influences from Italy which appear in the later French sculpture of the Giusti.

The first work which can be connected with the family is the tomb of Thomas James in the cathedral of Dol, finished in 1507, which has already been mentioned as an early example of Italian decoration in France.

Much more important and original is the tomb of Louis XII at St Denis (Plate 14), commissioned by his successor Francis I, probably in 1515, and finished in 1531. It bears the name of Giovanni only, but is often said to be a work of both brothers working in collaboration. The arrangement with the kneeling figures above links the design with the tomb of Charles VIII, and the placing of the *gisants* in an arcaded enclosure below follows the usual fifteenth-century disposition. In all other respects, however, the tomb marks an innovation in French practice. First of all, the enclosure of the *gisants* is now almost a small chapel open at the sides and the ends. This feature, combined with the allegorical figures of the Virtues at the corners and the apostles in front of the arcade, suggests that we may have here a remote echo of Michelangelo's first scheme for the tomb of Julius II. But the actual form is different, in that the 'chapel' is opened by ar-cades, and for this the Giusti probably followed another model, the tomb of Gian Gale-azzo Visconti, which Commynes had admired in the Certosa at Pavia.[41] In the sculpture several different hands can be distinguished. Two groups – the apostles and the Virtues – seem to be Florentine in derivation and apparently connected with the style of Andrea Sansovino. The apostles are dull but competent imitations of his statues in the chapel of S. Giovanni in the cathedral of Genoa (finished in 1503), the Virtues very coarse ver-sions of his later manner in the tombs in S. Maria del Popolo, Rome (1505–9). These two groups can almost certainly be attributed to members of the Giusti family. The bas-reliefs round the base seem also Florentine in style and indicate an artist trained in the studio of Bertoldo. On the other hand, as suggested by Vitry and Pradel, the kneeling figures of the King and Queen on the top of the tomb are likely to be by a French artist of the circle of Colombe. The most remarkable and at the same time the most puzzling group consists of the two *gisants*. In certain respects the heads of the two figures are classi-cal; in particular that of Louis XII is like the well-known heads of the Emperor Augustus (Plate 13). But the traces of French Gothic are strong. The lines of the eyes have a sweet-ness to be found in French fifteenth-century painting; and, by contrast, the grimness of Late Gothic sculpture can be seen in certain naturalistic details, particularly the rendering of the incisions and stitching made in the process of embalming the bodies. The naturalistic treatment of the open mouth showing the teeth, and the hollowing out of the cheeks reminds one in some respects of French fifteenth-century portraiture as it can be seen in the head of the donor in the Avignon Pietà. On the whole, therefore, it seems likely that these figures are by a French artist with some knowledge of Italian sculpture rather than by an Italian sculptor, who could hardly have absorbed these local elements.[42] But, whoever the artist may have been, the statues are unquestionably among the most remarkable works of the period. The sensitiveness of their modelling and the liveliness of their conception are shown up by the contrast with the heavy proportions and coarse modelling of the statues round the base of the tomb. The latter are only interesting as being among the few surviving examples of Italian High Renaissance sculpture which reached France at this period, though they cannot have given Frenchmen much idea of what was being produced at the period in Italy.[43]

The works which we have so far considered have been either exclusively or predominantly Italian. But it must be remembered that one French sculptor of great celebrity was still active at this time, namely, Michel Colombe. The greater part of his career falls outside our period, for he was born about 1430–5 and is last recorded in 1512. But we have almost no information about his work till the early years of the sixteenth century, when his name occurs in connexion with two important works: the tomb of Francis II, Duke of Brittany, in Nantes Cathedral, and the altar-relief of St George at Gaillon.

The tomb of Francis II (Plate 12B) is a work of collaboration, the story of which is complex and in many points obscure. In 1499 Anne of Brittany was collecting marble for the tomb of her father, and in January 1500 the Italian sculptor, Girolamo da Fiesole, was commissioned to carry out at any rate some part of the work. At the end of the same year Anne seems to have turned towards French artists, and we find her approaching Colombe and Perréal on the subject. Work seems actually to have been started by these two artists in 1502, apparently with Perréal in charge and supplying the general design and Colombe working out the detail of the sculpture. It is, however, likely that the sarcophagus was made by an Italian. The tomb was finally erected in 1507.

The general design with altar-tomb and *gisants* is the usual translation of the Late Gothic tomb into Italian terms, with the small difference that it combines the arches of the Orleans tomb with the roundels of the monument to Charles VIII. At the corner stand four allegorical figures of Virtues, an arrangement which may be regarded as a variation on Burgundian tombs like that of Philippe Pot. Vitry has argued convincingly that these figures and the *gisants* are the work of Colombe and his studio, and that except in certain points of iconography they show little direct Italian influence. They are far from the tortured Burgundian Late Gothic style, and belong in their calm to the style of the Loire, in which Colombe had grown up. They are idealized, but their idealization is different in character from that of the Italian Renaissance. In fact they belong to a French Late Gothic style, classical in its calm, but not in its forms, more individual and more harmonious than anything produced by the Italian sculptors imported into France.[44]

The altarpiece of St George for Gaillon (Plate 16), now in the Louvre, was executed by Colombe in 1508–9, and the frame for it carved by Jérôme Pacherot, the Genoese sculptor whom we have already noticed working at Gaillon. In this relief we find stronger traces of Italian influence than are usual in Colombe. Iconographically it does not go back, as is usually said, to Donatello's relief on Or San Michele, but more directly to various reliefs of the subject produced by the Gaggini family in Genoa.[45] Colombe, however, has not slavishly imitated the Italian work. In the latter the landscape is treated in a schematic manner, with the rocks reduced to geometrical forms, whereas Colombe has rendered with great care every incident of rock, pebble, or plant. Moreover, his dragon is entirely his own, with a Gothic combination of imagination and homeliness.

Colombe occupies a unique position among French artists of the early sixteenth century. He rarely borrows directly from Italian models, yet he adapted his art to suit the ideals which were coming into France from the south. His work is always distinguishably French, but it has deeper affinities with the sculpture of the Italian High Renaissance than many works which imitate the forms of the latter.

The monument to the children of Charles VIII is, like that of Francis II of Brittany, a work in which the style of Colombe and that of the Italians can be seen side by side. Girolamo da Fiesole was engaged to execute the tomb in 1499, and he is probably responsible for the sarcophagus, which is of elaborate and original design.[46] An unusual iconographical feature is the presence among the acanthus reliefs of scenes from the lives of Samson and Hercules, strangely inappropriate, one would have said, to the tomb of two young children. The figures of the latter clearly belong to the same school as those on the Nantes tomb and can with great probability be attributed to the studio of Colombe.

The last and most complicated monument of this period is the tomb of the two Cardinals of the Amboise family in Rouen Cathedral (Plate 15). The tomb was begun in 1515 and in its first form probably finished by 1522.[47] At that stage it contained only one statue, that of the elder Cardinal, now the left-hand of the two figures. The master mason was Rouland le Roux, who was probably also responsible for the design. Four sculptors are named: Pierre des Aubeaulx, Regnault Thérouyn, Mathieu Laignel,[48] and André le Flament. Vitry has pointed out that the spelling of the names in some of the inscriptions indicates that Italian craftsmen took part in the work, but their share was probably limited to the purely decorative passages. The design of the whole and the execution of the figure sculpture are certainly not Italian. The tomb is a variant of the Gothic form, with an altar-tomb set in a niche, but with the figure kneeling instead of recumbent. Much of the detail is evidently French and specifically Norman, for instance the finials and pendentives, which are like those of Hector Sohier at St Pierre at Caen. But Flemish influence is to be seen in the series of Virtues below the kneeling figures, which can be closely parallelled in the painting of the school of Antwerp, particularly in their unusual head-dresses. They may perhaps be connected with the name of André le Flament. This tomb is the last expression of the experimental spirit which animated the early years of the sixteenth century in France. In its general form it is Gothic, in its wildness it is Flamboyant, in its detail it is Italianate; and yet as a whole it is unmistakably in the style which we call 'François I'.

PAINTING

Bourdichon, Perréal

The position of painting in France at the beginning of the sixteenth century was very different from that of architecture and sculpture. In the two latter arts a vigorous medieval tradition survived which was capable of absorbing influences from abroad. Painting was, on the other hand, at a much lower ebb, although in the last two decades of the century it had produced a brilliant burst of inspiration in the works of the Maître de Moulins. After 1500, however, there are few signs of real activity in painting proper, though certain works to be found in the eastern provinces of France suggest that there may have existed there a competent school of religious painters yet to be rediscovered and isolated from contemporary Flemish work.[49]

Only two names of importance survive from this period. With one, Jean Bourdichon, can be connected a number of works; about the other, Jean Perréal, there is much contemporary evidence, but modern scholarship has not reached any agreement about the paintings that can be attributed to him.

Bourdichon was probably born about 1457 and seems to have spent most of his life in Touraine. He worked in turn for Louis XI, Charles VIII, Louis XII, Anne of Brittany, Charles of Angoulême, and his son Francis I, and died in 1521. He is known from records to have painted portraits and religious pictures, but apart from one triptych in Naples recently identified as his,[50] the only works which can be certainly attributed to him are manuscript illuminations. Of these the most important series and the one of which the authorship is proved beyond doubt is the *Hours of Anne of Brittany* in the Bibliothèque Nationale, finished in 1508. The illuminations of this manuscript allow us to define Bourdichon's position fairly clearly. In many respects he follows the Late Gothic tradition of fifteenth-century illuminators, and the miniatures illustrating the months show no novel features except a curious tendency to allow the figures to be cut off at the waist by the frame, a trick which at a later date we should call Mannerist. Another series of miniatures in the book reveals an astonishing naturalistic power in the rendering of plants and insects, a naturalism still essentially within the Gothic field but carried to a hitherto unknown pitch of perfection.

In the paintings representing the scenes from the New Testament and lives of the saints, however, a more mixed style is visible. In many the architectural setting shows unmistakable Italian influence. This was not new in French illumination, for since the time of Fouquet details of Italian decoration had been relatively common. It is, however, of some interest to notice that certain features in Bourdichon's designs can be traced directly to Bramante's work in S. Maria presso S. Satiro at Milan, particularly the shell-niches which appear in several miniatures, and the coffered vault in the 'Annunciation'. But it is also noticeable that the figure types and compositions are influenced by Italian models. Many of the heads are reminiscent of Milanese painting, notably of Foppa, but more remarkable is the unquestionable influence of Perugino. The miniature of St Sebastian (Plate 17A) is in almost exactly the pose of Perugino's figure of the saint in the Louvre and other paintings of the 1490s; [51] and in many of Bourdichon's compositions we find heads unmistakably Peruginesque in origin. It is not clear how the influence came to be transmitted, since we have no evidence that Bourdichon visited Italy. But the variety of Italian influences in his work points strongly to a visit, and seems to indicate that he went not only to Milan [52] but to other parts of Italy. [53] It is characteristic of Bourdichon that he should have been primarily influenced by large-scale Italian painting and sculpture rather than by miniatures. Many of his designs – for instance the 'St Sebastian' – look in reproduction like altarpieces rather than miniatures; and to this extent his art represents the decay of true illumination.

Jean Perréal, or Jean de Paris, seems to have commanded even more than Bourdichon the admiration of his contemporaries. We do not know the date of his birth, but it cannot have been far from that of Bourdichon, that is to say, in the second half of the 1450s. By 1483 he was in the service of the city of Lyons; soon afterwards we find him working for the Duc de Bourbon; and later he was in the service of the Kings of France, Charles VIII, Louis XII, and Francis I, till his death in 1530. He visited Italy on three occasions, accompanying Charles VIII to Naples in 1494, and going on Louis XII's campaigns of 1502 and 1509. His activities were varied: he was a specialist in the preparation of those triumphal entries which played such a considerable part in public entertainment in the fifteenth and sixteenth centuries; he was called upon to draw up programmes for big undertakings in sculpture, such as the tomb of Francis II of Brittany at Nantes and those erected by Margaret of Savoy in the church of Brou, though his precise share in each of these is obscure. [54] We know further that portraiture was one of his principal interests, and here we are on rather more certain ground. We know that he designed the medals struck for the entries of Charles VIII and Louis XII into Lyons in 1494 and 1499, which contain their portraits in profile. [55] Further, one painted portrait has been attributed to Perréal with a considerable degree of probability, namely the 'Louis XII' at Windsor (Plate 17B), which was almost certainly sent by the King to Henry VIII during the negotiations for Louis's marriage with Henry's sister Mary in 1514. [56] The style of this painting fits with what we know of Perréal's training; for, though in type it still belongs to the fifteenth-century tradition, it reveals in its modelling a knowledge of Milanese painting with which Perréal came in contact during his three journeys to Italy. [57]

From the beginning of his reign Francis I aimed at collecting Italian paintings and at attracting to his court some of the great masters of Italy. In the former project he was successful, and by the time of his death the Royal collection included important paintings by Raphael, Titian, and many other painters of the High Renaissance. But he found it harder to persuade the artists themselves to come to France. Leonardo da Vinci accepted his invitation and spent the last three years of his life (1516–19) in France. Andrea del Sarto came, but stayed only for one year (1518–19).

Francis I seems, however, to have set his heart above all on obtaining works by Michelangelo. The fame of this artist must have been known early in France, for the 'Pietà' in St Peter's, executed in 1498, was commissioned by a French cardinal, Jean de Villiers de La Groslaye, for the chapel of the King of France, and in 1508 the bronze 'David' was presented to Florimond Robertet. The King sent a message to Michelangelo asking for a work by him, but this desire was not satisfied till 1529, when his agent, Giambattista della Palla, was able to buy the 'Hercules',[58] with which Filippo Strozzi probably parted only in the hope of winning the support of the King for Florence against the Emperor. In the same year Michelangelo fled to Venice to escape from the siege of Florence, apparently with the intention of going on to France. He was, however, prevented from carrying out his plan by the pressure of his Florentine friends, who represented to him that this action would be regarded as treason to his native city. The last chapter of this story brings us to the year 1546, that is to say, nearly to the end of the reign, when Roberto Strozzi presented to Francis I the two 'Slaves' from the tomb of Julius II which the King passed on to Montmorency who set them up at Écouen.[59]

Curiously enough, however, the presence in France of the great masters of the Italian Renaissance or of their works seems to have exercised almost no effect on French art, and it was not till the arrival of Rosso and Primaticcio that Italian influence began to take root in French painting. But then it swept everything aside and founded a totally new school without links with any local tradition.

CHAPTER 2

THE MIDDLE YEARS OF FRANCIS I
1525 – 1540

HISTORICAL BACKGROUND

THE short period with which we are now concerned was one of almost continuous disturbance. Beginning with the defeat of Francis I by Charles V at Pavia (1525) and the captivity of the French King in Spain, it closed inconclusively with the interview of the King and the Emperor at Aigues Mortes (1538) and the curious journey of Charles V through France to suppress the revolt of the burghers of Ghent (1540). The diplomacy of Francis I during these years was notable neither for integrity nor consistency. His immediate repudiation of the Treaty of Madrid, his subsequent reconciliation with the Emperor, the constantly changing alliances between France, the Pope, England, and the smaller European states make up a picture of vacillation and confusion. But in spite of this confusion the decades before the middle of the century were important and productive for France in the political, social, and intellectual fields.

The wars, which mostly took place abroad, only affected the border provinces, and in the rest of France trade, industry, and agriculture continued to develop, bringing increasing prosperity, especially to the middle classes. While the landed aristocracy found itself in financial difficulties owing to the changes in the purchasing power of money, those involved in commerce were able to adapt themselves to these fluctuations and even to derive profit from them. In addition, their position was greatly strengthened by the formal recognition of usury through the establishment in 1522 of *rentes*, that it to say, loans guaranteed by the city of Paris and paying a high rate of interest, which were to be for several centuries the basis of *bourgeois* investment. At the same time the middle classes consolidated their position by establishing the right to bequeath municipal and legal posts from father to son, so that a new hierarchy sprang up in the towns, the *noblesse de robe*, despised by the *noblesse d'épée* but gaining steadily in real power.

In the administration of the kingdom Francis I pursued after his return from Madrid the policy of centralization which had been sketched out in the preceding decades. The *Conseil des Affaires*, which gradually supplanted the *Conseil Étroit*, depended solely on the King and became the chief weapon of his increasingly autocratic direction of the Government. In finance he gradually replaced the remains of the medieval system with one which depended entirely on the central government. He continued the policy of weakening the power of the nobles by reducing their rights to administer justice and by skilfully enlarging the *domaine royal* at the expense of the other feudal estates.

In fact, from this time onwards the nobility gradually lost the function and position which it had held under the feudal system and began to take up its new status as a court aristocracy. This evolution did not reach its final phase till the reign of Louis XIV, but it can be seen in its early stage under Francis I. In his reign the nobility still took an active part in the government as advisers to the King; the *Conseil des Affaires* consisted mainly of members of the old families; and the most powerful figure in the middle years of the reign was the Constable Anne de Montmorency. But the primary employment of the nobles grew to be attendance on the person of the King. After the return of Francis from Madrid the Court was reorganized on a grander scale than ever before, and around the Household, properly speaking, the King created a large floating population of nobles attached to his person and living on gifts and pensions from him. Naturally in order to house this increasing Court new and larger palaces were needed, and, as we shall see, the King was active in building them.

In the field of religion there is a sharp difference between the periods before and after Pavia. The Reformation had taken shape as a major European fact on which it was no longer possible to avoid taking sides. The 'liberal' Reformers, such as Lefèvre d'Étaples, found themselves squeezed out by the extremists, just as Contarini and Pole ultimately found themselves impotent in Italy. The spirit of Luther began to dominate French Protestantism, and the Affair of the Placards of 1534 and the persecutions which followed it give the tone of the new period. As early as 1528 at the Council of Sens the Gallican Church organized itself to resist the schismatics, in the spirit which was to be shown by the whole Roman Church nearly two decades later at Trent. The position of Francis himself in these struggles was unsteady. Swayed towards sympathy with the Reformers by his sister Margaret of Navarre, he was sometimes pulled equally strongly in the opposite direction by political necessity, such as a new alliance with the Pope, or by fear, as after the Affair of the Placards. In general, however, he tended more and more to identify himself with the party of orthodoxy, and the persecution of the Protestants grew more violent as the reign went on.

In the literary field no new figure of importance appears in poetry. Marot's style developed under the influence of Italian models in the direction of greater simplicity, and he dropped more and more in his later works the complex poetical tricks which he had inherited from the Rhétoriqueurs. French prose, however, produces at this period one writer of genius in François Rabelais, whose *Pantagruel* appeared in 1532, to be followed by *Gargantua* in 1534, and the *Tiers Livre* in 1546. Here, for the first time in France, humanist erudition is used by a writer who had a positive attitude towards life, even a philosophy, to propose and who, though soaked in the classics and in Italian literature, is original and wholly French.

In the visual arts, as we shall see, the same stage was reached at this time, but unhappily with no figure of the calibre of Rabelais to focus the movement into works of genius.

ARCHITECTURE

The Châteaux built for Francis I in the Île-de-France:
Madrid, Fontainebleau, etc.

The fact that on his return from Madrid Francis I made Paris his regular headquarters necessarily brought about a change of centre for artistic activities, and it is notable that whereas before 1525 the Loire valley had been the most advanced region of France, this now drops behind and becomes provincial, while the lead passes to the Île-de-France. In the period with which we are now concerned the major architectural undertakings may be divided into two groups of royal palaces, all of which are within a relatively short distance of Paris. The first consists of the châteaux of Madrid, St Germain, La Muette de St Germain, and Challuau; the second of Fontainebleau and Villers-Cotteret.[1] Of these, only St Germain, Fontainebleau, and Villers-Cotteret survive, and those only in much altered form.

The châteaux of the first group are closely related in style, though it is not possible to say that they are all designed by the same architect. Indeed, it is not certain who was responsible for the plans of any of them. In the Château de Madrid (Plate 18A), which was begun in 1528, those mentioned as engaged on the building were Pierre Gadier, Gatien François, and the Italian Girolamo della Robbia. The last was responsible for the terracotta decoration, but the accounts show that he was also in charge of building operations, and some critics have maintained that he was the designer of the whole château. However, it is too unlike any Italian architecture in its general lay-out and elevation for this to be possible. For St Germain and La Muette we know that the master mason was Pierre Chambiges from the beginning of the work in 1539 till his death in 1544, when Guillaume Guillain and Jean Langeois took over, completing the work in 1549. About Challuau we have no documents, but the name of Chambiges is traditionally and plausibly connected with it. It seems safe to conclude that the original design of each château is due to a Frenchman, probably to Chambiges for St Germain, La Muette, and Challuau, and perhaps to Gadier or François for Madrid, but that in this last case the Italian artist may have modified certain details.

All these buildings are of very singular design, unlike anything else in French architecture. They are all of unusual height, decorated with external galleries running between turrets. In certain features Madrid differs from the others. It has, for instance, a high-pitched roof, whereas all the others had flat terraces.[2] It has true *loggie*, while in the others the openings are only deep window bays, as at Blois. In this respect its design is more Italian than the others, and we may well see here a detail of arrangement introduced by Girolamo della Robbia; but the high-pitched roof is essentially French and must be attributed to the local master-masons.

The appearance of Madrid is preserved for us in the engravings of du Cerceau, which may be supplemented by the description of Evelyn, who saw the château in 1650: ''Tis observable onely for its open manner of architecture, being much of tarraces and galleries one over another to the very roofe, and for the materials, which are most of earth painted like Porcelain or China-ware, whose colours appeare very fresh, but is very fragile. There are whole statues and relievos of this potterie, chimney-pieces and columns both within and without.' This sentence evidently refers to the contribution of Girolamo which can be seen on the outside in the form of medallions and friezes, but which also included mantelpieces like that shown in a more detailed drawing of du Cerceau, which bears the Salamander of Francis I (Plate 18B). The effect of this coloured terra-cotta decoration applied to interior decoration on this scale must have been startling and somewhat barbarous, but it provides an interesting prelude to the decoration which Rosso and Primaticcio were to create at Fontainebleau a few years later. The novelty of the latter lay in the combination of painting with high-relief sculptured ornament, and in a sense Girolamo's work may be said to combine the methods of the two arts even more completely, since the reliefs are themselves executed in colour.

The decoration of the interior of Madrid was fantastic in form as well as in colour and material, but in a new way. It is no longer the almost Flamboyant fantasy of the early years of the century but one based on Early Italian Mannerism. The forms are those familiar in the late 1520s in decorative engravings and in Florentine small sculpture in stone or wood,[3] particularly the motive of caryatids which turn into architectural features, such as consoles or foliated balusters. The decoration of this château seems to have been an important source for later French artists, and many motives which we associate with the second half of the century are already to be seen here. In one respect the decoration is simpler than in the previous period: the dormers no longer have the complicated open-work designs to be found at Blois or Chambord. In general, they are covered by straight pediments, a form so far unknown in France, but connected with the new methods which were being evolved simultaneously by Gilles Le Breton at Fontainebleau.

In plan the Château de Madrid is of importance (cf. Figure 2), and, like Chambord, is ultimately connected with Poggio a Caiano. It consists of pairs of *appartements* connected by public rooms or *salles*, and du Cerceau explicitly praises the manner in which each *appartement* is arranged to be a self-contained unit with its separate entrance by a spiral staircase. The difference between Chambord and Madrid is that Chambord is the more compact and symmetrical plan, the whole building being contained in a square, whereas at Madrid the design consists of two square blocks linked by the narrower *salles*. La Muette and Challuau are known to us through the engravings of du Cerceau,[4] but they were little more than ingenious variants on the basic theme of Madrid, without the terra-cotta decoration. St Germain, which survives, though altered by Louis XIV and then put back somewhat ruthlessly to its former state in the nineteenth century, shows certain characteristics which distinguish it from the other members of this group.[5] On both the court and the outside façades it has on one floor a form of window hitherto unknown in France, consisting of a round-headed arched opening over which is a straight pediment; and a similar form, but with a curved pediment, is used in some of the doors in the turrets. This formula is common about 1500 in the architecture of Venice and its territories on the mainland, but is hardly found in other parts of Italy, and it may not be fanciful to connect its appearance at St Germain with the tradition recorded by Félibien in the seventeenth century that Sebastiano Serlio was responsible for at any rate some

Figure 2. Château of Madrid: Plan

work on the château, for he was trained partly on Venetian models, and reproduces in an engraving to his treatise the probable ancient source for the form in question in the Porta dei Leoni at Verona.

*

There is a striking contrast between the style of the châteaux just discussed and the work carried out at Fontainebleau between 1528 and 1540. Whereas the former buildings all look back to Blois and Chambord in the complexity of their design and decoration, the architecture of Fontainebleau is marked by great simplicity, which leads the way towards the classicism of the next generation.

In 1528 Francis I decided to make certain improvements in the medieval castle of Fontainebleau, which had up till then been no more than a hunting lodge.[6] Unfortunately, as in so many of his building undertakings, he began with the idea of making small alterations. By the time he had developed a scheme for total transformation, everything had been confused by attempts to incorporate old parts and to add wings here and there. The result is that, though charming and picturesque, Fontainebleau is one of the most inconsequently designed châteaux in France.

The work with which we are now concerned was carried out in almost every case under the master mason Gilles Le Breton. From the uniformity of style in different parts of the building it is reasonable to suppose that he was the designer as well as the executant, though some critics have maintained that another hand, perhaps even an Italian, was responsible for the original conception. The manner is, however, unmistakably French, and, if it is more classical than what went before, this classicism is an evolution within a French idiom, and is not due to the importing of new Italian motives.

From the contract signed by Le Breton in 1528 we know that the first plan of Francis I included the following modifications and additions: the building of a new entrance, the Porte Dorée (Plate 20A), to the court of the old castle, the Cour de l'Ovale; the addition of a gallery stretching behind the keep, and later called the Galerie François I (Plate 22A); and the construction of two short blocks at an obtuse angle to link the new entrance to the keep. In addition, the north side of the Cour du Cheval Blanc or Cour des Adieux (Plate 19B) probably dates from this period, though it differs in style from the other buildings. The reason for this difference may be that it was not part of the château proper but housed the monks who served the small church on the site of the present chapel of the Trinity. Of these buildings the Galerie François I has been completely remodelled externally, and the wings facing the Cour de l'Ovale are undistinguished. The most interesting is, therefore, the Porte Dorée, in which the new style of Le Breton appears clearly. Fundamentally it is, like the entrance to Gaillon, the fortified gate to a castle flanked by two towers, translated into a partly Renaissance idiom. But here the idiom is much simpler than at Gaillon. The decoration is limited to the application of flat pilasters on each floor and to the windows, which are topped with straight pediments. This simplicity was no doubt partly imposed on the architect by his material, which is the hard local *grès*, of great beauty and variety in colour but resistant to fine carving.

The most striking feature of the Porte Dorée is the series of three open bays one above the other in the middle. This may be an echo of certain Italian gates, such as Luciano Laurana's entrance to the Castel Nuovo at Naples, of which drawings might well have been brought back to France, or of the same architect's façade to the palace at Urbino. But, if the source is Italian, the treatment is French. First of all, the design is in several respects asymmetrical; the right tower is slightly broader than the left, and the middle peak of the roof is arbitrarily placed, a detail which no Italian architect of this generation would have overlooked. Secondly the windows in each tower are linked up in a vertical strip by the device of making the pediment of one window cut into the support of the one above or into the entablature of the main Order, an arrangement which we have already noticed at Gaillon and elsewhere, and which is still a trace of the Gothic love of the vertical. Finally the arches over the middle bays are slightly flattened, and the capitals are of a Quattrocento type which was already out of fashion in Italy.

The north side of the Cour du Cheval Blanc is even simpler in style and material. It is composed of brick pilasters and mouldings against a white plaster wall, an arrangement which was to be widely followed in châteaux all over France.[7] Here again no strict attention is paid to symmetry, for instance in the placing of the windows. The same point might be made about the east side of the court, but in this case the irregularities are due to subsequent alteration. The parts due to Le Breton, and built at various dates between 1528 and the death of Francis I, are in general distinguishable by being constructed in plaster with quoins and pilasters of *grès*, whereas the later parts are executed in a finer cream-coloured stone, more like that used in the châteaux of the Loire.

Of the many other works carried out by Le Breton at Fontainebleau almost all have been altered or pulled down; but one must be mentioned, even though as it stands to-day it is only a fragment. This is the portico and staircase in the Cour de l'Ovale, begun in 1531, of which a reconstruction is shown in Figure 3.[8] This design is so original that again critics have attempted to prove that it cannot be by Le Breton but must be by an Italian.[9] In fact, however, it is typical of his work, though much more inventive in conception than usual. The form of the staircase with double flight leading to a single flight bridging an arch to the first floor of the building is in the late medieval French tradition, and follows examples at Montargis and in the Palais of Paris,[10] but a closer model for the lower part was to be found at Bury (Plate 8A). Le Breton, however, has translated the model into his own terms.[11] The middle arch has exactly the form which we see on the outer side of the Porte Dorée, and the mouldings and capitals are similar. Le Breton is here more correct in his use of the Orders, especially in the upper floor, but he could well have acquired his new erudition from reading one of the editions of Vitruvius by then available. The staircase is the first of a great series of similar schemes, of which the two most celebrated were also to be built at Fontainebleau: Philibert de l'Orme's, known to us from du Cerceau's engravings and closely dependent on Le Breton's, and Jean du Cerceau's, which replaced it and which still stands in the Cour du Cheval Blanc.

The tendency towards a more classical style noticeable in Le Breton was the beginning of a movement which gathered strength during the 1530s. In various parts of France we find châteaux and town houses in which simplicity of form and decoration is

Figure 3. Reconstruction of staircase in the Cour de l'Ovale, Fontainebleau

accompanied by a stricter use of the classical Orders. In the Loire valley the châteaux of Champigny-sur-Veude (probably finished before 1543), Villandry (1532) (Plate 19A), and Valençay (c. 1540) all have affinities with Le Breton's manner,[12] though the last two still show traces of the earlier style in the use of round towers or fretted dormers. Further south at Assier, in the Lot, the two doors added in 1535 show a better knowledge of the use of the Orders and a more monumental feeling which prepares the way for de l'Orme and Bullant. In Normandy another artistic personality appears in Blaise Le Prestre, who was responsible for the Hôtel d'Écoville at Caen (1535–8) (Plate 20B) and the north wing of the château of Fontaine-Henri (c. 1537–44). These two buildings have in common a new formula for linking superimposed windows or niches into a vertical strip, which is here achieved by the use of full columns carrying the eye emphatically upwards. At the Hôtel d'Écoville the sculpture is also of a much more advanced type, classical in its detail and in its emphasis on the frontal view.[13]

Church architecture during this period was in the main limited to additions and alterations to existing buildings, but it produced one complete work of great interest, the church of St Eustache in Paris (Plate 21A). The foundation stone was laid in 1532; but the building was not finished till more than a century later, though the original design seems to have been generally followed. It is to be expected that Gothic tendencies should survive longer in ecclesiastical architecture than in secular, and this is amply borne out by St Eustache. It represents, however, a remarkable compromise between new and old, quite different from St Pierre at Caen. Here the plan, structure, and proportions are nearer to High Gothic than Flamboyant. The plan is almost exactly that of Notre Dame, with double aisles and chapels running round nave and choir, and transepts which do not project beyond these chapels. In the interior the arches are tall and narrow, and, although in general they are round-headed, those in the apse are stilted and pointed. The proportions of the nave again recall the thirteenth rather than the fifteenth century. This Gothic structure is, however, clothed in Renaissance forms, but not, as at St Pierre, covered with Italianate low reliefs. The ornament at St Eustache is, on the contrary, very simple, and the Italian impression depends only on the use of classical pilasters instead of Gothic. The Orders are, it is true, used in a way to horrify any classically trained architect. In some piers, for instance, the four main faces are decorated with Corinthian pilasters, the height of which is perhaps twenty times their breadth, and the corners of the pier are filled by three columns standing one on top of the other, all of somewhat bastard design. And yet, in spite of these eccentricities, the interior of St Eustache has a grandeur of space and proportions not to be found in any other sixteenth-century church in France. It is true that in these features it follows a medieval rather than a contemporary tradition, and it must also be noticed that the church was to have no influence on the general evolution of French architecture; but as an isolated work it remains of great importance.[14]

From the many additions made to existing buildings during this period one curious general feature emerges. Whereas decoration in the style of 1500–25 could be added to a Flamboyant Gothic building without any incongruity, as at St Pierre at Caen, the classical manner of the 1530s falls more readily into place in a context of Romanesque architecture. So, for instance, the strange tower added by Jean de l'Espine just before 1540 to the west front of Angers Cathedral, though it may be unhappy in its overcrowding, does not clash in style with the Romanesque façade. The same feature appears in a different way in the doors of St Michel at Dijon, built between 1537 and 1540 (Plate 21B). Seen from a distance these look like some kind of freak Romanesque porches with later detail added, although in fact they all date from the sixteenth century. It is typical of the increasing classicism of French architecture in the 1530s that it should be thus more closely related in character to Romanesque than to Late Gothic.

In certain French churches of this time we find additions made in a style directly deriving from Italy and without any real French admixture. Such, for instance, is the façade of the cathedral of Annecy (1535), which follows the style of Biagio Rossetti of Ferrara.[15] Another instance is the cylindrical chapel added to the cathedral of Vannes by archdeacon Jean Danielo in 1537.[16] Danielo had spent some years in Italy, and probably brought back designs based on the work of Antonio da Sangallo the elder, whose style seems to appear here, though coarsened by the execution of French masons.

After the return of Francis I from captivity French architecture makes a crucial advance towards freeing itself from Gothic influences. Certain medieval elements, such as the high-pitched roof, remain – and were indeed to remain for more than a century longer – but in general French style changes, so that borrowings from Italy can now be absorbed and not merely applied to the surface of what are still fundamentally Late Gothic buildings. A certain degree of simplicity and a respect for the surface of the wall bring French builders closer to their contemporaries in Italy, and, although they still do not seem to have understood the lesson of the High Renaissance in Italy, the way was opened for such an understanding by the next generation.

DECORATIVE SCULPTURE AND PAINTING
Rosso and the early work of Primaticcio

All the works which we have considered up till now, though they may have great charm and inventiveness, have been either hybrid or provincial. And it is not till we come to the style of decoration evolved at Fontainebleau in the 1530s that we find a real contribution being made in France to the main European artistic tradition. One must speak of a contribution made in France rather than a French contribution, for the artists responsible for the new manner are Italian; but the difference is that up till this moment the Italians who had settled in France and established their influence there had all been second-rate figures, whereas now two artists of real merit and of great invention appear on the scene. These are Giovanni Battista Rosso and Francesco Primaticcio.[17]

Much of the work which they carried out at Fontainebleau has been destroyed or ruined by injudicious restoration, but we can still form an idea of their achievement from the Galerie François I and the Chambre de la Duchesse d'Etampes, which survive, though much altered, and from drawings and engravings. In these two surviving rooms we see that brilliant combination of painted panels with stucco sculpture in full relief which is the characteristic of Fontainebleau decoration.

A word must be said first of the previous training of the two artists. Rosso was the elder and was born in Florence in 1494. In his extreme youth he seems to have been concerned with decorative painting, but his earliest surviving works are a series of religious pictures executed between 1517 and 1523, which express with great intensity the somewhat neurotic religious sentiment prevalent in some Florentine circles at that time. In 1523 he moved to Rome, where he turned to designing compositions of mythological subjects, which were engraved. At the Sack of 1527 he fled from Rome and spent three years moving from place to place, getting apparently into increasing difficulties from which he was saved by the summons to France in 1530. During these last years in Italy he was mainly occupied with paintings for churches, though he designed for Aretino the engraving of Mars and Venus which foreshadows to some extent the style which he was to develop in France.

Primaticcio's career was entirely different. He was born in Bologna in 1504 or 1505, and in 1526 joined the studio of Giulio Romano, who was engaged in decorating for the Gonzagas the Castello and the newly built Palazzo del Tè in Mantua. He stayed there till his departure for France early in 1532. Mantua was the ideal place for a young artist to receive training in decoration. Giulio Romano had transferred from Rome the tradition of mural painting and stucco work which had been created by Raphael, and he had been given by the Duke an opportunity of displaying his ability on the grand scale. We do not know exactly which rooms Primaticcio helped to decorate, but Vasari tells us that he executed the classical friezes in the Sala degli Stucchi in the Palazzo del Tè, and the old guides plausibly attribute to him the Sala di Cesare in the same building and the Sala d'Apollo in the ducal palace.[18] In any case, whether or not Primaticcio actually took part in the decoration of these particular rooms, he was able to watch the evolution of the decorative style of Giulio Romano and to learn a manner of combining painted with stucco decoration.

There is much doubt about the precise shares of Rosso and Primaticcio in the invention of the new manner. Most writers tend to give the credit to Rosso, chiefly on the grounds that he was the older artist, that he arrived first, that he was more highly paid, and that he had more assistants. But Vasari says explicitly, speaking of Primaticcio's arrival: 'And although the year before that the Florentine painter Rosso had gone into the service of the same King, as has been related, and had executed many works there, and in particular the pictures of Bacchus and Venus, Psyche and Cupid, nevertheless the first works in stucco that were done in France, and the first labours in fresco of any account, had their origin, it is said, from Primaticcio'.[19] It is intrinsically probable that Primaticcio rather than Rosso should have suggested the manner of combining painting with stucco, since he had been trained in this work, whereas Rosso was, as far as we know, trained as a painter only. Neither artist could have known in Italy exact models for the style evolved at Fontainebleau, for no decorative schemes of this kind appear to have been executed there before their departure. Those which come to mind as similar – the Sala Regia in the Vatican, the gallery in the Palazzo Spada, and certain rooms in the ducal palace in Venice – are all later.[20] The style current in Rome before 1530 was that practised by the studio of Raphael in the Sala dei Pontefici of the Vatican or in the Villa Madama, in which the relief was low and the disposition classical. In certain of the Mantuan rooms the relief is higher though the compartments are still rigid; but here Primaticcio could have found a model from which to evolve the more luxurious manner used at Fontaine-bleau.

It seems likely, therefore, that, although Rosso held the senior post at Fontainebleau, Primaticcio made a vital contribution to the style practised there. This should not be taken to mean that Rosso was lacking in originality, because when we examine the manner in which he applied the style we find that his work has great individuality and can be clearly distinguished from that of his colleague.

Rosso's main work, the Galerie François I, survives, whereas all the decoration executed by Primaticcio during Rosso's lifetime, that is to say, before 1540,[21] has perished except for the upper part of the fireplace from the Chambre de la Reine,[22] though we know something of his decoration of the Chambre du Roi and other rooms from his drawings. Probably both these groups of works were begun about 1533; Primaticcio's two rooms mentioned above were finished by 1537, and the gallery was apparently not quite finished at the time of Rosso's death.

Primaticcio's style, as it can be seen from his drawings for the Chambre du Roi and from the mantelpiece from the Chambre de la Reine (Plate 22B), is still connected with Mantua. The fruit swags on the mantelpiece recall those in the Sala del Zodiaco in the Palazzo del Tè, and the sphinxes are cousins of those in the Sala di Fetonte. The general design is classical in its emphasis on circular and square panels, but the proportions of the figures are elongated like those in the stuccos on the vault of the Sala degli Stucchi. The whole effect, moreover, is richer than anything to be seen in Mantua, mainly because of the higher relief.

In judging the Galerie François I (Plate 22A) we must remember that it has been seriously altered. Originally there were windows down both sides, except for one bay in the middle of each where a door opened into a small cabinet. The ceiling was lower by the height of the present cornice, so that the beams rested directly on the top of the stucco decoration. Apart from these structural alterations, the whole gallery was drastically restored under Louis Philippe, the paintings being entirely done afresh on the old designs and the panelling, that masterpiece of Francis I's best woodcarver, Scibec de Carpi, being replaced with new wood, presumably also following what was left of the old.

In spite of this, however, the gallery remains impressive as a decoration. In richness, variety, and ingenuity it has no predecessor and few successors. The walls are divided into two more or less equal parts, of which the lower is occupied by panelling and the upper by stucco and painting, a novel arrangement, but one which may be regarded as an extension of the deep frieze used in many Italian decorative schemes of the Quattrocento, such as the rooms of Isabella d'Este at Mantua. The spaces between the windows are all treated differently. Each has a central painted panel, but some are flanked by stucco figures, others by painted figures framed in stucco, and others by stucco cartouches. These plaster decorations again show great variety. In some the figures are Michelangelesque nudes (Plate 23), in others herms; some are dominated by *putti*, others by fruit garlands. Rosso's invention never flagged in producing new motives. But the hall-mark of the whole decoration is the use of strap-work, that singular form of decoration in which the stucco seems to be copied from pieces of leather rolled and folded and then cut into fantastic shapes. The origin of this device is not altogether clear, but Rosso probably derived it from Italian engravings.[23] But what had been merely a minor incident in a corner of a design is made by Rosso into a recurrent theme, worked into every part of the stucco. The success of this motive was enormous, and it was copied not only by French artists but all over Europe, first in Italy[24] and then in England, Flanders, and Germany, and so became a regular part of the vocabulary of Mannerist decoration.

The work of Fontainebleau must be classed as a variety of Mannerism and not of the High Renaissance style. It has nothing in common with the classical decoration of Raphael's *Loggie* or the Villa Madama. There stucco and painting are subordinated to the logic of the structure and follow the surface of the wall without interrupting it. Panels are enclosed in frames which themselves have simple geometrical forms; and the fields of stucco and paint are distinct. At Fontainebleau we find the opposite principles displayed. The wall surface is concealed behind the varied relief of stuccos; figures break over frames; cartouches disappear behind swags; the forms are complex rather than clear; everything tends towards ingenuity rather than logic. In fact France has passed from imitating a Late Quattrocento style in the earlier part of the reign to experimenting in Mannerist principles, skipping High Renaissance decoration just as she had skipped Bramante's style in architecture.

The decoration of the Galerie François I is purely Italian, but the room to which it is applied is quite different from the usual Italian form. This is the earliest surviving example of the Gallery which was to become a regular feature of French châteaux, and was also popular in England,[25] and it is sometimes argued that this essentially northern form is not suited to the decoration. But this argument is fallacious. It might be true that High Renaissance decoration would not fit a long, tunnel-like gallery of this kind, since it is designed to cover the surface of a classically proportioned room. But the variety of depth and design, which is one of the chief features of the Fontainebleau style, is admirably adapted to a long gallery to be read, so to speak, panel by panel, and to be seen often in sharp perspective.[26]

We shall follow the career of Primaticcio and study his later works at Fontainebleau in the next chapter, but Rosso's life closes with the year 1540, and of his other decorative work nothing remains. We need only add that he executed for the Constable Anne de Montmorency the 'Pietà' in the Louvre (Plate 24).[27] Since its recent cleaning this picture has recovered its startling but impressive colour, and shows that to the end of his career Rosso was still capable of rendering an intense and dramatic kind of religious emotion.

Many engravings were made of Rosso's designs during his lifetime and the years following his death, mainly by Domenico del Barbiere, Fantuzzi, and Boyvin, and these spread the knowledge of his style throughout France and abroad. It was mainly due to them that the influence was so extensive, not only in painting and engraving, but also in the decorative arts. Tapestries were woven after his designs, the most famous being the series after the panels in the Galerie François I, now in the Kunsthistorisches Museum in Vienna. These give perhaps a more complete idea than the Gallery itself in its damaged state of the original splendour of Fontainebleau.[28]

PORTRAIT PAINTING
Jean Clouet

Italian taste swept the board in architecture, sculpture, and decorative painting during the reign of Francis I, but in portrait-painting a completely different tradition prevailed. We have already seen that Perréal's portraiture, as far as we can judge it, was still deeply rooted in a local tradition, and the same is true of the great representative of this art in the next generation, Jean Clouet.

Much mystery surrounds this painter; we have few certain facts about him, and critics have shown little restraint in making up for this lack by ingenious hypotheses. The matter is still far from being cleared up, and it is intended to give here only those points on which there is general agreement.[29]

Jean Clouet, or Janet as he is often called, was not French by birth and remained a foreigner all his life, though his son was naturalized. His place of birth is not certainly established, but he may have been the son of Jan Cloet, a painter of Brussels, who is recorded as working for the Duke of Burgundy in 1475 and for the city of Brussels in 1499. He is first mentioned in a poem of Lemaire de Belges, written in 1509, in which he is praised in company with Gentile Bellini, Perugino, and Perréal. Perréal was the close friend of the poet, and it seems at least likely that Clouet, mentioned in the same breath, should also have been a member of this circle and so have known Perréal. From 1516 Clouet's name occurs in the royal accounts. At first he gets a lower wage than Perréal and Bourdichon, but, with the disappearance of the latter in 1523, his position rises and he appears as the equal of Perréal. The accounts mention him solely for portraits, but from other documents we know that he also executed religious paintings and even designed embroidery. In 1539 he is again praised, this time by Clément Marot and in even more extravagant terms, for he is mentioned as the equal of Michelangelo. He must have died soon after, for he is referred to as dead in a document of 1541.

The works which can be attributed to him with even a reasonable degree of probability are very few. A series of portrait-drawings, mostly at Chantilly, are traditionally attributed to him, and in the case of one there is external evidence to support the tradition. We know that Clouet painted the portrait of Guillaume Budé, and among the drawings is one which certainly represents him.[30] A painting now in the Metropolitan Museum is based on this drawing and is therefore presumably by Clouet.[31] Other drawings can be selected which are evidently by the same hand as the Budé, and they can therefore be attributed to the artist with reasonable certainty. One of these again is the basis for a painting, the 'Man with a Petrarch' at Windsor (Plate 27A), which, though damaged, is perhaps Clouet's most sensitive surviving painting. Other drawings substantiate the attribution to Clouet of the painting at Antwerp of the Dauphin Francis,[32] of the miniature of the Comte de Brissac in the Morgan library,[33] of the portrait of Mme de Canaples in the National Gallery of Scotland (Plate 25A), and of the miniatures of the Preux de Marignan in the manuscript of the *Commentaires des Guerres Galliques* (1519) in the Bibliothèque Nationale.[34]

With this relatively small amount of evidence it is difficult to form a clear idea of Jean Clouet's style. The paintings listed above are not all consistent in style and are not all related in their conception of form to the manner of the drawings with which they are connected. The 'Budé' and the 'Man with a Petrarch' are largely Flemish in inspiration, whereas the 'Mme de Canaples' and the 'Dauphin Francis' are larger and more abstract in their forms, like the drawings. The miniatures, owing to the difference of scale and medium, have naturally a character distinct from the other paintings. In fact, so great is the variety among these painted portraits, although the drawings on which they are based are all identical in style, that the possibility must be borne in mind that the drawings may have been used by other artists as the basis for painted portraits.[35] Alternatively, Clouet's style in painting may have changed markedly during his career; but as we have no exact dates to go on, this point cannot be established.[36]

When, however, we come to study the drawings (Plates 25–27), we find marked and consistent characteristics which are perhaps best brought out by a comparison with Holbein. Both artists are, of course, masters of observation in all that concerns the human face; but their methods of recording what they see could hardly be more different. Holbein relies above all on an outline which is both beautiful in itself and precisely expressive of character as it is shown in individual features. Clouet, on the other hand, seems hardly interested in the outline; it is generally softened by being worked over several times and in a drawing like the 'Unknown Man' (Plate 26) it has neither decorative nor descriptive quality. Clouet conceives the head primarily in terms of solid form, and not as a flat pattern on the paper to which modelling is later added. In this way his chalk portraits are nearer to Italian models than to Holbein, and it has been said that there is something almost Raphaelesque in their simplicity. Moreover, there is one technical device which serves this plastic conception and which can be directly linked with an Italian source. In all the drawings reproduced the modelling is achieved by a system of parallel diagonal shading strokes which break off where there is a light and begin again when there is a shadow. This simple method, which gives an almost geometrical quality to the modelling, is one used by Florentine artists in the Quattrocento and brought to perfection by Leonardo. The latter, it is true, makes the most effective use of it when he is working in silver point, but he also shades in this way with chalk.[37] It is quite possible that Clouet would have known drawings by Leonardo who brought with him to France the accumulation of his studio which he bequeathed to his pupil Melzi; but in any case this link with the great Italian master is an indication that Clouet's eyes were not, as is often said, turned entirely north, but that in his grasp of form he is in many ways nearer to Italy than to Flanders, and that he must count as one of the few French artists who understood the aims of the High Renaissance.

CHAPTER 3

THE CLASSICAL PERIOD OF THE SIXTEENTH CENTURY
1540 – 1565

HISTORICAL BACKGROUND

THE middle decades of the sixteenth century in France showed a remarkable flowering in all intellectual fields. Writers and artists began to free themselves from the tutelage of Italy, and individual figures appear whose art is not only classical but genuinely French. Ronsard and the Pléiade on the one hand, Philibert de l'Orme and Goujon on the other, created the first really original and independent movements since the Renaissance had touched France.

All these activities are centred round the Court even more completely than before. In culture as in politics the centralization of France continued during the last years of Francis I and the reign of Henry II. We have already seen the attempts of the former to gather the whole power of the State into his own hands, and though his son was personally less active in this way, and indeed played little visible part in public affairs, the politicians who ruled France for him – Montmorency and the Guises – continued the policy of Francis and carried absolutism to a further point. The same was true of religion. The Crown now firmly identified itself with the cause of Catholicism, and, although the Protestant party grew greater in number and more efficient in organization, repression by the Government also grew in intensity, with the result that more and more supporters of the Reformation left France to take refuge in Geneva.

In literature the years round 1550 are marked by the birth of the new classicism. Du Bellay's *Deffense et Illustration de la langue françoyse* (1549), the first four books of Ronsard's Odes (1550), and Jodelle's tragedy *Cléopâtre* (1552) were the manifestos of the new movement which took the name of the Pléiade. Ronsard is the most typical figure of the period. He was a firm but not a fanatical Catholic, a monarchist, many of whose finest odes glorify the King, and a passionate believer in the glory of his country, which he set forth in his most ambitious, if not his best poem, the *Franciade*. He was soaked in Greek and Latin literature, but was not a pedant; he knew the Italian poets and learnt much from them, but without ever imitating them slavishly, because a vital article of his faith was that the French language was in itself as splendid as Latin or Italian, and that his business was to write essentially French poetry. He created new forms of verse capable of expressing ideas and feelings hitherto untouched by French poets. In his didactic Odes his ideas are clear and nobly expressed; in his shorter lyrics real feeling is compressed into the strictest forms. France had not before him produced a writer of genius who expressed himself within the conventions of classical poetry.

A similar spirit of inventiveness and independence appears in the visual arts. Fontaine-bleau continued to be the King's favourite residence, and it was there that the new style reached its finest flowering under Primaticcio. It was there also that were displayed the works of art which Francis had obtained from Italy. Among the most important for the future of French art were the bronze casts made from the moulds which Primaticcio brought back from Rome after his journey of 1540. Through these casts French artists were able for the first time to study such famous ancient statues as the 'Laocoon', the 'Apollo Belvedere', and the 'Marcus Aurelius', as well as the reliefs from Trajan's Column. A few original antiques were at Fontainebleau, and the 'Diana', now in the Louvre, was to be seen in the house of the Duchesse d'Étampes at Meudon. Modern sculpture was also represented, and, in addition to the marble 'Hercules' by Michel-angelo already mentioned, there were casts of his 'Pietà' in St Peter's and of his 'Christ' in S. Maria sopra Minerva. Among paintings, the most celebrated were Michelangelo's 'Leda', several works by Raphael and his studio, including the 'Belle Jardinière', the big 'St Michael', the 'Holy Family of Francis I', and the 'Joanna of Aragon', Titian's portrait of the King, and Leonardo's 'Mona Lisa', 'Virgin of the Rocks', and 'Virgin and Child with St Anne'. There was enough, in fact, to make it not unreasonable, allow-ing for the normal level of court flattery at the time, for Vasari to say that Fontainebleau had become a second Rome.

Under Henry II patronage and collecting continued, but, as in politics, the King him-self played little part. He seems to have taken a personal interest in the rebuilding of the Louvre, but the real dictator in this field was Diane de Poitiers, a woman of great intelli-gence and a good patron of Philibert de l'Orme, who built Anet for her and enlarged Chenonceau. The great nobles who were active in the conduct of government under Henry II also played their part in the arts: Montmorency at Écouen and Chantilly, the Guises at Meudon and in their Paris hôtel, and St. André at Vallery. In certain provinces, particularly in the east of France and in the south-west, independent centres of activity sprang up, but in general the style of the court was accepted as the standard for the whole of France. Henry II was, in fact, inaugurating in the arts the policy which was to be carried to its fullest development by Louis XIV.

ARCHITECTURE
Serlio, Lescot, Philibert de l'Orme, Primaticcio

The years 1540 and 1541 are crucial in the history of French architecture. In the latter year Primaticcio returned from his visit to Rome, bringing Vignola with him; in 1540 or 1541 Sebastiano Serlio was called to France by the King, and about the same time Philibert de l'Orme settled in Paris after his training in Italy. In these two years, there-fore, a new wave of Italian influence was felt in France; and, further, the style which was now brought back from the south was very different from that which had come in dur-ing the earlier part of the century. For the first time French architects became aware of the achievements of the High Renaissance in Italy, and the examples of Bramante,

Peruzzi, and Sansovino were held up to them. Meanwhile the study of Vitruvius had been spreading in France, where editions of his work had become available. These two influences combined to exercise pressure in the direction of classicism and, since the general state of mind among French artists and intellectuals was receptive to such an influence, they took root and produced the first great period of French classical architecture.

Of the artists mentioned above, Vignola is the least important in relation to France, since at the time of his visit his career as an architect had not yet begun and he came in the capacity of a technician, principally to help in the casting of bronzes from the moulds after ancient sculpture which Primaticcio had brought from Rome. We have no further record of his activities in France.

As is so often the case with Italian artists abroad, the less talented man exercised the greater influence, and it is to Sebastiano Serlio, not to Vignola, that we must look to find the main channel of Italian influence in France at this time.

Serlio was born at Bologna in 1475.[1] After a preliminary training in this town he moved to Rome, where he is traceable from 1514 till the Sack of 1527 as a pupil of Peruzzi, who bequeathed to him all his plans and sketches, of which Serlio later made extensive use. The years 1527–40 seem to have been mainly spent in Venice, partly in actual building, of which little trace remains, and partly in the preparation of the treatise on architecture. The first section to be published was the fourth book, which appeared in 1537. Serlio sent a copy to Francis I through Georges d'Armagnac, Bishop of Rodez and ambassador in Venice, asking at the same time to be taken into the French King's service. The latter promised a gift of 300 crowns, which seems to have been slow in arriving, but, in spite of this, Serlio dedicated the next section, Book 3, to the King when it was published in 1540. This apparently produced the intended effect, and Serlio was called to France and put in charge of the building operations at Fontainebleau.[2] His position in relation to the royal palaces is not altogether clear, but he seems to have acted primarily in an advisory capacity, and none of the executed buildings can be attributed to him. Meanwhile he continued work on his treatise, of which Books 1 and 2 appeared in 1545, Book 5 in 1547, and an *Extraordinario Libro* in 1551. Books 6, 7, and 8 were still unpublished at the time of his death in 1554.

During his time in France Serlio seems to have carried out only two buildings: the house of the Cardinal of Ferrara at Fontainebleau, known as 'Le Grand Ferrare', of which only the gate survives, and the château of Ancy-le-Franc near Tonnerre in Burgundy. In addition, he made designs, which were not executed, for the rebuilding of the Louvre, for a pavilion and a *loggia* at Fontainebleau, for a merchants' *loggia* or stock-exchange at Lyons, and for a château in Provence.[3]

These works, executed or designed, were of great importance for the later development of French architecture, but in certain ways Serlio's influence was even greater through his treatise, which was issued in many editions and was translated into most European languages.

Serlio's treatise enjoyed this success because of its entirely new plan. Previous writings on architecture – and they were not many – had been almost purely theoretical. Vitruvius had gone through many editions, some illustrated, and had already been the subject of learned exegesis. Alberti's *Architecture* was lighter reading but still in the first place theoretical, and it was not illustrated till the edition of 1550. Serlio planned to produce for the first time an illustrated handbook for architects. His aim was essentially practical, and the value of the book was to depend more on its plates than on its text. It was to be a pattern book in which the architect could find solutions for all sorts of problems.

Serlio's practical aim appears in every part of the treatise. The first two books deal with geometry and perspective, which are essential to the architect, if he is to be distinguished from the mere builder. On the other hand, Serlio warns the reader that he is going to avoid all theoretical speculation on these two branches of mathematics, and will concentrate instead on their practical application. Book 3 contains plates and descriptions of the finest works of ancient architecture, to which Serlio adds some of the most important modern buildings by Bramante and Raphael. Such models are useful for architects living far from Rome, either in France, which Serlio already had in mind as his goal, or in Venice, where he actually composed this book. Book 4 deals with the five Orders, but without the erudite detail which the commentators on Vitruvius loved. Book 5 shows twelve designs for churches, mostly of ingenious forms, circular, oval, polygonal, or variants of the Latin cross. The real Book 6 dealt with palaces, but it was left in manuscript,[4] and the old collected editions put in its place the *Extraordinario Libro*, containing fifty designs for doors according to the different Orders. Book 7 is concerned with *Accidenti*, or miscellaneous problems which may present themselves to the architect. These include, for instance, plans for houses on irregular sites, designs for chimneys, schemes for systematizing older and asymmetrical buildings. Finally Book 8 was devoted to military architecture. Each book consists primarily of a series of plates to which the text acts as a commentary. In the early folio editions the woodcuts are of excellent quality, but the later quartos are illustrated with coarse reduced copies, of which the blocks are often ruined by overprinting.

Serlio was not an artistic genius, but he had one quality which must have helped towards his success in France: he was extremely adaptable. In fact he is in this way an exception to most of the Italian artists who went abroad in the sixteenth century, for his style grew more and more French the longer he stayed north of the Alps. This can be seen in his treatise as well as in his executed works.

Naturally the two books published before his removal to France are entirely Italian in character. His main sources are ancient remains and the work of modern Roman architects such as Bramante, but many of the designs are clearly Venetian in origin and show the influence of Sansovino. Books 1 and 2, published in 1545, only deal with architecture incidentally, but the buildings which appear in them are almost all Italianate in feeling, and Book 2 ends with three plates giving Peruzzi's designs for the tragic, comic, and satirical stage. The preface to the *Extraordinario Libro* warns us that we may expect a change, for in it Serlio apologizes for the freedom of the designs which it contains, excusing himself on the grounds that men naturally like novelty and asking the reader to remember in what country he is working. He adds that he purposes not to wander far from the precepts of Vitruvius, to whom be all praise. But when we look at the plates we cannot help feeling that the Roman architect would hardly have approved the fantastic designs with which we are presented. Some of the doors are still irregular in an Italian way, making play with complicated rustication in the manner of Giulio Romano. Others exploit a broken silhouette in a more Venetian style. But some are altogether personal in their licence as for instance the Ionic door in Figure 4. Instead of columns running up to the entablature supporting the pediment, this design shows them stopping at the spring of the arch, so that Serlio has to fill in the upper part of the sides with another Order of diminutive columns, in quite incorrect proportion to the Order

Figure 4. Serlio: Ionic Door, from the Sixth Book

below. Above this second Order are two decorative panels incorporating the crescent moon of Henry II or Diane de Poitiers, and in the middle is a simple pediment raised un-expectedly on a rectangular insertion, in which is an oblong panel. The whole door is thus broken up into loosely related fragments in a manner quite contrary to the principles of High Renaissance design. Other plates in the book are even more fanciful, but this one has been chosen because it happens to have been imitated closely by a French architect, Lescot, in the château of Vallery.[5]

In the true sixth and in the seventh book the French influence is more tangibly apparent. In the preface to Book 7 Serlio explicitly states that he is going to present some designs 'in the Italian manner' and others 'according to French custom'. When, for instance, he deals with fireplaces he gives two sets, one in a more or less Venetian style, and the other with picturesque French forms. In the same way the designs for windows include some which are of traditional classical type and others which represent Serlio's version of the French dormer. Many of the elevations of houses include the high-pitched French roof, which the author praises in the text for its practical value.

Serlio's later style as we see it in the illustrations to the last books is a curious mixture. The Italian manner which he brought with him to France was in itself not purely classical. Although he greatly admired Bramante, his real master in Rome was Peruzzi, who was less Vitruvian in outlook, and was notable for the ingenuity of his planning rather than for the correctness of his elevations. Further, Serlio's style was affected by his stay in northern Italy, and in Venice he picked up many tricks which tended to make his manner less Bramantesque, so that he came to France with a style freer and more picturesque than was normal in Rome at this time. It stands apart from the main stream of Italian Mannerism, since Serlio seems to have been quite unaffected by the element of conflict in the work of men like Michelangelo or Giulio Romano, and his deviations from Bramantesque classicism are rather towards a general enrichment of outline and detail. This tendency was fortified by the influences to which he was subjected in France, and his later designs mark an important stage in the development towards the style which is commonly called French Mannerism.

Of the two works which he actually carried out in France, the 'Grand Ferrare' (built 1544–6) has disappeared except for the entrance door, but we know its general character from drawings and engravings, most accurately from the drawing in the Columbia manuscript (Figure 7). The house consisted of a main block, or *corps-de-logis*, containing a single flight of rooms, from which stretched forwards two narrower wings, one with minor rooms and the other with a gallery. The court thus formed was closed by a wall, broken in the middle by the door which still stands. This plan was in one sense an adaptation of the design of Bury to a town house, but in another way it was an Italianate, regularized version of earlier French town houses, such as the Hôtel de Bernuy at Toulouse or the Hôtel d'Écoville at Caen, where the main *corps-de-logis* faced on a court closed on one or two sides by a screen wall. It is of great importance since it remained an almost standard form for the hôtel for more than a century. As far as we can judge, the building was simple in appearance, with a single slightly raised floor, covered by a high roof in the French manner. In one scheme, recorded in the Munich manuscript, Serlio proposed to add to the *corps-de-logis* an open portico, which was no doubt condemned as not suitable to the climate of Fontainebleau. In front of it was to be a terrace, in the middle of which Serlio introduced Bramante's circular steps for the Belvedere, a theme which he uses in several of his engraved plates.

The château of Ancy-le-Franc (Plate 28) survives complete, though it underwent many alterations during the period when Serlio was in charge of the building and some after his death. The building was probably begun in 1546, the date cut over the door on the south front, and Serlio's original designs are preserved in the Columbia manuscript (Figures 5 and 6). These show an entirely Italianate building with rusticated ground floor and four low square towers at the corners, in the manner of early Renaissance villas on the Venetian mainland. Along the middle section of the main storey ran an order of Doric pilasters enclosing an alternating series of windows and niches. Above this and below the low roof was an arcade, almost like a machicolation, which Serlio tells us was the personal invention of the owner, who later gave it up, perhaps under pressure from the architect. Two sides of the court were composed of double *loggie*, conspicuously north Italian in character and suggesting models by Falconetti.[6] In the Munich manuscript Serlio tells us that after the building was begun the owner decided to decorate it with pilasters on all

Figure 5. Serlio: Ancy-le-Franc: North Front

the floors, and we therefore know that this important change was made during the architect's lifetime and under his direction. It was accompanied by other changes for which he is almost certainly also responsible and which appear in the engravings of du Cerceau published in 1576. These include the abandoning of the niches in the bays between the windows. Later these bays were pierced with windows, producing the present arrangement. Another alteration for which Serlio is probably responsible is the addition of the high roof with dormers. At the same time the arrangement of the court was changed, the

Figure 6. Serlio: Ancy-le-Franc: Section

number of the bays was reduced, and the regular repetition of an arch was replaced by the motif of Bramante's Belvedere with its more varied disposition of double pilasters enclosing a niche between the arches. The result of these alterations was that the building ceased to be a masculine design, a real Italian *castello*, and became almost effeminate in its delicacy. At the same time it became markedly French, with its high roof and the flat patterning of the walls, which is familiar from châteaux such as Villandry.[7]

43

Of the various designs made by Serlio for specific buildings but never carried out, one must be mentioned. The Columbia manuscript contains a plan for a palace of the King, and this can be shown to be a project for the rebuilding of the Louvre, which Francis I had been considering since 1527. The plan was apparently rejected in favour of Lescot's, but indirectly it exercised an influence as great as his, because it contains the germs of those ideas for the completion of the building which were to be discussed for several centuries to come, and when we have to consider the various projects put up to Louis XIV we shall find that even then Serlio's plan was not forgotten, and that some architects were ready to borrow from it more than they admitted.

Serlio played an important part in the development of French architecture, because he accustomed the French to the idiom of the early sixteenth-century Italian masters. But his artistic personality was not strong enough to impose a style on the country of his

Figure 7. Serlio: Le Grand Ferrare: Plan

adoption. His treatise was used, so to speak, as a dictionary by many architects, particularly in the provinces, but, though they often copied the individual words, they had no idea how to put them together to form a sentence. For instance, the picturesque screens enclosing the forecourt of the château of Fleury-en-Bière are mainly composed of elements lifted from Serlio's engravings, but nothing could be more provincial or less Italian than the result produced by the French architect.[8] In a town like Toulouse, where the general understanding of architecture was higher, the borrowings are more intelligent, and Bachelier's door to the Capitole, for instance, now in the Jardin des Plantes, is a very competent version of one of Serlio's models.

*

The two great French architects of the middle of the sixteenth century, Pierre Lescot and Philibert de l'Orme, form a remarkable contrast. De l'Orme was primarily an engineer, with a love of ingenious structure and with great inventiveness in plans and architectural forms. Lescot's art was essentially decorative, and it is significant that in all his major works he appears as the close collaborator of the greatest sculptor of the time, Jean Goujon.

Lescot (born between 1500 and 1515, died 1578) was a quite different kind of man from the Le Bretons and the Chambiges, the master masons of the earlier part of the century. He came from a well-to-do legal family, and from his youth gave himself up to the study of mathematics, architecture, and painting, so that, unlike his French predecessors, he was a man of general education and of learning. There is no documentary evidence to show that he visited Italy in his youth, though he seems to have been sent to Rome on an official mission in 1556, that is to say after the completion of all the buildings which we know to be by him. The style of his work tends to confirm the view that he did not cross the Alps earlier, for though his designs are in many respects classical they show no specific likeness to Italian models, and they lack conspicuously the monumentality which was the mark of Roman architecture in the generation after Bramante. It seems much more likely that Lescot derived his knowledge of architecture from the study of illustrated books on the subject, with perhaps some first-hand contact with Roman remains in France.

Lescot's reputation rests mainly on his rebuilding of the Louvre. Of his other works the screen of St Germain l'Auxerrois (1554) has been destroyed, except for some of Goujon's reliefs preserved in the Louvre; the Hôtel Carnavalet (c. 1545–50) has been altered three times since his death; the Fontaine des Innocents (1547–9) has been totally reconstructed, and the château of Vallery is only a fragment.[9] The façade of the Square Court of the Louvre, on the other hand, survives complete, though many of the decorative reliefs have been recut. The story of this building has been worked out in the greatest detail,[10] but we need only notice here the principal stages of its construction.

In 1527 Francis I declared himself dissatisfied with the medieval palace of the Louvre and announced his intention of rebuilding it on up-to-date lines. He pulled down the keep which blocked a great part of the Square Court of the old château, but for many years nothing more was done. In 1546, however, he commissioned Lescot to erect a new building on the site of the west wing of the old château. Lescot's first project was to build a *corps-de-logis* of two floors only with a projecting central pavilion in which he placed the staircase. On either side of this there was to be a big room for public occasions. During the following five years, however, the plan and elevation were both altered. The staircase was moved to the north end of the wing, leaving space for a single much grander *salle* on each floor; but this move necessitated the addition of two more projecting pavilions at the ends, one of which had to house the new staircase. Finally the façade was heightened by the addition of an extra floor (Plate 29A), perhaps in order that the wing might not be overpowered in the view from the outside by another new building, the Pavillon du Roi, which had been added in the south-west corner facing the river. Originally the plan had only been to rebuild this one wing or at most to carry on the same scheme round the existing court; but at some date between 1551 and the death of Henry II in 1559 it was almost certainly decided to embark on a more ambitious plan and to build a court enclosed by blocks double the length of Lescot's executed wing. This plan was not carried out till the reigns of Louis XIII and Louis XIV, but all the documents of this later period give the credit of the original idea for the extension to the architect of Henry II, that is to say, Lescot.

In the context of French architecture of the middle of the 1540s the first feature which strikes one about Lescot's façade is its classicism. The Orders are of a correctness undreamt of by Le Breton, and though Serlio was in theory capable of producing such accurate imitations of antiquity, he had not apparently done so in practice. But, having noticed this correctness of detail, we are at once almost equally struck with the un-Italian character of the whole design. If we compare Lescot's front with the closest parallel in contemporary Roman architecture, Sangallo's court of the Palazzo Farnese, the contrast is startling.[11] The Roman building depends for its effect on simple masses of almost undecorated masonry, on the exact repetition of a standard arch along each floor, and on the clear demarcation of one floor from the next by the unbroken horizontal lines of the entablatures. Lescot's design has none of these qualities and in some cases displays their exact opposites. The effect is one of ornamental beauty rather than of monumentality. Apart from the pavilions, the façade is entirely articulated with pilasters and not with half-columns, and these pilasters are of the most decorative Orders, Corinthian and Composite, in contrast to the Doric and Ionic of the Farnese Palace. The pediments over the windows are alternately straight and rounded and are filled with reliefs.

Still more different is the general disposition of the façade. Lescot has carefully avoided the exact repetition on which Sangallo relies. The pavilions differ from the wings joining them, and each pavilion is itself divided into a wide central bay and two narrow flanking ones. Each floor has, further, a different system of fenestration; on the ground floor segment-headed windows[12] set behind round-headed arches; on the first floor pedimented openings; and in the attic windows crowned with crossed torches. Again, the pavilions have windows different from those in the rest of the façade. Finally notice how deliberately Lescot breaks the horizontals and emphasizes the verticals. Not one of the horizontal mouldings is allowed to run unbroken through the whole width of the front. On the ground floor the base of each pilaster breaks forward, whereas the entablature only does so in the pavilions, where, however, it has a return in the middle bay. On the first floor the pilasters rest on a more or less continuous base, except in the pavilions,[13] and the entablature breaks forward for the pavilions but does not return in the middle, as on the ground floor. On the other hand, the three pavilions form marked vertical elements, emphasized by the lines of the double columns which carry the eye upwards almost as in the façade of Fontaine-Henri.[14] In fact the triple repetition of the pavilion seems to be an echo, probably unconscious, of the late medieval château façade divided by three round towers, to be seen for instance at Josselin or Martainville. There is thus in this design a mixture of classical features with others which derive from the French tradition; but here the two elements are for the first time fused, so that it is possible to talk of Lescot's style as a form of French classicism, having its own principles and its own harmony.

The decoration of the interior of the new wing of the Louvre was also revolutionary. The *salle* on the ground floor was ornamented at one end with a gallery supported by Goujon's four caryatids, a form hitherto almost unknown in France and not, so far as I can trace, used on a monumental scale even by Italian Renaissance architects.[15] Lescot was no doubt inspired to use them by the description in Vitruvius, and he may also have seen them either in illustrated editions of his works or in Italian engravings, such as that by

Marc' Antonio based on Pierino del Vaga's decorations on the lower parts of the walls in the Stanze.[16]

At the south end of the *salle* a bay was cut off and formed into the Tribunal, which was separated from the main room by sixteen Doric columns, arranged in groups of four. As usual with Lescot, these columns are richly decorated, but they have a monumentality rare in his work.[17] In both these designs, as well as in the façade itself, the decoration was executed by Goujon, and there is little doubt that the sculptor must have been a collaborator with the architect on more or less equal terms, so that it is hard to say where the share of one ends and the other begins. The question is, however, hardly a real one; for Lescot's architecture was perfectly conceived to display sculpture, and Goujon's reliefs or caryatids were planned to decorate a building, so that the two men worked in full harmony, almost as one mind.

In one case we find Lescot using another collaborator. This is for the wooden ceiling in the *Chambre* of Henry II, that is to say the King's bedroom in which all State business was carried on. This ceiling survives, though moved to one of the rooms behind Perrault's colonnade, and it marks an epoch in French interior decoration. Previous ceilings had been of the traditional French pattern with beams running across them, decorated usually with painted motives. But in the ceiling for the Louvre Lescot and his Italian wood-carver, Scibec de Carpi, have rivalled the most elaborate southern designs of the period, even those of Venice. We can be certain that the design is here due to Lescot and not to the carver, partly because the documents indicate it,[18] and partly because Scibec de Carpi's other work, such as the panelling in the Galerie François I at Fontainebleau, based on Rosso's patterns, or the ceiling in the Salle de Bal of the same palace designed by Philibert de l'Orme, are entirely different in character.

Lescot is almost certainly responsible for the Hôtel Carnavalet begun *c.* 1545, the only example of a Paris house which survives from the middle of the century (Plate 29B).[19] The building has been much altered, but certain parts of the original survive: the main façade on the court with the sculptures of the four seasons from the studio of Goujon, the turrets which flank it, and the entrance, also decorated by Goujon. From the contract of 1548 it appears that the gallery along the left-hand side of the court was not built as early as the main block, but it was probably part of the original scheme. It was originally covered by a high-pitched roof with dormers, and the present first floor was added in the seventeenth century by François Mansart.[20]

In its general plan the Carnavalet follows Serlio's 'Grand Ferrare', except that the side towards the street is closed by a block containing stables and kitchen instead of a simple wall. The most interesting feature is the decoration of the façade on the court with Goujon's reliefs. This arrangement, which was to be widely followed later in Paris,[21] was not entirely new, since it is found in the earlier Hôtel d'Écoville at Caen. Goujon spent his early years in Normandy, and it may be that he knew this building and suggested the idea to Lescot.

There are still many points about the career and achievement of Lescot which need clarifying. Of his personality we know almost nothing, and even our records of his professional career are very incomplete. We have no evidence of his activity before 1544, and after the death of Henry II in 1559 he again disappears, though he lived nearly twenty years longer. But his position is assured as one of those who laid the foundations of the classical tradition of French architecture which was to produce its greatest representatives in the seventeenth century.

*

Lescot is, however, overshadowed by the figure of Philibert de l'Orme, beside whom he seems no more than a talented amateur. De l'Orme is the first French architect to have something of the universality of the great Italians. He combines the engineering skill of the French mason with the learning of the Renaissance artist. Like Lescot, he is classical without being merely an imitator of the Italians; but whereas Lescot can only play in one key, Philibert is master of a vast range of harmony.

He was born in Lyons, probably about 1510, and was the son of a master-mason. About 1533 he visited Rome, where he apparently spent three years. There he was noticed by Marcello Cervini, later Pope Marcellus II, and also by Cardinal du Bellay, who was at that time in Rome, accompanied by his secretary, François Rabelais. After three years spent in studying, measuring, and even excavating the antiquities of Rome and, we may suppose, enjoying the conversation of the humanists whom he must have met through the Cardinal, we find him back in Lyons in 1536. Here he executed his first known work, the house of Antoine Bullioud.[22] About 1540 he was called to Paris by du Bellay, who commissioned him to build a château at St Maur-lès-Fossés, near Charenton. Through the Cardinal he was introduced to the circle of the Dauphin and Diane de Poitiers, and in 1547 he was commissioned by the latter to build her château at Anet, which was completed about 1552.[23] When the Dauphin ascended the throne as Henry II de l'Orme was immediately appointed superintendent of buildings, and during the whole reign he remained the most powerful figure in the arts in France. For the King he designed the tomb of Francis I at St Denis, a chapel at Villers-Cotteret, and the Château-Neuf at St Germain. On the death of Henry II he was immediately dismissed, and seems for a short time to have been exposed to serious maltreatment from his enemies, of whom he had made many by his arrogance.[24] After four or five years, however, he was again taken into favour by the Queen Mother, Catherine de' Medici, who ordered him to build the palace of the Tuileries and to prepare new plans for completing St Maur, which she had bought from the heirs of Cardinal du Bellay.

During his years of disgrace he composed two works on architecture from which we learn much about him as a man and as an architect. The first, entitled *Nouvelles Inventions pour bien bastir et à petits frais* (1561), was a practical treatise on the construction of vaults and roofs and embodies the engineering aspect of Philibert's thought. The other and much more considerable work, the *Architecture*, in nine books was published in 1567. It was to have been followed by a second volume dealing with Divine Proportion, but Philibert was prevented from publishing this by his death in 1570.[25]

De l'Orme naturally makes use in the composition of his treatise of the obvious models, Vitruvius and Alberti. But his work is original both in plan and in treatment. It is not so speculative as Alberti, nor is it a mere illustrated compendium like Serlio. It combines the theoretical and practical aspects of architecture in a remarkable manner. The main reason for this seems to be that the author writes from his own personal experience. He emphasizes this point explicitly, and throughout the book he quotes in support of his suggestions some work which he has executed or some incident, often disagreeable, which has happened to him in connexion with a patron or a mason. This personal element gives freshness and solidity to his writing and prevents him from ever copying, parrot-like, Vitruvius or any other authority. On the other hand, the book is not solely made up of reminiscences or of practical hints; for Philibert was a man of education, with a desire to find a rational basis for his art. But here again his approach is personal and the theory is deduced from experience and observation.

His attitude appears in the general plan of the treatise. The first two books deal entirely with practical questions, such as the relations of the architect to the patron, the choice of the site, the effect of climate. The third and fourth are concerned with arithmetic and geometry, but again from a strictly practical point of view, to enable the architect to make good plans, to work out the structure of vaults, to use a plumb line, and so on. Books 5 to 7 are devoted to the Orders, and the last two books cover architectural details and decorative features such as doors, windows, and mantelpieces.[26] It is apparent from this arrangement that de l'Orme gives priority to the practical side of architecture, and he tells us this explicitly on several occasions: 'It would be much better, in my opinion, for the architect to fail in the ornamentation of the columns, in the proportions and in the treatment of façades (to which those who proclaim themselves architects devote most study) rather than that he should desert Nature's excellent rules which concern the comfort, convenience, and advantage of the inhabitants, and not the decoration, beauty, and richness of houses, made only to please the eye, and not for any benefit to the health and life of men.'[27]

But if the architect must bear in mind practical considerations, he should always act according to the dictates of reason, and not blindly without knowing what he is doing. Philibert attacks those who pile up ornament 'without reason, proportion, or measure, and more often by mere chance, without being able to say why they did it'.[28] Therefore the architect must be equipped with some theoretical knowledge. He should know the relevant parts of mathematics, have some notion of natural philosophy or, as we should say, science, and a smattering of music so that he can deal with questions of acoustics. On the other hand, de l'Orme differs from Vitruvius in that he does not consider it necessary for the architect to be versed in law or rhetoric. Here again we see his practical sense leading him to disagree even with the most revered of authorities.

The architect and the patron must plan everything before they actually start building. The patron must consider whether he can afford to erect the projected house, whether it is suitable to his station, and whether its upkeep will ruin him. He must then select his architect with care, but having chosen him he must give him a free hand, not interfere with him at every step, and not change his plans as the building grows.[29] The architect must work out his plans and models in detail before he actually starts, so that the patron may know exactly what is proposed and so that the cost of the building can be accurately estimated. In preparing these models and plans he must beware of using painters who embellish the architect's true plans, and so give a false impression to the patron.[30] As far as possible the architect must lay in a store of materials in advance so that he may not be compelled to change in the middle of the operations.[31] On one point Philibert is very firm, coming back to it continually, namely that the architect must resist if possible the idea of incorporating in his projected building fragments of older work existing on the site.[32] He quotes his own difficulties in this matter at Anet, and he may also have been thinking of the confusion introduced into so many of the buildings of the earlier part of the century, such as Fontainebleau, by the patching up and extension of earlier work. On the other hand, he is not adamant on this point, and in Book 3 puts forward an ingenious plan for regularizing a château of which two older parts survive.[33] But he does this only under protest, again advising the architect to avoid the problem if possible.

After considering these basic practical matters, Philibert goes on to the question of ornament. This he admits is necessary but it must above all be applied properly, 'as is necessary and reasonable', not merely to give an effect of richness. Generally speaking, he is opposed to richness of either decoration or material, except in the case of a royal palace or a public building to which it is appropriate.[34] In particular he is against the reckless use of marble, and laughs at those who think that nothing worth while can be built except in Italian marbles. He maintains, on the contrary, that the different kinds of stone to be found in France are as good as marbles brought from Italy and more suitable to the climate of the country.[35]

This is an instance of de l'Orme's national pride, which is an underlying theme in the whole of his writings. His independence of Italy and even of the ancients is one aspect of this, and he constantly attacks those who blindly follow these models, pointing out incidentally that in so doing they often fall into the trap of copying a good original for use in a different setting or on a different scale, which makes it look ridiculous.[36] But there is a more positive side to this doctrine. Philibert sets up by implication a standard which was new in France, that of reason as opposed to conformity to a model, classical or Italian. He judges every problem on the basis of his own experience and understanding, learning what he can from his predecessors but not following them blindly. This independence of mind makes him a worthy contemporary to the poets of the Pléiade, and a true representative of the first period in which France may be said to have produced her own classical style. We shall see that it is as much a characteristic of his buildings as of his writings.

His independence, his national feeling, and his practical sense all appear in their clearest form in the section of the treatise in which de l'Orme puts forward his proposal for a new French Order to be added to the five Orders of Greece and Rome.

His argument is double, theoretical and practical. On the theoretical side he argues that the Greeks and Romans invented Orders which satisfied their particular needs, so why should not the French, an equally great nation, invent an Order in accordance with their problems? The practical argument is also cogent. The Greek and Roman Orders were invented in countries in which marble is the natural material, whereas in France most buildings are made of stone. Now, it is difficult to obtain a shaft of stone long enough to make a large column in a single piece, and, further, in a shaft of this length stone will not bear the strain put on it. Therefore, generally speaking, stone columns have to be built in drums laid one on top of the other. The disadvantage of this is that the joints between the drums are visible and are disfiguring to the columns. De l'Orme therefore proposes a French Order in which the column is broken at intervals by bands of horizontal decoration which serve to cover these joints. Finally he extends the idea by applying it to the classical Orders and illustrates French versions of, for instance, the Doric and Ionic Orders,[37] distinguished from their classical prototypes by the bands of decoration round them.

When we come to examine the works actually carried out by Philibert de l'Orme we find the same qualities as in his writings. Unfortunately almost all that he built has been destroyed, and apart from sections of Anet and the tomb of Francis I, we have to rely on engravings.

The château of St Maur, probably begun in 1541 (Plate 31A), has not the individuality of his mature works, but taken in its context it is an important, even a revolutionary building. Philibert himself boasts, not unreasonably, that it was the first building in France 'to show how the proportions and measures of architecture should be observed',[38] and it is certainly true that it set a new standard of classicism for its date, which was, we must remember, the year of Serlio's arrival in France. The original plan and elevations are given in the treatise,[39] but only the main corps-de-logis was carried out according to them.[40] The design is reminiscent of the Palazzo de Tè, in that it consists of one floor only and that the rooms are arranged in a single suite round a square court. But it follows the French tradition in that the side opposite the corps-de-logis is lower than the other three and that the two wings at right angles to it project beyond it to form pavilions on the main façade. On the garden side de l'Orme planned a horseshoe staircase leading up to the first floor, the earliest example of this form in France. The elevations were simple. Round the court ran a single Order of coupled Corinthian pilasters, and in the middle of each side was a door flanked by columns.[41] Over the main door to the corps-de-logis were panels with inscriptions and reliefs in honour of Francis I. The main block of the entrance front had an almost similar arrangement, but the corner pavilions, and probably also the other outside façades, were decorated with rusticated pilasters, as opposed to plain pilasters in the court. This design for St Maur is remarkable in that it is the first attempt in France to decorate a complete building with a single Order of classically regular pilasters, disposed in the manner of the Italian architects of the High Renaissance. The result is hardly Italian, partly because of the use of certain French features such as the mullioned windows; but it justifies its author's boast about its novelty.

Though the greater part of Anet has been destroyed, its three essential features have survived: the avant-corps or frontispiece from the main block, which now stands sadly in the court of the École des Beaux-Arts (Plate 30B); and the chapel (Plate 32) and entrance gate (Plate 31B), which are still in situ, though the chapel now stands free instead of being, as it originally was, veiled by the porticoed east wing of the court.

The frontispiece, which probably dates from the late forties, is a splendid example of de l'Orme's new conception of classicism. In form it is a development of the medieval

French château entrance which had already been modified and Italianized to different degrees at Azay-le-Rideau, Fontainebleau, and Assier. But here the transformation is more fundamental. First of all the Orders are far more correct than in any of the earlier examples and are applied in their correct sequence – Doric, Ionic, and Corinthian – one above the other, as in the Septizonium in Rome. But, more important, the design has a monumentality which we have seen glimmering in French architecture of about 1540, but never with this grandeur or completeness. This quality is particularly apparent if we compare the fragment with one of Lescot's Louvre pavilions (Plate 29A). The choice and the massive proportions of the Orders, the severity of the mouldings, the boldness of the bases for the coupled columns, and the discreet use of the ornament are all in a spirit entirely foreign to Lescot. De l'Orme's design is classical but does not go back directly to any Roman model; it has the grandeur of Sangallo but is not copied from him. Not till the time of François Mansart was any further advance to be made in the designing of this favourite motive in French architecture.

The chapel [42] is even more remarkable. Apart from the apparently solitary experiment of the chapel at Vannes,[43] this is the first chapel in France in which is applied the Renaissance principle that the circle is the perfect figure, and therefore suitable for the house of God. It is applied, moreover, with great originality. Not only is the central domed space circular, but the side chapels are so shaped that the outer contour of the whole building is a circle, interrupted only by the right angles of the two sacristies. Further, the pattern of the marble pavement is composed entirely of arcs of circles, which are the projections of the coffering of the dome.[44]

This emphasis on the circle is in accordance with the practice of Bramante, but Philibert's application of it is quite different from his. In the Tempietto, Bramante chooses the simplest combination of the mathematically pure forms of circle, cylinder, and sphere, whereas de l'Orme, with an almost naïve enthusiasm, seeks a much more complex solution. The chapel lacks, therefore, the purity of the Tempietto, but it has its own brilliance. It is also important for one structural innovation. Instead of arches in one plane linked to the circular base of the dome itself through pendentives, the arches in this chapel are inscribed on the surface of a cylinder, not in a plane; that is to say the actual profile of the soffit describes a three-dimensional curve.[45]

Finally we must consider the entrance, probably built in 1552. This astonishing structure has, so far as I know, neither predecessor nor successor. It is designed almost without the use of classical elements except for the Doric columns round the actual door, and is thought of as a series of blocks of masonry, playing against each other almost in the manner of functionalist architecture. A sequence of rectangular blocks builds up to the central feature, surrounded by consoles and flanked by two rounded masses which support little terraces. The culmination of the whole design is the clock consisting of a bronze stag surrounded by hounds, which move at the striking of the hours, a piece of mechanical ingenuity typical of the architect. On each side, at the ends of the lower terrace, are four sarcophagi adding a touch of richness to the design, which, however, is mainly enlivened by the elaborate open-work balustrades running round the whole structure. An element of colour was formerly given by an inlay of black marble in the entablature of the Doric Order and by Cellini's bronze relief of Diana, now replaced by a plaster copy. This entrance is perhaps the most striking example of Philibert's ability to think in monumental terms while at the same time remaining free from any tendency to imitate models of the Italian High Renaissance.[46]

The two works executed for Henry II are less startlingly original than Anet, and both show more Italian influence than is usual with de l'Orme. The tomb of Francis I (Plate 34), begun in 1547, is his solution to the problem of producing a classical version of the type of tomb invented by the Giusti for Louis XII. It is in general design a Roman triumphal arch with the side arches set back from the plane of the principal front. The detail is pure and the use of coloured marble skilful, but the tomb has the disadvantage from the practical point of view that little of the *gisants* can be seen except their heads or their feet.[47]

The Château-Neuf at St Germain, or, as it was more properly called in the time of Henry II, the *Théâtre*, was begun in 1557. The contract proves that it was to consist of a central one-storeyed *corps-de-logis* to the corners of which were attached four pavilions. It was preceded by a court, enclosed simply by a wall and intended as a setting for festivities.[48] The unusual form of this court, a square with an apsed bay on each side, seems to be derived from a part of Hadrian's Villa which was being excavated in the sixteenth century and was then thought to have formed a symmetrical open court, though later excavations have shown that it was in reality a covered dining-hall with a strong longitudinal axis.

De l'Orme's last two designs were prepared at the request of Catherine de' Medici. In 1563 she acquired the unfinished château of St Maur and ordered the architect to make plans for its completion for her son, Charles IX, on a grander scale than originally proposed. A series of drawings by du Cerceau in the British Museum appear to embody de l'Orme's new project (Plate 31A).[49] The main difference from the first design lies in the doubling of the pavilions adjacent to the *corps-de-logis*, thus enabling the architect to put an extra *appartement* in each wing and so to enlarge the accommodation of the château. This arrangement was to be widely followed in the seventeenth century, for instance by Salomon de Brosse at the Luxembourg, although it had the disadvantage of making the side elevation asymmetrical. In spite of this enlargement the château was to remain a one-storey building with a flat roof. Its treatment externally was to consist of a series of rusticated pilasters, which hardly disturbed the simple grouping of the masses.[50]

The second commission for Catherine de' Medici was much more important. In 1563 and 1564 the Queen was acquiring land outside the walls of Paris with the intention of building herself a palace separate from the Louvre but conveniently near to it. This was to be the palace of the Tuileries. Philibert de l'Orme was commissioned to produce the designs, and he refers frequently in his treatise to the work that he was doing there for the Queen Mother. At the time of his death, however, only a very small part of the building had been completed; the lower section of a central pavilion containing a spiral staircase without support in the middle, and two wings, one on either side of it. We have little certain evidence about his intentions for completing the palace,[51] but it is clear from what was carried out that it would have been somewhat different in style from his usual work. He himself suggests the reason for this in references to the Tuileries in his treatise, for he labours the point that he followed in every detail the wishes of the Queen, adding that she demanded certain rich ornaments and materials and implying that he himself would have preferred to have made them simpler.

In view of the uncertainty which surrounds the designs for the Tuileries and the later plans for St Maur, it is difficult to give any precise characterization of de l'Orme's last style, but it is possible that he may have been moving away from the monumentality of his earlier works towards a more Mannerist style. There are details in the elevation of the Tuileries which are certainly due to de l'Orme and which foreshadow the innovations of Bullant. The most significant is the manner in which the dormers are overlapped by the pedimented panels between them, causing a blurring of each unit which would not be found in the architect's more classical works. In fact it seems that de l'Orme, having contributed more than any other architect to the creation of a truly French classical architecture, was towards the end of his life preparing the way for the succeeding generation.

*

In spite of the fact that he was Italian and senior to the architects whom we have just considered, it is convenient to take the work of Primaticcio in architecture at this late stage, because he did not become active in this field till towards the end of his career. He seems, as we should expect, to have approached architecture through decorative sculpture, and the first works which can plausibly be attributed to him are on the border line between the two arts. These are the grotto of the Jardin des Pins at Fontainebleau (Plate 37B; c. 1543),[52] the grotto at Meudon (c. 1555), and the gate in the Cour du Cheval Blanc at Fontainebleau (after 1561), of which the fragments are now incorporated in the lower storey of the so-called Baptistery. All these show him influenced by the rusticated work of Giulio Romano. The conception of the Grotte des Pins, with its giants emerging from a rocky background, suggests that Primaticcio knew sketches for Giulio's frescos of the Fall of the Giants in the Palazzo de Tè, although the actual frescos were executed just after he left Mantua.

More important and more strictly architectural is Primaticcio's other addition to Fontainebleau, the Aile de la Belle Cheminée, built in 1568 (Plate 37A). This is a colder, more academic work, from which we may conclude that Primaticcio had been influenced by the buildings of Vignola which he must have seen on his visit to Bologna in 1563. The general lay-out with the double flight of steps is impressive, but the detail is dry and strangely in contrast with the picturesque rustication of his earlier experiments in architecture.

Primaticcio's name must also be closely associated with the mausoleum which Catherine de' Medici designed for her husband, Henry II, herself, and her sons. This was the Chapelle des Valois, a circular building to be added to the end of the north transept at St Denis (Plate 36B). In the middle was to stand the tomb of the King and Queen, which was begun in 1563 on Primaticcio's designs, the sculpture being carried out by Germain Pilon[53] (Plate 35). The tomb was Primaticcio's solution to the problem tackled by the Giusti and de l'Orme in the monuments to Louis XII and Francis I. As in the former of these, we seem to have here an echo of Michelangelo's first design for the tomb of Julius II, but one which shows at any rate a slightly closer understanding of the original in the placing of the columns and statues at the corners of the whole structure. As a result of this disposition Primaticcio's tomb seems to be conceived more completely in the round than de l'Orme's, which is designed to be seen only from the front or from the side, but not from any intermediate position. This more plastic conception was no doubt due in part to the position for which the tomb of Henry II was destined, that is to say, the centre of a circular chapel, where it would have been seen from every angle.

The question of the authorship of the chapel itself is more complicated. The documents and the evidence of Vasari prove beyond doubt that the original plan was due to Primaticcio,[54] but very little seems to have been actually erected by the time of his death in 1570. In 1572 Jean Bullant was put in charge of the work, and remained connected with it till his death in 1578, when he was succeeded by Baptiste du Cerceau. The building was carried up to the top of the second Order by 1585, but was then abandoned.[55] It fell into decay, and was finally pulled down in the early eighteenth century.[56]

In its general design the Valois Chapel goes back to Italian models such as Bramante's Tempietto or Michelangelo's plans for S. Giovanni dei Fiorentini, though it differs from any previous buildings of this type in having six chapels instead of the usual four or eight, this number being dictated by the necessity of supplying four chapels for the four sons of Henry II and two more for the altar and the entrance. The division of the chapel externally into two storeys, each with its Order, from which emerges the drum carrying the dome itself, recalls Sangallo's design for St Peter's, which Primaticcio could have seen on his visit to Rome in 1540–1. All these links with Roman models tend to prove that Primaticcio's designs were followed fairly closely by his successors, but it is possible that Bullant may have been responsible for some of the detail, since the application of the Orders is consistent with his other work. Nothing in the chapel, however, suggests the intervention of Baptiste du Cerceau, who has sometimes been credited with an essential contribution to its design.

*

The four architects so far considered in this chapter all worked primarily in the Île-de-France; but the middle decades of the century were also a time of great activity in the provinces. It would be impossible to give even a brief account of the innumerable châteaux, churches, and town houses which were built or enlarged at this time all over France. But one or two centres call for special mention.

In the south-west of France a group of buildings can be distinguished as showing a style which is probably connected with the influence of a particular architect, Guillaume Philandrier or Philander. Philander was originally a classical philologist and in architecture was more notable for his learning than for his practical skill. Born about 1505, he accompanied Georges d'Armagnac, Bishop of Rodez, when he went as ambassador to Venice in 1536.[57] There he became a pupil of Serlio, who probably inspired him with the idea of working on Vitruvius. In 1543 he published a translation of this author and the next year a long and erudite commentary on him. On his return to Rodez in 1544 he was given charge of the structure of the cathedral, and about 1562 added to it the remarkable gable of the west front (Plate 36A). Here we see clearly Philander's strength and weakness; for he has simply planted a complete Roman church front on top of a tall plain Gothic façade. In its detail the design is remarkably pure and rather advanced for its date, even on Italian standards. But in its context it is preposterous. All sense of scale and appropriateness seems to have deserted Philander, and he has fallen straight into the trap against which de l'Orme warns architects.

But Philander's knowledge of classical architecture and his more scholarly attitude towards the use of the Orders seem to have had their effect on architects in the Rouergue,[58] and we find several châteaux in which an interesting kind of classicism is visible, different from that of northern France. The most important of these is Bournazel, of which the earlier and less important north wing was built in 1545 and the impressive double-arcaded screen on the east about 1550 (Plate 38A).[59] This arcade has something of the monumentality of de l'Orme, but is not imitated from his style. It is actually more Italianate, and it seems likely that this feature is due to the influence of Philander. The design has, on the other hand, several strictly French characteristics. The decoration, particularly in the metopes, reflects the style of Fontainebleau, and one feature in the application of the Orders is also irregular according to Italian standards but frequently found in France. The entablature of the upper Ionic Order is unbroken in spite of the fact that the columns are full and free-standing. This is a usage hardly ever to be found in Italy and is explicitly condemned by Alberti.[60] It is possible that it was derived by French architects from a celebrated Roman building, the so-called Temple of Diana at Nîmes, which, we shall see, was taken as a model in at least one other work.

Another centre of radiation for the new classicism, though not of quite so pure a kind, was Toulouse, a city proud of its independence in politics through its Parlement and in learning through its university. Humanists like Jean des Pins, Bishop of Rieux, rebuilt their houses there in the new manner as early as 1530. Though little remains of this work to-day, we can form some idea of the manner current at that time in Toulouse from the Hôtel de Bernuy of 1530 (Plate 38B), in which traces of Gothic influences are still visible, but which is strikingly original in its design. The important personality of the middle of the century is Nicolas Bachelier, who built some of the outstanding private houses of the town.[61] He began as a sculptor, and his works in architecture bear the marks of this early training. His door at the Hôtel de Bagis (1538; Plate 40B), with its ingeniously arranged supporting herms, is conceived essentially as a work of sculpture. The entrance to the Hôtel d'Assézat (1555) is more the work of an architect, but is still picturesque in its use of rustication and surface decoration. The application of Italian motives in it is quite personal, and the design has little in common with what was being produced farther north.

There is no clear evidence about the authorship of the court of this hôtel, the most original work produced in Toulouse at this time (built between 1552 and 1562; Plate 40A). Lavedan [62] argues convincingly that it is too classical for Bachelier, but can make no alternative suggestion. The only point that can be established is that the architect was familiar with the treatise of Serlio, since the elevation is largely composed of elements borrowed from the plates of Book 4. Whoever the architect may be, however, he must rank with Lescot and de l'Orme as one of the creators of the classical style of the middle of the century, and his influence seems to have been wide among architects in Toulouse.

Apart from these centres two single buildings deserve special mention. The first is the château of La Tour d'Aigues near Aix-en-Provence. The main building of the château was probably put up about 1560, and is a direct adaptation of Lescot's Pavillon du Roi at the Louvre. Much more remarkable, however, is the triumphal arch erected as the main entrance to the château and dated 1571 (Plate 39A). This displays some of the points which we have seen in the architecture of the south-west, monumentality and the use of the unbroken entablature over full columns. But its general character is quite different. La Tour d'Aigues is within easy reach of the most important Roman remains in Provence, and it is no doubt from the study of these that the architect derived his style. The rich frieze carved with trophies, the exceptionally fine and correct capitals of the Corinthian pilasters, and the elaborate carving of the cornice all suggest a careful study of Roman originals, not merely a casual acquaintance with them through drawings or engravings. In fact La Tour d'Aigues has more than any other French building of the century the character of a real Roman triumphal arch.[63]

The second building, the chapel at Champigny-sur-Veude, is equally remarkable. The chapel itself was begun in the early part of the century, and is an interesting example of Late Gothic with Italianate decoration. But in about 1570 the Duc de Montpensier added at its west end a narthex of very unusual form, built, according to Hautecœur, by Toussaint Chesnau (Plate 39B). It consists of a barrel-vaulted porch at right angles to the axis of the nave. The walls are decorated with two Orders of full columns, Ionic and Corinthian, each supporting an unbroken entablature. The decoration is fanciful, and entirely French, but the main design of the narthex may go back to the temple of Diana at Nîmes, which has the same form, though the barrel-vault is there supported by a single Order.[64]

The same tendencies can be seen in other examples of ecclesiastical architecture of the middle of the century, but generally only in parts added to existing buildings. The application of columns and pilasters to doors and porches becomes more and more monumental, as at Le Grand Andely.[65] Towers are decorated with Orders repeated in correct sequence one above the other, as at Gisors and in St Michel at Dijon (Plate 21B).[66] Screens were added in a strictly classical idiom, one of the finest being that at Arques-la-Bataille.[67] In other cases, for instance Le Mesnil-Aubry, the whole nave is built with classical columns, but the principles of the structure remain medieval and the columns support Flamboyant vaulting.[68] There is only one example of a whole chapel which embodies the principles of the new manner and which can compare in importance with provincial secular work like Bournazel or the Hôtel d'Assézat. This is the chapel of All Saints in the cathedral at Toul, apparently mainly erected before 1549.[69] This chapel is octagonal in plan, with two superimposed Orders supporting a coffered dome. The feeling of the design and detail is entirely Italian, and very advanced for this date, but it is impossible to point to any exact analogy among Italian buildings.

These scattered examples confirm the conclusion which was to be drawn from secular building that the new classicism created by the great architects of the court, Serlio, de l'Orme, Lescot, and Primaticcio, was accompanied by parallel and often independent movements in the provinces, which sometimes, as in the Hôtel d'Assézat and the châteaux of Bournazel and La Tour d'Aigues, produced buildings of real originality.[70]

PAINTING AND ENGRAVING

Primaticcio, Niccolò dell'Abbate, François Clouet, Jean Duvet

Rosso was responsible for the style of decoration which we connect with the school of Fontainebleau, but it was Primaticcio who created the manner of figure drawing which was to become the most recognizable characteristic of French painting for the rest of the sixteenth century.

This he achieved during the decade after his visit to Rome and the death of Rosso, in which period he planned some of the most important decorations at Fontainebleau. Most of these have disappeared or suffered from drastic restoration, but the preparatory drawings which survive give us an idea of Primaticcio's style and methods at this time. The panels for the Cabinet du Roi decorated between 1541 and 1545 and known from drawings (cf. Plate 42) are still in the tradition of Giulio Romano, and remind one of the seated allegorical figures in the Stanza di Costantino. The Chambre de la Duchesse d'Étampes (Plate 41) of the same years is much more important, and here the stuccos at least are fairly well preserved, though the paintings as we see them date entirely from the reign of Louis Philippe.[71] However, the finished drawing for one of them, the Masquerade (Plate 43B), shows that Primaticcio's style was undergoing a change. To some extent this transformation can be attributed to the effect which must have been produced on the artist by his first sight of ancient sculpture in Rome, and the nudes in the foreground suggest that something of the delicacy and softness of Late Hellenistic work was now qualifying the more masculine and sometimes inflated manner of Giulio. But in the Mannerist attitude of the figure bending down in the right-hand corner of the foreground and in the types of girls' heads on the right there is proof of a different influence, that of Parmigianino, which was to be the essential factor in transforming Primaticcio's style. It is likely that Primaticcio knew his work more through copies, drawings, and engravings than through paintings, but this was enough to make him realize the elegance and refinement of the artist's style and to enable him to absorb elements of it into his own art. The change is most clearly visible in the stuccos of the Chambre de la Duchesse d'Étampes, where the caryatids have the characteristics of Parmigianino's female figures: long tapering limbs, thin necks, small heads with exaggeratedly classical profiles. In the decorative part of the stuccos the influence of Rosso's Galerie François I is still evident, both in the fruit garlands and the strap-work, but the character of the figures is quite different from his. Rosso sometimes elongates his figures, but he does so in order to give them a sort of spiritual intensity, and the elongation is combined with an angular disposition of the limbs which heightens this effect. With Parmigianino and Primaticcio the forms are long and delicate, and are disposed with the utmost ease, never with abruptness. The figures in the Chambre de la Duchesse d'Étampes were the first examples of this formula which was to have such success in France and was to be imitated by other countries during the later sixteenth and early seventeenth centuries.[72]

The most important examples of this style were the two galleries at Fontainebleau which occupied the later part of Primaticcio's career, the Galerie Henri II or Ballroom, and the Galerie d'Ulysse. The former survives, much restored; the latter was destroyed in the eighteenth century, but much of its decoration is known from drawings and engravings.

The Salle de Bal is not of a form conveniently designed for painted decoration. Built between 1540 and 1550, with immensely thick walls, leaving deep window embrasures, the room was originally to have been vaulted, and the consoles to support the vaults survive. But under Philibert de l'Orme the plan was changed in favour of the existing coffered wooden ceiling. This left for the main frescoes somewhat awkward spaces composed of spandrels linked together over the slightly flattened arches. These zones and the spaces under the window embrasures were decorated by Primaticcio probably between 1552 and 1556. Owing to the condition of the paintings themselves, we shall form a fairer idea of their qualities from the surviving drawings (Plate 43A). Here Primaticcio has been visibly inspired by the example of Raphael's decorations in the Farnesina, the classic models for decoration within the difficult space of the spandrel; but his slightly broader fields have forced him to enlarge the compositions from the two or three figure-groups of Raphael to whole scenes. However, although compositions and many of the figures come from Raphael, all are changed in character and conform to the canons of proportions employed by Parmigianino.[73]

The second great decorative scheme, the Galerie d'Ulysse, was far more complex and took many years to complete. The gallery was of immense length, and filled the whole side of the Cour du Cheval Blanc on the first floor. It was probably begun soon after 1541, and by the death of Henry II the painting of the walls and vault was complete. The additions made by Charles IX consisted mainly of the decoration of the window niches and the paintings over the five fireplaces. The walls were decorated with a series of paintings illustrating the story of Ulysses which, as far as we can judge from the drawings and engravings, show Primaticcio as a master of academic design in a style more affected than previously by Michelangelesque influence, particularly in the scenes of violent action. In the gentler subjects, however, the style of Parmigianino dominates, and we can form some idea of what they must have been like from an oil-painting of Ulysses and Penelope, probably by Primaticcio himself, which is based on one of the panels (Plate 44B). A striking feature here is the group of small figures in conversation in the background, their lean silhouettes forming with the foreground group a contrast which in its dramatic quality recalls Rosso.

The vault was decorated with grotesques, among which were interspersed small panels of figures. The general disposition of one bay of this design is recorded in an engraving by du Cerceau (Plate 44A). This shows that Primaticcio drew his general idea from the frescoes attributed to Pierino del Vaga in the Salone di Studio of the Cancelleria in Rome, which he could have seen on his visit of 1540. In both decorations the effect depends principally on the great variety of forms given to the panels [74] and on the ingenious way in which they blend with the grotesques surrounding them.

The general plan of the bays seems to have been the same all through the gallery, but a difference is to be traced in the designs of the actual figure panels. In the earlier bays these seem to have been in the style of the Ballroom or the Chambre de la Duchesse d'Étampes. But from the middle of the gallery onwards there is a strong tendency to introduce illusionism. So, for instance, in the octagonal fresco of the fourteenth compartment which shows Jupiter and Juno surrounded by the Olympians, the figures are arranged in a steep perspective system such as Correggio used in his dome designs. In other panels the illusionism is contrived with the help of foreshortened architecture, recalling Tibaldi, as in the panel of Minerva visiting Jupiter and Juno in the thirteenth compartment. In the tenth bay, perhaps the boldest of all, the chariot of Apollo is depicted from exactly below, so that all that can be seen is the bellies of the horses.[75]

This change of conception may have been due to a development in the style of Primaticcio, but it can be more probably explained by the intervention of a new artist in the direction of the gallery. This was Niccolò dell'Abbate (c. 1512–71), a painter who was born and trained in Modena and is first traceable at Fontainebleau in 1552. He arrived with a wide experience of north Italian illusionist painting as it had sprung from the experiments of Mantegna and Correggio and been continued by the Mannerists. Niccolò himself had executed illusionist decoration in Italy: a frieze in the Palazzo Poggi in Bologna, an octagonal ceiling design of the Boiardo family now in the museum at Modena, and a complete ceiling in the Municipio of the same town.[76] He was therefore more deeply versed than Primaticcio in the latest devices of this kind of decorative painting, which the latter could not have seen till his visit to Bologna in 1563, when the vault of the gallery was already finished. It is therefore reasonable to suppose that this change is due to Niccolò, though it would not be safe to conclude from this that the drawings for all such illusionist panels in the gallery were prepared by him. Primaticcio, who had shown after his visit to Rome in 1540 that he was capable of absorbing new ideas and putting them to good use, may well have benefited by Niccolò's suggestions and incorporated them in his own designs.[77]

The last decorative work planned by Primaticcio was the chapel for the Hôtel de Guise. From a letter of 1555 we know that he recommended Niccolò to carry out the work, but it is generally assumed that the drawings are from his own hand.[78] In any case the designs show the illusionist methods of Niccolò in a high degree, especially the fresco over the altar which represented the Star of the Magi supported by angels. The general style of this composition recalls Correggio, but the immediate model seems to be the central panel of the Sala dei Pontefici in the Vatican, probably by Pierino del Vaga.[79]

Niccolò's personality seems to have been partly submerged in that of Primaticcio after his arrival in France, but the 'Continence of Scipio' (Louvre), which is almost certainly datable to that period, shows him as a quite independent designer of figure compositions. This is a typical work of North Italian Mannerism, not deriving, like Primaticcio, from the Roman tradition of Giulio Romano, but ultimately from Correggio via his imitators in Emilia. In the types, in the non-linear conception, and in the softness of the handling it is characteristically Modenese, and not Mantuan.

In one other field – that of landscape – Niccolò was an innovator in France. He had already evolved in Italy a style of landscape-painting based on that of Dosso, of which typical examples are to be seen in the Borghese Gallery. The 'Landscape with Orpheus and Eurydice', now in the National Gallery in London (Plate 45B), and the 'Rape of Persephone' in the Louvre were executed in the same style, probably in France.[80] Niccolò's style differs from that of Dosso in that it reveals more evident traces of the influence of Flemish landscape as it had been evolved by Patinir and his followers. The panoramic coast view, the fantastic buildings, the artificial disposition of the colour in tones of brown, green, and blue are all marks of the Antwerp school. Niccolò probably first came into close contact with this tendency in France, but its effect is already to some extent evident in the two Borghese landscapes which seem to have been executed in Italy.[81]

*

The Fontainebleau school as it was represented by Primaticcio and Niccolò dell'Abbate was the central stream of French painting during the period which we are considering, but there were artists working in the provinces who were hardly affected by their style. Unfortunately we are very ill-informed about these subsidiary groups, and till further research is carried out we are only in a position to indicate a few scattered instances of what may have been taking place in many districts in France.

The most important of the painters working independently of the Fontainebleau school is the elder Jean Cousin, whose identity and career are beginning to take shape owing to the discoveries of Maurice Roy.[82] He was a native of Sens, and is recorded there from 1526 onwards. In about 1538 he moved to Paris, where he evidently made for himself a highly successful career as a painter and designer of stained glass, and died in 1560 or 1561, leaving considerable property. Little work survives which can with any certainty be ascribed to him, but we can safely accept the traditional attribution to him of the 'Eva Prima Pandora', probably executed in Sens before 1538 and now in the Louvre, since the tradition can be traced almost to his own lifetime. Apart from this, the only solid fact is the contract of 1543 which proves his authorship of the tapestries of the life of St Mammès, of which three survive, two still in the cathedral of Langres for which they were woven, and one in a private collection.[83]

From these works we can deduce that Cousin, while conscious of contemporary art in Italy, did not draw his knowledge of it entirely from Fontainebleau. The 'Eva Prima Pandora' (Plate 46A),[84] though it shows the influence of Rosso in the head of the figure and to some extent in the drawing of the nude, differs entirely from anything produced at Fontainebleau in the setting with its rocky cave and dramatic silhouettes of trees, suggesting a knowledge of Leonardo in the use of light and of Dürer's engravings and woodcuts in the forms of the trees.[85]

It is known that Cousin designed much stained glass, and two windows in the cathedral of Sens are traditionally attributed to him. One, representing Augustus and the sibyl (1530), has been so much restored that no firm conclusion is possible; the other, of the life of St Eutropius (1536), is quite consistent with his style as far as it is known to us.

Cousin is not altogether typical of the provincial artist of this period, because he left his native town for Paris and there made his career. In the neighbouring Auxerre we find an example of an artist who seems to have worked solely for local patrons and never to have established contact with the tradition of the capital. This is Félix Chrétien, whose career as a painter was devoted to the service of François de Dinteville, bishop of Auxerre.[86]

By far the most striking work attributed to Chrétien is the painting of 'Moses and Aaron before Pharaoh', recently bought by the Metropolitan Museum (Plate 46B). This composition was painted as a pendant to the 'Ambassadors' of Holbein, commissioned by Jean de Dinteville, brother of the bishop, and depicting him with his companion, Georges de Selve. The 'Moses and Aaron', which is dated 1537, shows various members of the Dinteville family enacting the parts of the Hebrew prophets.[87]

Stylistically the picture has no parallel in French painting. The composition, with its almost life-size figures filling the whole height of the panel, is German rather than Italian in type. To some extent it must also have been directly influenced by the 'Ambassadors' to which it was a companion. In colour, too, the influence of Holbein is apparent. The flat treatment of the strong local colours in the robes and the jewelled painting of decorative borders all suggest that Chrétien had been put on his mettle by the challenge of the German artist. The result is in some parts crude, but the technical brilliance is startling, especially in the painting of the glassy substance of which the rod-serpent is composed. Chrétien's interest in Italian painting is visible in the drawing of the nude, and the combination of northern and southern elements makes up a whole which has a definitely French flavour, though this particular mixture cannot be found elsewhere in the country at the same period.[88]

Another group of provincial work shows direct contact with Italy. This is the series of frescoes illustrating the Trojan War in the château of Oiron (Deux-Sèvres) (Plate 45A). The contract for these paintings which was known in the nineteenth century shows them to have been painted in 1549 by Noël Jallier, an artist otherwise unrecorded. These frescoes are damaged but are being restored and will probably count among the most impressive decorations of the period. They show many elements of the Fontainebleau style, but they also reveal a knowledge of Roman decoration of the later 1540s, particularly of Daniele da Volterra's stucco frames in the Sala Regia of the Vatican [89] and Salviati's decorations of the Palazzo Sacchetti.[90]

*

Parallel with these schools of decorative painting the art of portraiture continued to flourish in France. Indeed, the middle of the sixteenth century is a period of unusual activity in this field, and the fashion for collecting portrait-drawings led to the setting up of regular factories for supplying them. Various attempts have been made, principally by Dimier and Moreau-Nélaton,[91] to put order into this mass of material, but it must be confessed that the problem is still to a large extent unsolved, and the greater part of the drawn and painted portraits of the period cannot be attributed with any certainty to named artists. The following summary will give what facts are tolerably certain, and will not include any attempt to deal with the problem of the anonymous works.

Two names occur frequently about the middle of the century in connexion with portraiture, François Clouet and Corneille de Lyon. About the former we have a few solid facts on which to base an account of his works; but in the case of Corneille there is no single work which can be authenticated by anything like contemporary evidence.

François Clouet was the son of Jean and often used his nickname of Janet. In 1541 after the death of his father he was appointed by Francis I to succeed him, and we must therefore suppose that he was already an artist of established reputation. On these grounds the date of his birth must be placed not later than 1510 and probably rather earlier. He died in 1572. He is recorded as executing various works now lost, but the earliest surviving painting which bears his signature is the portrait of his friend, the apothecary Pierre Quthe in the Louvre, dated 1562 (Plate 49). This portrait at once indicates that a principal source of inspiration for François Clouet must have been Florentine painting; for the type conforms to one in regular use by painters like Pontormo, Bronzino, and Salviati.[92] The pattern with the figure leaning one arm on a table and a curtain cutting off the corner of the composition is purely Florentine in origin, and the naturalism in the face and in the treatment of drapery is close to the early work of Bronzino or to the portraits of Salviati.[93] It is an altogether unpredictable work in French painting of this time, and points to the conclusion that the author must have paid a visit to Italy, for models of this type were not, as far as is known, available in France.[94]

A second portrait bearing his name is the life-size full-length of Charles IX in the Vienna gallery (Plate 47).[95] Here the main influence seems to be from Germany. The stance of the figure and the flat, almost heraldic treatment of the elaborately embroidered dress, though they have certain affinities with Florentine portraiture, are closer to portraits by Seisenegger dating from the 1530s.[96] Clouet's 'Charles IX' is more hieratic than contemporary Flemish portraiture, of which the leading exponent was Mor, and even Bronzino would appear naturalistic beside it. It conforms to a type of international Mannerist portraiture which spread over Europe in the second half of the sixteenth century, producing an exact parallel in Sanchez Coello in Spain and ending with the style of the Pourbus family at the turn of the century.[97]

For this portrait a drawing exists in the Hermitage which provides the basis for attributing to François Clouet a series of similar sketches (cf. Plate 50B) of which the greater part are in the Musée Condé at Chantilly. These show traces of influence from the elder Clouet, but with important differences. The technique is much more meticulous, the attention to accidents of feature and surface is greater, and, as a result, the emphasis on simple geometrical volume is much less apparent. Whereas Jean Clouet's drawings were in the tradition of the Italian High Renaissance, those of his son belong to the world of northern-European naturalism.

One painting signed by François Clouet stands apart from those so far considered. This is the 'Lady in her Bath' (Plate 48) formerly in the Cook collection, traditionally identified as a portrait of Diane de Poitiers, but more probably, as suggested by Irene Adler, of Marie Touchet, the mistress of Charles IX. Here again Italian motives dominate, for the conception and pose of the half-length portrait are taken directly from one of the so-called 'Monna Vanna' portraits emanating from the studio of Leonardo, of which the finest is the cartoon at Chantilly.[98] Clouet may have known one of these Italian originals, but he may equally have come to know the design through the adaptations of it frequently made in the circle of Joos van Cleve.[99] The latter hypothesis is perhaps supported by the somewhat Flemish flavour of the painting and by the resemblance of the composition as a whole to certain paintings by Joos van Cleve representing half-length groups, usually of the Holy Family, behind parapets on which are depicted a dish of fruit and other objects.[100] There may also be a faint echo of Titian in the presence of the maid-servant in the background, but there is no stylistic link with Venetian painting.[101]

The problem of Corneille de Lyon is, as has already been said, unusual in that, although we have many contemporary references which show him to have been a portrait painter of great repute, we have no work which we can attribute to him with certainty. The documents prove that he was of Dutch origin and was born in The Hague, that he was painter to the Dauphin, later Henry II, from 1540 onwards, and that he was naturalized French in 1547. In 1551 the Venetian ambassador, Giovanni Capelli, describes a visit to his studio, where he saw little portraits of all the members of the French Court. After the death of Henry II he continued in favour with his successors. He abjured Protestantism and joined the Roman Church in 1569, and the last record of him dates from 1574.

It is traditional to assign to him a group of small portraits of French sitters which are clearly distinguishable from the style of the Clouets and which suggest a Flemish origin (cf. Plate 50A). There is nothing to prove that they are from his hand, but the hypothesis is perfectly plausible.[102] These portraits are characterized by their small size, their sensitive naturalistic modelling in a northern manner, and usually by a green background. We have no evidence of the artist's early training, but there is nothing in Dutch portraiture of the time to suggest that he learnt his art in his own country. Closer links can perhaps be seen with Antwerp, more precisely with Joos van Cleve, whose portraits, though larger in scale, have very much the same modelling in thin glazes which give variety of light and texture to the features rather than plasticity. This influence may have been reinforced when the Flemish painter visited the French Court, probably soon after 1530, to paint the portraits of Francis I and his second wife, Eleanor of Portugal.[103]

★

If we turn to engraving we come upon an artist who forms in every respect a contrast to all that we have so far found in France during the sixteenth century. The painting of the period was a court art, almost exclusively associated with the King himself or with the great noble families; and it showed in the most highly developed form the characteristics of such an art: elegance, sophistication, and refinement. With the engravings of Jean Duvet (Plate 51), above all with his illustrations to the Apocalypse, we are confronted with the works of a religious mystic which sweep us at once into a world far removed from the Court of Fontainebleau and carry us back in some ways into the Middle Ages.

We know little of Duvet's life beyond the facts that he was a goldsmith, that he was born in 1485, that he lived mainly in Langres and Dijon. He may have spent some years in Geneva, but he died in France after, but probably not much after, 1561. His earliest dated engraving is an 'Annunciation' (R.D.5) of 1520. This does not foreshadow his mature style, but it is a startling work for its date, owing to the pure Italian style which it displays. The architectural setting is more accurately classical than anything to be found in contemporary French work; the figure of the Virgin has an almost Correggesque sentiment; and the angel reveals a knowledge of current Roman painting. An engraving for the 'Judgement of Solomon' (R.D.64), undated but probably early, is based on Raphael's cartoon of Elymas the Sorcerer and also incorporates borrowings from North Italian engravings. Duvet may have known the Raphael design from the engraving of Agostino Veneziano, but the real understanding of High Renaissance Italian design displayed in these and other early works leads to the conclusion that he must have visited Italy and have seen the works of Raphael and his contemporaries for himself. It is otherwise hard to see how he should have an understanding of them so much in advance of his fellow countrymen.[104]

Apart from the 'Apocalypse', the most famous engravings by Duvet are the Unicorn series, which may be tentatively dated to the 1540s.[105] Stylistically they show a further approach towards the manner of the 'Apocalypse'. The compositions are crowded, space is no longer clearly defined; the heads tend more towards the grotesque; elements, such as *putti*, borrowed from Italy, are transformed more and more into a personal idiom.[106]

It is, however, in the twenty-four engravings illustrating the 'Apocalypse' that Duvet's full imaginative power is seen (Plate 51B). The set was published at Lyons in 1561, but the first plate, with a self-portrait of the artist, bears the date 1555, and others may well have been executed before this time. In these compositions Duvet borrows extensively from Dürer's woodcuts of 1498, and it could even be said that his whole project is based on that of his predecessor. But it is the variations from Dürer rather than the resemblances that are interesting.

The approach of the two artists is entirely different. Dürer aims at the greatest clarity in his designs, at perspicuity in his setting out of the narrative, at making the supernatural stories seem, at least, to conform to the laws of nature. He compresses the spiritual significance of the subjects within this severe framework, and in the process gains the concentration which is one of the most marked characteristics of his engravings. Duvet accepts from the outset the purely visionary nature of his material and plans his compositions on that basis. All attempt to make them plausible is abandoned. Space is not a matter of interest; relative scales of figures or of figures to buildings are arbitrary; the human figure can be distorted to any degree if by so doing it becomes more expressive of the symbolical action it has to perform; clarity is no object in itself in a subject where commotion and turmoil are the central themes. Duvet accepts the dictation of the text with the utmost literalness. If St John speaks of a voice 'as it were of a trumpet', Duvet shows an actual trumpet blowing into the saint's ear. In the sealing of the hundred and forty-four thousand, whereas Dürer with typical moderation represents those sealed by a group of about a score, Duvet shows an innumerable crowd vanishing in confusion into the far distance. He is completely uncompromising in his methods; he does not shrink from rigid and monotonous symmetry when it is demanded, as in the

'Fountain of Living Water' (R.D.49), nor from the grotesque, as in the 'Fall of Babylon' (R.D.44), where the woman seen in the previous plate seated on the Beast is depicted tumbling down in an attitude which trembles on the borderline of comedy. But in all these designs there is an urgency and a conviction which make us forget the confusion and the technical incompetence. We feel only that here is an artist who has penetrated the visionary world described by St John and has translated his experience into appropriate terms, even if those terms are at variance with all the canons of classical art.

Duvet may seem at first sight an inexplicable phenomenon in French art of the sixteenth century, but this is not the case, if we examine more closely the circumstances in which he lived. Although we know little of his own life, we have some information about the atmosphere of Langres in his time. The religious activity of the town was dominated by the personality of the bishop, Claude de Longwy, Cardinal de Givry, who was appointed to the see in 1529.[107] The Cardinal belonged to the group of churchmen who recognized the abuses in the Catholic Church and wished to reform them, but were passionately opposed to the doctrines of Luther and the Protestants. Although himself a powerful figure in the Church, he was never a politician, and his reforms were aimed at producing a change of heart, not of constitution. In his diocese he inaugurated a movement of real enthusiasm, one manifestation of which was the foundation of many new confraternities for charitable and devotional purposes. Of these the most important was that of the Holy Sacrament, founded in 1548, to which we know that Duvet belonged.[108]

It was against the background of this emotional religious movement that Duvet's 'Apocalypse' was produced, and it is this atmosphere that it reflects. His art, therefore, offers a close analogy to some of the early manifestations of Mannerist painting in Italy, particularly to the work of Rosso and Pontormo in Florence in the 1520s, produced in a similar atmosphere of religious excitement.[109] The stylistic analogies with the art of these Florentine painters are obvious: the arbitrary proportions of the figures, the crowding and lack of space, the borrowings from Dürer, the revival of Gothic elements. The last feature is naturally more evident in the work of the Frenchman than in that of the Italians, since France had not yet fully thrown off the habits of medieval art. Duvet is also more specifically mystical than the southerners, who should rather be described as dramatic in their treatment of religious emotion. But in general the parallel is close, and the contrast between Duvet and the art of Fontainebleau is in almost every respect like that between the religious art of Pontormo and the official style of the Medici Court.[110]

Duvet is an appropriate artist with whom to end the chapter on the classical art of the mid sixteenth century, because in a sense he links the periods which precede and follow this classicism. We have already seen that in certain respects he springs from the Middle Ages; in others the mystical and agitated quality of his work foreshadows the art produced in the later part of the sixteenth century during the Wars of Religion.[111]

SCULPTURE

Goujon, Bontemps, Domenico del Barbiere

In the field of sculpture, as in that of painting, we find a great Italian playing his part in the development of the art in France; but in this case the exact share of the artist – Benvenuto Cellini – is very hard to define. For of the works which he executed during the five years of his stay – 1540 to 1545 – only two survive: the bronze relief of the Nymph of Fontainebleau and the gold salt-cellar executed for Francis I. We know from his autobiography that he also made models for a series of twelve silver statues of gods and goddesses, of which only the Jupiter was finished;[112] that he began a fountain with a colossal statue; and that he made two bronze busts and a number of silver vases. But of all these nothing survives. Even the 'Nymph of Fontainebleau', as we see it, is only a fragment of a scheme for reconstructing the whole of the Porte Dorée at Fontainebleau with supporting satyrs at the sides and a new disposition of the architectural surround.

There can, however, be no doubt that Cellini's work made a deep impression in France. Local artists must have been first of all struck by his dazzling technical skill; the types of nude to be seen in the salt-cellar probably influenced Primaticcio;[113] and, as we shall see, Cellini's treatment of drapery must have had an effect on Jean Goujon, the artist who dominates French sculpture in the middle of the sixteenth century. Goujon created the style current in Paris and widely imitated in the provinces, and invented a form of Mannerism as exquisite as the finest production of the school of Fontainebleau in painting and decoration, but flavoured with a personal type of classicism.

Goujon's birth and early career are a mystery.[114] The first trace of him is from the year 1540, when he is mentioned as making the columns supporting the organ loft in the church of St Maclou at Rouen. These columns are so remarkable for their date that they lead to two conclusions: first, Goujon must have been a fully formed artist when he designed them, and cannot therefore have been born later than about 1510; and secondly, it is hard to believe that he could have made so pure a classical design without a visit to Italy and first-hand experience of Roman architecture.[115] From this first work and from the payments to him by the authorities of the cathedral of Rouen we know that Goujon was as much an architect as a sculptor at this time, and this is confirmed by a later reference to him as having been 'architecte' to the Constable Anne de Montmorency.

One other work in Rouen has been generally attributed to Goujon, namely the tomb of Louis de Brézé, husband of Diane de Poitiers, in the cathedral (Plate 52). We do not know the exact date of the monument, but Brézé died in 1531, and the tomb is believed to have been put up by his widow, probably in the following years. But from the variation in style of different parts it seems that its construction took some time. Two decorative features in the tomb can be linked directly with works certainly by the sculptor;[116] and it is hard to imagine any other artist of the time in Rouen, or indeed in Paris, capable of designing the caryatids, which foreshadow those later designed by Goujon for the Louvre.

It is not, on the other hand, by any means certain that Goujon was responsible for the whole tomb. The panels with inscriptions are in the style of the school of Fontainebleau, and though they may possibly represent the manner of Goujon in the thirties, we have no evidence to support this view. The equestrian statue is cruder and more archaic than the rest of the sculpture, and the coarse but detailed vegetation behind it recalls the local school which produced the carvings under the vault of the Grosse Horloge and the reliefs in the Lady Chapel at Valmont. Moreover, the awkward placing of the figures at either side on the lower stage suggests that a change of plan was made in the course of construction, and therefore that more than one artist may have been involved.

In general conception, however, the tomb is original and impressive. It is an adaptation of the type of château entrance with an equestrian figure which goes back as far as Louis XII's wing at Blois and reappears in more classical form at Assier. But applied to a tomb it seems unique. Those parts of the decorative sculpture which can be attributed to Goujon are of high quality. The upper frieze is of ingenious design, with a repeating pattern of a winged genius crowning two gryphons, for which no parallel exists in France at this time. The caryatids are free and vivacious in conception and modelling, far in advance of anything which even the most competent Italians in France could have invented; and their heads and drapery both show a greater knowledge of classical models than was possessed by any contemporary sculptor in France.[117]

By 1544 we find Goujon in Paris at work on the first sculpture in which his mature style is displayed, the Rood Screen of St Germain l'Auxerrois. The transition to this major work may perhaps be formed by the much-disputed reliefs from the altar of the chapel at Écouen, now at Chantilly, which show links with the Brézé tomb and also with the Fontainebleau decorative style of the 1530s, but which include bas-reliefs of the four evangelists directly foreshadowing those on the screen.[118]

The Rood Screen of St Germain l'Auxerrois, of which the principal panels are preserved in the Louvre, was executed in collaboration with Lescot. Its sculptured decoration consists of a central panel of the 'Pietà', flanked by four smaller reliefs of the evangelists. The 'Pietà' (Plate 55A) is based on various Italian motives; the pose of the dead Christ is from an engraving of Parmigianino, and other elements come from Rosso, particularly the figure of the fainting Virgin and the close-cropped curls with which almost all the characters are equipped. The drama of the theme is expressed in an idiom borrowed from Rosso, but diluted through the emphasis laid by the artist on decorative beauty. The most striking feature of the relief is the patterning of closely repeated parallel folds against the plain ground of the panel, a treatment of drapery inspired partly by Cellini, whose influence seems to be mainly responsible for Goujon's change in style after his arrival in Paris. But his manner has also evolved in the direction of a greater classicism, especially in that the draperies now reveal the form under them. The panels of the evangelists show the same qualities, above all an exquisite sense of surface pattern and texture; but here the poses and types derive rather from Michelangelo than Rosso.

Goujon's most celebrated and most mature works date from the years about the middle of the century. They are the decorations on the Fontaine des Innocents and the work executed with Lescot at the Louvre.

The Fontaine des Innocents was built and decorated during the years 1547–9. In its original form it was a rectangular building on a corner, presenting façades of two bays on one street and one bay on the other. At the end of the eighteenth century, however, it was reconstructed as a free-standing square block. Its sculptured decoration, most of which is now in the Louvre, consisted of six tall, narrow reliefs of nymphs (Plate 53), three long reliefs with nymphs and tritons (Plate 55B), three more with *putti*, and, finally, Victories filling the spandrels. The long reliefs of nymphs and tritons show more clearly than any other of Goujon's works the influence of Cellini's 'Nymph of Fontaine-bleau', particularly in the drapery, which is disposed in close parallel folds and floats as a background to the nudes without any functional connexion with them. The figures themselves, however, have a lightness and delicacy far beyond Cellini's, recalling rather the drawings of Primaticcio. Once again, however, Goujon's sense of surface decoration is the source of the real beauty of these panels. Here the patterning of the drapery is supported by new elements, such as the scales of the sea-monsters and the picturesque effect of the shells on which float the nereids.

The upright panels of the nymphs are more restrained in style. The drapery is strictly classical in its manner, but Goujon allows himself a certain richness by adding to the plain classical dress jewelled girdles and patterned borders. The figures show a remarkable variety of poses, each adapted so that the raised arms holding the urns ingeniously fill the corners of the narrow panels. The elongation and the elegant attitudes are reminiscent of Primaticcio's form of Mannerism, but the classicism of the actual drapery gives the figures an entirely different character. For the first time in Goujon's work the artist seems to be in complete command of his medium, and to be able to express within the restricted formula of the bas-relief the most complicated *contraposto* of the figures, whereas in the earlier works, notably in the 'Virtues' on the Écouen altar, there was an element of uncertainty in the treatment and an abruptness of transition from the parts shown full face to those which appeared in complete profile.[119]

The work on the Louvre was far more extensive than that on the Fontaine des Inno-cents, but it was so completely restored in the nineteenth century that it is impossible to judge of more than its general disposition. Apart from purely architectural decoration such as friezes, Goujon's sculpture on the palace consisted externally of standing figures flanking the *œils-de-bœuf* on the ground floor and a series of reliefs on the attic. As re-gards the date of this work, we know that by 1549 Goujon had executed the figures round the middle *œil-de-bœuf* and signed the contract for the other two pairs. The reliefs on the attics were executed in 1553.

Stylistically the decorations on the ground floor display much the same qualities as those on the Fontaine des Innocents, except that they show a tendency for the draperies to form a broken, fan-like silhouette not to be found in the more classical reliefs of the Fontaine.[120] The reliefs on the attic floor are more remarkable, because they show great freedom in their relation to the architecture. The upper figures break out of the field of the pediment, and those at the side come over the zone of the capitals. Owing to their restored condition, it is unwise to draw any conclusion about their original quality.

The other important work for the Louvre was the decoration of the Salle on the ground floor of Lescot's wing. Here Goujon's main contribution is the gallery supported by four caryatids (Plate 30A). Compared with those on the Brézé tomb, these are markedly more classical in style, though it is impossible to say how much they may owe this character to the nineteenth-century restoration.[121] In any case, however, the conception of the gallery with caryatids is quite new in French architecture.[122]

Goujon's name continues to appear in the royal accounts till 1562, presumably for work on the Louvre, but after that date it is no longer to be found. According to some critics, the reason is that Goujon left France in 1563 on account of being a Protestant, and took refuge at Bologna and died there in or before 1568. It is not, however, quite certain that the Bolognese documents actually refer to him, and for the present Goujon's last years must remain to some extent a mystery.

*

This is the most convenient point to consider what was for long regarded as one of Goujon's most famous works, the 'Diana of Anet' (Plate 54). Maurice Roy[123] showed conclusively that the attribution to Goujon was of recent origin and without stylistic support, and proposed instead the name of Cellini. But most critics have rejected this view and hold to the old tradition to the extent of maintaining that the sculptor must be a Frenchman, though no new name has been as yet put forward.[124]

The work presents a puzzling problem. The date of its execution is not known, but it is first mentioned in 1554. It is by a sculptor of high quality and individual style, who has one gift which Goujon never possessed, the power to conceive a statue completely in the round. It is less classical than Goujon's mature style, and springs more directly from the art of Primaticcio, though perhaps with some influence from Cellini's Salt for Francis I. It is, however, essentially a product of the late school of Fontainebleau. The head, of exquisite if over-refined accomplishment, is characterized by the elaborate treatment of the hair, the small and delicate features, and the mannered drawing of the eyes.

There is only one group of works in French sculpture of the period in which the same qualities are to be seen, namely some of the reliefs on the tomb of Henry II, which are early works of Germain Pilon. In the panel of 'Faith', for instance, the head shows a very close resemblance to that of the 'Diana', and the drawing and pose of the figure have the same origin in Primaticcio. The mannered drawing of the eyes is typical of most of Pilon's mature works and the fluent modelling of the hair can be paralleled even in so improbable a context as the gisant of Valentine Balbiani (Plate 65).[125]

These similarities are not strong enough to justify a firm attribution of the 'Diana' to Pilon,[126] but they indicate that the statue should be placed in the circle in which his early work was produced rather than in the group round Goujon or Cellini.[127]

The only other sculptor of note among the contemporaries of Jean Goujon in Paris is Pierre Bontemps, a master of decoration rather than of monumental sculpture. He was probably born about 1505–10 and died in 1568. He is first traceable working on decorative sculpture at Fontainebleau under Primaticcio in 1536. From 1540 onwards he was engaged on making casts from the moulds after Roman statues which Primaticcio had brought back from Rome. By 1550 he was established in Paris, and about this time was given by Philibert de l'Orme important commissions in connexion with the tomb of Francis I at St Denis. The documents found by Roy[128] prove that he was responsible for most of the work on the *gisants*,[129] and executed the whole of the bas-reliefs round the base of the tomb, the contracts for which date from 1551 and 1552.

That Bontemps' real talent was for decoration is evident from his monument for the heart of Francis I, also now at St Denis (Plate 56B). Here he worked under the close direction of Philibert de l'Orme, with whom he signed a contract for the monument in 1550; but there is every reason to believe that the real invention of the decoration is due to the sculptor rather than the architect. The round urn standing on a tall rectangular base is one of the finest examples of the decorative style of the Fontainebleau school. The reliefs[130] representing the arts and sciences, which the King had so generously patronized, are of far more sophisticated design than those on the tomb. The round panels on the urn bear witness to the influence of Primaticcio on Bontemps, for the nymphs on them have the elongated forms of his figures; but the more masculine style of those on the pedestal recalls the manner of Rosso, while certain heads remind us that Bontemps had been engaged on the casts of ancient sculpture. Some of the details, such as the design of skulls and bones at the base of the whole monument, reveal real decorative invention.

The one other known work by Bontemps is the curious tomb of Charles de Maigny now in the Louvre, executed in 1557. Maigny, who was captain of Francis I's guards, is represented seated, in full armour, holding a pike, but asleep, with his head leaning on his left hand. This curious attitude may depict the sleep of the just, but in conjunction with the otherwise martial appearance of the figure it probably has some special significance, for other similar representations are known, though none of them has been satisfactorily explained.[131] The monument is again principally remarkable for its decorative charm, as displayed in the rendering of the armour and the stool on which Maigny sits.[132]

*

Outside Paris great activity existed in decorative and religious sculpture in the middle decades of the sixteenth century. Many town houses and châteaux still show fine roundels with busts in full relief which derive in many ways from the Italian lower relief medallions of the earlier parts of the century, but have a refinement and delicacy which is peculiarly French. The museum of Lyons contains a fine example (Plate 56A), which comes from the façade of a house at Vienne. It probably dates from just before the middle of the century but still shows traces of the manner of Francesco Laurana, who had worked in Provence at the end of the fifteenth century. Tombs, Easter Sepulchres, and carved screens were set up in many churches; but it is only in the eastern provinces that we can at present identify individual artists of importance, though there may well be others still awaiting discovery. The first of these was an Italian, Domenico del Barbiere, called in France Dominique Florentin. He was born in Florence in 1506, and came to France with Rosso in 1530. He worked on stuccos at Fontainebleau and elsewhere under both Rosso and Primaticcio, but in 1541 settled in Troyes, where he enjoyed great success as a sculptor for churches. His style is based on a mixture of the Florentine classicism of Sansovino and certain Mannerist devices. In general, the types of heads and the style of the drapery come from Sansovino, but in figures such as the 'Charity' in St Pantaléon at Troyes[133] there is a *contraposto* which implies a knowledge of the work of Michelangelo, and a relief from the tomb of Claude de Lorraine, Duc de Guise (d. 1550) now at Chaumont,[134] suggests in its composition the influence of Rosso and even of Salviati. Domenico's last work was the base of the monument for the heart of Henry II, of which the whole design was commissioned from Primaticcio about 1560 and the figures executed by Pilon.[135] He died at an unknown date between 1565 and 1575.

The second figure of importance is the Lorraine sculptor, Ligier Richier, who was born at St Mihiel about 1500 and spent the greater part of his life in the service of the Dukes of Lorraine. The Easter Sepulchre in the church of St Étienne in his native town[136] shows a mixture of Gothic naturalism and Italianate treatment of the draperies which is characteristic of much French sculpture at this period. Much more personal is the recumbent effigy of Philippe de Gueldres, Duchess of Lorraine (d. 1547) from her tomb, now in the church of the Cordeliers at Nancy.[137] Here the Italian elements are scarcely visible and are replaced by a grim naturalism in the rendering of the wrinkled face. This grimness rises to the macabre in the famous skeleton on the tomb of René de Châlons now in the church of St Pierre at Bar-le-Duc (Plate 57).[138] The attribution to Richier is not based on documents and is by no means certain, but the statue is evidently the work of an artist of Lorraine, and other examples of the same manner are to be found in the eastern provinces.[139] The revival of the Late Gothic love of skeletons is here evident, but the treatment is different. The edge is taken off the horror by the manner in which the shreds of flesh and skin which partly clothe the bones are made into decorative patterns like torn parchment; and the virtuosity of the performance distracts one from the grisly theme. Richier was evidently much affected by the disturbed religious atmosphere of the eastern provinces at this time, and he ended by becoming a convert to Protestantism and flying to Geneva where he died in 1566 or 1567.

French sculpture of the middle of the sixteenth century did not show the same range and inventiveness as the architecture of the period, nor did it produce any single personality of the calibre of Philibert de l'Orme; but it can claim to display more completely than contemporary painting the ideals of French society. Painting remained till long after the death of Henry II dominated by the Italians, whereas sculpture freed itself more rapidly; and Goujon is as emphatically a French artist as any produced in the whole century.[140]

CHAPTER 4

THE WARS OF RELIGION
1560–1598

HISTORICAL BACKGROUND

THE last forty years of the sixteenth century nearly witnessed the complete destruction of all that had been achieved by Francis I and Henry II during the first half of the century. The centralized and autocratic system of government which they had built up was almost submerged in the civil and religious wars with which France was torn during the reigns of the three sons of Henry II, Francis II (1559–60), Charles IX (1560–74), and Henry III (1574–89), and the first years of their successor, Henry IV (1589–1610).

The history of the Wars of Religion is confused, but the general issues which emerge are clear. Above all, it must be realized that the conflict was social as much as religious. Ostensibly the struggle was between the Calvinists and the Catholics; but the motives which led individuals and families to take part in it and to support one party rather than the other were often more political than theological. The great noble families saw in the wars a means of regaining the position and power which they had lost under the previous reigns. In the anarchy which inevitably accompanies civil strife they saw a chance of making their own advantage against the Crown, whose position was naturally weakened by the situation. Certain families joined one faction because their traditional enemies and rivals had joined the other. The house of Lorraine identified itself early with the cause of Catholicism, and this must undoubtedly have been an incentive to their rivals, the Bourbons, to favour the Protestant cause.

The manifestos of the two sides are often phrased in curiously similar terms. It is particularly significant that both parties refer to the reign of Clovis as a sort of Golden Age which they would like to revive. In fact, they look back nostalgically to the limited monarchy of medieval France with the throne supported by a strong nobility and a powerful clergy.

The religious struggle had not always had this aristocratic character, and in the early days the Protestant movement was mainly supported by the artisan classes in the towns, but by the second half of the century the nobles had taken charge of the conflict, and both parties, Catholic and Protestant, were dominated by their aristocratic leaders. It is, for instance, typical that by the Edict of Amboise (1563) Condé, the Protestant leader, extracted from his opponents terms which amounted to the right for the seigneur to worship as he liked – and for his dependants to worship in the same way – with no equivalent right of the Protestant dependant of a Catholic seigneur and only the most limited rights for the Protestant in a town.

It is, of course, true that the towns played an important part in the struggle. In the early stages they saw a hope of regaining their ancient liberties which had been en-croached upon by Francis I and Henry II, and they were therefore willing to engage in the struggle against the Crown. Later, however, the richer *bourgeoisie* gradually realized that they stood to lose more than they would gain by the weakening of the Crown, since it would involve the strengthening of the feudal nobility.

In the last stages the issues became even clearer. The succession of the Protestant King of Navarre as Henry IV gave the Catholic party, now organized under the Guises as the League, their finest opportunity. They were able to capture Catholic opinion in the towns, notably in Paris, and even to make the Parisians accept the help of Spain and a Spanish garrison. But when the King declared his conversion to the Catholic faith they found their position weakened. Generally speaking the *bourgeoisie*, represented by the Parlement, turned against the League, on the grounds that Henry IV was the legitimate successor to the throne and that his conversion had removed the last obstacle to acknow-ledging him. Mayenne, the brother of the murdered Duc de Guise, was determined to continue the struggle, and attempted to do so with the support of a few fanatical preachers who were still able to influence the people of Paris in favour of his cause. But eventually the feelings of patriotism and royalism triumphed, and the gates of Paris were opened to the King by members of the Parlement. The party of the moderates, of the *Politiques*, who put peace above religious fanaticism, had triumphed.

It is only to be expected that this atmosphere of violence should be reflected in the literature and the art of the period. The religious feeling is to be seen directly in the writ-ings of the Protestant poets, Agrippa d'Aubigné and du Bartas, who deal with explicitly theological subjects. The long philosophical poem of du Bartas, the *Semaines*, contains a complete view of the universe according to the Calvinist doctrine, written in turgid but forceful verse which moved Milton to approval. D'Aubigné's *Tragiques* shares with the *Semaines* the element of violence, but contains vivid descriptions of the state of France during the Wars of Religion which have real dramatic qualities. Both poets, however, are far removed in style from the classical principles of Ronsard; both indulge in com-plex allegory, in an uncontrolled use of metaphor, and in descriptions of immoderate length. The Catholic party did not produce anything comparable to these poets, and the only important religious poems which expressed their views are the last works of Ron-sard, in which, with much more restraint and in nobler form, he sets forth his own deep faith in the Catholic Church. But Ronsard was a man of the previous age, whose voice sounds like that of an elder statesman to whom no one has time to pay attention in the fury of civil war.

In spite of the almost ceaseless disturbance of the period, the court of the last Valois Kings continued to be a centre of cultural activity. In fact, Henry III was as great an enthusiast for letters as any of his predecessors. The atmosphere of his Court was, how-ever, very different from that of Francis I or Henry II. Henry III was a neurotic whose sensibility was heightened to an unhealthy degree. He demanded pleasures of the most sophisticated kind. Elaborate court ballets were succeeded by religious exercises of great severity, and the King's appetite was evidently excited by the contrast between the sumptuous ball dress worn one evening and the hair shirt put on the next day. His religion was perfectly sincere; but it was of a kind which revelled self-indulgently in mortification without precluding any forms of sensual indulgence.[1]

The life of the Court is best reflected in the painting of Antoine Caron, which we shall consider later, and in the poetry of Philippe Desportes, the secretary of Henry III, and the most popular court-writer. His poems are almost a foretaste of *Précieux* verse of the next century, ingenious, *alambiqué*, full of conceits and antitheses, with only the thinnest of ideas to hold the structure together – exquisite nothings gratifying to a jaded palate.

The visual arts were affected as much as literature by this curious and strained atmosphere. The mood of the time appears in many different forms, but all the art of the period has in common the feeling of strain and conflict, the desertion of the principles of rationalism and classicism which had predominated in the previous decades, the preference for the ingenious and complex over the simple and direct; in fact all the elements which we regard as making up the more advanced forms of Mannerism.

ARCHITECTURE

Bullant, Jacques Androuet du Cerceau the Elder

The architecture of the period covered by the Wars of Religion is dominated by two figures, Jean Bullant and Jacques Androuet du Cerceau the Elder, very different in the character of their work.

The date of Bullant's birth is unknown, but the first mention of him is the registration of his daughter's baptism in Paris in 1550.[2] As an architect he does not appear till 1556, when he is referred to as being in the service of the Constable Anne de Montmorency at Écouen. These two dates indicate that he was probably born about 1520 or 1525 rather than in the years 1510–15, as is usually stated. The difference is significant, because in one case he would be the contemporary of Philibert de l'Orme, whereas the whole character of his work confirms the view that he belonged to a younger generation. He died in 1578.

He himself tells us in the preface to his *Reigle Générale d'Architecture* that he visited Rome, where he made drawings after ancient buildings of which he made use in the details of his own works. We may suppose that this visit took place about 1540–5.

The first part of Bullant's career is closely linked with the Constable Montmorency, for whom he worked at Écouen, Fère-en-Tardenois and Chantilly. Of his two published works, one, the *Petit Traicté de Géometrie et d'Horologiographie* (written in 1561 and printed in 1564), was dedicated to the Constable, and the other, the *Reigle générale d'Architecture des cinq Manières de Colonnes* (*privilège* of 1563), to his son.

The exact share of Bullant in the construction of Écouen is by no means easy to define; but most critics now agree that he probably had nothing to do with the west and south wings, which were presumably built about 1538.[3] It seems likely, however, that he was responsible for the north wing, the outer façade of which is decorated with two superimposed Orders, Tuscan and Doric, and with dormers of a more classical design than in the earlier wings. This wing, which bears the cipher of Henry II, was probably Bullant's first work at Écouen, and can be tentatively dated about the middle of the 1550s. To the last years of the same reign can be assigned the portico on the court side of the same front which still bears the King's insignia, and probably also the entrance wing now destroyed but known from engravings of du Cerceau (Plate 58A). Both these works show the dependence of Bullant on de l'Orme at this stage of his career. The entrance pavilion is a variant on de l'Orme's central motive at Anet (Plate 30B); but Bullant has made the whole effect bolder by the insertion of an arched opening on the middle floor which gives his design something of the character of the Porte Dorée at Fontainebleau. His principal object seems to have been to create a worthy setting for the equestrian statue of the Constable which was to fill a second arched opening at the top, an arrangement recalling Louis XII's entrance to Blois. From du Cerceau's engraving the statue seems to reproduce one of Leonardo's early *modelli* for the Sforza monument.[4]

By far the most original part of Bullant's work at Écouen is the pavilion added to the court side of the south wing (Plate 58B).[5] The essential novelty here is the use of the colossal Order instead of the two superimposed Orders of the other pavilions. This appears to be the earliest surviving example of its use in France, though we know that de l'Orme planned to introduce it in his scheme for the Cour du Cheval Blanc at Fontainebleau.[6] Its use had already been authorized in Italy by Michelangelo in the Capitol palaces; but Bullant's application of the device is quite different. In the Capitol palaces the emphasis is on the horizontal, which is brought out both by the proportions of the building and by the strong lines of the entablatures. At Écouen the shape enclosed by the Order is nearly square and the vertical lines dominate almost unchallenged. It was perhaps because of this strong vertical tendency that the colossal Order soon became popular in France, whereas in Italy it was little copied, except by Palladio, till the time of Bernini.[7]

The impressive effect of this Écouen pavilion depends to a great extent on the fine quality of its detail. Bullant has copied his Order from the portico of the Pantheon, which he reproduces in his *Reigle générale* after drawings made in Rome. It is characteristic of him that he should in a single building combine two apparently contradictory tendencies: almost pedantically accurate classical detail, and a clearly anti-classical use of the colossal Order.

The feeling for grand scale is seen even more clearly in the bridge and gallery which Bullant built for Montmorency at Fère-en-Tardenois (Plate 59A). The date of its construction is not known, but it must lie between 1552 and 1562.[8] Bullant has here taken advantage of an unusual site as skilfully as de l'Orme had used the position of Chenonceau to construct his bridge across the Cher. The deep valley is spanned by a row of simple monumental arches of enormous height, over which runs a gallery. The ornament is limited to flat mouldings on the gallery and to slight rustication on the voussoirs; and the whole effect is of a Roman aqueduct thrown across a gorge. The entrance to the gallery[9] is composed of Doric columns with a rich entablature.[10] An unusual feature is that the window over the main door cuts through the entablature and into the pediment, thereby foreshadowing the design of the Petit Château at Chantilly and showing a form of Mannerism typical of the architect.

Bullant probably built the Petit Château for Montmorency's castle at Chantilly about 1560[11] (Plate 59B). It shows a different aspect of his style. Seen from outside it consists of a long, rather low building linking two higher pavilions at right angles to it. Structurally it consists of two equal floors but their existence is in part masked by the arrangement of the pilasters which form a single Order, higher than the lower storey, but not so high as the two storeys together. The result is that the windows of the upper storey cut through the entablature, and there is set up a sort of syncopation, with the two small storeys playing against the single large Order. On the end façades the arrangement is even more complicated. The middle bay is like that at Fère, and at the sides the windows of the two floors are linked into a single vertical strip cutting through the entablature. This syncopation, which is characteristic of Bullant's style, can be regarded as a French form of Mannerism, analogous in certain respects to Palladio's use of interlocking Orders, as, for instance, on the façade of the Palazzo Valmarana at Vicenza or of S. Francesco della Vigna, Venice.[12] In his arrangement of the windows at Chantilly, however, Bullant is taking up again, perhaps unconsciously, a Late Gothic tradition, of which an example can be seen in the château of Josselin, in which the windows and dormers form vertical panels which are cut across at the middle of a window by the balustrade round the roof. Here we see the same kind of syncopation as at Chantilly; but with Bullant the state of mind is different, because he must have been consciously breaking rules governing the use of the Orders, of which the architect of Josselin would not have been aware. In the case of the later architect, therefore, the device can properly be called Mannerist.

We know almost nothing of Bullant's activities during the second half of the 1560s, when his work for the Constable seems to have been finished.[13] On the death of de l'Orme in 1570, however, he was appointed to succeed him as architect to Catherine de' Medici, and his last works were all connected with her. As has already been said, his contribution to the Chapelle des Valois cannot be exactly determined,[14] and the same is true of the wing which was added to the Tuileries to the south of de l'Orme's construction; for the decoration on it seems to have been added later.[15]

In 1572 Bullant was commissioned by the Queen Mother to build a house for her, later called the Hôtel de Soissons. This hôtel, known from engravings of Silvestre, belonged to a type to be found earlier in du Cerceau's *Livre d'Architecture*, published in 1559. Its one remarkable feature was the tall column used by Catherine as an observatory, which still stands beside the Halle au Blé.[16]

In the very last years of his life Bullant seems to have produced for the Queen Mother two vast schemes, of which only small parts were executed. At a date between 1575 and 1579 [17] Catherine decided to enlarge the château of St Maur, for which de l'Orme had, as we have seen, produced a grand design. It is to be supposed that the new design was commissioned from Bullant, who was her regular architect. The scheme, known from du Cerceau's engraving, consisted of an enlargement of de l'Orme's plan by the addition of a further storey. On the park front there was now to be a grotesquely wide pediment, crushingly heavy in comparison with the nine bays of the *loggie* below it. In these last years Bullant's desire for the colossal seems to have grown greater, and in this case it could not be happily harmonized with the existing building.[18]

Catherine's passion for building, however, was not assuaged by this plan, and in 1576 she decided to enlarge her château of Chenonceau,[19] which she had forced Diane de Poitiers to give up to her after the death of Henry II. Again, in the absence of positive evidence, we may suppose that the plan was due to Bullant. As recorded by du Cerceau (Figure 8), it was to have been a vast project. The architect proposed to alter Bohier's château so as to be symmetrical, to build a gallery over de l'Orme's bridge, and to add a vast forecourt on the north side, with semicircular colonnades leading to long wings splayed out towards the entrance. Of these additions the only parts built were the western arm of the forecourt and the gallery on the bridge.[20] The gallery is typical of Bullant's style. In its general conception it reminds us of Fère, and in the decoration of the upper floor it displays another variant of his Mannerism. The pediments which cover the windows overlap the panels filling the spaces between them, thus forming a horizontal interlocking system reminiscent of the vertical disposition at Chantilly.[21] In the interior two remarkable mantelpieces survive which show the same kind of complexity in design combined with Bullant's love of rich classical detail.[22]

Bullant's main contribution to French architecture was made when he was working for Montmorency. His style was formed on the lessons he had learned from antiquity and from the study of de l'Orme; but he soon moved away from the classicism which he had thus acquired and evolved a Mannerism which lasted to the end of his career. In his last works, however, designed for Catherine de' Medici, he shows a new fantasy of invention which brings him nearer in feeling to his rival du Cerceau.

*

Jacques Androuet du Cerceau the Elder was the first of a dynasty of architects and decorators which lasted almost till the end of the seventeenth century. He was probably born about 1520.[23] According to his eighteenth-century biographer, Dézallier d'Argenville, he was enabled to go to Italy by Georges d'Armagnac, whom he probably joined in Rome while Armagnac was there, as ambassador from 1539 to 1544 and from 1544 onwards as cardinal.[24] The earliest certain trace of him is supplied by his first volume of engravings which was published at Orleans in 1549. He was apparently still there in 1551, but his first book of architecture, which appeared in 1559, was printed in Paris and dedicated to Henry II. From this time onwards he seems to have enjoyed considerable favour at Court. For some years after 1560 he worked for Renée de France, Duchess of Ferrara, for whom he made additions to the castle of Montargis, and who appears to have saved him from persecution on account of his Protestantism. In the 1570s he was employed by Charles IX, and was supported by Catherine de' Medici, to whom he dedicated several of his books. He is last recorded in 1584.

Even in his lifetime he was more famous for his engravings than as a practising architect, and nothing now survives of the little he is known to have built. By far the greater part of his engravings are of decoration, in the form either of grotesques or of designs for furniture or architectural detail. In these he was mainly inspired by Italian sources, and many of them are copies of traceable originals.[25] They show a high degree of

CHENONCEAV
AVGMENTACIONS DE BASTIMENS DELIBERES
FAIRE PAR LA ROYNE MERE DV ROY
ADDITAMENTA ÆDIFICII QVÆ
REGINA MATER ÆDIFICARE
INSTITVERAT

Figure 8. Château of Chenonceau: Plan

fantasy in the treatment both of decorative detail and of architectural elements, and to this extent form part of the generally anti-classical tendency of French art at this time.

In his purely architectural designs a clear development can be followed. In the early works of about 1550 we see a variety of influences. The *Arcs* of 1549 contain free interpretations of Roman triumphal arches in the idiom of Lescot; the *Temples* of 1550 are more fantastic, and reveal North Italian influence, apparently both Milanese and Venetian; and the *Vues d'Optique* of 1551 consists of compositions in the manner of Jean de Gourmont. Within the following ten years, however, du Cerceau seems to have gained freedom and established a personal style. The result is apparent in the first *Livre d'Architecture* published in 1559.

This book contains fifty designs for town houses, which had not up till this time been systematically treated. The full title contains the following significant phrase: 'pour instruire ceux qui désirent bastir, soyent de petit, moyen, ou grand estat', and in fact the book presents plans for houses of all sizes, from one suitable to a merchant, to the grandest hôtel of a noble family. The smaller houses consist of a single block, usually of only one storey, but with great variety in the elevations. The surface is varied by stone quoins and window surrounds; the openings are of different forms; and the front is often broken by small pavilions containing *cabinets* and covered by separate roofs, so that the sky-line also is discontinuous. The basic element out of which the houses are made up is the *appartement*, which we first saw early in the century at Chambord. In du Cerceau's town houses it usually consists of the *chambre* accompanied by a *cabinet* and *garde-robe*, the luxury of an *antichambre* not being necessary in a small hôtel; and generally there are two *appartements* linked together by a *salle* or living-room.

Later in the book du Cerceau shows more splendid houses, and in these he uses plans which are based more on the country château, usually with a *corps-de-logis* flanked by pavilions and preceded by a court enclosed by galleries and a screen (Plate 60B). This arrangement is also related to Serlio's Grand Ferrare, but the form with separate pavilions at the corners makes it more like a château in the final effect. In some plans du Cerceau gives free rein to his fantasy, and designs houses round triangular or circular cores with radiating wings. But generally speaking the plans seem to be very practical, and there is reason to believe that they were widely copied in houses built in Paris during the later sixteenth century.[26] Very few of these survive, but some are known from engravings. The biggest must have been the Hôtel de Nevers, begun after 1572 for the Duc de Nevers on the site of the Hôtel de Nesle. The house was never finished, and was pulled down in the seventeenth century, but from Chastillon's engravings of the whole scheme, and from views of it in its unfinished state by Silvestre and Stefano della Bella, it seems to have followed the disposition suggested by du Cerceau in his thirty-eighth design; and many of its details can be paralleled in others of his schemes. In fact so close is the resemblance that it seems not unreasonable to suggest that he was actually the architect.[27]

Du Cerceau's last years must have been largely occupied with the preparation of the two volumes by which he is best known, *Les plus excellents Bastiments de France*, published in 1576 and 1579. They are our best source of information for many sixteenth-century houses that have since been altered or destroyed, although du Cerceau is often unreliable in completing unfinished buildings according to his own fancy[28] and in adding ornament of his own invention to existing structures.[29] The book was originally prepared for Renée de France, and the drawings in the British Museum contain several which were clearly intended for her special pleasure.[30] However, she died in 1575, and the books were dedicated to the Queen Mother.

While preparing the publication of these volumes, du Cerceau found time to design two important châteaux, Verneuil and Charleval.[31] Verneuil was begun for Philippe de Boulainvilliers about 1565, and continued for the Duc de Nemours, who acquired the estate in 1568, but it was probably not finished till the time of Henry IV, who presented it to Henriette d'Entraigues in 1600. Charleval was begun for Charles IX in 1571 on a vast scale, but very little of it was actually built.

In plan Charleval is the more remarkable (cf. Figure 9). The château itself was built round a square cloistered courtyard. In front stretched a vast forecourt flanked by wings which concealed two further pairs of courts. The outer lines of the area covered by these five courts were continued by porticos enclosing two gardens, and the whole square thus formed was surrounded by a moat. In certain respects this is a derivation from Serlio's plan for the completion of the Louvre, and it must have been thought of by du Cerceau as a rival to de l'Orme's scheme for the Tuileries and Bullant's for Chenonceau. The plan of Verneuil is relatively simple, a square court enclosed by three wings and a screen with a circular entrance in the middle.[32] Its principal merit was the advantage which the architect took of the sloping ground to introduce a semicircular grotto below the terrace outside the garden front.

The elevations of both Verneuil and Charleval are in the highest degree fantastic (Plates 61A and 60A). Classical forms are used in the most wanton manner. Windows or niches interrupt entablatures, pediments are broken in varied ways, voussoirs are twisted, rustication spreads over pilasters, and the whole surface is covered with grotesque ornament. Du Cerceau is as anti-classical as Bullant, but he destroys classical principles mainly by breaking up smaller architectural features and by covering the surface of the building with his uncontrolled ornament. Compared with Bullant's subtle infringement of the rules, du Cerceau's Mannerism seems almost barbarous. We are reminded by Verneuil and Charleval of the fact that du Cerceau was above all a decorator, and not an architect. Nevertheless, his work was to have great influence in France for more than half a century.

We shall have occasion to examine the work of several of his descendants and followers in a later chapter, but his eldest son, Baptiste (c. 1545–90), must be mentioned here. He was probably responsible for the Hôtel d'Angoulême, later the Hôtel de Lamoignon, built in 1584 by Diane de France, illegitimate daughter of Henry II (Plate 61B). In style this house seems to derive rather from Bullant than from the elder du Cerceau, particularly in the use of the colossal Order of pilasters and in the breaking of the entablature by the dormers. Though much neglected, it is structurally the best preserved late sixteenth-century house in Paris.

In the provinces again we find movements parallel with those taking place in the capital, but with local variations. In the north-east of France, Flemish influence is naturally strong, for instance in the wing added by Tesson in 1572 to the town hall of Arras,[33] or in the Halle Échevinale at Lille, built in 1593 by Fayet.[34] Generally speaking, provincial architects of this period indulge in a great variety of surface effects, particularly through rustication and high relief sculpture. This can be seen in buildings such as the château of Pailly in the Haute Marne, attributed traditionally to Nicolas Ribonnier of Langres.[35] It reached its finest expression in Burgundy in the hands of Hugues Sambin (1515/20–1601/2) and his school. The most famous example of this manner is the Maison Milsand at Dijon (c. 1561) (Plate 62), which shows admirably the free use of fanciful sculpture on a small façade.[36] Rustication was carried to its highest point in the Petit Château at Tanlay[37] begun in 1568, on the ground floor of which every stone is cut into a sort of lace-work pattern of vermicular rustication.[38]

SCULPTURE

Germain Pilon

After the disappearance of Goujon about 1563 his place was taken by an artist of very different type, Germain Pilon. Pilon was born in Paris about 1530.[39] In 1558 he is mentioned as receiving payment for eight statues for de l'Orme's tomb of Francis I, which have since disappeared. Two years later, in 1560, he is found working for Primaticcio on the monument for the heart of Henry II, the base of which was executed by Domenico del Barbiere.

These two documents are of importance, because they point to the influences under which Pilon developed. One would expect him to have been strongly affected by his great predecessor Goujon, but there is hardly a trace of his style to be seen in Pilon's work. His first manner seems to be formed on quite different models: the stucco-work of Primaticcio at Fontainebleau (Plate 41), the figure-sculpture of Domenico del Barbiere and the reliefs of Bontemps, the sculptor of the monument for the heart of Francis I (Plate 56B).

The effects of the first two of these models can be clearly seen in the monument for the heart of Henry II, of which Pilon's three figures of the Graces and Barbiere's base are in the Louvre, the urn itself being a nineteenth-century restoration (Plate 63). In its general scheme this monument is a direct imitation of the incense-burner designed for Francis I, known to us from the engraving by Marc' Antonio.[40] But Marc' Antonio's three classically proportioned figures with their Roman draperies are translated into Fontainebleau nymphs with the long necks and small heads of Primaticcio's stuccos in the Chambre de la Duchesse d'Étampes (Plate 41). The fluent drapery suggests the influence of Domenico del Barbiere,[41] and in no way recalls either the engraving or the much more linear idiom of Goujon.

The transition to Pilon's later style can be seen in the tomb of Henry II and Catherine

CHARLEVAL

PLANVM TOTIVS ÆDIFICII AT QZ HORTORVM VT COEPTA
SONT OMNIA A KAROLO HVIVS NOMINIS NONO

LE PLAN TANT DV BASTIMENT QVE DV IARDIN AINSI
QVIL A ESTE COMMENCE PAR CHARLES 9

Figure 9. Jacques du Cerceau the Elder: Château of Charleval: Plan de' Medici, executed under the direction of Primaticcio between 1563 and 1570 (Plate 35). The four bronze figures of Virtues at the corners of the monument, of which the models were ready for casting in 1565, still have much the same character as the Graces on the earlier work, though the movements of torso and limbs are freer and the forms of the drapery more plastic. The reliefs round the base are exquisite variations on the types of figures used by Primaticcio in the decorations of the Ballroom at Fontainebleau,[42] and recall in general character the Bontemps panels on the monument for the heart of Francis I (Plate 56B).

When, however, we come to the kneeling figures of the King and Queen on the top of the tomb and the *gisants* under the canopy, we find Pilon in a quite different mood. The kneeling figures are in a sense bronze versions of the stone statues of Louis XII and Francis I and their families on their tombs nearby, and they conform to the French tradition of realism in such works. But they also embody new qualities, greater freedom of movement in the poses, strong feeling for the material used and, in the figure of the Queen, skill in the rendering of details of dress and jewellery. This was no doubt mainly due to the example of Cellini, whose Nymph must have constituted a spur to rivalry for any French sculptor in bronze. But Pilon never allows himself to be distracted by virtuosity from his main purpose.[43]

In the two *gisants* (Plate 64) the naturalistic element has been intensified. For these statues Pilon had several models available. He clearly studied the *gisants* on the tombs of Louis XII and Francis I and, in the case of the Queen, he had before him a marble statue which Girolamo della Robbia had been commissioned to prepare for the tomb.[44] Pilon has, however, provided a very personal solution to the problem. He has avoided the grim details, such as the embalming stitches in the Louis XII or the protruding ribs of della Robbia's statue, but he has rendered the complete relaxation of death with great poignancy. The modelling of the two figures is surprisingly different, the Queen's rounded and generalized, the King's fluid and very sensitive. Most striking of all is Henry's head, thrown back and seen in profile, his coarse features here acquiring a fineness which makes one think that the sculptor had been studying the St Peter's 'Pietà' of Michelangelo, of which a cast existed at Fontainebleau.[45]

No large-scale work by Pilon survives dating from the 1570s, but he was active during this period in making portrait busts and medals. The marble busts of Henry II, Francis II, and Charles IX now in the Louvre,[46] probably executed in the reign of the last-named king, are less interesting than the bronze of Charles IX in the Wallace Collection, London,[47] which reveals again Pilon's broad treatment of the metal. These busts suggest that the artist was well acquainted with contemporary Italian sculpture, the closest parallel being with Leone Leoni. The bronze bust of Jean de Morvilliers (after 1577) prepares the way for the more dramatic style of the 1580s.[48] In the same years Pilon made a set of large portrait medals representing Henry II and his three sons, which are remarkable for their psychological insight as much as for their technical brilliance.[49]

During the 1580s Pilon was mainly engaged on two schemes: groups for the Valois Chapel, and tombs of the Birague family.

When Catherine de' Medici commissioned the tomb of Henry II, her plan was to set it up in the central space of the chapel which Primaticcio was to build for her at St Denis.[50] At the same time she instructed Pilon to prepare for the smaller chapels various other groups which were not begun till about 1583. One of these groups was to represent the Resurrection, and fragments of it are in the Louvre and the church of St Paul-St Louis.[51] It shows more than any other work of Pilon a debt to Michelangelo. The two soldiers have his full *contraposto*, and the Christ is based on his cartoon of the 'Noli me tangere' of 1531. The 'Virgin of Pity' (Plate 66),[52] also for the chapel, is the first instance of Pilon's late style, which we shall see fully illustrated in the Birague statues, while the 'St Francis in ecstasy', now in the church of St Jean-St François,[53] almost foreshadows the Baroque in the relaxed open gesture of the arms and hands, very different from the tension usual in Mannerist renderings of religious feeling.

Even more impressive is the group of works from the chapel of René de Birague in the church of Ste Catherine du Val-des-Écoliers in Paris. Birague, a Milanese by birth, was chancellor of France from 1573 to 1578. After the death of his wife in 1572 he took orders and was made a cardinal; he himself died in 1583. Before his death he commissioned from Pilon the tomb of his wife, Valentine Balbiani, and his own monument was executed by the same artist at the expense of his heirs. The tombs were much damaged in the eighteenth century and at the Revolution, but the Louvre has preserved the kneeling bronze figure of Birague himself (Plate 67), the recumbent marble statue of his wife,[54] as well as her *gisant* in bas-relief (Plate 65).[55]

The statue of Birague is a development from the bronzes on the tomb of Henry II. But the conception is grander and the treatment broader. Pilon has placed the figure in profile kneeling at a prie-Dieu with his robes hanging in heavy folds and forming a long train behind him.[56] All decorative detail has been eliminated, except for the indications of fur on the hood, which are sharply incised in the clay. Pilon has here exploited to the full the heavy monumentality of bronze, and has deliberately left the surface rough and unpolished. The head and the hands show intense observation and great directness of rendering. The tomb of Valentine Balbiani is altogether different. The marble recumbent effigy shows that Pilon was still capable of virtuosity in the carving of detail, and its very richness heightens the contrast with the grim *gisant* on the sarcophagus below. Here for the first time we see Pilon using naturalism to stimulate emotion. In this relief he has sought all the effects which he deliberately avoided in the *gisant* of Catherine de' Medici. The figure is emaciated, the bones stick through the flesh, the hands are those of a skeleton, as in the work of the naturalistic sculptors of the Late Gothic period. This is the first instance in French sculpture of the phenomenon common in Mannerism, a return to the Middle Ages. The treatment of the figure, however, is far from being Gothic. On the contrary, the modelling shows Pilon's fluid conception of form carried even farther than in his earlier works. The relief is very low, and the forms seem to flow loosely over the ground. This is the same conception of modelling which we saw in the *gisant* of Henry II, but developed and applied to the different problem of low relief carving.

The bronze relief of the Deposition (Plate 68) now in the Louvre comes from the same church as the Birague tombs and probably formed part of the same decorative scheme. There is no evidence about its date, but its style is so close to that of the *gisant* of Valentine Balbiani that it must have been executed within a year or two of the tomb. It has not the same grimness of detail, but it comes close to it in its dramatic intensity and in the treatment of relief. There are strong traces of Italian influence here, principally of Michelangelo and his school.[57] The closest parallels are to be found in Bandinelli's reliefs of the same subject in the Louvre and the Victoria and Albert Museum.[58] But the treatment is entirely personal. It is interesting to compare this relief with Goujon's treatment of the same subject (Plate 55A). The comparison shows up not only the difference in the technical methods of the two artists and their opposed conceptions of modelling; but it also reminds us that the whole feeling of the period had changed. In Goujon the emotion is there but it is expressed in symbols which conform to canons of classical beauty. Pilon does not hesitate to use gestures and features that are almost grotesque in order to heighten his effect. Goujon is typical of the classical period in the middle of the century; Pilon embodies the emotional state of mind which marked the decades of the Wars of Religion.

It is not surprising that the personal and emotional qualities of Pilon's art were not copied by his successors. But most French sculptors of the last decades of the sixteenth century were much influenced by his earlier manner. The most interesting of these followers was Barthélemy Prieur (active 1573–1611), who made the sculptures on the monument for the heart of Constable Montmorency, now in the Louvre, of which the architectural parts were designed by Bullant.[59] The central part of the composition is a twisted or 'Salomonic' column, probably the earliest imitation in French architecture of the columns in St Peter's said to come from the Temple of Jerusalem, popularized through engravings after Raphael's cartoon of 'Elymas'.[60] Round the foot of this column stand three life-size bronze Virtues which are variants of Pilon's corner figures on the tomb of Henry II.[61] Other examples could be found all over France of allegorical sculpture in the same style, and also of kneeling tomb figures deriving from Pilon's Henry II, Catherine de' Medici and Birague, which may be said to have set a fashion lasting well into the seventeenth century.[62]

PAINTING

Antoine Caron, Jean Cousin the Younger, and the Portrait Painters

There are few periods at which French painting was at a lower ebb than the last quarter of the sixteenth century and the first quarter of the seventeenth, and few periods about which we are more ignorant. In the reigns of Charles IX and Henry III only two painters, Antoine Caron and Jean Cousin the Younger, stand out as recognizable personalities; a few portrait painters, hardly above the level of mediocrity, can be isolated; and for the rest we know some names of artists to whom no works can be assigned and a vast number of works – mainly portrait drawings – to which no names of artists can be attached, at least with any certainty.

Antoine Caron,[63] who is at present enjoying a rather exaggerated popularity, is of interest in that he reflects vividly the peculiar atmosphere of the Valois Court during the Wars of Religion. We know that he died at the age of seventy-eight, probably about 1600, and we may therefore conclude that he was born in the early 1520s. He is first recorded as working under Primaticcio at Fontainebleau before 1550, and he later became painter to Catherine de' Medici. We know, further, that Caron was closely connected with the Catholic League, and was a friend of Louis d'Orléans, the poet and pamphleteer of that movement.

Caron's themes fall into three main categories. The first are allegorical subjects which in presentation recall the festivities for which the Court of the last Valois was famous. His paintings of the 'Triumphs of the Seasons', for instance, include *fêtes galantes*, water-parties, picnics, and orchestras with an allegorical procession in the foreground illustrating the season in question, apparently based on the ballets which had become a favourite pastime of the Court. The two large sets of drawings – the 'Histoire des Rois de France' and the Artémise series – belong to the same category. They reflect court ceremonial rather than court ballets, but the spirit is the same; in the latter the allusion to Catherine de' Medici in the person of Artemisia is clear.

In these two sets of drawings the theme of battles also occurs, and provides a link with the next type of subject treated by Caron, that of the Massacre. The signed painting in the Louvre represents the relatively rare subject of the 'Massacres under the Triumvirate', and it has often been pointed out that this must be understood as a direct reference to the bloodshed which characterized the Wars of Religion during which the picture was executed. The violence of this painting reflects an aspect of life as typical of the period as the court ballets shown in the first group.

Finally two paintings show a more fantastic approach: the 'Astrologers Studying an Eclipse' and 'Augustus and the Sibyl' (Plate 70A) bring out the love of predictions, horoscopes, and anything on the borderline of magic which was current in the late sixteenth century, and particularly in the circle round Catherine de' Medici.

In his subjects, therefore, Caron is typical of the most sophisticated Court Mannerism, with its emphasis on external ceremonial and elaborate allegory and its love of the fantastic or irrational. In treatment this Mannerism is even more apparent. The most obvious characteristic of Caron's style is the elongation of his figures, a device which he learnt from Niccolò dell'Abbate, but which he greatly exaggerated.[64] From him also he learnt their strange twisted attitudes and tapering limbs.[65] His long, pin-headed figures are then placed in a space which is intentionally too large for them, so that they seem lost and insignificant in it. This space is usually defined by architecture, drawn in sharply exaggerated perspective and composed of the most fantastic fragments which Caron could find in the designs of du Cerceau, combined with schematic versions of Roman ruins or sometimes with a landscape, again based on Niccolò. To this must be added a colouring dominated by unexpected rainbow contrasts, often against an almost white ground in the architecture. The sum total of these elements of content and form is to produce what is perhaps the purest known type of Mannerism in its elegant form, appropriate to an exquisite but neurotic aristocratic society.[66]

In his own time Jean Cousin the Younger must have enjoyed a great reputation, since his name is mentioned with reverence by contemporary writers; but his work has mostly disappeared. He was the son of Jean Cousin the Elder, was born in Sens about 1522, lived most of his life in Paris, and probably died about 1594. His *Livre de Fortune* (1568), a series of emblem drawings, shows him as a continuer of Rosso's decorative style.[67] Two engraved designs of the 'Brazen Serpent' and the 'Conversion of St Paul' indicate that he was influenced by Florentine Mannerism. In particular the 'St Paul' belongs to a type of composition used by Salviati in his painting in the Doria Gallery[68] and his fresco in the Cancelleria.[69] Cousin's most important surviving work is the 'Last Judgement' in the Louvre, engraved under his name in 1615 (Plate 69A). Here he is playing, like Caron, on the theme of the puniness of humanity, which is made to swarm over the earth like worms. But his formula is a Florentine one, and seems to be derived from Bronzino's 'Descent into Limbo' in the Colonna Gallery,[70] although the actual types of figures suggest a Flemish influence. Cousin's main field of activity may have lain outside painting properly speaking, as he is known to have designed widely for book illustrations and for stained glass.[71]

One series of drawings must be mentioned here as throwing an interesting light on the taste of the time. These represent the tournament held at Sandricourt in the year 1493. The drawings which are in the Louvre are probably by Jérôme Bollery (died soon after 1600).[72] It is unexpected to find an artist commissioned at the end of the sixteenth century to make drawings of a famous feat of chivalry of a century earlier,[73] but the subject may well have appealed to a certain section of the aristocracy which looked back with nostalgia to the days of feudalism.[74]

Portraiture continued to be one of the most popular forms of art in France in the later sixteenth century, and in particular the vogue of portrait-drawings grew even greater. In this genre the two eldest members of the Dumonstier family, Étienne and Pierre the Elder, were among the most distinguished, but they hardly did more than carry on the tradition of François Clouet. The same may be said of Benjamin Foulon and François Quesnel, whose drawings are more polished, but less vigorous than those of the two Dumonstiers. Among the few painted portraits of the period which can be attributed to named artists one of the most interesting is that of Mary Ann Waltham, signed with the initials of François Quesnel and dated 1572 (Plate 69B). This is typical of the last phase of French sixteenth-century portraiture, when the naturalism of François Clouet has been stylized so that the modelling almost disappears and the portrait is dominated by the flat linear pattern. Marc Duval showed greater boldness in his full-length life-size portrait of the three Coligny brothers, known from copies and an engraving. To the same category belongs the anonymous portrait of Catherine de' Medici and her children which was burnt in the fire at Castle Howard.[75]

One novelty was introduced into French painting in the last decades of the sixteenth century, namely the treatment of domestic subjects, or at any rate subjects which were neither religious nor classical.[76] The favourite themes of artists in this field are scenes from the Commedia dell'Arte, such as the 'Woman Choosing between Youth and Age' (Plate 70B), or court balls, such as those of the Duc de Joyeuse, at Versailles, and of the Duc d'Alençon in the Louvre.[77] All these paintings show strong Flemish influence, and it is quite possible that they were the work of Flemish painters living in France.[78] Compositions of the same type, but usually with a more satirical tendency, are to be found in the engravings of the period, many of which were devoted to political satire by both factions in the time of the League. Here again Flemish influence is evident, and engravers seize on the idiom of Bruegel to satirize their religious and political opponents in the same spirit as he had used it in Flanders.[79]

CHAPTER 5

HENRY IV AND THE REGENCY OF MARIE DE' MEDICI
1598 – 1630

HISTORICAL BACKGROUND

WHEN Henry IV entered Paris in 1594 and was acknowledged king by the great majority of his subjects, he found a country worn out with a civil war which had been intensified by religious fanaticism and confused by foreign intervention. The trade and industry of France were almost ruined, her administration was dislocated, and her population impoverished. During the first few years of his reign Henry devoted himself to driving out the Spaniards, coming to terms with the remaining rebels, and finding a religious settlement. These aims had been achieved by 1598, when the Peace of Vervins brought freedom from the invaders, and the Edict of Nantes gave the world the first proof that religious toleration could be the basis of sound state policy. As regards the rebels, even Mayenne, the most recalcitrant Leaguer, had made his peace with the King well before this date.

From 1598 onwards, therefore, Henry and his minister Sully were able to devote their whole attention to the problem of internal reconstruction. The situation could hardly have been more serious. In the country the peasantry had, as always, suffered more than any other section of the community from the civil war and the increased taxation. The nobility were greatly impoverished, partly owing to the expenses of the war and partly through the alteration in the value of money, which lowered the effective value of rent-rolls. The inhabitants of the towns had suffered from the interruption of trade due to the general insecurity of the kingdom. The *bourgeoisie* was, however, in a much better position to recover than the aristocracy, whose income depended entirely on their land, who were forbidden to engage in any kind of trade and who, incidentally, had tasted the pleasures of court life during the latter part of the sixteenth century and were reluctant to go back and look after their estates.

The reforms of Henry and Sully were mainly directed towards improving the catastrophic financial position of the Crown and restoring the general prosperity of the kingdom by the revival of agriculture, trade, and industry. To attain the first of these objects Sully tried to free the Crown lands from mortgage and to bring some order into the system of taxation. He could do no more, however, than remove some of the grosser abuses in the system of farming out taxes, so that the actual yield to the Crown was increased; but he never tried to change the system itself. His encouragement to agriculture was more effective; and his attempt to break down the rigidity of the guild system did something to free small-scale industry. Trade was helped by his improvement of communications, but was still hindered by internal customs barriers.

Henry IV's most effective reforms were probably in the field of administration; for he was able to restore to the Crown the power which it had held under Henry II, but which it had almost entirely lost during the Wars of Religion. Learning from the experience of his predecessors he refrained from calling the States General and did everything to strengthen the administration which depended directly on the Crown. The Council, which in effect governed the kingdom, was reduced to twelve members appointed by the King, and as a matter of policy the Princes of the Blood and the great nobles were excluded from it. Realizing that the provincial governors had now become dangerously powerful and capable of using their power in their own interests rather than in those of the Crown, Henry limited their authority by removing from them the control of taxation and justice, and by appointing his own nominees as governors of the provincial fortresses. With regard to the towns his policy was like that of Francis I, a mixture of cajolery and bullying which extracted from them important concessions and decreased their separatist potentialities.

The policy of Henry IV and Sully was notable more for its solid common sense than for any profound theoretical doctrines about government. But the result of this practical régime was that at the time of Henry's assassination in 1610, France was once more in a position to take her part in the affairs of Europe as one of the great powers. Unfortunately, however, during the minority of his son Louis XIII, who was only nine when he came to the throne, the regency was in the hands of Henry's widow Marie de' Medici, who handled the affairs of state with such indecision that the work of her husband was greatly jeopardized. Seeing the weakness of her Government, largely directed by her unscrupulous and incompetent favourite Concini, the Princes of the Blood and the nobles, led by Condé, Soissons, and Bouillon, did their utmost to regain the position which they had lost under the previous reign. At the same time the Parlement challenged the Crown on every possible issue, above all on the recurrent problem of the *Paulette*, the arrangement which enabled the members of the Parlement to hand on their posts to their children, and so establish the hierarchies which gave them social position and freedom from taxation. This double opposition to the central power might have proved fatal, but for the appearance of a new figure capable of dealing with both. Richelieu, who had been made a Secretary of State in 1616 and had risen by 1624 to be the head of the Council, was to be the continuer of the policy of Henry IV and the final consolidator of the centralized autocracy of France.

In the intellectual field the first three decades of the seventeenth century were a time of considerable activity. They witnessed a religious revival of which the leading representatives were Cardinal de Bérulle, St François de Sales, and St Vincent de Paul. The particular character of this revival gave the tone for religious thought through almost the whole century in France. It was profoundly sincere, but lacked the ecstatic and mystical quality of contemporary movements in Italy and Spain with their love of self-mortification. Instead these French enthusiasts taught a practical doctrine which could easily be harmonized with ordinary social existence. The movement led to a general raising of the religious life of the community, and, in the case of St Vincent, to the first great charitable undertakings.

At the same time the development of a purely secular morality was fostered by the revival of Stoicism due to Guillaume du Vair, one of the leaders of the moderate party or *Politiques* at the time of the League, and Pierre Charron. The latter's famous treatise *De la Sagesse*, published in 1601, was used as a handbook by the sceptics of the next generation, but also influenced the stream of Stoicism which was ultimately to unite with Christianity in the thought of Pascal.

In literature two strongly conflicting tendencies are apparent. On the one hand, a very fantastic style flourished, which appealed primarily to the aristocratic taste of which the law-giver was Mme de Rambouillet with her circle of *Précieux*. This public enjoyed the long pastoral novels, such as d'Urfé's *Astrée*, deriving from Italian and Spanish models and a brand of Mannerist poetry which specialized in epigrams, madrigals, anagrammatic verses and tortured sonnets. On the other hand, Malherbe introduced his reform, and so laid the foundations of French classical verse. His rational approach to literature, his common-sense purification of the language, his demand that poetry should be clear, easily intelligible, and carefully chiselled, put him in complete opposition to the fantastic school of Maynard, Racan, and Voiture, the poets admired by the *Précieux*. These qualities also explain why he was the favourite poet of Henry IV.

ARCHITECTURE

The Replanning of Paris, the Younger du Cerceau, Le Muet, Salomon de Brosse

The buildings for which Henry IV was directly responsible must be considered in two groups: the additions to the royal palaces, and the improvements to the city of Paris.

Of the former the finest example is the Stable Court at Fontainebleau (Plate 71B), built probably by Rémy Collin round a square court open on one side towards the Cour de l'Ovale.[1] The great entrance, which bears the date 1609, is a translation into French terms of Bramante's Belvedere niche. The architect has relied for a great part of his effect on the variety of surface produced by the rustication and by the different colours of the hard local *grès*, which Serlio had used in a similar spirit in the door of the 'Grand Ferrare'. The niche form of entrance is echoed in the semicircular bay in the middle of the opposite side of the court.[2]

Far more revolutionary are Henry IV's improvements to the city of Paris. It was in accordance with his general policy that he should want to embellish his capital, and in keeping with his character that his improvements should be of a very practical kind. In the short space of about ten years he completed the Pont Neuf, built the Place Royale and the Place Dauphine and began the Place de France, created the Hôpital St Louis and laid the foundations of the Collège Royal. In these works Henry IV brought town-planning to a new stage and established certain principles which were to influence the development of Paris for several centuries. In some cases we shall find that he was taking up ideas which had been suggested in the sixteenth century, but the manner in which they were carried out bears the clear stamp not only of the later period, but also of the character of the King himself. For many of these buildings we do not even know the names of the architects who seem to disappear behind the personality of the King. We know that Henry took a close personal interest in these schemes, and they all have so much in common that we must suppose Chastillon, Louis Métezeau, or Baptiste du Cerceau, whose names appear in some confusion in the accounts, to have been above all builders acting under the direction of a single mind, that of the King himself.

In 1599 Henry IV took up the building of the Pont Neuf which had been begun under Henry III in 1578, but interrupted by the civil war. As originally planned, the bridge was to be a somewhat fanciful affair with houses on it, and at each end triumphal arches, which were to serve purposes of defence as well as of ornament. Henry IV simplified the scheme, and eliminated the houses and the triumphal arches. The purpose of the bridge was to link the southern part of Paris, containing the university, with the business and administrative quarters on the Cité and the right bank. In order to deal with the traffic which this new communication would create, Henry further planned the rue Dauphine cutting through the maze of small streets on the left bank. In this way traffic coming from the north bank could communicate not only with the university quarter but with the Faubourg St Germain, which as a result of this scheme became more accessible and was later to be developed as a rich quarter.

In 1604 Marie de' Medici offered to present to the city of Paris an equestrian statue of the King to be set up at the point where the Pont Neuf cut the end of the Cité. The statue, commissioned from Giovanni da Bologna and completed by Tacca, was not set up till 1614, but the project evidently influenced the development of the site; for in 1607 Henry IV decided to build the Place Dauphine to cover the triangular space at the end of the island, facing the point where the statue was to be set up (Figure 10). The Place consisted of two ranges of buildings on the equal sides of an isosceles triangle, leaving openings at the apex and in the middle of the base. The houses were of standard design, with pairs of arched openings for shops on the ground floor, separated by narrow doors leading through a passage to the small court at the back, from which a steep staircase led to the living quarters above. The outside was of simple design, very similar to the Place Royale (cf. Plate 71A), and of cheap materials, brick decorated with quoins and *chaînes* in stucco. Henry IV was here following up an idea suggested in the previous century, for du Cerceau publishes at the end of the second volume of his *Plus Excellents Bastiments* a line of buildings 'recently erected' between the Petit Pont and the Hôtel Dieu, which in their general disposition with arcaded shops separated by doors on the ground floor are exactly like those of the Place Dauphine. But it is characteristic of the more advanced thought of Henry IV that, whereas his predecessors had planned a single block of such buildings, he should have extended the idea to a whole square which in its turn was part of a larger scheme of town-planning.

The Place Royale, or Place des Vosges as it is now called (Plates 71A and 72A), was conceived in 1603 and carried out from 1605 onwards. It was built on the site of the old royal palace of the Tournelles, which was abandoned by Catherine de' Medici after the death of Henry II in the tournament held there. Four years later, in 1563, she put forward a

PONT NEUF

CHEVAL DE
BRONZE

PONT NEUF

QUAI DES ORFÈVRES

QUAI QUI REGARDE LA MÉGISSERIE

RUE DE HARLAY

Figure 10. Place Dauphine: Plan

plan to make on the site a Place de Valois, surrounded by houses of standard design, but the Wars of Religion interrupted the project. The idea in Henry IV's mind is clearly expressed in the instrument drawn up for the execution of the project. The square was to provide a *promenoir* for the people of Paris and a place for them to assemble on occasions of public rejoicing. At the same time it was to contain houses suitable for the well-to-do. The King let the plots round the square at a nominal rate on condition that the buyer built according to the agreed plan. Henry himself built the two central pavilions on the north and south sides, called the Pavillons du Roi et de la Reine, which are taller than the rest of the houses and more elaborately decorated. The normal plot sold consisted of four bays, which made a house of respectable, but not excessive size. The result was that, though the great noble families continued to build private houses on larger and freer sites, the less rich members of the aristocracy and the wealthier *bourgeois* flocked to the Place Royale, and made it the centre of a quarter, called the Marais, which remained fashionable for the rest of the seventeenth century, till it was gradually displaced by the Faubourg St Germain.

The style of the houses was of the same simplicity as in the Place Dauphine. Instead of the shops on the ground floor of the latter we find here an arcaded cloister which was an essential part of the King's plan; but in the upper storeys the elevation is similar, with stucco *chaînes* against the brick, and very simple dormers. On the two main floors the architect has used French windows, opening right down to the floor, which were apparently a novelty.[3]

In the last of Henry IV's great town-planning projects, the Place de France (Plate 72B; designed in 1610), the practical and symbolical sides were both clearly emphasized. Only a small part of the scheme was carried out, but we know the whole from the engraving prepared by Claude Chastillon, who in the legend tells us that he and the engineer Jacques Alleaume were responsible for the design. It consisted of a semicircular space closed along the diameter by the walls of Paris between the Porte St Antoine and the Porte du Temple. In the middle of this diameter was a new gate, the Porte de France. Round the circumference were seven buildings for markets and other public services, separated by roads leading radially from the Place itself. These roads were cut by an outer ring of streets, some distance behind the market buildings. Each street bore the name of a French Province, so that the whole plan was a symbol of national as well as civic pride. Stylistically the buildings are like those of the Place Royale and the Place Dauphine in their simplicity, but they are more archaic in one detail, namely in having turrets at the corners of the pavilions which thus look almost like Flemish town-halls of the later middle ages.[4]

It would be hard to over-estimate the importance of Henry IV's public works in Paris for the history of town development, so advanced were they for their time. Italy had produced open spaces such as the Capitol and the Piazza of St Mark's surrounded by some of the great public buildings of the city symmetrically disposed; and in Flanders and north-eastern France towns like Antwerp, Brussels, or Arras could show squares on which stood houses of the guilds or the richest citizens. But Henry's *places* were the first to combine the regularity of design of Italy with the Flemish grouping of small houses.

They were the first examples of that most characteristic expression of *bourgeois* pride and practical sense, the regularly designed series of living houses disposed on a geometrical plan and carried out in simple materials, unostentatious but comfortable.[5] The idea was soon copied. Elsewhere in France examples are to be found built at Charleville (1608) by Charles de Gonzague, Duc de Nevers, at Henrichemont by Sully (1608), at Montauban (1616) by the municipality and at Richelieu (*c.* 1632) by the cardinal.[6] But the idea was soon to spread outside France. In England Covent Garden (*c.* 1630) is a direct imitation of the Place Royale, which may therefore be regarded as the ultimate ancestor of the square development in London, Bath, and elsewhere. And in other forms the idea took root in Holland, Germany and, later, even in Italy.

In Paris itself, as has already been indicated, Henry IV's improvements led to the development of several new quarters. It became fashionable to build round the Place Royale, and the bolder spirits soon began to take advantage of the new bridge to buy sites in the almost deserted Faubourg St Germain. In 1608 the contractor Marie acquired the right to let off the whole of the Île Notre-Dame, now the Île St Louis, to which he agreed to build the bridge bearing his name. During the following decades some of the finest private houses in Paris sprang up on this island, which still preserves its rigid layout with one street from end to end, crossed by three at right angles to it. At about the same time a further area north of the Louvre and the Tuileries gardens was enclosed within the walls of Paris. There Richelieu built the Palais Royal, and a little later Mazarin his house, now the Bibliothèque Nationale, and round this nucleus sprang up yet another quarter.[7]

In all these newly developed areas those who could afford the larger free-standing type of hôtel gave to the architects of the time an opportunity to display their skill in planning and decoration.

In 1605 Charles, Duc de Mayenne, reconciled with the King after his activities in the League, began an hôtel in the rue St Antoine, not far from the Place Royale.[8] The house, which still stands, though much altered, was built by Jacques Androuet du Cerceau the Younger and is a variant of the type known in the sixteenth century in the Hôtel Carnavalet, consisting of a main *corps-de-logis* and wings leading to a street façade of two pavilions joined by a lower section containing the entrance.[9]

During the regency of Marie de' Medici many hôtels were put up particularly in the Marais of which the finest surviving example is the Hôtel de Châlons-Luxembourg, probably built soon after 1623.[10] The house itself is a narrow building in brick and stone standing behind a court, the entrance to which is formed by a magnificent door (Plate 76B), originally free-standing. This is a fine example of the more fantastic style which was current in Paris in the period after 1620.

The most important designer of private houses during this period was Jean du Cerceau, son of Baptiste, who was born about 1585 and died about the middle of the seventeenth century. He was responsible for the two most typical private houses of the reign of Louis XIII, the Hôtel de Sully and the Hôtel de Bretonvilliers. The former, built in the rue St Antoine for a rich financier, Mesme Gallet, between 1624 and 1629, was bought in 1634 by Sully, the minister of Henry IV. It still stands (Plate 74B), decayed but not much altered externally, except that, as at the Hôtel de Mayenne, the middle of the street façade has been filled in.[11] The plan follows that of the Hôtel de Mayenne, and the real novelty is to be found in the richness of the decoration. The façades on the court are ornamented with allegorical figures in niches which are an echo of Goujon's decorations on the Hôtel Carnavalet. All the windows are covered by sculptured friezes and pediments containing masks or shells. The dormers are also of unusually elaborate form with carved scrolls at the sides and friezes and masks over them. The style of these carved decorations is one which does not seem to be traceable in Paris at an earlier date, but it is remarkably like that practised by Hugues Sambin in Dijon almost half a century earlier, and may be a derivation from it.

Figure 11. Jean du Cerceau: Hôtel de Bretonvilliers: Plan

Jean du Cerceau's other hôtel was also built for a rich financier, Ragois de Bretonvilliers, between 1637 and 1643 on the newly developed Île St Louis.[12] It was pulled down in the nineteenth century, but we can form a fair idea of its appearance from the engravings of Silvestre and Marot. It must have derived much of its beauty from its position on the eastern point of the island with views up the river. The exterior seems to have had sculptured decoration very like that on the Hôtel de Sully, and its chief originality lay in its plan (Figure 11) in which two novel features appear. The first is the ingenious use of the site. The main entrance from the street led into a court of the usual form with the *corps-de-logis* facing the visitor, but to the left through an arched opening was another smaller court containing the stables. On the garden side the architect has taken advantage of this extra width to enlarge the façade which has eleven bays, the middle one being blind to cover the fact that the two façades on court and garden are not co-axial. The garden, which filled the space down to the point of the island, was open to the river on the south and east sides, but protected from other buildings on the north by a gallery which ran out from the main building. The second novelty is the placing of the staircase. In the Hôtel de Sully, and as far as we know in most Paris houses of the time, the staircase occupied the middle of the main block,[13] an inconvenient arrangement because it broke the flight of principal rooms. At the Hôtel de Bretonvilliers du Cerceau has placed the staircase in the corner of the court, so that it actually occupies a space in the left-hand wing. In this way he is able to give it a bigger space than it could have in the middle of the main block, and at the same time to allow for a continuous row of reception rooms on the first floor. A vestibule in the middle of the ground floor gives access to the rooms on either side, and also provides a passage to the garden. In order to preserve symmetry in the court another entrance is made in the right-hand corner which leads to the rooms in the corresponding wing.[14]

The principles on which private houses were built during this period are laid down in two books. The first is the *Architecture Françoise* of Louis Savot, first published in 1624, in which the author discusses the practical conditions of building in Paris, including the various laws and regulations governing private houses, and the nature and price of materials. The second is the *Manière de bien bastir pour toutes sortes de personnes*, published by Pierre Le Muet in 1623, and again in an enlarged edition in 1647. This treatise is an up-to-date version of du Cerceau's first book of architecture, in that it provides designs of houses for different categories of owners. But Le Muet goes much farther down the social scale than his predecessor. His smallest houses are for a street frontage of only twelve feet, with just enough room on the ground floor for one small room and a narrow passage leading through to the staircase and the tiny court. From this smallest model, built almost without ornament and in the simplest materials, Le Muet takes the reader on to larger houses, mainly in the current brick-and-stone manner.[15] In the second half of the book, which was only added in the edition of 1647, he is more ambitious and gives plans and elevations of a few very grand hôtels which he actually built. Most of them were erected after the period which we are now considering, but they belong in character to the generation of the younger du Cerceau, for Le Muet, who was born in 1591, but lived till 1669, formed his style in the 1620s and never fully assimilated the classicism of the succeeding generation. The most important of the surviving houses is the one built for the Président Duret de Chevry in 1635, enlarged for Tubeuf in 1641, later sold to Mazarin, and now forming part of the Bibliothèque Nationale (Plate 75).[16] This building shows the architect's love of complicated rustication, of stone *chaînes* and quoins and of unusually shaped pediments filled with low reliefs. His other Paris houses, dating from the 1640s, reveal Le Muet in more classical mood, but there are always some Mannerist features which appear through the surface regularity.[17]

In the château building of the early years of the seventeenth century we find the same conflict of styles. In the reign of Henry IV the greater part of the castles and country houses built conform in materials and manner to the brick-and-stone work of the Place Royale, but in the years after 1610, and even in some cases earlier, architects make an even greater display of fantasy here than in the Paris hôtel.

Of the simple style a fine example is Grosbois (Plate 78B), of which the central pavilion is said to have been built by Raoul Moreau, a financier and civil servant who owned the estate from 1562 till 1616. The exact date of the building is unknown, but it cannot be far off 1600. The four pavilions attached to the central *corps-de-logis* and the two wings leading to the pavilions at the entrance of the court are said to have been added by the Duc d'Angoulême, natural son of Charles IX, who bought Grosbois in 1616; but the difference in style is hardly perceptible.

Grosbois consists of a building round a court with doubled pavilions at the corners of the principal *corps-de-logis*. It has, however, one very unusual feature, the apse-shaped centre to the main block. This relates it to de l'Orme's Château-Neuf at St Germain; but the closest parallel for it is the stable-yard at Fontainebleau.[18] Allowing for the difference in materials the two buildings are also very alike in general conception and their designs must spring from the same architect or circle of architects. Grosbois is built of the materials usual in the simpler Henry IV châteaux, but they are applied in an original manner. The surface of the walls is of white plaster which is relieved with quoins and *chaînes*, but in this case the quoins are of stone, whereas the *chaînes* are of brick, an arrangement which gives an effect of variety to the elevation without any use of ornament.[19]

The same simple manner can be found all over the country. But on the whole the provinces favoured a more fantastic style. When, for instance, in 1606 Charles de Cossé, Duc de Brissac, decided to rebuild the château of Brissac, near Angers, he used the foundations of the medieval castle and began to build on them a structure which in its proportions and its detail is a complete contrast to all that had been put up in the Île-de-France (Plate 77). As it stands to-day the château is only a fragment, and the main façade is still squeezed between two medieval towers, which were to have been pulled down so that the front could be made symmetrical. Its enormous height – on the north side where the ground falls away it rises to six storeys – and its unusual, compact plan make it look more like a castle than the house of a country gentleman; but we must remember that the Wars of Religion were only just over and that Brissac had taken an active part in them. The surface of the building is restlessly broken with long-and-short borders to the windows, rusticated *voussoirs* and pilasters, and in the central pavilion elaborate Late Mannerist carved decoration. In many details, too, the arrangement is Mannerist in feeling. Notice, for instance, the double dormers with curved pediments enclosed under a single straight one, and on the same floor in the middle pavilion the two pediments interrupted by the intrusion of the window of the floor above.[20]

So far no mention has been made of the most distinguished architect of the period, Salomon de Brosse, but he is conveniently considered at the end of this section because more than any of his contemporaries he prepares the way for the next generation and the introduction of classicism. His father was an architect of some distinction, and his mother was the daughter of the elder Jacques du Cerceau. He was born in 1571 at Verneuil, and presumably brought up in the circle of late du Cerceau activities there. After the Edict of Nantes his family, who were Protestants, moved to Paris, and from about 1610 onwards he seems to have enjoyed considerable success as an architect. During the next few years he was commissioned to build three great châteaux: Coulommiers in

1613 for Catherine de Gonzague, Duchesse de Longueville; Blérancourt (Plate 79A), finished before 1619 for Bernard Potier; [21] and the Luxembourg (Plate 74A) in 1615 for Marie de' Medici.[22] In 1618 de Brosse began his two major public commissions, the rebuilding of the Salle in the Palais of the Paris Parlement, and the construction of the palace for the Parlement of Brittany at Rennes (Plate 79B). In 1623 he rebuilt the Protestant Temple at Charenton, after the first Temple built in 1606 – perhaps also after his design – had been burnt.[23] He died in 1626.

Of the three châteaux the Luxembourg and Coulommiers are in many ways traditional. In plan they are variants of the well-established form with *corps-de-logis*, two wings and a screen enclosing a court. The Luxembourg (cf. Figure 12) is the more

Figure 12. Salomon de Brosse:
Luxembourg: Plan

mature with its double pavilions at the corners of the main block, each pavilion providing a complete *appartement* on every floor. On the other hand, this plan has the disadvantage that its side elevation is asymmetrical.[24] At Coulommiers[25] de Brosse gets over this difficulty by doubling the pavilions at the ends of the wings as well as those on the *corps-de-logis*. This arrangement is an exact reproduction of Jacques du Cerceau's first plan for Verneuil, which de Brosse must have known from childhood.

The essential contribution of de Brosse to the development of French architecture at this moment lies in the fact that he was the first architect since Philibert de l'Orme to think in terms of mass, and not of decoration of surface. All the members of the du Cerceau family were essentially inventors of ornament, and even Bullant, though a more intellectual designer, designed primarily patterns playing on the surface or porticos applied to a building.

De Brosse's sense of mass can be seen most clearly in the two later châteaux, the Luxembourg and Blérancourt (Plate 79A). In Coulommiers it is less in evidence, partly because the more elaborate dormers, still in the du Cerceau manner, blur the edges of the roof, and partly because the walls facing the court are articulated with a system of coupled full columns on each floor, based on Lescot's design for the Louvre. In the Luxembourg the dormers are replaced by an attic floor under a cornice which leaves an almost unbroken edge at the spring of the roof. Much greater emphasis is also placed on the *corps-de-logis* itself, conceived as a complete symmetrical unit, to which the wings, being lower and narrower, are clearly subordinated. The articulation with columns used at Coulommiers is also given up, and both the court and the exterior façades are now covered with a uniform and rather light rustication, which does not break the clarity of outline of the blocks.[26]

In one respect the Luxembourg follows the design for Coulommiers, and even the earlier example of Verneuil, namely in the design of the entrance front which has as its central element a sort of rotunda. It is noticeable, however, that de Brosse's design is far more restrained than du Cerceau's. His rotunda goes back to the Valois Chapel and Bramante's Tempietto as models rather than to the Mannerist fantasies of Verneuil.

At Blérancourt de Brosse's plastic conception is even more apparent, because the château has no wings, but is reduced to the *corps-de-logis* with four flanking pavilions. This is an important step, leading up to the classical conception of the château as it was evolved by François Mansart, and bearing a closer relation to the ideals of the Italian Renaissance than any earlier buildings in France. This free-standing symmetrical block, designed to be seen from all sides, is of the same family as Bramante's House of Raphael or Peruzzi's Farnesina. But apart from de l'Orme's Château-Neuf at St Germain, it was a novelty in France, where up to this time the château had either been built round a court or on a straight plan with pavilions and wings. De Brosse introduces at Blérancourt another feature which adds to the compactness of the whole. In his two other châteaux he had used the traditional high-pitched roof, though at the Luxembourg he had altered it to the extent of cutting off the apex; but at Blérancourt he adopts for the pavilions the square domes used by Jacques du Cerceau at Verneuil, though he makes them even lower, so that they bring the roof into easy relation with the main mass of the pavilions below.

As far as we can judge from the engravings, Blérancourt was a revolutionary building in another respect. Its application of the Orders was far more correct than in the other works of de Brosse or the buildings of his contemporaries. The Orders chosen were the two most severe, Doric and Ionic, and the walls are decorated by them alone without any further ornament. In the pavilions which still stand at the corners of the forecourt we can see also how finely classical was the design of the windows, far in advance of anything else which was being done in France at this time. The interlacing pattern of the balustrade was one copied by François Mansart and used in France at any rate till the generation of Jacques-Ange Gabriel. The same classicism is to be seen in the façade of the Palais du Parlement at Rennes (Plate 79B),[27] where de Brosse's feeling for sharply defined mass, for the simplicity of the wall and for delicacy of classical detail appears at its clearest. Here he anticipates many of the features to be developed later by François Mansart.

The name of de Brosse is also traditionally associated with the most important piece of church architecture of the period, the façade of St Gervais (1616; Plate 80B).[28] This design is a novelty in ecclesiastical architecture, for it is the application to a church façade of the three superimposed Orders regularly used for the entrance to a château. The closest model is de l'Orme's frontispiece at Anet, to which de Brosse has simply added a straight pediment over the main door and a curved one at the top of the whole structure. In this way de Brosse has invented a French form of the current Roman church façade. His problem is different, however, because in the case of St Gervais the church to which the façade was being added was a tall Late Gothic building, and this necessitated the use of three floors instead of the two usual in Roman fronts of the same type.[29]

The chapel of the Trinité at Fontainebleau supplies a good example of the interior decoration of the period. The main ornamentation of the ceiling dates from the reign of Henry IV, and consists of a combination of stucco frames and painted panels in the manner to be seen in all parts of the palace, though with rather more advanced details of ornament. Over the altar and the royal gallery, however, Marie de' Medici added two big stucco groups of angels supporting her coat of arms (Plate 73) in the new style which was to be current in France during the period c. 1615–35. This is a variant of the strapwork invented by Rosso at Fontainebleau, which had in the interval been imitated and transformed by Florentine architects such as Buontalenti, who had given it a more curvilinear and three-dimensional quality. Instead of curving over like pieces of cut leather, its forms are now more like a shell or even the lobe of an ear.[30] This form of decoration was widely used during the regency of Marie de' Medici, in stone or wood work, as for instance in the door of the Hôtel de Châlons-Luxembourg (Plate 76B), and can even be traced in the early work of architects of the next generation – for instance, in Mansart's Church of the Visitation and in private houses by Le Vau.

French architecture during the reign of Henry IV and the regency of Marie de' Medici reflects the conflicting tendencies visible in all fields of French culture at this time. Henry IV himself was responsible for works revolutionary in their rational conception and their simple execution. On the other hand, private patrons were still indulging in the fantasies of Late Mannerism, not, it is true, quite as wild as those of the previous decades, but still ignoring the logical style encouraged by the King. Salomon de Brosse alone understood the simplicity of the great royal ventures and added to it a monumental sense which prepared the way for the greatest figure of the next generation, François Mansart.

PAINTING AND SCULPTURE

The Second School of Fontainebleau – the Mannerists of Nancy: Bellange and Callot –
Late Mannerism in Paris – Vignon – Biard

Henry IV devoted considerable energy to the decoration of the royal palaces, but unfortunately few of the paintings which he commissioned survive, and we are therefore
badly informed about the so-called Second School of Fontainebleau, which was responsible for them.

The name is generally applied to three painters: Ambroise Dubois (1542/3–1614),
Toussaint Dubreuil (1561–1602), and Martin Fréminet (1567–1619), who may be said
to have revived the function of their predecessors at Fontainebleau – Rosso, Primaticcio,
and Niccolò dell'Abbate – after the Wars of Religion had interrupted large-scale painting
in France. Unfortunately, however, these three artists lacked the imaginative invention
of the earlier group, and, as far as we can judge their work, its level is one of even
mediocrity.

The oldest of the three members of the school, Ambroise Dubois,[31] was born in Antwerp, and apparently came to France as a youth. Before leaving his native town he
seems to have acquired the international Mannerism current there, based on a mixture
of local Flemish elements with a variety of Italian styles introduced mainly by the great
engraving firms, such as that of Jerome Cock.

His most important work in France, the decoration of the Gallery of Diana at Fontainebleau, was destroyed in the nineteenth century and is now mainly known from descriptions and copies. But many paintings survive from the other cycles executed in the
same palace, illustrating the story of Clorinda from Tasso, and Heliodorus' novel,
Theagenes and Chariclea (Plate 81A). Of the former series, painted for the Queen, three
are known, of which the 'Baptism of Clorinda' in the Louvre is typical; of the latter
almost the whole series has escaped destruction and is still to be seen in the Salle Ovale at
Fontainebleau.[32]

Toussaint Dubreuil, who died at the age of forty-one in 1602, seems to have been an
artist of greater sensibility whose style was formed more on French models. His paintings in the Petite Galerie of the Louvre, now the Galerie d'Apollon, were destroyed in
the fire of 1661, and his decorations at Fontainebleau have also disappeared without
trace. From the series of compositions at St Germain one survives in the Louvre (Plate
81B) while others are known from drawings; and further several tapestries of the history
of Diana are known from his designs.[33] In these his manner is based primarily on Primaticcio. He makes use of certain Italian Mannerist devices, such as the cut-off half-figures
in the foreground, but in general the style is of great restraint and lacks the extremes of
elongation usual in the generation of Caron. In fact, Dubreuil forms a link between Primaticcio and the classicism of Poussin in the following century.

On the death of Dubreuil in 1602 Henry IV summoned to Paris Martin Fréminet who
had spent the previous fifteen or sixteen years in Italy, first in Rome and later in Venice

and Turin. In Rome he had been in close contact with the Cavaliere d'Arpino, by whose style he was much influenced. Of his few surviving works the most important is the ceiling of the chapel of the Trinité at Fontainebleau, begun in 1608.[34]

While painting in Paris was in this state of general mediocrity, Nancy was the scene of a remarkable revival of artistic activity and produced a group of artists celebrated in their own time far beyond the frontiers of Lorraine: Jacques Bellange, Jacques Callot, and Claude Deruet, who represent in their several ways the last stage of Mannerism in Europe.

Bellange is an artist who has only been disinterred from neglect during the last few decades, and we still know very few facts about him.[35] He is recorded in Nancy between 1600 and 1617 as painting portraits, executing wall decorations in the ducal palace, and preparing scenery and machines for theatrical performances, but little survives from his hand except drawings and engravings.[36] It is generally supposed that he visited Italy, and although there is no external testimony for such a visit, the internal evidence points strongly to his presence in Rome in the last decade of the sixteenth century.

The etchings of Bellange are the last in a long evolution of that particular type of Mannerism in which a private mystical form of religious emotion is expressed in terms which appear at first sight to be merely those of empty aristocratic elegance. The founder of this tradition was Parmigianino, who invented many of the formulas used by his successors, such as the elongation of the figures, the small heads on long necks, the sweeping draperies, the strained, nervous poses of the hands, and the sweet ecstatic smile which those of Protestant upbringing find it hard not to think of as sickly and insincere, but which incorporates a particular kind of mystical feeling. This type of Mannerism, which flourished in the smaller towns of Italy in the sixteenth century and expressed a religious mood very different from that of official religious circles in Rome, came to Bellange through its exponents in the last decade of the century, Baroccio and his two Sienese followers, Francesco Vanni and Ventura Salimbeni. If he visited Rome he would have known their works through his compatriot, the engraver and publisher Philippe Thomassin, but many of them were in any case accessible through engravings. Vanni and Salimbeni added to what they learnt from Baroccio certain stylistic elements which are strictly Sienese and derive ultimately from Beccafumi. To these Italian sources must be added that of Flemish engraving which would have been known to Bellange in Nancy.[37] Out of these varied elements Bellange created a style which is intensely personal and which can be seen at its best in the etching of the 'Three Marys at the Sepulchre' (Plate 84). The most immediately striking characteristics of the etching are the strange poses and forms of the three women, their long, sweeping draperies,[38] their swan necks and tiny heads with hair strained up from the nape of the neck, and their elongated nervous fingers. At first one is tempted to feel that they are merely ladies of the court walking in the ducal garden, but such an interpretation would miss the essential point of the work. True, the forms are those of a hyper-sophisticated court society, but the neuroticism which they display has taken a religious form, as it often did at the time of the Counter-Reformation. This state of mind may be complex and remote from modes of religious feeling current to-day, but it is not for that reason any the less sincere; and it would be as false to call Bellange unreligious as it was when, thirty years ago, critics made the same accusation against El Greco.

To create the mysterious atmosphere of his compositions Bellange uses every trick known to his predecessors. His distortions in attitude and feature have already been mentioned, but he has many other shots in his locker. In the 'Three Marys', for instance, he places the three principal figures in the very foreground, but turns them round so that they all face away from the spectator and into the composition. Almost the same device is used with great effect in the 'Carrying of the Cross'. The composition is based on Schongauer's engraving of the same subject, but the two soldiers on either side of Christ in his design are brought forward and made into huge *repoussoirs*, leading the eye into the picture and towards the central figure which appears between them. In this case Bellange uses another familiar trick, for between the two soldiers there projects into the composition the figure of a woman cut off at the waist by the edge of the picture. This device goes back to some of the earliest works of Italian Mannerism, the Certosa frescoes of Pontormo, who, perhaps like Bellange, borrowed it from Dürer. In the etching of the 'Three Marys' Bellange has shown a typically cavalier attitude towards the question of space. Sometimes he deliberately makes the space vague, as in the great 'Annunciation' (Plate 83A), but in the case of the 'Three Marys' he chooses a viewpoint so high that the ground is tipped up, and the spectator seems to be looking down on the principal figures. Bellange has sought other effects of surprise in a spirit very typical of a Mannerist. For instance, he has chosen the unusual course of representing the action as seen from the inside of the cave, and has broken the unity of time by showing the Marys twice over, once in the foreground and again in the mouth of the cave in the background.[39]

Bellange's most important works all deal with religious themes (cf. Plate 83A); but he also designed a few *genre* compositions of which the most remarkable is the 'Hurdy-gurdy Player' (Plate 83B). Here Bellange shows an interest, exceptional for him, in the ugliness and deformity of the blind beggar; but, as we shall see with Callot, there is nothing unusual in this simultaneous inclination towards the opposite extremes of elegance and repulsiveness.

Jacques Callot was born at Nancy in 1592 or 1593. His family had been connected with the ducal court for several generations and his father was King-at-Arms to Duke Charles III. In 1607 Jacques was apprenticed to a Nancy goldsmith, Demange Crocq.[40] At some time between 1608 and 1611 he left Nancy for Rome, where he joined the studio of his compatriot, the engraver Philippe Thomassin, who has already been mentioned in connexion with Bellange. There he learnt the current technique of line engraving and practised his hand at copying compositions by Flemish artists such as Sadeler, and Late Mannerist works in Roman churches. At the end of 1611 he moved to Florence, where his real artistic career begins. He was immediately attached to the court of the Grand Duke, Cosimo II, who was a patron of the arts and above all a lover of every kind of festival and celebration. In 1612 Callot was commissioned to engrave a series of plates recording the memorial ceremonies for the death of the Queen of Spain, and soon afterwards another on the life of Ferdinand I of Tuscany, the latter mainly after the designs of Florentine painters. But he was to achieve his greatest success in engraving those public festivities with which the Grand Dukes sometimes amused the people of Florence, and of which the invention was usually due to Giulio Parigi. Parigi provided the fantastic cars and allegorical figures of the *Guerra d'Amore* or the *Intermezzi*, but it was Callot who found the brilliant idiom for rendering the action of those taking part. The idiom can be seen applied to a slightly different subject in the background of the etching of the 'Two Pantaloons' (Plate 87A), which dates from this period. In this case the people represented are not the members of a pageant, but the ladies and gentlemen of Florence out walking. In the sophisticated Medici Court, however, the borderline between *festa* and daily life was very vague, and here the courtiers are behaving almost as if they were taking part in a ballet. It is this swaggering, dance-like action that Callot renders with such vividness, adopting for the figures poses which go back to Late Gothic models, seen through the eyes of Flemish Mannerists such as Goltzius. But affected though their movements are, Callot's figures are based on close and witty observation; they combine artificiality with naturalism in a manner only excelled by Watteau. Some of them even take up the poses of the little figures in the fantastic engravings after Bosch and Bruegel which were common in Italy.[41] Callot seems to have been influenced by these artists in the way in which he builds up his innumerable figures into a single composition. In the 'Two Pantaloons' the problem is relatively easy; but in the huge plates like the 'Florentine Fête' (Plate 86) the actors taking part in the scene run into hundreds, and Callot displays incredible skill in forcing them into a coherent pattern.

The 'Two Pantaloons' shows another important aspect of Callot's work, namely his love of the grotesque. Even in Rome he had begun to imitate the engravings of beggars and deformities by artists like Villamena and Agostino Carracci, who in their turn had derived the idea of such studies from Flemish artists of the sixteenth century. Callot made a speciality of this kind of subject, and his *Gobbi* (hunchbacks) and *Beggars* are still among his most popular works. In the 'Pantaloons' he borrows his grotesque characters from a source to which he often turned, the *Commedia dell'Arte* or Italian Comedy. In the 'Two Pantaloons', however, Callot not only depicts these grotesque figures, but shows them side by side with his elegant courtiers. It is typical of the Mannerist state of mind that the artist should turn, in his reaction against the norm of classical beauty, towards the two extremes of affected elegance and sheer ugliness, and should find a further piquancy in the juxtaposition of the two.[42]

In 1621 the Grand Duke died and his widow, who became regent, introduced economies, which included the cancellation of Callot's pension. The artist therefore left Florence and returned to Nancy, where he soon became one of the leading figures in the artistic life of Lorraine.

In Nancy he carried on the various types of etching with which he had established his reputation in Florence. In 1627, in continuation of his fêtes series, he engraved the celebrations in honour of the visit of the Duchesse de Longueville during her exile from Paris; in 1622 he produced the finest of his studies in the grotesque, the 'Gipsies'; and in the 'Fair of Gondreville' (1624) he repeated the Italian 'Impruneta'. These last two etchings show signs, however, of a new tendency in his art which appears after his return to Nancy, an interest in the objective rendering of everyday scenes which are neither swaggeringly elegant nor grotesquely ugly. In the 'Gipsies' he still shows his interest in the grotesque though much less than in the 'Hunchbacks', and in other etchings his rendering is much more objective.

This difference of tone is part of a general change of attitude, which can be described roughly as an increasing seriousness. The old elements of court Mannerism still occur, but parallel with them others gain ground. For the first time, for instance, Callot makes drawings and etchings of landscape for its own sake. Plate 85A of the 'Agony in the Garden' shows his feeling for the rendering of natural scenery, though here it is used as a setting for a religious subject; but there are many dozens of drawings and etchings executed by Callot at Nancy in which the landscape is the real theme. Generally speaking, these follow the Mannerist tradition as it had developed in the Low Countries from the inventions of Bruegel, whose engraved landscapes Callot must certainly have known. The convention is fairly rigid and can be seen in Plate 85B: a dark tree in the very foreground, the recession based on an alternation of light and dark passages, arranged in wings as on a stage, aided by an exaggerated perspective established either by the sharply converging lines of buildings or the sudden diminution in the scale of the figures, as in the 'Agony'. The stage properties which Callot employs are arbitrary and often repeated – fantastic rocks, broken-down cottages, decaying châteaux – but he uses them with such skill and variety that their artificiality is not disturbing.

A marked change can be seen in the religious etchings of Callot during the Nancy period. In Florence he had designed many compositions of religious subjects in the current style of the Late Florentine Mannerists without any personal addition, and without great depth of feeling. But in the Nancy designs such as the 'Great Passion', for which Plate 85A is one of the preparatory drawings, a real sense of drama appears.[43] Here Callot uses the devices of Mannerism to give poignancy to the story. The artist brings out the sense of tragedy by isolating the tiny figure of Christ in one of the suddenly lit passages in the middle distance; by contrast the approaching soldiers appear in the shadow, half cut off by the edge of the hill. That is to say, the tricks of scale and of lighting are used for dramatic and not for purely formal purposes.

In 1625 Callot was called to Brussels to collect material for his huge 'Siege of Breda', commissioned by the Infanta Clara Eugenia, and in about 1629 Richelieu invited him to come to Paris in order that he might celebrate the capture of La Rochelle and the island of Ré in a similar manner. These three siege compositions are among his most dazzling performances from the technical point of view, in the brilliant grouping of their hundreds of small figures and the inventiveness of their decorative borders. While in Paris he also made some of his most celebrated topographical landscapes, including the two views of the Seine.

He returned to Nancy about 1631, and the remaining four years of his life were marked by Richelieu's invasion of Lorraine in 1633, the capture of Nancy and the ignominious surrender of the Duke. We do not know how far Callot was directly involved by these events, but they must have affected his life, and his reaction is to be seen in his last great work, the 'Grandes Misères de la Guerre', executed in 1633.

It has frequently been pointed out that these etchings must not be connected too

closely with the actual campaign in Lorraine because some of the scenes which they contain had already been introduced by Callot into earlier works, notably the 'Siege of
Breda', and that some of the 'Misères' themselves were begun before the attack on
Nancy. But this does not affect the real point. Lorraine was near enough to the Empire
to have been in contact with the horrors of the Thirty Years War for fifteen years;
Callot himself had been forced to study the sieges of Breda and La Rochelle, even if only
after the event; and the 'Grandes Misères' may therefore be regarded as a precipitation
of his general feelings about war, brought to a head by the invasion of Lorraine.

In the manner of presentation Callot brings all his previous experiments to bear on
intensifying the horror of the story which he has to tell. In the etching in which the ban-
dits are hanged (Plate 85c), the traditional dark tree in the foreground is replaced by a
group of the priest giving absolution to a man about to join the row of gallows-birds
in the centre of the composition. The tree from which they hang is isolated in the middle
of a wide circle of soldiers, reduced by distance to minute scale. In the figures of the
hanged men Callot has expended as much observation and as much finesse as in all his
sketches of the courtiers of Florence. The result is strangely grim, and gives the lie to
those who maintain that Callot was a purely detached observer, recording the scene of
hanging without emotion as if it had been the Fair of Gondreville.[44]

One painter active in Paris before the return of Vouet in 1627 must be mentioned,
namely Claude Vignon (1593–1670), who represents a phase of European art which
otherwise hardly penetrated to Paris. He was born in Tours, and probably began his artistic education in Paris in the current Late Mannerist style of Lallemant and Fréminet. But
his style was really formed in Rome, where he seems to have spent roughly the years
1616–24. There he seems to have come under all sorts of influences, including that of the
followers of Caravaggio; but the artist to whom he owed most was Elsheimer. He must
have studied his works directly, but he no doubt also knew those of Elsheimer's younger
followers such as Lastman. The composite nature of his style is well seen in the 'Death
of a Hermit' (Plate 88; painted after 1620). Here marked traces of Late Mannerism
can be seen in the heads of the angels, and of Caravaggesque naturalism in the still-life;
but the most noticeable feature of all is Vignon's use of that rich and almost tortured
quality of paint which Lastman learnt from Elsheimer and transmitted to the young
Rembrandt. In colour the same mixture exists: the subdued grey-browns in the monk's
habits – recalling Zurbaran – are strikingly interrupted by the almost rainbow sequences
in the wings and robes of the angels. In certain works of the 1620s, such as the 'Queen
of Sheba' in the Louvre, the closeness to the early Rembrandt is even greater. Nor is it
entirely accidental, because we know from a letter that the two artists were at any rate
acquainted and that Vignon, who seems to have been a dealer and valuer of pictures as
well as a painter, sold works of Rembrandt in France.[45] Vignon lived long enough to become a foundation member of the Academy, but like his contemporary Le Muet in
architecture he never understood the new classicism, and his later style is only a dilution
of his earlier manner with the Mannerist features somewhat reduced.[46]

Objectively the most important artistic event in Paris during the period which we are
considering was the decoration of the gallery of the Luxembourg for Marie de' Medici

by Rubens in the years 1622-5, though it is a fact, frequently commented upon, that these masterpieces of Baroque painting exercised almost no influence on French art till the end of the seventeenth century, so contrary were they to the current conventions of Late Mannerism and to the new canons of classicism which were about to be imposed.

Portraiture during the reign of Henry IV and the regency of Marie de' Medici was entirely dominated by the Flemish artist, Frans Pourbus the Younger(1569-1622).[47] Trained by his father, Frans the Elder, he achieved European reputation as a court portrait painter, first in Brussels and then, from 1600 to 1609, in Mantua. In the latter year, after passing through various other cities, he was called by Marie de' Medici to Paris, which he had visited for a short time in 1606, and where he was to remain till his death in 1622.

Pourbus brought to France the tradition of portraiture of which Mor had been the founder and greatest exponent in the Low Countries, but which had evolved since his death towards a greater degree of formalism, with more emphasis on outward show and on the depiction of rich dresses and jewels. By the turn of the century this manner had become almost universal and is to be found as much in Spanish painters, such as Coello and Pantoja de la Cruz, as in the earliest works of Rubens.

The most important commissions which Pourbus received in Paris were for state portraits of Henry IV, Marie de' Medici, and the Dauphin, later Louis XIII. The portrait reproduced on Plate 89 shows the impressive quality which he was able to give to his sitters, though in this case he has left out many of the enrichments which he uses for the portraits of the Royal Family. On the other hand this representation of the Duc de Chevreuse reveals a different side of Pourbus's talent, namely his naturalism in the painting of both the head and of the stuff, a quality which is frequently obscured under the formality of the state portraits.[48] This type of portrait was to be the basis of the style of Philippe de Champaigne, and is therefore important for the whole later development of the *genre* in France.

★

French sculpture produced little that was notable during this period. The most important monuments were erected by foreigners and have since been destroyed, namely the equestrian statues of Henry IV on the Pont Neuf and of Louis XIII in the Place Royale.[49] Of the former, begun by Giovanni da Bologna and completed by his pupils, the only parts surviving are the slaves round the pedestal by Pierre Francheville, a Fleming, who after being influenced by Adriaen de Vries became an assistant to Bologna.[50]

The most important French sculptor of the period was Pierre Biard (1559-1609) whose work has disappeared for the greater part. Of his tomb for the Duc d'Épernon and his wife at Cadillac the bronze 'Fame' is preserved in the Louvre and shows Biard to have been a more robust artist than the followers of Giovanni da Bologna who surrounded him. In 1606 he was commissioned to complete the screen of St Étienne du Mont by carrying it across the aisles. Here again the statues show a masculine but not very brilliant personality.[51]

CHAPTER 6

RICHELIEU AND MAZARIN
1630–1661

HISTORICAL BACKGROUND

DURING the ministries of Richelieu and Mazarin – that is to say, roughly between 1630 and 1660 – France finally established her position as a great power in Europe. In foreign policy these years mark her victory in the struggle with Spain and the Empire, and internally during the same period the last forces of discord, social and religious, were crushed. The outward glory of France was greater in the decades which followed, when Louis XIV laid down the law to Europe, but there is something more heroic in the preceding phase, which is the age of achievement as compared with that of enjoyment.

In external affairs Richelieu and Mazarin did little more than follow the lines of policy which had become traditional in France since the time of Francis I, but, with a richer and more united country behind them, they were able to follow them with greater success. Richelieu managed to inflict serious wounds on Spain and the Empire, while at the same time exposing France as little as possible to the horrors of war. His practice of subsidizing the enemies of the Habsburgs – even when, as in the case of Gustavus Adolphus, they happened to be Protestant – proved extremely profitable, and his diplomatic skill often caused serious defeats to the enemy without costing France a single man. Mazarin had only to continue along the same lines, although he was forced to come into the open and declare war on Spain. However, his diplomatic skill enabled him to extract at the Peace of Westphalia (1648) advantages out of all proportion to the sacrifices France had made. The same technique led to the final humiliation of Spain at the Peace of the Pyrenees in 1659.

Of even greater importance were the internal reforms carried out by the two ministers. Here their techniques were wholly different, Richelieu using open and ruthless methods, Mazarin going about his work in a more subtle and indirect manner; but the results were the same.

To Richelieu goes the credit for solving the problem of religious unity. After defeating an open rebellion of the Protestants in 1629, he had the wisdom to leave them complete liberty of conscience, while at the same time destroying them as a political force. His attitude towards Rome was equally skilful, though somewhat surprising in a cardinal. By playing ingeniously on the Gallican tendencies of the Parlement he managed to restrict Papal interference to the minimum. At the end of his life he could reasonably have said that, although there might be differences of doctrine in the field of religion in France, there was unity of loyalty.

His struggle with the socially dissident elements was far more difficult. The Wars of

Religion had weakened and impoverished the feudal nobility, but had by no means destroyed their power. They soon realized that Richelieu intended to finish the work and, led by the princes and princesses of the blood, organized a series of plots, all of which failed owing to their habit of including in each conspiracy Gaston d'Orléans, the King's brother, who invariably betrayed it. These plots were seized on by Richelieu as opportunities to strike at the nobility, and were followed by executions and the razing of castles. Even when not engaged in such violent attacks, Richelieu continued his policy of weakening the nobility by other methods, such as steadily undermining the position of the provincial governors and transferring as much as possible of their power to the central authority. In the same way he continued the old policy of reducing the Parlements and the provincial États, though here he was not always successful, because he was dependent on them for a part of the state income.

The death of Richelieu at the end of 1642, followed by that of Louis XIII himself early in 1643, seemed for a moment to endanger the whole of the work that had been achieved. The nobility were quick to realize the weakness of the Crown, owing to the fact that the King was a minor, and they were deceived by the apparent benignity of the new minister, Mazarin. Instantly the old plots began again and it was evident long before the outbreak of the Fronde in 1648 that Mazarin would have trouble with these traditional enemies of the Crown.

The great blunder made by Mazarin was his estrangement of the *bourgeoisie*. Like Richelieu, Mazarin had somewhat primitive ideas about finance, and, provided that money was available for present needs, he did not enquire too closely into the methods by which it was obtained or the possible implications for the future. This lack of foresight, combined with the corruption of the financiers who worked for him, created a series of grievances in the minds of the *bourgeoisie*. New taxes were added which hit them particularly; the sale of offices was increased, which lowered the effective value of those already in existence; and, most serious of all, the payment of *rentes* became extremely irregular and the rate of interest insecure. The result was that the middle classes were, almost against their will, forced into hostility towards the Crown as it was represented by Mazarin, and, when the nobles came into the open against the minister, they could count on support from this unexpected quarter.

The story of the Fronde (1648–53) is one of confusion, but the main implications of it are clear and important. The nobility went into it hoping to regain the power which they had seen slipping from them. The *bourgeoisie* took part, as has just been said, for much more temporary reasons, and they soon realized that they stood to lose more by the victory of their allies, the nobility, than by the triumph of their nominal enemy, the Crown. The situation was fundamentally the same as that during the Siege of Paris under the League, and the evolution of thought was the same. The *bourgeoisie* gradually came to its senses, and the basic differences which separated it from the nobility were given greater prominence by the injudicious use which the latter made of a powerful but dangerous weapon: their ability to rouse the Paris mob against the *bourgeoisie* when the latter was recalcitrant. After the people of Paris had burnt the Hôtel de Ville at the incitement of Beaufort, the *bourgeoisie* realized that they had chosen the wrong allies. The

Fronde collapsed partly because of the futility, internal quarrels, and lack of policy of the nobles, and partly because the *bourgeoisie* saw where their real interests lay.

The Fronde is of immense significance because it led to a re-alignment of parties within the kingdom which lasted for more than a century. The power of the nobility was finally and completely broken, and the way was open for Louis XIV to distract them from noticing that they no longer performed any function by giving them that most expensive of toys, the Court of Versailles. The middle classes finally accepted the fact that they could best achieve their aims by submitting to the wise dictation of a central authority. Luckily Colbert was sufficiently intelligent to conduct autocratic government so that the middle classes really obtained the benefits for which they had hoped.

One feature of this period, which is of particular importance for the development of the arts, is the enormous increase in the wealth and power of the middle classes. We have seen that throughout the sixteenth century they had been establishing their position, but it was under Richelieu and Mazarin that their rise took a steeper upward curve. The methods by which they attained their wealth were mainly disreputable, largely through the exploitation of the loose financial administration of the Government, but the result was remarkable in many ways. It is hardly an exaggeration to say that during this period, apart from works ordered by the Crown, the first minister, or by one or two princes of the blood, such as Gaston d'Orléans, every commission of importance comes from a *bourgeois*. Whereas in the late sixteenth and the early seventeenth centuries the names of the great French families occur frequently in art history, if we list those who employed François Mansart or Le Vau, Poussin or Vouet, we shall hardly find one name belonging to the *noblesse d'épée*. The period ends characteristically and spectacularly with the career of one of the greatest of all *bourgeois* patrons, the Surintendant Nicolas Fouquet. Fouquet gained immense wealth by methods no more corrupt than those of his colleagues, and he used his money with exceptional taste. He collected round him a team of architects, sculptors, painters, poets, dramatists, and musicians, who made of Vaux-le-Vicomte the greatest art centre of its period and who after his disgrace were to become the nucleus of the culture of Versailles.

Artistically the period of Richelieu and Mazarin saw the rise of French classicism. This was true in all the arts, literary as well as visual. We shall see later the parallel which exists between the classicism of Poussin in painting and that of Corneille in tragedy, and both artists are characteristic of a wider movement. This is not the occasion to analyse the French classical spirit. It will be enough to recall that in these years there flourished perhaps the most uniformly brilliant group of Frenchmen in all fields that has ever appeared at one time. In philosophy it was the age of Descartes, in religious thought that of Pascal, in drama that of Corneille, in painting that of Poussin and Claude, and in architecture that of François Mansart.

But though classicism and rationalism were the great invention of the age, French culture at the time was not uniform. We shall examine the different tendencies which exist, for instance, in the field of painting, ranging from the pure classicism of Poussin to the naturalism of Louis Le Nain, but the same variety can be found in literature. While all progressive sections of Paris were applauding the heroic tragedies of Corneille, Mme de Rambouillet and her circle of *Précieux* were still playing elegant games with madrigals and anagrammatic verses.[1]

In the field of the visual arts the variety is further complicated by outside influences. Many French artists visited Italy, where Rome was their principal goal, but they were also more deeply affected than is generally realized by Venetian art. At the same time Paris was open to influences from Flanders and even Holland, which led some painters in the direction of naturalism. Fortunately the French spirit was strong enough to make out of these elements an art which, though varied, is yet united in its fundamental principles.

ARCHITECTURE

Lemercier, François Mansart, the early work of Le Vau

French classical architecture was the creation of three men: Jacques Lemercier, François Mansart, and Louis Le Vau. Of very different character, of talent varying in degree and kind, they yet each made a distinct contribution to the evolution of the style and were to influence their successors for more than a century.

Jacques Lemercier was the eldest and certainly the least talented of the three. He was probably born about 1580–5, the son of a master mason who worked on the church of St Eustache. It may be assumed that he obtained his first training in his father's workshop till, at a date before 1607, he went to Rome, where he seems to have stayed till about 1614. In 1615 he is mentioned in the royal accounts, but we have no record of any work by him till 1624, when he was commissioned to carry out Louis XIII's new plans for extending the Louvre. His career was, however, to depend above all on the favour of Richelieu, for whom he built the Palais Cardinal, later called the Palais Royal (begun 1633), the Sorbonne (begun 1626),[2] the château and church at Rueil, and the château and new town at Richelieu (begun 1631). In addition to these buildings for the Cardinal, he probably carried out town and country houses for the Duc de Liancourt and the Hôtel d'Effiat,[3] and he was involved in the building of three great Paris churches, the Oratoire, St Roch, and the Val-de-Grâce, but in the first two cases his share is impossible to determine.[4]

Lemercier's style is composed of two elements which he never succeeded in completely fusing; the first is the current French manner of the first years of the seventeenth century, and the second consists of the idiom which he learnt in Rome.

It will be convenient to consider the second aspect first, because it can be found in isolation in Lemercier's church designs. The three churches for which he was entirely responsible were two small buildings at Rueil and Richelieu and the more ambitious church of the Sorbonne begun in 1635 (Plate 90; Figure 13).[5] All three show a Roman form of front with two superimposed Orders facing the nave, this higher central part being linked by volutes to the lower sections closing the aisles. This Roman front had only been seen once before in Paris in the Noviciate of the Jesuits built by Martellange in 1630,[6] which was an almost exact copy of Giacomo della Porta's S. Maria dei Monti.[7] From the general character of Lemercier's three façades it is clear that he has studied the same type of model, and has followed Giacomo's method of articulating the wall principally with pilasters.[8] The alternating rhythm of wide bays with doors or windows and narrow ones with niches could also be paralleled in the churches of Giacomo and the other members of this academic late sixteenth-century group.

The Sorbonne, however, leads us to a more precise source and even to a possible master for Lemercier in Rome. The plan (Figure 13) is an unusual one, consisting of a central dome, round which are grouped a nave and choir of equal size and two shallow transepts, the corners between the arms of the cross being filled with four rectangular chapels each of two bays. The only asymmetrical element in the plan – apart from the north porch, to be considered later – is the shallow bay containing the altar. Now, this plan is a close imitation of Rosato Rosati's church of S. Carlo ai Catinari in Rome, which was begun in 1612; that is to say at a time when Lemercier was in Rome.[9] Even

Figure 13. Lemercier: Church of the Sorbonne: Plan

more striking, however, is the resemblance of the two domes. The drum of the Sorbonne dome differs from the conventional Roman design of the late sixteenth or early seventeenth centuries in that it is articulated with clustered pilasters, between which are round-headed windows; and both these features occur in S. Carlo, but, as far as I know, in no other dome of the period.[10]

Now, the dome of S. Carlo was not completed till 1620, that is to say, about six years after Lemercier left Rome, and one is forced to the conclusion that he must have known Rosati's plans; hence that he must have had access to his studio; and therefore that possibly this architect may have been his master. In any case, Lemercier's relation to Roman architecture can be precisely defined; he brought back to France the academic style inaugurated by Giacomo della Porta and continued after his death by a few architects, of whom Rosati was one, who resisted the movement of Maderna towards the Baroque. In this way his function in relation to the development of French art is analogous to that of Vouet, who brought back the idiom of painting current in Italy just before the flowering of the Baroque.

There is, however, one original feature in the Sorbonne. The church had to present two important façades: the main front towards the street, and another on the north towards the court of the college. In order to make the latter front impressive Lemercier added to the north transept a free-standing classical portico with a triangular pediment enclosing a cartouche with the arms of the Cardinal, which makes an impressive and unusual end to the courtyard.[11]

Towards the end of his career Lemercier had one further opportunity to design a dome, when he took over the construction of the Val-de-Grâce from Mansart in 1646 (Plate 91).[12] Here Lemercier continues to use pilasters for the drum, but by doubling the number of piers he strengthens the effect of upward movement, which is carried on in the statues and candelabra round the base of the dome.[13] The result is to make the Val-de-Grâce the most dramatic and impressive seventeenth-century dome in Paris.

Lemercier received his most important royal commission in 1624, when he was ordered to continue the Square Court of the Louvre according to the scheme conceived in the sixteenth century. This involved doubling the existing wing on the west side of the court and inventing a centre for the now enlarged building. For this centre Lemercier built the Pavillon de l'Horloge, of which the three lower stages are simply an adaptation of Lescot's design. Over the latter's attic, however, Lemercier adds a full storey of his own invention with caryatids supporting a complex pediment, above which rises a square dome of the kind used by J. A. du Cerceau the Elder and de Brosse, which Lemercier was to repeat constantly, for instance at Richelieu. The only trace of Roman feeling in this design is in the curious repetition of the pediments, a straight within a curved within a straight pediment, which is an extension of the method used by della Porta on the façade of the Gesù. The caryatids after the designs of Sarrazin are an ingenious solution to the problem which faced later architects in continuing the court;[14] that is to say, the difficulty of knowing what Order to use in the top floor, since the lower floors are decorated with Corinthian and Composite, above which, according to classical precept, no proper Order of columns may be placed.[15]

Of Lemercier's smaller domestic works in Paris only one need be mentioned in detail, the Hôtel de Liancourt.[16] In 1623 the Duc de Liancourt bought the Hôtel de Bouillon, built by de Brosse in 1613, and enlarged it to almost double its size on the designs of Lemercier.[17] The enlargement of the site gave the architect the opportunity of an ingenious piece of planning (Figure 14). Seen from the street, the left half of the site was occupied by a base-court and a small garden, and the right half by a court forming the main approach to the house. The *porte cochère* was flanked on the court side by two quadrant wings with niches, an arrangement probably surviving from de Brosse's building[18] which was to be much imitated by later architects. More remarkable, however, was the disposition of the principal *corps-de-logis* which ran along the whole width of both courts, presenting on the garden side a front of fifteen bays, with pavilions at the ends and a portico with three openings in the middle. From the court the entrance to the house lay in the corner; it opened on the staircase and led through it to the vestibule on the garden.[19] In this way Lemercier managed to produce the maximum grandeur on the garden side while leaving ample room for the stables and offices, and at the same time concealing the difference of axis between the court and garden fronts. This type of solution was to be used by almost all his successors in Paris.

Of the three country houses, Rueil, Liancourt, and Richelieu, built by Lemercier, practically nothing remains. Rueil was a modest house with elaborate gardens. Liancourt is known to us through engravings which show it to have been a variant on the standard

Plan du rez de chaussee de l'Hostel de Liancourt
Au fauxbourg St. Germain à la rue de Seine

Figure 14. Salomon de Brosse and Lemercier:
Hôtel de Liancourt: Plan

pattern of three wings round a court, differing from the normal in having the right-hand wing missing except for the end pavilion, thus giving a view from the court over the elaborate gardens at the side of the château.

The château of Richelieu (Plate 92A) was on a scale quite different from the houses so far mentioned.[20] In conception it is reminiscent of Charleval. The château itself was of the usual form round three sides of a square court, with a low closing wall on the fourth;

but in front of this spread a forecourt enclosed by two lines of offices. This forecourt opened out again into a still wider space, of which the middle formed the main approach to the house, while on each side was a base-court concealed behind a rusticated wall. Finally came the entrance gate itself, set in a semicircular wall with pavilions at the ends. The main lines of the design were carried on into parterres behind and on the north side of the château. Of all this there remain only two small garden grottos, the entrance gate, and one domed pavilion of the office block. Plate 92A, which represents the château from the garden side, gives an idea of the general character of the ensemble, with the buildings of the office block and one base-court disappearing into the distance on the left. It also shows, however, that Lemercier was ill at ease when designing on this scale. In particular, the garden front is composed of a series of almost unrelated sections: a heavy central pavilion and two smaller end pavilions, against which nestle, as it were, four mean little turrets, in two cases supported on *trompes*. In this additive method of designing a façade, Lemercier has made no advance on the architects of the previous generation; and much of the decoration is also archaic, particularly the elaborate dormers. From contemporary descriptions we learn that the effect of the exterior depended largely on the statues and busts which filled niches all round the court and a few on the garden front. These were nearly all antiques, except for the two Michelangelo Slaves which were moved here from Écouen. The interior was richly decorated with paintings and tapestries.[21]

The Cardinal's ambition was not, however, limited to the building of a château at Richelieu. He wished also to found a town which should bear his name, and he therefore ordered Lemercier to prepare a completely new scheme according to which the village of Richelieu would be enlarged to a township planned and executed according to the most rational principles. This project was carried out, and Richelieu still stands to-day (Plate 92B) as one of the most consistent examples of town-planning on a small scale. The town forms a rectangular grid with a main street forming the long axis and connecting two squares, and the houses are of uniform design, built of brick with stone quoins. The project is in fact an extension of Henry IV's ideas for the Paris *Places*. But Richelieu lacked the common sense of Henry; he overlooked the fact that there was no good economic reason why there should be a town on that particular site, and though he used every means to persuade people from neighbouring districts to migrate to Richelieu, he had little success, and the town seems always to have been as deserted as it is to-day.

*

François Mansart was in almost every way a complete contrast to Lemercier. Lemercier was no more than a competent designer, whose importance lies in his introduction of a new foreign idiom. Mansart was an architect of almost unparalleled subtlety and ingenuity who learnt little from his contemporaries abroad, but brought a genuinely French tradition to a high level of perfection.

We know surprisingly little about Mansart's life.[22] According to Perrault, he was born in Paris in 1598. His father was a master carpenter who died when he was quite young, and François is said to have been trained by his brother-in-law, Germain Gaultier, who had collaborated with de Brosse at Rennes. Mansart himself probably worked under de

Brosse at Coulommiers,[23] and the style of his early works proves beyond doubt that this architect was the real formative influence on him. There is no evidence to show that Mansart ever visited Italy,[24] and the purely French character of the greater part of his works is strongly against it. As we shall see, however, he instinctively understood some of the essential qualities of Italian classical architecture more profoundly than some of his contemporaries who mastered the Italian idiom of detail.

If 1598 is the correct date for his birth, Mansart must have been unusually precocious, because he appears in 1623 as a well-established architect, and by 1635 his reputation must have equalled that of any rival, since he was called on to plan the château of Blois for Gaston d'Orléans, the King's brother, as well as to build several important private houses in Paris. In 1646 he suffered a severe setback over the building of the Val-de-Grâce, a commission given to him in 1645 by Anne of Austria. As a result of his difficult character, his recklessness with regard to expense, and his habit of changing his plans as he went along, he was deprived of the job, which was given instead to Lemercier. The same difficulties continued to surround him, and towards the end of his life prevented him from obtaining important commissions, such as the construction of the east front of the Louvre, so that when he died in 1666 he had grown to be somewhat neglected in favour of younger and more flexible men.

As far as we can judge his character, he was arrogant, obstinate, intolerant, difficult, and probably dishonest, but these qualities were only the unattractive reverse of his high feeling for his own calling and his justifiable confidence in his ability as an architect. He made many enemies, who attacked him during his lifetime on all scores, charging him with incompetence as well as corruption. The latter charge may be true, but posterity has not ratified the former.

We have records of three buildings for which Mansart was responsible before 1630, and from these we can form some opinion of his early style and its sources. These are the façade of the church of the Feuillants in Paris (1623),[25] and the châteaux of Berny (designed in 1623),[26] and Balleroy (begun about 1626).[27]

The façade of the Feuillants, as it is known to us through the engraving in Blondel, brings out clearly Mansart's dependence on de Brosse in his early years. It is an almost exact copy of the two top storeys of St Gervais (Plate 80B), with the addition of certain ornaments deriving from French Mannerism of the late sixteenth century.[28] That is to say, it is less classical than the model on which it is based, so that Mansart's position at this time can be defined by saying that though he based his style on de Brosse, he had not yet understood the significance of his last classical phase, as it is shown at Blérancourt and Rennes, but dilutes his borrowings with decorative elements from the tradition of the du Cerceau.

The same features can be seen in the château of Berny, of which part of one wing on the court side still stands (Plates 93A and B), and of which the general lay-out is preserved in the engravings of Silvestre and Pérelle.[29] The form of the house was unusual. Seen from the court, it presented a main *corps-de-logis* of two storeys rising to a three-storeyed pavilion in the middle covered by a high-pitched roof. Two short wings sprang forward on either side of this main building, ending in the façade shown in plate 93B[30] and joined to the central block by quadrant arcades like those at Coulommiers. Outside these two pavilions were two others covered with low square domes, another reminiscence of de Brosse, though taken this time from Blérancourt.[31]

This disposition, composed of an agglomeration of almost independent units, shows that Mansart was trying to conceive the château as a free-standing plastic unit but that he had not yet mastered the method of so doing which de Brosse had used with such success at Blérancourt. The surviving fragment shows, however, that he was already evolving a personal style. There are still many traditional Mannerist passages, such as the heavy voussoirs of the dormer, and the consoles of the window and door, but certain details, above all the niches and the palms at the top of the ground-floor panels, foreshadow the classicism of Mansart's mature style.

In Balleroy (Plate 94), near Bayeux, built for Jean de Choisy,[32] Mansart has overcome the immaturity visible in the design of Berny. In general character and materials the château is like the country houses of Henry IV's time, and depends for its effect on its massive blocks, composed of the rough, brownish-yellow local stone, with quoins and window-surrounds of dressed white stone. The main design of the court side is like the middle of Berny, but Mansart has omitted the wings, and ends the building with low one-storey blocks. The grouping of the main masses is much clearer and more harmonious than at Berny. On the court side it depends on the simple relation of the three main blocks, which are almost in the same alignment, while on the garden side the central block breaks forward more markedly, leaving room for small terraces on either side.

One of the most striking features of the whole design of Balleroy is the forecourt. This is surrounded by a low terrace on which stand two small pavilions, as at Blérancourt. The court itself is raised above the approach, from which it is reached by a flight of steps copied from Bramante's scheme for the Belvedere, but made oval in plan instead of circular. This staircase is echoed in three other oval flights, of which two lead from the forecourt to the terrace and the third to the front door. One result of this series of rises in level is that the simple masses of the château seem to tower over the visitor arriving from the village and crossing the moat.[33] At Balleroy, in fact, we may say that Mansart appears for the first time as an independent artist. He has now realized the implications of the classicism of de Brosse in his last phase, and has combined the manner of his master with another tradition which can also in a sense be called classical, namely the brick-and-stone style of Henry IV.[34]

The two patrons who commissioned the châteaux just discussed must have prepared the way for contact with those who were to employ the architect during the rest of his career. Choisy, the owner of Balleroy,[35] was chancellor to Gaston, Duc d'Orléans, brother of Louis XIII, and it was no doubt he who obtained for Mansart the commission for the rebuilding of Blois for the Duke. Nicolas Brulart de Sillery, who began Berny, was chancellor of France, and therefore belonged to the class which was to provide Mansart's best patrons, the great officers of the Crown, particularly those who were connected with the Treasury. La Vrillière, Longueil, Duplessis-Guénégaud, Fieubet, La Basinière, the men whose names recur most frequently in the career of the architect, all belonged to this class of *bourgeois* who had enriched themselves, often with suspicious rapidity, in the service of the State and the collection of taxes. Not once do we come upon the name of a great noble family on Mansart's books; and although he was occasionally to receive commissions from the King and the Queen Mother, he was never successful in these, and his achievement was entirely fostered by the *parvenus* – 'avortons de fortune', as Sauval calls them – who were intelligent enough to understand his sophisticated but luxurious classicism, and rich enough to indulge his extravagant whims.

During the years from 1630 to the beginning of the construction of Maisons in 1642 Mansart's personality continues to affirm itself more and more clearly. This is the period

Figure 15. François Mansart: Visitation: Plan

of the purest classical works, such as the new wing at Blois, in which the subtlety of the architect's methods reaches its fullest expression and his treatment of detail its greatest refinement. The characteristics of his style during these years are the pursuit of clearly defined forms in plan and in elevation the increasingly correct use of the Orders and a great respect for the flat surface of the wall.

In the earliest of the works now to be considered these features are only partially apparent. The church of Ste Marie de la Visitation in the rue St Antoine was begun in 1632 at the expense of Noël Brulart, a relation of the builders of Berny, and consecrated in 1634. The plan (Figure 15), strictly central in conception, consists of a domed circle round which are grouped three curved chapels, recalling de l'Orme's design for Anet.[36]

These are covered with oval domes into which strong light falls from a tall lantern, producing an effect which anticipates that of the cut-off domes used by Mansart later in his career. The decoration of the interior shows the transition through which the architect was passing. The main Order of the pilasters and the decoration up to the cornice are strictly classical and conceived in terms of flat panels which hardly disturb the surface of the walls, and the same method can be seen in the panelled design on the domes of the chapels (Plate 96B), but in the latter case there is superimposed on this panelling fantastic Late Mannerist high-relief decoration of scrolls and cherubs' heads, which seems in comparison a pure archaism.[37]

In 1635 Mansart received his first recorded commission for a private house in Paris from Louis Phélypeaux de la Vrillière, and designed for him what was to be a model for the classical type of hôtel for many decades (Plate 93C).[38] The main part of the building follows the usual form, and consists of three wings round a court closed by a wall,[39] but Mansart has given a classical simplicity and harmony to the whole design. All the elements – the main corps-de-logis, the central pavilion, and the wings – are clearly defined masses, almost unbroken by ornament, and each harmoniously related to its neighbours. The windows are rectangular openings surrounded by the simplest mouldings. The division into floors is the same the whole way round the court, but monotony is avoided by subtle variations in the pitches of the roofs, all of which incidentally are lower than was normal at the time, and therefore more easily brought into harmony with the masses which they cover. The garden front was of about double the width of the court side, and was not coaxial with it, but Mansart has disposed his rooms with great ingenuity to conceal this irregularity. On the garden side La Vrillière planned a grandiose extension, consisting of two wings, longer than those on the front court, to run back at right angles to the garden front. Only one of these was built, and even over this Mansart was nearly frustrated by the cutting of a new road across the back of the site. But he characteristically got over the difficulty by making the end of the gallery overhang the street on a trompe, an arrangement which was greatly admired by his contemporaries. The ceiling of the gallery was painted between 1645 and 1650 by François Perrier,[40] who collaborated with Mansart on other occasions,[41] and the walls were ornamented with a series of large classical compositions by Guercino, Guido Reni, Poussin, and other painters.[42]

In the Hôtel de la Vrillière, Mansart showed how his classical style could be applied to a town house;[43] at Blois (Plate 95) he had an even finer opportunity of showing its potentialities in a great château.

Had it been completed Blois would have been a grander and more monumental version of the Luxembourg. It was to consist, like the latter, of a court with main corps-de-logis, double pavilions, wings, and closing side with a rotunda entrance. But it was to have been extended beyond this by a forecourt leading down towards the town on the east and by terraced gardens stretching over the sunk road to the west.[44] The main door to the corps-de-logis was approached by two quadrant colonnades, a more classical version of the arcades at Coulommiers and Berny. The plan was full of the kind of ingenuity which has already been noticed in the Hôtel de la Vrillière. Not only were the axes of the court and the garden façades different, but the latter was on a higher level than the former. Mansart, however, has skilfully masked these differences by his disposition of the staircase in the central pavilion.[45] The two wings were to contain long galleries, which were no doubt designed to house the Duke's collections, including his antiques and his natural history specimens, and on the north-west side the gallery was to be doubled by a huge *salle des fêtes*, which would have projected some thirty feet beyond the wing of Francis I on the cliff overhanging the town.

Figure 16. François Mansart: Hôtel de la Vrillière: Plan

Of all this vast project only the central block and the quadrant colonnades were built,[46] but this fragment is one of Mansart's purest works. Blois is the direct descendant of de Brosse's design for Blérancourt. The masses have the same grand simplicity, and Mansart follows his master's use of the superimposed Orders to articulate them. In this case, however, the problem is less easy because of the difference of level between the two sides of the block. Mansart, however, gets over this by using on the court side the Doric for the ground floor, Ionic for the main storey, and a truncated Corinthian for the attic,[47] while on the other front he replaces the Doric by a low, unarticulated basement. In this way a particular Order is always to be found on the same level on both fronts of the block, a fact which shows that Mansart, unlike most of his French contemporaries, thought of his buildings in the round, and not merely as composed of a series of disconnected fronts.[48] But Mansart eliminates the curved roofs of Blérancourt and substitutes for them a continuous high-pitched broken roof of the kind which bears his name.[49] He has further sharpened the definition of the edges of his buildings by bringing the pilasters right to the corners of the block, whereas de Brosse always sets them slightly back. This clarity of disposition, the harmonious proportions of the masses, and the restrained details which hardly break the surface of the walls[50] combine to make this one of Mansart's most completely satisfying designs. His style was to become more plastic and more dramatic later in his career, but never again was it to be so placid.

Very different qualities are, however, revealed by the one part of the interior to be actually executed, the grand staircase. Even this was not completed in Mansart's time. The panels on the walls still await their decorative sculpture, and the steps themselves, based on those at Maisons, were put up in this century. In plan the staircase follows the type which Mansart had used at Balleroy and at the Hôtel de la Vrillière, with three flights round the sides of a square. But it is in the treatment of the upper part of the space that Mansart's boldness appears (Plate 96A). The staircase itself only leads to the first floor, but the cage runs through the whole height of the building. At the top of the first floor it is covered by a coved ceiling, which supports a gallery allowing communication between the top floor rooms on either side of the stairs. The central panel of the ceiling, however, is open, so that the eye passes right through to the upper storey, which is covered by a dome supported on pendentives and ending in a low lantern. This arrangement is in a sense a development of the device used in the smaller domes in the Visitation. There the rim of the cut-off dome stands out dark against the strongly lit lantern, but in the staircase at Blois this effect of contrast is much intensified by the fact that there are windows on the second floor which are not visible from the staircase itself, but which throw light on the dome above. In this way a practical necessity – the communication between two parts of the château – is made the excuse for an arrangement almost Baroque in its use of directed light.[51]

The decoration of the staircase is also in some ways related to that of the Visitation. The dome is panelled in much the same way; above the panels and in the shallow lantern is decoration composed of Mannerist scroll-work and masks mixed with more classical garlands. The classical tendency is more apparent in the low reliefs on the panels, in the *putti* and trophies below the cornice, and in the panels, again with arms, on the cove below, though in the last there appear again Mannerist elements in the form of masks. The whole of this decoration seems to be in the manner of Simon Guillain, who is known to have been working in Blois in 1637–8, and to whom the groups which once stood on the colonnade on the court side have always been attributed.

During the 1640s a change comes over Mansart's style. His buildings become freer in planning, more plastic in conception, and more classical in decoration. This is also the period when he seems to approach most closely the ideals of High Renaissance architecture in Italy, sometimes through direct borrowing, but sometimes apparently unconsciously.

In this decade Mansart embarked on his two most important undertakings in church architecture, the Val-de-Grâce (Plates 91 and 101) and the chapel at Fresnes (Figure 17). The Val-de-Grâce was begun in 1645 by Anne of Austria in fulfilment of a vow made before the birth of the Dauphin, later Louis XIV. Mansart was commissioned to build a

Figure 17. François Mansart: Chapel of Fresnes: Plan

church and a convent, but, as has already been said, after little more than a year's work he was dismissed and Lemercier appointed to complete the work. The history of the building is complicated,[52] but it is certain that Mansart was responsible for the plan of the church and for its construction up to the entablatures of the nave and the lower storey of the façade. The remainder of the structure was designed by Lemercier;[53] the sculptured decoration of the interior was carried out by Michel Anguier between 1662 and 1667 and the dome was painted by Pierre Mignard in 1663.

The exact date of the building of the chapel of Fresnes is not known,[54] but it cannot be far off that of the Val-de-Grâce to which its plan (Figure 17) is closely related, though on a miniature scale.[55]

The essential feature which the two plans have in common is the dominant central domed space, surrounded by three equal apses for the choir and transepts.[56] This arrangement is quite unlike anything that had been built in France up to this time, and seems to derive from Palladio's Il Redentore in Venice.[57] The source is important, for the plan of the Redentore is one of Palladio's most classical designs, in which the principles of the High Renaissance are carried out with great consistency in the play on circular forms and the repetition of the same elements three times in the choir and the transepts. In plan, therefore, the Val-de-Grâce and Fresnes provide evidence of the way in which Mansart seems to approach the methods of Italian High Renaissance architects at this stage in his career. The treatment of the interior of the Val-de-Grâce is also highly classical, though less Italianate than the plan.[58] The main Order of Corinthian pilasters and the fine but severe entablature are due to Mansart, and although the decorative reliefs in the spandrels and pendentives on the vaulting were only executed after his retirement they carry on perfectly the combination of richness and severity which is characteristic of the whole design. Externally the lower storey of the façade with its massive portico is an instance of Mansart's fully plastic style in the 1640s. In the Feuillants and the Minims he had used columns against the wall of the façade, and in the Visitation they are to be found flanking the door. But at the Val-de-Grâce the whole portico projects, supported by half-columns against the walls and full columns standing some feet in front of them. This portico is perhaps an adaptation of Lemercier's on the north side of the Sorbonne, but it is a novelty in Mansart's work, and its simpler arrangement of the heavy columns in pairs gives it a grandeur and a monumentality lacking in Lemercier's portico, just as it makes his upper storey above look light and almost over-delicate by comparison.[59]

During the period 1640–55 Mansart built a series of private houses in Paris, some of which survive and some of which are known from engravings. In the Hôtel du Jars, begun in 1648,[60] he made an important innovation in planning (Figure 18). The site was narrow, and in order to take full advantage of it he arranged the principal rooms in two parallel ranges, with the staircase at the right-hand end of that on the court side. This freer disposition in depth enables him to give greater variety of shape and size to the rooms and at the same time to arrange convenient access to all of them. It was to be followed in most of the later developments of the hôtel design. In the Hôtel Carnavalet, which he remodelled in 1655,[61] he made a further unusual disposition by carrying the principal rooms on the first floor round all four sides of the court, instead of interrupting them on the street front as was normally done. This meant that the façade on the street was all of the same height, instead of consisting, as usual, of two high pavilions joined by a lower central section.[62] In the side pavilions (Plate 100B) Mansart has produced one of his subtlest designs, a delicate arrangement of Ionic pilasters above a rusticated ground floor, with detail of the greatest restraint.[63]

Figure 18. François Mansart: Hôtel du Jars: Plan.

The château of Maisons, or Maisons-Lafitte, as it has been called since the nineteenth century, is the most complete work surviving from the hand of Mansart and gives a better idea than any other of his genius as an architect. In 1642 René de Longueil, later to be called the Président de Maisons, decided to build a new château on his estate and, having called in Mansart, appears to have given him a completely free hand.[64] The main structure seems to have been finished in 1646 and the decoration was probably carried out in the immediately succeeding years.

The plan is a variant on themes with which Mansart had played in his earlier châteaux. It consists of a free-standing block, like Berny, with a prominent central frontispiece, flanked by two short wings of the same height as the main block which are continued in two projecting blocks of one floor only. Each part of the building is composed of rect-angular masses, which are as clearly defined as at Blois but more complex. The relations of the main blocks are simplified by the elimination of the quadrant colonnades used at Blois, so that the two wings project in unbroken rectangular sections from the main front. The same principle can be seen in the design of the frontispiece on the entrance side (Plate 99), which grows out of the main wall in a series of shallow layers. The plane of the main wall of the façade is carried on upwards in the top storey of the frontispiece which is decorated with Corinthian pilasters only. In front of this stands a layer con-structed with columns – Doric below, Ionic above – and on the ground floor there pro-jects from this yet another block, slightly narrower than the other panels and articulated with Doric pilasters. Behind this frontispiece and behind the wall of the main façade stands an attic supporting a high-pitched roof. The central part of the frontispiece is broken in varying ways on different floors. The entablature over the Corinthian pilasters at the top is completely interrupted; that over the Ionic columns breaks back over the central window, and that over the Doric pilasters on the ground floor is continuous. In this way there is built up a structure of blocks each clearly defined, each different from its neighbour and each seeming to grow logically out of the whole setting. This is per-haps the purest example of the plasticity of Mansart's architecture in the 1640s.[65]

Maisons is the only building by Mansart in which the decoration of the interior sur-vives. The entrance vestibule (Plate 98) is a magnificent example of his severe richness – a design of Doric columns and pilasters, with allegorical reliefs on the vault and eagles on the entablature, but all kept in restraint by being executed in stone without either gilt or colour. Most splendid of all, however, is the staircase (Plate 100A), the finest surviving specimen of Mansart's work in this field. It mounts in four flights round the sides of a square of which the central part is open, following in this way the plan which he had already used at Balleroy and Blois. The whole space is covered with a dome, below which runs a narrow oval gallery serving the same purpose as the coved open ceiling at Blois, namely to allow communication between the two ends of the building on the second floor. But the gallery at Maisons, having no window above it, does not produce the light contrasts so carefully calculated at Blois, and, being narrower, it interrupts less sharply the continuity of the space. In fact in its spacing and lighting the staircase at Maisons is more classical than that at Blois.

Its decoration is particularly fine. As at Blois, the walls are ornamented with panels, on which sit groups of *putti* representing the arts and sciences.[66] Even more remarkable, however, is the balustrade (Plate 97B), which is composed of interlocking curved blocks of great complexity, topped by a rich bunch of acanthus decoration.

These are all examples of the more playful and freer type of decoration at Maisons. In other parts it takes on a more severely classical character which almost reminds one of the style of Louis XVI, particularly in the sphinxes on the side pavilions, in the draperies over the main entrance, and in the flaming urns flanking the classical medallions on the top section of the frontispiece.

Maisons suffers sadly from the fact that the estate was broken up at the end of the nineteenth century. The château is now surrounded by main roads and villas instead of the terraced gardens made for it by Mansart, but in spite of this lack of charm in setting, it remains one of the most remarkable works in the whole range of French architecture.

The alterations to the Hôtel Carnavalet are the latest surviving work by Mansart, but there are records during the last ten years of his life of other projects, of which two were not even begun and the third, the least important, has been destroyed. We are left therefore with the impression that Mansart was somewhat neglected during his last years, owing, no doubt, partly to changes in taste but partly also to his difficult character. The drawings of these last years themselves confirm what we are told by his contemporaries that he was incapable of producing and keeping to any final plan for a building, and in the case of the projects for the Louvre, we know that it was for this reason that he finally lost the commission.

In 1664 Colbert, who was considering the completion of the Square Court of the Louvre by the building of its eastern wing, asked Mansart to produce designs for the work.[67] Mansart's drawings are preserved in the Bibliothèque Nationale but have never been fully studied. Even a cursory examination of them, however, brings out the immense fertility of Mansart's invention at this time. There are only about half a dozen sheets of plans, but to each of them is attached a series of flaps incorporating variants, these flaps again having other flaps, so that for certain parts of the buildings there may be two, four, eight, or even sixteen possible combinations. In some the façade is planned with Orders on each floor, in some with a colossal Order, in some with no Order at all. Sometimes Mansart uses pilasters, sometimes half columns, sometimes full columns, and often a combination of all these forms. In the arrangement of the interior also there is great variety: oval, octagonal, or square vestibules, with or without columns; and staircases in single flights round a square, in two flights which lead to one, or of one flight dividing into two. And, as at the Carnavalet, Mansart shows respect for existing work, incorporating the design of Lescot and Le Vau as far as possible.

In 1665, Colbert evolved another scheme to the glory of Louis XIV for which he again seems to have asked Mansart to produce designs. This was to be a chapel for the tombs of the Bourbon dynasty at St Denis to outshine the unfinished Valois Chapel there.[68] The chapel, which was to be of vast dimensions – its diameter was almost the length of the whole church – represents Mansart's last researches into the problem of the centralized building. But it is conceived on very different lines from the Visitation. The central domed space was to be supported on full columns, and round it were to be grouped chapels which in the plans take on a confusing variety of forms, so that evidently Mansart was here 'thinking aloud', as he was in the Louvre sketches. One of the designs has an unexpected feature, namely that each chapel is covered by a separate dome visible from the outside, which produces an effect of small independent units clustering round a large one reminiscent of the church projects of Leonardo.[69] Mansart also makes use here of a device which we have found several times in his domestic architecture: the cut-off dome. In this case the principal dome of the chapel is truncated, so that the eye can see through to an outer shell, on which presumably there was to be frescoed decoration.[70]

In 1665 Mansart designed a staircase for the Hôtel d'Aumont, of which the main part had been built nearly twenty years before by Le Vau.[71] The staircase, which is known from the engraving in Daviler (Plate 97A), is an interesting example of Mansart's ingenuity in his last period. He has exploited brilliantly the possibilities of the limited available space by putting the bottom steps of the flight in the middle of the opening leading to the staircase, and then moving the succeeding steps to one side, at the same time narrowing them, so that when they turn round for the last part of the flight they are only of half the width of the whole space. However, this transformation is so subtly done that it would hardly have disturbed anyone going up the stairs. The staircase is preceded by a shallow vestibule with full Doric columns and a deep niche on each side, which provides a dramatic and plastically conceived approach to the main flight. The balustrade seems to have been as ingenious as that of Maisons.[72]

Mansart must be regarded as one of the artists who expressed most purely and completely the French classical spirit of the seventeenth century. His works show in the highest degree the qualities generally associated with this spirit: clarity combined with subtlety, restraint with richness; obedience to a strict code of rules coupled with flexibility within them; and concentration by the elimination of inessentials. His style has not the heroic quality which is to be found in the more classical paintings of Poussin and in the great tragedies of Corneille, but he worked for patrons who demanded luxurious settings for their lives and would not altogether have appreciated the stoical grimness of Poussin's most severe works. But with that difference it is fair to say that his style is the equivalent in architecture of the classicism which grew suddenly to dominate French culture in other fields during the minority of Louis XIV. Voltaire has summed up the qualities of this art in lines which are believed to refer to Maisons:

> Simple en était la noble architecture;
> Chaque ornement en sa place arrêté
> Y semblait mis par la nécessité:
> L'art s'y cachait sous l'air de la nature,
> L'œil satisfait embrassait sa structure,
> Jamais surpris et toujours enchanté.

*

François Mansart may have been the most subtle architect of his generation, but he was not the most successful. Louis Le Vau seems to have been temperamentally much better suited to the demands of his patrons and, whereas Mansart threw away commissions owing to his obstinacy and arrogance, Le Vau was adaptable enough to fit in with what was demanded of him. He seems to have lacked the scrupulous artistic conscience which was the most marked quality of Mansart. Le Vau is, on the contrary, an artist careless of detail and thinking always of a general effect, inconsistent in his use of the Orders, but brilliant in decoration. Mansart walked alone; Le Vau was the head of a team of craftsmen – painters, sculptors, stucco-workers, gilders – who combined to produce effects which come nearer to the Baroque than any other architectural work in France during this generation. He was a great *metteur-en-scène* rather than an intellectual artist.

We know almost nothing of his life.[73] He was born in Paris in 1612, and his father was a master-mason also called Louis. From about 1639 onwards he seems to have been financially interested in the development of the Île St Louis. He built a house there, where he lived with his father, and it was there that his most important private commissions in Paris were carried out: houses for Lambert, Hesselin, Gruyn des Bordes, Sainctot, Gillier, and other wealthy patrons. He and his father seem to have done a little speculation in buying and selling plots as well as being concerned with the actual building. His first patrons come from a class closely related to those who employed Mansart, but with a slight difference. Both architects worked for the recently enriched financiers, but whereas Mansart also built for the great officers of the Crown, Le Vau was more favoured by the members of the Parlement. It was not till he was noticed by Fouquet in about 1655 that he moved into the higher circle, but he made much better use than Mansart of his newly gained position and managed after the fall of Fouquet to obtain the favour of his rival, Colbert, and through him that of Louis XIV. His works at the Louvre and Versailles, executed between 1661 and his death in 1670, belong therefore to the next phase in French history, and will be considered in a later chapter. For the moment we are only concerned with his buildings for private patrons, almost all of which date from before 1661, and which may be conveniently considered under the two headings of Paris houses and country châteaux.

We have no information about Le Vau's early training, though we may assume that it was begun under the instruction of his father. The earliest work attributed to him, the Hôtel de Bautru, built between 1634 and 1637, in the latter of which years Le Vau was only twenty-five,[74] shows him beginning in the picturesque style of the last du Cerceau, and using the pointed roofs, the ornamental dormers, the rich rustication, and the ingeniously curved entrance doors which they favoured. From the very beginning, therefore, the contrast with Mansart is visible. Mansart derives from de Brosse, the most monumental architect of the previous generation; Le Vau bases his style on the decorative tradition.

Very soon, however, Le Vau gave proof of greater individuality, and in two hôtels which were almost certainly begun before 1640 he made a real contribution to the designing of the Paris house. The Hôtel Tambonneau was built by Le Vau for a rich and debauched Président de la Cour des Comptes on a site in the rue de l'Université, bought in 1639, when the Faubourg St Germain was still almost deserted. It is known from the engraving in the *Grand Marot* (Plate 104A). This, one may feel, is Le Vau's answer to Mansart's Hôtel de la Vrillière, that is to say, it is his first version of the classical hôtel design. It is still traditional in plan, with one-storeyed wings on each side of the court, but its proportions are less Mannerist and its decoration more restrained than in the Hôtel de Bautru. It includes one motive which Le Vau was to use in different forms for the rest of his career, the triple-arched portico on two floors as the central element of the main block. No plan of the house survives, but it seems fairly certain that on the ground floor this entrance led, as it always does in Le Vau's later works, to a shallow, oblong vestibule through which the visitor reached the central salon on the garden front. Blondel tells us one fact about the house which is also typical of Le Vau's style: the garden façade was decorated with a colossal Order of Ionic pilasters, whereas on the court side there is no Order on the main block and two small superimposed Orders in the central portico. This inconsistent employment of the Orders emphasizes once more the contrast with Mansart, and shows that Le Vau thought of his buildings rather as a series of separate façades than as solid blocks of which the whole surface had to receive a consistent articulation by means of the Orders.

The Hôtel Hesselin was among Le Vau's first commissions in connexion with the Île St Louis. The site was bought in 1639, and the house was under construction in 1642; it was pulled down in 1931, but is recorded in engravings and in photographs.[75] This house shows Le Vau's ability to make a plan to suit unusual circumstances. Since the hôtel faced on a quiet quay, and not on a noisy street, there was no need for the usual arrangement of a court to set the main rooms well back from the entrance. Le Vau has, on the contrary, placed the part of the house used for living purposes in the block on the river, from which there would have been a fine view across to the University and up-stream towards the Salpêtrière. A further piece of ingenuity appears in the disposition of the river façade, for Le Vau had also been commissioned to build the house on the next site for Sainctot, and he managed to combine the two fronts so that they make an almost symmetrical whole. We have no records of the appearance of the interior, but we know that Le Vau was already using here the team of artists who were to work for him for most of his career: as painters Le Sueur, Bourdon, Lebrun, and Dorigny; as sculptors Sarrazin, Guérin, van Obstal, and Le Hongre, whose carved wooden doors are the only surviving part of the hôtel.

At almost exactly the same time Le Vau received the far more important commission to build a house for Jean Baptiste Lambert.[76] The plot was bought in 1639, and the owner moved into the house in 1644, though the decoration of the interior continued probably for another ten years. The site was one of the best on the island, on the eastern point facing up the river, parallel with the Hôtel de Bretonvilliers and separated from it by the main street which formed the axis of the island. It was, on the other hand, curious in shape (Figure 19), and Le Vau has made brilliant use of its possibilities. The entrance from the street leads to a court of which the curved end facing the visitor (Plate 102A) contains the staircase. The wings on each side of the court are composed of two sets of private rooms, which are approached from the staircase through an oval and a circular vestibule respectively. The right-hand vestibule also gives access to a wing which runs parallel with the street towards the point of the island. On the first floor this contains a long gallery with windows on one side looking over the garden and ending in a bow with a magnificent view up the river, with the Arsenal in the foreground.

Plan du Second étage de la Maison de Mr le Président Lambert.

Cour

Chapelle

Gallerie dont le plafond representant l'apotheose d'Hercule
est un des plus beaux ouvrages de Charles le Brun.

Vestibule

Grand Escalier

Anti chambre

Chambre

Cabinet des murs
peint par E. le Sueur

Cabinet

Garderobe

Corridor

Chambre pour les
domestiques
malades

Garderobe

Antichambre

Cour   Garderobe

Chambre

Cabinet

Cabinet

Oratoire

Anti chambre

Chambre

Mariette exud.

133

Figure 19. Le Vau: Hôtel Lambert: Plan of second floor

Externally the Hôtel Lambert shows features which we have already found in Le Vau's buildings. The entrance from the court to the staircase is composed, as at the Hôtel Tambonneau, of porticos of three openings on two storeys; but here the bays have flat entablatures instead of being arched. In this way the design is more classical than in the earlier building, but in other details we can see how free Le Vau is in his treatment of the Orders. The upper Ionic Order appears too small for the Doric below it, partly perhaps because of the high isolated bases of the latter, which make the columns look even taller than they are; and the architect is further incorrect in carrying on the Doric entablature right round the court, even though there are neither columns nor pilasters to support it. On the outside of the gallery, moreover, he introduces a colossal Order, thus once more showing his lack of feeling for the plastic unity of the whole.

The importance of the building, however, depends, apart from the brilliant use of site, on the disposition and decoration of the interior. The staircase is a highly personal invention, conceived on almost theatrical principles entirely opposed to those applied by Mansart in his staircase at Maisons. There the visitor realizes at first glance the whole plan and spacing of the staircase; at the Hôtel Lambert these are only gradually revealed as he goes up the steps, encountering as he does so a series of surprises. After going up a few steps from the court the staircase divides into two flights, of which that on the left leads only to the lower of the two main floors, while that on the right, after taking the visitor to this level, doubles back and leads him to the upper floor. Gradually, as he goes up this second stage, he moves from the narrow confined flight into the main cage of the staircase, three times the width of the flight, lit by big windows on the next floor and continued upwards past a gallery through the whole height of the building.[77] The effect is of emerging from a dark tunnel into a well-lit, open space. The contrast is deliberately prepared and ingeniously carried out in an almost Baroque spirit.[78]

Much of the decoration of the interior survives.[79] The Cabinet de l'Amour, decorated c. 1646–7, has suffered most severely, for it has been stripped of its panelling and its paintings, which are now for the greater part in the Louvre. Its original appearance, however, is preserved in an engraving by Picart (Plate 104B). The walls were divided into almost equal parts, consisting of a dado and frieze, almost as in sixteenth-century French rooms. The dado was decorated with landscape panels by the elder Patel, Swanevelt, and Jan Asselyn, and the frieze with mythological subjects by Perrier, Romanelli, and Le Sueur, who was also responsible for the figure panels in the ceiling. The Cabinet des Muses survives in better condition, though it was altered in the eighteenth century[80] and its paintings have been removed to the Louvre. It is probably a few years later, though it must have been begun before 1650, the year of Perrier's death, since he painted the decorations on the cove of the ceiling. It presents an advance on the Cabinet de l'Amour in the general disposition of the decoration, since the walls are no longer divided into equal dado and frieze, but are treated as wholes with a single central painting by Le Sueur, above and below which are narrow decorative panels of grotesques.

The gallery is even more striking (Plate 105A). Mention has already been made of the skill with which the architect has designed it with an eye to the view which it overlooks, and his abilities are no less apparent in its decoration. It is by far the finest room of this period to survive, and although many Paris houses had galleries of this type,[81] the enthusiasm of early writers justifies us in assuming that this must always have been an exceptional example. The walls are decorated with a series of stucco reliefs, bronze and gold in colour, by van Obstal, representing the Labours of Hercules, to whom the room is dedicated. On the side opposite the windows these reliefs alternate with landscapes by Rousseau. The ceiling was painted by Lebrun, who continued the story of the hero in a huge decoration which was in its time the most ambitious piece of Baroque illusionism to be executed in France. Le Vau was presumably the controlling mind behind this magnificent scheme, and it shows his real qualities at their best. As a purveyor of this kind of grand and highly coloured setting Mansart could not hold a candle to him; his ambitions lay in other fields.[82]

Le Vau's most important building before he gained royal favour was the château of Vaux-le-Vicomte, but before he undertook this task he had already built at least one other major country house, Le Raincy, designed before 1645 for Jacques Bordier, Intendant des Finances.[83] The plan was a usual one: a main block with slightly projecting pavilions at the end of the forecourt; but the novelty was the introduction of a great oval vestibule in the centre which made a curved projection in the middle of both garden and court façades.[84]

It was, however, in 1657 that Le Vau had his great opportunity, when he was commissioned by the Surintendant des Finances, Nicolas Fouquet, to plan for him on his estate at Vaux-le-Vicomte the most splendid château and gardens to be found in the whole of France (Plate 103). The building was carried out at unparalleled speed; the roof was already being put on before the end of 1658, and the decoration of the interior was almost complete by the time of the fête of 1661.

The plan of the château (Figure 20) was an adaptation of that of Le Raincy, varying externally only in that it has double pavilions and no forecourt. It is, therefore, a completely free-standing block in the tradition of Blérancourt and Maisons. As at Le Raincy, there is a projection in the centre of each façade, but with a slight difference. Instead of a single oval vestibule, the middle of the block is occupied by a rectangular vestibule which leads to an oval salon lying across the main axis of the building. The staircases are fitted into the spaces at the sides of the vestibule,[85] and the two wings contain each a splendid *appartement*, one on the east side for the King and one on the west for the owner of the house.

The vestibule itself is of an unusually masculine style for Le Vau, and its sole ornament is a row of detached Doric stone columns. His favourite motive of the triple opening is here carried right through the building, for the transitions from court to vestibule, from vestibule to salon, and from salon to garden are all made through three arches. The salon is again relatively staid in its ornament, white stucco composite pilasters below and stucco caryatids above; but the ceiling was to have had frescoes by Lebrun which would have added greater richness.[86] The other rooms are elaborately decorated, some with painted grotesque panels, others, like the King's bedroom (Plate 102B), in a style new to France which Lebrun had brought from Italy. This is based on a combination of stucco, gilding and painting, which Lebrun seems to have learnt from studying Pietro da Cortona's

Cabinet

Chambre

Garde-robe

Anti-chambre

Grand Sallon

Vestibule

Antichambre

Chambre

Cabinet

Bains

Coste du Jardin

Coste de la Cour

Figure 20. Le Vau: Vaux-le-Vicomte: Plan

136

rooms in the Palazzo Pitti. In the King's *appartement* Le Vau and his team of collaborators, Lebrun for painting, Guérin and Thibault Poissant for sculpture, invented the
style which was to be used in the decoration of Louis XIV's first rooms at Versailles;
that style which at first sight seems to be Baroque, but which is always more restrained
than its counterpart in Italy.[87] It uses the Baroque combination of all the arts in one
striking general effect, but it eschews the more ingenious tricks of illusionism and foreshortening which the Roman Baroque decorators loved. The line of demarcation between painting and sculpture is kept clear, and figures are not allowed to wander from
one into the other. It is, in fact, a compromise, a Baroque tamed by the French classical
spirit.

Externally the architecture of Vaux shows only too clearly Le Vau's weaknesses as a
designer. There is the looseness in the use of the Orders which we have found in almost all
his works; but there is also a great indecision in the grouping of the main masses. On the
garden side the projection made by the oval salon is not brought into any relation with
the remainder of the façade, and to it is applied, as the centre for the whole design, what
is in effect the frontispiece of the Hôtel Tambonneau. It may be said in defence of Le
Vau that he must have been working under great pressure of time and that he could not
work out details such as these as carefully as he may have wished; but the fact remains
that his artistic conscience did not prevent him from producing these ill-digested features.

It is, however, unfair to cavil at details, because the general impression of Vaux is
triumphantly successful, and this was certainly what mattered to Le Vau and to Fouquet.
The combination of château and gardens has hardly its peer in France, and although this
must be largely attributed to the skill of Le Nôtre, who here appears for the first time
as a garden designer, there can be little doubt that Le Vau must have had the main direction of the lay-out, and that the admirable relation of the buildings to the whole must
be due to him. The approach to the house from the road slopes slightly down, flanked
by the two base-courts, built of brick and stone, in contrast to the milky stone of the
château itself. As the visitor walks down he is able gradually to see the gardens stretching
away beyond the house itself. The terraced parterre slopes slowly down again till, half
a mile away, it reaches the canal and the grotto, beyond which the ground rises again in
a long grass stretch between trees. Fountains, terraces, grottos, canal, *tapis-vert*, all the
elements of Versailles are already there, and on a scale which might well have made the
King jealous when he saw it.

The last chapter in the story of Vaux is well known. On 17 August 1661, Fouquet
entertained there the King, the Queen, Mlle de la Vallière, and the whole Court. After a
supper prepared by Vatel, they were offered a new comedy-ballet, *Les Fâcheux*, composed for the occasion by Molière, with décor by Lebrun and music by Lully. La Fontaine, Fouquet's poet, was in the audience, and wrote a description of the evening, which
ended with a splendid firework display. Three weeks later Fouquet was arrested for em-
bezzlement; all his property was confiscated; and his enemy and destroyer, Colbert,
took over his artists to work for the King. In the most literal sense, therefore, Vaux was
the preparation for Versailles. Colbert needed only to transport to Paris the team of
architects, sculptors, painters, composers, and poets to have, ready-made, a means of

flattering the King's taste for splendour. Colbert was not the man to miss such an opportunity because of any of the scruples which a more sensitive character might have felt. It may, however, be thought that he went unnecessarily far in actually transporting to Versailles the best statues and the rarest trees with which Fouquet had ornamented his park.

From 1661 onwards Le Vau becomes the servant of Colbert and the King, and, as has already been said, his work for them will be considered in the next chapter.[88]

French architectural style of the mid seventeenth century was formed by Mansart and

Figure 21. Antoine Le Pautre: Hôtel de Beauvais:
Plan of ground floor

Le Vau, but among their contemporaries were many artists of considerable talent, who produced work with individual characteristics.

The most original of these was Antoine Le Pautre (1621–81).[89] Before 1650 he had already built the monastery of Port-Royal, which still stands, and at least one private house, the Hôtel de Fontenay-Mareuil.[90] But his reputation rests on the Hôtel de Beauvais, erected between 1652 and 1655, on the rue St Antoine, which survives to-day, though in sad condition. This house is the most ingenious of all the solutions found by French architects for the problems presented by difficult and irregular sites (Figures 21 and 22). In this case Mme de Beauvais had bought two plots, one facing the rue St Antoine and the other the rue de Jouy. Though contiguous, the two sites formed together an area with re-entrant angles and with no side parallel to any other side. Le Pautre has planned a deep *corps-de-logis* on the rue St Antoine, with shops on the ground floor and a *porte-cochère* in the middle leading to a circular vestibule where the visitor got out of his coach and walked into the staircase on the left. Beyond this main block the architect has contrived to fit in a court which is symmetrical in spite of the small amount of space available on the left. The court ends in a sort of apse, from which the coach-house opens,

Figure 22. Antoine Le Pautre: Hôtel de Beauvais:
Plan of first floor

while to the right a covered way leads out beside the stables to the rue de Jouy. If we compare the plan of the first floor with this disposition of the space below we shall see yet further proofs of Le Pautre's boldness. In the main *corps-de-logis* the rooms correspond very roughly to those below them; but in the rest of the plan they go their own way without consideration for what is underneath. Over the stables and the passage to the rue de Jouy, and at right angles to them, Le Pautre contrives a long gallery, a hanging garden, and an *appartement*, while over the coach-house there is a terrace and a chapel. The detail of the Hôtel de Beauvais is disappointing in comparison with the general plan, though the staircase is skilfully designed and richly decorated with stuccos by Martin Desjardins (Plate 106).[91]

Of Le Pautre's other executed works we know little,[92] but more light is thrown on his methods by the volume of engravings which he published in 1652. In these he presented to the public the designs for country and town houses which he had not been able to execute. That he had found no patrons bold enough to undertake them need not surprise us, if we look at their vast scale and fantastic qualities (Plate 105B). In these plates, unrestrained by the ties of practical considerations – which, however, as we have seen in the Hôtel de Beauvais, he was well able to deal with – Le Pautre gives free rein to his imagination, and creates a series of designs which have hardly any parallel in French architecture. Some depict vast rusticated châteaux; others show villas almost Palladian in plan, but with porticos supported by huge figures totally foreign to the spirit of Palladio; yet others derive their inspiration from nearer home and are adaptations of designs by Le Vau. The château illustrated in plate 105B, for instance, recalls Le Raincy in its use of the colossal Order intermingled with rusticated wall surfaces. But in its general conception it is far freer than anything that Le Vau created. Le Pautre alone among French architects could have thought of the semicircular concave bays which link the end pavilions to the centre and to which the drum over the middle section forms a contrast of convex curves.[93] Internally the plan is wholly fantastic. The middle three sections of the building are occupied by the vestibule and the staircase, and only the two wings contain living-rooms; but even here half of each wing is taken up with a huge columned salon. It was a splendid invention, and one from which later theatrically-minded architects[94] were able to derive useful ideas, but hardly, as it stands, a practical design for a country house.

Generally speaking, however, the architects of Le Pautre's generation had their feet firmly on the ground. They knew exactly what their patrons wanted, and they were able to satisfy equally their practical demands and their desire for display. Even, for instance, Jean Boullier of Bourges, an almost unknown architect by whom only one work is recorded, seems to have been completely successful in the field of private house designing. His one work, the Hôtel Aubert de Fontenay in Paris (or Hôtel Salé, as it was called, after the source of the owner's wealth, the Gabelle), built in the years 1656–66,[95] presents to the street a fine classically conceived façade with discreet use of rustication in the manner of Mansart.[96] In the interior Boullier has taken up Mansart's idea of a double row of rooms which has enabled him to introduce a magnificent staircase on an unusual plan (Plate 107A), consisting of a single flight starting up the middle of the cage and turning back on itself, instead of dividing into two, the third section of the whole space being filled with a gallery which leads to the rooms at one end of the house. The effect of the staircase depends as much on its decoration as on the plan, particularly on the fine stuccos and the splendid forged-iron balustrade. In interiors such as this the style of Versailles seems once more to be foreshadowed.

Pierre Cottard (?–1701) is also remembered for one building, the Hôtel Amelot de Bisseuil, better known as the Hôtel des Ambassadeurs de Hollande, on which he worked from 1657 to 1660. Here the decoration, both internal and external, rather than any skill in planning, is the most striking feature, and the house presents to the street one of the finest of Parisian *portes-cochères* (Plate 107B).[97]

A more puzzling figure, of whom too little is known, is Gérard Desargues (1593–1661), who worked at Lyons as well as in Paris. He was a mathematician and engineer rather than an architect, and his achievement lies in the field of construction. In the rue de Cléry he built for M. Roland a house with a staircase of great originality (Figure 23).[98] The staircase is placed in the corner of the court and set diagonally. A few steps lead to an oval vestibule from which the first flight goes straight up, to divide into two flights, each at an angle of 45° with the first flight. Desargues was probably led to this

Figure 23. Desargues: House of Monsieur Roland: Plan

unexpected plan by his interest in structural problems, but the result was a type of staircase which was taken up again by architects of the early eighteenth century when they were seeking original forms and trying to break away from the strictly rectangular plans of the seventeenth century.

Mention must also be made here of Jean Marot (c. 1619–79), since he was also a designer of private houses, though he is chiefly remembered for his volumes of architectural engravings, notably the *Grand Marot* and the *Petit Marot*, which have often been referred to in these pages. The only works which he is known to have carried out are the Hôtels de Pussort, de Mortemart, and de Monceaux, all of which are engraved by him, but we can also learn something of his style from his plates after his own unexecuted projects. These show him to have been an eclectic with little originality and with a rather dry manner. He picked up ideas from all his major contemporaries, particularly Mansart and Le Vau, and on the whole added little to them. He is more personal when he is designing decoration or triumphal arches or working in any field which is not strictly architectural.[99]

One of the few public buildings put up in Paris during this period is the Hall of the Marchands-Drapiers (Plate 108), designed in about 1655–60 by Jacques Bruant, the elder brother of Libéral, the builder of the Invalides.[100] The only part which survives is the façade which was transported in the nineteenth century to the Carnavalet museum. In certain respects the design derives from Mansart's frontispieces at Blois and Maisons, particularly in its application of the three Orders, with a truncated Corinthian for the attic. But the general character is entirely different, since Bruant's frontispiece is conceived primarily as a setting for sculptured decoration, which centres on the arms of Paris flanked by two caryatids.[101]

The middle decades of the seventeenth century were also a period of activity, though not of great progress, in church-building. We have already considered the major works produced – Mansart's Visitation, Lemercier's Sorbonne, and the Val-de-Grâce – but besides these a number of other churches of quite different character were erected. In most cases they were long in building and there were several changes of architect, so that it is difficult to determine the real authorship of any part of the design. But they all have one feature in common: they represent an attempt to reconcile the new classical forms with traditional church-planning. Notre-Dame des Victoires (begun 1629), St Jacques-du-Haut-Pas (begun 1630), St Sulpice (begun 1645), St Roch (begun 1653), St Nicolas-du-Chardonnet (begun 1656), St Louis-en-l'Île (begun 1664) are all built on a Latin cross plan with aisles and ambulatory like Gothic churches. In some there are even more curious reminiscences of medieval architecture. In St Sulpice, for instance, the curve of the vault is so much higher than the semicircle that it looks almost like pointed groining, and many of these churches have a rib along the ridge of the vault which again produces a Gothic effect. Externally some of them, for instance St Nicolas-du-Chardonnet and St Sulpice, present what can almost be described as a chevet with buttresses, classical in their moulding but Gothic in their structure.

The period of Richelieu and Mazarin was in French architecture, as in other fields, one of great individualism. François Mansart, Louis Le Vau, Antoine Le Pautre were personalities who left their mark on the art of their time and on that of succeeding generations. They all contributed to the creation of the French classical style, but their contributions were distinct, marked by the idiosyncrasies of their makers. Colbert and Lebrun had not yet imposed the uniform excellence which marked all the visual arts under the personal reign of Louis XIV. Architects could still be difficult, even preposterous; they were not and could not be courtiers. They still had the calibre of the men who fought, however futilely, in the Fronde. Life at Versailles under Louis XIV may have been much more polished than it had been in Paris in the time of Retz and Mlle de Montpensier, but it must have been much duller. The same is true of the art of the two periods.

Painting

Vouet and early Italian Baroque

As we have seen, French painting was dominated by a form of Late Mannerism throughout the first quarter of the seventeenth century. The event which inaugurated the new movement was the arrival in 1627 of Vouet, who had been in Italy for fifteen years and brought back a style of Italian painting which was up till then unknown in France.

Vouet was born in 1590.[102] At the age of fourteen he is said to have come to England to paint the portrait of a French lady, and in 1611 he accompanied the French ambassador to Constantinople. From there he made his way to Italy, arriving in Venice in 1613. By 1615 he had moved to Rome, which seems to have remained his headquarters till his return to France in 1627, though he may have visited Naples in 1620 and certainly spent a period during 1621-2 in Genoa, visiting several towns, including Modena and Bologna, on his way back.[103] In 1624 he was elected President of the Roman Academy of St Luke. He is again traceable in Venice in 1627, presumably en route for France. On his arrival in Paris he immediately scored a great success, receiving commissions for the decoration of private houses and churches on a great scale. The arrival of Poussin in 1640 was a threat to his monopoly, but when the latter returned to Rome in 1642 Vouet was left again in almost unchallenged supremacy, though in his last years advanced opinion probably began to turn against him and in favour of a more classical style. But he seems to have enjoyed wide popularity till his death in 1649.[104]

During his Roman period Vouet was much influenced by Caravaggio, as we can see in his earliest known work, the 'Birth of the Virgin' in the church of S. Francesco a Ripa (Plate 110), and in the scenes from the life of St Francis in S. Lorenzo in Lucina.[105] The 'Birth of the Virgin' is an unusually original version of Caravaggio's style, novel in its broad, low composition, bold in its foreshortenings, and striking in its handling of drapery. In fact it shows a vitality which Vouet was soon to lose. It reveals a curious feature of the artist's style at this period, for one detail, the head of the maid-servant in the middle, is taken directly from Michelangelo.[106] An analogous point occurs in the 'Temptation of St Francis' in S. Lorenzo, where the figure of the saint is borrowed from Michelangelo's model of a river-god in the Accademia. This combination of Michelangelesque and Caravaggesque elements gives an unusual flavour to Vouet's naturalistic work of this time.[107]

Vouet seems, however, soon to have deserted this style for a more eclectic manner, and the surviving works of the Italian period show him as an eclectic fluctuating between the early Baroque manner of Lanfranco and Guercino and the more classical styles of Domenichino and Guido. The altarpiece of the Virgin appearing to St Bruno, painted in 1620 for the Certosa of S. Martino at Naples (Plate 109), shows most of the tendencies in his work at this time. The sentiment, marked above all by the atmosphere of ecstasy, is already Baroque, though it is still restrained; in the same way the composition, with its strong diagonal, is typical of the transitional stage towards the full Baroque movement of a Pietro da Cortona. On the other hand, the firm modelling and the almost Domenichinesque type of the Madonna show that the artist has not altogether thrown off the classical tradition. The influence of Reni is visible in many of the compositions engraved after Vouet by Mellan, such as the 'Lucretia'. At the same time he painted portraits of a swaggering, bohemian type which in the treatment of light and colour remind one that he had also passed through Venice.[108]

On his arrival in Paris, Vouet seems at first to have been mainly occupied with painting religious subjects, and in this field the style which he brought from Rome was bound to be successful with the French public. The Mannerist upbringing of Parisian connoisseurs would have prevented them from appreciating the naturalism of the Caravaggesques, and the religious atmosphere was not sufficiently enthusiastic and emotional for them to have stomached the full Baroque. But Vouet's compromise manner, Baroque still qualified by a classical tradition, was exactly in tune with the needs of a society whose religion was that of St François de Sales, of Bérulle, and of Olier. For the rest of his career Vouet was overwhelmed with commissions for altarpieces in the churches of Paris, whether for the various orders – the Jesuits at St Paul-St Louis and at their Noviciate,[109] the Minims, the Carmelites, and the Oratorians – or for the parish churches such as St Eustache and St Merri. One of his most successful altarpieces was the 'Presentation in the Temple', commissioned in 1641 by Richelieu for the high altar of the Noviciate of the Jesuits (Plate 111B). The general principles of design are still the same as in the early painting at S. Martino, with the strong diagonal emphasis. But the space is now more carefully defined by means of the architecture, which also gives stability to the pattern by its strong verticals. That is to say, the composition is slightly more classical than in the S. Martino painting, whether it is considered in two or three dimensions. In the same way the modelling is firmer and the drapery more statuesque. The colour is colder, and perhaps shows the influence of Philippe de Champaigne. In the treatment of the subject there is also a change. The presentation is more rational, with less emphasis on the supernatural and emotional sides of the theme. The figures swoon less, and the angels appear in more human guise without the aid of clouds and mystical light. In fact in both form and content this altarpiece shows that Vouet after his return to France moved farther away from the Baroque and nearer to the type of classical painting of which Poussin was beginning to set the standard.

At the same time he began to try his hand at poetical and allegorical composition. The first large series in this genre is one illustrating Tasso, executed for Bullion in 1630,[110] in which the artist applies his Roman style to this new kind of subject. More personal are the allegorical panels executed for the various royal palaces, of which a series is in the Louvre and a fine 'Allegory of Peace' at Chatsworth (Plate 111A). This work, which is probably very late,[111] shows that Vouet did not always carry on the classical tendencies visible in the 'Presentation'. The design is freer, the modelling looser, and the whole picture is conceived more in terms of light and colour, reminding us of the fact that Vouet in his youth studied not only in Rome but also in Venice, where he must have learnt the style of colouring which he here displays, a rather pallid version of Veronese's tones.

Vouet's most important innovations, however, lie in the field of decorative painting, in which he founded a tradition destined to dominate French painting for a century.

His earliest decorative schemes were carried out in conjunction with the sculptor Jacques Sarrazin, and consisted of painted panels surrounded by stucco.[112] In the ceilings each panel was depicted in steep perspective, but there was no attempt to create a consistent illusion linking up the different parts of the decoration.[113] A second group of decorations is mainly made up of panels of grotesques with landscapes and small figure groups set among them. The most important of these were two for Anne of Austria at Fontainebleau (1644) and the Palais Royal (between 1643 and 1647), now destroyed and only known from engravings,[114] but a similar series, probably by Vouet and his pupils, survives, though much restored, at the Arsenal, where it was executed for the Maréchal de la Meilleraye about 1637.[115]

It was, however, at the Hôtel Séguier that Vouet received his greatest opportunity. There he painted the chapel (1638), the library (finished by 1640), and the lower gallery, which was left incomplete at his death in 1649.[116] In the first two of these Vouet introduced methods of decoration which were up till then unknown in France. Or rather, to put it more precisely, he grafted new wood on an old tree, and revived with fresh ideas a tradition which had been founded by the school of Fontainebleau, but had died out in the early seventeenth century.

It will be remembered that in the Galerie d'Ulysse at Fontainebleau, Primaticcio and Niccolò dell'Abbate had included illusionist panels in steep perspective and that the method had been carried even further in the chapel at the Hôtel de Guise.[117] The second school of Fontainebleau had not continued the tradition,[118] but Vouet took it up, adding to it the methods which he had learnt in Italy. In the library at the Hôtel Séguier the ceiling seems to have been completely painted, without stucco but with a background imitating gold mosaic. The individual compositions are in steep perspective, some of them based on Guercino's 'Aurora', but others showing Vouet's debt to Venetian painters. Some of the big oval designs have architectural backgrounds which derive directly from the ceilings of Veronese, whose works, we are told by Amidei, Vouet had particularly studied in Venice.

In the chapel ceiling he went a step further, and decorated it with a fresco of consistent illusionism. The subject was the Adoration of the Magi (Plate 112A), and Vouet disposed the procession of the Kings and their attendants in a sort of frieze round the cove of the vaulting, so that the figures seem to stand on the cornice. As Sauval points out, he has followed the example of Primaticcio and Niccolò, who used the same arrangement in the Guise Chapel. But, whereas the sixteenth-century artists organize their figures into a continuous bas-relief, Vouet is far freer in his disposition. All but the central figures of the Kings and the Holy Family are arranged behind a balustrade, which must have looked like a continuation of the wall architecture into the ceiling, and behind the groups are indications of further architecture, carrying the composition into depth. In details the figures again recall Veronese, but the general scheme of the fresco is closer to the two first examples of this type of illusionism, Correggio's dome in the cathedral of Parma and Giulio Romano's ceiling of the Sala di Troia in the Palazzo del Tè.[119]

In this fresco Vouet introduced a form of illusionist decoration which was not to be followed up in France till almost the end of the century,[120] for the ceiling decorations of the next decades are based on the illusion created by means of painted architecture, and therefore derive from a different tradition, that of the Farnese Gallery.

Vouet's influence on French painting was greater than his real quality as an artist might lead one to expect. His success depended on his bringing in a suitable new Italian idiom at the moment when it was needed, and on his skill in undertaking all sorts of tasks. Historically his position is parallel to that of Lemercier, but in temperament he reminds one more of Le Vau. He was supple, brilliant, rapid, adaptable. Like Le Vau's, his artistic conscience was not very sensitive, and his works suffer from a certain superficiality. But he brought new life to French painting when it was at a very low ebb; he introduced a solid tradition of competence; and he managed to inspire a generation of pupils who were to carry on his work in a remarkable way. Almost all the artists of the middle of the century – François Perrier, Le Sueur, and Pierre and Nicolas Mignard – passed through his studio, and his influence was felt even farther through the most important of them all, Charles Lebrun. Theoretically Poussin represented the ideal which the Academy set itself to follow in the later seventeenth century, but all its members, starting with Lebrun, sacrificed as often, though with less ostentation, at the altar of Vouet.[121]

Among Vouet's contemporaries were several artists who, like him, drew their inspiration from Italy and who continued to paint up to the middle years of the century without being affected by the new classicism introduced by Poussin. They are not artists of great calibre, but they are typical of one aspect of French taste at this period.

Vouet's collaborator, François Perrier, is still a somewhat hazy figure. Born, according to Dézallier d'Argenville,[122] in 1590, he went young to Rome, and returned to France in 1629, painting for the Charterhouse at Lyons in that year and joining Vouet at Chilly in 1630. He then settled in Paris and executed a number of works, including a series for Bordier at Le Raincy. He made a further journey to Rome, returning in 1645. In the same year he was commissioned to paint the gallery at the Hôtel de la Vrillière, his most important work, replaced by a copy when the gallery was rebuilt in the nineteenth century. At about the same time he decorated the cove of the ceiling in the Cabinet des Muses at the Hôtel Lambert, and perhaps executed some of the panels on the walls of the Cabinet de l'Amour.[123] He became a foundation member of the Academy in 1648, and died two years later.

Perrier's style seems to have been formed in Rome on the study of the Carracci and of Lanfranco, in whose studio he actually worked. His 'Acis, Galatea, and Polyphemus' (Plate 113B) in the Louvre is based on Lanfranco's treatment of the subject in the Palazzo Doria Pamphili, but is treated in a much more picturesque and less classical manner. In his decoration of the La Vrillière gallery he used a compromise between the decorative methods of the Carracci and those of the early Baroque. A part of the ceiling was divided up by ribs painted in imitation of architecture, against which were set pictures in trompe l'œil gilt frames, flanked by satyrs and nudes; but the middle section was opened up to a vista of open sky, across which the chariot of Apollo was seen advancing. The walls of the gallery were completely redecorated in the eighteenth century, so that the general effect of the room is hardly as it was intended by Perrier and Mansart, but even in its present state it is still possible to realize the importance which it must have had in the development of French decoration. It must not, moreover, be forgotten that Lebrun, who applies the same method in the gallery at the Hôtel Lambert, worked for a time in the studio of Perrier before he joined that of Vouet.[124]

Jacques Blanchard is a more easily intelligible figure. He was born in 1600 and was brought up, presumably in the Late Mannerist tradition, by his uncle, the painter Nicolas Bollery.[125] In 1620 he went to Lyons, where he worked for a time under Horace Le Blanc, and in 1624 attained what was no doubt his original goal, Rome. Here he only stayed for eighteen months, and at the end of 1625 moved to Venice, where he spent two years, mainly studying Veronese. In about 1628 he returned to Paris, stopping on the way to carry out commissions in Turin and Lyons. In the remaining years till his death in 1638 he seems to have achieved a certain success in painting small religious and mythological subjects, though he also undertook the decoration of two galleries, one for Bullion, in whose house Vouet was also working.

The dominant influence on his formation was certainly the painting which he saw in Venice, and above all that of Veronese, whose cool colours and silvery light he imitates more successfully than Vouet. He seems to have specialized in painting such subjects as 'Charity' (Plate 112B), of which many different versions exist, all showing the particular type of rather delicate sentiment which appears in almost all his work. In this painting the influence of Veronese is visible not only in the light and colour, but also in the architectural background and in the classical building up of the group. In other probably earlier paintings, such as the 'Medor and Angelica' in the Metropolitan Museum, New York, he is more Mannerist, borrowing his compositional method from Tintoretto and his treatment of trees from Paul Brill. In yet other paintings, notably the 'Cimon and Iphigenia' in the Louvre, his model is evidently Rubens, whose late nudes he must have known. Blanchard is also a sensitive painter of portraits, as can be seen from that of the sculptor Duquesnoy in the Czernin collection, Vienna.[126] This portrait must have been painted in 1624–5, when Blanchard was in Rome, and it is interesting as showing that he must have known Poussin there, since Duquesnoy and he were close friends at this time. There is, however, no trace either then or later of influence from Poussin's work on Blanchard, who seems to have been always loyal to the Venetian-Flemish tradition.

A more interesting painter, of greater individuality and range, is Laurent de la Hyre. He was born in Paris in 1606,[127] and worked for a short time in the studio of Lallemant. His main training, however, consisted of studying the works at Fontainebleau, particularly, his biographers say, those of Primaticcio, but no doubt also those of Dubois and the other painters of Henry IV's time. The effect of this training can be seen in his earliest surviving works, the two altarpieces painted for the Capuchins in the Marais, representing the 'Adoration of the Shepherds' and 'Nicholas V before the Body of St Francis',[128] dated 1630 (Plate 114), in which the architectural setting, seen in sharp perspective, is used very much as it had been in the ceiling panels of the Galerie d'Ulysse at Fontainebleau. On the other hand, his figures have none of the characteristics of Mannerism, but are, on the contrary, staid and realistic, unlike the work of any other religious artist active in Paris at that time. We must therefore suppose that La Hyre had also seen more classical and naturalistic models. We know that he did not visit Italy, but he could have found inspiration for this style in the Venetian paintings in the royal collection and in certain private collections in Paris, particularly that of the Duc de Liancourt, who had an important series of paintings by Titian and Veronese.[129] In La Hyre's works of about 1635–7[130] this Venetian influence is even more apparent, both in the classical arrangement of the space defined by the architecture and in the treatment of light and colour. About 1638 La Hyre appears to have come under the influence of Poussin's earlier style, of which he produced a personal variant. The 'Mercury giving the Infant Bacchus to the Nymphs' in the Hermitage at Leningrad (Plate 113A), dated 1638, is typical of this phase. The romantic treatment of the ruins is close, for instance, to Poussin's 'Adoration of the Magi' at Dresden, but La Hyre adds to the architecture broken fragments of sculptured heads and bas-reliefs, a device which he frequently uses at this time.[131] The figures, moreover, are in a personal style, independent of Poussin, and the landscape, with its romantic view on a river valley, is one of the earliest examples in La Hyre's art of his individual contribution in this field.

In his last years, from about 1648 till his death in 1656, La Hyre's paintings fall into two categories. His figure compositions become colder and more classical, under the influence apparently of Poussin and of Philippe de Champaigne.[132] In these works the artist seems to be adapting himself not altogether happily to the new fashion, and the result is something impersonal and not deeply felt. At the same time, however, he continued to develop his interest in landscape, and it was in these years that he produced his most original works in this field. Sometimes he models himself on Flemish masters, such as Foucquier, who was then working in Paris,[133] though modifying their naturalism into a slightly more generalized formula. At other times, as in the 'Landscape with the Arcadian Shepherds' at Orleans, he adopts the luminous qualities of the early Claude and uses them to create a poetical setting for a nostalgic classical theme.

La Hyre is far from being a great master, and his influence was never considerable; but he is typical of a phenomenon which was to become increasingly common in France from this time onwards, namely the artist with minor talent who managed to make a personal contribution to a school of painting more notable for its steady level of quality than for the giants which it has produced. La Hyre embodies in a small way the good sense and the good taste of French seventeenth-century culture.[134]

So far in this section we have considered those painters of the mid-seventeenth century who were dominated by the influence of Italy, and it will be appropriate therefore to end it with a mention of the few Italian artists of importance who actually visited France during the decades in question.

One of these, the engraver Stefano della Bella (1610–64), spent the years 1639 to 1650 in Paris. He was a pupil of Callot, and benefited from the popularity of Callot's work in France. His extremely delicate topographical and decorative etchings had much success in Paris, and the latter probably exercised some influence on engravers of the next generation, like Jean Le Pautre.[135]

The appearance in Paris of the celebrated Roman decorative painter, Giovanni Francesco Romanelli, the ablest pupil of Pietro da Cortona, naturally created a more lasting effect. Romanelli paid two visits to Paris. The first took place in 1646–7, when he painted for Mazarin the Galerie Mazarine which survives in the Bibliothèque Nationale, and also for the Président Lambert in the Cabinet de l'Amour. The second was in 1655–7, when he decorated the rooms of the Queen Mother, which also survive, though radically altered, on the ground floor of the Louvre.[136]

In the Galerie Mazarine Romanelli created a type of decoration blending in a novel manner classical and Baroque elements. The painted mythological scenes are enclosed in well-defined stucco frames, partly gilt, the panels themselves being mainly treated without illusionist foreshortening. This is a method which had been frequently used in both countries, but with the difference that the panels here are much larger than usual and their forms simpler and more rectilinear, producing therefore a less broken and more unified effect. Romanelli may be said to have combined the classical pattern of the Farnese ceiling with the rich stucco effects achieved by Pietro da Cortona in the Palazzo Pitti, the Baroque character of the latter being thus adapted to a more classical canon, which, as Romanelli no doubt realized, would be palatable to a French public.[137] The scheme was to have its influence on the most important decorations of the next generation, particularly on Lebrun's Galerie d'Apollon in the Louvre.[138]

Philippe de Champaigne and Flemish Influence

Although French artists turned more regularly to Italian art for inspiration than to any other school during the seventeenth century, there were always certain groups whose interests were directed northwards to Flanders. We have already noticed the small amount of influence exercised on French painting by Rubens' Marie de' Medici cycle, but his manner and technique were to a certain extent introduced to France by a much less considerable master who, however, by adapting himself completely to French taste, established a more important position than Rubens in the development of French art in the mid seventeenth century.[139]

This artist was Philippe de Champaigne. He was born in Brussels in 1602 and trained there, mainly as a landscape painter under Jacques Foucquier or Foucquières.[140] In 1621 he came to Paris, perhaps with his master, who arrived in the same year. He worked with various painters, including Lallemant, on whose designs he executed a portrait group of the aldermen of the city of Paris.[141] At about the same time he met the young Poussin, with whom he collaborated on decoration for Marie de' Medici in the Luxembourg under the landscape painter, Nicolas Duchesne.[142] In 1627 he paid a short visit to Brussels, but returned at the beginning of the next year to Paris to succeed Duchesne as painter to the Queen Mother. In 1628 he began for her a series of paintings in the convent of the Carmelites in the rue St Jacques.[143] At the same time he seems to have gained the favour of Louis XIII, for whom, presumably, he painted the portrait in the Louvre showing the King crowned by Victory with a background composed of a view of La Rochelle, where the Protestants had been besieged and defeated in 1628. Six years later, in 1634, he executed a picture for Notre Dame showing Louis XIII offering his crown to Christ at the foot of the Cross. In 1636 Champaigne was commissioned by one of the canons to design two tapestry cartoons of the Life of the Virgin for the cathedral.[144]

Before 1635 Champaigne had also attracted the attention of Richelieu,[145] for whom he decorated one gallery at the Palais Royal and painted a series of portraits of great men for another.[146] The Cardinal also commissioned him to execute the frescoes in the dome of the Sorbonne and to paint his own portrait (Plate 116A). Of his other recorded works of this time we have no trace, except the composition painted in 1634 to celebrate the reception of the Duc de Longueville into the Order of the Saint-Esprit, a huge formal design now at Toulouse.[147]

As far as we can judge him in this early period, Philippe de Champaigne stands in the same relation to Rubens as did Vouet to his Italian masters. That is to say, he succeeds in moderating a Baroque idiom to a more restrained and classical form in which it was acceptable to the French public.[148] The 'Adoration of the Shepherds' in the Wallace Collection (Plate 115) shows the artist in this phase.[149] The handling and the lighting have been learnt from the early Rubens,[150] and even the colour and the composition are derived from him, but they have been transformed in the borrowing. Champaigne has checked the strong movement which Rubens introduced into the group, and he has modified the colour in the direction of cold and strong local colour, almost unbroken and unblended. There are still Baroque traces in the conception of the subject, particularly in the miraculous lighting and in the *putti* which fly in at the top. But Champaigne's personal style is already apparent in the naturalistic treatment of the shepherds, who are unlike Rubens' figures and at the same time quite unclassical.[151]

The only portraits of this period about which we have any certain knowledge are those of Louis XIII and Richelieu.[152] The allegorical portrait of the King after the siege of La Rochelle (1628) is probably the earliest of the series, and embodies the type used in all the later portraits, but Champaigne has evidently not felt at home in the rendering of the Victory, a trace of Baroque machinery which does not harmonize with the straightforward rendering of the King. In a fine version of Louis XIII belonging to the Comte de Paris one source of Champaigne's portrait style is evident, for he has here borrowed the pattern used by Pourbus for his state portrait of Henry IV in the Louvre and also for that of the Duc de Chevreuse, except that he has modified the perspective, presumably because the picture was intended to be seen from below.[153]

The portraits of Richelieu show, on the other hand, his links with Rubens and van Dyck. The full-length (Plate 116A) is based on a pose much used by van Dyck in his Genoese portraits, and borrowed by him from Rubens. On the other hand, the modelling of the robes is much more classical and even sculpturesque, a fact which suggests that Champaigne had been studying Roman statues and that he was moving towards the imitation of them at the same time as Poussin, but independently of him.[154]

In 1643, or soon after, there occurred the most important event in Champaigne's life: he came in contact with Port Royal and the doctrines of Jansenism.[155] Like so many serious men of his time, he was evidently attracted by the sincerity of the Jansenists, their severe way of life, their devotion to their beliefs, and their complete rejection of everything that was worldly. For the rest of his life Champaigne was in close relation with the convent, for which he painted several of his most important works. But the effect of their teaching can be seen in everything that he produced, whether religious or secular.

In the religious works of his later period Champaigne rejects the elements of the Baroque which he had retained in the earlier. There are no radiances, no *putti*, no ecstasies; everything is carefully stated in clear and intelligible terms which appeal to the reason as much as to the emotions. In the big compositions, such as the series illustrating the lives and martyrdoms of St Protasius and St Gervasius (1655),[156] the result is sometimes cold and uncomfortable. Champaigne here abandons his near-Baroque energy, but never quite attains the classicism of Poussin, at which he seems to be aiming. The compositions are cold rather than lucid, and the figures rigid rather than statuesque. But in the scenes which admit of more restrained treatment the effect is of real intensity. Among the finest is the 'Crucifixion' in the Louvre, painted by Champaigne in 1674, the year of his death, and bequeathed by him to the Charterhouse of Paris. Here the simplicity of the presentation is dramatically effective – the cross standing in isolation, seen frontally with a classically constructed view of Jerusalem in the background.[157]

The most important works of this later period, however, are the portraits, in which Champaigne attains to real originality. He occasionally continues to produce the more or less show-pieces, such as the portrait of the Président de Mesme (1653) in the Louvre, in which he still uses a modification of the Rubens–van Dyck formula. But his real invention is the half-length portrait of a much simpler type (Plate 116B) which he uses to depict his Jansenist friends, and also a series of ecclesiastical and *bourgeois* patrons. The formula is a simple one, based on the Venetian sixteenth-century type of figure behind a parapet. But in the example here illustrated he has modified the pattern by representing his model actually sitting in a window on the sill of which he leans his hand. In this he may have had in mind certain Dutch models, either paintings of Frans Hals or etchings by Rembrandt. But the treatment is highly personal; the sharp observation and the severe naturalism of the portraits are all Champaigne's own. In colour one can almost say that these portraits are Jansenist in their extreme restraint. Champaigne's sitters usually wear black, and there is little to relieve the severity of the whole, since they are shown against a grey background and behind a stone-coloured parapet. In pose they are again as classical as possible, with the head and body almost frontal, and no suggestion of movement or contraposto. In these portraits, in fact, Champaigne creates a French equivalent for the *bourgeois* portraiture which flourished in Holland at the same period.

On three occasions Champaigne was also commissioned to paint the official portrait group of the mayor and aldermen of the city of Paris.[158] One of these groups, for the year 1648, exists in the Louvre (Plate 117A). As in the case of the Saint-Esprit commemorative pictures, the artist here had to follow a rigidly established formula. The individual heads are painted with great naturalism, but the figures kneel in almost hieratic poses on either side of a small altar, on which is the figure of St Geneviève, the patron saint of Paris. The severity and rigidity of the design are in keeping with the dignity of those who ruled over the city at this time and who, from what we know of them, took their duties seriously and proudly maintained the independence of their municipality.

All Champaigne's qualities are concentrated in the masterpiece of his later period, the votive picture for the curing of his daughter (Plate 117B). The story of the miraculous cure is well known. Champaigne's daughter, who was a nun at Port Royal, was attacked in 1660 by paralysis, which by the end of 1661 had made it impossible for her to walk at all. The prioress, la Mère Agnès Arnauld, then declared a *novena* in the hope that she might be cured, and at the end of it she found that she was suddenly and miraculously enabled to walk. In thanksgiving for this cure Champaigne painted the votive picture of the miracle, which he presented to the convent. In it he depicted his daughter stretched on a chair in her cell, while the prioress kneels in prayer beside her. The composition is of the simplest, with the two figures set in almost geometrically related poses at right angles to each other against the plain background of grey walls. The colour is limited to greys and blacks, with only two strong notes of red in the crosses on the nuns' habits – and even one of those is partly obscured. The indication of the miraculous event is limited to the ray of light which falls between the two figures. In its restraint and simplicity this painting is as typical of the Jansenist approach to a miracle as Bernini's 'St Theresa' is of the Jesuit.[159]

Philippe de Champaigne is important not only as an original artist but also as summing up one aspect of French art in the middle of the seventeenth century. His portraits and his later religious works are as true a reflexion of the rationalism of French thought as the classical compositions of Poussin in the 1640s. One uses the formula of Roman republican virtue to express his beliefs, and the other that of Jansenism, the most severe and heroic of all forms of Catholicism in the seventeenth century.

It is a considerable drop from Champaigne to the remaining portrait painters of this period, but some of them must be mentioned. In their own day the cousins Henri (1603–77) and Charles Beaubrun (1604–92) enjoyed a great success, especially among the society of the *Précieux*. Their style was a continuation of the Late Mannerist formula of Pourbus in a less sensitive manner, and their portraits have little value except as records (cf. plate 148B). Louis Elle (1612–89), son of Ferdinand, was of the same type, though he sometimes enlivened his portraits by a pose borrowed from van Dyck. Justus van Egmont (1601–74), a pupil of Rubens, spent the years *c.* 1628–48 in Paris, where he painted many of the most important members of the Court, using a moderated version of Rubens' style.[160]

The only member of the group to attain distinction was the draughtsman and engraver, Robert Nanteuil.[161] He is in engraving what Philippe de Champaigne was in painting, and it is no chance that he should have engraved so many heads after his Flemish contemporary. Technically he was a master of his craft, and his original engraved portraits reveal an acute power of observation (Plate 147). His works give us the most complete view which remains to us of the great figures of the middle of the century.

The Caravaggesques

The influence of Caravaggio never penetrated as far as Paris, but in the provinces his style enjoyed a considerable vogue. We have already seen that Finsonius practised it with success in Provence, and in the next generation the tradition was carried on by a far more sensitive painter, Nicolas Tournier of Toulouse (1590–after 1660),[162] who specialized in Caravaggesque religious and genre scenes (Plate 119A), but who also painted a vast 'Victory of Constantine', now in the museum of Toulouse. His naturalism is always qualified by a slightly Mannerist elegance in the poses of his figures and by his preference for rather elegant types, as opposed to the coarse peasant heads of most Caravaggesques.

It was, however, in Lorraine that the influence of the master produced its most interesting results, and in Georges de la Tour we find a personal interpretation of the convention not to be paralleled elsewhere.

La Tour was born at Vic-sur-Seille in 1593.[163] By 1620 he was established as a master in Lunéville, one of the most prosperous towns of the duchy, which he seems to have made his headquarters for the rest of his life and where he died in 1652. Records show him to have been successful in his career and to have accumulated enough wealth to arouse jealousy among his fellow townsmen. Quite early in his career, in 1623–4, he received commissions for two works from the Duke of Lorraine, but there is no evidence that the favour of the Prince was continued. In 1639 he is mentioned as having the title of *Peintre du Roi*, and it is known that Louis XIII owned a painting by him of St Sebastian. Some five years later he caught the attention of the Duc de La Ferté-Senecterre, who had been made French governor of Lorraine in 1643, and who managed to persuade the town of Nancy to present him with several works by the artist. In fact La Tour's links seem to have been not with the Court of Lorraine itself, but with a *bourgeois* circle in Lunéville and with members of the French administration at Nancy. It is, therefore, to be expected that his style should not be like the court Mannerism of his immediate predecessors and contemporaries at Nancy, Bellange, Callot, and Deruet, but should strike out on quite different lines. We know further that he was connected with the religious revival which took place at this time in Lorraine, and it has been plausibly suggested that his painting reflects the feeling of the Franciscans who were the leaders of it.

La Tour's artistic education has been the cause of much speculation. What appears to be the artist's earliest work, 'The Cheat', in the Landry collection, shows no direct evidence of Caravaggesque influence, but is an exercise in a manner which had been practised in Nancy by Callot in etching and by Jean Leclerc in painting.[164] But a series of paintings which I believe can be assigned to the 1620s, including the 'St Jerome' (Plate 119B), show that La Tour soon came into contact with the style of Caravaggio. Most writers have assumed that he went to Italy and picked up the tradition as it was continued in Rome by Manfredi and Valentin. The particular form of naturalism in the 'St Jerome', however, seems to suggest not so much direct knowledge of Caravaggio's own painting and that of his Italian imitators, as acquaintance with his Dutch followers. The closest parallel is to be found in Terbrugghen's works, such as the four evangelists at Deventer painted in 1621, a time when La Tour might well have visited Utrecht. In these one finds the curious clay-like handling of the flesh and the emphasis on the dry wrinkles which are so characteristic of the 'St Jerome'. In this phase La Tour is naturalistic in the sense that he describes minutely the incidents on the surface of the bodies which he paints. Only in the cardinal's hat in the background is there a trace of the generalized treatment which was to be the hallmark of his later style. The other works which I believe to be of the same date all have the same picturesque, rugged, descriptive quality, for instance the 'Hurdy-Gurdy Player' in the museum at Nantes, which is the equivalent in a modern subject to the 'St Jerome', and painted from a very similar model.[165]

A painting, representing 'Job and his Wife', at Épinal marks the transition to the next phase. It is still conceived in the same spirit of descriptive naturalism, but it has one important difference: it represents a night scene, illuminated by an unshaded candle held by Job's wife. This is yet another link with the Dutch followers of Caravaggio who were the real exponents of this treatment of light. This method is used with great originality in almost all La Tour's later works, but in various different ways. In the recently discovered 'Penitence of St Peter',[166] dated 1645, and in the 'Christ and St Joseph in the Carpenter's Shop' (Plate 120), in the Louvre, the warm, almost coppery tones suggest the influence of Honthorst's mature work, which La Tour may have seen if he made a second journey to the Low Countries, as is possible, in the years 1639-42, when he is not recorded in Lunéville. But in another group, the latest of all, the use of candle-light effects is far more personal, and it is here that La Tour shows his true qualities. These can be grouped round the 'Denial of St Peter' at Nantes, dated 1650,[167] and include the 'St Sebastian' (Plate 121) in Berlin and the Rennes 'Nativity' (Plate 122A). Here at last La Tour has broken away from the descriptive style of his earlier period and, avoiding all disturbing detail, reduces individual forms to almost geometrical terms, and relates them to each other in compositions of equally mathematical clarity. The result is a monumentality which has no parallel among the other followers of Caravaggio, an impressive simplicity which converts the formula of naturalism into something classical.

The style of Caravaggio admits of two different, one can almost say opposite interpretations. Some of his followers, particularly the Neapolitans, emphasized the dramatic and horrific qualities in his painting, and adapted the manner to gruesome renderings of martyrdoms in which every unpleasant detail is recorded with fidelity and heightened by chiaroscuro. La Tour in his mature works seeks in Caravaggio exactly the opposite qualities. He does not imitate his rendering of detail, and he avoids the depiction of the disagreeable details. Notice, for instance, that in the 'St Sebastian' there is no blood and no anguish; the saint lies motionless and apparently dead, but with hardly a trace of his martyrdom. The forms are generalized to their greatest simplicity, and all violence, all movement even, are eliminated, so that the picture takes on a quality of stillness and of silence rarely to be found in the visual arts. In this calm, detached interpretation of Caravaggesque naturalism La Tour comes near to the classicism of Poussin and to the nobility of the finest compositions of Champaigne. The art of La Tour is as far removed as it can be from the Mannerism of the Court of Nancy, but it has qualities in common with the style which was being evolved as a reflexion of *bourgeois* culture in Paris at the same time.

The Le Nains

More ink has been spilt over the 'Le Nain Problem' than over any other question in French seventeenth-century art; to some effect, however, since, although many points remain obscure – and are likely to do so for a long time – it is now possible to give in outline a solution.

The problem itself can be easily and shortly stated. There were three brothers called Le Nain, all painters and all born at Laon. The eldest, Antoine, was probably born in 1588; the next, Louis, in 1593; and the youngest, Mathieu, in 1607. The two elder brothers both died in 1648, but Mathieu survived till 1677. From early accounts we know a few facts, including the point that the brothers may on occasions have collaborated on the same canvas. About fifteen signed and dated pictures survive, but the signatures simply read 'Le Nain', without christian name, and the dates are all between 1641 and 1648, when all three brothers were active. There is therefore no solid starting point for distinguishing the works of the three brothers. On the other hand, stylistic analysis has shown that there are three main groups, each with a distinct character, to which the names of the three brothers have been convincingly attached. The border-lines between the groups are, of course, liable to provoke incidents between critics, and there is endless room for speculation on the possibility of collaboration in any one painting.[168]

Antoine, we are told, 'excelled in miniatures and portraits in small'. By 1629 he had moved from Laon to Paris, and was made master painter to the Abbey of St Germain des Prés. To him are attributed a series of small pictures, mainly on copper (Plate 122B), depicting groups of diminutive figures, painted in strong and pure local colours, and naïvely placed with no great care for calculated composition.[169] Most of these groups are portraits of *bourgeois* families, either of Laon or of Paris, shown in the surroundings of their own houses. But some of Antoine's compositions – for instance, the small picture in the National Gallery – represent peasant families. The origins of Antoine's style are obscure. He was trained in his native town, and the tradition which he would there have picked up must have been a late form of Netherlandish sixteenth-century naturalism, such as that practised by Adriaen Pietersz. van der Venne, or Hendrik Averkamp.

Louis, the second brother, is a far more considerable artist; indeed, it is because of his achievement that the family is worthy of the attention which it has received. Of his life we know only that, together with his brothers, he was installed in Paris by 1630, but that, unlike Antoine, he was still at that date an apprentice. Eighteenth-century writers describe him as 'Le Romain', and, although this evidence is too late to be conclusive, it points strongly to a visit to Rome. The paintings associated with his name are quite different from those of Antoine (Plate 123A). They are larger in scale, impressive, and almost classical in composition, and subdued in colour, being mainly painted in a narrow range of cool greys, grey-browns, and grey-greens. They mainly depict scenes of peasant life, but occasionally, as in the Louvre 'Adoration of the Shepherds', Louis tried his hand at a religious subject.[170]

In the case of Louis it seems possible to explain the origins of his manner more fully than for Antoine. The writers of the seventeenth century describe him as a painter of *bambochades*, that is to say as an imitator of the Dutch artist Pieter van Laer, or Bamboccio as he was called in Rome, who specialized in small pictures of low life. Louis Le Nain could have learnt from Bamboccio not only the type of composition which he painted but also his colouring, for Bamboccio, too, based his palette on a limited range of colours near to grey. Further, we know from Sandrart that van Laer, who was born in Haarlem in 1592 or 1595, came through France on his way to Rome, which he reached in 1626. It is therefore possible that Louis Le Nain could have known him in Paris, and perhaps have continued the acquaintance in Rome.[171]

Whatever his sources, Louis Le Nain had mastered by the early 1640s a style which enabled him to paint his remarkable peasant scenes (Plate 123A). In a sense these pictures belong to the tradition of Dutch *bamboccisti*, but with the very important difference that the artist never satirizes his sitters, nor draws out their grotesque or amusing qualities. He paints the peasants with complete sympathy, but at the same time he resists the desire to idealize them. He steers, that is to say, a course midway between the boors of Brouwer and the pious simpletons of Millet's 'Angelus'. This detached observation is coupled with a mastery of a classical type of composition which intensifies the calmness of the presentation. The figures are grouped without obvious thought, but in fact on a carefully worked-out method of frontal positions and balancing half-views, strangely like that used by Philippe de Champaigne in the votive picture. Here we find again that recurrent phenomenon in French art of this period, a classicism which does not use the outward forms of Greek or Roman formulas, but attains to the clarity and calm which are the more fundamental qualities of the style. Louis Le Nain is classical in his approach to life and to painting, even though he never turned to mythology for his themes.[172]

Mathieu Le Nain was a quite different character. In 1633 he became master painter to the city of Paris, and he seems to have made for himself a successful career through his municipal connexions. He became a lieutenant in the city militia, was made a *chevalier*, probably of the Order of St Michael, called himself 'Seigneur de la Jumelle', from a farm which he owned near Laon, and had an expensive funeral at St Sulpice. Like his elder brothers, he was a member of the Academy, but, unlike them, lived long enough to enjoy the privileges which it afforded.[173]

The paintings connected with the name of Mathieu reflect his character. Among the earliest is probably the 'Corps de Garde' (Plate 123B), dated 1643, which is also perhaps his masterpiece. It shows a scene almost certainly taken from Mathieu's life in the Paris militia, and represents a party of officers sitting round a table, drinking and attended by a Negro servant. The scene is lit by a candle standing on the table, and the effect is therefore immediately reminiscent of the Dutch Caravaggesques, whose works Mathieu must have known. Essentially his style is made up of elements learnt from his brother Louis,[174] to which is added a finish of handling which again suggest contacts with the Dutch school. Appropriately to his swaggering subjects, Mathieu makes his compositions more lively and more Baroque than those of Louis. One is not tempted here to seek comparisons with the classical artists of the century.[175]

The Le Nain brothers present one further important problem: who were their patrons? We have seen that Antoine's groups are mainly portraits and were no doubt commissioned by modest *bourgeois*. Mathieu evidently also had a regular clientèle of a slightly richer *bourgeois* class who bought his composite portraits such as the 'Corps de Garde' and the Louvre group which evidently represents a party of intellectuals. The difficult case, however, is that of Louis and his peasant scenes. Clearly they were not bought by the peasants whom they represented. Nor can one argue entirely on the analogy of Dutch painting and say that they would naturally have appealed to a middle-class town public; for, as we have already seen, Louis's paintings lack the comic or bohemian side which made such subjects interesting to the townsman. One might hope to find a parallel in the literature of the period; but there is none that really fits. The novelists of the time, such as Scarron and Charles Sorel, often describe peasants and country life but always with the intention of making them grotesque; and La Bruyère and his famous description of the French peasant are still fifty years off. We have no record of any collector who owned peasant scenes by the Le Nain in the artists' life-time, nor indeed till the later eighteenth century, when interest was revived in them under the influence of Rousseau's doctrines and the belief in the nobility of the simple life. It is probably safe to guess that the aristocracy did not interest themselves in Louis's painting, since their inclination seems to have been in the direction of a much more Mannerist type of art. Rather, we may believe, some sober magistrate might have been attracted by the classical distinction and the severe dignity of Louis's finest compositions, remembering perhaps also his own origins in the peasantry which may not have lain so many generations away. But this is pure speculation.[176]

Naturalism produced one other remarkable artist in this period, the engraver Abraham Bosse (1602–76).[177] Bosse is generally studied purely as a recorder of life and manners, but he is also an artist of high quality. He began as an illustrator of novels and religious works and as a copier of the Late Mannerists. But in the 1630s he developed an independent and very personal style. His subjects are either taken from contemporary life, as in the 'Mariage à la Ville' (Plate 124B) and the 'Mariage à la Campagne' series (1633), or are clothed in the forms of his own period as in the 'Wise and Foolish Virgins' (c. 1635) (Plate 124A). Bosse always gives a clear idea of the life of his day; but the kind of life which he describes is a limited one, that, namely, of the well-to-do *bourgeoisie*. In the 'Mariage à la Ville' this is particularly clear. The characters are all the dignified members of the *noblesse de robe* and their families. The scenes illustrated are the practical events associated with a *bourgeois* marriage – the signing of the contract, the return from the baptism, and so on. The artist takes no stock in the personal aspect of the theme, nor in the romantic – or falsely romantic – love-making which played so important a rôle in the aristocratic-intellectual life of the Hôtel de Rambouillet and the circle of the *Précieux*. In most of the engravings the lovers play a quite minor part and always behave with unemotional decorum. When aristocratic figures appear in Bosse, as they do on occasions, they are usually slightly caricatured as in the 'Noblesse Française à l'Église', or made to symbolize the morally less respectable part of society. For instance, in the engravings illustrating the Parable of Lazarus the 'Rich Man's Feast' is shown attended by over-dressed fashionable figures, whereas in the 'Prodigal Son' the father wears the clothes and has the appearance of a respectable magistrate.

When Bosse renders a biblical subject such as the 'Wise and Foolish Virgins' he makes the parable the means of conveying a moral dear to the serious hearts of his audience, and at the same time gives yet another series of scenes from *bourgeois* life. In the engravings of the 'Wise Virgins Watching' (Plate 124A) we see his narrative and descriptive skill, but at the same time his mastery of technique. His detached naturalism in the rendering of the subject brings him close to Louis Le Nain, and he has further in common with him a fine grasp of classical composition, coupled in this case with a Caravaggesque use of lighting. His qualities are the opposite to those of Callot – solid technical ability and clear composition, as opposed to wit and brilliance of touch – so that to a certain extent he represents the classical phase of French art engraving just as Callot embodies the Mannerist stage.[178]

Nicolas Poussin

By a curious freak, French painting of the seventeenth century produced its most remarkable and its most typical works not in Paris but in Rome, since it was in Rome that Poussin and Claude spent almost the whole of their active lives. In one sense these artists belong not to the French school, but to that of Rome or the Mediterranean. Seen from another point of view, however, Poussin at least is the key to the whole later evolution of French art. In him are summed up all the qualities traditionally associated with French classicism; and his influence was to be predominant in French art from his own time up to our own, in the sense that many artists took him as their ideal, and an almost equal number reacted against him with a violence which was in itself a tribute to his importance.[179]

Nicolas Poussin was born in 1593 or 1594 of a peasant family in a hamlet near Les Andelys in Normandy.[180] In 1611 he had his first taste of painting when Quentin Varin came to Les Andelys to execute a series of altarpieces for the church there. Varin (*c.* 1570–1634)[181] was a minor Late Mannerist who worked mainly in the north-east provinces of France. As his surviving paintings at Les Andelys and elsewhere show, he was an eclectic of mediocre quality, combining some knowledge of late sixteenth-century Roman painting with an inherited Flemish style. He can have done little more than whet Poussin's appetite, but he did this to such a degree that the boy left home in the next year, apparently going first to Rouen, where he worked under Noël Jouvenet, and then to Paris. We know almost nothing of his activities between his arrival in Paris about 1612 and his arrival in Rome in 1624, although some writers have filled the gap with great ingenuity by invention. He studied for a short time with the Flemish portrait painter Ferdinand Elle and probably also with Lallemant. We know too little of these artists to be able to deduce what he would have learnt from them, but it is safe to guess that he would have absorbed a style close to that of the Second School of Fontainebleau. In addition to these models, however, he had access to others better suited to his taste. He was able to work in the Royal Library, where he studied engravings after Raphael and Giulio Romano, and in the collection of sculpture, where he formed his first acquaintance with Roman statues and reliefs. It is to be supposed that he also had access to the royal collection of paintings, and so began to know Raphael and Titian. He made several attempts to reach Rome, the first two being abortive and taking him only as far as Florence and Lyons respectively. He also travelled about France executing works of which little trace remains.[182]

In Paris he met Philippe de Champaigne, as we have seen, and worked with him for the Queen Mother at the Luxembourg. It was perhaps at her Court that he found his first real patron, the Italian poet Marino, who was attached to Marie de' Medici as her laureate. During the years 1615–23 Marino enjoyed a great success in Paris, particularly at the Hôtel de Rambouillet, where we may picture him reading parts of the *Adone*, his most important work, published in Paris in 1622. He may even have introduced Poussin to this circle, and we know at any rate that he commissioned from the young artist a series of drawings illustrating Ovid's *Metamorphoses*, which are the only works before 1624 certainly attributable to him.[183] They confirm the view suggested above that Poussin started as a follower of the Second School of Fontainebleau, and as a not very distinguished member of that school. They are coarse and vigorous, full of Mannerist tricks of drawing and composition, and of borrowings from the approved authorities. They give no indication that their author was to become a great artist.

In 1624 Poussin succeeded, at the third attempt, in reaching Rome, spending a few months in Venice on the way.[184] Unfortunately for him, his one friend in Rome, Marino, left within a few months for Naples, where he died in the next year. But before leaving he had introduced Poussin to Marcello Sacchetti, through whom he met Cardinal Francesco Barberini, the nephew of the recently elected Pope Urban VIII.

Poussin's first five years in Rome were a time of experiment. After a period of real poverty he obtained several important commissions, some for the Cardinal personally and one for an altarpiece in St Peter's, and he seemed set for a successful career as a painter of large altarpieces and classical compositions. It is difficult to define his style at this stage, because he tried his hand at so many different things, changing his manner with each new type of commission. His very first works in Rome – two battle scenes from the Old Testament[185] (Plate 125A) – still show the influence of his study in Paris of engravings after Giulio Romano and Polidoro, although his imagination had been refreshed by contact with the antique sarcophagi which he would have seen in Rome. These two battle-pieces are, however, still Mannerist, in that their composition is constructed in terms of high relief, without any real space in which the figures can exist and move.[186]

Soon after his arrival in Rome, Poussin is known to have worked in the studio of Domenichino, and to have copied his 'Martyrdom of St Andrew' in S. Gregorio al Celio. The influence of this artist is more apparent in his work of the 1630s, but it can be traced in the general design and the cool colouring of paintings such as the 'Triumph of David' at Dulwich[187] and the 'Parnassus' in the Prado.[188]

In the last years of the 1620s Poussin carried out several large-scale compositions, mainly, we may suppose, on commission. The most important was the altarpiece of the 'Martyrdom of St Erasmus' (Plate 126) for St Peter's, for which he obtained the commission in 1628 through Cardinal Barberini. This was, of course, the chance for which every young artist in Rome longed, but there is some reason to think that Poussin did not profit much by it from the point of view of his own career. In any case, it remained his only public picture painted in Rome, and we can feel in Sandrart's account of its reception that many critics disapproved of it, and preferred its pendant, Valentin's 'Martyrdom of St Processus and St Martinianus', for its colour, its naturalism, and its vigour. The truth seems to be that Poussin already felt ill at ease in these big compositions in which the Baroque painters scored their great successes, and his attempt to produce a design which should be in accordance with his own principles and at the same time fulfil the needs of an altarpiece for St Peter's led to a compromise which satisfied neither condition.

In one other painting of this period, the 'Madonna del Pilar' in the Louvre,[189] Poussin is more frankly Baroque. In others, such as the 'Massacre of the Innocents' at Chantilly,[190] painted for Giustiniani, he is more Caravaggesque. In the 'Marriage of St Catherine'[191] he adapts a Venetian type, derived from Veronese, to the solution of the same problem. In the 'Inspiration of the Poet' in the Louvre (Plate 127), Poussin attains complete originality. Here the classicism is so marked that many critics have dated it much later, but although in the pose of the Muse the artist uses an ancient model with a directness unusual at this period, the pale, cool colour, the luminous modelling, and the free handling, which are Venetian in origin and recall Veronese, point to this short phase in Poussin's career.[192]

About 1629 or 1630 a crisis seems to have occurred in Poussin's life. One cause may have been the relative failure of the St Peter's picture; another may have been the severe illness from which he suffered at this time. But whatever the reason, he seems suddenly to have changed direction. He abandoned the arena in which the artists of Rome were competing for the public commissions for churches and palaces, and from now onwards paints only relatively small pictures. His patrons, moreover, were no longer the princes of the Church or members of the wealthy Roman families. He seems to have been dependent for the next ten years on a small circle of *cognoscenti*, of whom the most important was the Commendatore Cassiano del Pozzo. This attractive character was secretary to Cardinal Francesco Barberini, and Poussin no doubt knew him from his first years in Rome. Cassiano was a serious patron of the arts and the friend of Pietro da Cortona, Lanfranco, Testa, Mola, and many other artists. But his dominating passion was the study of antiquity. With apparently limited means, he brought together a collection of material designed to illustrate every aspect of life in ancient Rome. Original ancient marbles were for the most part beyond his purse, but he made up for this by commissioning a team of artists to draw for him every fragment of classical sculpture, every piece of ancient architecture, and every relic of Imperial Rome that was dug up. The volumes containing this collection are now at Windsor, and they give one a singularly vivid idea of the atmosphere in which Poussin moved at this time. Cassiano was evidently not a man who took advantage of his position to intrigue for promotion in the political world, and we can rather imagine him surrounded by his friends and collaborators, poring over his drawings and documents illustrating the ancient world.[193]

It was in this backwater of scholarly and sensitive archaeological study that Poussin produced his paintings in the 1630s. In those dating from the years 1629–33 a complete change of subject and style is visible (Plate 128). During these years Poussin hardly treats religious subjects; his themes are taken from ancient mythology, and from Tasso. The stories of Bacchus, Narcissus, Apollo and Daphne, Venus and Mercury, Rinaldo and Armida – these are the stock-in-trade of the artist at this time.

One of the earliest of these *poesie* must be the 'Rinaldo and Armida' at Dulwich (Plate 125B). The colouring and the juicy handling of the pigment are Venetian and close to the 'Marriage of St Catherine'; the closed sculptural oval of the figures recalls the 'Massacre of the Innocents'; but the feeling is new in Poussin. His intention here is to render the dramatic moment in the romantic story: the *coup de foudre* as Armida falls in love with Rinaldo just as she is about to kill him. Even the usually artificial *putto* here plays a real part, as he holds back the arm which is about to raise the dagger. Poussin's rendering is effective by its very literalness.

Among the classical compositions, the slightly later 'Arcadian Shepherds' (Plate 128) is exceptional, since it is not taken directly from an ancient author, but its theme – the presence of death even in Arcadian happiness – is based on classical ideas. It shows clearly the change in Poussin's approach. The picture derives in its conception and its execution from models quite other than those on which Poussin had hitherto drawn. Above all, the influence of Titian is manifest. Poussin must have seen the works of Titian when he passed through Venice in 1624, but, as far as we can judge from his works, he was not deeply influenced by him at that time. We know, however, that in Rome he studied attentively the Este 'Bacchanals', which were at that time in the Villa Ludovisi,[194] and it is these *poesie* that we find reflected in Poussin's paintings of this time.

In a few instances Poussin actually borrows figures direct from Titian,[195] but generally speaking he imitates the atmosphere, the colour, and the light of his model. In the 'Arcadian Shepherds' the most obviously Titianesque element is the treatment of the trees and the sky. Poussin has taken over Titian's play of dark tree-trunks and light leaves against the stormy sky, and has caught the romantic atmosphere created by these means. Unlike Poussin's works of the late twenties, it has a warmth and a richness of colour which are again due to Titian, for whom in this respect he has forsaken Domenichino and even Veronese. Above all, however, it is in his attitude towards antiquity that Poussin has learnt from the great Venetian. His approach is poetical, and not archaeological; there are none of the outward signs of classicism which were favoured in Rome at that time, and which were later to be much used by Poussin himself. The painter has sunk himself in the atmosphere of Ovid and his interpretation of mythology, and has produced this personal version of it in paint.

The 'Arcadian Shepherds' was painted as one of a pair, the pendant being a picture representing Midas washing in the Pactolus to rid himself of the gift which he had begged of Bacchus that everything he touched might turn to gold.[196] These two pictures are typical in their rather melancholy, disillusioned themes of the tone of Poussin's painting at this time. Even his love-stories are usually sad – Narcissus, Apollo and Daphne, Venus and Adonis. They are not treated philosophically nor with great earnestness; they are taken rather as excuses for elegies designed to provoke agreeably and romantically melancholy thoughts.[197] When religious themes occur, they are treated in exactly the same elegiac spirit; and it is characteristic that the dead Christ in the Munich 'Entombment'[198] is identical with the young hunter in the 'Death of Adonis' at Caen.[199]

About 1633 another change begins to take place in Poussin's style. The turning point is marked by the 'Adoration of the Magi' in Dresden, dated 1633,[200] which provides a basis for distinguishing a group of paintings and assigning them to the years 1633-7. In these Poussin no longer concentrates on poetical and mythological themes; his preference is rather for subjects which offer a good pageant. From the Old Testament, for instance, he likes scenes from the wanderings of the Children of Israel, the 'Golden Calf' (Plate 129A),[201] or the 'Crossing of the Red Sea';[202] from ancient history the 'Rape of the Sabines'[203] or the 'Saving of Pyrrhus'.[204] This is also the time of the great Bacchanals, notably those painted for Richelieu,[205] which are more elaborate and spectacular than the earlier paintings of the same kind.

The 'Golden Calf' shows clearly the qualities of Poussin's painting at this period. Certain elements remain of the earlier manner. The landscape is still Titianesque, the colour is warm, and the small figures in the background are still treated with the rough free handling of the 'Arcadian Shepherds'. But the feeling has changed. The influence of Titian has been to a great extent replaced by that of Roman sculpture and of the late Raphael and Giulio Romano. The group of dancing figures, for instance, can be traced from Roman reliefs through paintings by Mantegna, Giulio Romano, and Taddeo Zuccaro to Poussin, that is to say, through a linear and sculptural tradition quite different from that of Titian. Poussin has, moreover, arranged this group strictly in the form of a basrelief. As far as possible each figure is turned so that its whole movement is in a single plane, parallel with that of the picture, and in almost every case the head is seen in profile. For the first time in Poussin's work the figures have that frozen appearance which is often to be seen in marble figures of dancers, as if they had been turned to stone in the middle of their action; and this quality is yet further evidence for the fact that Poussin was now studying ancient reliefs more and more closely.

A similar change can be seen in the modelling of individual figures. It is perhaps clearest in the foreground group of a mother with two children. Ultimately this group is derived from one in Raphael's 'Mass of Bolsena', and Poussin has attempted here to imitate to some extent the generalized modelling of Raphael, though he has emphasized more than his predecessor the sharp edges of the folds in the drapery. But he is now evidently thinking in plastic terms, and no longer in the colourist idiom of Titian.

One further point must be noticed. Poussin has here taken great pains to make the various actors in the scene show their emotions and explain the part which they are playing by means of their gestures and their facial expression. This was later to be for him a point of cardinal importance, but even at this stage he exploits it to a considerable extent.

The rejection of Venetian colouring, the sharper modelling, and the evolution of a composition based on carefully balanced movements are more apparent in a small group of works which must be dated just after the 'Golden Calf'. The most important are the 'Nurture of Jupiter' at Dulwich[206] and the 'Kingdom of Flora' formerly at Dresden (Plate 129B).[207] In no other pictures did he attain to such light-hearted delicacy. The composition of the 'Flora' is built up of a complex play of diagonals, all in planes parallel with the picture, so that once more the whole group occupies a shallow stage, behind which the pergola and the rocks form a sort of drop-scene. The poise of the composition is exquisite but never too obvious. Echo and Narcissus form a closed oval group in the foreground, while Ajax on their left balances in his death-movement Flora scattering flowers on the right. Clytie follows Apollo with her eyes – the only movement in depth in the whole composition – and on the right the other pairs of lovers give stability by their vertical and horizontal poses to what might otherwise be a too lively whole.

In the paintings of the very last years of the thirties the tendencies which we have noticed in the immediately preceding period are intensified. The influence of Titian disappears, while that of Raphael and of antiquity increases. The compositions become more carefully planned; forms are more plastically modelled; colour is more local and less broken. Generally speaking, Poussin shows a leaning towards a psychological interpretation of his themes, and the emphasis on gesture and expression becomes increasingly marked. This is made very clear in the letter with which he accompanied the painting of the 'Israelites collecting the Manna' when he sent it in 1639 to the patron in Paris who had ordered it. He explains that his intention is to 'represent the misery and hunger to which the Jews had been reduced, and at the same time their joy and delight, the astonishment with which they are struck, the respect and reverence with which they feel for their law-giver; with figures of women, children, and men of different ages and temperaments, all which things, if I am not mistaken, will not be displeasing to those who can read them'.[208] Notice his use of the verb *read* in the last sentence. This brings out his real intention, that the spectator should study every group in the composition and be able to decipher the exact feelings of each figure and his function in the action as a whole. This is, of course, carrying the psychological and literary conception of painting very far, and the dangers of the method were to become only too obvious in the next generation when the Academy transformed it into a system.

At the same period, although Poussin continued to paint subjects from the *Metamorphoses*, he turned also to classical allegory and executed for instance the 'Dance of Time', now in the Wallace Collection in London,[209] which foreshadows to some extent the more philosophical classical paintings of the next decade. It was also in these years that he painted for Cassiano del Pozzo the series of the 'Seven Sacraments',[210] which came to England in the eighteenth century, and of which five are still in the collection of the Duke of Rutland. In the 'Ordination' (Plate 130B) the influence of Raphael is once again apparent, since the design and the types are taken closely from the tapestry 'Feed my Sheep'. But it is important to notice that Poussin is now turning to the more classical Raphael of 1515 and not to the style of the master's very last years.

In 1640 Poussin set out for Paris. For nearly two years the Surintendant des Bâtiments, Sublet des Noyers, had at the command of the King and Richelieu been trying to persuade the artist to return to his native country. The offers made to him were in many ways tempting: good salary, honourable position, lodgings in the Louvre, and so on. But Poussin clearly did not want to give up his quiet existence in Rome, where he could devote all his energy to his work. However, the pressure became too great to resist, and eventually he had to give in.

His first letters from Paris were cheerful. He was well received by Sublet des Noyers, Richelieu, and the King, who, on his being presented, made the not very generous comment: 'Voilà Vouet bien attrapé', which Poussin, with even less generosity, retailed to his correspondent, Cassiano del Pozzo, in Rome. But very soon the trouble began. He was commissioned to carry out two altarpieces, two large allegories for Richelieu, and to plan the decoration of the Long Gallery of the Louvre. It would have been hard to find tasks worse suited to Poussin's talent and method of working. He was used to painting small canvases on which he could work at his leisure and without the help of assistants. Here he was being made to work in a hurry and on a scale which made it inevitable that the execution should be mainly left to assistants. In addition, he had to face the intrigues of artists whose position in Paris had been threatened by his arrival, above all Vouet, but also men like Foucquier, who had been commissioned to decorate the Long Gallery with landscapes, and saw a dangerous rival in Poussin. He made a further enemy in Lemercier, whose decorations for the Gallery he criticized mercilessly in a letter to des Noyers.

The paintings which Poussin actually executed during this visit to Paris are among the least satisfactory that came from his brush. The altarpieces and the allegories are cold and empty. Poussin had never been addicted to such compositions, and he had lost whatever skill he may once have had for them.[211] We can only form a partial idea of the decoration of the Long Gallery,[212] but although it was much admired in its day and exercised considerable influence for half a century in France, Poussin's real gifts did not lie in this field. In fact, the most successful works produced on the visit were probably the designs for three frontispieces for books to be printed by the Royal press: a Bible, a Virgil, and a Horace. These are all competent, classically conceived compositions, which to some extent lead on to the work of the next years.

In September 1642, having been in Paris just over eighteen months, Poussin set out again for Rome, nominally to fetch his wife, but quite certainly with the determination not to return. He reached his real home before the end of the year, and never left it again till his death in 1665.

From the point of view of his official mission, therefore, Poussin's visit to Paris was a failure. But in other ways it had consequences of the greatest importance for his development. While in Paris he established contact with a circle of friends whom he had begun to know during the last years of the 1630s, when some of them had visited him in Rome. Not only were these men to be his best patrons for the latter part of his life, but they were to influence his whole intellectual outlook, and so to have an important bearing on his evolution as an artist.

Poussin's new friends belonged to a clearly defined class, and, as we have come to expect in this period, it is from the bourgeoisie that they sprang. But they were not the same as those who commissioned their houses from Mansart or Le Vau. They came of more modest but more solid stock. They were not so rich as the Lamberts nor so powerful as the Longueils, but their money had been gained by more honest means, and they were less ostentatious in spending it. Poussin's most regular patrons and most intimate friends were merchants, minor civil servants, and small bankers. The circle extended into the legal world, but on the whole only to the more modest sections of the Parlement, and although one or two names occur which are already familiar to the reader as among the richest men in Paris – La Vrillière, Jabach – they stand out as exceptions.[213]

One of Poussin's Paris friends must be mentioned more specifically, because after 1640 he played a part as important as Cassiano del Pozzo's had been before that date. This was Paul Fréart de Chantelou, a civil servant, secretary to des Noyers. He seems to have been the first Frenchman to 'discover' Poussin, and it was for him that the artist painted the 'Manna' despatched to Paris in 1639. In the next year Chantelou was sent by des Noyers to Rome to bring Poussin to Paris, and in Paris it was he who looked after the artist during his stay[214]. After Poussin's return to Rome the two friends continued to write to each other regularly, and this correspondence, of which luckily Chantelou kept the part which he received, gives us the most interesting details which we have about Poussin's life and works in the last twenty years of his life. Chantelou was probably not as intelligent a man as Cassiano, but he was devoted and patient, and it is clear from Poussin's last letters to him that the artist felt a deep debt of gratitude towards him. Other members of this circle also corresponded with Poussin and visited him on their business journeys to Rome,[215] but our knowledge of their relations with the artist is fragmentary.

For these Paris intellectuals Poussin produced during the ten years after his return to Rome the paintings which were regarded in his own time as his most perfect, and which are now considered to be among the purest embodiments of French classicism (Plates 131–133).

In treatment of subject and in formal conception they reveal the fact that a revolution had taken place in the artist's outlook. Poussin's choice of theme is significant. He continues to treat religious and classical subjects, but in both his attention is differently directed. In the field of religious painting his preference is now for the New Testament rather than the Old, and in the New he turns to the central themes, to those which have always occupied great religious artists – the Holy Family, the Crucifixion, the Entombment. He again takes up the theme of the Seven Sacraments, but he treats it with a quite new solemnity. When he uses Old Testament stories, it is no longer the pageant scenes from the book of Exodus that he selects, but those which admit of more dramatic or psychological interpretation: the Judgement of Solomon, Rebecca and Eliezer, Esther before Ahasuerus, the Finding of Moses. In the classical field he completely abandons Ovid and the loves of the gods, and turns instead to the Stoical historians for his matter. Coriolanus, Scipio, Diogenes, Phocion are his heroes. In all these he expounds moral themes in accordance with Stoical philosophy, all variations on the central problem of the victory of the will over the passions: Coriolanus sacrificing himself for his country; Scipio overcoming his sexual desires out of generosity; Diogenes giving up his last tie with material things; Phocion suffering death for his refusal to conceal the truth. We have already seen that the revival of Stoicism in France was fostered by the middle classes, and no doubt Poussin's *bourgeois* friends found these stories exactly to their taste. It is also important to notice that in certain respects they correspond to the stories of

Corneille's classical tragedies of the same decade: in *Horace* the sacrifice of personal interests to the safety of the state; in *Cinna* the victory of moderation over the desire of vengeance; in *Polyeucte* the sacrifice of one's life for religious beliefs; in the earlier and more romantic *Le Cid*, the willingness to sacrifice love to a code of honour.

On the other hand, the parallel between Poussin and Corneille must not be pressed too closely, for there is an essential difference between their approaches. Poussin's conception of his stories is fundamentally human and rational; Corneille's heroes are superhuman, and often defy the dictates of reason. They pursue *la gloire* with an enthusiasm which takes on the character of a pure and uncontrolled passion, and actions such as the murder of Camille by her brother in *Horace* have an almost monstrous quality which sets them apart from the moderate behaviour of Poussin's Greeks and Romans. In this respect Corneille is more Baroque than classical.[216]

Poussin's presentation of his themes is, however, curiously like Corneille's. Both aim at perfect clarity, at an exposition which states everything essential and leaves out everything incidental. Both work within very strict rules – in the one case the Unities, in the other a canon of classical forms – but both derive extreme subtlety from this very limitation. Both aim at concentration rather than richness, and both may be said to limit their vocabulary to the minimum. Each, we are led to feel, could have explained exactly why he used a particular phrase or selected a particular pose. Neither ever gives his audience the unexplained shock of revelation which is the characteristic of the opposite Shakespearian type of art; but both lead the spectator by an infallibly calculated series of steps to the exact point at which they aim.

In order to see how Poussin achieves these effects, it is necessary to examine some of the paintings of the period in greater detail. The method becomes apparent if we set paintings of this time beside those of similar subjects from Poussin's earlier years. Compare, for instance, the two versions of the 'Arcadian Shepherds' (Plates 128 and 131B), the first painted, as we have already seen, about 1630, and the second probably executed about 1650. One is immediately struck by what Poussin has sacrificed in the second version – warmth of colour, freedom of handling, dramatic effect as expressed both in the action and in the setting. All sense of urgency has gone, and, instead of rushing forward to decipher the inscription, the shepherds stand motionless in contemplation of what they have read, absorbed by the thoughts which it arouses. As befits this new conception of the subject, Poussin has eliminated all movement, and has changed the diagonal arrangement of the figures of the earlier version for a nearly frontal disposition. The figures themselves are more strictly classical in their poses, types, and drapery, and Poussin has clearly been studying ancient sculpture with renewed interest and with the intention of imitating it more closely than before. The landscape is calm and without the contrasts which give its particular character to the Devonshire version. In fact, where one version is spontaneous, lively, and poetical, the other is calculated, calm, contemplative, and philosophical.

The same change of feeling can be seen in the religious paintings. The second series of Sacraments executed for Chantelou between 1644 and 1648 (Plates 130A and 131A) have a solemnity wholly lacking in the more picturesque first series. This is perhaps most apparent in the 'Eucharist' (Plate 131A), one of Poussin's most severe compositions. The scene is set in a room of the utmost simplicity, without ornament, and articulated only with plain Doric pilasters. The apostles are shown lying on couches round the table – a point of archaeological accuracy to which Poussin attached great importance – and are dressed in Roman togas. The artist has chosen a moment which enables him to combine the two main themes which the subject involves: the dramatic and the sacramental. Christ has given the bread to the apostles and is about to bless the cup, but on the left of the composition we see the figure of Judas leaving the room. That is to say, Poussin represents primarily the institution of the Eucharist, but at the same time reminds the spectator of Christ's words: 'One of you shall betray me'.[217] The double theme is made even clearer in the actions of the apostles, which are defined with great precision. Some are engaged in eating the bread, others show their realization of the significance of what is taking place by gestures of astonishment, while St John shows from his expression of sorrow that he is still thinking of Christ's words about Judas. It is typical of Poussin's humanist religious belief at this time that he should combine in this way the transcendental and the dramatic elements of the story.

Formally Poussin has concentrated his group into a symmetrical relief pattern. His choice of a low view-point has enabled him to foreshorten the front apostles, so that they form a compact group with those on the other side of the table.

In this respect, however, we can see Poussin's new method even more clearly by a comparison of the two versions of the Sacrament of Ordination (Plates 130A and B). In the first the apostles are arranged in a long row in the very front of the composition with the principal group, consisting of Christ and St Peter, on the extreme left. Behind them the landscape closes the picture like a backcloth. In the second version Poussin has used a quite different compositional method. Christ stands in the middle of the picture with St Peter kneeling at his feet and facing into the composition. The apostles are arranged in two groups at the sides and form a sort of avenue, leading up to the central group and also establishing a much greater depth in the composition than in the earlier version. Behind them is a landscape which is no longer a backcloth, but is planned in three dimensions. To the left is a hill crowned with buildings, and on the right a temple surrounded by smaller buildings. These two blocks, defining the middle distance, are joined by a bridge, which runs parallel with the picture plane and almost closes the composition. Not completely, however, for over it the eye can see two rows of buildings stretching still farther back. That is to say, the landscape, punctuated by architectural features, is a three-dimensional space, analogous in its form to the groups of the apostles in the foreground. This more spatial conception of composition is a method regularly used by Poussin during this period, and is one of the indications that his mind was turning not only to classical antiquity but also to the most classical works of the High Renaissance in Rome, Raphael's frescoes in the Stanza della Segnatura. For this is merely an extension of the principles of composition displayed by Raphael in the 'School of Athens'.

Another example of this method of space composition, and one which further illustrates Poussin's link with High Renaissance art at this time, is the 'Holy Family on the

Steps' (Plate 132) of 1648. The Madonna and the Child are based on Raphael's 'Madonna with the Fish', and the pyramidal formation of the whole group was perhaps suggested to Poussin by Andrea del Sarto's 'Madonna del Sacco'. But the essential features of the composition are of Poussin's own invention. The whole space of the picture is organized in purely geometrical terms. The figures are placed in a setting defined by the simplest planes: the wall, the side of the temple, and the steps themselves, which carve out the space into a series of rectangular blocks. This obvious emphasis on the mathematical structure of the space composition reminds one that Descartes was a contemporary of Poussin, and that he conceived the physical universe as being subject to the laws of mathematics. It is by no means certain that Poussin actually read Descartes, but it is still true to say that his conception of space composition is based on the same mathematically rational principles which governed Descartes' view of the material world.

The same fact is apparent in another group of Poussin's paintings. In the second half of the 1640s he began, rather unexpectedly, to turn his attention to landscape, a field in which he had hitherto shown little interest. In doing so, however, he applied the same method which he had used for his figure compositions. The most impressive examples are the pair of landscapes illustrating the story of Phocion, a theme taken from Plutarch (Plate 133).[218] Round the story of the collecting of the hero's ashes by his wife after his unjust condemnation to death Poussin has built up a landscape of the greatest solemnity, suitable to the subject with which he is dealing. The calm and sombre scene, with the city of Megara in the background, has just the heroic character which the story demands. But the most interesting feature of the picture is that Poussin has managed to apply to the confusion of inanimate nature the same principles of mathematical order which he introduced into, say, the 'Holy Family on the Steps'. The space composition is as carefully planned and as mathematically lucid as the architectural setting of the latter. Poussin has achieved this by a judicious introduction of architecture into the landscape and by treating the natural features with a monumental simplicity which reduces them to the same clarity. In the foreground the line of the wall crossed by that of the path leads the eye into the middle distance, fixed by the line of the river, which runs parallel with the plane of the picture. Behind this rises the city in which houses, temples, and rocks all conform to the same principles of clarity and parallelism. Even the sky falls into the same scheme: it does not lead the eye off to infinity, but is closed by layers of clouds, which recede one behind the other like the more tangible elements in the foreground and middle distance.

How complete was the identity of his treatment of animate and inanimate nature can be seen from the remarkable 'Finding of Moses' painted for Raynon in 1651 (Plate 134A). Here the figure groups in the foreground and the rocks and buildings in the middle distance are all handled as masses to be fused into a single spatial scheme almost without distinction. The caesura in the middle of the figures is echoed in a break through the landscape, which leads the eye to the distant vista of the town. This picture also illustrates a feature which was to become more important in Poussin's last period. Up to this time he had always made his figures express their meaning by gesture or facial expression. Here he manages to produce the sensation of excitement at the discovery of the child to a great extent by the fluttering effect of the draperies in the left-hand figures, contrasted with the static quality of those on the right.

Since it was in the period 1643–53 that Poussin's art attained its greatest maturity, and his ideas their greatest clarity, it may be worth while to consider for a moment what we know of his method of work and the principles which underlay it. In his letters he often emphasizes points which have been made in the foregoing pages. Painting, he says, deals with human action, and above all with the most noble and serious human actions. It must present these according to the principles of reason; that is to say, it must show them in a logical and orderly manner, as nature would produce them if she were perfect. The artist must seek the typical, and the general. Painting should appeal to the mind and not to the eye; hence it must not bother with trivialities, such as glowing colour, which is only a sensuous attraction, but must only use colour and light as means of expressing the action of the picture.

One form which this doctrine took with Poussin was the well-known theory of Modes. According to this, each subject demands a particular kind of treatment, just as, according to the ancients, different Modes in music expressed different characters of themes, the Dorian heroic, the Lydian melancholy, and so on. The principal result of this view was that if the artist was treating a harsh and solemn subject his painting would also have to be harsh and solemn, and it would be wrong for him to introduce into it any sweetness or charm. Poussin was consistent in applying this doctrine, with the result that many of his paintings of this period are remarkably lacking in attraction to the eye, and appeal to the emotions only through the mind and the reason.

Of Poussin's method of work we have some knowledge from accounts left by his contemporaries. When a subject was suggested to him, he began by reading carefully all that he could find about it. Then he made a rough sketch of the projected design. For the next stage in the evolution of the design he made small wax figures, which he dressed with linen draperies and put them into a sort of peep-show, or miniature stage, to which he could control the lighting and in which he could put a backcloth to represent the landscape. Then, having arranged the figures to his satisfaction, he would make another sketch. If that did not seem right he would again move his puppets and make a new sketch; and so on, till he found the grouping which satisfied both his desire for harmony and his principle of the greatest clarity of exposition. We can actually watch this process taking place, for in some cases – for instance the 'Baptism' belonging to the second series of Sacraments – enough drawings survive to show us half-a-dozen stages in the game.[219]

When the figure composition was fixed in this way, Poussin made bigger models, and again covered them with draperies. From these he executed the actual picture, never painting direct from life, but going to look at real figures when he felt the need to do so. The proportions and types of the lay figures from which he actually painted were based on his long study and intimate knowledge of ancient statues, and it was to these that he looked as the ideal for his own compositions. He felt that if he painted from life he would lose his image of this ideal. This unusual method explains many of the features of Poussin's style: its classicism, its marble-like detachment, and also its coldness, which at some moments comes near to lack of life.

In the last twelve years of his life (1653–65) Poussin's style changes again, and in a rather curious way. By this time his position in Rome was unique. His reputation was European, but he had never played an active part in the official artistic activities of the city. He had become something of a hermit, revered by many, but seeing only a small circle of intimate friends. We have the impression that he now worked more to satisfy his need to paint, and less to please anyone else. His last works are, therefore, highly personal, and represent the researches of the old artist in the privacy of his studio rather than his reaction to any outside impulse.

In the figure compositions of his last phase certain features present in the previous years are intensified, such as the almost puritanical simplicity and severity of the compositions, and the elimination of all picturesque ornament. But there are new qualities. In the 'Rest on the Flight', finished in about 1658 (Plate 134B), for instance, the calmness has been carried to a much higher pitch. Action and gesture have disappeared, and even facial expression is reduced to the minimum. The composition is as clear as in the works of the 1640s, but even simpler in that it is based entirely on horizontals and verticals, with hardly a diagonal movement. The whole painting is typical of the method of expressive understatement which Poussin uses so much in the last period.

The 'Rest on the Flight' also contains another typical feature. The details of Egyptian architecture and customs in the background were taken, as Poussin himself indicates in a letter, from the Roman mosaic at Palestrina which represents scenes from Egyptian life.[220] We have seen that in earlier periods Poussin paid attention to details of classical archaeology, but he is here doing more. Up till now he had been content with a generally antique setting for such a subject, but now he seeks greater precision and wants the details to be correctly Egyptian.

The same motionless quality which we have noticed in this composition is to be found in the few classical paintings of the last years, such as the 'Achilles on Scyros', painted in 1656, and now only known from engravings,[221] and even more clearly in the 'Holy Families'. The most striking of these is one with almost life-size figures in the Hermitage, probably finished about 1655 (Plate 135). The last vestiges of action and expression have gone. The only figure to make any gesture at all is the infant St John, who holds out his hands. The other figures are lost in a marble stillness, which gives a sort of abstract grandeur to the composition.

Poussin also returned in his last years to the painting of mythological stories, but in a spirit entirely different from that in which he had treated them in his early years. Now he makes the stories in Ovid symbols for some general truth which he wishes to convey. His gods and goddesses have the same abstract qualities as the figures in the 'Holy Family'. Moreover, they are usually placed in a landscape, and the two together are used to convey the allegory. It has been shown, for instance, that the 'Landscape with Orion' in the Metropolitan Museum is an allegory on the origin of clouds,[222] and the 'Birth of Bacchus' in the Fogg Museum symbolizes the contrast between the forces of life and death.[223] In these paintings it is noticeable that nature itself takes on a character new in Poussin. Instead of being orderly and subject to the laws of reason, it has a grand wildness quite unexpected in his work. Even in the 'Apollo and Daphne' (Plate 136), left unfinished at his death, we feel that nature has this character. The exact meaning of the subject here is not clear,[224] but there is little doubt that Poussin has combined in it various different mythological stories to symbolize some special idea which eludes us. In any case, it sums up all the strange features of his last phase: the wildness and grandeur of inanimate nature, the impassive calm of the human actors, here more than ever like wax images, and the other-worldly atmosphere in which they live. These are no longer the gods and goddesses of Ovid, subject to the passions of the flesh. They are symbols created by the mind of the artist, existing in a world of pure intellect, into which it is not always easy to penetrate.

Poussin's last phase is a logical development from his earlier work. The whole of his œuvre is based on the assumption that the processes involved in the creation of a work of art are essentially rational. Poussin himself possessed a powerful imagination, without which his works would, of course, be insignificant; but he regarded this as something to be assumed and not to be talked about or deliberately cultivated. The business of the artist, according to him, was to mould his imaginative conceptions into forms of perfect clarity, which should, further, conform to certain canons derived from classical art and should produce an internal harmony almost musical in quality. These were the conscious aims of the artist and they could be attained by Reason. In concentrating so exclusively on this aspect of art Poussin was inevitably led to sacrifice certain opposite qualities: spontaneity of design, freedom of handling, richness of colour, beauty of matière; and he ran the risk of inhibiting the free working of his imagination. His art may, therefore, be said to lack the ease and directness essential to man's very greatest imaginative expressions. But if Poussin fails in this, he attains other qualities only one degree less important: the invention of visual forms limited in range but perfectly adapted to their purpose, a concentrated pointedness in expression, an integrity which seems both intellectual and moral, a high seriousness and a harmonious calm which are hardly excelled save in the frescoes of Raphael and the sculptures of fifth-century Greece.

Landscape Painting : Claude Lorraine and Gaspar Dughet

As we have seen, Poussin, following the example of Annibale Carracci and Domenichino, experimented in classical landscape, but it was Claude Lorraine who did for Roman and French painting what, much earlier, Altdorfer had done for Germany, and Patinir and Bruegel for Flanders, that is to say, established landscape as a means of artistic expression as subtle and varied as the older genres of religious and historical painting.

Claude Gellée, known to the French as Le Lorrain, and to the English as Claude Lorraine, was born in the village of Chamagne, not far from Nancy, in 1600.[225] At a very early age, probably when he was about twelve, he went to Freiburg-im-Breisgau and thence to Rome, to follow the favourite trade of the Lorrainers, that of a pastry-cook. In this capacity he obtained employment in the house of the landscape painter Agostino Tassi and, gradually turning himself from cook into apprentice, learnt from him the rudiments of painting. At an uncertain date, probably about 1623, he made a visit to

Naples, to study under the Flemish artist known in Italy as Goffredo Wals. We know too little of the work of this painter[226] to be able to estimate his influence on the young Claude, but the visit to Naples produced one result which affected Claude for the rest of his life. He was haunted by the beauty of the Gulf of Naples, and to the very end of his life we find him reproducing the coastline from Sorrento to Pozzuoli and the islands of Capri and Ischia.

In 1625 he left Rome and, passing through Loreto, Venice, Tyrol, and Bavaria, returned to Nancy. There he worked for a time as assistant to Deruet, painting architectural backgrounds to his ceiling paintings for the Carmelite church, now destroyed. By the end of 1627, however, he had again abandoned his native country and returned to Rome, travelling this time through Marseilles and Civita Vecchia. As far as the records tell us, he never again left the city, though it is hard to believe that he did not revisit Naples to revive in his mind the image of the bay.

By the end of the 1630s he had established a considerable reputation as a painter of landscape. We know that about 1634 another artist, Sébastien Bourdon, thought it worth while to imitate his style and pass off a painting of his own as a work of Claude; and before the end of the decade he had attracted the attention of Béthune, the French ambassador, Cardinals Crescenzio and Bentivoglio, and finally Urban VIII, all of whom had commissioned paintings from him. From that time onwards patrons were never lacking, and the measure of Claude's success in later life is the fact that he felt it necessary to record his compositions in drawings, forming the *Liber Veritatis*,[227] to guard against imitations and forgeries. He died in 1682, a respected member of the colony of foreign artists in Rome.

Whereas the landscape of Poussin derives from the line of Bellini, Titian, Annibale Carracci, and Domenichino, Claude's roots are in a quite different tradition, that of the Northerners established in Rome. Apart from his master Tassi he learnt his art in the first instance from studying the works of Paul Brill and Elsheimer.[228] Brill and Tassi had implanted and developed in Rome the style of Late Mannerist landscape, with its artificial disposition of dark-brown foreground, lighter-green middle distance, and blue hills on the horizon, each stage being marked by wings as in a theatre, starting from a dark tree in the foreground. This artificiality of design was coupled with a stylized treatment of the detail, the trees in particular being painted in a set formula of frond-like branches. Elsheimer had used this Mannerist idiom of landscape, but in a wholly different spirit; for he had understood the poetical possibilities of light enveloping the whole of a landscape, of an infinite vista contrasted with a filled foreground, and of the evanescent effects of dawn and twilight.

In his earliest paintings Claude imitates the more prosaic of these models, and, for instance, in the 'Mill', dated 1631 (Plate 139A), he follows closely the example of Brill. There on the left is the regulation dark tree; the foreground is filled with incidents of the kind which Brill loved – boats in construction, fragments of ancient columns, and small figures, in this case artists sketching; on the right is a picturesque tower; behind it the trees form the next stage, and the hills close in the background. The Mannerist scheme is carried out even to the formula for the tree silhouettes. Of Elsheimer we can see little, except that there is some feeling for the enveloping quality of light, which gives a more definite mood to the picture than would be found in Brill. This is the only fore-taste of the poetical qualities of Claude's mature style. In the etchings of the same period the influence of Elsheimer is more evident, and through their technical incompetence there shines a glimmer of real imagination.[229]

During the years 1640–60 Claude developed his full mastery in every type of landscape painting, and we may therefore consider the general characteristics of his style as it is manifested in those years.

The first problem to be considered is the actual content of his paintings. I say *content* rather than *subject* because it has long been realized that it was not of primary importance to Claude whether he depicted in a painting the Flight into Egypt or Cephalus and Procris. He did not, like Poussin, evolve his composition logically from the particular theme of the painting. On the other hand, it is quite wrong to jump from this argument, as some have done, to the conclusion that Claude was not concerned with subject, but merely painted light or pursued some abstract quality in his art. He was, on the contrary, deeply interested in the content of his paintings, but this content was something different from the theme set him for any particular work.

As a first approximation we may say that the content of his painting was the beauty of the countryside round Rome. This was actually in itself a novelty in landscape painting. The south German and Austrian painters had discovered the beauty of the Danube valley; the Umbrians had realized the pure clarity of their hills; the Venetians had ren-dered the romantic quality of the plains of the Veneto and foothills of the Alps. But be-fore Claude the Roman Campagna had generally been an object of interest rather than of aesthetic admiration to artists. Many Northerners had drawn it for the ruins which covered it; but no one had noticed its pictorial possibilities. It had been studied with the eyes of curiosity; Claude saw it with the eyes of wonder.

We know from the artist's early biographers of his constant excursions from Rome, wandering over the whole range of the country, sketching it with the pen, in wash, and even, we are told, in oils. His surviving drawings confirm the extent and the subtlety of his observation. But even in the finished pictures we can see his knowledge incorpor-ated, though in more generalized form.[230] Sometimes he paints the Tiber valley with Soracte in the distance, sometimes the more deserted Campagna south of the capital. He is equally at home in the olive-groves of the Sabines, and among the vines and lakes of the Albans. Pines, oaks, and feathery poplars all take their place in his scenes; and sometimes he fills the middle distance with the citadel of an Etruscan town (Plate 138A). Always there recur the memories of the bay of Naples, the rock arch of the School of Virgil (Plate 138B), the caves in the cliffs of Capri,[231] the coastline leading out to Ischia (Plate 138B), or the harbour itself (Plate 139B), though here no doubt he fused with Naples reminiscences of Civita Vecchia and Genoa also seen in youth.

But it is not only the topographical appearance of the Roman country that Claude paints. The scenes which he chooses are given significance and poetical quality by his understanding of the light which bathes them. Here he follows Elsheimer, though with a difference. Generally speaking, the German artist preferred the exceptional light effects –

moonlight, or a dark twilight. Claude sometimes selects these, but his normal tendency is towards the more typical effects, a cool early-morning light, the hot noonday, or the warm glow of evening. To our northern eyes his light often appears artificial and exaggerated, but in reality he renders effects which can be seen daily in the country which he painted.[232] Like Elsheimer, he uses light to impose imaginative and visual unity on his compositions; but whereas Elsheimer tends to work with a dramatic intention and to seek strong chiaroscuro, Claude aims rather at serenity, and therefore avoids contrasts. This is a tendency which becomes more marked in his later period, but it is also true of his maturity. Even when he paints ships and buildings directly against the light of the setting sun (Plate 139B), he minimizes the contrasts of value in order to preserve the calm unity of the whole.

For Claude, however, the Roman countryside was not empty. It was filled with associations and memories of antiquity. But the aspect of antiquity which fascinated Claude was very different from that which inspired Poussin. He had no mind to revive the virtues of Republican Rome or the splendours of the Imperial city. His antiquity was the pastoral life described in the bucolic poems of Virgil, the first poet to record the beauty of Italian landscape. Claude loved first of all the life which Virgil and his contemporaries led on their villas, and secondly he was inspired by the earlier epoch which the poet described, the Golden Age of the time when Aeneas landed and founded Rome. Some of his paintings actually illustrate themes from those passages in the *Aeneid* which describe this part of the hero's life,[233] and many are filled with the same atmosphere.[234] Claude's Campagna is peopled with the shades of Aeneas and his companions, and with the gods which Virgil describes in the *Georgics*, not the great gods but the little ones, 'Pan and old Sylvanus and the Sisterhood of Nymphs', and 'the tutelary spirits of country folk'.

The poems of Virgil were evidently Claude's main source of inspiration in these paintings, but from all accounts he was not himself a Latin scholar. He is more likely to have absorbed the atmosphere of the pastorals through Italian translations and through the conversation of his more learned friends, such as Cardinal Massimi. I believe, however, that he also derived ideas – and this time directly – from visual sources in ancient art. We know that the Vatican Virgil was much studied in the circles in which Claude moved,[235] and it is quite likely that some of the illustrations of pastoral subjects in it may have suggested ideas for his compositions. He no doubt also knew Roman frescoes of landscape subjects in which architecture and country scenes are mingled,[236] in a form of composition which he used extensively, for instance in the paintings entitled 'The Decline of the Roman Empire'[237] in which the arches and aqueducts of ancient Rome rise from the Campagna. But Claude differs from his ancient models in one important respect: his buildings in these cases are in ruins, and it is an essential part of his intention to create a feeling of nostalgia for past greatness.

We may say, in short, that the content of Claude's paintings is a poetic rendering of the atmosphere of the Roman countryside, with its changing lights and its complex associations. This is as different as could be from the content of Poussin's heroic landscapes, which, as we have seen, are built up round a stoical theme according to a series of logical calculations. It follows that the means of expression chosen by Claude must also differ radically from those of Poussin.

In certain very rare cases the two artists seem to approach each other. In paintings like 'The Mill' in the National Gallery, London,[238] or even in the 'Port Scene' (Plate 139B), Claude uses a symmetrical composition in which the clear recession by stages reminds one of the method of Poussin. But this is the exception, and in general it is the contrast, and not the similarity between the two artists that strikes one. Instead of Poussin's hollow box-like space filled with solid objects which recede in well-defined steps, Claude creates a much looser space, almost always leading the eye to infinity at some point, and often with a wide line of horizon. This space is filled with atmosphere which penetrates the trees standing in it and forms the continuum of the picture (cf. Plate 137). Recession is established often without the use of linear perspective, by the subtle degradation of colour, usually in objects such as trees which have no sharp outline. Moreover, these objects may be disposed on a horizontal plane, as are, for instance, the trees covering the valley in the 'Erminia' (Plate 137), in which the eye is led from the river to the extreme distance simply by the change in colour of the groves. When he paints water, Claude can be even bolder, and in the late 'Perseus' (Plate 138B) we see at its most daring a method which he uses frequently in the works of the middle years. Here Claude carries the eye over the unbroken surface of the sea right to the horizon, with no external aids, by means of colour and tone changes, coupled with the slight variations in the frequency of the waves which pattern the surface. In the early works he makes use of the *repoussoir* trees in the foreground which we have noted in 'The Mill', but in the paintings of the middle and later years he frequently throws away this too obvious help, and for instance in the 'Apollo' of 1654 (Plate 138A) the composition consists of two masses of trees and a town all rising like blocks from a composition primarily planned on the horizontal plane.

This freely invented atmospheric space is then filled with trees and buildings through which the air flows so that they hardly seem to interrupt its continuity. Claude's branches have none of the marble solidity of Poussin's. They wave in the moving air and reflect the flickering light. Nothing in Claude is fixed; everything is about to change. Compare, for instance, his treatment of water with that of Poussin. The latter rarely represents water at all, but when he does it is the unruffled surface of a river which reflects as steadily as possible the surrounding scene.[239] Claude, on the other hand, prefers the sea, and in the sea he loves to render the perpetual movement of the waves – or rather ripples, because they never take on the romantic grandeur of waves. Like his trees, they primarily perform the function of reflecting the changing light.

Even in their use of architecture the methods of Poussin and Claude are different. Poussin gives us structures of the simplest cubical forms, every detail of which could be justified on archaeological grounds. Claude chooses buildings with varied and picturesque surfaces, preferably ruined, sometimes Gothic, and almost always fanciful and mixed in their styles. Poussin's buildings are solid blocks of masonry; Claude loves open porticos seen against the sun, or towers that lose their substance in the mist (Plate 139B).

We can learn as much about Claude from his drawings as from his paintings. Turning through the volumes of sketches in the British Museum, we realize the range and intensity of his observation. Here we have the first records of those wanderings over the Campagna of which Sandrart and Baldinucci tell us. The variety of the drawings is endless. Some are prosaic notes of a building or a prospect, put down in a hard pen outline. Others are more carefully studied descriptions of a section of the landscape. Others are the immediate record of a suddenly perceived *contre-jour* effect (Plate 141). In some (Plate 142A) all these qualities are combined, and we have the poetical rendering of a startling visual impression – the hillside of Tivoli seen against the light. Before Claude no one had ventured to tackle such a subject, and since his time few have done so with success. In order to render precisely the complexity of the light effects with the echoing reflexions in the valley, Claude has allowed the solidity of the hills to disappear, so that the town seems almost to float in the air.[240] How completely he was prepared to make this sacrifice can be seen in the drawing of trees (Plate 142B), which, as has frequently been said, has an almost Chinese appearance.

In addition to these magically fresh notes, Claude also used drawing as a means of preparing his compositions. Many finished preparations for painted compositions exist,[241] and in some cases we can follow the artist in the evolution of a design. For the 'Apulian Shepherd', for instance, there are several preliminary sketches which show that Claude played about with his trees and hills in the same calculating spirit that Poussin moved his puppets on his toy stage.[242]

In the last fifteen or twenty years of his life Claude's style changed, and he produced some of his most remarkable and daring compositions. In certain respects the tendencies visible earlier were simply intensified. The boldness of asymmetrical composition, the modulation in the horizontal plane, the emphasis on the open and the infinite can all be seen in their finest form in paintings such as the 'Perseus' of 1674 (Plate 138B). Never did Claude invent a more unconventional composition: a flat surface from which rise a tree and a rock arch. Never was he bolder in his light effects with the dark arch against the pale moonlight.

One new tendency can be seen in this picture. The human figure is now reduced to insignificance. Naturally human beings had never played an important part in Claude's conception of painting, but in the earlier works they had held their place with some dignity.[243] Now they have become puppets, completely dominated by the natural scenery which surrounds them. In some cases, for instance in the 'Ascanius' painted in the year of his death (Plate 140), this puniness of men is emphasized by placing the figures beside a huge piece of architecture.[244] This painting reveals all the qualities of the artist's last phase. Claude has now entered a dream-world comparable with Poussin's realm in the 'Apollo and Daphne'. All the obvious methods which he had used in his earlier periods are rejected. The range of colour is reduced to its utmost limits: silvery green trees, pale grey-blue sky, grey architecture, and neutral-coloured dresses for the figures. The trees are now so diaphanous and the portico is so open that they hardly interrupt the continuity of the air. The figures are thin and elongated, so that they, too, have the immaterial quality suited to this fairyland.[245] All the elements of Claude's poetry are here in their most naked form, but combined in a magical way which defies analysis.[246]

Claude's position in European painting is clear. At the moment when Dutch painters were applying to nature their principles of realism, Claude showed that the methods of French classicism can also be used to extract the poetry of inanimate nature. Just as Poussin is the last stage in the rational treatment of landscape, so Claude, starting from a different tradition, carried to its furthest point the study of light and atmosphere as a means of creating both pictorial and imaginative unity. In this sense he represents the end of a development which reached its first peak in Umbria in the person of Perugino. But Claude is bolder; he confined the infinity of nature within the rigid boundaries of classical composition.

*

Claude and Poussin represent the two great tendencies in French classical landscape in the seventeenth century, but there were among their contemporaries several painters who enjoyed not unmerited success in this field.

The most distinguished of them was Poussin's brother-in-law, Gaspar Dughet (1615–75), who took to calling himself Gaspar Poussin. We know singularly little about his life and the chronology of his works is still a matter of speculation.[247] What are probably his early paintings[248] show him working in a rather romantic style, deriving from the tradition of Elsheimer and Brill, with a preference for storm scenes, abrupt contrasts of light and arbitrary Mannerist compositions, but by the later forties, when he painted the frescoes in S. Martino ai Monti and the Palazzo Doria Pamphili, Rome, he was already undergoing the influence of his brother-in-law and turning to a more classical form of landscape. His most familiar style, which probably represents the works after about 1650, can be seen in many examples of which plate 143A is typical. His formula here is a compromise between the extremes of Poussin and Claude. His space composition is less rigidly geometrical than Poussin's, but more finite than Claude's. He lacks Claude's fine perception of light, but is more generous in his treatment of it than Poussin. He conveys well, but without poetry, the character of certain parts of the country round Rome, particularly the Sabine hills. His main importance historically is that in the eighteenth century he was greatly admired by English painters such as Richard Wilson and by the supporters of the Picturesque movement, and his compositions were taken by them as models for landscape gardens and parks.[249]

The Minor Classical Painters: Le Sueur and Bourdon

To complete the account of painting before the reorganization of the Academy by Colbert and Lebrun in 1663 something must be said of a group of painters who either died before this event or remained little affected by it.

The most important of them is Eustache Le Sueur, who was born in 1616 and died young in 1655.[250] At an early age, probably about 1632, the boy entered the studio of Vouet. His first recorded works are a series of designs for tapestries illustrating the *Hypnerotomachia Poliphili*, for which Vouet received the commission about 1637, but passed it on to his pupil.[251] These paintings show that Le Sueur had fully learnt the manner of his master, but had as yet established no independence.[252] The 'Presentation of the Virgin' in the Hermitage (Plate 144A), probably painted in the early 1640s, is still full of reminiscences of Vouet, but it has also features which are more individual. The types are still those of the master, but the modelling is firmer and the design slightly more rigid and classical.

About 1646–7 Le Sueur embarked on his first major work, the Cabinet de l'Amour at the Hôtel Lambert. The importance of this room as a decorative whole has already been discussed in connexion with the architecture of Le Vau. Le Sueur's share was a series of panels illustrating the story of Cupid which ornamented spaces in the ceiling and on two sections of the walls. The influence of Vouet is still visible, though there is a certain lightness in the drawing and a calmness in the composition which distinguish these works from the decorations of the older artist. The second series of paintings for Lambert, in the Cabinet des Muses, show greater independence (Plate 144B). They were probably carried out about 1647–9, and they reveal for the first time the influence of the two painters who were to dominate Le Sueur's last years, Poussin and Raphael. In this case the influence of Raphael is the more marked, though he is seen through the eyes of Romanelli. Le Sueur presumably studied his work in engravings since he never went to Rome – a fact which all his early biographers deplore, while at the same time quoting him as an example of how successful an artist can be without making such a journey. The poses and types of the Muses in the principal panels tell us that Le Sueur has had before his eyes the 'Parnassus' and perhaps the roundels from the ceiling of the Stanza della Segnatura, from which he has learnt a fullness of form lacking in his earlier figures.

There is a tradition recorded in the eighteenth century that Le Sueur came to know Poussin intimately when the latter was in Paris in 1640–2. The story has been scouted by most recent critics, but there is reason to believe it, because we know of a painting executed by Le Sueur after a drawing by Poussin made during the visit to Paris.[253] In any case Le Sueur's style was profoundly affected by the study of Poussin's compositions of the 1640s. The works in which this influence appears most clearly are those illustrating the life of St Bruno, painted for the Charterhouse of Paris, probably about 1648,[254] and now in the Louvre. The 'St Bruno in his Cell' here illustrated (Plate 145A) did not actually form part of this series,[255] but it displays their salient qualities. From Poussin Le Sueur learnt a new interest in the psychological aspect of his subjects and also a new classicism of composition and modelling. But here, and in all Le Sueur's best paintings of this time, there is a reflective religious atmosphere, a tone of *recueillement*, which is not to be found in Poussin. It is personal to Le Sueur, but it seems also to be the direct expression of the cloistered way of life which the Carthusians were among the few religious houses in Paris to follow in the seventeenth century. We know nothing of Le Sueur's own religious views, but it is hard to doubt that there existed a real sympathy between him and the monastery for which he painted the St Bruno series.[256]

In the last years of his life Le Sueur's style underwent yet another change. The certain works of this period[257] indicate that the artist had been deeply impressed by Raphael's tapestry designs. In fact the 'St Paul at Ephesus' of 1649 (Louvre) is little more than a series of quotations from them. In the works of the 1650s, however, the interpretation is freer though hardly more successful. Le Sueur caricatures the plastic grandeur of Raphael's forms and turns them into inflated and often meaningless shapes.[258]

In his own day Le Sueur was much admired, and throughout the eighteenth century his reputation in France was almost as great as that of Poussin. A certain *tendresse* which distinguished his work from that of his more heroic rival appealed to an age when sensibility was the fashion.

Sébastien Bourdon (1616–71), the exact contemporary of Le Sueur, was capable of imitating almost any style, and giving it a personal flavour, but he never evolved one of his own. Born at Montpellier, he moved at the age of seven to Paris, at fourteen to Bordeaux, and in 1634 reached Rome. There he spent three years imitating the work of the Bamboccisti and Castiglione, and he continued to follow their styles in the years after his return to Paris in 1637.[259] In 1643 he was commissioned to paint the *Mai* for Notre Dame, which was to represent the 'Martyrdom of St Peter'.[260] This is an ambitious Baroque composition with a Venetian looseness of handling.[261] A series of lively compositions of the same type, such as the 'Caesar before the tomb of Alexander' in the Louvre, probably date from about this time.

In 1652 Bourdon was invited by Queen Christina to come to Sweden as her court painter. During the two years which elapsed before her abdication in 1654 he painted portraits of the Queen and various members of her Court,[262] but apparently no history paintings. In 1654 he returned to Paris, where he continued to enjoy great success as a portrait painter (cf. Plate 148A). Soon after his return he executed a 'Martyrdom of St Andrew' for the church of that name at Chartres,[263] in which the energy of his earlier Baroque style has been restrained under the influence of Poussin.[264] About 1659 he went to Montpellier, where he painted for the cathedral a vast 'Fall of Simon Magus' in the same style. He was violently attacked by rival local painters and returned to Paris in 1663 after having executed a series of tapestry cartoons and seven canvases of the 'Acts of Mercy' in an increasingly Poussinesque manner.[265] On his return to the capital he undertook the decoration of the gallery of the Hôtel de Bretonvilliers, which as far as one can judge from surviving drawings was again in the manner of Poussin.[266] It was no doubt during his last years in Paris that he carried out his most characteristic works, which show the strong influence of Poussin, but yet have a certain rather sweet charm, which seems to have appealed to his contemporaries. The 'Holy Family', reproduced on plate 146A, is an unusually fine example of what must be considered his best and most personal manner. In it elements from Poussin's 'Holy Families' are translated into a more elegant form and treated with a cool colour which is entirely Bourdon's own.[267]

Le Sueur and Bourdon still belong to the group of individualists who followed their own inclinations in painting. The next generation was to take a different course and was to work under the advantages and disadvantages of an intelligent dictatorship.

Sculpture

Sarrazin, François and Michel Anguier

French sculpture in the middle of the seventeenth century has neither the quality nor the range of the architecture and painting of the same period. It produced no artist of the first rank, but a number of craftsmen of high ability, whose work is worth studying as being typical of the artistic taste of the period and as preparing the way for the movement in the following decades. Stylistically sculpture presents much the same problems as contemporary painting. A local tradition survives from the end of the sixteenth century, and on this are grafted influences from Italy and Flanders. The result is a series of works which vary in their mixture of classical, naturalistic, and Baroque elements. The scale of variation is not so great as in painting, and there is nothing comparable to the gap which separates say Poussin from Vouet, or La Tour from Le Sueur; but the constituents are the same in the two arts.

The two artists who were least affected by foreign influences were Simon Guillain (c. 1581–1658) and Jean Warin (1604–72). Guillain[268] spent a short time in Italy, returning in 1612, but his style was probably more deeply affected by the work of his father, Nicolas Guillain (d. 1639),[269] and by the bronze sculpture of Pilon. His only important surviving work in sculpture properly speaking is the monument erected on the Pont-au-Change in 1647, of which a relief and the three bronze figures of Louis XIII, Anne of Austria, and the young Louis XIV are in the Louvre (Plate 149A). In their treatment of the metal they are a direct continuation of the method of Pilon, though the vitality of the Mannerist has given place to a rather conventional academic treatment of the drapery, analogous to that of Vouet. In the same way, the heads lack the earlier artist's psychological insight and are conceived in a dull semi-classical formula.[270]

Warin is a more subtle artist, and in a work such as the bust of Richelieu (Plate 149B) he is not entirely unworthy to bear the comparison with the portraits of the same sitter by Philippe de Champaigne. He combines with the traditional methods of Pilon some knowledge of Baroque busts, such as those by Bernini and Algardi, although he never seems to have visited Italy. He was the most brilliant medallist of the century, and reorganized the French Mint, of which he was appointed head in 1646.[271]

The most important figure of the period is Jacques Sarrazin (1588–1660),[272] who created the style which dominated the middle of the century, and through whose studio most of the sculptors of the next generation passed. After a preliminary training under Nicolas Guillain, Sarrazin went to Rome, where he spent the years 1610–c. 1627. His personal and stylistic contacts in Rome were with the group of classicizing artists who immediately precede the rise of the Baroque: Giacomo della Porta, for whom he worked at Frascati, Domenichino, and in sculpture Francesco Mocchi, Pietro Bernini, and François Duquesnoy.[273]

The influence of his Roman training can be seen in the first works which Sarrazin executed on his return to Paris, such as the altar in St Nicolas des Champs and the sculpture for the château and nymphæum at Wideville. But a more personal manner appears in his first royal commission, the decoration of Lemercier's Pavillon de l'Horloge at the Louvre (1636) (Plate 150A). Sarrazin's caryatids may claim to be the first works of French classicism in sculpture, and are thus the exact parallel to the work of Poussin and François Mansart at the same moment in the other two arts. From the frontal poses, the archaeological accuracy of the dress, and the treatment of the draperies we can see that Sarrazin has not taken his classicism entirely second-hand through the artists he had known in Italy but has also looked directly at ancient Roman statues.[274]

Between 1642 and 1650 Sarrazin directed the decoration of Maisons for Mansart (Plates 98 and 100). Here a great variety in style is displayed, probably because Sarrazin only supplied small models and exercised a general supervision of the decorations which were carried out by his pupils Guérin, Buyster, and van Obstal.

Sarrazin's last work was the monument erected to Henri de Bourbon, Prince de Condé, father of the great Condé, in the church of St Paul-St Louis. It was begun in 1648, interrupted by the Fronde and only taken up again after the Peace of the Pyrenees, so that the monument was not finished till 1663, three years after the artist's death.

In the nineteenth century it was moved by the duc d'Aumale to Chantilly and reconstructed in a wholly new setting, with the result that in its present form only the individual groups, and not the general arrangement represent the original intention of Sarrazin.[275] The groups, however (Plate 151A), reveal the importance of this late stage in Sarrazin's evolution; for here we see in fully developed form the style which was to dominate the sculpture of Versailles for the next two decades. It was Sarrazin who invented in sculpture the peculiar mixture of classicism and Baroque which was to fit with the doctrine of Lebrun and to play its part in the style of Louis XIV. The iconography is classical, though embellished with later Italian glosses. The sentiment lies between the cold rationalism of the purely classical artists of the time and the ecstasy of the Baroque. The poses are clear and almost frontal, but the movement is free. The drapery is based on ancient Roman models, but not interpreted in the almost puritanical spirit with which Poussin viewed them. The bronze is not fretted as it would have been by a Mannerist, but flows in agreeably ample folds. The features are classical, but there are reminiscences of the School of Fontainebleau in the columnar elongation of the neck. These figures could be transferred to the parterre of Versailles, and not look out of place; and it is only appropriate that Sarrazin should figure among the artists who took part in the first decoration of the gardens there, even though his 'Sphinx and Children' was only carried out from his designs after his death.[276]

The brothers François and Michel Anguier represent a tendency in French sculpture of the middle of the seventeenth century which is independent of the Sarrazin group. Both brothers were born at Eu in Normandy, François probably in 1604 and Michel in 1613.[277] François Anguier is said to have worked in his youth in Abbeville, Paris, and England; Michel moved to Paris in 1627 or 1629 and worked under Simon Guillain on the altarpiece of the Carmelite church near the Luxembourg. The two brothers seem to have gone together to Rome in about 1641 and to have joined the studio of Algardi. François returned to France in 1643, but Michel stayed in Italy till 1651. On his return he joined François who was engaged on the Montmorency tomb at Moulins (1648-52; Plate 150B).

This tomb reveals the new Roman influence which the Anguiers introduced into France. The model for the monument as a whole is to be sought early in the century in Giacomo della Porta's Aldobrandini tombs in S. Maria sopra Minerva, although Anguier has enriched the design by sculptured decoration. The style of the figure sculpture is a variation of that which the artists would have learnt in the studio of Algardi in the 1640s, that is to say, a form of Baroque less extreme than Bernini's, and therefore more easily acceptable than his to the classically minded French public. The figure of the Duke shows clearly the combination of influences present here. The pose is one traditional in France since the early seventeenth century, but the twist on the body, the undercut curls of the hair, and the lively treatment of the drapery all betray a Roman origin. In the figure of the Duchess classical influence is more visible, and this is even more clearly the case with the allegorical statues at the side of the main group which were executed by pupils. Michel Anguier's share seems to be limited to the seated Hercules below on the left, antique in conception but with some Baroque movement in the pose of torso and head.

In their later periods the paths of the two brothers diverge. François continues along the lines indicated in the Montmorency monument,[278] while Michel on the whole tends more towards classicism. In the years 1655–8 he decorated the rooms of the Queen Mother in the Louvre in collaboration with Romanelli.[279] Here his immediate model was the decoration of the Palazzo Pitti by Romanelli's master, Pietro da Cortona,[280] which he could have seen on his return journey from Rome; but he translates the heavy Baroque stucco figures of his original into more elegant classical terms. His works at the Val-de-Grâce show the last form which the struggle of Baroque and classical tendencies took in him. The reliefs in the spandrels and on the vault of the nave (Plate 101) are as classical as any work of the time, but in the group of the 'Nativity' for the high altar, now in St Roch (Plate 151B),[281] Baroque movement asserts itself. The mood which it expresses, however, is not the ecstasy of the Roman Baroque but a sort of pathos which is purely French[282] and, like Le Sueur's religious sentiment, seems to prepare the way for the eighteenth century.[283]

His only important official commission after 1661 was the decoration of the Porte St Denis (1674), which came to him because Girardon to whom it had been entrusted was called back for more important jobs at Versailles.[284] His work on the arch must have seemed almost archaic to the public of the 1670s in spite of his attempt to add richness by effects of high relief to his severely designed classical trophies.[285]

Many sculptors of this generation survived long after the beginning of the personal reign of Louis XIV, but they found themselves, like Michel Anguier, pushed aside in favour of the younger generation.[286] It is a curious fact that whereas the period which we have been studying excelled in the arts of architecture and painting and was weakest in sculpture, the next phase, the era of Versailles, was to shine most conspicuously in that field. Poussin and François Mansart were never forgotten, even during the later years of Louis XIV, but the reputations of Sarrazin and the Anguiers disappeared under the glory of Girardon and Coysevox.

CHAPTER 7

LOUIS XIV AND COLBERT
1660–1685

HISTORICAL BACKGROUND

ON 9 March 1661 Cardinal Mazarin died, and the next day, to the surprise and even the amusement of his courtiers, the young King announced that he would not take another First Minister, but would himself govern France. This decision opens the most spectacular period in French history. In two decades a series of successful wars gave France the most powerful position among European countries; skilful development of her natural resources supplied her with apparently inexhaustible wealth, and the whole nation united to glorify the King, who believed himself to be the greatest monarch of the century, and was determined to demonstrate the fact to any who might doubt it.

Louis was fortunate – or perhaps wise – in his choice of the man who was to carry out his policy. Jean-Baptiste Colbert, whom Mazarin had bequeathed to the King as his ablest assistant, was to be till his death in 1683 Louis' adviser on all matters of importance, whether political, economic, religious, or artistic, and the engineer of the State machine on which the greatness of the King was based.

Under the inspiration of the King, and with the skilful organization of Colbert, the finishing touches were given to the centralized autocracy for which the way had been prepared by Henry IV, Richelieu, and Mazarin. Internally the last vestiges of opposition to the central power were destroyed. The administration was a pyramid of which the apex was in reality as well as in theory the King, whose power was exercised through a hierarchy of Secretaries of State and councils at the centre and an efficient body of *Intendants* in the provinces. In this way an almost uniform system, dependent on the central authority, was imposed on all activities throughout France.

This direction from above was carried by Louis XIV and Colbert into all fields. In industry, for instance, which the latter was particularly successful in fostering, strict regulations were imposed on each trade and the authority of the guilds replaced by that of the State. This reorganization, which was coupled with improvements in agriculture and internal communications and with the building up of a merchant fleet, greatly increased the national wealth, and brought prosperity to the industrial and trading sections of the middle classes, who heartily supported Colbert's régime, except on those occasions when their particular privileges were threatened.

Colbert's achievements were, however, restricted by two factors: his inability to put real order into the finances of the kingdom, and his limited economic outlook. His ideas in the latter field were based on the principle that France should aim at being self-supporting, should import as little and export as much as possible, and should destroy by tariffs and if necessary by war all rivals to her commerce and industry, and so accumulate herself the greatest reserves of bullion, for him the only measure of wealth. This rigid mercantilist point of view prevented Colbert from making the best use of the material resources of France which he so ably developed. At the same time it involved him in wars, for instance with Holland, which, though practical in their aims, led in fact to the weakening of France rather than to her real profit.

Louis XIV and Colbert carried their principles of national power and unity into the intellectual as well as the practical field. The thought as well as the actions of all Frenchmen must follow the State plan. In religion, for instance, the independence of the Gallican Church was fiercely and successfully upheld against the demands of the Pope, who was also deliberately humiliated by the King over the affair of the Corsican guards. At the same time tendencies towards internal disunity, such as the Jansenist movement, were severely suppressed.[1]

Naturally the fine arts were not exempt from this universal direction, and their history in this period is that of the closest and most complete State control ever exercised before the present century. Colbert managed to get into his own hands all the key positions in relation to the arts. In 1664 he became Surintendant des Bâtiments; in the Academy he held successively the posts of Vice-Protector (1661) and Protector (1672); and as Controller-General of Finance all important projects had ultimately to be dependent on his goodwill.

Colbert believed that, like all other activities, the arts should serve the glory of France. To do this efficiently their practice had to be organized on the same basis as industry and their theory established in a body of accepted dogma. The practical side of this scheme was secured by the foundation of the Gobelins, and the theoretical by the establishment of the various academies. Just as Louis XIV had need of Colbert to find the means of executing his plans for the State, so Colbert had to find a pro-consul who would act for him in the field of the arts. Once again exactly the right man was to hand in the person of Charles Lebrun (1619–90), who was to be, till the death of Colbert in 1683, dictator of the arts in France. Lebrun was not a great imaginative artist, but he had exactly the talents required for the particular situation: flexibility, power of organizing, the ability to inspire and control a team of artists, untiring energy, and patience in the face of a changeable and difficult patron. His range of knowledge was vast. He could design a painting, a piece of garden sculpture, the lock of a door, the border of a tapestry, all with equal ease, and all in a style which made them suit their function and harmonize with each other. Lebrun produced no single work which one is tempted to linger over, to study, and to analyse, but in creating an ensemble such as the decoration of Versailles he was a master.

This was, of course, what Colbert needed; for the end to which the arts had to be applied was the glorification of the King and the creation of a suitable setting for him. Louis' conception of himself as the greatest monarch in Europe naturally led him to demand the most magnificent surroundings for himself and his Court, which were also designed to serve a political purpose and to be a distraction for his nobles. The elaborate hierarchy and complicated etiquette of the Court itself had to be reflected in a palace which by grandeur of scale and richness of decoration was to be the visible embodiment of the power of the Sun-King.

The organization of the Gobelins factory was typical of Colbert's methods. The buildings in which it was housed were those of a tapestry factory which had been established in the fifteenth century, but the scope of Colbert's scheme was far wider than the mere weaving of wall-hangings. The official title of the factory was *Manufacture royale des meubles de la Couronne*, and, as this implies, it was planned to produce everything necessary to the furnishing of the royal palace. Lebrun was appointed director in 1663, and under him worked an army of painters, sculptors, engravers, weavers, dyers, embroiderers, goldsmiths, cabinet-makers, wood-carvers, marble-workers, and even mosaicists. The entire production, which involved some two hundred and fifty workmen, was controlled by Lebrun, who supplied the designs for every section. These were worked up into cartoons or models by assistants, and were then translated into their final form; but at each stage Lebrun kept a close eye on the work. The well-known tapestry showing the visit of the King to the factory (Plate 152B) gives some idea of the variety of its productions. Carpets, silver basins, inlaid tables, and a hundred other articles of luxury are being brought out for the King to inspect, and on the wall in the background hangs one of Lebrun's own cartoons for the series of tapestries illustrating the life of Alexander the Great.

The Gobelins was, however, more than a universal factory, it was also a school, and in its constitution, drawn up in 1667, much attention was paid to the training of apprentices. It is interesting to notice that they were first of all to be given a grounding in drawing, and only when they were competent in this field could they begin the study of any particular craft. In this, as in many other details, Colbert's regulations differ markedly from the old-fashioned methods of the guilds which were still organized on almost medieval principles. Moreover, all artists connected with the Gobelins were given exemption from the demands of the guilds, and enjoyed the same freedom as the artists who had lodgings in the Louvre and were directly employed by the King.

The system of production set up at the Gobelins created the high level of technical skill and the uniformity of style which were requisites of the products demanded by Colbert and Louis XIV for the royal palaces. Individual inventiveness was at a discount, but it was Lebrun's great achievement to canalize the energies of so many craftsmen into a single channel. Versailles is one of the supreme examples of what team-work can do in the arts.

For the theoretical organization of the arts Colbert naturally turned to the system of academies which had already been successfully used for this purpose in Italy and which had been introduced into France during the previous régimes. In 1635 the French Academy had been founded to establish the true doctrine in the field of literature, and thirteen years later a similar organization had been set up for the visual arts. In its original form the Royal Academy of Painting and Sculpture was a means used by artists employed by the King to gain independence from the guild and to establish their social position. In Italy the principle had been laid down that the liberal arts, including painting, sculpture, and architecture, should be organized into academies, leaving the guilds to handle the mechanical arts only. French artists were therefore only following an Italian precedent in claiming to practise a liberal art, and therefore to have a right to an academy. As in earlier academies, the foundation members of the French Academy of Painting asserted the principle that their art should be taught on a theoretical basis, and not by mere practice, like the manual crafts. For this reason they insisted that, in addition to the life-class for the students, lectures should be held in which the truth about the arts should be expounded. In practice, however, it was found that the artists were reluctant to lay down the law in this way, and at first the lectures seem rarely to have taken place.

The Academy, however, offered to Colbert and Lebrun just the weapon which they needed, and after a thorough reorganization in 1663 it was turned into another part of the State art-machine. A hierarchy was established descending from the Protector through the Director (Lebrun) to professors, members, associates, and students. Teaching was carried out according to rigidly laid down principles; theory was expounded by the now compulsory lectures followed by discussion. In due course the system was extended. In 1666 a French Academy was founded in Rome under the directorship of Charles Errard for the training of young artists sent there from Paris. Academies were also established for the other arts: dance in 1661, science in 1666, music in 1669, and architecture in 1671.

The teaching and doctrine of these academies naturally varied according to the particular art concerned, but certain principles underlay the work of them all. In the case of the visual arts there was much in common between the practice of the Academy of Painting and Sculpture on the one hand and that of Architecture on the other. In each case it was assumed that the practice of the art could be learnt by the application of certain precepts, and that these precepts could be discovered by a process of rational analysis, that they could be exactly expressed in words and that they could be conveyed to any intelligent person. We shall examine later the methods used in the two academies; for the moment it will be enough to notice that their theory and practice represent the most fully developed form of academic training known in Europe, and the most thorough application of the principle that the arts can be learnt by taking thought.

The position with regard to literature was somewhat different. Racine, Molière, and La Fontaine all enjoyed great favour at Court, but were not entirely dependent on it. For them the Paris public was as important as that of Versailles, and they were therefore saved from being absorbed into the machine. Boileau, it is true, laid down the law as rigidly as Lebrun, but he did not have the economic control over writers which the latter could exercise over artists. Consequently we find in literature a far higher degree of individual talent than prevailed in the visual arts. With the possible exception of Bossuet none of the great writers of the period devoted the best of their talent to the glorification of Louis XIV or the success of his arms and policy. It is true that Racine wrote, under royal command, the *Précis des Campagnes de Louis XIV*, but no one would maintain that either this piece of historical eulogy or Charles Perrault's *Siècle de Louis le Grand* ranks as one of the masterpieces of the period. It is not for works such as these that the reign of Louis XIV is remembered as one of the high points in the history of French literature, but rather for *Phèdre* or *Le Misanthrope*, both works produced in Paris and admired at Versailles less than the now-forgotten tragedies of Quinault.[2]

The style produced in the visual arts under the dictatorship of Colbert is a curious compromise. Naturally the Baroque appealed to Louis XIV by its richness and its command of grand scale. On the other hand, he could not take over, lock, stock, and barrel, a style which had been developed so largely to satisfy religious needs. The more dramatic qualities of Roman Baroque – its use of directed light in architecture, its rendering of swooning ecstasy in painting and sculpture – could not be employed in the Versailles of the great period, which required a more secular and a more rational style. Moreover a tradition of classicism was by now ingrained in the French and made them naturally opposed to the more bizarre qualities of the Italian Baroque. Consequently French artists produced during this period a series of compromises in which the lessons of the Italian Baroque were tempered by *le bon goût*.

Owing to the dictatorship of Colbert and Lebrun this style was imposed uniformly all over France. In the period which we are now considering everyone accepted the official doctrine about the arts; all were orthodox, and there were no heretics.[3] All the great commissions emanated from the Crown, and any artist who aspired to success had to obtain such a commission, which generally speaking only came through the official channels of the Academy or the Gobelins. The standards of Paris and Versailles were accepted all over France, and we find little independent initiative in the provinces during this period. When great cities wanted to carry out any important work they usually tried to get a design from the capital, and, if they failed, they compelled their own craftsmen to follow the Parisian models as closely as possible.

But the domination of the taste of Versailles spread further than the borders of France. All western Europe began to imitate the Court of Louis XIV in its manners, its etiquette, and its art, and even countries like England and Holland, which were politically opposed to France, were influenced by her taste. Significantly the artistic relations between France and Italy began to change. Up till this time Rome had been the unchallenged capital of the artistic world, looked up to by all countries, including France. Students were sent to Rome to study, and the aim of most French kings and ministers was to attract to their own country the best available Italian artists. The first indication that this situation was changing was the failure of Bernini's grandiose visit to Paris to design the new Louvre. The rejection of his plans by the King may have been partly due to the intrigues of Charles Perrault, but it was fundamentally the expression of a new fact: that French architects could now supply what was demanded, and that there was no need to call in a foreigner, even if he was the most celebrated Roman artist of the day.[4] Other small indications point in the same direction. Poussin and Vouet had held or been offered the post of President of the Academy of St Luke in Rome, but they were both Romans by adoption; and it was a far more significant event when in 1675 Lebrun was awarded this privilege, the highest artistic honour in Rome, although he had not been there for thirty years. Moreover, Italian writers on art began at this time to dedicate their works to French patrons. For instance, Malvasia's *Felsina Pittrice* (1678) has on its title-page the name of Louis XIV, and Bellori's *Vite de' Pittori* (1672) that of Colbert. Such a tribute

LOUIS XIV AND COLBERT

might have been paid to Francis I, but it would be hard to parallel in the intervening period. Before the end of the century the rising position of France in the arts was to be demonstrated in a more positive manner. There is clear evidence of influence going from Paris to Rome instead of only in the other direction. In what one may call the International Late Baroque of Maratta and Carlo Fontana there are elements which can only be accounted for by a conscious imitation of French models. In fact it was due to the work of Louis XIV, Colbert, and Lebrun that in the eighteenth century Paris replaced Rome as the artistic capital of Europe and attained the peculiar eminence which she has never lost to this day.

ARCHITECTURE AND THE DECORATIVE ARTS

The Louvre, Versailles – Le Vau, Perrault, J. H. Mansart, Le Nôtre –
Blondel and the Academy – L. Bruant – the Decorators

Versailles is the great monument of Louis XIV's reign, but he did not at once decide to make it the seat of his Court. Colbert did his utmost to persuade the King not to desert Paris, and during the 1660s he devoted his energies to completing the Louvre in the hope that it would remain the principal royal palace.

Before Colbert's accession to power work had been continued steadily on the Square Court, first by Lemercier and then after his death in 1654 by Le Vau,[5] who carried on the building to the east side.

In the 1660s Le Vau had designed for the executors of Mazarin's will the Collège des Quatre Nations (Plate 153A), for the foundation of which the Cardinal had left a large sum.[6] The building, now the Institut de France, was placed on the south side of the Seine on the axis of the Square Court of the Louvre and was conceived as part of the same grand scheme. It is of importance in French architecture of this period as being one of the few buildings to embody some of the principles of Roman Baroque architecture. The domed church flanked with wings curving forward combines motives from Pietro da Cortona[7] and Borromini,[8] and presents a dramatically effective ensemble not to be paralleled in French architecture of the seventeenth century. Le Vau's plan included a bridge which was to link the college with the Louvre. This was not built till the nineteenth century, and then only as the meagre Pont des Arts; but even this allows one to appreciate the effect which the architect intended to be produced on the visitor as he walks across the river towards the college with its semicircle spread symmetrically before him.

This bold piece of planning, together with his other public works, the château of Vincennes,[9] and the hospital of the Salpêtrière,[10] clearly designated Le Vau as the architect best suited to construct the great front facing St Germain l'Auxerrois which was to close the Louvre on the east. He had already prepared several plans for this part of the palace; but he was prevented from carrying them out by the appointment of Colbert as Surintendant des Bâtiments in January 1664. The exact reasons for Colbert's animosity towards

Le Vau are obscure,[11] but whatever the cause, he immediately set about finding an alternative architect.

He first applied to François Mansart, who failed to get the commission because he refused to be tied down to an agreed design.[12] Foiled here, Colbert submitted Le Vau's plans to the criticism of all the architects of Paris and then asked them to propose their own designs. As a result projects were sent in by various architects which are known to us from engravings.[13] Still dissatisfied, Colbert decided to appeal to Italy. At first he planned to ask the best Roman architects to criticize Le Vau's projects, and then, changing his mind, determined to ask them to make their own designs.

Of the four architects who actually submitted designs only two need concern us: Carlo Rainaldi and Bernini.[14] Rainaldi's drawings[15] show a palace of a curious type, Italian Baroque in elevation, but ending in high roofs in the French manner, with three domes of fantastic shapes unknown to either Italian or French architecture. They convey the impression that Rainaldi was trying to suit his design not only to the exigencies of a northern climate but also to a taste which he believed to be fantastic and untrained in the rules of classical architecture. If so, he had misjudged his audience, and his project does not seem to have had any success in Paris.

The fate of Bernini's designs is a more complicated story.[16] From Rome he sent drawings for a building (Plate 155B) which, like Rainaldi's, would have been a Baroque palace, with an oval pavilion in the middle from which projected two elliptical wings ending in corner pavilions, the whole front being decorated with colossal pilasters.[17] Colbert sent his comments and criticisms of this project to Bernini, who prepared a second design much in the same spirit. At this stage he was called to Paris, and arrived in June 1665, after an almost royal progress through France.[18] Once arrived, he prepared yet a third scheme, much wider in its scope, since it involved remodelling or encasing the whole of the Square Court and not merely completing the east wing.

This third scheme is preserved in the engravings of Marot (Plate 155C and Figure 24). It shows a colossal block-like palace, with a flat roof and a balustrade ornamented with statues, the walls being again articulated with a colossal Order, this time of half-columns and pilasters. In this design Bernini made no concessions to French taste, but presented a vast mass of plastically conceived masonry in the tradition of Caprarola or his own Montecitorio. On the river front its height – a whole storey greater than Le Vau's façade – would have crushed the two existing galleries. Inside the court nothing would have remained visible of the buildings of Lescot, Lemercier, or Le Vau which would have been hidden behind double *loggie*, with staircases in the corners. Most important of all, the plan was open to very serious criticism on the score of convenience in its internal arrangement. Colbert's final comment was that although it provided admirable space for ballrooms, staircases, and grand approaches, it left the King no better housed than before.

The arrogant attitude towards French traditions implied in Bernini's design was maintained by the artist in his personal relations with French artists and administrators. He very soon made himself unpopular by criticizing everything and by always making unfavourable comparisons with Rome. It was easy, therefore, for Charles Perrault, Colbert's main assistant in the Surintendance des Bâtiments, to organize feeling against

Bernini, and before the latter left for Rome in October 1665 there were many in France who realized that his plans would never be carried out.[19]

Not only, however, was his project never realized, but his visit exercised no serious influence in France. The only work which he actually executed while in Paris was the bust of the King;[20] but his opinion was also asked by a number of individuals in connexion with works of architecture which they had in hand.[21] In some of these cases we know positively that his advice was rejected,[22] and nowhere was any visible mark left to show that it was followed. At the most it may be said that in a few altarpieces his Baldacchino in St Peter's was an inspiration to French artists, but this was already well known through engravings. It was a meagre result for so pompous and much-heralded a visit.

In the spring of 1667 Louis XIV, having finally decided to abandon Bernini's plans, created a council of three men who were to collaborate in preparing an alternative project. The team consisted of Le Vau, who was still First Architect and enjoyed the confidence of the King, if not that of Colbert, Lebrun as First Painter, and Claude Perrault, brother of Charles. The choice of Perrault seems at first sight curious. He was a doctor by profession whose interest in architecture was purely amateur. That his qualifications were serious, however, is proved by his edition of Vitruvius,[23] and his scientific training, which extended to engineering, was to be of great use in the Louvre project.

In April 1667 this commission presented two alternative schemes of which the King selected one for execution. Within three years the Colonnade as we know it to-day was more or less complete (Plate 154).[24]

Since the time of its erection arguments have raged about the real authorship of this building,[25] some claiming that the essential contribution was made by Perrault, others that it was due to Le Vau.[26] The most probable solution seems to be that the work is the result of real, though no doubt reluctant, collaboration, and that all three artists concerned made their particular contribution to the final result.

Stylistically the building is complicated. The flat skyline and the continuous tall Order on a high stylobate derive from an Italian tradition, going back to Michelangelo's design for the Palazzo dei Senatori, and perhaps taken over directly from Pietro da Cortona.[27] The coupling of the columns can perhaps be linked with the name of Le Vau, who had used coupled colossal pilasters in the garden front of the Hôtel de Lionne.[28] On the other hand, the strictly Roman details of the Orders and the conception of the colonnade as the peristyle of a Roman temple are features not to be found in either Italian architecture or the work of Le Vau. They are probably due to Perrault, who was the one member of the commission with pronounced archaeological leanings. It was no doubt his engineering skill which made it possible to solve the practical difficulties involved in bridging the wide intercolumniation and the distance between the colonnade and the back wall.[29]

The Colonnade has no exact parallel in French architecture, but it is the first example in this art of the style of Louis XIV. In certain respects it is Baroque: the scale of the Order, the depth given by the free-standing colonnade, the variety of rhythm due to the coupling of the columns. In other ways it is more strictly classical than earlier French work: the clear and simple definition of the masses, the straight line of the front (in contrast to the curves of most of the Italian designs and even Le Vau's first scheme),[30] the

Plan du Chasteau du Loiure
Ou Desseing du Caualier Bernim

grandes Galleries

4
Entrée du Costé des Tuilleries

Cour

Cour

Petit Jardin
du Roy

Cour

2
Entrée du costé
de la Riuiere

Cour

3
Passage

Rue St

henoré

Cour

Cour

1
Principale entrée du
Costé de St Germain de Lauxerois

Figure 24. Bernini: Third project for the Louvre: Plan

severe and almost unbroken entablatures, and the purity of detail in the Order and the mouldings.[31]

Before the Colonnade of the Louvre was completed Louis XIV had made it clear to Colbert and to the world that he intended to transfer his Court from Paris to the palace which he had begun to build at Versailles, and which was to become the symbol of his greatness.

The history of Versailles is long and complicated and has been written in full detail.[32] In 1624 Louis XIII had built there a small château [33] of brick and stone consisting of a court surrounded by three wings, the inner façades of which still survive, though somewhat altered, in the existing Cour de Marbre (Plate 156B). Louis XIV had early developed an affection for Versailles, and soon after taking over the reins of government had ordered Le Vau to make some small alterations in it and to enlarge it by the addition of two wings of *communs* in the forecourt. In 1668, however, after the Peace of Aix-la-Chapelle, he began to plan much more serious changes, and for a time intended to pull down the existing buildings and begin on an entirely new plan.[34] In 1669, however, it was finally decided to carry out Le Vau's scheme for enveloping the old château in a new building which completely hid it on the garden side but left the original court fronts exposed. As seen from the gardens the new building (Plates 156A and 158) presented a vast block of twenty-five bays, of which the middle eleven on the first floor were set back behind a terrace. The articulation of the building was almost Bramantesque, the ground floor being treated as a rusticated base, the first being decorated with an order of Ionic pilasters and columns, above which came an attic forming a straight skyline broken only by statues.[35] More than any other building by Le Vau Versailles shows a real grasp of the principles of classical architecture and at the same time a feeling for grand scale. The blocks are clearly defined and conceived in cubical terms, the two side sections standing out from the recessed centre in the simplest manner, their surfaces being broken only by the projecting central frontispieces with coupled columns. It is hard for us to judge the real quality of the building because the effect of varied depth was destroyed by the filling in of the terrace in the middle of the façade when J. H. Mansart made the Galerie des Glaces, and the scale ruined by the addition of Mansart's vast wings to north and south. But, as far as we can imagine it from the existing building and from engravings of its original state, it proves that Le Vau rose finely to an opportunity far beyond anything which had confronted him earlier in his career.

The effect of the outside depends, of course, to a great extent on the setting and on the gardens which were planned and made by Le Nôtre during the 1660s. Silvestre's engraving (Plate 156A) gives a good idea of the main terrace which led from the palace downwards towards the gardens on the west side. It shows Le Nôtre's skill in taking advantage of the accidents of the ground and yet at the same time forcing them into a coherent and clearly comprehensible design. As at Vaux-le-Vicomte nature was the raw material from which he was to make his effects, but nature had to be tamed and forced into a pattern suitable to man's use and to the ideas of order on which man's whole existence depended in this most highly regulated of societies. The rationalism which underlay Boileau's poetry, Colbert's economic plans, or Bossuet's theology was also the basis of

Le Nôtre's garden designs. The symmetry and order of the palace were extended to the gardens, which were planned with hedges cut to regular shapes, paths following geometrical patterns, and fountains flowing along prearranged channels. In this formal layout statues and pieces of architecture take their place with perfect ease.[36] This conception of a garden is the exact reverse of that with which the Englishman is now familiar, and it requires as much effort for us to recognize its qualities as to see the beauties of Racine if we have been wholly brought up on Shakespeare.

The gardens and courts of the palace were the scene of the great out-of-doors fêtes given by Louis XIV. In 1664 the 'Plaisirs de l'Île Enchantée', lasting three days, were given in honour of Mlle de la Vallière, and in 1674 even more splendid celebrations were prepared to celebrate the reconquest of the Franche-Comté.[37] On these occasions all the arts combined, and the achievements of Fouquet at Vaux were imitated and excelled. Quinault and Molière collaborated with Lully in the writing of ballet-comedies and operas, for which Gissey and Berain supplied the settings and dresses. Temporary theatres were set up in the gardens; firework displays were given round the fountains; and torchlight suppers were prepared in the Cour de Marbre (Plate 156B).

But, however grand the outside and the gardens of Versailles may be, it was on the interior that Louis XIV lavished his chief care. It was here that he had to appear on the most important ceremonial occasions; it was here that he received the ambassadors of foreign Powers; and it was here that the full complexity of court life was displayed.

The new style of interior decoration was actually first used not at Versailles, but in the Galerie d'Apollon at the Louvre. After the fire of 1661 the gallery was rebuilt by Le Vau, and Lebrun was commissioned to decorate it in 1663.[38] The decoration is based on the mixture of stucco decoration and painted figure compositions and arabesques which the artist had used at Vaux, but the scale is bigger, the forms more complex and the reliefs richer. It is an altogether royal gallery and is the first instance of Lebrun's use for the King of the teamwork which he had inaugurated at Vaux. He himself made the sketches for all parts of the decoration, but in the execution he was assisted by a host of artists and craftsmen.[39]

The first rooms decorated at Versailles were probably in the same style, but they have all disappeared. However, those forming the *Grands Appartements* of the King and Queen, decorated under the direction of Lebrun between 1671 and 1681, survive, though not in their original splendour (Plate 152A). The ceilings of these rooms are decorated with the same combination of stucco and paint as in the Galerie d'Apollon, but in some cases there are illusionist panels in the corners, most effectively in the Salle des Gardes de la Reine, where groups of spectators look down into the room from behind painted balustrades, a device much loved by Baroque architects, which had been widely used in Italy since it had been introduced by Veronese in the Villa Maser.[40]

The decoration of the walls was entirely different from the traditional type based on painted panelling which had been used at Vaux and in the Louvre. In some rooms the walls were covered with patterned velvet, usually crimson or green, on which were hung Italian paintings from the royal collection. In others, such as the Salon de Vénus and the Salon de Diane, they were panelled in different-coloured marbles, a material much favoured by Italian Baroque architects, but here disposed in classical, rectilinear patterns.

At the time of their greatest splendour the effect of these rooms must have been even more remarkable than it is at present. The floors were paved with different-coloured marbles, and the furniture consisted of inlaid tables and cabinets, stools covered with cut velvet or tapestry, and gilt-bronze *girandoles*. In the Salon de Mercure, which was the state bedroom, there was in addition a complete set of silver furniture, including a balustrade round the alcove,[41] eight candlesticks, each two feet high, four silver basins, three feet high, two pedestals with perfume burners, a pair of fire-dogs, and a chandelier. All this luxury was of short duration, for the marble floors had to be removed in 1684 for practical reasons and the silver furniture was sent to the mint in 1689 to be melted up during the financial crisis of the war of the League of Augsburg.[42]

The iconography of these rooms was based on the theme of Apollo or the Sun, with whom Louis had by now identified himself.[43] The seven rooms of the King's *Appartement* were named after the seven planets, culminating in the Salon d'Apollon, which was, appropriately enough, the Throne Room. In each Salon the particular attributes of the planet in question were set forth in fables or allegories alluding to the great kings of the past. In the Salon de Vénus the influence of love on kings was expounded; in the Salon de Mercure the theme is the wisdom of kings; in the Salon de Mars the great warrior kings of antiquity.

These rooms, in which all the great festivities of the Court took place, were approached by the most spectacular of all the inventions of this period at Versailles, the great staircase or Escalier des Ambassadeurs (Plate 153B). This was designed by Le Vau, but was only begun in 1671, the year after his death, by his collaborator d'Orbay.[44] The form of the staircase was novel[45] and filled a long, narrow space. A short, broad flight led to a landing, where it divided into two flights following the long wall of the cage. The whole staircase was lit by an opening in the middle of the coved ceiling. The decoration, planned by Lebrun, was of the greatest splendour. The sides of the flights were panelled with marble, and above them the main wall was painted with sham architecture, composed of an order of Ionic columns, the gaps between which were filled with imitation tapestries illustrating the victories of Louis XIV, and open *loggie* in which stood figures symbolical of the four continents. The ceiling was covered with a huge fresco in which the symbolism of the continents was carried on, combined with allegories in praise of the virtues and achievements of the King.

This staircase was the finest example of the co-operation between Le Vau and Lebrun, and proved how brilliantly these two artists could adapt themselves to the needs of the new epoch. It opened the way for the second stage in the creation of Versailles, in which the name of Le Vau is replaced by that of Jules Hardouin Mansart.

Jules Hardouin, to call him by his proper name, was born in 1646, and was the great-nephew of François Mansart, from whom he is said to have received his first training and whose name he later added to his own.[46] He must have been precocious, because when he was only twenty-eight he was commissioned by the King to rebuild the little Château du Val in the forest of St Germain. Two years later he received a more important commission, the reconstruction of Clagny for Mme de Montespan, the King's mistress, and before 1670 he had built several private houses, including the Hôtel de Noailles at St Germain and the Hôtel de Lorge in Paris.[47] These buildings show that the architect had learnt more from Le Vau than from his great-uncle. They have in common with the former many details of planning and elevation,[48] and in some cases a similar sense of the *mise-en-scène*.[49] They also reveal certain qualities which were not to be typical of Mansart's mature works, notably ingenuity in planning and inventiveness in the shape of rooms. In the Château du Val, for instance (Figure 25), the right wing consists of four rooms of different and unusual shapes, grouped so that they can all be heated by a single stove fitted into the space left in the middle of the group.[50] This tendency is of importance, since it foreshadows the development of architecture in the first years of the eighteenth century, when Mansart's pupils were responsible for introducing the more comfortable type of private house which we associate with the rise of the Rococo style. Another feature in Mansart's houses indicates a similar tendency. All the early buildings mentioned above, except the Hôtel de Lorge, show an emphasis on the horizontal quite unusual at the time. Both the Hôtel de Noailles and the Château du Val have only one full floor, and, though Clagny has two storeys, its length is so huge that the effect of the horizontal is even greater there than in the other houses. This is again a tendency which was taken up in the early eighteenth century.

Mansart was already working at Versailles in 1673, but in a quite minor capacity. It was not till after the Peace of Nijmegen in 1678 that he was put in charge of the vast extension of the palace which the King planned. The project consisted of the construction of the Galerie des Glaces and the two salons adjacent to it, the addition of the wings to the north and south of the central block, and certain modifications to the Cour de Marbre.

Externally these alterations were disastrous. The construction of the Galerie des Glaces involved filling in the terrace in the middle of Le Vau's garden façade, thereby destroying, as has already been said, an essential part of the design. The addition of the two wings more than trebled the length of the garden front; but Mansart simply repeated the existing elevation along his addition, with the result that Le Vau's Ionic Order on the principal story, which was rightly proportioned to his short façade, looks mean when repeated over the six hundred yards of the extended front (cf. Plate 158).[51]

Internally, however, Mansart and Lebrun created the most effective ensemble in the whole palace and the work in which the style of Louis XIV is most completely summed up, the Galerie des Glaces (Plate 157) and the two rooms which led to it: the Salon de la Guerre (Plate 159) and the Salon de la Paix.[52] There is nothing essentially new in the design or decoration of these rooms. In form and decoration the Gallery is basically a repetition of the Galerie d'Apollon, except for the mirrors from which it takes its name and the marbling which has a parallel in the earlier rooms of the *Grand Appartement*. The Salon de la Guerre is more original in being decorated almost entirely in terms of sculpture. The centre of interest is the white plaster panel by Coysevox of the King triumphing over his enemies, round which are reliefs in gilt bronze and bronzed stucco.

But if the principles are not original, the application of them is so brilliant as to produce quite new results. The scale, the richness of the materials, the delicacy of the detail, the ingenious relation of the three rooms to each other, all make of this suite something far more impressive than any earlier work in the style. But once again we must remember that what we now see is only a fragment. Here, even more than in the *Grand Apparte-ment*, the effect depended on the silver furniture which was on a yet grander scale – tables, standing candlesticks, and hanging candelabra – all alas! melted down in 1689.

In relation to the earlier rooms there is a significant change in the iconographical scheme. It was at first proposed to devote the room to Apollo, but this deity was soon abandoned in favour of Hercules, whose achievements were to symbolize those of Louis himself. But finally he also was dismissed, and Lebrun was ordered to paint on the ceilings the life of the King himself. The taste of the time compelled the use of allegory for such representations, and the result is a mixture somewhat confusing to the modern mind. Louis appears dressed as a Roman Emperor, performing the acts of his reign sur-rounded by the gods and goddesses of antiquity, and by figures symbolizing his enemies.[53] In spite of this indirect method of representing contemporary events it is typical of the confidence and pride of the high period of the reign that Louis XIV should have chosen such themes.

Once again these rooms present a compromise between the principles of the Baroque and of classicism typical of the art of Louis XIV. The general disposition of the suite, and particularly the approach through the arches joining the gallery to the two Salons, has a parallel in the Salone of the Palazzo Colonna in Rome, the type of Late Roman Baroque interior.[54] But in all details the French gallery is the more restrained: the ceiling is less illusionistic, the compartments of the walls are more rectilinear, the carved trophies more classical. This is as far as the French could go towards the Baroque at this period.

Apart from these modifications to the palace itself, Mansart was responsible for cer-tain other buildings of importance connected with it. The stables, built between 1679 and 1686, formed part of the extension of the palace towards the east. They filled the gaps between the three avenues which spread fan-wise from the open space in front of the palace. On the garden side Mansart replaced Le Vau's Orangery by a larger and grander building (1681–6).[55] In 1687 he again replaced a building of Le Vau's, the Trianon de Porcelaine, by a new and more extensive structure, the Trianon as we know it to-day, a curious one-storeyed building of which the most original feature is the open colonnade in the middle linking the two wings.[56] The Trianon was a retreat where Louis could take refuge from the publicity of official court life. For the same purpose he began in 1679 the château of Marly, now destroyed, but known from drawings and engravings (Plate 160A).[57] It was planned by Mansart on a completely novel principle. The central feature of the design was a square block for the King, in front of which, flanking the parterre, stretched a double row of smaller pavilions for the courtiers, separated from the main building.[58] The great charm of Marly evidently lay in its skilful lay-out and in the inti-mate relation which was created between these relatively small buildings and the foun-tains, parterres, and canal which surrounded them. It was a colony of gazebos rather than a palace.

In this respect Marly shows in exaggerated form the characteristics of the art of Louis XIV. As pure architecture even Versailles cannot rank high. The story of its building,

Figure 25. J. H. Mansart: Château du Val: Plan

197

with the many changes of plan, in part accounts for this; but there is a more fundamental reason. The interests of Le Vau and J. H. Mansart, and above all those of the King, lay in other directions. What Louis XIV wanted, and what the two artists so brilliantly supplied, was a setting for the Court. In the previous generation architects such as François Mansart were devoted to the abstract qualities of the art, and his patrons were sufficiently sensitive to encourage him to develop these interests. To Louis XIV fine points of proportion, subtleties in the use of the Orders, or the exact quality of moulding were matters of indifference; and neither Le Vau nor J. H. Mansart was sufficiently devoted to them to pursue them without encouragement. The result is that Versailles with its splendour internally, its vast size externally, its magnificent park and its enchanting garden pavilions, presents a whole of unparalleled richness and impressiveness; but it offers little in either painting, sculpture, or architecture which is of the first quality in itself. Louis XIV aimed first and foremost at a striking whole, and to produce it his artists sacrificed the parts.

Mansart's other additions to Versailles belong to the end of the reign, and will be considered in the next chapter. But there are some less prominent figures among his contemporaries who must receive notice here.[59]

The most distinguished of these was Libéral Bruant (c. 1635–97), younger brother of Jacques.[60] He never attained the success which his talent merited, and only secured one of the many public commissions of the day, namely the building of the Invalides (Plate 160B). The vast construction, planned to house disabled soldiers, was begun in 1670 and finished in 1677, apart from the domed church added later by J. H. Mansart. It was designed in the form of a grid, like the Escorial or Serlio's scheme for extending the Louvre. The external elevations are undistinguished, but the arcaded courts have a severe gravity reminiscent of a Roman aqueduct.[61] The same impressive simplicity is evident in an even higher degree in the chapel which Bruant designed about 1670 for the Salpêtrière, the hospital founded by Mazarin for the sick and destitute of Paris (Figure 26). Here Bruant has shown great inventiveness in planning a building with a number of almost separate compartments to accommodate the various sections of the community occupying the hospital, while producing at the same time a highly original variant of the centralized church plan. Round the central octagon are grouped four identical rectangular members and in the spaces between them four smaller octagonal chapels. All these subsidiary parts are connected with the central octagon by small bays, almost like apses cut off in the middle, so as to leave a narrow arched opening. The unusual forms so created are treated with extreme simplicity as regards decoration, and the result is an interior which shows a feeling for hollow enclosed space almost unique in French architecture of the seventeenth century. To twentieth-century eyes Bruant had the qualities essential to an architect in a higher degree than J. H. Mansart, but he lacked entirely the sense of the spectacular without which none could achieve success at Versailles.[62]

While all this activity was taking place in the field of architecture, the Academy was keeping an eye on theory. Its doctrine is to be found set out in the minutes of the weekly meetings held by this body[63] and also in certain full-dress treatises of which the most important is the *Cours d'Architecture* of François Blondel, originally given as lectures to the students, but published in volume form between 1675 and 1698.[64]

Blondel expounds a strictly classical and rationalist doctrine. Architecture must follow the laws of nature and reason rather than fantasy. One of the manifestations of reason is orderliness, which alone makes architecture apprehensible to the human mind. From reason certain rules can be deduced, which are of absolute validity. They apply in particular to proportions; for instance, the proportions of the five Orders are deduced from those of the human body, and must never be altered. The student can shorten the process of learning these principles by studying and imitating those works in which they have been most perfectly embodied, that is to say, in the first place the buildings of classical

Figure 26. Libéral Bruant: Salpêtrière chapel: Plan

antiquity,[65] and secondly those of the great masters of the Italian Renaissance. In short, the old academic doctrine: reason, rules, and the best masters.

This rigid doctrine corresponded exactly to Colbert's desire for orthodoxy, and it was generally accepted, till the whole system of values on which it was based was challenged in the Quarrel of the Ancients and Moderns. But it cannot be said that it was precisely in conformity with the practice of architects such as J. H. Mansart, whose style showed a greater degree of richness and less attention to the rules of Vitruvius than would have pleased Blondel.[66] We shall find the same phenomenon in the painting of the period, for not even Lebrun could carry into his work at Versailles the strict classicism which he preached in the Academy. It would, however, be wrong to suppose that there was any sense of conflict over the difference; the fact is simply that it is easier to be strictly rational in theory than in practice.

Painting and Sculpture

Lebrun and the Academy – Mignard – Girardon – Coysevox

The great achievements of painting during this period lay in the large-scale decoration already considered; but French artists naturally continued to produce easel pictures, and the theoretical teaching of the Academy was more appropriate to small-scale classical composition than to heroic frescoes.[67]

The views of the Academy of Painting and Sculpture are in essence closely related to those of their architectural colleagues and can be summed up in the same formula: reason, rules, and the best masters. But naturally the application to the representational arts involves many differences of detail.

The foundation of their doctrine is the proposition that painting[68] appeals to reason or the mind, and not primarily to the eye. It is therefore an intellectual and a learned art, intended for educated people. The Academicians accept the traditional definition that painting is an imitation of nature, but this imitation must only be carried out according to the laws of reason. The artist must choose from the variety and disordered richness of nature the most beautiful parts, that is to say, those parts which accord with reason.[69] In other words, the artist must reduce nature to the laws of reason, i.e. the rules of proportion, perspective, and composition. Further, he must concentrate on the permanent aspects of nature – form and outline – and not devote too much attention to those elements, such as colour, which are ephemeral and which, incidentally, appeal to the eye and not to the mind.[70]

On this basis the Academy worked out in its lectures a system of rules as complicated as any that have ever been devised to govern the art of painting. The painter must only choose noble subjects. Like the dramatist, he must observe the unities of time, place, and action, though he may be allowed certain liberties in the matter of time to suggest what immediately precedes and succeeds the actual moment depicted. He must observe the proprieties; there must be nothing 'low' in his compositions, and everything must be suitable to the theme chosen.

The Academicians, however, were not content with such general indications, but set out their decisions in rigid form. Lebrun produced his famous treatise on the expression of the passions[71] in which he gives the student exact instructions how to represent any particular state of emotion, and, lest the written word should not be explicit enough, accompanies each chapter with a diagrammatic drawing. Henri Testelin, the secretary of the Academy, extended this method, and in his *Sentiments des plus habiles peintres*, published in 1680, tabulated the agreed views of the Academy on the subjects of drawing, expression, proportion, chiaroscuro, composition, and colour.

To these rules were added equally strict instructions on the suitability of different artists as models for the young student. The Academy arranged its hierarchy of merit as follows: first, the Ancients;[72] secondly, Raphael and his Roman followers; thirdly, Poussin. The student was specifically warned against the Venetians, since they led to a too great interest in colour, and against the Flemish and Dutch artists, since they imitated nature too slavishly, without discrimination.[73]

These precepts were naturally supplemented by practical instructions, which followed the same principles. On arrival at the Academy's school the young student was set to copy the works of the approved old masters, first in drawing and then in painting. Next he was made to copy casts from the antique. After this preliminary training he was allowed to draw from life, since by then, it was believed, his taste would have been sufficiently formed by his study of the masters for him to be able to select from the model before him according to taste and reason.

The reader will not be surprised to learn that this restrictive teaching did not produce remarkable or individual artists. The painters trained in the Academy under the direction of Lebrun are uniformly competent, but rarely more; and when they show character it is usually by breaking the rules which had been inculcated into them.

Lebrun himself was an artist of great natural talent. Born in 1619, he was first trained under Perrier and Vouet, and while still in the studio of the latter produced a painting of Hercules and Diomedes (Plate 161), which reveals a vigour of design and handling entirely lacking in his later works.[74] In 1642 he went to Rome, where he worked for four years, partly under the instruction of Poussin, and partly studying contemporary Roman art. Returning to Paris in 1646, he at once obtained commissions for decorative and religious paintings. His reputation was established by his decorations in the Hôtel Lambert and at Vaux in the later 1650s.[75] In 1661 he was given his first commission by the King, for 'The Family of Darius before Alexander' (Plate 164A), in which the qualities of the artist's mature style appear fully developed. The traces of Poussin's influence are still visible in the classical detail and in the attention paid to gesture and facial expression. But Lebrun has taken the edge off Poussin's style. The composition is freer and more picturesque; the setting is richer and more striking;[76] the subject is pathetic rather than heroic.[77] Finally, the hero is Alexander, with whom Louis XIV was known to admit to some similarity, and who was to be the theme of the next series of works commissioned by him from Lebrun.[78]

The 'Tent of Darius', as it was called, established Lebrun's position with the King. From this moment he obtained, as we have seen, every post of importance in the arts, and supplied designs for all the great decorative schemes in the royal palaces.[79] We have already noticed that in these works he was compelled by the nature of the task to be less strictly classical than in his theories, and the same phenomenon appears in the few easel pictures which he produced during the period of his success. A typical example of his style is the painting of 'Louis XIV adoring the Risen Christ', painted for the chapel of the Mercers' Company in 1674, and now in the museum of Lyons (Plate 162). The first impression is of a lively Baroque composition, such as Pietro da Cortona might have produced for a Roman church; and it is only on careful examination that we notice the other elements. The types are more Raphaelesque and the presentation of the figures is more frontal than would be the case in a contemporary Roman composition. But the fact remains that the altarpiece is closer in its general effect to the Baroque artists whom Lebrun condemned than to Poussin, whom he set up as the ideal model.[80]

In the bottom right-hand corner of this painting we see the figure of Colbert, modestly placed and realistically painted, which may serve to remind us of the fact that Lebrun was also a portrait painter of distinction. His portrait of his first protector, the chancellor Séguier, at the entry of Louis XIV and Marie-Thérèse into Paris in 1661 is a fine solution to the problem of producing a classical version of the life-size equestrian portrait (Plate 163A). The group is treated like a frieze with the horse seen exactly from the side and the pages arranged in a row, the one on the extreme right turning back to close the composition. This is the French classical answer to the challenge of Rubens' 'Buckingham' or van Dyck's 'Charles I', the great Baroque models for this kind of composition, and, though it lacks their vigour, it has a stateliness suitable to its time and place. But even here Lebrun is not entirely true to his own principles; for, though the composition is classical, the naturalistic treatment of the embroidered dresses and the warm colouring of the whole picture show that he had borrowed from the Flemish tradition of van Dyck, which in his lectures he was so strongly to condemn.

Lebrun's dictatorship lasted till the death of Colbert in 1683; but the latter's successor, Louvois, had for many years been a supporter of Lebrun's rival, Pierre Mignard, by whom the first painter found himself gradually displaced. Till his death in 1690 he continued to receive marks of favour from the King himself, but they were in reality consolation prizes. The important commissions went elsewhere, and Lebrun's last years were mainly occupied with the execution of small easel pictures which were graciously received by the King and put away in some little-used room.[81]

The personal rivalry between Lebrun and Mignard must not lead us to assume that they represented opposing styles. On the contrary, the paintings of Mignard fit in with the teaching of the Academy even more fully than those of Lebrun. Born at Troyes in 1612, Mignard studied first under Jean Boucher of Bourges and then in the studio of Vouet in Paris. In 1636 he reached Rome, where he lived till 1657 with only a short interruption in 1654–5 for a visit to Venice and other towns in the north of Italy. In Rome he formed his style mainly on the study of Annibale Carracci, Domenichino, and Poussin,[82] and although he later supported the claims of the Venetians in the quarrel about drawing and colour, he seems to have done so from a desire to oppose Lebrun rather than from any real admiration, for it is hard to see any trace of Venetian influence in the colour or handling of his own work.[83]

In 1657 he was summoned back to France at the command of Louis XIV and attained considerable success primarily as a portrait painter, but also in the execution of decorations for private houses and churches. In the latter field his two most important commissions were the painting of the dome of the Val-de-Grâce for Anne of Austria in 1663 and the decoration, now destroyed, of the gallery and salon at St Cloud for Monsieur, the King's brother, in 1677. Neither work shows great originality, the dome being a direct imitation of the type originated by Correggio and re-introduced in the seventeenth century by Lanfranco, and the St Cloud decorations being hardly distinguishable in design and conception from the works of Mignard's rival at Versailles. In all his historical and religious paintings the most striking feature is the coldness of colour and handling derived from the tradition of Domenichino and Poussin. In 1689 Louvois brought to a head the rivalry between his favourite and Lebrun by commissioning from the former a 'Tent of Darius' (Plate 164B) in direct competition with the latter's acknowledged masterpiece. Mignard's painting was at the time much admired, though to us it seems tired and hollow, lacking the gusto of Lebrun's design and missing equally the classical poise and harmony of Domenichino and Poussin, the two models whom Mignard seems to have followed. And once again the 'colourist' Mignard turns out in practice to be more classical and more linear than the official leader of the party in support of drawing.

The only field in which Mignard shows any originality is that of portraiture. He did not follow the usual French formula derived ultimately from the north, and practised by Philippe de Champaigne or Claude Lefèvre, but imported a manner based partly on Roman work,[84] and partly on contemporary Venetian artists such as Forabosco. The result was the well-known kind of court portrait with which Mignard's name is principally associated.[85] He also revived allegorical or mythological portraiture, which had been popular in the sixteenth century and had enjoyed some favour in *Précieux* circles,[86] but was not widely used till the second half of the century. 'The Comte de Toulouse as Cupid asleep' (Versailles), 'The Marquise de Seignelay as Thetis' (Plate 166A) are typical of his work in this manner, and it is seen in slightly different form in the equestrian portrait of Louis XIV at the Siege of Maestricht (1673) (Plate 165). Here the King appears dressed as a Roman Emperor on a prancing horse while a Victory flies down to crown him with laurel. In this case Mignard is competing directly with Baroque artists, with Bernini in the pose of the horse, and with Rubens in the whole conception of the portrait. The result proves how unwise it was for a classically trained painter to attempt the vivacity of movement which was the natural idiom of a Baroque artist. As in many of his works, Mignard has fallen between all the stools; and has failed to achieve what his less ambitious rival, Lebrun, did so well in the Séguier portrait, to find a classical solution to the formal equestrian portrait.

At the end of his life Mignard's ambitions were satisfied, and he obtained the official recognition which he had so long sought. On the death of Lebrun in 1690 the King, at the instigation of Louvois, made him his First Painter and sent word to the Academy that they were to appoint him director and chancellor of their body. And so, in a single sitting, Mignard was made Associate, Member, Rector, Director, and Chancellor. His triumph over his dead rival was complete.

★

The principal rôle assigned to the sculptors of the period was their share in the decoration of the gardens and rooms of Versailles, and their work in this field has already been referred to in considering the general architectural problems of the period. But some of them stand out as individuals of such significance that they call for separate study, in particular François Girardon (1628–1715) and Antoine Coysevox (1640–1720).[87]

Girardon[88] was a close collaborator of Lebrun and embodied in his works the classical theories of the Academy. Like Lebrun, he was a *protégé* of Séguier, who sent him to Rome for a short visit, probably between 1645 and 1650. On his return the artist continued his training in the school of the Academy, of which he became a member in 1657.

His few surviving early works[89] show that he learnt the current style based on Sarrazin. From 1663 onwards he played a part in the decoration of the royal palaces, particularly in the Galerie d'Apollon, and in 1666 he received the commission on which his fame principally rests, the group of 'Apollo tended by the Nymphs' for the grotto of Thetis at Versailles (Plate 167). It is hard now to judge this work because not only was it moved in the late eighteenth century to a new 'picturesque' setting of rocks and ruins designed by Hubert Robert, but the arrangement of the figures in the group was altered.[90] The engraving on plate 166B shows the original disposition of the group in an enclosed niche, which was flanked by two other similar niches containing the horses of Apollo carved by Guérin and the Marsy brothers. This idea of continuing the action through several different parts of the building and so linking them up is a Baroque device. It is certainly part of Lebrun's general project; for Girardon's group itself is the most purely classical work in French seventeenth-century sculpture. The direct inspiration of Hellenistic work is strikingly evident in the types, the modelling of the nude and the treatment of the draperies, and can be accounted for by the fact that the artist paid a special visit to Rome during the execution of the group in order to refresh his memory of ancient sculpture there.[91] The main problem which faced Girardon, however, was not the treatment of the individual figures, but the manner of linking them into a coherent group. Antiquity provided no model to guide him here,[92] and Girardon was not prepared to use the methods evolved by Baroque sculptors with such success for their fountains or altar-groups. He therefore fell back on a quite different source, the paintings of Poussin. The late classical compositions of this artist are conceived so much in terms of solid objects set up in space that Girardon needed only to translate them into sculpture.[93] In its original form the group must have satisfied in a high degree the canons of classical composition. The central figure, closely imitated from the Apollo Belvedere, is seen frontally in a classical pose; the nymphs are placed symmetrically round him, but with such variety and contrast in their poses and gestures that monotony is avoided.

Girardon's other sculptures for the gardens of Versailles are not outstanding,[94] except for two: the relief on the 'Bain des Nymphes',[95] which can almost be described as a seventeenth-century version of Goujon's reliefs on the Fontaine des Innocents, and the 'Rape of Persephone' (Plate 169A).

In the Apollo tended by the nymphs Girardon had tackled the problem of separate figures forming a group to stand in a niche. The 'Persephone' is a free-standing group, composed of three entwined figures carved out of a single block. Girardon is therefore here directly challenging comparison with Bernini's treatment of the same theme and with Giovanni Bologna's 'Rape of the Sabines'. Once again the statue does not now stand in the position for which it was originally designed. At present we see it standing in the middle of the circular Colonnade, facing the entrance but inviting the spectator to walk round it and view it on all sides. It was planned, however, to form one of a quartet of groups at the four corners of the Parterre d'Eau.[96] We do not know exactly how it was to be placed, but it would certainly have been set on a definite axis, so that it presented one principal aspect. Girardon has taken this fact into account and has designed the group with a marked emphasis on frontality. This feature is brought out most clearly by a comparison with the two Italian groups. Bologna's version presents a satisfactory composition from whatever angle it is seen, but does not finally arrest the spectator at any one point. Bernini's is evidently meant to be studied primarily from one view, with the body of Pluto seen frontally, but there is such a wealth of cross-movement in depth that it can in fact be examined from many sides. Girardon has concentrated everything on one view, to the extent that he has almost designed the statue as a high relief. Pluto stands, stepping forward, so that the plane formed by his two legs defines the main aspect. His head is turned to be seen full face. Persephone, although she writhes into a twisted contraposto, does so in such a way that the main axis of her body remains in a plane parallel to the principal aspect. The same is true of the figure of her sister, Cyane, who appears below the other two.[97] Once again it is to Poussin that Girardon has turned for inspiration, and in the two versions of the 'Rape of the Sabines'[98] he found the formula that he needed; for in these groups Poussin had solved the problem of forcing figures in violent movement into groups which fitted into his classical scheme of composition in planes parallel with that of the picture.

Apart from these sculptures for Versailles, Girardon received many other commissions, both private and public, in which the same tendencies are visible. In the monument to Richelieu in the church of the Sorbonne (1675-7) (Plate 168) he provides the classical type for the free-standing altar-tomb. Like all Girardon's works, it was carefully designed to suit its position, which was originally the middle of the choir on the main axis of the church.[99] Here it would have presented two principal aspects, one towards the altar, the other towards the north, from which side it would be approached by those who came into the church from the university. The latter would see the full-length recumbent figure of the Cardinal exactly from the side, except that the upper half of his body is turned so as to face towards the spectator; while the mourning figure at his feet would be seen exactly from behind.[100] From the altar the group is again coherent with the mourning figure leading straight back to the dead man, who turns his head so as to look up at the altar and is supported by the allegorical figure of Piety whose gaze follows his.

Girardon's one commission for the city of Paris, which was also the most important work of his later period, was the equestrian statue of Louis XIV, prepared in the years 1683–92 for the Place Vendôme, but destroyed at the Revolution. Here again both Girardon's natural tendency and the nature of the problem provoked a classical solution; for the statue was to stand on the axis of the Place facing down the street connecting it with the rue St Honoré. But in this case the artist had no need to turn to Poussin for inspiration. The ancient model lay ready to hand in the statue of Marcus Aurelius, and Girardon made full use of it in his design. The pose of the horse and even the King's outstretched arm are copied almost literally from the Roman model. The artist has only made a few concessions to contemporary taste in the naturalistic treatment of the saddle-cloth and the skirt of the armour.

Girardon did not die till 1715, but his most important work was executed well before the end of the century. There is no direct evidence to show that he lost the favour of the King, but it is certain that by the 1690s the taste of the latter was moving away from the

classical manner, of which Girardon was the most distinguished exponent, and beginning
to favour a more Baroque style.

It is partly for this reason that the position of Girardon's rival, Coysevox, improved
as that of Girardon became weaker. For classicism never came easily to Coysevox,
whereas even in his early years leanings towards the Baroque are clearly apparent. He
was born in 1640 at Lyons,[101] came to Paris in 1657, and studied at the Academy school
and under Lerambert for at least six years. His earliest surviving work, a 'Madonna' in
Lyons,[102] shows the influence of Michel Anguier, but he certainly also learnt much from
studying Sarrazin. By 1679 he was working at Versailles, which was to be the scene of his
most spectacular successes.[103] His sculpture there can be divided into two categories. In the
statues and fountains in the forecourt and gardens he attempts to follow the classical
manner of Girardon, but with little success; for they are either heavy and lifeless, like
'La France triomphante',[104] or pure pastiches of the antique, like the 'Nymphe à la
Coquille'.[105] Where Coysevox excels is in the decoration of the later rooms in the palace,
particularly the Galerie des Glaces (Plate 157), the Escalier des Ambassadeurs (Plate 153B),
and the Salon de la Guerre (Plate 159). His free invention, his love of rich materials, and
his technical virtuosity make him the ideal counterpart of Mansart, just as Girardon was
of Lebrun. The most splendid piece of real sculpture, as opposed to decoration, in these
rooms is the stucco relief of the victorious Louis XIV in the Salon de la Guerre. Here
Coysevox does brilliantly what Mignard so signally failed to do in his equestrian portrait (Plate 165). The chief reason for the sculptor's success is that he has approached
the matter in the spirit of the Baroque. He makes no attempt to restrict the violence of
the action in order to conform to classical canons. On the contrary, he emphasizes the
movement across the surface of the relief and in depth into it. The body and head of
the King are boldly turned, his arm projects out into space, and the fallen soldiers below
are arranged so as to lead the eye into the composition. Yet another less obvious device
is used for the same purpose. Although the horse is seen from the side, the relief becomes
higher towards the right, so that the head and forequarters of the animal project farther
than the hind-quarters and one foreleg is actually free of the relief. This arrangement
gives variety to the whole effect, and breaks up any trace that might remain of classical
emphasis on the plane of the relief itself. In fact, this panel is the most Baroque piece of
sculpture produced by any of the Versailles team up to its date.[106]

Coysevox's most original works are his busts, but they belong mainly to the later part
of his career, and will be dealt with in the next chapter. For the moment it will be
enough to notice that even his earlier busts, such as the bronze of Louis XIV, dating
from about 1680, in the Wallace Collection (Plate 170), are free in their movement and
startling in the skill of their modelling. In this field, however, Coysevox had the advantage of knowing one great Baroque original, Bernini's bust of Louis XIV, which stood
at Versailles. His own works look calm and almost severe beside the swirling rush of the
Roman sculptor's marble, but the existence of Bernini's bust helps in part to explain the
curious paradox that whereas Girardon, who twice visited Rome, showed no sign of
even being aware of the Baroque, Coysevox, who as far as we know never went to
Italy, comes closer in feeling to his Roman contemporaries than any other Frenchman.[107]

CHAPTER 8

THE DECLINE OF LOUIS XIV
1685 – 1705

HISTORICAL BACKGROUND

THE death of Colbert in 1683 is a convenient event from which to date the change in the position of France and the beginning of the decline which marked the last years of Louis XIV's reign. But even before the minister's death his power was declining and he was beginning to be eclipsed by his rival, Louvois, whose personality was to dominate France during the eight years that he survived his predecessor, and whose policy was to be continued in many ways after his own death, partly because it was largely based on a desire to flatter the King and indulge his personal inclinations.

To put it very shortly, the change from the régime of Colbert to that of Louvois was marked by a tendency towards purely aggressive, useless, and ruinous wars, which strained the financial system and brought out the faults inherent in it. The result was increase in taxation, with even greater injustice in its distribution and corruption in its collection; and the more oppressive the taxation grew the more inflexible the administration had to become in order to enforce it. Meanwhile the increased autocracy in the political field was accompanied by a similar movement in religion, of which the Revocation of the Edict of Nantes in 1685 was the most significant example.

Of the various campaigns before the Treaty of Nijmegen in 1678 it could always be said that, though often unjustified in an ethical sense, they were directed towards practical ends, such as the advancement of trade or the strengthening of natural frontiers. But the wars of the last part of the reign were of a quite different kind. That of the League of Augsburg may have been declared to forestall attack, but that attack would have been provoked by Louis XIV's obvious intention to attain domination of the continent of Europe. The War of the Spanish Succession was legally justified, but only a megalomaniac would have taken up the testament of Charles II of Spain, and taken it up in such a provocative manner.

The result of these two wars on the state of France is too well known to need much emphasis. The misery to which the peasantry was reduced is a common theme of writers of the time; the greater nobility were busy ruining themselves at Versailles; the smaller lived in obscurity and relative poverty on their estates; the solid *bourgeoisie* suffered from the irregular payment of *rentes* and from the interruption of trade; and, as usual in such disturbed circumstances, the only section of society which prospered was a small group of financiers who made and often lost again vast fortunes at spectacular speeds.

The power of the King himself became in effect more and more absolute. Although it had always been so in name, under the guidance of Colbert it had been exercised with greater discretion and in a less arbitrary manner. With increasing age the King became less and less able to brook opposition, either from his ministers or his subjects. The function of the latter became to pay and obey blindly, and of the former to endeavour to find out beforehand what advice the King wanted to be given in order to gain favour by giving it. In effect, therefore, the entire government of the country depended on the personal whim of the King; and the King had become a megalomaniac and a bigot.

The blame for his bigotry is usually placed too exclusively on Mme de Maintenon, for in fact other advisers, such as Louvois, probably had as much to do with it. And in any case his reactionary policy in religion was only the counterpart of his attitude in politics. It could even be said that his reasons for fearing the Huguenots were as much political as religious; for the threat of the 'State within the State' was still a living memory. One thing is certain, that he became much more *dévot*, and that his particular form of religion partook of the pietistic enthusiasm of seventeenth-century Catholicism, as embodied in the doctrines and methods of the Jesuit order, to which his confessor, the Père La Chaise, belonged. That his relations with the Papacy remained strained was due to the political necessity of maintaining as far as possible the privileges of the Gallican Church.

However, as the government became more and more reactionary, there grew up an increasing resistance to it, though this opposition was of necessity more intellectual than practical. The new rationalist and independent thought which led the way to the eighteenth century was born well before the end of the seventeenth. It was not at Versailles but in Paris, or even in exile, that men like Fontenelle and Bayle were preparing the challenge to all authority, whether religious, philosophical, or political, which in the hands of the Encyclopaedists was actively to further the break-up of the old régime.

Within France itself one of the most significant manifestations of the new spirit was the Quarrel of the Ancients and Moderns, to which Fontenelle made a vital contribution by his new doctrine of progress but which in the field of the arts and literature can be said to date in its active form from the publication of Charles Perrault's *Siècle de Louis le Grand* in 1687, which was followed in the years 1688–96 by the even more explicit *Parallèles des Anciens et des Modernes*. Perrault's thesis was that the blind adoration of the ancients taught by the French Academy and the Academy of Painting was irrational. The moderns, he said, had made great advances on the ancients not only in science but also in the arts. They could draw on new styles and could use methods such as perspective which were unknown to the Greeks and Romans. This view was, of course, a direct attack on one of the cardinal principles of the Academy of Painting, for whom ancient art was the absolute standard by which all contemporary work was to be judged. The issue was confused, because although the doctrine of the moderns was revolutionary and in the end helped to destroy the dictatorship of the Academies associated with the régime of Louis XIV, Perrault, who was a skilful controversialist, pointed to Lebrun and Racine, the two stoutest supporters of the ancients, as the examples of contemporary artists who had excelled these very ancients. In the same way he maintained that Louis XIV was himself a proof that kings were as great in the seventeenth century as they had been in antiquity. Nevertheless, the supporters of the ancients were not deceived by this simple piece of tactical manoeuvring and fully realized the danger of the attack on their position.

Parallel with the Quarrel ran another which affected only the field of painting, but within that sphere was of even greater importance. This was the Quarrel of Colour *versus* Drawing.

This quarrel arose out of the gradually increasing admiration of certain French artists for Venetian painting. We have seen that even in the earlier part of the century some painters, such as Vouet and Jacques Blanchard, had profited from the example of Titian and Veronese, but it was not till the publication of C. A. Dufresnoy's poem, *De arte pingendi*, in 1667 that any theoretical defence of the importance of colour and the Venetian conception of painting was put forward. Dufresnoy was, however, very tentative in his statements, and it was rather in the notes to the poem by Roger de Piles that a real assertion of the value of colour was to be found.

The matter came to a head in 1671 in the Academy itself. In that year Gabriel Blanchard, the son of Jacques, read a lecture attacking Philippe de Champaigne, who, in spite of his Flemish origin, had just made a highly doctrinaire statement of the views of Lebrun and the majority of the Academy that colour was altogether inferior to drawing. There followed a violent discussion which was nominally closed by Lebrun in an *ex cathedra* statement of the official doctrine in favour of drawing in a lecture given in January 1672.

But the matter was not to rest there, for Roger de Piles, who, though not a member of the Academy, had been taking an interest and probably an actual part in the discussions, began to publish his views in a series of theoretical pamphlets.[1]

Fundamentally his arguments are much the same as those of Blanchard, and the problem can be summarized as follows. The orthodox Academicians maintained that drawing was superior to colour because the former was a purely intellectual matter and appealed to the mind, whereas colour appealed only to the eye, that is to say to one of the senses.[2] Put otherwise, drawing is to colour as the soul to the body.

To this the defenders of colour replied as follows. The principal aim of painting is to deceive the eye, and colour achieves this more fully than drawing. This doctrine was in many ways revolutionary, for although the Academy would have agreed that the purpose of painting was to imitate nature, they would not have allowed the use of the word *deceive*, and they would immediately have qualified their statement about imitation by saying that the artist must, of course, select from nature and only imitate the most beautiful parts of it. The view of the colourists was therefore a statement of a much more complete naturalism than had hitherto been formulated in France. But they went even further, and directly attacked the rationalism of academic teaching. Drawing, said the Academy, imitates the real, whereas colour only represents the accidental. On the contrary, said their opponents, colour represents truth, whereas drawing only represents reasonable truth, that is to say truth altered to suit the demands of reason. This was again heretical, because it implied that reason was not the ultimate standard of judgement in the arts. Finally, they said, drawing appeals only to the learned and the expert, but colour appeals to everyone, thereby asserting an almost democratic conception of art and challenging the view generally accepted since the early Renaissance that painting is an art appealing to the mind and only to be enjoyed by intellectuals.

This dispute involved, therefore, attacks on a number of the most important props of the academic position, and, quite as much as the Quarrel of the Ancients and Moderns, served to undermine its authority. For gradually the view of the Colour party came to be accepted, and by the end of the century, though the battle had died down, it was the colourists who were left in possession of the field.

The later stages of the discussions centred round the importance of a single artist, Rubens. It is a fact, on which all historians of French art have commented with surprise, that the great cycle painted by Rubens for Marie de' Medici in the Luxembourg exercised almost no influence in French painting for more than half a century. What is even more curious is that the discovery of his importance was made not by practising artists but by the critic Roger de Piles.[3] By the middle of the 1670s de Piles was already advising the Duc de Richelieu, who was re-forming his collection, to buy Rubens, and in his later theoretical works Rubens plays a more and more prominent part.[4]

For Roger de Piles the first quality in Rubens was that he was a naturalist. This view may seem strange to us, but was reasonable in the context, because Rubens was the means of escaping from the imitation of classical art which Poussin had inaugurated and which the Academy had codified into a soulless system. Rubens, moreover, had all the other qualities necessary to the great artist, such as invention, knowledge of allegory, power of composition, and so on. In one quality only was he deficient, namely drawing – to us also a curious opinion, but we must remember that for even the opponents of the Academy drawing meant the drawing of Raphael and Poussin.[5]

It is not surprising that, with this highly complicated historical background and the break-up of the whole academic structure, we should find in the actual practice of the arts a great variety of tendencies all active at the same time. The changed state of mind of the King and the Court provided the background necessary for the appearance of a strong Baroque movement in France, and this is in fact one of the most striking features of official art of the later 1680s. The rise of La Fosse and a little later of Jouvenet in history painting, the establishment of Largillierre and Rigaud as the most popular portrait painters, the belated success at Versailles of Puget, the gradual supersession of the classical Girardon by Coysevox in sculpture, and the increasingly Baroque elements in the architecture of J. H. Mansart – all these phenomena occur within a few years of 1685 and mark the change in the taste of the Court.

Parallel with this transformation, however, there occurred another, also within the Court, but starting a little later in date. The younger members of the royal family – the Dauphin, the Duc de Chartres (son of Monsieur, the King's brother), and the Duchesse de Bourgogne (the wife of his grandson) – began to grow bored with the formality and pomposity of the academic style, as it was interpreted by the followers of Lebrun, and demanded a gayer type of decorative painting of which the subjects were the lighter themes from classical mythology treated in a more frivolous style. This tendency was one of the main factors which led the way towards the Rococo.

At the same time, however, there grew up in Paris a style independent of Versailles and in many ways opposed to it. Among artists, among their personal friends, and among a small group of *bourgeois* admirers there was developed a real taste for naturalism.[6] Even the portrait painters, such as Largillierre and Rigaud, who for their smart patrons could produce all the tricks of the Baroque, worked in a quite different style when painting for their own pleasure or that of their friends. Formal classical portraiture was superseded by intimate portraits based on the models of Flanders and sometimes of Holland, and even in small religious pictures painted for this circle the old tradition of Poussin and Lebrun began to give way to a more naturalistic and picturesque manner.[7]

These confusing and conflicting tendencies naturally manifested themselves differently in each of the three arts, but basically the same kind of variations of taste can be seen in all of them.

ARCHITECTURE

The later work of J. H. Mansart – Bullet

The architecture of the last decades of the seventeenth century must be considered in two parts: public and private buildings. In the public works the tendencies towards the Baroque which we have seen latent in the architecture of the high period of the reign are suddenly given free rein. In the private houses the opposite characteristics come to the fore, and practical convenience rather than a desire to impress is the primary object sought.

Till his death in 1708 Mansart continued to control all the public works, whether executed at the direct order of the King or by some public body in his honour. The most important of these are the two chapels for the Invalides and Versailles, and the two public squares in Paris, the Place Vendôme and the Place des Victoires.

As early as 1676 Louis XIV had decided that Bruant's chapel at the Invalides was not worthy of his greatness, and planned to build a second one on a grander scale. We know just enough about this first scheme to be certain that it was quite different from the chapel finally erected (Plate 172),[8] the plans of which were prepared in 1680, although the actual building was only completed in 1691, and the decoration of the interior lasted until after Mansart's death in 1708.

In certain respects the chapel springs from the French seventeenth-century tradition. Its plan, a Greek cross with circular chapels in the corners connected with the central space by low, narrow openings, is taken directly from François Mansart's designs for the Bourbon Chapel at St Denis;[9] and the lower part of the façade, constructed in rectangular blocks, recalls the same artist's church of the Minims.[10] But in other respects the design reveals features which could not be found in France before this date. Even the lower part, though classical in its rectilinearity, is Baroque, in that it builds up towards the centre by means of a series of breaks forward, culminating in the pedimented frontispiece. But the design of the dome is even more singular. Ultimately it derives from St Peter's, but with suprising variations. Mansart has broken away in two respects from the usual arrangement, namely a regular disposition of windows, each separated from the next by a buttressing pier, with a window on the main axis of the church; for he has placed alternately one and two windows between his pairs of piers, and on the main axis he has set neither a window nor even a buttress, but the pier with two half-columns which forms the centre of each two-windowed bay between the buttresses. This un-expected placing of a solid instead of a void on the principal axis is quite unclassical, but it is repeated in the lantern, which is square in plan but is set with a corner on the main axis. Further, there is a greater emphasis on the vertical than in the classical models for this kind of church, the Sorbonne or the Val-de-Grâce. The lines of the columns in the portico are carried up through the piers of the drum, along the consoles and the heavy ribs of the dome, to be interrupted for a moment by the projection at the bottom of the lantern, but to be taken up again strongly through the lantern and so to continue up to the unexpected climax, the obelisk which tops the whole design.[11] A Baroque richness is given to the whole effect by the gilt trophies which fill the areas of the dome between the ribs, so that seen across Paris the Invalides stands out in isolated Baroque splendour be-tween the simplicity of the two earlier domes and the conscious coldness of Soufflot's Panthéon.[12]

The interior is as Baroque as the exterior.[13] Its general character is set by the main Order of vast free-standing columns, supporting a rich and deeply projecting entabla-ture. Compared with the boldness of this conception the Sorbonne seems timid and the Val-de-Grâce modestly classical. Between the columns are openings to the side chapels, above which are stone reliefs of unusually free conception, like Bernini's *Loggie* in St Peter's, but in white stone instead of coloured marbles. In the dome itself Mansart has again taken up an idea of his great-uncle for the Bourbon Chapel, for it is cut off so that the spectator looks through it to an outer shell on which is painted a heavenly glory. This is lit by windows concealed in the upper part of the drum.[14] The Baroque character of the interior is completed by the high altar, which consists of a variation of Bernini's St Peter's Baldacchino, with black marble columns, standing out dark against the opening which leads through to the older church.[15]

The chapel of the Invalides demonstrates, therefore, the tendency towards the Baroque which became so strong in religious architecture at the end of the century. The same mood dominates Mansart's other important work in this field, the chapel at Versailles (Plate 173).[16] There had been several chapels at Versailles before this one, but all had been regarded as more or less temporary. In 1688 Louis XIV decided to build one worthy of the palace, and commissioned Mansart to prepare plans. Work was started on the build-ing in 1689, but the war of the League of Augsburg interrupted it almost at once, and the project could not receive attention till after the Peace of Ryswick. In 1698, however, Mansart was ordered to take up the work again, and in the next year building operations were resumed, on slightly modified plans. By 1703 the structure was finished and by 1710 the decoration of the interior was complete.

The chapel presented a special problem, in that it had to consist of two storeys, of which the upper containing the royal pew had to be made the more important. Man-sart's solution to this was to make a low arcaded ground floor, for the courtiers and the public, and a high colonnaded first storey, with the royal pew at the west end communicating directly with the King's *Appartement*, and a spacious gallery for his immediate suite. The result of this arrangement was to make the chapel of great height in relation to its breadth, so that the proportions of the interior are those of a Gothic chapel rather than of a classical building.[17] Moreover the colonnade on the first storey creates variations in depth and contrasts of light which are quite unclassical in feeling. But the most Baroque part of the whole chapel is the ceiling, which is covered with an illusionist fresco by Antoine Coypel (1708–9) (Plate 187).[18]

It is to be expected that these two chapels should be the most Baroque works produced at the end of Louis XIV's reign, because they embody the two ideas which lead most usually to this style: a heightened religious atmosphere and an autocratic rule, coupled in this case with a strong belief in Divine Right on the part of the ruler. But if, seen in the context of French seventeenth-century architecture the chapels of Versailles and the Invalides appear Baroque, compared with the Italian churches of the High Baroque they seem very restrained. Walls are never curved, entablatures are rarely broken, pediments are straight, plans are simple. The French did not follow the Baroque principle of fusing the three arts of architecture, sculpture, and painting into one; they never used directed light with the dramatic force of a Bernini; and they rarely employed coloured marbles for decoration.[19] In fact, their tendency towards the Baroque was always checked by the tradition of classicism, even in these last decades of the seventeenth century.

This fact is even more apparent in the two squares built at the same period in Paris, the Place des Victoires and the Place Vendôme. The former was planned in 1685 by the eccentric Duc de la Feuillade as a piece of exaggerated flattery to the King. He commissioned Desjardins to make a statue of Louis as the centre of the square; but the statue pleased the King so much that the Duke presented it to him and ordered the artist to make another. Meanwhile Mansart was commissioned to design an appropriate setting, and produced a plan for a circular Place with four huge standard lamps which were to burn always before the statue of the King, as if before a holy image. These were removed in the eighteenth century, and since that time the whole Place has suffered increasing depredations, so that it is now hardly possible to imagine its original appearance.[20]

The Place Vendôme, however, can still give us a true idea of Mansart's ability in this field (Plate 174). In 1685 the King bought the site of the Hôtel de Vendôme from the bankrupt owner, the Duc de Vendôme, with the intention of making an arcaded square with buildings to house the royal library and the various royal academies.[21] Once again, however, financial difficulties necessitated a change of plan, and in 1698 a new project was devised. The idea of housing the library and the academies was dropped, the arcaded ground floor was given up in order to make fuller use of the available space, and the King made over the whole site, together with the buildings which had been begun on it, to the city of Paris, on the following terms: the authorities would erect the façade as planned by Mansart, but they might sell the plots behind the façade to private individuals to build on as they wished.

As finally completed the Place Vendôme is a square with the corners cut off, closed except for two openings which form its main axis. On the axis stood Girardon's equestrian statue of the King, facing one of the openings.[22] The buildings which surround the

Place were decorated with a colossal Order of pilasters, broken by frontispieces with half-columns at the centres of each side and at the cut-off corners.

The Place Vendôme must inevitably suggest comparison with the Place Royale (or Place des Vosges) of the first years of the century (Plate 72A), and the differences are very revealing. The Place Royale was designed by Henry IV for a practical purpose, to provide decent houses for the moderately well-to-do and a covered promenade for the people of Paris. The Place Vendôme, as originally planned, was intended to house the establishments dependent on the King's bounty and to form a suitable setting for the King's statue. That is to say, it was designed for the greater glory of the King and to display his beneficence to the arts. In the form which it ultimately took the nobler part of this scheme was abandoned; the setting for the statue survived; and the houses were handed over not to the useful citizens who inhabited the Place Royale but to the excessively wealthy and somewhat ostentatious financiers who built their hôtels round it.[23]

In its general conception, as a piece of scenic architecture rather than a practically designed domestic scheme, the Place Vendôme is close to Roman Baroque architecture which could offer a brilliant solution to this type of problem in the Piazza of St Peter's. In detail, however, it is restrained and relatively classical, so that once more we find a compromise between the two opposites, classicism and Baroque, though here the Baroque element is less marked than in the two chapels discussed above.

It would, however, be wrong to regard Mansart in his last years as entirely a protagonist of Baroque ideas. In the field of domestic architecture his work has a quite different character. During the last decade of the century a number of rooms at Versailles, Trianon, and Marly were redecorated under his direction, and for them a new style was evolved which marks the first stage towards the Rococo.[24] Panelling became lighter, looking-glasses replaced overmantels, cornices became less monumental; in fact, everything was done to make the decorations of the walls lighter and more elegant (cf. Plate 175A).

From the same period we know of one project by Mansart for a private house (Figure 27).[25] This design is full of unusual features. In addition to the main door in the middle of the corps-de-logis, there is a second entrance in the right-hand corner of the court, which creates an asymmetrical arrangement. Inside the house the staircase and vestibule form a single space, which is again contrary to the usual practice of the time. Mansart also breaks away from the conventional rectangular shapes for his rooms, for the dining-room to the right of the vestibule and the salle above it both have rounded ends, and the secondary staircase in the corner of the court is also curved in plan. In elevation there is one surprising and unclassical device; for on the garden front, instead of the usual arrangement of a central projecting pavilion and two others, one at each end, there is a colonnaded portico on the ground floor in the middle with two pedimented frontispieces, one on each side, separated from the portico by one window bay.[26] This disposition completely breaks up the centralized symmetry of the traditional garden façade and foreshadows the less rigid designs of the early Rococo.

From the time of his appointment as first architect to the King, and even more after he became Surintendant des Bâtiments in 1699, Mansart was occupied with so many

Plan au rez de chaussée d'une Maison à bâtir à Paris sur les desseins de Mr Mansard premier Architecte et Surintendant des Batimns. du Roy

Jardin   *Jardin*

Grande Salle   Anti=Chambre   Grand Cabinet   Cabinet   Ariere Cabinet

Passage

Grand Escalier   Vestibule   Salle à Manger   Anti Chambre   Chambre à Coucher   Garderobe   Petitte Gardorobe   Petitte cour

Escalier

Remises   Cour des Ecuries   Ecuries

Grande Cour   Passage

Salle du Comun   Remises   Cour des Jumiers

Cuisine   Ecurie   Lieux

GardeManger

Logem.t du Suisse   Porte   *Rue*

1 2 3 4 5   10   15 Toi.

Gravé par P. le Pautre

Figure 27. J. H. Mansart: Plan of a house

different jobs that he cannot possibly have attended personally to every detail of each of them. Some of his contemporaries, including Saint-Simon, who hated Mansart, explicitly accuse him of having kept one or more young architects in the back room, who did all the essential work but got none of the credit. Several modern critics have developed this theory, and there is no question that for the decorative side of the work Mansart relied to a great extent on his two ablest assistants, Lassurance and Pierre Le Pautre.[27] Indeed, it would probably be fair to say that they, rather than Mansart himself, were responsible for the steps which led towards the invention of Rococo decoration. On the other hand, no analogous evidence has as yet been produced for the strictly architectural side of the designs.[28] It is true, as we shall see, that in the buildings which can be certainly attributed to him Lassurance shows skill in design and is at least abreast of the times in this field. But the facts are not enough to prove that Mansart was dependent on him for this side of his work. On the contrary we have already seen that in his very first works, executed in the 1670s, when he certainly did not have an organized office, Mansart showed marked talent as a planner. That these gifts were not particularly displayed in the work at Versailles is due to the nature of the commission rather than to the character of the architect. Versailles called forth Mansart's other great gift, his sense of the dramatic and of the appropriate setting for the King; ingenuity of planning was not demanded here. When, however, he had occasion towards the end of his life to design once more a private house, then these talents, long buried, manifested themselves again.[29]

Mansart will probably always be the subject of dispute. His meteoric career reasonably aroused jealousy among his contemporaries and less reasonably arouses suspicion among modern critics. He did not have the concentrated intellectual qualities of his great-uncle, and he was always working in a hurry and in circumstances which prevented him from achieving a particular kind of excellence. But his enemies have gone too far in denying him real ability as an architect. He served the needs of his time perfectly, and applied to them vast talents: an exceptional sense of grandeur, great skill in directing a team of craftsmen, and, when it was called for, considerable mastery of the strictly practical side of the architect's profession.

The crucial steps in the development of decoration were made at Versailles and the other royal palaces, but the revolution in planning was carried out in Paris. Mansart, as we have just seen, played a part in this, but equal importance must be attached to the work of an architect who was his exact contemporary, Pierre Bullet (1639–1716).[30] Bullet was a pupil of Blondel and began his career by carrying out some of his designs such as the Porte St Denis (1671). As a result of this work he was himself commissioned to build another gate, the Porte St Martin, for the city of Paris (1674). During the 1680s he was responsible for a number of designs for private houses[31] which show him to be a supporter of the classical tradition of the previous generation, and little affected by the innovations of Mansart at Versailles.[32]

In the very first years of the eighteenth century, however, he built two houses of great novelty. The rich financier Crozat the elder bought two of the sites at the corner of the Place Vendôme and commissioned Bullet to construct on them houses for himself (finished 1702) and for his son-in-law, the Comte d'Évreux (1707) (Figures 28, 29, and

Plate 175B). The irregularity of the site of the Hôtel d'Évreux, of which the street frontage consists only of four out of the five bays of the cut-off corner of the Place Vendôme,
has provoked a brilliant solution, including a diagonal approach to the courtyard,
through a circular *porte-cochère*. With an ingenuity as great as that of Antoine Le Pautre
at the Hôtel de Beauvais, Bullet has managed to form a symmetrically disposed court,
rounded at one end and closed by a portico at the other (Plate 175B).[33] The Hôtel Crozat[34]

Figure 28. Bullet: Hôtel d'Évreux: Plan of first floor

presented a more regular site, but Bullet has been no less clever in using it. The most remarkable feature of this plan, however, is the great variety in the shapes of the rooms.
On the first floor the gallery, the *antichambre*, and the front bedroom all have rounded
ends; the Cabinet is equipped with a niche-shaped protuberance which allows access
from two doors; and the vestibule, squeezed between two spiral staircases, has the shape
of a T, with an oval dome at the crossing of the two axes. Here the method which we
saw hinted at in Mansart's early design for the Château du Val is fully developed, and we

are near to the complete freedom and fantasy which the architects of Louis XV show in the shapes of their rooms.[35]

The late work of Mansart and that of Bullet lead up directly to the eighteenth century, and the innovations of these two architects are taken up by the younger generation. Pierre Cailleteau, called Lassurance (?–1724), was the most important pupil of Mansart in this field. In the first decade of the century he built a series of houses in which the new tendencies are developed.[36] Several of these have the long low elevations which were first introduced by Mansart at Le Val and Clagny; all have a freedom of planning, which is derived partly from the same source, and partly from Bullet. Other architects who were not direct pupils of Mansart show the same tendencies: Dulin (c. 1670–1751) in the Hôtels Dunoyer (1708) and Sonning; Jean Sylvain Cartaud (1675–1758) in the house of the younger Crozat (1704); Pierre Alexis Delamair (1676–1745) in the complex of the Soubise and Rohan hôtels (before 1706); and Claude Mollet (1660–1742) in the Hôtel d'Humières (1700).[37] But with the works of this generation we have left the Grand Siècle and have crossed the threshold of the Rococo.[38]

SCULPTURE

Puget – The later work of Coysevox

If we were to follow the strict order of dates, Pierre Puget would have been treated in the previous chapter, since he was of the same generation as Lebrun and Girardon.[39] Logically, however, he fits in at this point in the history of French sculpture, for the first half of his career belongs to the story of Mediterranean art, and he does not come into the main stream of French culture till the middle of the 1680s. Moreover his sudden if short-lived success at this moment is one of the most striking examples of the change of taste in favour of the Baroque.

Puget was born in 1620 at Marseilles. He spent the years 1640–3 in Rome and Florence working under Pietro da Cortona, principally on the decoration of the rooms in the Palazzo Pitti. During the years 1643–56 he divided his time between Marseilles and Toulon, where he was engaged in designing the decoration of warships and in executing paintings for local churches.[40]

In 1656 he received his first important commission, for the door of the Hôtel de Ville at Toulon (Plate 176A). The general scheme of this door was one already current in Italy,[41] but in the treatment of the figures Puget shows great originality. In the freedom of their movement and in the fluidity of their modelling they are far more Baroque than anything of the period in the Parisian tradition. It is usual to say that in works such as these Puget was imitating the manner of Bernini; but this is not the whole truth, nor even the essential point. Puget's style here springs from the Roman Baroque, but not in the first place from Bernini. There is no work of Bernini which attempts to convey the feeling of anguish, which is the principal characteristic of Puget's Atlantes. In this way they mark rather a direct return to the 'Slaves' of Michelangelo, who was at all times an important inspiration to the artist. But there are also models for them to be found nearer at hand,

Figure 29. Bullet: Hôtel Crozat: Plan of first floor

in Puget's own master, Cortona. One of the novelties of the latter's ceiling in the Palazzo Barberini is that in the painted corners the entablatures are supported not, as in the Farnese Gallery, by nonchalant athletes in classically calm poses, but by struggling figures oppressed by their loads.[42]

Puget's figures have, however, a character quite distinct from any Roman work. The sense of strain in them is more intense than in Cortona's, and is expressed in a different way. They display in their faces anguish of mind as well as of body; [43] in fact they almost remind us of the damned souls in Michelangelo's 'Last Judgement'. Bernini's figures often express equally strong emotion, but of another kind – mystical ecstasy in the 'St Theresa', nervous tension in the 'David'. They never show this particular mood, which is personal to Puget.

In 1659 Puget was called to Paris on a commission which must have seemed to him the beginning of real success. He was invited by Claude Girardin, one of Fouquet's chief assistants, to make two statues for his château of Vaudreuil in Normandy.[44] As a result of this he came to the notice of Fouquet himself, and received a commission to make for him a Hercules resting.[45] Puget went himself to the Carrara mountains to choose marble for this statue, and settled in Genoa to execute it; but before it was finished he heard of the fall of Fouquet, and his hopes of success collapsed.

For the next twenty years Colbert kept Puget away from Versailles and prevented him from obtaining any really important commissions. This is often said to be due to the fact that the artist had worked for Colbert's enemy Fouquet, but the connexion with the latter did not prevent the minister from taking over all the other artists who had worked at Vaux. There may have been some element of personal feeling in the matter, because Puget was a man of violent temper certainly not made to get on with the sober and calculating Colbert, to whom he probably failed to pay his court.[46] But there is no need to postulate such personal differences. Colbert was quite right in thinking that Puget was not a suitable artist for the work to be carried out at the Court. His leanings were far too clearly towards the Italian Baroque; he was not formed in the classical school; and he was an individualist, who would not have submitted to the tyranny of Lebrun. In the statues produced for Girardin and Fouquet he had tried to moderate his violence and to give them an appearance of classicism, but the effort was too visible and the result was not successful.[47]

On the disgrace of Fouquet Puget decided to stay in Genoa, and within a very short time he had established a reputation there as a sculptor. His most important works in Genoa were two statues of St Sebastian (Plate 176B) and the Blessed Alessandro Sauli, made for the Sauli family to decorate the niches in the crossing piers of S. Maria di Carignano, Genoa.[48] In these works Puget comes nearer than at any other time to the feeling of Roman Baroque sculptors and even to Bernini. In fact the likeness of the 'St Sebastian' to the latter's 'Daniel' in the Chigi Chapel is so great that one is tempted to think that Puget must have known this work.[49] However, the differences which exist between the two statues are significant. Bernini's 'Daniel' is more plastic in its conception than Puget's 'Sebastian'. Daniel surges forward in the movement of prayer, right out of the niche; St Sebastian falls in a pose contained by the plane closing the front of the niche. This refusal of the full Baroque three-dimensional movement is typical of Puget and distinguishes his work from that of Bernini.[50]

In 1667 Puget returned to France and apart from an occasional visit to Genoa, and one to Versailles, the rest of his life was spent at Toulon and Marseilles. He was engaged on various tasks, including the decoration of ships and architectural work for the town of Marseilles. But in spite of difficulties of every kind he continued to produce sculpture.

In 1670 he found in the dockyards at Toulon two blocks of marble which had been abandoned there, and after some difficulty he got Colbert's permission to use them for statues. From them he carved the 'Milo of Crotona' (Plate 179A) and the relief of 'Alexander and Diogenes' (Plate 178).[51]

The 'Milo' is perhaps Puget's most remarkable work. It has the qualities of emotional intensity which were already apparent in the door of the Hôtel de Ville at Toulon and the 'St Sebastian', but in addition it has a concentration and a geometrical regularity which are almost classical. In the 'Milo' Puget invented a truly French Baroque.

The statue is Baroque in its violence of movement, in the sharp twist of the arm and head, in the naturalism of the tree trunk, which indicates that the artist must have known Bernini's 'Apollo and Daphne'. But the movement is so carefully controlled that, seen from the front as it is meant to be seen,[52] the whole statue forms a simple silhouette composed of two sets of parallel axes: the legs and left arm forming one set, and the torso, drapery, and tree trunk forming the other. If this pattern is compared with, say, the 'David' of Bernini, which also depicts great strain, the difference is evident. In the 'David' there is the maximum of contraposto, so that no straight line or plane survives; in the 'Milo' the whole statue is based on straight lines and planes. And just as the physical strain is concentrated into a rigid and mathematical scheme, so the emotional expression is made to conform to a classical formula. For the head and the mask are based on the 'Laocoon' and have the degree of restraint apparent even in that most Baroque of ancient groups. Again this feature is brought out most clearly by a comparison with the 'David', with its tense lips and down-drawn eyebrows.

The 'Milo' was taken to Versailles by Puget's son, François, and arrived there in 1683. After a moment of doubt it was approved by the King and given a prominent position in the gardens at Versailles. What was almost more important, it was admired by Louvois, and when a few months later Colbert died, Louvois wrote to the artist in the most flattering and encouraging terms. Puget reacted immediately to this display of interest. He continued the 'Alexander and Diogenes' and the 'Perseus and Andromeda', the latter of which was well received at Versailles in 1684;[53] he probably made the 'Triumph of Alexander' at this time,[54] and he planned various other works for Versailles: a colossal 'Apollo' for the canal, an equestrian statue of the King, an 'Apollo and Daphne', an 'Apollo and Marsyas'.[55]

The 'Alexander and Diogenes' is the most important marble relief which came from the hand of Puget.[56] It bears the same relation as the 'Milo' to Roman Baroque. The work with which it most obviously challenges comparison is Algardi's relief of the 'Meeting of Leo I and Attila' in St Peter's. But once again the differences are more striking than the similarities. Whereas Algardi lays the emphasis on movement into depth, Puget keeps everything in a series of planes near the surface of the relief and parallel with it. Algardi breaks into the middle of his composition with a vista leading to an indefinite distance, whereas Puget carefully closes his background with an architectural setting. The movement of Algardi's figures is sinuous and full of contraposto; Puget's figures make a series of straight diagonals across the surface of the marble. In fact he seems to turn back once more to his first master, Pietro da Cortona, and to have translated into high relief the latter's angular, diagonal compositions, such as the 'Bronze Age' and the 'Iron Age' from the Pitti frescoes.[57]

Puget's last years – he died in 1694 – were embittered by renewed failures at Court. The 'Alexander' never reached Versailles; his last work, the relief of 'St Charles Borromeo in the Plague at Milan' was refused by the King;[58] and he had the greatest difficulty in getting payment for those works which had been accepted. Some part of his failure was due to the intrigues of rivals;[59] but Puget could never have been a successful court artist. With the help of Louvois he was able to come in for a moment on a wave of taste; but when Louvois was gone he could no longer hold his own. The famous and arrogant memorandum, in which he set out to Colbert the terms on which he would work for the King, gives the measure of his discretion as a courtier, for the words *je veux* occur with a frequency and an emphasis unknown at Versailles. His recurrent quarrels with the authorities in the shipyard at Toulon and with the town council of Marseilles confirm that he was headstrong and difficult. In fact he had almost the temperament of a Romantic artist,[60] of which the fine side appears in his enthusiastic letter to Louvois, written at the age of more than sixty in 1683, in which he exposes his plans and which contains the celebrated phrase: 'Je me suis nourri aux grands ouvrages, je nage quand j'y travaille; et le marbre tremble devant moi, pour grosse que soit la pièce'.[61]

We saw in the last chapter that in his work at Versailles under Lebrun and Mansart Coysevox showed a greater tendency towards the Baroque than his collaborators, and in many of his later works, such as the kneeling statue of Louis XIV set up in Notre Dame in 1715,[62] this tendency persists. In others, notably the 'Duchesse de Bourgogne as Diana' (Plate 179B), there is a lightness and a delicacy which point towards the Rococo.

But it is in the busts of the later years that the real novelty of Coysevox's style lies. For those of the King and the great dignitaries of the Court Coysevox continues to use the formula which he had evolved as early as 1680 (cf. Plate 170). But when he came to portray his personal friends he dropped all formality and swagger and replaced them by penetration of character and naturalism of rendering. We find this tendency as early as the 1670s in his busts of Lebrun (Plate 171).[63] Here, beneath the classical drapery, there appears the pleated linen shirt of the day; and in the rendering of the mask itself the sculptor makes no attempt to reduce the features to classical canons.[64] But the last works, such as the bust of Robert de Cotte (1707; Plate 180), are even more revolutionary. This portrait is both more vivid and more intimate than any earlier French sculpture.[65] The bust has been reduced so that there is nothing to distract the eye from the head itself, which is shown in the action of turning sharply round as if the sitter's attention had suddenly been attracted to his right. Bernini had used this device in a lesser degree to give liveliness and movement to his figures, and Coysevox himself had adopted it in his earlier formal busts. But never before did the gesture have such alertness, never had the twist of the neck and the tilt of the head been so expressive. This seizing of the character-istic movement is supplemented by a minute observation in the rendering of the features, which again convey with great vividness the character of the sitter. In its freshness and spontaneity this bust seems to foreshadow the work of Houdon.

Coysevox's later work is typical of the varied and contradictory tendencies of the period about 1700. His marble groups and busts for Louis XIV are still in the half-classical, half-Baroque convention which he had evolved in the 1680s; for the younger generation at the Court he produced figures which are already *dix-huitième*; [66] and for his personal friends, among artists and *bourgeois*, he invented a quite new kind of naturalism.[67]

PAINTING

La Fosse, Jouvenet, Antoine Coypel – the Portrait Painters: François de Troy, Largillierre, and Rigaud – Desportes

The historical complexity of the last decades of the century and the variety of conflicting tendencies in the arts are most clearly visible in the painting of the time. The Baroque invades religious and historical subjects; mythological themes are treated with a freedom from classical rules which eventually turns into a Rococo lightness; portraiture fluctuates between bombastic variations on the methods of Rubens and van Dyck on the one hand and naturalistic experiments in the vein of Rembrandt on the other; landscape is mainly based on the idealization of Claude, but Desportes makes sketches from nature which foreshadow the intimate observation of the English water-colourists.

In the time of Colbert religious painting had taken a quite secondary place, since painters were required above all to celebrate the successes of the King in war and peace. After the middle of the 1680s this situation is reversed. There were fewer victories to celebrate, and the contemporary events which are chosen for record are royal marriages, the reception of ambassadors and other formal incidents of this kind.[68] Generally speaking artists were encouraged by the King to paint allegorical paintings on general rather than topical themes, and the changed attitude of the Court towards religion naturally gave rise to a revival in the painting of altarpieces and decorations for churches. It is typical of the periods before and after 1683 that the representative decorative work of one should be the Galerie des Glaces, and of the other the church of the Invalides.[69]

Of the various artists who were responsible for the transformation of French painting at this time the most original was Charles de la Fosse (1636–1716).[70] He began his train-ing under Lebrun, but his evolution was much more deeply affected by his visit to Italy, where he spent the years 1658–60 in Rome and the following three years in Venice, also visiting Modena and Parma. He returned to France armed with a knowledge of the latest Roman manner, that of Pietro da Cortona and his followers, but with a stronger leaning towards North Italian artists, particularly Veronese and Correggio. The results of this training can be seen in his diploma piece, the 'Rape of Proserpine' (1673; Plate 181A), in which the landscape is purely Venetian in feeling while the figures derive from the late Poussin, and in the 'Finding of Moses' (Plate 182A),[71] in which the general plan of the composition and the picturesque treatment of the dresses recall Veronese, the figures are reminiscent of the Roman Baroque of Pietro da Cortona, and the trees show that La Fosse was already studying the landscapes of Rubens.[72] In the fresco executed in 1676 for the dome of the church of the Assumption,[73] his model was Correggio, though again a flavour of the Roman style can be seen in the types of the figures.

During the later 1670s La Fosse was mainly occupied as assistant to Lebrun, first at the Tuileries and then at Versailles, where he was responsible for part of the painted decoration in the Salon de Diane and the whole of that in the Salon d'Apollon. Here his tendencies towards a light and rather free style were held in check by the control of Lebrun, and the panels which he painted for these rooms are the most classical works which he produced.[74]

In the 1680s, however, his leanings towards the party in favour of colour against drawing, already indicated by his admiration for Venetian painting and Correggio, took a new turn, and he suddenly entered the field as the first French artist to make full use of Rubens as a model and an inspiration. The effect of this admiration, no doubt due to the influence of Roger de Piles who was a close friend of La Fosse, has already been noted in the landscape of the 'Finding of Moses'. It is also evident in the figures of the 'Sacrifice of Iphigenia' over the mantelpiece of the Salon de Diane at Versailles,[75] but it is in the 'Presentation of the Virgin' (Plate 181B), dated 1682, that the full effects of his new taste appear. This picture is closer to the mature manner of Rubens and more fully Baroque in its conception than anything that had been produced in France up to this date. The pattern is ultimately Venetian and one which had already been imitated in France since the days of Vouet; but it is seen through the eyes of Rubens, who had invented variants of it which must have been known to La Fosse.[76] Moreover, the types and the swelling draperies are in a spirit unknown in France and directly taken from Rubens.

This sudden irruption of the style of Rubens into French art is somewhat surprising, even after the preliminary 'softening up' of de Piles, and it is worth noticing that the 'Presentation' was commissioned by a church in Toulouse and not for either Paris or Versailles. It may be that in this work La Fosse felt free from the trammels of the Academy and therefore able to indulge his enthusiasm for Flemish art to a degree which he would not have dared in the metropolis.[77] But the painting was executed at the exact moment when Puget was beginning to be accepted at Versailles and when taste at the Court was swinging over towards the Baroque.

In the other two major commissions of his career, La Fosse was only one of a team of artists collaborating on a large scheme of decoration, although he seems to have shown greater invention than his competitors. The first of these was the series of compositions ordered in 1688 by Louis XIV for Trianon. To suit the informal character of this palace the subjects dictated to the artists were chosen from mythology instead of history or allegory, and the style in which they were executed was altogether lighter than anything that had hitherto been usual at the Court. Many of the pictures are now scattered or lost, but a few remain in place and can give us an idea of the conception of the whole. La Fosse's 'Apollo and Thetis' over the mantelpiece of the Chambre du Couchant takes up a theme which had been used in the Grotte de Thétis two decades earlier, but treats it in a much lighter vein. In the Grotto, as we have seen, Girardon made of the story a pure classical group, but La Fosse gives to his nymphs a slender elegance and a rosy flesh-colour which foreshadow Boucher. In fact, this series of paintings, which included also works by Bon and Louis de Boullongne the Younger, is the first in which something of the lightness of the Rococo can be traced.

But the taste of the King did not long continue to lead him in this direction, and this was the last occasion when any subjects so frivolous were chosen even for the decoration of an informal retreat. The increasing piety of the King and the influence of Madame de Maintenon are more evident in the other great joint commission of the last years of the reign, the decoration of the Invalides.

In 1692 La Fosse, who had been working for the Duke of Montagu in London since 1689,[78] was called back to Paris to undertake the decoration of the church which Mansart had just added to the foundation.[79] At first he was commissioned by Mansart to paint the whole building, but gradually other patrons pressed the claims of their favourite artists – Michel Corneille the Younger, Jouvenet, Noël Coypel, Bon and Louis de Boullongne – and the share of La Fosse was reduced to the painting of the outer dome (Plate 182B) and the four pendentives.

The subject of the dome fresco is 'St Louis presenting to Christ the sword with which he has vanquished the enemies of the Church', a theme which combines Louis XIV's new religious enthusiasm [80] with the veneration for his great ancestor, who is depicted in royal robes and in the likeness of the donor. La Fosse has based his design on Correggio, but he has greatly lightened his model by putting all the figures near the edge of the circle and so leaving the middle of the field for the open sky. In this way he gives a certain Rococo lightness to what is basically a Baroque composition.[81]

In La Fosse are summed up almost all the tendencies of the last decades of the century: interest in Venetian and Flemish colour, a tendency towards Baroque composition, and in his last phase a foreshadowing of the Rococo. And in most cases he seems to have been first in the field with his methods. The other artists who collaborated with him at Trianon and the Invalides show both less originality and less variety.

The most distinguished of them is Jean Jouvenet. He was born in Rouen in 1644 and joined the studio of Lebrun soon after his removal to Paris in 1661. His decorations in the Salon de Mars at Versailles are pure imitations of his master, and all his early works [82] seem to have been based on the study of Lebrun and the artists whom he recommended, particularly Le Sueur and the Roman followers of the Carracci. Jouvenet's 'St Bruno in Prayer' (Plate 183A) illustrates well his relation to Le Sueur. In type the two figures of the saint are closely similar; but the feeling is different. In Le Sueur's version he stands in an attitude of *recueillement* before the altar on which are a cross and a skull. In Jouvenet he clutches a crucifix, almost in a swoon. Jouvenet, that is to say, gives to the scene a tone of Baroque emotionalism which Le Sueur has avoided. The pattern is correspondingly altered. Le Sueur's is static and composed of verticals; Jouvenet's is based on the strong diagonal of the saint's body, crossed by the swaying figures of the two monks in the background.

In his later work the Baroque tendency is even more marked. His most important series of canvases consisted of the four colossal pictures of the 'Miraculous Draught of Fishes' (Plate 184), 'The Resurrection of Lazarus', 'Christ driving the Traders out of the Temple', and 'Christ in the House of Simon', painted for St Martin des Champs and put in place in 1706.[83] Most writers attribute the Baroque quality of Jouvenet's later style to the influence of Rubens; but this seems rather wide of the mark. Jouvenet never uses the composition in depth of Rubens, nor does he imitate his types or his Baroque drapery. His manner is rather a free and more lively version of the style which Lebrun had used in his big classical and religious compositions, and is derived ultimately from the late work of Raphael. Jouvenet makes greater use than Lebrun of the Baroque implications in the latter, but his manner is still far from the full Baroque. His relation to it is comparable with that of Puget. His compositions are primarily planned as high reliefs, and the movements are in sharp diagonal straight lines rather than in curves. The drapery is based on the Raphaelesque convention, though it is treated with a greater consideration for deep shadows than was the case with Poussin or even Lebrun. In colour, too, Jouvenet never follows the Flemish manner, but is always closer to Lebrun.[84]

In one respect, however, he differs from most of his rivals in religious painting. There is in his work a strong element of naturalism on which his early biographers comment. In the 'Miraculous Draught', for instance, the piles of dead fish in the foreground are given a prominence and are treated with a relish which would have shocked the Academy in Lebrun's time; and we are told that, in order to paint the picture, Jouvenet made a special journey to Dieppe to study similar scenes on the spot. The same naturalism is to be seen in Jouvenet's choice of types for the same picture, in which the apostles are the coarse fishermen which a Caravaggesque might have selected.[85]

Jouvenet's relation to the Baroque is therefore somewhat different from that of La Fosse. Whereas the latter's brand of Baroque was essentially taken from Rubens, Jouvenet evolved an indigenous form of the style, based on a blend of French and Raphaelesque elements, to which he added a type of naturalism Flemish in character, but not directly derived from Rubens.[86]

The third important representative of the Baroque in French painting of this period was Antoine Coypel (1661–1708).[87] He was younger than both La Fosse and Jouvenet by half a generation, and comes later into the movement. He was something of an infant prodigy, and at the age of eleven accompanied his father, Noël Coypel, as a student when the latter was appointed director of the French Academy in Rome. After spending three years in Rome, where he was commended by Bernini, and one in the north of Italy, where he studied Correggio, the Bolognese, and the Venetians, he returned to Paris in 1676 and was received as a member of the Academy in 1681, giving as his Diploma piece 'Louis XIV resting after the Peace of Nijmegen' (Plate 185B). This painting, which has already been referred to as an example of the emptiness of allegorical compositions of this period, is of interest in showing the influence of the later seventeenth-century Bolognese imitators of Albani, partly in the exaggerated sweetness of the expressions and partly in the light and gay colouring, which differs from both the cold classical tones of Poussin and from the warmth of the Venetian key. It is nearer to the gaiety of the Rococo. In others of his early works, however, such as the 'Liberation of St Peter', known from an engraving by Château, he shows a stronger leaning towards the style of Poussin, and it is clear that he began his career with the eclecticism typical of his generation, mixing elements from the classical and the colourist tradition.

Coypel, however, was a close friend of Roger de Piles, and gradually the colourist tendency in him triumphs. By the early 1690s he appears as one of the most whole-hearted admirers of Rubens, and his 'Democritus' of 1692 in the Louvre (Plate 186A) is little more than a pastiche of the master. During the later 1690s he practised a style in which he aimed at combining certain Baroque qualities taken from Rubens with the taste and psychological approach of a Poussin and a Domenichino. The result is the series of vast biblical compositions which were among Coypel's most celebrated works in his own time, but which to us combine the bombast of the Baroque and the pedantry of the classical style without the virtues of either.[88]

At about the same time Coypel was taken up by the Grand Dauphin, by Monsieur (the King's brother), and by his son, the Duc de Chartres, who later succeeded his father as Duc d'Orléans and was Regent during the minority of Louis XV. For the Dauphin Coypel painted at Meudon in about 1700 a series of panels illustrating the story of Cupid and Psyche, in which he did his best to introduce a certain degree of Rococo lightness,[89] but in general he continued to work in a more explicitly Baroque manner.

In 1702 the Duc d'Orléans, who had recently succeeded his father, began extensive alterations to the Palais Royal and commissioned Coypel to decorate the big gallery with scenes illustrating the story of Aeneas. The gallery has been destroyed, but a few of the wall panels and the sketch for the ceiling survive.[90] The former are in Coypel's most bombastic manner, though with more vitality and less melodrama than in the biblical series; but the ceiling is important as being one of the most completely Baroque schemes to be found in the whole of French art. A huge piece of false perspective architecture opens out in the middle to allow the eye to sweep through to the sky in which the apotheosis of Aeneas is taking place.

Even bolder in the same manner is the ceiling of the chapel of Versailles (Plate 187), painted in 1708. It is significant that Roger de Piles disapproved of this work, for in it Coypel turns his back on Rubens and follows a Roman Baroque model, Baciccia's ceiling for the Gesù,[91] with which de Piles would not have been in sympathy. Coypel follows his original closely, in the general principles of the design which depends on the most melodramatic forms of *trompe-l'œil*, and on the creation of the effect that the celestial world is literally bursting through the vault into the chapel itself. Coypel has even extended the *trompe-l'œil* because, whereas in the Gesù the fresco is surrounded with real stucco decoration, at Versailles the architectural setting to the composition is entirely painted, in imitation of real vaulting and relief.

As regards the quality of his work, Antoine Coypel cannot rank high even among artists of his own generation, but his importance historically is considerable, partly as representing a taste which was at first in opposition to that of the King, but which eventually conquered even the Court, at any rate enough to gain for the artist the commission for the ceiling of the chapel. Stylistically he is significant as having produced the two most completely Baroque decorations to be found in French art of this period.

We have already noticed the tendency towards the elegance and lightness of the Rococo in the mythological paintings executed for Trianon in 1688,[92] and the fact that after this date Louis XIV himself could hardly have continued to favour this type of work. He did, however, allow and even encourage it in works not executed for his own use, for instance for the decoration of the Ménagerie, which he ordered to be undertaken in 1699 for the Duchesse de Bourgogne, who had completely won his heart and had brought into the Court of Versailles the only lightness and gaiety to be found there in the King's last years. His comment on the first project shows his aim: 'Il me paroist ... que les sujets sont trop sérieux ... il faut qu'il y ait de la jeunesse meslée dans ce que l'on fera'.[93] And it is indeed in the works ordered for the younger members of the royal family that the tradition is carried on.[94]

La Fosse and Antoine Coypel, as we have seen, had a considerable share in the creation of this new style, but other artists such as Bon and Louis de Boullongne the Younger devoted themselves almost exclusively to it.[95] Compositions such as Bon's 'Triumph of Amphitrite' at Tours, probably exhibited in the Salon of 1699, or his 'Hippomenes and Atalanta' in the Hermitage (Plate 185A) mark the transition between a light Italianism in the manner of Albani and Maratta[96] and the full Rococo. It was from this tradition that sprang François Lemoyne (1688–1737), the next link in the chain, and the master of Boucher.

A different aspect of the nascent Rococo is to be seen in the work of J. B. Santerre (1651–1717),[97] who was principally known in his own day as a painter of portraits, usually in an allegorical convention, but whose importance historically depends rather on his few religious compositions. In 1709 he painted for the chapel at Versailles a 'St Theresa' which caused a scandal by its almost erotic interpretation of the saint's mystical ecstasy. This picture is lost, but we can form an idea of its character from the artist's Diploma piece, the 'Susanna' of 1704, now in the Louvre.[98] This nominally religious painting in fact represents a classical nymph – a devotee of Venus rather than of Diana – in an attitude of provoking coyness, designed for the titillation of the spectator's senses rather than for his edification. Santerre's 'Susanna' foreshadows not only the shepherdesses of Boucher but even more the provocative nudes of Fragonard or Baudouin. Stylistically the 'Susanna' is also interesting in that it marks a revival of Mannerism, which was to be a phenomenon connected with the Rococo in several ways. In this case the return is to Primaticcio, from whom Santerre has taken the delicate, elongated forms of his nude, and the studied affectation of the pose.

Like religious and mythological painting, portraiture enjoyed a considerable success during the last years of the century. During the glorious decades of 1660–80 few painters had devoted themselves exclusively to this genre, which was considered of secondary importance. The great personages of the time liked if possible to be shown in action, for instance as the victorious general, or at least surrounded by appropriate and allegorical embellishments. The straightforward naturalistic portrait, in which Champaigne excelled, had almost disappeared, except in the hands of Mignard, and even his portraits, though not always allegorical, have usually an element of flattery which takes them out of the category of naturalism.

But after about 1685 several important artists appear who specialized in portraiture and who created a new fashion in this field. The essential novelty of their style is the introduction of the technique and patterns of the Flemish school, particularly of van Dyck. We have already had occasion to notice that Philippe de Champaigne learnt from Rubens and van Dyck; but he radically transformed what he borrowed, stamping it with the mark of his own austere and classical personality. The generation of the end of the century tried, on the contrary, to imitate the very qualities in van Dyck which Champaigne avoided, the Baroque sweep of the draperies and his mixture of impressiveness and intimacy.

The oldest but the least talented of the portrait-painters whom we have to consider was François de Troy (1645–1730), father of the more celebrated Jean François.[99] Some of his portraits, such as that of the Lute-player Charles Mouton of 1690 in the Louvre,[100] suggest an awareness of Italian seventeenth-century portraiture, but his more typical portraits of women show him as an imitator of the free movement and the loosely painted drapery of the Flemish tradition (Plate 190B).[101]

François de Troy was, however, soon outshone by the two more brilliant portrait painters of the same generation, Nicolas de Largillierre (1656–1746)[102] and Hyacinthe Rigaud (1659–1743). Many of the works by these two artists belong in spirit and in date to the eighteenth century, but both made important contributions to the development of French painting well before 1700, and they must be considered as helping to create the transition from one century to the other. Both contributed to the elimination of the style of the Grand Siècle, both belonged to the party of Colour; but in certain other respects they are sharply opposed: in their *clientèle*, their naturalism, and in their relation to the painting of the Netherlands.

Largillierre's early life and training were exceptional.[103] He was born in Paris, but his parents moved to Antwerp when he was a child. At an early age he entered the studio of Antoine Goubaud, a painter of still-life and peasant scenes, and in 1672 was received Master in the guild of Antwerp. Soon afterwards he moved to London,[104] where he was encouraged by Lely, for whom he probably worked from about 1674 to 1680. His particular job was the painting of drapery and of still-life accessories, and no doubt many of the elaborate vases of flowers in the backgrounds of Lely's late portraits are from his hand.[105] In 1682 Largillierre settled in Paris, where he remained for the rest of his life, except for a short visit to England in 1685 to paint the portraits of James II and Mary of Modena. Either on this occasion or before his return to France in 1682 he also painted two portraits of members of the Warner family. All these portraits are lost but are known from engravings,[106] which prove that Largillierre had absorbed the style of Lely in his last years, and was not entirely unaffected by other artists working in England, such as Soest, Wissing, and the early Kneller.

That is to say, Largillierre started his career in France with the particular variation of the idiom of the Netherlands which was current in England about 1680, and during the first twenty years after his transfer to Paris we find him adapting it to suit the taste of his country. In some portraits, such as those of three members of the Lambert family,[107] he applies the English convention directly, but in most cases he combines elements from it with other devices. For instance, in the portrait of a tutor and his pupil (Plate 188),[108] dated 1685, the angular draperies of the pupil and the schematic drawing of his face belong to the English convention, whereas the head of the tutor is in a quite different vein of naturalism, suggesting rather a knowledge of Dutch painting. The pattern itself, with the two figures cut off at three-quarter-length, is a formula derived from van Dyck and much favoured by his English followers. But the affectation of the boy's pose and the unexpected placing of the dog in the foreground, facing into the composition, distinguish the painting from English models.

In 1684 Largillierre was received into the Academy, and in 1686 he submitted as his Diploma work the portrait of Lebrun, now in the Louvre (Plate 190A). In this work he applies his Flemish methods to producing what is one of the most typical portraits of the Grand Siècle. He creates a new genre, the state-portrait of an artist. Up till this time artists had usually painted themselves without any particular setting or apparatus. Some Flemish and Dutch painters are shown at work in their studio, surrounded by the actual furnishings of the place. Poussin had created a unique classical model with a background of mainly blank canvases, a sort of abstraction of a studio. Largillierre depicts Lebrun surrounded not by the actual appurtenances of a studio, but by objects symbolical of his achievement – the classical casts on which he based his style, the sketches for or engravings after his most celebrated works – just as in a royal portrait the King is shown with the attributes of the Monarchy. This is indeed the true portrait of the dictator-artist, appropriate to the régime of Colbert; but it is paradoxical that the spirit of the time should have been so richly presented by an artist who, as much as anyone, was to help to replace it by a freer and more individual type of painting.

By the end of the 1680s Largillierre had established a considerable reputation among the richer *bourgeois* of Paris from whom he had received regular orders for portraits; but in 1687 he received a new type of commission, for one of the portrait-groups which the City of Paris caused to be executed to commemorate certain solemn occasions. In this case the theme was the banquet given by the Échevins to the King when he made his first formal visit to the Hôtel de Ville, as a gesture of forgiveness to the city for their part in the Fronde. The painting was destroyed at the Revolution, but is known from several sketches.[109] Largillierre shows the Échevins seated in front of a table deliberating on the statue of the King to be erected at the Hôtel de Ville to celebrate their pardon. In the middle of the table is a bust of Louis, and on the wall behind hangs a vast canvas of the banquet itself. The whole is a Baroque version of the Dutch corporation group, with the naturalism and psychological insight of the latter abandoned in favour of freedom in gesture and movement and dramatic effect in grouping.

Nine years later, in 1696, Largillierre executed a second commission of the same kind of which the finished picture happily survives (Plate 189). It was ordered by the city for the church of Ste Geneviève to commemorate the intervention of the patron saint to end a drought in 1694. In this composition the artist has combined northern and southern methods. In the poses and draperies of the lower figures Largillierre follows the portrait convention with which he had already scored such success; but in its general conception the composition is an adaptation of a much-used formula for Baroque altarpieces in which saints are replaced by the Échevins and the Virgin by Ste Geneviève. In this painting portraiture is blended with religious art, in a whole which is one of the most completely Baroque works of the period. Largillierre achieves what Antoine Coypel attempts with such moderate success in the chapel ceiling, and here the heavenly world bursts wonderfully and effectively into the real world, streaming down on the Échevins who might well be kneeling in the setting of Mansart's chapel. In this painting Largillierre looks not only back to Baroccio but forward to Tiepolo.[110]

The contrast between this composition and Philippe de Champaigne's Échevin group of 1648 (Plate 117A) gives the measure of the change in spirit between the two periods. The earlier group is still archaic both in its pattern and in its severe draperies, and it expresses the traditional dignity of the city fathers; in the later version we feel the ostentation of a *bourgeoisie* no longer independent in its power or its thought but tied to the Court and aping its manners. To such patrons the brilliant Baroque rhetoric and the rich Flemish colouring of Largillierre's composition would appeal instantly.[111]

Rigaud scored his success in a different field and by different means.[112] He was born in Perpignan in 1659 and his artistic training was begun in the south. In 1674 he went to Montpellier, where he studied under the little-known artists, Paul Pezet and Antoine Ranc, and later moved to Lyons with Henri Verdier, a fellow-pupil in the studio of Ranc. We can form little idea of the style which he would have learnt in this way, but we may suppose that it was rather more Baroque than the official manner practised in Paris at the same time.

In 1681 he reached the capital, and for a few years seems to have devoted himself to painting portraits of other artists and members of the *bourgeoisie* in a manner close to that of François de Troy.[113] But a new field was opened for him by receiving in 1688 a commission to paint the portrait of Monsieur, the King's brother, and in the next year another for that of his son, the Duc de Chartres.[114]

From this time onwards Rigaud dropped his Parisian clients and became almost exclusively a court painter. His sitters in the 1690s and the first year or two of the eighteenth century included most members of the royal family, the great generals (Luxembourg, Villeroy, Vauban), visiting Princes (the Crown Prince of Denmark, the Count Palatine Christian of Zweibrücken), diplomats (Lord Portland, his son, and Matthew Prior), and more or less everyone of distinction at Versailles.

For this *clientèle* Rigaud naturally evolved a formula different from that invented by Largillierre for his aldermen and financiers. His patterns are usually based on van Dyck, but he combines with this manner certain features taken from the French tradition, and he gives to the resultant mixture a clearly aristocratic elegance which contrasts with the rather *bourgeois* bombast of Largillierre.

Perhaps his most typical works are his military portraits (cf. plate 191A). For these his regular formula is to present the figure in modern armour in three-quarter or full-length, against a landscape background which usually shows a battle in progress.[115] This is quite different from the convention of the previous generation, when generals preferred to be shown in the dress and action of a Roman Imperator. Rigaud's portraits depend on van Dyck, but in the introduction of the battle scene in the background he is following a tradition already familiar in France, for instance in the portraits of Philippe de Champaigne.[116] Stylistically, too, he combines features from these two sources; for though in the brilliance of the armour painting and the richness of the floating draperies we are made to think of van Dyck, there is in the poses and gestures a certain stiffness which is foreign to him and more akin to the archaism of Champaigne.[117]

The same fusion is to be seen in Rigaud's state portraits, of which the best known is that of Louis XIV painted in 1701 (Plate 191B), the most Baroque representation of a King of France up to this time. The general conception follows the Baroque convention with column and draperies as a background; the figure has a fully Baroque swagger and contraposto; and the ermine cloak, thrown nonchalantly back, cuts through the space in a complexity of Baroque curves. But there are qualifications to this abandon. The pose, as has been pointed out,[118] has affinities with van Dyck's 'Charles I Hunting' in the Louvre; but it is at least as like Champaigne's 'Louis XIII in Armour'. Though the cloak swirls about, it does so in folds which are modelled with a linear sharpness again nearer to Champaigne than to van Dyck. The colour is strong and owes much to the lessons of the Flemings, but it is applied with a coldness of touch which would have pleased the followers of Lebrun. In short, Rigaud has produced a Baroque version of the French state portrait, combining the severity of the old tradition with something of the liveliness of the new, and adding, incidentally, a point of elegance and affectation – notice the ballet pose of the feet – which is specifically French and reminds us that we are on the threshold of the eighteenth century.[119]

There is, however, in the art of Rigaud as it was developed by the end of the seventeenth century the same kind of division which we noticed in the sculpture of Coysevox. For parallel with the series of Baroque portraits the artist also produced others of a much more intimate and naturalistic type. This other style appears to some degree in his family groups, such as that of the printer, Pierre Frédéric Léonard, with his wife and daughter,[120] in which, although the draperies are still Baroque, the figures are painted with a much closer observation of character than is usual in Rigaud's formal portraits. But the new tendency is most clearly apparent in the famous double portrait of his mother, painted in 1695 for the marble bust which the artist commissioned from Coysevox (Plate 192A). In this strikingly observed portrait there are echoes of van Dyck and Champaigne, if only in the placing of the two heads on a single canvas; but the real source is a different and a new one. The whole conception of the portrait, the attention with which the wrinkles of the skin are painted, the meticulous handling of the cap, and the dry painting of the white bodice, all combine to prove that Rigaud was here taking as his model Rembrandt's early portraits of his mother. We know that he admired Rembrandt, since the inventory of his pictures, taken at the time of his wedding in 1703, includes seven paintings by the master and two copies by Rigaud after him.[121] In the eighteenth century the art of Rembrandt was to have a wide success in France, but Rigaud was the first French artist since Vignon to study his works, and the first without exception to find in him an inspiration towards naturalism and psychological subtlety. It is typical of the contradictions of the period that the same artist should have produced on the one hand some of the most Baroque formal full-lengths and, on the other, the first in a long line of intimate portraits which was to be carried on throughout the eighteenth and even into the nineteenth century.

The naturalism which was latent in so many branches of art in the last decades of the seventeenth century attained its most striking and revolutionary manifestation in the field of landscape. It did not, however, have a monopoly here any more than in the other genres of painting, and the ideal landscape of Claude was continued by painters such as Étienne Allegrain (1644–1736) and the younger Pierre Patel (1648–1707), who added to it a new type of artificiality almost eighteenth century in character.

But one artist, François Desportes (1661–1740), breaks entirely new ground. Desportes was the son of a peasant and was born in Champagne. At the age of twelve he was sent by his father to Paris and entered the studio of Nicasius Bernaerts (1620–78), a Fleming and a pupil of Snyders who enjoyed considerable success as a painter of animals. After the death of his master Desportes studied at the Academy and for a time seemed to be settling down to a career as a portrait painter, in which capacity he spent the years 1695–6 at the Court of Poland. On his return to Paris he began to devote his attention to the painting of animals, in the form either of hunting scenes or of still-life composition with dead game. It was for these works that he was celebrated in his own day, and they were bought by all the most important patrons of the day, headed by Louis XIV, who commissioned hunting-scenes, portraits of his favourite dogs, and pictures of rare animals for Marly and the Ménagerie at Versailles.

But as a preparation for the landscape backgrounds of his hunting scenes Desportes made a series of studies (Plate 192B) in oil on paper, which reveal an entirely novel approach to nature. They are direct notes of views which he saw in the neighbourhood of Paris and in the Seine valley, put down with sensitiveness and humility, with no desire to improve the actual scene so as to make it fit in with a preconceived idea either of what nature should be or how a composition should be constructed. In some cases the designs are simple, in others they have unexpected features, such as the intrusion of a reed or a tree-trunk into the very foreground, which almost recall the conscious snapshot effects of the Impressionists. In colour they are subdued, painted in the quiet light of the Île-de-France, which no one else rendered so faithfully till the time of Corot.[122]

Desportes' nephew gives the following account of his uncle's method, startling in the late seventeenth century when artists never thought of actually painting in the open air in front of the scene itself:[123] 'He used to take out into the country his brushes and his palette ready loaded with colours, in zinc boxes; he had a walking-stick with a long steel point, which held it firm when stuck in the ground, and on the handle, which opened, there hinged with a screw a little easel of the same metal, to which he fixed the drawing-board and paper. He never visited his friends in the country without carrying this little bundle; with it he was never bored and he never failed to make good use of it.'

Desportes lived till 1743, and many of his works belong to the eighteenth century in character, but the habit of making these landscape sketches seems to go back to before 1700.[124] In spirit, on the other hand, it looks even further forward, to the methods of the English water-colourists and of the Barbizon school.

POSTSCRIPT

The Transition to the Eighteenth Century

It would be foolish to try in a concluding section to look back over the whole period dealt with in this book and to summarize the already too short and simplified account which has been given of the movements in French art through two hundred years. But it may be worth while to add a word about the transition to the next century.

In the preceding chapters attention has been drawn to various tendencies in artists who were already mature before 1700 which lead on to the Rococo. But about the turn of the century a younger generation sprang up which prepared the way for the next stage even more clearly. In the year 1699 the Academy revived the habit of holding exhibitions of works by its members, which had lapsed since 1683. Five years later, in 1704, the experiment was repeated, and from the catalogues of these two Salons we can learn much about the new atmosphere in painting. The Salon of 1699 contained works in the traditional academic manner, others by the representatives of the Baroque movement, and yet others in the lighter mythological style of the Boullongnes. But in 1704 a new tone appears. For the first time the exhibition included playful genre-paintings in the style of the small Dutch masters. This tendency was in a sense an extension of the naturalism which we have seen latent in several artists of the older generation; but it catered for a new *bourgeois* taste for small and intimate works, suitable for the informal rooms of the early eighteenth century rather than for the great galleries of the seventeenth.

At the same time, but outside the Academy, Claude Gillot (1673–1722) was evolving a more fantastic style, and in his scenes from the Italian Comedy was reviving the spirit of Callot, which had been dormant for several generations.

From these ingredients the new style was to be born. The colour of Rubens, the light-heartedness of La Fosse, the naturalistic observation of the followers of the Dutch school, the fancy of Gillot – these were the elements from which the early Rococo was to be made up. It needed only the genius of Watteau to bring them all together into a new synthesis; or rather it needed the genius of Watteau and the care and support of his sensitive Parisian friends, Julienne and Crozat. For it must never be forgotten that Watteau was essentially a product of Parisian society, which in him, as fully as in Voltaire, asserted once again its independence of the Court of Versailles and its determination to follow its own way.

NOTES

CHAPTER I

p. 2   1. We do, however, know that in 1498 the Maréchal de Gié asked the Signoria of Florence for seven Roman busts which had belonged to Lorenzo de' Medici. Gié's taste must have been in advance of that of his compatriots, for a little later he also begged for a copy of Donatello's bronze David. Instead Michelangelo was commissioned to make a work of the same subject to his own design; but owing to the disgrace of the Marshal, the Signoria eventually sent the statue to his successor in the favour of Louis XII, Florimond Robertet, who built the château of Bury, where the statue stood for many years. See J. Wilde, 'The Hall of the Great Council of Florence', *Journal of the Warburg and Courtauld Institutes*, VII (1944), 76.

p. 3   2. His followers continued the tradition of using such detail and transmitted it to miniaturists like Bourdichon (see p. 18), who incorporated it in a wider scheme of Italianization.

3. He was also responsible for the altar now in St Didier, Avignon.

p. 4   4. All these examples are illustrated in Henry Martin, André Blum, &c., *Le Livre Français des origines à la fin du second Empire* (Paris, 1923).

5. Cf. p. 14.

p. 5   6. Reproduced in Hautecœur, *Architecture*, I, 95. The frame of the Sepulchre bears the date 1496, but as Pradel (*Michel Colombe*, 32) points out, the arms indicate that the monument must have been begun before 1495.

p. 6   7. Cf. P. Vitry, *Michel Colombe*, 276.

8. P. Vitry (*Michel Colombe*, 191) reproduces two fragments of terra-cotta pilasters which may be part of Charles's decoration.

9. Except for certain details in the cornice and dormers.

10. Cf. E. Mâle, *La Cathédrale d'Albi* (Paris, 1950), 37 and plates 54 ff.

11. Cf. M. Dumolin, *Le Château d'Oiron* (Paris, 1931), 12.

12. P de Cossé Brissac, *Châteaux de France disparus*, 28 ff. Fragments of the sculptured decoration survive in the museum of Poitiers (cf. P. Vitry and G. Brière, *Documents de Sculpture Française*, plates 30 and 31).

13. Screens similar in form are to be found in S. Petronio, Bologna. The fantastic and endlessly varied columns recall the Cappella Colleoni at Bergamo, and the open-work panels above derive directly from the sacristy of S. Maria presso S. Satiro at Milan by Bramante and ultimately from Donatello's panels in the Old Sacristy of San Lorenzo. This is one of the few imitations of Bramante's work to be found in France.

14. For a full account of the tomb and the chapel in which it stands see G. Durand, 'Les Lannoy, Folleville et l'art italien dans le nord de la France', *Bulletin Monumental*, 70 (1906), 329.

15. Reproduced in Hautecœur, *Architecture*, I, 89.   p. 7

16. The apse of St Pierre was widely imitated, for instance at St Sauveur at Caen (1546). Hautecœur (*Architecture*, I, 160) gives a full list of such imitations.   The type of pendentive used in the ambulatory is to be found in many churches in Normandy, e.g. Le Grand Andely, Verneuil-sur-Avre, Tillières-sur-Avre.

17. E. Chirol in the most recent work on Gaillon (*Le Château de Gaillon* (Rouen and Paris, 1952), 60) relates this contract to another fountain for the gardens, but the style of the fountain here illustrated points conclusively to Gaggini as its author. A similar fountain was set up in the château of Oiron (now in the church of the same village) by a member of the Gouffier family, probably Artus, nephew of Cardinal Amboise (cf. M. Dumolin, *Le Château d'Oiron* (Paris, 1931), 68). Montaiglon (*Gazette des Beaux-Arts*, I, 1876, 560) attributes it to the Giusti, but it probably dates from a period before the connexion of their family with Oiron.

18. For a full account of Pacherot see P. Lesueur, 'Remarques sur Jérôme Pacherot, et sur le Château de Gaillon', *Bulletin de la Société de l'Histoire de l'Art français* (1937), 67.

19. A portrait of the Cardinal's brother, Charles,   p. 8 in the Louvre, is traditionally attributed to Solario, though the attribution has been challenged.

20. Reproduced in G. Huard, *L'Art en Normandie* (Paris, 1928), figure 251. The interior of Gaillon is described in the earliest account of the château, written in 1510 by Jacopo Probo d'Atri (cf. R.

Weiss, 'The Castle of Gaillon in 1509–10', *Journal of the Warburg and Courtauld Institutes*, XVI, 1953, 1, 351).

p. 8 21. The earliest traceable example of the use of Italian ornament in Paris is in the Hôtel de la Trémouille, which formerly stood in the rue des Bourdonnais and of which the entrance door is now set up in the court of the École des Beaux-Arts (rep. in C. Martin and C. Enlart, *La Renaissance en France*, first series, II (Paris, 1911), plate lxxxv). The exact date of the door is not known, but it seems to belong to the same phase as Gaillon. The sculptors responsible for it were no doubt brought back by Louis de la Trémouille, the general of Louis XII and Francis I, who was active in all the Italian campaigns and was killed at Pavia.

p. 9 22. The best account of Blois is in F. and P. Lesueur, *Le Château de Blois* (Paris, 1914), 21.

p. 10 23. Cf. p. 123.

24. A more regular version of the repeated *loggie* motive occurs in the court of the château of La Rochefoucauld, probably built between 1525 and 1533 (cf. Gébelin, *Les Châteaux de la Renaissance*, 125).

p. 11 25. Letter of 3 Sept. 1663; cf. *Œuvres de J. de La Fontaine*, IX (Paris, 1892), 244.

26. L. H. Heydenreich (*Leonardo*, Berlin, 1943, 159, and 'Leonardo da Vinci, Architect of Francis I', *Burl. Mag.*, XCIV, 1952, 277), following Reymond ('Léonard de Vinci architecte du Château de Chambord', *Gazette des Beaux-Arts*, I, 1923, 337), maintains that Leonardo was responsible for the conception of Chambord, but the arguments in favour of this view are not quite conclusive. On the other hand, it is certain that Leonardo designed the château which Francis I intended to build for his mother at Romorantin, for which drawings survive. *See* Heydenreich, *loc. cit.*, and the article by C. Baroni, *Leonardo als Architekt*, in the commemorative catalogue of the Leonardo exhibition in Milan, 1939 (German edition, 239 ff.). Baroni also reproduces drawings for a double spiral staircase which may be connected with Chambord.

p. 12 27. The nearest parallel is Vincennes.

28. Félibien's drawings are reproduced and the whole problem of Chambord fully discussed in P. Lesueur, *Dominique de Cortone dit Le Boccador*, chapter 4. Domenico seems to have been active for the greater part of his career in France as a woodcarver rather than as an architect, and the only other building which he is known to have designed is the Hôtel de Ville in Paris (1532), but here again his plans were altered in the course of execution.

29. Reproduced in H. Willich and P. Zucker, *Die Baukunst der Renaissance in Italien* (Potsdam, n.d.), 190.

30. A close imitation of the Orleans town-hall p. was erected more than two decades later (1525) at Beaugency.

31. Illustrated in Martin and Enlart, *La Renaissance en France*, II, plates 47–57.

32. Almost all the towns of France which were of importance in the early sixteenth century have houses of this kind, notably Orleans, Rouen, Tours, Amboise, Toulouse, and Bourges; but the two mentioned here may be taken as typical. A curious offshoot of French architecture at this time can be traced in the circular chapel built on the site of S. Luigi dei Francesi between 1518 and 1525, of which carved fragments are incorporated in the later church. The architect is named by Vasari as a Frenchman called Jean, not otherwise identifiable. The fullest information about the chapel is given in C. Ricci, 'Il Tempietto di San Luigi de' Francesi', *Rivista dell' Instituto Nazionale d' Archaeologia e Storia dell' Arte*, N.S., 1, 1952, 317. There seems, however, little justification for the reconstruction shown on p. 325, which shows a Bramantesque structure which no French architect of the time was, as far as we know, capable of conceiving. The building is likely to have been much nearer to late French Gothic architecture in character.

33. For instance, the sculpture at Solesmes and the p. work deriving from it (cf. P. Vitry, *Michel Colombe*, chapter 8. For eastern France, cf. H. David, *De Sluter à Sambin, La Renaissance*).

34. An important example is the tomb of Charles IV of Anjou (d. 1473) in Le Mans Cathedral. It has been attributed to Francesco Laurana because the dead man was the brother of King René, for whom this artist worked, but on stylistic grounds it is far more likely to be a product of the studio of Antonio Rossellino.

35. One of the artists who collaborated in this tomb, Girolamo Viscardi, also received the commission for the marble sarcophagus and figures in the abbey church at Fécamp (cf. p. 6).

36. Cf. A. Venturi, *Storia*, VI, 768 ff., and A. Pettorelli, *Guido Mazzoni da Modena* (Turin, 1925).

37. Reproduced in P. Vitry, *Michel Colombe*, 183.

38. Reproduced in P. Vitry, *op. cit.*, 169.

39. For instance San Zaccaria, Venice (cf. Venturi, *Storia*, VI, figure 306).

40. Cf. Montaiglon, 'La famille des Juste en p. France', *Gazette des Beaux-Arts* (1875), 2nd period, XII, 401.

41. Erected 1493–7 by Giovanni Cristoforo

Romano. The sarcophagus was only inserted in the sixteenth century. Another possible Milanese source may be found in the designs of Agostino Busti (Il Bambaja) for tombs, including that of Gaston de Foix which would certainly have been known in France.

16   42. Pradel (*Michel Colombe*, 85 ff.) believes the *gisants* to be definitely French and attributes them as well as the kneeling figures to the atelier of Guillaume Regnault. He tentatively revives the theory that the conception of the whole monument may be due to Perréal. Its likeness to the Visconti tomb in Milan to some extent confirms this, since Perréal must have seen the latter on his visits to Italy.

43. Other examples are the two statues of saints by Girolamo Viscardi at Fécamp, which also betray the influence of Andrea Sansovino.

44. Of the plans of Perréal and Colombe for the tombs of Brou we know virtually nothing, for there is every reason to think that no part of them was incorporated in the scheme as finally executed by the Flemish sculptors called in by Margaret of Savoy after she had dismissed the French artists. Colombe was responsible for one further tomb now destroyed but known from a drawing (cf. Pradel, *op. cit.*, plate XIV, 1). It was erected between 1510 and 1517 for Guillaume Guegen, bishop of Nantes. Its decorative elements are once again fully Italianate, but the *gisant* seems to be still in the style of the Loire School.

17   45. Several of these reliefs are reproduced in the *Burl. Mag.*, XVIII (1911), 325 ff. The Gaggini family were closely connected with France, and one member of it at least, Pace, came to the country. It is therefore quite possible that Colombe would have known one of the Genoese prototypes. One of them, indeed, existed on the fountain at Gaillon, sent from Genoa in 1508.

46. It seems to combine features of different Florentine models: Desiderio's Marsuppini tomb, Verrocchio's sarcophagus for Giovanni and Piero de' Medici in S Lorenzo, and Antonio Pollaiuolo's bronze tomb of Sixtus IV.

47. Cf. L. Le Gendre, *Vie du Cardinal d'Amboise*, II (Paris, 1724), 240.

48. Laignel is also known as an independent artist. He executed the tomb of Cardinal Hémard de Denonville (1543) in Amiens Cathedral (reproduced in G. Durand, *Monographie de l'église Notre-Dame Cathédrale d'Amiens*, II (Amiens, 1901–3), plate xcii) and almost certainly that of François de Lannoy (before 1545) at Folleville (reproduced in G. Durand, 'Les Lannoy, Folleville et l'art italien dans le nord de la France', *Bulletin Monumental*, 70, 1906,

plate opposite 400). Both tombs have features in common with the Amboise monument, but are more strictly Italianate, particularly in their decoration.

49. An altarpiece of the life of St Jerome, dated   p. 18
1518, in the museum at Brou, for instance (reproduced in J. G. Lemoine, *Bourg et l'église de Brou* (Paris, 1948), 60–2), and one at Autun, dated 1515, representing the Last Supper in the middle panel and on the wings the Manna, and Abraham and Melchizedek (reproduced in L. Réau, *Les Richesses d'Art: La Bourgogne, La Peinture* (Paris, 1929), 22–4), may be genuine French products; but our present knowledge is too incomplete for any definite statement.

50. See G. Ring, *A Century of French Painting, 1400–1500*, plate 155 and page 241, No. 319.

51. E.g. the altarpiece from S. Domenico, Fiesole,   p. 19
now in the Uffizi, and the single figure in the Louvre. In the Brunswick *Hours of Henry VIII*, also attributed to Bourdichon, a more complicated borrowing from Perugino occurs. The artist has used for his version of the Pietà the lower figures in Perugino's painting of the subject in the Accademia, Florence (reproduced in W. Bombe, *Perugino* (1914), 26), and has copied the head of the Blessed Giovanni Colombini from the same painting for his St Sebastian in another miniature of the same book. It is interesting to notice that Perugino is placed among the great living Italian artists by Jean Lemaire de Belges in his poem, *La Plainte du Désiré*, 1509 (cf. E. Moreau-Nélaton, *Les Clouet et leurs émules*, I, 48).

52. In Pavia he could have seen one work of Perugino, the altarpiece of which three panels are now in the National Gallery, executed in 1498.

53. Some borrowings suggest that he visited Tuscany and Bologna. For instance, the miniature of Peter Martyr in the *Hours of Anne of Brittany* recalls a painting by Francia of c. 1490, now in the Borghese Gallery (reproduced in A. Venturi, *North Italian Painting of the Quattrocento, Emilia* (Paris, 1931), plate 62), and the St Francis in the *Hours of Henry VIII* is based on Benedetto da Maiano's relief on the pulpit of S. Croce (reproduced in L. Dussler, *Benedetto da Majano* (Munich, 1925), figure 12). The 'St Mark' in the *Hours of Anne of Brittany* is related to the seated figure in Jacopo della Quercia's tomb of Galeazzo Bentivoglio in Bologna (reproduced in I. B. Supino, *Iacopo della Quercia* (Bologna, 1926), plate 62), but it is more likely to derive from a southern source. Similar arrangements occur in works in Sicily (e.g. the arch in S. Francesco, Palermo) by Francesco Laurana, who spent some years in France, and by Antonio Gaggini (cf. a

similar arch in S. Zita, Palermo), who was related, though possibly not very closely, to the Gaggini family of Genoa, who worked for Cardinal Amboise.

p. 19 54. Mlle Huillet d'Istria has tried to prove that Perréal executed the frescoes in the cathedral library of Le Puy (*Gazette des Beaux-Arts*, I, 1949, 313 ff.), but her arguments are not convincing.

55. Reproduced in G. F. Hill, *Medals of the Renaissance* (Oxford, 1920), plate xxv, 2, and G. Ring, *op. cit.*, 189.

56. Cf. J. Dupont, 'A Portrait of Louis XII attributed to Jean Perréal', *Burl. Mag.*, LXXXIX (1947), 235.

57. Perréal is mentioned in Leonardo's notes as having given him certain technical hints (cf. Dupont, *loc. cit.*). For the latest view of the problems connected with Perréal, see G. Ring, *op. cit.*, 242, No. 331; G. Ring, 'An Attempt to Reconstruct Perréal', *Burl. Mag.*, XCII (1950), 255; and Mlle Huillet d'Istria, 'Au sujet d'articles récents sur Jean Perréal', *Gazette des Beaux-Arts*, II, 1952, 57.

58. This statue was set up in the Cour de la Fontaine at Fontainebleau and can be seen there in seventeenth-century engravings. p. .

59. For Michelangelo's relation with France see L. Dorez, 'Nouvelles Recherches sur Michel-Ange et son entourage', *Bibliothèque de l'École des Chartes*, LXXVIII (1917), 193 ff.

CHAPTER 2

23 1. Villers-Cotteret is not really an example of the
new style, but is rather a final flowering of the manner current in the previous period. The decoration
in the chapel and on the vault of the staircase is remarkable and inventive, but belongs in feeling
rather to the period of Chambord than to the year
1539 from which it appears to date (illustrated in
F. Gébelin, *op. cit.*, figures 118, 126 ff.).

2. The roof of La Muette was to have been flat,
but the design was altered by Philibert de l'Orme.

24 3. For instance in furniture or stone capitals.

4. *Les plus excellents Bastiments de France*, I, and II
respectively.

5. Illustrated in Gébelin, *op. cit.*, plate lxiii.

26 6. For a complete history of Fontainebleau see
F. Herbet, *Le château de Fontainebleau* (Paris, 1937).

27 7. A good specimen is Fleury-en-Bière not far
from Fontainebleau, illustrated in E. de Ganay and
E. Pilon, *Châteaux et Manoirs de France, Île-de-
France*, I, plates 41 ff. Hautecœur (*Architecture*, I,
326) appears to accept the quite untenable attribution of this building to Lescot. Soulange-Bodin's
suggestion of Gilles Le Breton (quoted by Hautecœur) is far more plausible.

8. This staircase has had a singularly unhappy
history. Before 1579 the outside steps were removed and new flights arranged within the building. Henry IV caused the surviving parts to be
taken down and reconstructed in alignment with
the wing to its left, and at the end of the nineteenth
century it was declared dangerous and completely
reconstructed in new materials.

9. It has even been attributed to Serlio, but the
now established date of 1531 for the staircase rules
him out, as he did not arrive in France till 1540 at
the earliest. It is, however, interesting to notice that
one of the staircases in his Treatise (ed. Venice,
1600, Book II, 42) is in its general form taken from
Le Breton's design.

10. For Montargis cf. the engravings of du Cerceau in the *Plus excellents Bastiments*, I.

11. The Italian examples which offer the closest
parallels are actually all later, e.g. Michelangelo's
staircases outside the Belvedere Niche and the
Palazzo dei Senatori, and Vignola's at Caprarola.
Falconetti's in the villa at Luvigliano is contemporary (between 1529 and 1534), but it is very unlikely
that Le Breton would have known it.

12. The arches of the *loggie* facing the courts at p. 28
Villandry and Valençay have the form used by Le
Breton in the Porte Dorée and elsewhere at Fon-
tainebleau.

13. One group of houses at Orleans presents a
curious problem, to be seen at its clearest in the
Hôtel Toutin, sometimes called the Maison de
François I, built 1538–40 (cf. *Archives de la Commission des Monuments Historiques*, IV (Paris, 1855–72),
17, also described and illustrated in *Congrès Archéo-
logique*, 1930, 159 ff.). The house consists of two
corps-de-logis linked by a double *loggia* running along
the side of the court. In its arrangement and in its
forms this *loggia* is more Italianate than anything
else to be found in France at this date. Other details
of the building, such as the windows and door on
the front *corps-de-logis*, narrow down the source to
Venice or the surrounding territory. On the other
hand, the detail is in many respects too free to be by
an Italian architect (cf. for instance the irregular
Doric entablature). It seems likely, therefore, that
the building is by a French architect acquainted with
the palaces of Venice and its neighbourhood.

14. It is possible that when complete the abbey p. 29
church of Valmont, near Fécamp (before 1540),
may have had something of the character of St
Eustache, though it is broader in its proportions
(illustrated in G. Huard, *L'Art en Normandie* (Paris,
1928), figure 74).

15. The façade of Annecy is reproduced by Hautecœur, *Architecture*, I, 106, and S. Pietro, Modena, on
which it seems to be based, in A. Venturi, *Storia*,
VIII, I, figure 397.

16. Illustrated in G. Duhem, *Les Églises de France,
Morbihan* (Paris, 1932), plate opposite 208.

17. The sculptor Giovanni Francesco Rustici spent p. 30
the years *c.* 1528–1554 in France, but no trace survives of his work or influence there.

18. Some critics believe that this room is later, but p. 31
I cannot agree with their arguments.

19. Vasari's statement is probably reliable because
he was at one period in correspondence with the
artist and probably met him in Rome. The evidence
of the payments made to the two artists in no way
contradicts his assertion, and in fact the earliest records are for schemes which were conducted by
Primaticcio and not Rosso, though this is no certain
guide since the records are incomplete.

R   239

p. 31   20. The only earlier example with the same high relief is one which neither Rosso nor Primaticcio is likely to have known, namely the frieze by Domenico Paris in the Palazzo Schifanoia at Ferrara (illustrated in A. Colosanti, *Volte e Soffitti Italiani*, (Milan, 1923), plate 22).

21. The correct date of Rosso's death has been established by M. Roy, *Artistes et Monuments de la Renaissance Française*, 150.

22. The lower part is a nineteenth-century addition.

p. 32   23. Kusenberg indicates as early examples engravings by Zoan Andrea, Nicoletto da Modena, and Agostino Veneziano, which are reproduced in R. Berliner, *Ornamentale Vorlageblätter*, plates 18, 19, and 23.

24. Examples of it occur in the last plate of Serlio's fourth book of architecture, published in Venice in 1537.

p. 33   25. Hautecœur, *Architecture*, I, 54, lists the earlier examples which have disappeared. It was also copied in Italy (cf. the Galleria della Mostra in the Palazzo Ducale at Mantua).

26. The iconography of the paintings in the Galerie François I has so far defied elucidation. The latest attempt by Sven Lövgren ('Il Rosso Fiorentino à Fontainebleau', *Figura*, I, 1951, 57) has not supplied any solid foundation for an interpretation. The themes include a mixture of mythological, allegorical, and historical subjects, and the relation between them is obscure.

27. He may also have designed the tomb of Alberto Pio, in the Louvre (cf. M. Roy, *op. cit.*, 138 ff.). If we accept Roy's conclusions, which seem convincing, we have in this tomb an explicitly Michelangelesque design of Rosso, deriving from the Medici chapel sculptures (cf. also his design based on the monument of Julius II, Kusenberg, *op. cit.*, plate 75).

28. Reproduced in H. Göbel, *Die Wandteppiche und ihre Manufakturen in Frankreich, Italien, Spanien und Portugal*, II, plates 21 ff.

A chapter on the decoration of this period cannot end without reference to an artist who though he worked in a minor field reached the highest degree of skill in it, Geoffroy Tory (*c.* 1480–1533), to whom must go the credit of printing some of the finest illustrated books of the Renaissance. He was a keen humanist and a friend of Robert Étienne; he made more than one journey to Italy and studied Roman antiquities with a care which was new in a Frenchman. It is therefore not surprising that in this humanist atmosphere he should have produced designs which are closer in feeling to Italian High Renaissance work than almost anything else produced in France in the sixteenth century. His reform dealt with typography as well as with the decoration of the page, and he was one of those responsible for the introduction of a good Roman type into France. He was a true humanist turning to Greece as his ultimate inspiration and believing that proportion should be based on the human figure, as can be seen from the title of his treatise printed in 1529: *Le Champfleury, auquel est contenu l'art et la science de la deue et vraye proportion des lettres attiques qu'on dit autrement antiques et vulgairement lettres romaines proportionées selon le corps et visage humain*. For an account of Tory's work, cf. Lieure, *La Gravure dans le livre et l'ornement* (Paris, 1927).

29. The main arguments are summed up in Dimier, *La Peinture de Portrait*, and E. Moreau-Nélaton, *Les Clouet et leurs émules*.

30. Reproduced in Moreau-Nélaton, *op. cit.*, plate p. 10.

31. I have not seen the picture, and cannot therefore judge whether it is a copy or an original, but A. E. Popham (*Burl. Mag.*, XLII, 1923, 129) accepts it. Since this article was written the picture has been cleaned and the false inscription removed.

32. Reproduced in Moreau-Nélaton, *op. cit.*, plate opposite 57.

33. Moreau-Nélaton, *op. cit.*, plate opposite 53.

34. Moreau-Nélaton, *op. cit.*, plates opposite 48, 49. The attribution of these miniatures to Clouet has been even more frequently contested than in the case of most works ascribed to the artist, but the theory that they were by a Godefroy who signed some other miniatures in the manuscript is now generally abandoned.

One famous painting frequently attributed to Clouet must be mentioned, namely the half-length portrait of Francis I in the Louvre (reproduced in Moreau-Nélaton, *op. cit.*, plate opposite 52). This bears little resemblance to Clouet's style and can hardly be by him. It has been suggested that it is by a Flemish artist, but this also seems unlikely, and its affinities seem rather to be with German painting. The nearest parallels are portraits like Holbein's 'Guildford' at Windsor or his 'Morette' at Dresden. It may possibly, therefore, be by a South German or Swiss artist influenced by Italian painting.

35. If this is the case, then logically the argument for attributing any of these works, paintings or drawings, except the painting of Budé, falls to the

ground, since the drawing of Budé need not be by the same hand as the painting, and so the essential link with the other works is broken.

36. The only reasonably firm points are the following. The miniatures of the *Preux de Marignan* occur in a manuscript written in 1519. The portrait of the Dauphin Francis (born 1517) can be dated a little after 1520 on the age of the sitter. The same argument would place the miniature of Brissac (born 1505) to a date rather before 1530, and the portrait of Budé (born 1467) to the late 1530s. If these dates are approximately correct, they would indicate that Clouet developed from the monumental style apparent in the miniatures, and even more marked in the portrait of the Dauphin (and that of Mme de Canaples, which may date from the end of the 1520s) to a late manner far more Flemish in character, represented by the 'Budé', with which the 'Man with the Petrarch' (Plate 27A) could also be associated. The portrait of Madame Madeleine, daughter of Francis I, in the Edouard de Rothschild collection (published by Dimier, in the *Gazette des Beaux-Arts*, II, 1933, 100), which appears from a photograph to have a good claim to be a work of Jean Clouet, would belong to the early group, since it is datable on age to about 1522–3.

37. Cf. for instance A. E. Popham, *The Drawings* p. 35 *of Leonardo da Vinci* (1946), plates 157, 173.

p. 39   1. For the latest account of his life and details of his printed and manuscript works see W. B. Dinsmoor, 'The Literary Remains of Sebastiano Serlio', *Art Bulletin*, XXIV (1942), 55 ff.

2. In an article to appear in the *Journal of the Warburg and Courtauld Institutes* M. Jean Adhémar will produce evidence to show that Serlio was originally brought to the notice of Francis I by Aretino.

3. This château, of which Serlio gives the designs at the end of Book 7, is called by him *Rosmarino* and said to be designed for a Provençal gentleman whom he met at Lyons. It has, however, never been identified.

p. 40   4. It is known from two manuscripts, one at Columbia University and one in Munich; see Dinsmoor, *op. cit.*, who gives a full account of both manuscripts and reproduces many of the illustrations. In this article the author promises a full publication of the manuscripts. Book 8 exists only in the Munich manuscript.

p. 41   5. See below, note 9. The arcade at Vallery is reproduced in *Châteaux et Manoirs de France, Île-de-France*, I, plate 9.

p. 43   6. In his seventh book Serlio reproduces, very inaccurately, a work of this architect, the Casino of Luigi Corner at Padua, and other designs in the treatise suggest his influence.

7. Serlio's design for Ancy seems to have been little imitated in France. One adaptation of it, however, is to be seen in the château of Petit-Bourg, known from the engraving by Pérelle before its rebuilding in the eighteenth century. The garden front seems to be an almost exact copy of one of the Ancy façades, but Petit-Bourg differs from its model in that it consists of three wings only and not of four completely enclosing a court (Blomfield, *A History of French Architecture, 1661–1774*, II, plate 109, reproduces Pérelle's engraving, but attributes the château as shown there to Lassurance, who rebuilt it in the eighteenth century). Ancy was also sometimes imitated in the Lyons district, for instance in the château of the Villeroy family at Neufville-sur-Saône and that of Tours at Crèches-sur-Saône.

p. 44   8. The doors at the château of Kerjean, most of which are variations on designs by Serlio, are somewhat less provincial.

p. 45   9. Of these works, the Carnavalet, the Fontaine des Innocents, and Vallery are not completely documented as being by Lescot, but the reasons for their attribution to him seem to me sufficient. For Vallery see P. du Colombier 'L'Énigme de Vallery', *Humanisme et Renaissance*, IV (1937), 7. For the Fontaine des Innocents and the Carnavalet, see pp. 47, 69.

10. See L. Hautecœur, 'Le Louvre de Pierre Lescot', *Gazette des Beaux-Arts*, I (1927), 199; L. Batiffol, 'Les premières constructions de Pierre Lescot au Louvre', *op. cit.*, II (1930), 276; and C. Aulanier, 'Le Palais du Louvre au 16e siècle', *B.S.H.A.F.*, (1952), 85.

11. The comparison is with the two lower floors p. only of the Farnese, not with the top one added by Michelangelo.

12. These windows were to become almost standard in France for about two centuries.

13. The extension down to the floor level of the middle window in each side wing is a later alteration.

14. Cf. p. 28.

15. Caryatids occur in Italy in designs for fireplaces, woodwork, &c., but only on a small scale. They are also to be found in painting (cf. Daniele da Volterra's Cappella Orsini in SS. Trinità dei Monti of 1541, destroyed but known from drawings and engravings). In France they are to be found on the tomb of Louis de Brézé in Rouen Cathedral, which is earlier in date and also probably designed by Goujon (*see* plate 52).

16. Delaborde, *Marc-Antoine Raimondi* (Paris, p. 1888), No. 214.

17. This is perhaps the only design of Lescot which seems to go back directly to an Italian model, for both in their grouping and in their proportions the columns closely recall those in Giulio Romano's portico on the garden side of the Palazzo del Tè at Mantua.

18. M. Roy, *op. cit.*, I, 419.

19. M. Roy (*op. cit.*, II, 490 ff.) challenges this traditional attribution, on the grounds that Lescot's name does not appear in the contracts. But in his recent book about Goujon, Pierre du Colombier (76) declares his belief in Lescot's authorship.

20. The engravings in Marot show the original state of this wing, and prove that the dormers were

of the same type as those on the block over the street (certainly built by 1558) and that therefore the two buildings were probably designed at the same time.

21. For instance, in the Hôtel de Sully.

48 22. This contains a typical experiment in structural ingenuity, three *trompes* supporting a gallery.

23. Cf. P. Héliot, *Mémoires de la Société Nationale des Antiquaires de France*, lxxxii (1951). From 1556 to 1559 he built for Diane de Poitiers the bridge of the château of Chenonceau.

24. Cf. M. Roy, *op. cit.*, I, 381.

25. The *Architecture* enjoyed so much success in France that a second edition was issued the next year, and it was again republished in 1648. It was also read outside France and a copy in the British Museum has the autograph of Vincenzo Scamozzi. Lord Burghley ordered a copy from Paris apparently as early as 1568 (Cf. H. A. Tipping, *English Homes*, Period III, II, 315).

49 26. In the later editions the *Nouvelles Inventions* of 1561 are added as Books 10 and 11.

27. Book 1, chapter 6. The same view is repeated in chapter 8 of the same book.

28. Book 1, chapter 8.

29. Book 1, preface and chapters 1–4.

50 30. Book 1, chapter 10.

31. Book 1, chapter 13.

32. Book 1, chapter 2.

33. Chapter 8.

34. Book 1, chapter 8, and Book 5, preface.

35. Book 1, chapter 15. We are reminded of the lines of Joachim du Bellay, nephew of de l'Orme's patron the Cardinal, published in 1558:

Plus me plaist le séjour qu'ont basty mes ayeux,
Que des palais Romains le front audacieux:
Plus que le marbre dur me plaist l'ardoise fine.

36. Book 6, preface. He may have had in mind the work of pedants such as Philander, who was guilty of just this blunder. See p. 56.

51 37. Book 7, chapter 11 ff.

38. Book 11, chapter 11.

39. The plan in book 1, chapter 7, and the elevations of the outside and the court façades in book 8, chapters 14 and 15.

40. Even this was not completed, for the steps were not built and the design was altered after 1563 by the insertion of the gallery shown in du Cerceau's engraving.

41. The original court front can be seen in plate 31, since it was embodied in the second scheme there illustrated. The balcony on short pillars was, however, an addition at the second stage.

42. Built *c.* 1549, the decoration completed in p. 52 1552.

43. See p. 29.

44. Surprisingly, Palladio seems to have imitated this plan in his chapel at Maser, undated but certainly later than Anet. It remains uncertain how he knew it, since it does not appear to have been engraved till 1579, when it appeared in the second volume of the *Plus excellents Bastiments*. But de l'Orme was studied in Palladio's circle (cf. above, note 25).

45. The only other chapel by de l'Orme of which we have any knowledge, built *c.* 1550 in the park of Villers-Cotteret, also played elaborately on the theme of the circle, but here in the form of a trefoil. It was also important for two novelties: the use of de l'Orme's French Order and the addition in front of the main chapel of a free-standing classical portico (illustrated in Hautecœur, *Architecture*, I, 428).

46. On the basis of similarity of style one work p. 53 must be closely connected with the entrance of Anet and even tentatively attributed to de l'Orme. This is the decorative part of the screen in the church of St Étienne-du-Mont, Paris (Plate 33). It has been proved that the main structure of the screen dates from the time of the completion of the choir, i.e., *c.* 1538 (cf. C. Terrasse, 'Le Jubé de St Étienne du Mont', *Revue de l'Art Ancien et Moderne*, II, 1922, 165 ff.), but this argument only applies to the structure of the main arch, and not to the balustrades, which would be extremely advanced at such an early date. They were, however, probably executed before 1545, when the contract was signed for the balustrade of the gallery which leads from the screen round the choir. In style the pierced balustrades of the *jubé* and the spiral staircases are very close to those at Anet, and in the absence of any other indication of date or author it seems reasonable to suggest that they may be by the same architect. One detail confirms this attribution. The bases and capitals of the columns on the spiral staircases are sloped, a very unusual feature, but one which de l'Orme specifically recommends in his treatise, in a passage where he reproves Bramante for not having done it in the spiral staircase in the Belvedere (Book 4, chapter 19).

Echoes of the style of Philibert de l'Orme at Anet are also sometimes to be found in the provinces, for instance in the château of Maillé near Morlaix, built probably after 1577 by a family remotely connected with Diane de Poitiers' husband.

p. 53   47. The tomb is very like a design in Serlio, book 7, chapter 52; but it is impossible to say whether de l'Orme knew and used Serlio or whether the latter incorporated de l'Orme's model in his book.

48. Cf. L. de la Tourrasse, 'Le Château-Neuf de St Germain-en-Laye', *Gazette des Beaux-Arts*, I (1924), 68, and Roy, *op. cit.*, I, 375.

49. The plans had been finished by 1567, since they are frequently referred to by de l'Orme in the treatise.

50. This design seems to have been soon abandoned in favour of one probably by Bullant, cf. p. 77.

51. It is generally assumed that the designs preserved by du Cerceau in his *Plus Excellents Bastiments*, and in the drawings in the British Museum (reproduced in H. W. Ward, *French Châteaux and Gardens in the Sixteenth Century*, plates xviii–xx), embody Philibert de l'Orme's scheme accurately. But it is very doubtful whether this is really the case. The various plans and elevations are not consistent with each other, and several of them do not agree with those parts which were executed and which we know in their original state from seventeenth-century engravings. Moreover, certain of these varying details of decoration are suspiciously close to the style of du Cerceau; and the oval halls in the side courts in the British Museum drawing (Ward, *op. cit.*, plate xviii) are also very similar to pavilions in one of du Cerceau's ideal plans (*ibid.*, plate xxvii). It seems likely that the designs as given by du Cerceau are his own variants on de l'Orme's projects, and in the present state of our knowledge there is no certain method of distinguishing clearly the earlier architect's work.

p. 54   52. The attribution of this grotto to Primaticcio is due to Dimier and, though not certain, is very probable.

53. Cf. p. 82.

p. 55   54. Dimier, *Le Primatice* (1900), 359, has established Primaticcio's claim in spite of the fact that Félibien and Brice attribute the chapel to Philibert de l'Orme.

55. Its state in that year is known from a drawing made by van Buchel in his diary for September 1585 (cf. *Mémoires de la Société de l'Histoire de Paris*, XXVI, 1899, plate opposite 128). Silvestre (Faucheux, No. 64, plate 28) shows it in the same condition.

56. It is always stated that some of the columns were taken and re-erected round the lake in the Parc Monceau, but if this is the case their whole arrangement must have been much altered in the process.

57. From Philander's work at Rodez it is safe to assume that he also visited Rome.

58. And perhaps farther north in Saintonge; for p. the strange monument at Moëse, which dates from 1563, is an example of the archaeological spirit of which Philander was the most eminent exponent (reproduced in *Sites et Monuments*, *Angoûmois et Saintonge*, Paris, N.D., 73).

59. The château has been attributed by the local historian Gaujal (cf. Gébelin, *op. cit.*, 62) to Guillaume de Lissorgues, who was born in the village of Bournazel and built the nearby château of Graves (reproduced Gébelin, *op. cit.*, figure 67). Gébelin rejects this attribution, but on stylistic grounds it is plausible in connexion with the north wing, which has many features in common with Graves. The east wing is much more monumental, but there are so many details of decoration common to both wings that it is hard to believe that they are by different hands. The unusual frieze of the Ionic Order is to be found almost exactly repeated on the entrance gate on the south side of St Sernin at Toulouse. Another example closely related in type is on the choir screen of the cathedral of Rodez, dated 1531, of which the surviving fragments have been moved to a side chapel of the choir. It seems likely that the same team of decorative sculptors must have been working on these three friezes.

60. Book 4, chapter 12.

61. The following are documented as by him: Hôtel de Bagis, 1538; Hôtel Buet, 1540; parts of Hôtel d'Assézat, 1555. To these can be added on grounds of style the Hôtel du Vieux Raisin or Beringuier-Maynier, after 1547. Outside the town the château of St Jory is certainly by him (1545), and that of Pibrac (*c.* 1540) is plausibly ascribed to him (cf. *Congrès*, 1929, 134 ff.).

62. *Congrès* (1929), 154.

63. Another fine and little known house in the p. south is the château of Marsillargues (Hérault), mainly built in the reign of Henry II on an unusual plan, and with fine carved decoration in the Fontainebleau style.

64. A similar arrangement with a single Order is to be found in Italy in the vestibule of the sacristy of S. Spirito, Florence, by Giuliano da Sangallo and Cronaca. This may also be based on the temple at Nîmes, which was certainly known in Italy by the early sixteenth century.

65. Door to north transept, c. 1555–70, illustrated in Hautecœur, *Architecture*, I, 378.

66. The tower at Gisors was built after 1559. Those at St Michel, Dijon, were probably begun about 1560, but were not finished till the seventeenth century (cf. Hautecœur, *Architecture*, I, 390, 392).

67. Illustrated in Hautecœur, *Architecture*, I, 406. Its date is not known, but on grounds of style it can be placed soon after the middle of the century.

68. Illustrated in Hautecœur, *Architecture*, I, 403. The author illustrates many other specimens of the church architecture of the period, 374–421.

69. This chapel is illustrated in Hautecœur, *Architecture*, I, 163, who however wrongly describes it as the chapelle des Évêques, an earlier chapel in the same cathedral. The classicism of the chapel, somewhat unexpected in so unimportant a centre, may perhaps be connected with the presence there earlier in the century of Jean Pélerin, alias Viator, whose treatise on perspective published in 1505 showed him to be well versed in classical architecture.

58 70. Reference must be made in this section to a character who, though not a practising architect nor even an original writer on the subject, yet played a part in the development of architectural doctrine and methods in the sixteenth century. This is Jean Martin, a professional translator through whose work a number of important architectural writings became widely known in France. From 1545 onwards he was concerned with the French versions of Serlio; in 1546 he published a French translation of the *Hypnerotomachia Poliphili*, with new engravings by French artists. In 1547 there followed a Vitruvius with plates and commentary by Jean Goujon, and in 1553 Alberti's *Architecture*. For a full account of his work see Pierre Marcel, *Jean Martin* (Paris, 1927).

71. The room had already suffered by being transformed into a staircase by Louis XIV.

59 72. The influence of Parmigianino must have been reinforced by that of Cellini, who was in France from 1540 to 1545 (cf. p. 67). The figures on the salt-cellar made for Francis I have the same characteristics as Parmigianino's nudes.

73. According to Sauval, Primaticcio also designed the decoration of a gallery in the Paris house of the Constable Anne de Montmorency. This decoration is known to us from the engravings of Guérineau, which for some reason Dimier regards as not revealing the style of Primaticcio. They seem, however, to fit exactly with his manner at the time of the Ballroom, containing Raphaelesque elements,

in this case from the sibyls in S. Maria della Pace, Rome, adapted to the style of Parmigianino. From Sauval we know that, as was often the case, the actual execution was entrusted to Niccolò dell'Abbate. The same was true of the Ballroom.

74. They even have in common the unusual hexagonal shape for some of the panels.

75. An Italian parallel for this is the fresco in the p. 60 Palazzo Chiericati, Vicenza, but it is probably too late in date to have been a model. Both, however, may derive from a common source, perhaps Michelangelo's 'Phaeton' drawings of 1533.

76. The first two reproduced in Venturi, *Storia*, IX, 6, figures 345, 352 f., and the last by F. Würtenberger, 'Die italienische Deckenmalerei in Mittelitalien', *Römisches Jahrbuch für Kunstgeschichte*, IV (1940), 72.

77. Two drawings by Primaticcio identified by Dimier (*Le Primatice* (1928), plate 32) as designs for the decorations of the Grotte des Pins also show the use of very steep perspective, but of a different type. The closest Italian parallels for them are in a fresco by Beccafumi in the Palazzo Comunale at Siena (cf. L. Becherucci, *Manieristi Toscani* (1944), plate 109) and by Luini at Saronno (cf. P. Toesca, *Affreschi Decorativi* (Milan, 1917), plate 128).

78. This is, however, far from certain; but the whole problem of the distinction between the drawings of the two artists has yet to be cleared up. For a full account of this chapel see C. Samaran, 'La Chapelle de l'hôtel de Guise', *Gazette des Beaux-Arts*, II (1921), 331.

79. Reproduced in A. Venturi, *Storia*, IX, 2, figure 343. Another possible source is one of Tibaldi's frescoes in the Palazzo Poggi at Bologna, begun c. 1554 (reproduced in G. Briganti, *Il Manierismo e Pellegrino Tibaldi* (Rome, 1945), figure 123), which may have been quickly known in France through the close Bolognese contacts of Primaticcio and Niccolò dell'Abbate. Primaticcio probably built other private houses in Paris which are now destroyed. One, in the rue des Bernardins, is mentioned in the minutes of the Academy of Architecture for 13.vii.1678 as being designed by him, and containing a gallery decorated with frescoes by Niccolò dell'Abbate after his designs (cf. *Procès Verbaux de l'Académie Royale d'Architecture*, I, 1911, 171).

80. The Louvre painting was in the Orleans col- p. 61 lection. Both may have belonged to the set of four large landscapes for Fontainebleau for which Niccolò was paid in 1557 (cf. Laborde, *Comptes*, II, 195).

81. One other major Italian artist, Francesco Salviati, also visited France during this period, but this stay lasted less than two years, 1554–6. His work at

Dampierre has vanished and his 'Deposition', now in the church of St Marguerite in Paris (reproduced in the catalogue of the exhibition 'Peintures Méconnues des Églises de Paris', Musée Galliera, 1946, No. 63), does not seem to have exerted much influence. In Rome he worked on the Palazzo Sacchetti at the same time as the mysterious French sculptor and painter Maître Ponce or Ponzio Jaquio, who is also traceable as an assistant to Primaticcio at Meudon and St Denis (cf. E. Hewett, 'La Décoration du Palais Sacchetti par Maître Ponce et Marc le Français', *Gazette des Beaux-Arts*, 1, 1928, 213). It is also worth remembering that Bronzino was represented in the Royal Collection by the Allegory, now in the National Gallery in London, which was presented by Cosimo I to Francis I shortly before the death of the latter.

Henry II and Diane de Poitiers seem also to have been interested in the work of Michelangelo, for a small portable altar at Wilton bearing their emblems is based on his 'Pietà' design known from engravings by Bonasone and Béatrizet. From the style of the panel and the decoration of the frame the altarpiece seems to have been the work of a Fontainebleau artist (reproduced in N. R. Wilkinson, *Wilton House Pictures*, II (London, 1907), plate opposite 32).

p. 61 82. For the fullest account of Cousin see Roy, *op. cit.*, I, I.

83. These were commissioned by the Cardinal de Givry (cf. p. 66).

84. The unusual subject, identifying the pagan Pandora with the biblical Eve, has not so far been adequately explained.

85. The St Mammès tapestries suggest different influences. In all of them the decorative borders are strictly in the manner of Rosso and show exceptionally complicated strap-work. The main panels, however, appear to be based largely on a knowledge of Italian engraving of the school of Raphael and Giulio Romano. Classical and Renaissance buildings, not always well understood, compose the settings, accompanied in the 'St Mammès preaching to the beasts' by a rather naïve representation of a country-side, based on Late Gothic conventions. The figures have the frozen quality of early Roman Mannerism seen through the medium of engraving rather than known in the original.

p. 62 86. The little available information about Chrétien is to be found in an article by M. F. S. Hervey and Robert Martin-Holland, 'A Forgotten French Painter: Félix Chrétien', *Burl. Mag.*, XIX (1911), 48, in which the artist's few certain works are repro-

duced. Chrétien may have accompanied his patron when the latter was in Rome as ambassador from 1531 to 1533, and was certainly with him when he went there again in 1539 to escape from difficulties which surrounded him at Court. Chrétien therefore had direct knowledge of Italian art, and must have had contact with the first generation of Roman Mannerists. This influence is apparent in the earliest of the three works traditionally attributed to him, the altar-piece of the life of St Eugenia in the church of Varzy, in which the muscular exaggeration of the imitators of Michelangelo is combined with a northern naturalism in the portraits of the members of the Dinteville family who are introduced into the story. The 'Stoning of St Stephen' in Auxerre Cathedral, dated 1550, indicates that the artist had stayed in Florence on his visit of 1539 to 1542, for here his style is influenced by Florentine Mannerists such as Bacchiacca and Granacci, and the treatment of the landscape is again Florentine deriving from Picro di Cosimo.

87. The painting probably has some reference to the position of the family in French politics at the time. They were active supporters of the Dauphin, later Henry II, and his mistress, Diane de Poitiers, against the party of Francis I and the Duchesse d'Étampes; and their situation was therefore in many ways delicate. Chrétien's painting may well have been a sort of manifesto, setting forth the importance of Jean as the political leader (Moses) and François as the religious power (Aaron). It has been suggested that Pharaoh represents Francis I, but the features show little resemblance to his, and the King would hardly have been flattered by being identified with the enemy of the chosen people, defeated by the skill and courage of his opponents, Moses and Aaron.

88. It recalls in some degree the style evolved earlier in Holland by Scorel. Another painting which may be tentatively attributed to Chrétien on the grounds of its similarity to the 'St Stephen' is the 'Martyrdom of the Theban legion', sold at Sotheby's from the Halsey collection, 5 December 1928, lot 43. Recently yet another work, a 'Judgment of Solomon', from the Erle-Drax collection, has been acquired by Mr Sidney Sabin (published in the *Connoisseur*, CXXXIII, 1954, 193) and plausibly attributed to Chrétien. Like the 'Moses' it seems to include portraits of the Dinteville family.

89. As the frames of the Sala Regia were not begun till 1546 at the earliest, it seems likely that Jallier visited Rome in the years 1546-9. Another imitation of the same frames is to be found in the outside

of the gallery at Chenonceau, built by Bullant (see p. 78). Three of the Oiron frescoes are reproduced by M. Dumolin, *Le Château d'Oiron* (Paris, 1931), 45 ff.

90. Farther south in Avignon a curious artist, Simon Mailly or Simon de Châlons, can be traced between 1535 and his death in 1561 or 1562. Born at Châlons-sur-Marne, he seems to have been trained in Flanders, for his few certain works show the influence of Antwerp painting of the 1530s. He was, however, also affected by Italian art, and his 'Virgin of Sorrows' in the Borghese Gallery, dated 1543, is a copy of the painting by Solario of the same subject. He seems to have executed many altarpieces for the churches of Avignon, of which the 'Adoration of the Shepherds' of 1548 in the Musée Calvet is typical in its mixture of Flemish with Italian elements. For further information about Mailly see the article in Thieme-Becker, and a short note by G. Frizzoni in *L'Arte*, II (1899), 154.

91. See L. Dimier, *La Peinture de Portrait*, and E. Moreau-Nélaton, *Les Clouet et leurs émules*. Both authors record the available facts, but both, and particularly Dimier, allow themselves to speculate with dangerous freedom in the field of attribution. A much more scientific approach is displayed in Irene Adler's article, 'Die Clouet', *Jb. der Kunsthistorischen Sammlungen in Wien*, New Series, III (1929), 201.

63 92. Cf. for instance L. Beccherucci, *Manieristi Toscani* (Bergamo, 1944), plates 50, 120, and 124; and A. Venturi, *Storia*, IX, 6, figure 13.

93. The most exact likeness is with Salviati's portrait of a man in Vienna, reproduced by Irene Adler, *op. cit.*, 232.

94. We must remember, however, that Salviati's portrait of Aretino, now lost, belonged to Francis I (cf. Vasari, *Vite*, VII, 19).

95. The date now reads 1563, but appears to have been altered from 1569. To fit with the King's age as given, it should be 1570.

96. For instance, the portrait of Archduke Ferdinand in Vienna of 1548.

97. On stylistic analogy with the Charles IX several other portraits can safely be attributed to François Clouet : for instance, the full-length Henry II in the Uffizi (reproduced in Dimier, *La Peinture de Portrait*, I, plate 16); the head of Henry II, dated 1559, of which versions exist at Versailles, at Windsor, and in the Pitti (cf. Dimier, *op. cit.*, II, 124, Nos. 493, 494). On the basis of drawings we may add the Claude de Beaune in the Louvre (Moreau-Nélaton, *op. cit.*, I, figure 29).

The Odet de Châtillon dated 1548 at Chantilly (Moreau-Nélaton, *op. cit.*, figure 27) presents a difficult problem. The drawing (Moreau-Nélaton, *op. cit.*, figure 30) is certainly by François Clouet, but the painting is more Italianate than anything we possess of his. If, however, the hypothesis of a visit to Italy is accepted, then we might expect Italian influence to be stronger in an early work such as this, than in his more mature portraits, and the attribution becomes more acceptable.

98. Cf. A. de Hevesy, 'L'Histoire véridique de p. 64 la Joconde', *Gazette des Beaux-Arts*, II (1952), 5.

99. Cf. M. J. Friedlaender, *Altniederländische Malerei*, IX (1931), plates 53, 63.

100. M. J. Friedlaender, *op. cit.*, plates 29, 31, 37, and 38. The nurse in the Clouet may have been suggested by the St Joseph in the composition shown on plate 38.

101. This composition was imitated several times. At Chantilly is an almost exact copy dating from the end of the century, and perhaps representing Gabrielle d'Estrées (reproduced in Moreau-Nélaton, *op. cit.*, II, figure 464). Another more individual interpretation at Dijon shows the maidservant in the background taking clothes out of a chest, a direct reminiscence of Titian. A double portrait of the same type exists in several versions and is said to represent Gabrielle d'Estrées and the Duchesse de Villars.

One composition which is in no sense a portrait is also attributed to François Clouet with some degree of probability, namely the 'Diana at her bath' of which versions exist at Rouen and in the possession of Messrs Wildenstein (the latter version was exhibited in the exhibition *Landscape in French Art*, Royal Academy, London, 1949, No. 11 and reproduced in the book of illustrations, plate 3).

102. Dimier's attempts to separate from him two artistic personalities closely related to him, whom he calls the 'Peintre de Rieux-Châteauneuf' and the 'Anonyme de M. Benson' are not convincing (cf. *La Peinture de Portrait*, I, 40 ff.).

103. Mlle Huillet d'Istria has recently put forward the thesis that the art of Corneille de Lyon derives from that of Perréal, a view with which I cannot agree (cf. *Arts*, 3 December 1948).

104. A. E. Popham in his interesting article on p. 65 Duvet (*Print Collector's Quarterly*, VIII, 1921, 123) has pointed out many borrowings of Duvet from Italian sources. He also makes the important point that his engraving after Raphael's Cumaean Sibyl (R.D.52) agrees with the original and not with any of the Italian engravings after it. Duvet must

therefore either have worked from the original or from a drawing brought back by another artist from Rome.

p. 65 105. It is said by all writers on the artist that this series refers to the loves of Henry II and Diane de Poitiers, but there seems to be no solid reason for this view. It is more likely that we have here a revival or continuation of the medieval theme of the hunting of the unicorn, though it is here interspersed with classical allusions, such for instance as the appearance of Jupiter with eagle and thunderbolt in the background of the 'Triumph of the Unicorn' (R.D.58). The exact significance of the series, however, still requires investigation.

106. In one of the set, 'The Unicorn purifies a spring with his horn' (R.D.59), a quite different spirit appears, and the composition is filled with animals rendered with a naturalism which is sometimes naïve, as in the almost heraldic lions, and sometimes reveals a startingly close observation, as in the foreshortened poses of the beasts.

One other engraving by Duvet probably dates from the same period (Plate 51A). It is usually called, not quite accurately, 'Moses surrounded by the Patriarchs' (R.D.2). Its theme is a variant of one common in medieval cathedral porches, the ancestors and antetypes of Christ, and the arrangement of the figures on truncated columns against a vaulted recess is also a direct echo of the practice of the Middle Ages. In certain details, moreover, the figures seem to go back to medieval models. The Abraham and Isaac group, and the Melchizedek, are both types best known in the north porch of Chartres, and some of the other figures with their cross-legged dancing poses almost suggest that Duvet had in mind models such as the sculptures of Moissac and Souillac.

p. 66 107. See the excellent account given by L. E. Marcel, Le Cardinal de Givry (Dijon, 1926).

108. L. E. Marcel, op. cit., I, 166. Duvet's exact religious position is uncertain. He seems to have become a Protestant and to have left France shortly before 1540. On the other hand in 1556 he reappears in France, apparently as a Catholic (cf. H. Naef, 'La Vie et les Travaux de Jean Duvet', B.S.H.A.F., (1934), 114). It must, however, be borne in mind that these facts may apply to two different artists of the same name.

109. There is also a parallel with the Oratory of Divine Love to which Contarini and Pole belonged. This coloured the later compositions of Michelangelo to which, particularly to the 'Last Judgment', Duvet's engravings also owe much.

110. Contemporary with the isolated figure of Duvet there flourished a school of engravers who specialized in the illustration of books, and who, while not attaining the perfection of Geoffroy Tory, yet kept up a good general level of technical competence and of invention. The best of these artists were Bernard Salomon (active 1540–69), who illustrated Petrarch and Ovid, and the elder Jean de Gourmont (c. 1483–after 1551), chiefly notable for his curious architectural and perspective fantasies. For a full account of these engravers, see F. Courboin, Histoire Illustrée de la Gravure en France. One painting by Jean de Gourmont, dated 1537, is known (Staedel Institute, Frankfort; reproduced in A. Malraux, Psychologie de l'Art, La Monnaie de l'Absolu (Paris, 1950), 24).

111. To the English student the comparison of Duvet with William Blake is inescapable. Both were visionaries; both were uncompromising in their determination to render exactly what they experienced; both are confused, technically incompetent, provincial even. But both have the supreme conviction of the mystic. One can, however, push the comparison further, for not only were their intentions similar, but also their choice of means for the expression of their ideas. Both have affinities with the artists of the Middle Ages, but both also borrow their idiom in part from the engravings of the High Renaissance, above all those after Raphael and Michelangelo, and both translate these models into Mannerist terms. Blake may have known the engravings of Duvet, for one was reproduced by William Young Ottley in his Facsimiles of Scarce and Curious Prints in 1826, which proves that the artist was known in the circle in which Blake moved. There are certain similarities between the designs of the two artists which are hard to explain except by direct influence.

112. A drawing for the Juno survives (reproduced p. 6 in the Life of Benvenuto Cellini written by himself, ed. J. Pope-Hennessy (London, 1949), plate 22).

113. Cf. above, p. 245, note 72. The stories of the rivalry between the two artists are probably exaggerated, and in any case would not prevent one from borrowing from the other.

114. For an excellent account of his life and work see Pierre du Colombier, Jean Goujon (Paris, 1949). The author has been particularly successful in clearing up the problems connected with the apocryphal works of Goujon and presents for the first time a completely consistent view of his personality and development.

115. The Corinthian capital is far more correct than

any to be found in the illustrated editions of Vitruvius published before that date. It agrees, however, exactly with one illustrated in a plate designed by Goujon for Martin's translation of 1547.

116. The capitals of the Corinthian columns are identical with those in St Maclou; and the very unusual frieze of the upper storey is almost exactly repeated in an engraving by Goujon for the 1547 edition of Vitruvius, in which the Corinthian capital is also engraved (45 v.).

68 117. The allegorical figure at the top of the whole monument, seated between columns, is similar in style to those on the Hôtel d'Écoville at Caen, and suggests that Goujon probably received his first training in Normandy. P. du Colombier also plausibly attributes to the Rouen period of Goujon the general design of the Chapelle de la Fierte de St Romain beside the cathedral, built in 1542-3 (op. cit., 30, and plate 32). Here again links with the Hôtel d'Écoville at Caen can be seen in the circular aedicules on the tops of the two structures.

118. Pierre du Colombier (op. cit., 41 ff.) argues that they date from 1545-7 and were executed by two different pupils after Goujon's design. I find it easier to believe that they were carried out about 1543, probably with the assistance of pupils. This theory does not conflict with the dates inscribed on various parts of the chapel, and is stylistically probable. The altar reliefs are related to the Brézé tomb in the treatment of drapery in the 'Virtues' and the 'Evangelists', and also in the naturalistic rendering of the shrubs in the relief of the 'Sacrifice of Abraham'. The 'Virtues' are based in their general design on Caraglio's engravings after Rosso's 'Gods', and the 'Evangelists' are enclosed between panels of Fontainebleau strap-work. These features all point backwards towards the thirties, but the actual designs of the 'Evangelists' panels are a direct preparation for those on the screen. The relief of the 'Sacrifice of Abraham' has incidentally one quality characteristic of Goujon's earlier work; namely the discomfort in reducing a figure to the convention of a bas-relief, which is particularly evident in the Abraham.

69 119. Goujon's reliefs on the Hôtel Carnavalet date from about the same period as the Fontaine des Innocents, and show the same stylistic qualities though on the whole in rather coarser form, owing probably to the collaboration of assistants.

120. The same tendency is to be seen in the relief of a Victory over a mantelpiece at Écouen which is traditionally ascribed to Goujon. The attribution is convincing, but the relief must be much later than the other work at Écouen, partly because of the connexion with the style of the Louvre reliefs, and partly because the mantelpiece almost certainly belongs to Bullant's part of the château, which probably dates from about the middle years of the fifties. The Victory is based on an engraving after Rosso (cf. Kusenberg, Le Rosso (Paris, 1931), plate lxii).

121. Du Cerceau's engravings show the draperies p. 70 as far more broken and less coldly neo-classical; but he is liable to alter such details in the direction of his own more developed Mannerist style, and is therefore not quite reliable as a witness. On the other hand, it should also be noticed that the caryatids in Goujon's own plate to Martin's edition of Vitruvius of 1547 are also much freer than those we now see in the Louvre.

122. Vitry and other critics attribute to Goujon the decoration of the chapel of Anet, but P. du Colombier (op. cit., 129 ff.) has convincingly shown that it is the work of an imitator.

123. Op. cit., I, 320.

124. Cf. M. Mayer, 'La Fontaine de Diane du Château d'Anet n'est pas de Benvenuto Cellini', Revue de l'art ancien et moderne, LXVIII (1935), 125. The arguments are summed up by P. du Colombier (op. cit., 132 ff.), who believes that the statue is by a French sculptor working on the indications of a painter who made the drawing now in the Louvre (reproduced, P. du Colombier, op. cit., plate 76).

125. One piece of external evidence supports the attribution of the 'Diana' to Pilon. We know that in 1558 he was working with Philibert de l'Orme, to whom he supplied statues for the tomb of Francis I (cf. Babelon, Germain Pilon, 33), and therefore collaboration with this architect at Anet is plausible.

A puzzling feature about the 'Diana' is that in its present state it differs from the engraving of du Cerceau and also from a sixteenth-century drawing after it in the Louvre (reproduced in Mayer, op. cit., 129), both of which show the stag's head and the left-hand dog in quite different positions from the group itself. It seems, however, that these two versions are not independent and that both embody the sort of alteration which du Cerceau often made. An unpublished drawing by Jacques Gentilhâtre of the first years of the seventeenth century (in a volume in the Library of the Royal Institute of British Architects) reproduces the group as it is at present.

126. The dates have been held to present difficulties for this view, because till recently Pilon was supposed to have been born in 1536 or 1537. MM.

Connat and Pierre du Colombier have, however, now proved that he cannot have been born after 1531 and was probably born a few years earlier (cf. 'Quelques documents commentés sur André et Germain Pilon', *Humanisme et Renaissance*, XIII, 1951, 196). The documents discovered by them also prove that in 1557 Pilon was already a master and was engaged with his father on major works of sculpture. It was previously known that from 1555 onwards he was supplying models for Paris goldsmiths.

p. 70   127. Another work from Anet, a relief of Diana now in the Cluny museum, is also usually attributed to Goujon but does not conform to his style (reproduced in P. du Colombier, *op. cit.*, plate 44). It may also be an early work of Pilon, though the style is rather more classical. The head is related to those of the standing figures of the monument for the heart of Henry II or the *châsse* of Ste Geneviève, both in the Louvre.

p. 71   128. Cf. Maurice Roy, *op. cit.*, I, 162 ff.

129. Reproduced in J. F. Noël and P. Jahan, *Les Gisants*, I (1949), plate 20.

130. Reproduced in P. S. Wingert, 'The funerary urn of Francis I', *Art Bulletin*, XXI (1939), 383 ff. The themes may have been suggested by the panels on the fountain designed by Cellini for Francis I (cf. *The Life of Benvenuto Cellini written by himself*, ed. cit., 284).

131. Cf. for instance the warrior in Valentin's 'Four Ages of Man' in the National Gallery, and Terbrugghen's 'Sleeping Mars' at Utrecht (reproduced by W. Stechow in 'Zu zwei Bildern des Hendrick Terbrugghen', *Oud Holland*, XLV (1928), 280).

132. Roy, *op. cit.*, I, 113, attributes to Bontemps the tomb of Admiral Chabot in the Louvre, and the monument to Guillaume du Bellay in the cathedral of Le Mans. These works form a complete stylistic unity with the Maigny tomb and there is every reason to accept their attribution to the sculptor, who thus appears as the most important carver of tombs about the middle of the century. In all these monuments the heads suggest the influence of followers of Michelangelo such as Bandinelli. The tomb of Guillaume du Bellay was erected in 1557 at the expense of his brother the Cardinal (cf. Heulhard, *Rabelais, ses voyages en Italie* (1891), 345-7).

Further works are ascribed to the artist by M.

Beaulieu in 'Nouvelles attributions à Pierre Bontemps', *Revue des Arts*, III (1953), 82.

There seems also to be a connexion between England and the atelier of Bontemps. The tomb of Sir Philip and Sir Thomas Hoby at Bisham (Berkshire), executed just after the death of the latter in 1566, has figures exactly in his manner (reproduced in *Country Life*, LXXXIX, 1941, 345). Sir Thomas Hoby knew France well and was ambassador in Paris at the time of his death. Bontemps was a Protestant, and a link between the two men is not at all unlikely.

133. Reproduced in M. Aubert, *La Sculpture fran* p. 72 *çaise du Moyen-Âge et de la Renaissance*, plate 55.

134. Reproduced in P. Vitry and G. Brière, *op. cit.*, II, plate CXXIX, No. 2.

135. Cf. J. Babelon, *op. cit.*, 58. For further details about Domenico del Barbiere, see R. Koechlin and Marquet de Vasselot, *La Sculpture à Troyes ... au 16ᵉ siècle* (Paris, 1900); and Venturi, *Storia*, X, 2, 578 ff.

136. Reproduced in M. Aubert, *op. cit.*, plate 58.

137. Reproduced in Vitry and Brière, *op. cit.*, II, plate CXIX, No. 5.

138. The setting, not shown in the plate which comes from a cast, and the little heart which the skeleton holds are later additions.

139. For instance a stone statue in the museum at Dijon and a small bronze of very fine quality in the museum at Strasbourg. The Cimetière des Innocents, Paris, also contained stone skeletons, one of which survives in the Louvre (No. 319).

140. One other work of sculpture, prepared by Italian sculptors for France in this period, but not actually delivered till much later, must be mentioned here, namely the bronze equestrian statue to Henry II which Catherine de' Medici invited Michelangelo to make in 1560. Michelangelo handed on the commission to Daniele da Volterra, promising to help him with advice. By the time of Daniele's death the horse was cast but not the figure of the King. The Wars of Religion prevented the continuation of the project, and the horse was only sent to France in the seventeenth century, when it was used for the statue of Louis XIII in the Place Royale (cf. p. 110). Vasari gives a full account of the part of this story which concerns Michelangelo and Daniele da Volterra (cf. *Vite*, VII, 66 ff.).

CHAPTER 4

75   1. For a vivid account of the activities of the Court of Henry III see F. Yates, *The French Academies of the 16th Century*.

2. Certain authors have attributed to Bullant the chapel built by Jean d'Amoncourt in the cathedral of Langres in 1549, but there is no evidence to support this theory (cf. Hautecœur, *Architecture*, I, 233 ; see also 371, where the date is given wrongly as 1543).

3. For the best account of Écouen see Gébelin, *op. cit.*, 87. The monograph by C. Terrasse (Paris, 1925) gives further details and illustrations.

76   4. The pavilion on the court side of the north wing is one of Bullant's clumsiest designs, at any rate in its present relation to the staircase to which it leads, though this may have been inserted later. The pavilion consists of two Orders, Doric and Corinthian, superimposed, the entablature of the upper Order being continuous, that of the lower breaking back over the two entrance doors. Above is a pair of dormer windows with round pediments, linked by a higher blind panel which has a straight pediment overlapping the two dormers, the whole design being reminiscent of de l'Orme's façade of the Tuileries. The Tuileries, however, is later. Bullant may have known the arrangement in an earlier work of de l'Orme now lost, but it is also possible that the older architect may in this case have been influenced by the younger.

5. The central pavilion on the outside of the north wing, apparently built after 1559, is, like that on the court front, a clumsy design, consisting essentially of two triumphal arch designs standing one above the other and supported on a ground floor pierced with four openings. This seems to be an instance of Bullant's using ideas which he had learned in Rome but not yet fully digested.

6. Cf. Gébelin, *op. cit.*, 101. It is sometimes said that an earlier example is to be found in the Petit Château at Chantilly, but apart from the uncertainty of the dates of the two buildings, the pilasters at Chantilly are not, properly speaking, colossal (see p. 77).

7. In certain respects Bullant's use of the colossal Order is closer to Palladio than to Michelangelo. The latter only uses it in the form of pilasters, whereas Palladio in the court of the Palazzo Porto-Colleoni (1552) uses full columns. The Loggia del Capitano provides an even closer parallel, but is too late to have influenced Écouen, since it was not begun till 1571.

8. Cf. Gébelin, *op. cit.*, 95.

9. Cf. a drawing by Blomfield, in his *History of French Architecture, 1494–1661*, I, plate 54.

10. The panels breaking into the entablature recall a similar arrangement in the portico on the court side of the north wing at Écouen.

11. Cf. Gébelin, *op. cit.*, 76.   p. 77

12. The dates make it impossible that there should have been any direct influence, and, as with the colossal Order at Écouen, this seems to be a case of parallel independent development.

13. In 1568, however, he was commissioned by the Constable's widow to design his tomb in the church of St Martin at Montmorency of which fragments survive in the Louvre (cf. R. Baillargeat, 'Étude critique sur les monuments élevés par les seigneurs de Montmorency', *B.S.H.A.F.* (1952), 107.

14. Cf. p. 55.

15. Marot's engraving shows the arms and initials of Marie de' Medici on the dormers of this section. The unusual niches with the two halves of a curved pediment interchanged can also hardly date from Bullant's time, since they were first used by Buontalenti in the Porta delle Suppliche in the Uffizi, which can be dated after 1580 (cf. Venturi, *Storia*, XI, 2, figure 433).

16. Hautecœur (*Architecture*, I, 543) confuses this Hôtel de Soissons, which he illustrates, with another in the rue de Grenelle nearby which was later bought and remodelled by the Duc de Bellegarde and Séguier (cf. Piganiol de la Force, *Description de Paris*, III (1742), 58 and 64).

17. Gébelin (*op. cit.*, 169) points out that the design includes the arms of Lorraine and must therefore be later than 1575, the date of Henry III's marriage with Louise de Lorraine; and the scheme is engraved in the second volume of the *Plus Excellents Bastiments*, which appeared in 1579.

18. This scheme was executed slowly, as we can see from Silvestre's engraving of the middle of the seventeenth century, which shows the façade half finished.

19. Cf. Gébelin, *op. cit.*, 83.   p. 78

p. 78   20. The wing of the forecourt appears in a drawing of du Cerceau in the British Museum (90) of before 1579, which, however, does not show the gallery. The latter must have been built after the drawing was made but before 1581, when it is mentioned in a letter (cf. Gébelin, *op. cit.*, 84). Bullant, who died in 1578, is therefore unlikely to have actually superintended its erection, but there is no reason to doubt that his plans were followed.

21. The model in this case is Daniele da Volterra's stucco frames in the Sala Regia of the Vatican, dating from after 1547.

22. Reproduced in *Châteaux et Manoirs de France, Région de la Loire*, III, plate 51. A rather similar mantelpiece is to be found at Écouen (reproduced in Gébelin, *op. cit.*, figure 153). Another piece of decoration certainly inspired by Bullant, and perhaps actually designed by him, is in the farmhouse of La Courtinière, not far from Chenonceau (reproduced in *Châteaux et Manoirs de France, Région de la Loire*, I, plates 82 and 83).

23. In his important and learned work on the du Cerceau family (*Les du Cerceau*), Geymüller proposes 1510–15 as the date of birth of Jacques the Elder. But this suggestion is based on the attribution to du Cerceau of certain drawings made in Rome *c.* 1532. There is, however, no reason to suppose that they are by him. As I hope to show, the later date of birth fits in far better with the known facts, the traditional account of his life, and the stylistic development. Geymüller also attributes to the architect many other drawings and also engravings which are probably not by him. In fact, the whole question of his work in these two media is still to be cleared up. I shall therefore limit myself as far as possible to the volumes of engravings which bear the name of the architect and to drawings directly connected with them.

24. In this case he would have met Philander, who was also in Armagnac's suite.

25. It is sometimes said that he was influenced by Flemish decorative engravers such as Vredeman de Vries; but if influence there was, it seems to have worked in the other direction. Many of du Cerceau's designs can, however, be traced to originals by Italians such as Enea Vico and Nicoletto da Modena (cf. R. Berliner, *op. cit.*, 54 and *passim*). Some of his designs for mantelpieces seem to have been inspired by those in the Château de Madrid.

p. 80   26. We have already seen that Bullant's Hôtel de Soissons was also related to du Cerceau's projects, and among surviving examples may be quoted the wing built by the Abbot of St Germain des Prés as

his private residence in 1586 (engraved in A. Berty, *Topographie, Bourg St Germain*, plates opposite 118, 120, and 122), and the Hôtel de Sandreville, 26 rue des Francs-Bourgeois (reproduced in G. Pillement, *Les Hôtels de Paris*, I, plate 2). Among the most important houses of the period must have been the Hôtel de Gondi, later de Condé, north of the Luxembourg, known from engravings by Marot and drawings by Gentilhâtre in the Royal Institute of British Architects volume. It was apparently built shortly before 1584, probably by Claude Villefaux, the author of the Hôpital St Louis (cf. M. Dumolin, *Bulletin de la Société historique du 6e Arrondissement*, XXVI, 1925, 19 ff.). Its style is surprisingly restrained and classical for the period.

27. The second *Livre d'Architecture* of 1561 is devoted to details such as mantelpieces and dormers, but the third of 1572 gives plans for country houses embodying the same practical spirit as the designs of 1559 for town houses.

28. As with the Tuileries, cf. p. 244, note 51.   p.

29. As in the fountain of Gaillon, cf. p. 7.

30. They are discussed and many of them reproduced in W. H. Ward, *op. cit.*

31. In neither case is there direct proof that du Cerceau is the architect, but in this case Geymüller's arguments seem convincing and have been generally accepted. For the few documents available about Charleval see Mme R. Lemaire, 'Quelques précisions sur le domaine royal de Charleval', *B.S.H.A.F.* (1952), 7.

32. The *Plus Excellents Bastiments* illustrates two schemes which differ in detail, particularly in that one has double, the other single pavilions.

33. Reproduced in Hautecœur, *Architecture*, I, 319. p.

34. Reproduced in P. Parent, *L'Architecture civile à Lille* (Lille, 1925), plates 2 and 7.

35. Cf. Hautecœur, *Architecture*, I, 313 and figure 223.

36. Sambin also built the Palais de Justice at Besançon, and published in 1572 a work on the use of caryatids illustrated with brilliant and fanciful engravings. For a full account of his work see H. David, *op. cit.*, 401 ff.

37. Reproduced in Hautecœur, *Les Richesses d'Art de la France, La Bourgogne, L'Architecture*, I, plate 40.

38. One of the most astonishing documents about provincial Mannerism at this period is Joseph Boillot's *Nouveaux Pourtraitz et figures de termes pour user en l'architecture, composez et enrichiz de diversité d'animaulx, representez au vray selon l'antipathie et*

contrarieté naturelle de chacun d'iceux, printed at Langres in 1592. It consists of a series of fantastic designs for terms, in which the entablatures are supported not by human figures, but by animals, grouped in pairs according to the 'antipathy' between them as indicated by the Natural History of Pliny and other ancient authors. One term, for instance, is formed of an elephant and a dragon, another of a bull, a lion, and a crocodile, and so on.

39. For the date of his birth, cf. above, p. 249, note 126. The fullest account of Pilon's life is to be found in J. Babelon, *Germain Pilon*, and in P. du Colombier, 'Germain Pilon et sa famille', *Humanisme et Renaissance*, v (1938), 100.

Recent research has shown that his father, André Pilon, was a sculptor of some distinction, and the important 'Entombment' at Verteuil is now regarded as a work from his atelier, perhaps executed with the help of his son (cf. R. Crozet, 'La Mise au Tombeau de Verteuil', *B.S.H.A.F.*, 1953, 19). According to Abel Lefranc ('Philibert de l'Orme, grand architecte du Roi Mégiste', *Revue du seizième siècle*, IV, 1916, 148), a Germain Pilon *imagier* was recorded as working at Fontainebleau before 1550. Now that the earlier date of birth has been established for the sculptor, this reference may well be the first record of his work.

40. Bartsch, 489. Reproduced in H. Delaborde, *op. cit.*, 237. The design is traditionally attributed to Raphael and must in any case emanate from his studio. It is always assumed that the engraving represents an incense-burner, but there is no indication of scale, and in view of the adaptation of the design to a large monument by Pilon it is permissible to wonder whether the original was not also planned to be on a monumental scale.

41. Cf. particularly the statues from the tomb of Claude de Lorraine at Joinville (reproduced in Vitry and Brière, *op. cit.*, II, plate cxxix, Nos. 3 and 4).

84 42. It is with the works so far mentioned that the 'Diana of Anet' is so closely related; see p. 70.

43. Another possible source of influence on these bronzes is Leone Leoni, whose standing bronze statue of the Empress Isabella of 1553 is in many ways like Pilon's Catherine (reproduced in E. Plon, *Leone Leoni* (1887), plate opposite 102). Leoni's relations with France are not clear, but we know from letters that he paid a short visit to Paris in 1549 and that he was in touch with Primaticcio in 1550 (*op. cit.*, 48, 61, 64, &c.). Leone's son Pompeo uses the convention of life-size kneeling bronze figures for the tombs of Charles V and Philip II (reproduced,

op. cit., plates opposite 230 and 232) in the Escorial, but these are later than Pilon's Henry II. The convention is, however, rare, and there appears to be no precedent for it in Italy; it is therefore possible that, whereas the elder Leoni influenced Pilon, the younger was in this respect influenced by him.

44. Now in the Louvre; reproduced in Vitry and Brière, *op. cit.*, II, plate cxxxiv, No. 5.

45. Cf. L. Dimier, *Le Primatice* (1900), 332. Some years later, in 1583, Pilon made two marble *gisants* of the King and Queen in coronation robes which are also at St Denis (reproduced in Babelon, *op. cit.*, figures 25–27). They have however none of the imaginative intensity of the nude *gisants* on the tomb.

46. Reproduced in Babelon, *op. cit.*, figures 42, 43, and 45.

47. Babelon, *op. cit.*, figure 44.

48. Babelon, *op. cit.*, figure 46.

49. Babelon, *op. cit.*, figures 57–60.

50. See p. 54.   p. 85

51. Babelon, *op. cit.*, figures 28–30.

52. The terra-cotta is in the Louvre (Babelon, *op. cit.*, figure 31) and the marble in St Paul-St Louis (Babelon, *op. cit.*, figure 32).

53. Babelon, *op. cit.*, figure 34.

54. Reproduced, Babelon, *op. cit.*, figure 38.

55. The original appearance of the tombs is known from sketches by Gaignières (Babelon, *op. cit.*, figures 77 and 78).

56. The pose and the relation of the figure to the tomb are reminiscent of the Amboise tomb at Rouen (cf. Plate 15).

57. The head on the extreme left seems to be an p. 86 idealized portrait of Michelangelo.

58. Reproduced in Venturi, *Storia*, x, 2, figures 166 and 167.

59. The monument is fully described and illustrated in C. Day, 'Le Monument funéraire de Montmorency', *Gazette des Beaux-Arts*, II (1928), 62.

60. Cf. J. B. Ward Perkins, 'The Shrine of St Peter and its twelve spiral columns', *Journal of Roman Studies*, XLII (1952), 21. In the sixteenth century they are rare even in Italy, though they can be seen in the Cortile della Mostra in the Castello at Mantua and in a grotto at the Villa d'Este at Tivoli. The idea of a central column flanked by figures is derived from Primaticcio's monument for the heart of Francis II, now at St Denis (reproduced in L. Dimier, *Le Primatice* (1928), plate 48). Salomonic

columns have a long previous history in French painting. They are used by Fouquet and in the sixteenth century by various draughtsmen and designers of tapestry cartoons.

p. 86   61. Mlle Lamy has also proved that the bust of Christophe de Thou in the Louvre is by Prieur (cf. *B.S.H.A.F.*, (1947–8), 65 f.).

62. Cf., for instance, Vitry and Brière, *op. cit.*, II, plates 175, 182–4, 189. Pilon's busts were also much imitated, cf. Vitry and Brière, *op. cit.*, plates 185–7.

63. There is as yet no *résumé* of the information available about Caron, which is contained in scattered articles. The most important are the following: C. Lebel in *B.S.H.A.F.*, (1937), 20; (1940), 7 and in *L'Amour de l'Art* (December 1937; September 1938); J. Ehrmann, in *B.S.H.A.F.*, (1945–6), 114 and (1949), 21; *Journal of the Warburg and Courtauld Institutes*, VIII (1945), 195, and *Burl. Mag.*, XCII (1950), 33; and Jean Adhémar in *Médecine de France*, XX (1951), 17.

Owing to our ignorance of the painting of this time there is at present a danger of attributing to him works displaying what may really be the characteristics of the period rather than of the individual painter. It may therefore be useful to set out the relatively certain facts about him.

As a basis for identifying his works we have the following evidence: a painting of the 'Massacres under the Triumvirate' in the Louvre signed and dated 1566; eight engravings, after his designs by his sons-in-law, Thomas de Leu and Léonard Gaultier, in Blaise de Vigenère's translation of Philostratus published in 1609; an equestrian portrait of Henry IV (1600), engraved by G. van Veen; and a drawing in the Louvre (No. 1956) with an early ascription to him. On grounds of style we may safely add to these the drawings made for Houel to illustrate the *Histoire des Rois de France*, edited by J. Guiffrey and published by the Société de l'Histoire de l'Art Français in 1920, and the greater part of those for the same author's *Histoire d'Artémise* (discussed and reproduced in M. Fenaille *État Général des Tapisseries de la Manufacture des Gobelins*, V, 113 ff. Almost all the drawings with small figures seem to be by Caron). A drawing in the National Gallery of Scotland, evidently by the same hand as these, allows us to add to his œuvre the designs of the Uffizi tapestries representing fêtes at the Court of Henry III for one of which it is a study. The following paintings show the characteristics displayed in the certain works of Caron: 'Augustus and the Sibyl' in the Louvre; the 'Triumph of Winter' in the René Holzer collection; the 'Triumph of Sum-

mer' belonging to Messrs Wildenstein; and the 'Astrologers Studying an Eclipse' in the writer's possession. The 'Triumph of Spring' is known from a copy. Of the other pictures ascribed to Caron by MM. Lebel and Ehrmann I feel that judgement should be reserved till we are better informed about the artist's contemporaries. In the case of the 'Triumph of Semele' and the 'Night Fête with an Elephant', for instance, which do not seem to be by the same hand as those discussed above, it is worth remembering that Nicolas Bollery (active 1585, died 1630) is said by van Mander to have painted 'Night scenes, masquerades, Mardi Gras' and similar festivities (cf. van de Wall's translation (New York, 1936), 407), which would exactly apply to these paintings.

64. Caron is by no means alone in using these proportions. They are to be seen, e.g., in the engravings of Bernard Salomon and Étienne Delaune.   p.

65. In the 'Augustus' the group of the Emperor and the Sibyl is taken almost directly from a composition by Niccolò, but Caron has greatly intensified the affectation of the gestures (cf. A. E. Popham and J. Wilde, *The Italian Drawings of the 15th and 16th Centuries at Windsor Castle* (London, 1949), 185, figure 19).

66. There must have been other French painters carrying on the manner of Niccolò dell'Abbate, for instance the author of the 'Threshers' at Fontainebleau (exhibited in *Landscape in French Art*, Royal Academy, London, 1949, No. 19, book of illustrations, plate 1).

67. Published in full by L. Lalanne (Paris and London, 1883).   p.

68. Reproduced in H. Voss, *Die Malerei der Spätrenaissance*, I, figure 87.

69. He may have known the pattern through Giulio Clovio's version which was engraved by Cort.

70. Reproduced in Venturi, *Storia*, IX, 6, figure 158.

71. The engravings to Ovid's *Metamorphoses* of 1570 and his *Epistles* of 1571 are attributed to him, and the stained-glass windows in St Gervais are said by Brice to be from his cartoons.

72. They are discussed and illustrated in P. Marcel and J. Guiffrey, 'Une illustration du Pas d'Armes de Sandricourt', *Gazette des Beaux-Arts*, I (1907), 277. The authors there attribute the drawings to the younger Bollery (active 1585, died 1630), but their style suggests an artist of an older generation.

73. The drawings are probably based on illuminated manuscripts of which several are known (see

the article quoted above), but they are treated in a more or less Mannerist idiom, with figures unexpectedly cut off in the foreground.

74. Of painting in the provinces at this time it is impossible to give any coherent account. A few isolated names and works can be identified but in most cases we know nothing at all of the artists concerned. A few individual works may be mentioned as typical:

(1) At Vitteaux in Burgundy a triptych dated 1592 and signed by Nicolas de Hoey, presumably a member of the family of Dutch artists of that name (reproduced in L. Réau, *Richesses d' Art de la France: La Bourgogne, La Peinture* (Paris, 1929), plates 17–19). For another member of the family, Jean de Hoey, see A. de Hevesy, 'Le premier garde des peintures du Roi de France', *Gazette des Beaux-Arts*, I (1950), 57.

(2) André Ménassier, of Montbard, who signed the frescoes in the chapel at Ancy-le-Franc in 1596 (reproduced *Gazette des Beaux-Arts*, I (1950), 14), and the altarpiece of the Trinity in the church of Semur in 1587.

(3) P. Mauroy, who signed a 'Golgotha', in a very Flemish style, belonging to Messrs Wildenstein (exhibited *Landscape in French Art*, Royal Academy, London, 1949, No. 12).

(4) Mathieu Beaubrun, who signed the altarpiece of the 'Last Supper' at Trilport-en-Brie about 1585 (reproduced in L. Dimier, *La Peinture de Portrait*, I, plate 63).

(5) Martin Noblet who signed a painting of Ceres dated 1576, which was acquired by the Louvre in 1938 and appears to be a copy after a design by Floris.

(6) In many châteaux decorative frescoes are to be found, e.g., in Tanlay (cf. L. Réau, *op. cit.*, plate 13), and Ancy-le-Franc (cf. *Country Life*, 4 September, 1937, 247 ff.).

A short summary of painting in the region of Troyes in the later sixteenth century is given by M. Mathey in 'La Peinture à Troyes au 16ᵉ siècle', *Combat* (i.ii.1954).

75. Reproduced in Dimier, *La Peinture de Portrait*, I, plate 23. The work of all these minor artists is discussed and illustrated in the two works of Dimier and Moreau-Nélaton already quoted.

76. For a summary of this early genre painting see J. Adhémar, 'French Sixteenth-century Genre Painting', *Journal of the Warburg and Courtauld Institutes*, VIII (1945), 191, and C. Sterling, 'Early Paintings of the Commedia dell'Arte in France', *Metropolitan Museum Bulletin*, New Series, II (1943), 11.

77. Others are in the museums of Rennes and Blois and at Penshurst.

78. L. Dimier, *La Peinture de Portrait*, I, 123, p. 89 attributes the court ball scenes to Hermann van der Mast, but without any very solid reasons.

79. Owing to lack of space the applied arts have been left out of this and the preceding chapters, but a good account of their development in the sixteenth century will be found in F. Gébelin, *Le style de la Renaissance en France*, which also has an excellent bibliography.

p. 93   1. Cf. F. Herbet, *op. cit.*, 351.

2. At St Germain Henry IV transformed the little theatre begun by Philibert de l'Orme for Henry II into an imaginative scheme of terraced gardens leading from the river to a casino, the whole design being strongly reminiscent of Italian gardens such as the Villa d'Este at Tivoli. This similarity to southern originals confirms the attribution of the design to Étienne du Pérac, the one architect of the reign who was well acquainted with the gardens of Rome and its neighbourhood (cf. L. de La Tourasse, 'Le Château-Neuf de St Germain-en-Laye', *Gazette des Beaux-Arts*, I, 1924, 68).

p. 96   3. The middle of the square was decorated in 1639 with the equestrian statue of Louis XIII, of which the horse was that made by Daniele da Volterra for the monument to Henry II (cf. above, p. 250, note 140) and the figure was added by Pierre Biard the Younger. The whole statue was melted down at the time of the Revolution.

4. The Hôpital St Louis, an isolation hospital outside the walls of Paris, begun in 1607, still survives almost unaltered. The main wards of the hospital are symmetrically disposed round a square court while other buildings, for the staff of the hospital, form the corners of an outer square and are linked by covered ways with the wards (engraved by Chastillon and Pérelle; photographs of it are reproduced in Louis Chéronnet, *Paris Imprévu*, plates 64–7).

The Collège Royal was only begun in the year of Henry IV's death and was not completed till the eighteenth century. Here the type of building demanded a slightly different style, and Chastillon's engraving shows a work in the Late Mannerist tradition of the du Cerceau family.

p. 97   5. As might be expected, the idea was foreshadowed in the most advanced city-state of the early Renaissance, Florence, and is to be found expressed in theoretical form in Alberti (*Architecture*, Book VIII, chapter 6).

6. Cf. Hautecœur, *Architecture*, I, 578. The model of Montauban was widely followed in its neighbourhood, for instance at Valence d'Agen and Lisle de Tarn.

7. These new quarters are referred to with wonder by Géronte in Corneille's *Le Menteur* (1643).

8. Cf. Hautecœur, *Architecture*, I, 541. Reproduced in G. Pillement, *Les Hôtels de Paris*, I, plate 8. The

middle part of the façade was filled in during the eighteenth century.

9. J. A. du Cerceau the Younger was also employed by the Duc de Bellegarde to alter the house which he had bought from the Duc de Montpensier in 1612. A few smaller hôtels survive which appear to date from the reign of Henry IV. The Hôtel d'Alméras (reproduced in G. Pillement, *Les Hôtels de Paris*, I, plate 11) is said to date from 1598; and a house at No. 7 rue des Grands Augustins, on the site of the Hôtel d'Hercule, seems on stylistic grounds to date from *c.* 1600, though the documentary evidence about its building points to a much later date.

10. In that year the site was bought by the *maître d'hôtel du Roi* called Perrochet, whose initials appear on the dormers.

11. This addition is now being removed.   p.

12. Cf. Hautecœur, *Architecture*, I, 501.

13. Savot in his *Architecture Françoise*, first pub- p. lished in 1624, states that the staircase should be in that position (ed. 1673, 49). However, it is possible that Lemercier's Hôtel de Liancourt and François Mansart's Hôtel de la Vrillière were earlier examples of the Bretonvilliers arrangement.

14. Jean du Cerceau is known to have altered the Hôtel de Soissons, later Bellegarde, when it was bought by Séguier in 1633 (cf. Hautecœur, *Architecture*, I, 543, who, however, confuses this house with the other Hôtel de Soissons built by Bullant for Catherine de' Medici). From their similarity in style to the Hôtel de Bretonvilliers it seems safe to attribute to Jean du Cerceau the two houses built for Falconi between 1637 and 1643 on the corner of the Quai Malaquais and the rue des Saints-Pères (cf. Dumolin, *Études*, I, 259) known from engravings by Marot.

15. A house at No. 6 rue de Seine, which can be dated *c.* 1622 (cf. Dumolin, *Études*, I, 187), is so like designs in Le Muet's *Manière de bien bastir* that it can reasonably be attributed to him.

16. For a detailed account of the building of this hôtel, cf. R. A. Weigert, 'L'Hôtel de Chevry-Tubeuf', *B.S.H.A.F.*, (1945–6), 18. Weigert proves that the actual builder of the house was Jean Thiriot, but it is more than probable that he was not the architect, and the traditional attribution to Le Muet seems on stylistic grounds to be correct.

17. The hôtels which can be attributed with reasonable certainty to Le Muet are the following: three

in the rue des Petits Champs next to the Hôtel Duret de Chevry, built for Tubeuf in 1642, now destroyed but known in one case from engravings in Le Muet's book (Plates 2–5); the Hôtel d'Avaux, 71 rue du Temple, engraved by Le Muet; the Hôtel Tubeuf at 16 rue Vivienne, built in 1649 and engraved in the *Perit Marot*; the Hôtel de l'Aigle, at No. 16 rue St Guillaume (cf. A. Mauban, *Jean Marot*, 246), and the Hôtel de Chevreuse, later de Luynes, in the Faubourg St Germain, now destroyed but engraved in the *Grand Marot*. The door of the Hôtel Comans d'Astry, 18 Quai de Béthume (Plate 76A), can also be ascribed to Le Muet on the grounds of its similarity to plate 8 in his *Divers traictez d'Architecture* (Amsterdam, 1646), the hôtel itself having been built in the next year, 1647 (cf. Dumolin, *Études*, III, 79).

18. It does, however, occur in one of the elder du Cerceau's engraved designs (*Troisième Livre*, plate vi) which may be the origin of both Grosbois and the Fontainebleau stables. R. A. Weigert, 'Jean Thiriot et le duc d'Angoulême', *B.S.H.A.F.*, (1953), 120, proves that the builder (and probably the designer) of the later parts of Grosbois was Jean Thiriot.

19. There are many other examples of this simple brick-and-stone style in the neighbourhood of Paris, such as Rosny (Plate 78A); Courances, *c.* 1624; Baville (*Châteaux et Manoirs de France, Île-de-France*, I, 35); Bombon (*op. cit.*, II, 40); Courquetaine (*op. cit.*, II, 28); Ormesson (*op. cit.*, II, 17); Grignon, between Versailles and Mantes.

20. This provincial style occurs in all parts of France: at the château of Beaumesnil in Normandy (reproduced in H. de Saint-Sauveur, *Châteaux de France, Normandie* (Paris, n.d.), plates 18–23), built between 1633 and 1640; at Cheverny, near Blois (cf. *Châteaux et Manoirs de France, Région de la Loire*, IV, 20), built in the same years; at Bussy-Rabutin as late as 1649. Le Muet built three châteaux which show the same manner: Pontz in Champagne and Chavigny in Touraine, both now destroyed, but known from the engravings in Le Muet's book, and Tanlay, near Tonnerre, which still stands (cf. L. Hautecœur, *Les Richesses d'Art de la France, La Bourgogne, L'Architecture*, I, plates 41–4).

21. Cf. Pannier, *Salomon de Brosse* (Paris, 1911), 45. The attribution to de Brosse goes back to 1619 when the château is described by Bergeron (quoted by Pannier). Charles Perrault (*Hommes Illustres*, I, 87) attributes it to François Mansart, who may have assisted de Brosse here as he did at Coulommiers (cf. p. 118).

22. Cf. A. Hustin, *Le Palais du Luxembourg* (1904), 3.

23. Other recorded works by him are as follows: a door for the Hôtel de Soissons, copied from Vignola; work on the Hôtel de Bouillon, later Liancourt, which probably included the principal court (datable 1613; cf. Berty, *Topographie, Bourg St Germain*, 239, note 2). The whole question of de Brosse's contribution to the building of Monceaux is at present under revision. For the problem of St Gervais, cf. p. 103.

24. In the nineteenth century two more pavilions were added on the garden front, and the whole façade was moved forward.

25. Now destroyed but known from engravings by Marot and Silvestre, the former showing the architect's original scheme, the latter what was actually carried out. A novelty in the plan of Coulommiers is the introduction of curved colonnades linking the *corps-de-logis* with the wings in the court.

26. This rustication seems to be the only element which survived in the finished buildings of Marie de' Medici's original project of constructing a palace in imitation of the Pitti. We know that she sent Métezeau to make drawings of the latter in 1611, but Salomon de Brosse certainly did not follow them in any important features of his design. p. 102

27. The plans and engravings given by Pannier, *op. cit.*, 76 ff., show that the main façade at least was executed according to de Brosse's design, and has only been altered since by the removal of the exterior staircase and the consequent alterations to the middle bay of the ground floor.

28. Brochard (*Saint Gervais*, Paris, 1938) has published documents which prove that the actual builder of the façade was Clément Métezeau, but the early guide books unanimously name de Brosse as the author of the design, and there seems to be every reason to believe their testimony. p. 103

29. In the case of St Paul-St Louis by Derand (Plate 80A) the church was of the same date as the façade, but the Gothic feeling for height survives in the proportions of the interior and forces the architect to adopt the three-storey type of façade. Generally speaking the church building of the period is *retardataire*, cf. St Étienne-du-Mont (1610) and other examples listed by Hautecœur (*Architecture*, I, 603 ff.). The Jesuits alone, through their leading architect Étienne Martellange (?1569–1641) produced an individual style (cf. Hautecœur, *op. cit.*, I, 558 ff., and P. Moisy, 'Le recueil des plans jésuites de Quimper', *B.S.H.A.F.*, 1950, 70 ff. and 'Martellange, Derand et la conflit du baroque', *Bulletin Monumental*,

cx, 1952, 237). In many of their chapels, e.g. at Rouen (begun *c.* 1610), pure Gothic structural forms survive combined with classical decoration. In addition St Joseph des Carmes, Paris (1615–20), must be mentioned as an early though elementary attempt to introduce a Roman manner in French church architecture (cf. Dumolin and Outardel, *Les Églises de France, Paris et la Seine* (Paris, 1936), 128.

The western parts of Brittany were the scene of great activity in church building during this period, but in a style essentially late sixteenth century in character. St Thégonnec, Guimiliau, Lampaul, and many other villages in Finistère can show churches, *ossuaires*, and calvaries, astonishingly rich and complex in their carved decoration, but many decades behind the taste of the capital, and coarse and heavy in execution.

An interesting but isolated example of the penetration of up-to-date Italian ideas into France occurs in the chapel of the Pénitents Bleus, now the church of St Jérôme, Toulouse. Its plan is composed of a series of circular and oval curves otherwise hardly to be found in French architecture. It was built between 1622 and 1625 by Pierre Levesville who came from Orleans and was trained in Italy. He is recorded in Rome, but it is likely that he also knew Milan, since the plan of the chapel is closer to the works of Francesco Maria Ricchino than to anything available at the time in Rome. For a fuller account of the church and the architect see the short article in Thieme-Becker and P. E. Ousset, *La Chapelle des Pénitents Bleus* (Toulouse, 1925).

p. 103 30. Hence the term *Ohrmuschelstil* given to this type of ornament.

p. 104 31. His real name may have been Bosschaert. The best account of his life is the article in Thieme-Becker, IX, 600.

32. The water-colour copies of the decoration in the Galerie de Diane by Percier in the library of the Institut de France give some idea of the decorative scheme but falsify the Mannerist character of the paintings. Two of them are reproduced in L. Dimier, *French Painting in the Sixteenth Century*, plates opposite 274 and 276. A few much-restored fragments of the originals are preserved in the Galerie des Assiettes at Fontainebleau.

For the Theagenes and Chariclea series see W. Stechow, 'Heliodorus' *Aethiopica* in art', *Journal of the Warburg and Courtauld Institutes*, XVI (1953), 144.

33. The identification of the St Germain series is due to L. Dimier (cf. *Les Arts*, 1905, 32, No. 46, and *Critiques et Controverses*, 1909, 39). The drawings are in the Louvre and are reproduced in the *Inventaire général, École Française*, by Guiffrey and

Marcel, V, 33. For the tapestries see Fenaille, *op. cit.*, v, 231 ff. Examples of the Diana compositions are in the Palace of Holyrood House, Edinburgh.

34. Two panels from the ceiling are reproduced in p. Dimier, *Histoire de la Peinture Française des origines au retour de Vouet*, plates 60 and 61.

35. The fullest account of his activity is given by F. G. Pariset in an article printed in the volume *Iacques Callot et les peintres et graveurs lorrains du dix-septième siècle*, published by the Musée Historique Lorrain at Nancy in 1935. His etchings are listed by Robert-Dumesnil, *Le Peintre-Graveur Français*, v, 81, and XI, 9. Reproductions of them are to be found in E. Tietze-Conrat, *Der französische Kupferstich der Renaissance*, and in the *Bulletin of the Museum of Fine Arts*, XI (Boston, 1942), 2 ff. Several drawings are reproduced by P. Lavallée, *Le dessin français du treizième au seizième siècle*.

36. I am greatly indebted to Dr Jan Lauts for calling my attention to a pair of paintings signed by Bellange, representing the Virgin and the Angel of the Annunciation, now in the Gallery at Karlsruhe (Plate 82). They were published by Anna Maria Ressner, in *Die Kunstinventare der Markgrafen von Baden-Baden* (Bühl, 1941), 62, 120, 187, and plate 14. Dr Grete Ring pointed out that the Virgin is a slightly altered version of Dürer's 'Fürlegerin' in Augsburg. This connexion confirms the fact that Bellange was inspired by earlier German art, as was already suggested by the use which he made of Schongauer's engraving of the 'Carrying of the Cross' in his own etching of the same subject. Other paintings attributed to Bellange in the museums of Nancy are published by Pariset ('Peintures de Jacques de Bellange', *Gazette des Beaux-Arts*, I, 1936, 238), but although all of them must be works of the Nancy School, their attribution to Bellange must remain in doubt.

37. Some of his figures recall the designs of Goltzius, Bloemart, or Jan Saenredam. The composition of his engraving of 'Christ carrying the Cross' (R.D.7; reproduced by Pariset, *op. cit.*, 52) is based on Schongauer's print of the same subject (B.21). The crowd pressing into the narrow gully on the left and grouped round a horse seen exactly from behind suggest the influence, probably indirectly, of Bruegel's 'Conversion of St Paul' in Vienna.

38. Reminiscent of Beccafumi; for instance the group in the foreground of the 'Esther' in the National Gallery, London.

39. Pontormo and other early Florentine Mannerists had revived this pre-Renaissance practice. p.

40. Cf. P. Marot, 'L'Apprentissage de Jacques Cal-

lot', in *Mélanges dédiés à la mémoire de Félix Grat*, II (Paris, 1949), 450.

07 41. Callot's 'Temptation of St Anthony' was an essay in the manner of Bosch.

42. Callot's technique in etching is highly personal. He found the current soft varnish inadequate to the delicacy which he sought and replaced it by the hard varnish employed by lute-makers, a habit in which etchers have followed him to the present day.

08 43. The whole set of these drawings, now at Chatsworth, is published by D. Ternois, 'La "Passion" de Jacques Callot', *Revue des Arts*, III (1953), 107.

09 44. The third member of the Nancy trio of artists, Claude Deruet (1588–1660), was in his day even more successful than the others. Of his representations of court festivities in the manner of Callot but lacking his finesse several survive (e.g., four panels of the Elements painted for Richelieu, now at Orleans, plate 87B), but he also practised portraiture in a rigid Late Mannerist style (cf. one at Strasbourg, probably representing Julie d'Angennes, the celebrated daughter of Mme Rambouillet, as Astrée, *c.* 1641). For an account of his work see F. G. Pariset, 'Claude Deruet', *Gazette des Beaux-Arts*, I (1952), 153.

Deruet's contemporary, Georges Lallemant (died 1635–7) left Nancy about 1601 and settled in Paris. He brought to Paris the manner of Bellange and seems to have popularized it there (cf. F. G. Pariset, 'Georges Lallemant émule de Jacques de Bellange' *Gazette des Beaux-Arts*, 1954, 299). One Echevin group documented as by Lallemant and datable to 1611 is in the Carnavalet Museum; another of 1614, probably by him, is at present on loan there from Versailles. For the third, designed by Lallemant and executed by Philippe de Champaigne, cf. below, p. 149. For recently discovered documents about Lallemand, see F. G. Pariset, 'Documents sur Georges Lallemant', *B.S.H.A.F.*, (1952), 169.

45. The available information about Vignon is to be found in an article by C. Sterling, in the *Gazette des Beaux-Arts*, II (1934), 123, 'Un Précurseur français de Rembrandt: Claude Vignon', and in the catalogue of the exhibition 'Les Peintres de la Réalité', held at the Orangerie in 1934. Like Deruet, Vignon was a favourite with the *Précieux*. He was also a remarkable etcher and his compositions in this medium, together with those of his contemporary, Pierre Brebiette (1598–1650), are among the most vigorous works of this rather spiritless period in Parisian art (cf. E. Tietze-Conrat, *op. cit.*, plates 36–42, and F. Courboin, *op. cit.*, I, plates 405–8, 413–14).

46. Mention must also be made here of the first group of imitators of Caravaggio connected with France. The first, Moïse Valentin, hardly concerns the history of French painting since he spent the whole of his active life in Rome. The second is a Fleming, Louis Finson or Finsonius (d. 1617), who lived for a number of years in Provence painting altarpieces in a style combining elements borrowed from Caravaggio, Elsheimer, and Late Mannerism. For both these artists see H. Voss, *Die Malerei des Barock in Rom* (Berlin, 1924), to whose account certain details have since been added by G. Isarlo in *Caravage et le Caravagisme Européen*. For Finsonius see also A. von Schneider, *Caravaggio und die Niederländer* (Marburg, 1933), 86 ff.

One other provincial painter of the period deserves mention. Jean Boucher of Bourges (1568–after 1628) painted altarpieces for churches in Berri several of which, ranging in date from 1604 to 1628, survive in the Musée Cujas at Bourges. His manner is composed of a mixture of Italian and Flemish Late Mannerist elements.

47. For a summary of all the available information about Pourbus see the article by L. Burchard in Thieme-Becker, XXVII, 315. p. 110

48. Pourbus also executed portrait groups of the Prévôt des Marchands and the Échevins (Lord Mayor and Aldermen) of the city of Paris, probably in 1614 and 1616. Fragments of one picture survive in the Hermitage at Leningrad. Similar groups were commissioned by other town councils, for instance at Narbonne, and at Toulouse where Jean Chalette (1581–1645) was employed for this purpose. Another popular portrait painter was Ferdinard Elle the Elder (b. before 1585, d. 1637), who painted a portrait of Mme de Châtillon at Hampton Court. The sixteenth-century style of portrait drawing continues in Daniel Dumonstier and in a series of highly naturalistic heads traditionally attributed to Lagneau.

49. Cf. above, p. 94 and p. 256, note 3.

50. For Francheville see R. de Francqueville, 'Documents inédits sur le sculpteur dit Francheville', *B.S.H.A.F.*, (1952), 158.

51. Other sculptors of this period, of whose work little survives, were Mathieu Jacquet, called Grenoble, who worked on the Belle Cheminée at Fontainebleau, and Barthélemy Tremblay, whose speciality was portraiture (cf. A. Michel, *Histoire de l'Art*, V, II, 743 ff.). In addition tomb sculpture continued to flourish all over the country, following the lines laid down by Pilon.

CHAPTER 6

p. 114   1. It can be shown that the *Précieux* also had a definite taste in the visual arts, and that they continued to admire Late Mannerism long after it was outmoded in other Parisian circles.

2. The correct dates are given by L. Batiffol (*Autour de Richelieu* (Paris 1937), 113 ff). The college was begun in 1626 and mainly finished by 1629 when the plans for the new church were prepared. But the building of the latter does not seem to have been started till 1635.

3. Marot names Lemercier as the final architect of the Hôtel de Liancourt begun by de Brosse. The fact that Lemercier was the duke's architect indicates him as the builder of the château of Liancourt (finished before 1637; cf. *B.S.H.A.F.*, (1918–19), 169), and this attribution is supported by its striking likeness to other works by him. Sauval attributes to him the Hôtel d'Effiat and the same patron's château at Chilly. Dézallier d'Argenville and Dulaure, however, ascribe the latter to Métezeau. The style of the château is not obviously related to that of either architect, but perhaps more closely to Métezeau's than to Lemercier's.

4. On the Oratoire, cf. Dumolin and Outardel, *B.S.H.A.F.* (1950), 80.

5. The churches of Rueil and Richelieu are reproduced by Hautecœur, *Architecture*, I, 650.

6. Engraved by Marot. Interesting but freer experiments in the same genre were the front of St Laurent, begun in 1621 (destroyed 1862, but reproduced in Dumolin and Outardel, *op. cit.*, 80) and François Mansart's façade of the Feuillants (cf. p. 119).

7. Reproduced in Venturi, *Storia*, XI, 2, figure 726.

p. 115   8. Only in the Sorbonne does he use full columns in the lower storey, and there it may be noticed he follows the sixteenth-century French manner of putting over them an unbroken entablature. In this he may also have had in mind Rughesi's façade of S. Maria in Vallicella, Rome (1605).

9. For a full account of this church see S. Ortolani, *San Carlo a' Catinari*, Rome. The façade was not carried out according to Rosati's design. The similarity between the two churches extends to the interior, where the barrel vault and the particular Order used are very alike.

10. The four small turrets round the base of the dome may have been suggested by the small domes on St Peter's.

11. Lemercier may have derived the general idea p. of the free-standing portico from Michelangelo's design for St Peter's, or he may have adapted it from Palladio's villa designs. There was, however, no actual model for it in Rome at his time. The placing of the cartouche in the field of the pediment was common in Rome, e.g. in della Porta's S. Luigi dei Francesi.

12. Cf. p. 125. The medal struck in 1650 proves that the dome is due to Lemercier (cf. A. Blunt, *François Mansart*, 15).

13. The influence of the dome of St Peter's is much more marked here than in the Sorbonne, though it cannot be said that Lemercier has borrowed directly from any one scheme. The drum is higher than in any of them; the hemispherical, ribbed cupola recalls Michelangelo's design as engraved by du Pérac; but it is capped by an unexpectedly light lantern. We know that Lemercier was interested in Michelangelo's later architectural designs since he engraved his model of 1559–60 for S. Giovanni dei Fiorentini when he was in Rome in 1607 (published by E. Panofsky, *Wasmuths Monatshefte für Baukunst*, V, 1920–1, Supplement, 35 ff.).

14. Cf. p. 281, note 66.

15. Their use in this position may possibly have been suggested by the Roman Palais des Tutelles at Bordeaux, which still stood in Lemercier's day, and was engraved in Claude Perrault's *Les dix livres d'architecture de Vitruve*, 219. According to Perrault's description, the Roman caryatids, like those on the Louvre, were unusual, in that they supported the entablatures of pilasters, not of columns. Those of Lemercier, however, seem to be unique in one feature: they occur in pairs, one farther back than the other, like stepped-back pairs of pilasters – an astonishingly Mannerist feature to appear at so late a date and in so apparently classical a form. At an unknown date, but certainly towards the end of his career, Lemercier produced a design for the east front of the Louvre, known from the engraving by Marot. He was also responsible for much of the decoration of the interior of the palace, including that of the Long Gallery. Cf. A. Blunt, 'Poussin's Decoration of the Long Gallery', *Burl. Mag.*, XCIV (1951), 369.

16. The Palais Cardinal was admitted by all, including Richelieu, to have suffered from being composed of a series of additions and, as far as we can judge from engravings, it must always have presented a confused appearance. The Hôtel d'Éffiat seems to have been a successful small house. It has been destroyed, but is reproduced from an old photograph in G. Pillement, *Les Hôtels du Marais* (Paris, 1945).

17. Cf. Berty, *Topographie, Bourg St Germain*, 239. Evelyn visited the completed house in 1644 (cf. *Diary*, under date 1.iii.1644, N.S.). It was pulled down in the first years of the nineteenth century, but is known from engravings by Silvestre and in the Petit Marot.

18. The exact share of the two architects is uncertain, but it seems likely that de Brosse was responsible for the lay-out of the principal court and the elevations of the buildings surrounding it, except for the dormers. Lemercier appears to have redesigned the interior of the main block, extended it and invented the whole garden front.

19. This vestibule with its triple opening was to be the basis of a favourite plan of Le Vau.

20. For details of the building and furnishing of Richelieu, see E. Bonnaffé, *Les Collections des Richelieu* (Paris, 1883). The earliest and fullest description of the château is in E. Brackenhoffer, *Voyage en France, 1643–4*, 219 ff.

21. In one room, for instance, the frieze was decorated with the paintings by Mantegna, Costa, and Perugino from the studio of Isabella d'Este at Mantua, with which the three Poussin 'Bacchanals' hung *en suite*.

22. The only early sources are the life in Charles Perrault's *Hommes Illustres*, published in 1696, and a violent satirical attack on Mansart in a broadsheet published in 1651 with the title of *La Mansarade* (reprinted in the *Archives de l'Art Français*, second series, II, 242). Though obviously prejudiced, this pamphlet gives a view of the architect's character which appears to have some foundation.

23. Cf. Perrault, *Hommes Illustres*, 87. He seems to have built there a small staircase in the left wing of the château (cf. *Bulletin Monumental*, 1853, 597).

24. In fact, Brice (*Nouvelle Description de Paris*, II (Paris, 1725), 317) specifically states that he did not go there.

25. All the old authorities from Sauval onwards agree in attributing this façade to Mansart. Mariette gives the date 1624, but Dumolin (*B.S.H.A.F.*, (1930), 18) gives 1623 without evidence. It is

engraved in Blondel's *Architecture Française*, Book V, No. 20.

26. Berny is attributed to Mansart in a contemporary poem in the *Recueil de Sercy*, third part (Paris, 1666), 222. Tallemant des Réaux (*Historiettes*, ed. Monmerqué, II (Brussels, 1854), 52), Mlle de Montpensier (*Mémoires*, ed. Chéruel, III (Paris, 1891), 372), and Merian (*Topographia Galliæ*, I (Amsterdam, 1660), 328) state that it was begun by Nicolas Brulart de Sillery, who died in 1624. It is described in some detail in the diary of Giovanni Francesco Rucellai for 1643 (cf. G. F. Rucellai, *Un' Ambasciata* (Florence, 1884), 117). The question of both authorships and date has recently been settled by the discovery in the Archives Nationales of the original drawing, dated 27 November 1623, and the contract which names Mansart as the designer (cf. *Arts*, 4.viii.1954, 8).

27. The attribution of Balleroy to Mansart is given by Perrault. The date, *c.* 1626, seems to be purely traditional, but is not contrary to the evidence of style.

28. The elaborate volutes ending in two fanciful obelisks recall Roman churches such as S. Maria dell'Orto in their function and sixteenth-century French models in their detail. Above the rounded pediment Mansart has added a panel, the top of which consists of a straight entablature breaking into an arch in the middle, a form which Mansart was to use regularly and which he derived from sixteenth-century models (cf., for instance, the entrance at Fleury-en-Bière). The door has three heavy voussoirs, a device which the architect frequently uses at this time (Berny and Balleroy) and which comes from the elder du Cerceau.

29. The two sets of engravings differ in material points. As far as it is now possible to check the matter, Silvestre seems to be the more reliable of the two artists.

30. The central window and the door have been partly bricked up.

31. Other borrowings from de Brosse are the circular dormers (Blérancourt) and the pedimented windows (Rennes) which do not occur again in the surviving work of Mansart. p. 120

32. For the plan and detailed illustrations of Balleroy see C. Gould and A. Blunt, 'The Château de Balleroy', *Burl. Mag.*, LXXXVII (1945), 248.

33. There are no measured elevations of the building available, but to the eye it looks as though Mansart has made the walls of the château slope slightly inwards, a device which would increase the apparent height of the building.

34. Balleroy seems to have been imitated by later

builders in Normandy. The principal façade of the château of Thury-Harcourt, for instance, which was destroyed in 1944, is almost a copy of Mansart's design (reproduced in H. Soulange-Bodin, *Châteaux de Normandie*, 1 (Paris, 1928), Plate xxv).

Brécy, near Bayeux, presents a more complicated problem. Soulange-Bodin (*op. cit.*, 23) and Blomfield (*A History of French Architecture 1494–1661*, II, 111) both accept the traditional attribution of the château and the gardens to Mansart, and it may indeed be that Mansart provided a general plan which was carried out by a not very competent local builder, assisted by an unusually good decorative sculptor, who showed real invention in the reliefs of the entrance and the statues in the garden.

p. 120   35. The builder of Balleroy may actually have been the father of the chancellor. Both were called Jean and the dates are somewhat obscure, but the father appears to have owned Balleroy in the late 1620s.

p. 121   36. A further similarity with Anet is the fact that the arches round the dome have three-dimensional curves.

p. 122   37. At the same date (1632) Mansart also built the other convent of the Visitandines in the rue St Jacques (now destroyed. Cf. *Commission du Vieux Paris* (1903), 52.). In 1636 Mansart designed the façade of the church of the Minims (cf. Dumolin, *B.S.H.A.F.*, (1930), 18) known from the engraving by Marot. Apparently, however, only the lower storey was erected from his designs. A small fragment still survives (cf. Yvan Christ, *Églises Parisiennes*, plate 83) and a plan exists in Stockholm (cf. *B.S.H.A.F.*, (1949), 29).

38. The fullest account of the building of this hôtel is given by G. E. Bertin in his 'Notice sur l'Hôtel de la Vrillière et de Toulouse', *Mémoires de la Société de l'Histoire de Paris*, xxvIII (1901), 1. It is described in great detail by Sauval (*Histoire et recherches des antiquités de la ville de Paris*, II (Paris, 1724), 226. The engravings of Marot show its appearance as left by Mansart, but the plan in Blondel dates from after the alterations of de Cotte, who completely changed the disposition of the interior. The manuscript plan in the Bibliothèque Nationale reproduced in Fig. 16 gives the original arrangement. Almost nothing now survives of Mansart's building which forms part of the Banque de France, but the gallery altered by de Cotte was reconstructed in the nineteenth century, and the ceiling of Perrier, executed in Mansart's time, was exactly copied.

39. This closing wall is curved on the inside, as at Lemercier's almost contemporary Hôtel de Liancourt.

40. Cf. *Mémoires Inédits*, I, 132.

41. For instance, at Fresnes and in the Visitation.

42. One of the novelties of the house, according to Sauval (II, 228), and as we learn from the plan, was the staircase, which occupied a square space with an open well in the middle. It is possible that de Brosse's staircase in the Luxembourg may have foreshadowed this form, but it seems to have been essentially a type used by Mansart. He had already introduced it at Balleroy, and at Maisons was to give it its finest form. In my book, *François Mansart* (35), I wrongly stated on the authority of Blondel that Mansart's staircase in the Hôtel de la Vrillière was in essentials preserved by de Cotte, but the plan here reproduced shows that it occupied a different position. Another important feature in Mansart's design is the entrance vestibule, a square room covered by a circular dome supported on full columns. Nothing of this sort seems to have existed in French architecture before this date.

Dumolin (*B.S.H.A.F.*, (1930), 20) adduces a payment by La Vrillière to Louis Le Vau in 1640 to prove that this architect must have finished the hôtel begun by Mansart, but the payment may refer to one of La Vrillière's other houses in the same quarter (cf. Bertin, *op. cit.*, 4).

43. During the 1630s Mansart also built other houses in Paris. The Hôtel de la Basinière, probably begun in 1636 (cf. Dumolin, *Études*, I, 250), is known from the engravings in the *Petit Marot*. It survives, completely remodelled, as part of the École des Beaux-Arts. The Hôtel de Chavigny was probably built between 1635 and 1641 (cf. Dumolin, *Topographie*, III, 297. Hartmann, *Commission du Vieux Paris* (1923), 6, gives the date 1631 for the acquisition of the site by Chavigny. The building is mentioned in the *Mansarade*.). Part of it survives, somewhat altered, in the second court of the Hôtel Poulletier, 13 rue de Sévigné (reproduced by G. Pillement, *Les Vieux Hôtels de Paris*, I, plate 14). It also appears in an engraving of Silvestre (Faucheux, *Catalogue raisonné de l'œuvre d'Israel Silvestre* (Paris, 1857), 49, No. 12) under the name Hôtel St Paul. The Hôtel d'Aubespine, described by Sauval (II, 202) may have been built before 1633, after which time its owner was in more or less continuous disgrace, but there is no certain evidence on this point.

44. The only drawings which represent the complete scheme (reproduced, Lesueur, *Le Château de Blois*, and A. Blunt, *François Mansart*, plates 29–31) do not date from the first stage of the designing of the château, but documents prove that Gaston planned some such general scheme from the beginning. It is quite likely that the plan reproduced by Lesueur, *op. cit.*, 112, may have been altered by Mansart at a

much later date, perhaps even in the 1650s. His first scheme may be recorded in the under-drawing in Blondel's plan of the château, reproduced by P. Lesueur, 'Un Ouvrage inédit de Jacques-François Blondel', *Gazette des Beaux-Arts*, II (1931), 363.

In my book *François Mansart* (62 ff.) I put forward the view that Mansart's surviving work at Blois was carried out in two different stages, the main building dating from 1635–38, and the staircase, the colonnade and the frontispiece on the court façade belonging to a much later period, probably the fifties. I am now, however, convinced that this hypothesis cannot be maintained. Documents published by Lesueur in the *Mémoires de la Société des Sciences et Lettres du Loir-et-Cher*, XXX (1938), 140 ff., prove that the colonnade was constructed during the first building campaign; an examination of the masonry establishes that the frontispiece was built at the same time as the main block; and a closer stylistic analysis of the decoration of the staircase shows, in my opinion, that it must date from the thirties rather than the fifties. The trophy reliefs on the cove are almost certainly designed by Guillain, and not by Sarrazin, as is usually said, for they are in many features nearly identical with the relief from the monument on the Pont-au-Change, now in the Louvre (1647, reproduced in Planat and Rümler, *Le Style Louis XIV* (Paris, 1912), plate 10). Guillain and his pupils are known to have been active at Blois in the years 1637–8 (cf. Lesueur, *Le Château de Blois*, 111 f.), but are not recorded there later. Moreover, the Blois reliefs have Mannerist details, such as the masks and certain parts of the scroll work, which point to their being earlier than the Pont-au-Change relief in which they are not present. It is hardly possible that Mansart, having decorated Maisons in the 1640s in the fully classical manner employed by Sarrazin and his assistants, should in the fifties have gone back to the much less advanced and more Mannerist style of Guillain.

123 45. There is some reason to think that he altered this arrangement during the execution of the building.

46. The colonnades were destroyed in the nineteenth century and later reconstructed but with a plain entablature.

47. It only develops into a full Order in the central pavilion.

124 48. We shall see that Le Vau was particularly weak in this matter.

49. In fact, as has frequently been pointed out, he did not invent it. His immediate model must have been de Brosse's roof at Rennes. According to the drawings, Blois was also to have an ornamental iron railing along the ridge of the roof as at Rennes.

50. The Orders are all pilasters which play a regular rhythm in very low relief, except on the southeast front, where the arrangement is made more elaborate, both on the flat and in depth, by the introduction of niches.

51. In the designs for the Bourbon Chapel (1664–6) the architect applied the same method to a church (cf. p. 129).

52. Cf. A. Blunt, *François Mansart*, 14 ff.   p. 125

53. Le Muet and Le Duc who were made architects in charge in 1655 and 1666 respectively do not seem to have altered the design of the church.

54. The château of Fresnes was near Meaux and p. 126 belonged to the Guénégaud family. An engraving of it is reproduced by Hautecœur (*Architecture*, II, 58), who, however, confuses it with the other Fresnes near Meulan, belonging to the O family. The early writers attribute to Mansart only the chapel, which is known from the engravings in Mariette, but the garden front shown by Pérelle is in his style, and it was probably he who made all the alterations which are known to have been carried out to the earlier château (cf. Piganiol de la Force, VIII, 164).

The question of dates is complicated. According to Huygens (*Gazette des Beaux-Arts*, II, 1937, 102) Guénégaud bought the estate about 1640. From the *Mémoires Inédits* we know that the chapel was decorated by Perrier, who died in 1650, and the author clearly implies that this work was carried out before 1645. This view is confirmed by the Life of Perrier by Caylus and Mariette (cf. *Archives de l'Art français*, 1913, 194). These facts cast some doubt on the traditional view, derived from Mlle de Scudéry, that Mansart executed at Fresnes the plans which he had been prevented from carrying out at the Val-de-Grâce, which would involve dating the chapel after 1646.

55. We know nothing of the external appearance of the chapel which according to Huygens (*loc. cit.*) was over the main entrance and was approached from two terraces. It must therefore have been placed like the rotundas at the Luxembourg or Blois. An even closer parallel is Monceaux, built by de Brosse, where a chapel occupied the same position.

56. In the Val-de-Grâce the crossing is preceded by a nave of three bays, whereas at Fresnes there was only a short nave of one bay.

57. The plan of Fresnes with its short nave may also be compared with Bramante's S. Biagio della Pagnotta (reproduced in G. Giovannoni, *Saggi sulla Architettura del Rinascimento* (Milan, 1935), 91).

58. Except for the baldacchino, which dates from 1663–67 and is probably from a design by Le Duc,

based on the baldacchino in St Peter's by Bernini, who may have had a share in modifying Le Duc's scheme during his visit of 1665 (cf. P. du Colombier, *L'Église du Val-de-Grâce* (Paris, n.d.), 10).

p. 126   59. The window in the upper storey is a characteristic borrowing of contemporary Roman forms by Lemercier.

60. Cf. Dumolin, *Études*, II, 281.

61. Dumolin, *op. cit.*, III, 329. Some alterations must have been carried out in the hôtel between the original building of the hôtel and the work of 1655, since the engravings in the *Petit Marot* which illustrate the state of the house before the latter date show certain details, such as the staircase and a circular room, which cannot possibly belong to the Lescot design. Some historians have believed that they were also by Mansart; there is no positive evidence for this, but it does not seem unlikely.

62. Mansart has preserved Lescot's entrance which was decorated with reliefs by Goujon.

63. The same sort of refinement was to be seen in the door of the Hôtel du Jars, known from a detailed engraving in Blondel. The door of the Hôtel de Conti, built soon after 1648 (cf. Dumolin, *Études*, III, 389), has equally fine detail but is more plastic in conception, being placed in a simply designed rusticated niche. The remains of a similar niche can be seen in the much-damaged front of the Petit Hôtel de Conti, which still stands at the end of the Impasse de Conti and forms part of the Monnaie.

During the period which we are now considering Mansart built two further houses for the Duplessis-Guénégaud family, one the Hôtel d'Albret, 31 rue des Francs-Bourgeois, begun in 1643 (cf. Dumolin, *Études*, III, 389) and now wholly altered, and the other at the corner of the rue des Archives and the rue des Quatre Fils, built between 1647 and 1651, which still exists and contains a fine staircase (cf. *Commission du Vieux Paris* (28 Feb. 1931), 57). The question of the Hôtel Fieubet on the Quai des Célestins is highly complicated, but I believe that the garden façade is due to Mansart (the rest was entirely altered in the nineteenth century). Even more difficult is the question of Mansart's possible contribution to the Hôtel Mazarin. R. A. Weigert has published a document (cf. *B.S.H.A.F.*, (1945), 6, 26 ff.) which proves that Mansart made internal alterations for Mazarin to the old Hôtel Tubeuf, and mentions his name as the original architect of the galleries added by Mazarin, but he points out that his name is struck out in the document, which leads one to suppose that, although he apparently received the original commission for the work, he may have been relieved of it owing to one of those

difficulties which seem to have arisen so frequently between him and his patrons. The style of the work at the Hôtel Mazarin amply supports this hypothesis, since it bears no resemblance to that of Mansart. Externally the galleries are a mere repetition of the work of Le Muet for Tubeuf, and internally the decoration is richer in detail and more Mannerist in design than any mature work of Mansart.

64. According to the author of the *Mansarade* the p. 1: architect pulled down a part of Maisons to rebuild it according to a better design. The same author states that the vestibule collapsed before it was finished. The fullest account of Maisons and its builder is to be found in J. Stern, *Le Château de Maisons* (Paris, 1934).

65. The same qualities can be seen in all parts of the building, for instance in the low pavilions projecting from the wings, which are composed of rectangular blocks of Doric pilasters, with an oval re-entrant bay on the outside. The frontispiece on the garden side is as ingenious as that on the entrance front, but with slight variations.

66. All the sculptural decoration of Maisons is p. 1 from the designs of Sarrazin, though it was mainly executed by his pupils, Guérin, Buyster, and van Obstal.

67. The story is told in full by Hautecœur, *Le Louvre et les Tuileries de Louis XIV*, 145 ff. Two of Mansart's drawings are there reproduced.

68. The drawings are reproduced and discussed by Hautecœur, *Architecture*, II, 70. There is no documentary evidence for Mansart's connexion with the chapel, but there is no reason to doubt that the drawings are by him.

69. For a fuller discussion of this point see A. p. 1 Blunt, *François Mansart*, 29.

70. As Hautecœur has pointed out, the younger Mansart used exactly this method in the chapel of the Invalides several decades later (cf. p. 212).

71. It is possible that Mansart also carried out the enlargement of the garden front, but, if so, he only modified and extended Le Vau's design (cf. below, p. 265, note 82).

72. Since it has long been customary to ascribe to François Mansart buildings of the mid seventeenth century for which no other name can be found, it may be worth adding a note on those works which are not discussed in the text. The following buildings can be ascribed to him on good evidence, although little or nothing now remains of them: the château of Gesvres (Charles Perrault, *Hommes Illustres*, p. 87); the Aubespine tomb in the cathedral of Bourges of which fragments survive in the museum

(cf. *Bulletin de la Société des Antiquaires de France*, XLVII, 1903, 329). Piganiol de la Force (III, 248) ascribes to him the high altar of the Filles Dieu, and that of St Martindes Champs (*op. cit.*, 376); Perrault further tells us that Mansart carried out unspecified work at Richelieu, Choisy, and Petit-Bourg.

Other traditional attributions can, however, be firmly rejected on documentary and stylistic grounds: the châteaux of Chamarande and Cany; the town halls at Troyes and Arles; the arch at Toulouse; the château of Bercy, which is by François Le Vau, and that of Canteleu near Rouen (referred to as Chantelou by Hautecœur, *Architecture*, II, 69), which is probably by his brother Louis. Hautecœur dismisses the following buildings which I have not seen: Daubeuf, La Ferté St Aubin, and the Hôtel des Rames at Abbeville. He leaves open the attributions of the châteaux at La Ferté-Reuilly and Dampierre (Aube), the chapel at Marines, and the church of the Annonciades at Tours. I have been unable to trace the source of Blomfield's statement (*A History of French Architecture, 1494-1661*, II, 68) that Mansart built the oval choir to the Oratoire. It seems to be without solid foundation. The question of the destroyed church of Ste Marie de la Visitation at Chaillot must remain open. Dézallier d'Argenville (*Voyage Pittoresque des Environs de Paris*, 2) and Blondel (*Cours d'Architecture*, II (Paris, 1771-7), 322) ascribe it to François Mansart, but Piganiol de la Force (*op. cit.*, II, 304) says it was entirely rebuilt in 1704. The engraving of the Order on the façade given by Blondel (*op. cit.*, plate 83c) does not supply enough evidence to settle the matter on stylistic grounds.

131   73. The few available facts have been collected by Dumolin in 'Notes sur quelques architectes du 17ᵉ siècle', *B.S.H.A.F.*, (1930), 12.

74. The house is shown in its original state in an engraving by Silvestre, copied in Merian. It was later altered by Colbert, who gave it the form which it has in the *Grand Marot* engravings. Marot, Mariette, and Florent le Comte (*Cabinet des Singularitez*, I, xxviii) all agree in attributing the building to Le Vau, and their testimony must be accepted in spite of the improbability of the commission being given to so young an architect. It is possible that he was here acting as assistant to his father, and the work may be the result of their collaboration. Later they certainly worked together in this way, as their names occur together in several of the contracts for houses in the Île St-Louis.

The Hôtel de Bullion is sometimes ascribed to Le Vau, but there seems to be no foundation for this attribution, which is even more difficult to accept

than that of the Hôtel Bautru, because it must have been finished by 1634, when Vouet began the decoration of one of the galleries (cf. Dumolin, *Topographie*, II, 388).

75. Plans and elevations in the *Grand Marot* and a   p. 132
general view of this part of the island in Pérelle. Photographs in Contet's *Vieux Hôtels de Paris, Île Saint-Louis* and in *Commission du Vieux Paris* (1931). For the dates cf. Dumolin, *Études*, III, 119.

76. The facts about the building are given in Dumolin, *Études* III, 90 ff. The house is engraved in Blondel's *Architecture Française*, and the painted decorations by Picart in *Les Peintures ... dans l'Hôtel du Chastelet* (Paris, 1746). Contet's *Vieux Hôtels de Paris* devotes a whole volume to the house.

77. The use of the gallery recalls Mansart's designs   p. 134
at Blois and Maisons.

78. The gradual change from the narrow and dark lower flight to the open luminous space at the top was developed by German Baroque architects, particularly by Balthasar Neumann at Bruchsal.

79. The interior has recently been brilliantly restored under the direction of M Jacques Dupont and the Monuments Historiques (cf. *B.S.H.A.F.*, (1946-7), 125).

80. Cf. L. Dimier, 'Une erreur corrigée touchant l'Hôtel Lambert', *B.S.H.A.F.*, (1927), 30.

81. Cf. p. 122.   p. 135

82. Apart from the smaller houses which he built on the Île St Louis, Le Vau also designed several other important Paris hôtels. For Scarron he built the house now known as the Hôtel d'Aumont, finished by 1649 (cf. C. Sellier, *Anciens Hôtels de Paris*, 196), later altered by Mansart (cf. above, p. 154); reproduced in Pillement, *Les Hôtels de Paris*, I, plate 17, and in the same author's *Hôtels du Marais*. The original state is shown in the engravings in the *Petit Marot*. The Hôtel Miramion on the quai des Tournelles is so similar to the Hôtel d'Aumont that it must be attributed to the same architect. In 1656 Le Vau built the Hôtel de Lauzun for Charles Gruyn des Bordes (cf. Dumolin, *Études*, III, 113), which survives, though the interior was over-restored in the nineteenth century. His last Paris house, the Hôtel de Lionne, built in 1662 (cf. Dumolin, *Études*, II, 229), is known from the engravings in the *Grand Marot*. Here Le Vau took up Mansart's idea of the double flight of rooms, and introduced an apsed vestibule which led through a columned opening to the staircase, a typically dramatic arrangement. On the exterior he again used small and colossal Orders indiscriminately.

83. Engraved by Silvestre and in the *Petit Marot*.

The upper limit of date is given by the fact that Perrier painted there before 1645 (cf. *Mémoires Inédits*, I, 132).

p. 135 84. Here again Le Vau is untidy in his use of Orders, applying a colossal Order to the end pavilions, the rest of the building being simply rusticated.

85. This arrangement of vestibule, salon and staircase was imitated in England, for instance by Vanbrugh at Castle Howard and Blenheim.

86. Cf. J. Cordey, 'Le grand salon ovale de Vaux-le-Vicomte et sa décoration', *Revue de l'Art*, XLVI (1924), 233.

p. 137 87. It is in itself typical that Lebrun should have chosen as his model the Pitti decorations and not the much more Baroque Barberini ceiling by the same artist.

p. 138 88. In addition to these major works, Le Vau made alterations to Meudon for Servien, who bought it in 1654 (its state after Le Vau's improvements is shown in Hautecœur, *Architecture*, II, 100). He was also involved in the building of several churches, including St Louis-en-l'Île and St Sulpice, but his share is hard to determine (Hautecœur, *op. cit.*, 94 ff.).

His younger brother, François (1613–76), was also an architect of considerable reputation. His certain works include the châteaux of Bercy, Lignières, and St Fargeau (Hautecœur, *op. cit.*, 114 ff.), and two buildings often attributed to Louis may actually be his, namely the châteaux of St Sépulchre, near Troyes, built for Hesselin (engraved in the *Grand Marot*) and of Sucy-en-Brie (cf. *Châteaux et Manoirs de France, Île-de-France*, II, plates 47–51; and *B.S.H.A.F.*, (1925), 32), built for Lambert about 1640. Both these designs have details, such as the breaking of the field of the pediment, which occur regularly in the work of François but are not found in the certain buildings by Louis. The little château of Suisnes (*Châteaux et Manoirs de France, Île-de-France*, II, plates 63–68) seems to be a provincial imitation of the style of Louis Le Vau.

89. For the facts of his career see Dumolin, *Études*, I, 378, and 'Notes sur quelques architectes du 17ᵉ siècle', *B.S.H.A.F.*, (1930), 15.

90. Both are engraved in his *Œuvres*.

p. 139 91. The house is well illustrated in Contet's *Vieux Hôtels de Paris, Le Quartier St Paul*.

p. 140 92. They are listed by Dumolin in the works quoted above and by Hautecœur, *Architecture*, II, 145 ff.

93. It seems possible that Wren may have had this engraving in mind when he designed the Great Model of St Paul's. The domeless drum may also have given Fischer von Erlach the idea for the Schwarzenberg Palais.

94. In England, for instance, Vanbrugh seems to have been influenced by the massing and rustication of Le Pautre's design at Blenheim and elsewhere.

95. Cf. Dumolin, 'Quelques artistes inconnus du 17ᵉ siècle', *B.S.H.A.F.*, (1928), 364.

96. As in the Hôtel Guénégaud in the rue des Archives or in the Hôtel du Jars. Mansart, however, would never have introduced the awkward relation of a big pediment over a small one which disturbs the harmony of the front.

97. Cottard also built the château of Villacerf (cf. Hautecœur, *Architecture*, II, 137) and published several series of engraved designs for architecture and decoration. Other minor architects who built private houses at this time are Adam Robelin, whose Hôtel de Léon in the rue de La Garancière has an unusual colossal Ionic Order of pilasters with rams' heads in the capitals (cf. Hautecœur, *Architecture*, II, 132), and Jean Richer, three of whose houses are engraved in the *Grand Marot*, but show little originality (Hautecœur, *op. cit.*, 124).

98. Desargues is named as the author of this house p. 1 by Lemaire (*Paris ancien et nouveau*, III, 30), Brice (*op. cit.*, I, 458), and Bosse, who was a personal friend and who engraved this staircase as well as another by the architect in the château of Vizille (1653), in his *Traité des Manières de dessiner les Ordres* (cf. G. Gaillard, 'Nouveaux documents sur la construction et la décoration du Château de Vizille', *B.S.H.A.F.*, (1951), 19). M. Roland's house is engraved in the *Petit Marot*, but without the name of the architect. Hautecœur reproduced the plan of his house (*Architecture*, II, 125, figure 116), but identifies it with a house by Richer in the same street (reproduced, *op. cit.*, figure 117).

99. Many buildings, such as the château of Turny p. 1 and the house of M. de Sainte-Foy, have been attributed to Marot for no better reason than that they appear in his engravings without the name of the architect. Stylistically they are quite unlike his documented works. The château of Lavardin, engraved in the *Grand Marot*, was ascribed to him in the eighteenth century (cf. Mauban, *Jean Marot*, 23.).

100. Cf. p. 198. Blomfield ascribes the building to the younger brother, but all the early authorities agree that it is by Jacques.

101. Hautecœur (*Architecture*, II, 130 f.) attributes to Bruant the château of Fayelles and the house of the banker Jabach in Paris, both engraved in the *Petit Marot*, but he gives no evidence for his view. Jabach's house is known to have been mainly built by Bullet (Hautecœur, *op. cit.*., II, 690), although

other architects may have had a hand in it earlier; but there is nothing to indicate that Bruant is one of these and the style is not at all like his. For details about Jabach's house see Grouchy, 'Everhard Jabach, collectionneur Parisien', *Mémoires de la Société de l'Histoire de Paris*, XXI (1894), 225 ff.

143 102. There is no systematic account of the whole of Vouet's career, though L. Demonts ('Essai sur la formation de S. Vouet en Italie', *B.S.H.A.F.*, (1913), 309) and J. Bousquet ('Documents sur le séjour de Simon Vouet à Rome', *Mélanges d'Archéologie et d'Histoire*, 1952, 287) have collected the information available about his Italian period. H. Voss ('Die Caravaggeske Frühzeit von S. Vouet und N. Regnier', *Zeitschrift für bildende Kunst*, LVIII, 1924, 56) has added certain further attributions. For Vouet as a portrait-painter, see A. Blunt, 'Some portraits by Simon Vouet', *Burl. Mag.*, LXXXVIII (1946), 268. The most useful sources for Vouet's activities are Félibien (*Entretiens*, III, 392), G. Lioni and Fausto Amidei (*Ritratti di alcuni celebri Pittori* (Rome, 1731), 53), and Dézallier d'Argenville (*Abrégé*, IV, 10).

103. It has been suggested that he visited Naples on the ground that two paintings by him are to be found in Neapolitan churches, the 'Virgin appearing to St Bruno' in S. Martino (Plate 109) and the 'Circumcision' in S. Angelo a Segno (reproduced in the catalogue of *La Madonna nella Pittura del '600 a Napoli*, Naples, 1954, plate 10). But the former is dated 1620 and the latter 1623, and it is easier to imagine that they were executed in Rome and sent to Naples than to suppose two visits to the city for which there is no other evidence. Demonts sees in the work of Vouet qualities which he attributes to the influence of Neapolitan painting but which seem to me traceable to Roman sources. His statement that Vouet was a friend and imitator of Bernardo Strozzi in Genoa and Venice seems to be based on the portrait engraved after Vouet in Venice in 1627, which, however, actually represents the poet Giulio Strozzi and not the painter.

104. Not 1641 as often stated. Cf. *Archives de l'Art français, Documents*, V (1857–8), 215.

105. Reproduced in Voss, *Malerei des Barock*, 139.

106. The head of the Virgin in the Doni Madonna.

107. Demonts (*op. cit.*, 58) quotes an engraving by Vignon after Vouet dated 1618, which represents a love scene and appears to be more purely Caravaggesque.

144 108. See A. Blunt, 'Some Portraits by Simon Vouet', *op. cit.*, 268.

109. It should be remembered that outside Italy the Jesuits did not foster the extreme forms of Baroque with which their name is so closely associated in Rome.

110. Now in the collection of M. Guyot de Villeneuve (cf. L. Demonts, 'Les Amours de Renaud et Armide', *B.S.H.A.F.*, (1913), 59).

A painting of 'Time defeated by Venus, Cupid and Hope', signed and dated 1628, is in the London art trade.

111. From the arms it seems to have been painted for Anne of Austria, for whom Vouet worked in 1644–9, and it may even refer to the Peace of Westphalia in 1648.

112. We know from Sauval's description (II, 192) p. 145 that the gallery in the Hôtel de Bullion, begun in 1634 (cf. *B.S.H.A.F.*, (1927), 179), was of this type. A similar scheme survives, though much damaged, in the grotto of Bullion's château of Wideville (reproduced in L. Dimier, *Histoire de la Peinture Française, 1627–90*, I, plates 4, 5). The main panels of the ceiling in the gallery at Chilly are known from the engravings of Perrier (painted 1630–2; cf. Félibien, *Entretiens*, III, 396), and from the description of Dézallier d'Argenville (*Voyage Pittoresque des Environs de Paris*, 242) it is clear that they were enclosed in stucco decoration. The centre panel from the ceiling of the chapel at Chilly, representing St Anthony received into heaven, is also engraved by Perrier, who seems to have assisted Vouet in the execution of all the work at Chilly.

113. For the panels of the ceiling at Chilly Vouet seems to have been inspired by Guercino's 'Aurora', as far as the presentation of the chariot is concerned; but he does not imitate Guercino's much bolder illusionist scheme for the whole ceiling.

114. The Fontainebleau series were engraved by Dorigny in 1644 (R.D. 94–9), and the Palais Royal set by the same artist in 1647 (R.D. 105–19).

115. Reproduced in Contet, *Vieux Hôtels de Paris, Quartier St Paul*, plates 25–33.

116. The chapel was engraved by Dorigny in 1638 (R.D. 56), the library in 1640 (R.D. 76–82), and the panels from the lower gallery in 1651 (R.D. 123–31 and 133). The latter, which can be identified from Sauval's description (II, 196), represent mythological subjects which have, however, reference to the career of Séguier's protector, Richelieu. So, for instance, Jupiter giving the reins to Phaeton symbolizes Louis XIII handing over the government to Richelieu; and the destruction of the daughters of Niobe represents the driving out of the English from the island of Ré.

117. Cf. p. 60.

p. 145   118. Though Fréminet's ceiling in the chapel at Fontainebleau contains illusionist panels.

119. This scheme was not used again in Italy till it was taken up afresh by Tiepolo.

p. 146   120. It was applied in a clumsy way by Walther Damery in his dome fresco in the Carmelite church, painted apparently in 1644. In the 1680s it was used by Lebrun and Houasse in the Salon de la Guerre, the Salon de la Paix, and the Salle de l'Abondance at Versailles (cf. p. 193).

121. Vouet's decorative ability appears also in the field of tapestry. Many of his designs were used with success by Comans and La Planche in their factory (cf. Fenaille, *op. cit.*, I, 303–47).

122. *Abrégé*, IV, 19. Félibien (*Entretiens*, IV, 203) gives no date of birth, nor do Caylus and Mariette in their joint life of the artist (*Archives de l'Art Français*, 1913, 186).

123. The early lives only mention the frescoes in the Cabinet des Muses which still exist, but the author of the introduction to Picart's engravings of the Hôtel Lambert states that Perrier also executed one of the wall panels in the Cabinet de l'Amour, which is generally assumed to be the painting of 'Aeneas and the Harpies' now in the Louvre.

p. 147   124. Though at an earlier date, in 1632.

125. For Blanchard's life see Félibien, *Entretiens*, III, 388, and Dézallier, *Abrégé*, IV, 49; for a list of his works, cf. L. Demonts, 'Deux peintres de la première moitié du 17ᵉ siècle', *Gazette des Beaux-Arts*, II (1925), 162.

126. Another portrait signed and dated 1631 is in the collection of Mrs John S. Newberry, Detroit (reproduced in the *Bulletin of the Detroit Institute of Arts*, XVI, 1937, 100).

127. The most useful early life is that in the *Mémoires Inédits*, I, 104.

128. The first, now at Rouen, reproduced in Dimier, *Histoire de la Peinture française, 1627–90*, I, plate 27.

p. 148   129. Cf. Bonnaffé, *Amateurs français au 17ᵉ siècle*, 185.

130. For instance, the *Mai* of 1635 now in the Louvre, of St Peter healing the Sick, and two paintings in the Hermitage at Leningrad, dated 1636 (one reproduced by Weisbach, *Französische Malerei*, 61). The *Mai* of 1637, representing the Conversion of St Paul, now in St Thomas d'Aquin (reproduced in *Peintures Méconnues des Églises de Paris*, Galliera Museum, 1946, No. 36), is La Hyre's most Baroque composition.

131. For instance in the 'Holy Family' (Nantes, dated 1641; other versions in the Louvre and Ber-

lin), the little Louvre 'Madonna' of 1641, and in the 'Scene from the Life of Abraham' in the Hermitage, which must date from about the same period.

132. The influence of Poussin can be seen most clearly in a painting of Job (sold at Christie's, 16 March 1945, lot 115), and that of Champaigne in the 'Supper at Emmaus' and the 'Noli me tangere' of 1656, painted for the Grande Chartreuse and now at Grenoble. The coldness is apparent in the 'Allegory on the Peace of Westphalia' (1648) in the Louvre.

133. For instance, in the landscape with shepherds of 1648, reproduced in *Les Peintres de la Réalité*, Orangerie, 1934, No. 41, and in the 'Landscape with Bathers' at Maisons-Lafitte.

134. A number of minor contemporaries of the painters discussed above deserve mention. Lubin Baugin (*c.* 1610–63), called 'Le Petit Guide', specialized in small Holy Families based on the designs of Parmigianino but incorporating also some of the sentiment of Guido Reni (cf. Plate 145B). He is not identical with the still-life painter of the same name (cf. below, p. 271, note 178). Nicolas Chapron (1612–1656), mainly known as an engraver, also painted small pictures of Bacchanals (cf. two in the Hermitage) in a manner which he probably learnt in Rome, where he went in 1642, from Poussin, Castiglione, and Andrea Podestà. Michel Corneille the Elder (1602–64) began in a style which has some relation to the Dutch group round Lastman and Pynas, but was later influenced by Vouet and Poussin. The brothers Jacques and Guillaume Courtois, born in Franche Comté, belong to the history of Italian art, since their whole active career was spent in Italy, where they italianized their name into Cortese, *alias* Il Borgognone.

To these must be added certain provincial painters who brought into France various Italian idioms. In the south Guy François of Le Puy (1580–1650) painted large altarpieces in a semi-Baroque manner (cf. *Les Peintres de la Réalité*, No. 44). At Toulouse Hilaire Pader executed huge religious and allegorical compositions for the town and wrote a long poem about painting (cf. P. de Chennevières-Pointel, *Recherches sur la vie et les ouvrages de quelques Peintres Provinciaux*, IV, I). At Aix-en-Provence a Fleming, Jean Daret (1613–64), settled, and decorated the churches and houses of the town (cf. Chennevières-Pointel, *op. cit.*, I, 41, and J. L. Vaudoyer, *Les Peintres Provençaux* (Paris, 1947), 54). In the north-east Philippe Quantin, at Langres and Dijon, represents the same phase as François in the south, and is just as provincial (cf. *Les Peintres de la Réalité*, No. 136, and Weisbach, *op. cit.*, 84 with reproductions; paintings in the museum at Dijon). Richard Tassel of Langres is a more elusive personality (cf. Plate 146B), who seems to have imitated Caravaggio, Rubens, Jan Lys, and many other artists, if, that is to say, all the works at present attributed to him are actually by him (cf. H. Ronot, 'La Vie et l'activité du peintre Langrois Richard Tasset dit Tassel', *B.S.H.A.F.*, 1947–8, 84, and C. Sterling, 'Richard Tassel et Jan Lys', *La Renaissance*, 1936, 53). At Troyes Ninet de Lestin (d. 1662), a pupil of Vouet, added a personal note of naturalism to his master's style. His works, which deserve more notice than they have received, are to be found in the museum and many churches of Troyes, particularly St Rémi. In the Loire district Jean Mosnier (1600–?50) produced in the château of Cheverny one of the most complete surviving decorative schemes of this period. He also worked for Marie de' Medici in the Luxembourg, where some of his paintings survive in the Chambre du Livre d'Or (cf. Chennevières-Pointel, *op. cit.*, II, 151).

135. For a short account of his life and work see A. Blunt, *The Drawings of G. B. Castiglione and Stefano della Bella at Windsor Castle* (London, 1954), 89.

49 136. The documents for the two visits are given in O. Pollak, 'Italienische Künstlerbriefe', *Jb. der Preuss. Ksts.*, XXXIV, Beiheft, 46 ff.; and in L. Hautecœur, *Le Louvre et Les Tuileries de Louis XIV*, 36 ff., where the two principal rooms are illustrated. For a general account of Romanelli, see Voss, *Malerei des Barock*, 548.

137. Particularly after Poussin had set up a new classical model in his decoration of the Long Gallery of the Louvre.

138. The rooms decorated for the Queen Mother on Romanelli's second visit were treated in the same way, though they presented an easier problem, since they were smaller and more compact in form, and so allowed the artist to arrange his panels to follow the lines of the structure.

139. One follower of Rubens, Pieter van Mol (1599–1650), practised the style of his master unchanged in France. Between 1631 and 1635 he decorated the chapel of Jacques d'Étampes in the Carmelite church in the rue de Vaugirard with a series of panels which are perhaps the most purely Baroque works painted in France in this generation (cf. Count Arnold Doria, 'Les Peintures religieuses de Pierre van Mol aux Carmes', *Revue de l'Art*, LXVII, 1935, 77).

140. The fullest early lives of Champaigne are those by Félibien (*Entretiens*, IV, 312) and in the *Mémoires*

Inédits, I, 239. A. Gazier's *P. et J. B. de Champaigne* (Paris, 1893) is still the only general monograph, but one by A. Mabille de Poncheville (Paris, 1938) has some useful plates. Félibien tells us that Champaigne could not afford to enter the studio of Rubens as he wished. For Foucquier see W. Stechow, 'Drawings and Etchings by Jacques Foucquier', *Gazette des Beaux-Arts* (1948), 419. Many interesting details will be found in the catalogue of the exhibition of Philippe de Champaigne held in the Orangerie, Paris, in the spring of 1952. In particular, several works of the artist's early period and examples of his landscapes (Nos. 30, 31) were here shown for the first time.

141. Mlle Hériard-Dubreuil has convincingly identified this with a painting now in the church of Montigny-Lemcoup (cf. *B.S.H.A.F.*, (1952), 14). She dates the picture 1625, but there are some reasons for supposing that it might be as late as 1636 (cf. A. Blunt, 'Philippe de Champaigne at the Orangerie, Paris', *Burl. Mag.*, XCIV, 1952, 174).

142. Almost nothing is known of Duchesne, whose daughter Champaigne later married. But a landscape with the marriage of Louis XIII belonging to Lord Elgin which comes from the Luxembourg may possibly be by him (cf. *Landscape in French Art*, Royal Academy, London, 1949, No. 358).

143. The 'Assumption' and the 'Raising of Lazarus' from this series are at Grenoble, and according to Félibien were executed by pupils. The 'Presentation' has often been identified with one at Brussels, but it does not agree in size with the others, and looks later in style. This is confirmed by the existence of a small version dated 1642 (Sotheby's, anon. sale, 17 July 1946, lot 131). It seems more likely that the Carmelite painting is that now in the Dijon museum (cf. Orangerie Exhibition, 1952, No. 5).

144. The cartoons are in the Louvre and the tapes- p. 150 tries at Strasbourg (cf. J. Lejeaux, 'La Tenture de la Vierge', *Gazette des Beaux-Arts*, 1948, 405).

145. He had already executed several portraits of the Cardinal by that date (cf. F. Boucher, 'Sur quelques portraits du Cardinal de Richelieu par Philippe de Champaigne', *B.S.H.A.F.*, (1930), 192).

146. The gallery was painted with mythological and allegorical subjects of a kind which Champaigne rarely treated, but nothing remains of it. The portraits of famous men included the 'Gaston de Foix', now at Versailles, based on the design by Giorgione. This series was carried out in conjunction with Vouet, and is engraved in *Les Portraits des Hommes Illustres* (Paris, 1650).

147. It is based on the pattern set by the seal of the

Order (see F. Yates, *op. cit.*, plate 15), and also used in a miniature of the first installation of knights (reproduced in Blum and Lauer, *La Miniature française aux 16ᵉ et 17ᵉ siècles*, plate 100), visible on the book on which Longueville takes the oath in Champaigne's painting. Champaigne repeated the pattern again when called upon to paint a similar ceremony of 1654 (Grenoble).

p. 150 148. The 'Adoration of the Kings' at Le Mans must be among Champaigne's first works, and shows him at his closest to Rubens.

149. It is tempting to identify this painting with the Carmelite picture of 1628–9; but, if so, it must have been considerably cut at the top and sides, which in fact seems quite likely.

150. Cf. for instance the painting of the same subject at Fermo (reproduced in H. G. Evers, *P. P. Rubens* (Munich, 1942), 38).

151. They include several figures which were to recur for many years in his painting, particularly the man with a big Roman nose, who can be found as late as the Louvre 'Last Supper' of 1648. The same modified Baroque style is to be seen in the tapestry cartoons of 1636 and in a different form in the 'Louis XIII offering his Crown to Christ', though here the artist seems to have had to fit in with an almost hieratic formula, as was the case with the Saint-Esprit composition of 1634.

152. I cannot myself accept the painting of a dead nun at Geneva, dated 1634, as a work of Champaigne. The portrait of a little girl with a falcon in the Louvre, on the other hand, seems to be authentic and must be early.

153. Another variant of this pattern, showing the King in robes of state, exists in a good studio version at Windsor.

154. The 'Three Heads', painted as a model for a marble bust, is in pattern an imitation of the van Dyck 'Charles I', which at this time was in Bernini's studio in Rome, and would therefore have been known to the maker of the projected bust, whether this was Bernini himself or, as is sometimes said, Francesco Mocchi.

155. By a curious irony he was introduced to Jansenism by Hardouin de Péréfixe, who was later identified with the persecution of the nuns of Port Royal (cf. A. Gazier, *Histoire du Monastère de Port Royal* (Paris, 1929), 94, 212).

p. 151 156. In the Louvre and at Lyons. A more successful example is 'Christ nailed to the Cross' at Toulouse.

157. It is typical of his careful attention to literal detail at this stage of his career that he should have copied the Temple of Jerusalem from the reconstruction given by Villalpandus in his commentary on Ezekiel.

158. Cf. A. Blunt, 'Philippe de Champaigne's Portraits of the Échevins of Paris', *Burl. Mag.*, LXXXII (1943), 83. A further fragment unknown to me at the time of writing this article is in a Swiss private collection, and is at present (1954) on loan to the Musée d'Art et d'Histoire at Geneva.

159. One lost painting must have presented almost p. the same dignity and simplicity in a different form. This is the 'Memento Mori' still-life engraved by Morin (Plate 118): in the middle a skull, seen frontally, on the right a vase of roses with one petal fallen, on the left a watch; the perfectly classical still-life, as impressive in its simple symbolism as those of Zurbaran. Another curious manifestation of Champaigne's art at the end of his life is to be found in the series of landscapes with hermits which he painted for Port Royal (two in the Louvre). In these he seems to be imitating Poussin's classical landscape of *c*. 1650, particularly that with the three monks.

160. None of these painters has received or deserves detailed treatment. They are mostly represented in the museum of portraits at Versailles, and the facts about them are in the relevant articles in Thieme-Becker. The Beaubrun are discussed by Weisbach, *op. cit.*, 264.

161. For Nanteuil, see C. Petitjean and C. Wickert, *L'Œuvre gravé de Robert Nanteuil*, with complete reproductions of his engravings.

162. For Tournier see R. Mesuret, 'L'Acte de p. baptême de Nicolas Tournier', *B.S.H.A.F.*, (1952), 13.

163. All the known information about La Tour is to be found in F. G. Pariset, *Georges de La Tour*. I have set out my reasons for disagreeing with many of the author's conclusions, particularly on the chronology of La Tour's works, in a review, *Burl. Mag.*, XCII (1950), 144. For illustrations and summary treatments of the artist see also Paul Jamot, *Georges de la Tour*, and S. M. M. Furness, *Georges de La Tour of Lorraine*.

164. On Leclerc, cf. Pariset, *op. cit.*, 117 ff.

165. To this must now be added the remarkable p. pair of paintings (known to me only in reproductions) of an old man and peasant woman in a Swiss private collection (published by V. Bloch, 'Georges de la Tour once again', *Burl. Mag.*, XCVI, 1954, 81). Iconographically these works seem to be unique in their period, in that they represent two single figures of peasants, not illustrating any specific theme or story, monumentally conceived and executed on a fairly large scale (nearly 3 ft high), without the element of the grotesque or the comic which usually

accompanies such themes (even in La Tour's 'Joueur de Vielle'). They raise in an even more acute form the problem considered in the text section in connexion with Louis Le Nain: what kind of patron could have been interested in these objective and almost heroic presentations of peasant types?

In the same article Mr Bloch refers to another newly discovered but as yet unpublished early work by La Tour, a 'Fortune Teller' in the possession of Messrs Wildenstein.

166. Reproduced in V. Bloch, *Georges de la Tour*, plate 18.

167. A work of not very high quality, and probably executed with the help of pupils, but important as being the only dated work of the last years.

168. The most useful biography on the Le Nains is that by Paul Fierens, *Les Le Nain*, in which a full bibliography is given. To this must be added V. Lazareff's monograph published in 1936 in Moscow, in Russian, and an article by George Isarlo, 'Les trois Le Nain et leur Suite', *La Renaissance*, 1 (1938), in which the author publishes, somewhat uncritically perhaps, a very remarkable series of works by or connected with the three brothers. Two articles by V. Bloch (*Burl. Mag.*, LXXV, 1939, 50, and XC, 1949, 352) represent the most recent appreciation of the three brothers.

169. The example illustrated here is the most accomplished of all this group, and its attribution to Antoine has for this reason been doubted.

170. This composition is probably now unique, since the 'Nativity' in the Hevesy collection (Fierens, *op. cit.*, plate 58) cannot be by any member of the family, and even the lovely 'Birth of the Virgin' in St Étienne-du-Mont (usually wrongly called the 'Holy Family') is hard to reconcile with their styles. Louis presumably painted other religious subjects, for the 'St Peter' offered to Mazarin in 1656 must almost certainly have been by him (*Procès-Verbaux de l'Académie Royale de Peinture*, I, 111).

171. A visit to Rome between 1626 and 1630 (when we know Louis was back in Paris) would also account for another puzzling feature in Le Nain's painting, the similarity to certain early works of Velasquez, who was in Rome in 1629-30. Not only is Louis's tonality very close to the Spanish master's, but there seems to be an almost direct echo of the composition and some of the types of the 'Borrachos' in Louis's 'Peasant Family' (Plate 123A).

An alternative but less satisfactory origin for Louis's style would be a visit to Haarlem, where he could have found painters working in the manner which he later used. There is, for instance, a picture by Jan Molenaer, signed and dated 1629, which has always been recognized as being very close to Louis in feeling (reproduced in Fierens, *op. cit.*, plate 3). This version is signed with a monogram, but another in the von Heyl collection, Worms, is fully signed. The influence of Orazio Gentileschi, who passed through Paris in 1626, has also been suggested (cf. *Les Peintres de la Réalité*, No. 99).

172. If, that is to say, the Reims 'Forge of Vulcan' is accepted as being by Mathieu and not, as some critics think, largely by Louis.

173. Antoine and Louis died within a few months of the foundation of the Academy.

174. Those are most evident in what must be one of his first experimental works, the 'Young Gamblers' (Buckingham Palace and Louvre; Fierens, *op. cit.*, plates 63 and 64).

175. The Le Nains were also portrait painters and two signed portraits survive, one of a lady at Avignon (Fierens, *op. cit.*, plate 59), and one of the Marquis de Troisvilles (*Les Peintres de la Réalité*, No. 65). Many others have been attributed to them, mostly irresponsibly.

176. For the official Academy view of the Le Nains see Félibien, *Entretiens*, IV, 215. They had at least one imitator in the seventeenth century, Jean Michelin (1623-96; see *Les Peintres de la Réalité*, No. 121). Wallerand Vaillant (1623-77) is sometimes classified with the French naturalist painters, but wrongly because he was born at Lille, which was not then French, trained in Flanders, and lived mainly in Holland and Germany. The Dutchman Jacob van Loo (c. 1614-70), however, should be mentioned, since he spent ten years of his life in Paris and painted *bambocciate*.

177. On Bosse see two works by A. Blum, *L'œuvre gravé d'Abraham Bosse*, and *Abraham Bosse et la Société française au 17e siècle*.

178. This is probably the most convenient place to mention a special manifestation of naturalism in France, the painting of still-life. Generally speaking, it was a much-despised form of art, particularly in the later part of the century under the influence of the doctrines of the Academy, by whom it was only tolerated as a form of decoration in the hands of painters like Jean Baptiste Monnoyer, better known as Baptiste (1634-99), who also painted in England. But in the earlier part of the century it was practised by Sébastien Stoskopf of Strasbourg (on whom see H. Haug, in *Trois siècles d'art Alsacien* (Strasbourg, 1948), 23) and several painters of whom little is known beyond their names and a few works: Baugin (certainly not the same as Lubin Baugin mentioned earlier in this chapter), Bizet, Gobin,

p. 157

p. 158

Linard, and Louise Moillon. On all these painters see *Les Peintres de la Réalité, passim,* and *La Nature Morte,* Orangerie, Paris, 1952, 72 ff.

p. 158   179. A Romantic painter of 1830 might well have written a pamphlet entitled *Poussin et Rubens* as a parallel to Stendhal's *Racine et Shakespeare,* except that it had already in effect been done before the end of the seventeenth century (cf. p. 210).

180. The most important sources for the life of Poussin are as follows: *Correspondance de Nicolas Poussin,* ed. Jouanny (a popular edition by P. du Colombier is useful but not quite complete); Sandrart, *Teutsche Academie,* 257 ff.; Bellori, *Vite,* 407; Félibien, *Entretiens,* IV, 3. Among modern monographs the most interesting is W. Friedlaender, *Nicolas Poussin.* O. Grautoff, *Nicolas Poussin,* contains the only recent attempt at a Catalogue Raisonné. Works discovered since the publication of his book are listed and reproduced in T. Bertin-Mourot, 'Addenda au catalogue de Grautoff', *Bulletin de la Société Poussin,* II (1948), 43. E. Magne, *Nicolas Poussin,* though quite uncritical, contains good plates and some useful references in the list of the artist's recorded works. The drawings are in the course of publication in *The Drawings of Nicolas Poussin,* by W. Friedlaender in collaboration with R. Wittkower and A. Blunt. Three volumes have so far appeared. Of the more recent monographs, mention must be made of those by André Gide, which contains good plates, and P. Jamot, which is a volume of reprints of his articles. Louis Hourticq's *La jeunesse de Poussin* contains in my opinion a wholly fanciful and incorrect reconstruction of Poussin's early life and work.

Two other works must be mentioned: J. Smith's volume on Poussin in his *Catalogue Raisonné of the Works of the most eminent Dutch, Flemish, and French Painters,* which will always remain the basis for any list of the artist's work, and A. Andresen's *Nicolaus Poussin, Verzeichniss der nach seinen Gemälden gefertigten Kupferstiche.*

Generally speaking, Poussin's works after 1640 can be dated with a fair degree of certainty on the basis of his letters and of the early biographies, but for the early period the evidence is much more indefinite. In a short summary such as this it is impossible to set out the arguments which depend on the evidence of drawings combined with that of the few documented pictures, and I have therefore simply given what I believe to be the correct chronology, indicating in footnotes cases where my views differ materially from those of other writers.

181. For Varin see Grautoff, I, 21, 334, and the article in Thieme-Becker.

182. The château of Mornay, in the Charente In- p. 1
férieure, had till recently a gallery with a series of canvases decorating the walls and an inscription: *Nicolas Poussin pinxit anno 1614.* Unfortunately the gallery was burnt in 1947, and only one of the two paintings traditionally ascribed to Poussin survives (reproduced by Grautoff, I, 344). It has recently been acquired by the French State. There seems quite good reason to suppose that it may be by him, and in any case the reason for which Grautoff (I, 342) rejects it is inadequate. He argues that because it is copied from a composition by Joseph Heintz it cannot be by Poussin, who would never have used such a model. But he forgets that in 1614 Poussin was a youth of twenty, and Heintz was the favourite painter of the Emperor.

183. Now at Windsor; see A. Blunt, *The French Drawings at Windsor Castle,* 33 and figures 14 ff.

184. Cf. D. Mahon, 'Nicolas Poussin and Venetian Painting; a new connexion', *Burl. Mag.,* LXXXVIII (1946), 15 ff.

185. Grautoff 4, 5.

186. Two important paintings are quoted by Grautoff and most other authorities as being certainly of this period, namely the 'Death of Germanicus' (Grautoff 10, formerly Barberini collection, Rome, now Corsini collection, Florence) and the 'Capture of Jerusalem' (Grautoff 11, Vienna). But in both cases the documents have been misinterpreted. The 'Germanicus' was probably executed after 1630 and the 'Jerusalem' probably about 1637-9.

187. Grautoff 6. The painting appears to have been carried out in two stages, and traces of a quite different background are visible under the present surface. It is possible therefore that it may have been altered in the 1630s.

188. Grautoff 8.

189. Grautoff 16.   p.

190. Grautoff 17.

191. Formerly Cook collection. Reproduced in the *Commemorative Catalogue of the exhibition of French Art* (Royal Academy, London, 1932), plate 37.

192. Moreover, in 1665 Chantelou told Bernini that it had been painted more than forty years before (cf. *Voyage du Cavalier Bernin en France,* 120). This must be an exaggeration, but it points to a very early date.

193. Cassiano was also much interested in natural science, and was secretary of the Lincei Academy. Several volumes of his scientific drawings are also at Windsor.

194. That is to say, the 'Feast of the Gods', begun p. by Bellini and finished by Titian (Washington), which Poussin copied (the copy now at Edinburgh),

the 'Feast of Venus' and the 'Andrians' in the Prado and the 'Bacchus and Ariadne' in the National Gallery, London.

195. The Cephalus in the 'Cephalus and Aurora' (Grautoff 47) is taken from the central figure of the 'Bacchus and Ariadne' (cf. Mahon, *op. cit.*, plate II). And the Narcissus in the Louvre painting (Grautoff 3, there wrongly dated 1623–6) is based on Bordone's 'Dead Christ' (Mahon, *op. cit.*, plate III).

196. Cf. A. Blunt, 'Poussin's "Et in Arcadia ego"', *Art Bulletin*, XX (1938), 96.

162 197. This melancholy aspect of Poussin's art in the early thirties must not be over-emphasized, as this is also the period of the first Bacchanals (e.g. National Gallery, No. 62) and the 'Triumph of Flora' (Grautoff 45). It does, however, distinguish the works before 1633 in comparison with those of the next few years.

198. Grautoff 20.

199. Grautoff 34.

200. Probably Poussin's diploma piece for the Academy of St Luke in Rome.

201. For an analysis of the 'Golden Calf' see the present writer's *Gallery Book* on it (London, 1951).

202. Grautoff 89, now in Melbourne.

203. Louvre, Grautoff 70. The other version, formerly in the Cook collection, now in the Metropolitan Museum (Grautoff 71), is slightly later.

204. Grautoff 57.

205. Grautoff 85, 86, 87, and perhaps 50. See M. Davies, *National Gallery Catalogues, French School* (1946), 40, No. 42. His arguments to prove that Grautoff 50 is not by Poussin are highly ingenious, but not conclusive.

206. Grautoff 63.

163 207. The drawing at Windsor for this composition (Blunt, No. 169) was certainly made about 1627–8, but the painting cannot be so early. There is evidence for believing that in his early years Poussin made designs which he did not have the opportunity of carrying out till many years later.

208. *Correspondance*, 5.

209. Grautoff 73.

210. Grautoff 92–6, 99. The seventh, 'Penitence', has disappeared and is said to have been destroyed in a fire in the nineteenth century. The 'Extreme Unction' was probably begun in 1636, and the 'Baptism', the last of the series to be executed, was sent off from Paris in 1642. It is now in the National Gallery, Washington.

164 211. The altarpieces were for St Germain-en-Laye (Grautoff 100) and the Noviciate of the Jesuits (Grautoff 101). The latter was a pendant to Vouet's 'Presentation', and it cannot be denied that in this competition Poussin is the loser. The allegories for Richelieu are Grautoff 104 and 106.

212. Cf. A. Blunt, 'Poussin's Decoration of the Long Gallery in the Louvre', *Burl. Mag.*, XCIV (1951), 369 and XCV (1952), 31.

213. The list is too long to give here, but it is p. 165 curiously consistent. For a discussion of some of Poussin's patrons and of their social and political views see M. Alpatov, 'Poussin Problems', *Art Bulletin*, XVII (1935), 5, and A. Blunt, 'The Heroic and Ideal landscape in the work of Nicolas Poussin', *Journal of the Warburg and Courtauld Institutes*, VII (1944), 160 ff. It is not possible to identify the exact style of architecture approved of by these friends of Poussin, because with the exception of the two or three wealthy ones they lived in houses of too little distinction to be mentioned in guide-books. From their addresses, however, something can be deduced. Many of them lived in the commercial district round the rue St Martin and the rue St Denis, no doubt in the tall standard street houses, many of which still exist, and a few, particularly the civil servants like Chantelou, lived in the smarter district round the Louvre, but again in standard houses, not in the great hôtels. Further details about Poussin's Paris friends can be found in Bonnaffé, *Amateur, français au 17e siècle*.

214. In 1665 he was given the same position when Bernini came to Paris (cf. below, p. 278, note 18).

215. Probably the other most intimate friends of the artist were the banker Pointel, for whom he painted the 'Rebecca', the 'Judgement of Solomon', several landscapes and one of the self-portraits, and Serisier, who commissioned the two Phocion landscapes, the 'Esther' and a lost 'Flight into Egypt'.

216. In the sense in which the word Baroque is p. 166 used in art-history; in literary history it is now used with a different meaning, more closely related to certain aspects of Mannerism.

Recent writers on French literature such as Nadal (*Le Sentiment de l'amour dans l'œuvre de Corneille*, Paris, 1948) and Bénichou (*Morales du Grand Siècle*, Paris, 1948) have emphasized the emotional and anti-rational element in Corneille and have identified it, perhaps too closely, with an aristocratic tendency in the dramatist's work. It is, however, certainly true that Poussin's paintings of the 1640s embody a much more strictly *bourgeois* spirit than Corneille's plays of the same period.

217. Poussin also includes a reference to the first p. 167 incident of the story, the washing of the apostles' feet, by showing on the right the basin and the towel.

218. Painted in 1648. The second composition is p. 168

known in several versions of which the original appears to be that belonging to Lord Plymouth (cf. T. Bertin-Mourot, *op. cit.*, plate 35).

p. 169   219. Cf. Friedlaender, *The Drawings of Nicolas Poussin*, I, Nos. 75–84.

p. 170   220. The copies of the mosaic made for Cassiano del Pozzo and no doubt used by Poussin are at Windsor.

221. Reproduced in Friedlaender, *Nicolas Poussin*, 260.

222. Cf. E. Gombrich, *Burl. Mag.*, LXXXIV (1944), 37 ff.

223. Cf. A. Blunt, 'Heroic and Ideal Landscape', and D. Panofsky, 'Narcissus and Echo', *Art Bulletin*, XXXI (1949), 112.

p. 171   224. Cf. E. Panofsky, 'Poussin's Apollo and Daphne in the Louvre', *Bulletin de la Société Poussin*, III (1950), 27.

225. The most important sources for the life of Claude are the biographies of Sandrart and Baldinucci. The most useful monographs on him are those by Mrs Mark Pattison, Walter Friedlaender, P. Courthion, and T. Hetzer. The unrivalled collection of drawings in the British Museum has been catalogued by A. M. Hind, who also wrote a short book on the artist's drawings in general. The drawings in the Louvre have been completely published and reproduced by L. Demonts, and the etchings by A. Blum. The drawings of the *Liber Veritatis*, preserved at Chatsworth, were reproduced in engravings by Earlom. Among the few works on the artist in English the following must be mentioned: the attacks of Ruskin in *Modern Painters*, a monograph by G. Graham, an essay by Roger Fry in *Vision and Design* (London, 1921), and an article by John White, *Burl. Mag.*, XCII (1950), 43.

p. 172   226. There are drawings attributed to him in the British Museum.

227. For a detailed discussion of the *Liber Veritatis* see M. Davies, *National Gallery Catalogues, French School*, 20 ff.

228. For the certain works of Claude's early period (before 1635) see W. G. Constable, 'The Early Work of Claude Lorrain', *Bulletin of the Museum of Fine Arts*, XLII (Boston, 1944), 69. To the paintings mentioned there two may be added:

1. 'Landscape with Shepherds', dated 1629. Formerly in the collection of the Marquis of Drogheda, Philadelphia Museum (reproduced *The Philadelphia Museum Bulletin*, XLV–XLVI, 1950–1, 46).

2. 'The Wood Splitters', dated 1635 (L. V. 21). Formerly Lord Granville and Sir George Leon. New York art trade.

The painting 'Blind Man's Buff' in Detroit, attributed by W. R. Valentiner to Claude and van Laer and given the date *c*. 1627, can hardly have any connexion with the former at least (cf. W. R. Valentiner, 'An Early Work by Claude Lorrain', *Institute of Fine Arts Bulletin*, XXI, Detroit, 1942, 58).

229. At about the same time Claude painted some   p. 17 almost topographical pictures: 'The Siege of La Rochelle' (Louvre, 1631) and the 'Campo Vaccino' (probably before 1636, Louvre), both of which suggest the influence of Tassi in the general scheme and of Callot in the figures.

230. In one case only can we identify a painting with a precise spot, namely the view of Tivoli at Windsor Castle (L.V. 89).

231. For instance the rock formation in 'The Temple of Apollo at Delphi' (L.V. 182) is closely reminiscent of parts of Capri.

232. It is only recently that we have been able to   p. 17 realize the variety of light effects in Claude. In the nineteenth century all Claudes were toned with coloured varnish till they appeared to represent a sunset, and it is only since they have been cleaned that we can realize that they depict different and clearly characterized moments.

233. The 'Landing of Aeneas', painted for Don Gaspero Altieri (L.V. 185), now in the collection of Lord Fairhaven, contains one curious feature worth noticing. The ship in which Aeneas sails flies a flag on which are the arms of the Altieri family. This is, of course, a piece of grotesque snobbishness on the part of Claude's patron, but it also indicates the degree to which the Romans of the seventeenth century still felt themselves to be the descendants of the ancient Romans and so, according to the tradition, of Aeneas and his companions.

234. The 'Peasant Dances' in the Louvre (L.V. 13) and the etching of the Goatherd (Blum 5, 6) might almost be illustrations to the end of the second *Georgic*.

235. The copies of the illustrations made for Cassiano del Pozzo are in the Royal Library at Windsor.

236. Many such paintings from Pompeii and Herculaneum are preserved in the Naples Museum, and similar works must have been available in the seventeenth century, since they were copied by the two Bartoli (cf. T. Ashby, 'Drawings of ancient paintings in English Collections, Part I, The Eton Drawings', *Papers of the British School at Rome*, VII (1914), plates vi and xiii. Claude himself made a drawing of the Roman fresco with a rock arch in the Palazzo Barberini (British Museum, Hind 249), and he must also have known the Palestrina mosaic of which Poussin made extensive use (cf. p. 170). He may also

have been influenced by descriptions of Roman wall decorations in the form of landscapes with architecture given by Pliny (*Natural History*, Book XXXV, chapter 116) and Vitruvius (Book VII, chapter 5).

237. The two most famous are L.V. 115 and 82 in the collections of the Duke of Westminster and Lord Radnor. The titles are later inventions, but they embody an idea which must have been intended by Claude.

238. L.V. 113. Claude's direct model here is Domenichino.

239. E.g. the river in the 'Phocion' (Plate 133), or more clearly that in the 'Man with a Serpent' in the National Gallery, London.

240. In the reflected light on the hill below the town Claude uses a method which he favoured at this time, of floating crimson wash into the warm bistre in which the rest of the drawing is executed.

241. Sometimes Claude seems even to have repeated a composition which he had already painted in a highly finished drawing, evidently intended to be complete in itself (cf. Blunt, *French Drawings at Windsor Castle*, 22, No. 48).

242. One peculiar method which he used was to trace part of a composition through on the back of the paper and then complete it in a different way (cf. Blunt, *French Drawings at Windsor Castle*, 21, No. 43). The whole question of Claude's drawings needs to be studied. Our knowledge of the development of his drawing style is still very incomplete.

243. It is known that Claude sometimes allowed other artists to add the figures to his compositions, but this happened more rarely than is generally suggested.

244. This is done with even more dramatic effect in the 'Expulsion of Hagar' at Munich (L.V. 173).

245. This is a deliberate intention of Claude, as is proved by the fact that in another case ('The Landing of Aeneas'), where the figures are equally elongated, a preliminary drawing exists (British Museum, Hind 303) in which they have normal proportions.

246. Notice that even here the coastline of Sorrento and Capri appears in the background.

247. The certain facts about him are set out by E. K. Waterhouse, *Baroque Painting in Rome*, 61; cf. also Weisbach, *op. cit.*, 332.

248. Certain of the landscapes in the Doria and Colonna palaces in Rome, and one now belonging to Mr Denis Mahon (cf. *Landscape in French Art*, Royal Academy, London, 1949, No. 47).

249. Jean François Millet (1642–79), also called Francisque, a Fleming who lived the greater part of

his life in Paris, applied competently, but with little imagination, the principles of Poussin's landscapes of the 1640s, and occasionally, as in 'The Storm' in the National Gallery, London, showed real originality (see M. Davies, 'A Note on Francisque Millet', Société Poussin, *Deuxième Bulletin*, 1948, 13). Jean Lemaire (1598–1659), who was a pupil of Poussin and called himself Lemaire-Poussin, specialized in architectural fantasies (cf. A. Blunt, 'Jean Lemaire', *Burl. Mag.*, LXXXII, 1943, 241). Pierre Patel the Elder (*c.* 1620–*c.* 1676) was principally famous for his landscape panels, which were incorporated into the decoration of rooms as in the Cabinet de l'Amour at the Hôtel Lambert. His compositions contain a mixture of architecture and pure landscape, and show that he had some understanding of Claude (cf. Plate 143B). Jacques Rousseau (1630–93) painted the landscapes in the gallery at the Hôtel Lambert, and in 1690 settled in England, where he painted decorative landscapes at Hampton Court and Montagu House. This period also produced one draughtsman and engraver of great distinction in landscape, Israel Silvestre (1621–91), whose topographical views are among the most sensitive works of the time.

250. G. Rouchès, *Eustache Le Sueur*, gives a full bibliography on the artist. The most important early sources for his life are the biographies in the *Mémoires Inédits*, and by Félibien. Much important material is brought together by Dussieux in 'Nouvelles Recherches sur la vie et les ouvrages de Le Sueur', *Archives de l'Art Français*, II (1852–3), I.

251. Three of these cartoons survive (cf. A. Blunt, 'The *Hypnerotomachia Poliphili* in Seventeenth Century France', *Journal of the Warburg Institute*, I, 1937–8, 117).

252. He seems to have been more personal as a portrait painter in these early years, as for instance in the portrait group in the Louvre (reproduced, *op. cit.*, plate 15), and in single portraits of men in the museums of Guéret and Marseilles.

253. The 'Holy Family' of which versions exist in the National Gallery, London, at Chantilly and at Pavlovsk. The drawing is at Windsor (cf. Blunt, *French Drawings at Windsor Castle*, 45, No. 213).

254. The exact date is uncertain. The inscription in the cloister gave the year 1648 which may refer to the beginning or the end of the work. The *Mémoires Inédits* say that Le Sueur executed the paintings in the period 1645–8, Félibien in 1649. Stylistically it seems certain that they cannot be earlier than the Lambert decorations discussed above and I am therefore inclined to accept 1648 as the date at which they were begun.

p. 178   255. In the seventeenth century it belonged to Bernard de Rozé (cf. Rouchès, *op. cit.*, 92).

256. The affinity with another great painter of Carthusian subjects, Zurbaran, is obvious.

257. 'Christ and the Magdalene' (Louvre), painted for the Charterhouse of Paris in 1651; the 'Adoration of the Shepherds' (La Rochelle, 1653; reproduced in R. Lécuyer, *Regards sur les Musées de Province*, I (1949), plate xx); 'St Gervasius and St Protasius' (Louvre); 'The Presentation' (Marseilles, painted for St Sulpice); four paintings for the abbey of Marmoutiers (1654–5), namely 'St Sebastian' and 'St Louis' in the museum at Tours, and 'The Appearance of the Virgin and other Saints to St Martin', and the 'Mass of St Martin' in the Louvre.

p. 179   258. The only exception is the 'Mass of St Martin' in which the style of the St Bruno series is carried on.

259. Examples of his Bambochades are in the Louvre, and in the Montpellier and Dulwich galleries. Imitations of Castiglione include an etching of 'Jacob's Journey' (R.D. 1), 'Rebecca and Eliezer' at Welbeck (*Seventeenth-Century Art*, Royal Academy, London, 1938, No. 327), and the 'Sacrifice of Noah' in the Louvre.

260. Louvre. A small version is at Chatsworth.

261. Bourdon passed through Venice on his return from Rome to Paris.

262. Portraits of the Queen are at Stockholm and in the Prado.

263. Now at Montpellier.

264. Other works in this transitional style are the 'St Paul and Barnabas' in the Prado and the 'Adoration of the Shepherds' in the Louvre.

265. The 'Acts of Mercy' are in the Ringling Museum, Sarasota.

266. Drawings by Michel Corneille after the principal panels exist in the Musée Atger, Montpellier.

267. Certain other painters of the same generation as Le Sueur and Bourdon deserve mention. Charles Alphonse Dufresnoy (1611–68), who spent the greater part of his life in Italy, combined a taste for Venetian painting with the study of Poussin, whose drawings he sometimes used as a basis for his compositions (cf. W. Friedlaender, *The Drawings of Nicolas Poussin*, II, 16). He is chiefly remembered for a Latin poem on painting which embodied in epigrammatic form the doctrine of the classical school, and which enjoyed a great success for a century after the author's death. It was translated into English by Dryden and later annotated by Reynolds. For Dufresnoy as a painter see L. Demonts, 'Deux peintres de la première moitié du 17ᵉ siècle',

Gazette des Beaux-Arts, II (1925), 162 ff; for his poem see A. Fontaine, *Doctrines d'Art en France*, 17. Jacques Stella (1596–1657) of Lyons began his career in Florence (1619) as an engraver in the manner of Callot, but in 1623 moved to Rome, where he became a friend and imitator of Poussin (see the article on him in Thieme-Becker). Louis de Boullongne the Elder (1609–74) and Nicolas Loir (1624–79) were both representatives of a kind of classicism which combined elements from the traditions of Vouet and Poussin. For Boullongne see *Mémoires Inédits*, I, 195, and Caix de St Aymour, *Les Boullongne*. For Loir see *Mémoires Inédits*, I, 337, and the article in Thieme-Becker.

A few provincial artists influenced by the Parisian-Roman classical school should also be mentioned here. Nicolas Mignard of Troyes (1606–68), who worked mainly at Avignon, was a successful painter of religious works in a style based on those of Vouet, Poussin, and the more classical Roman artists of the Seicento (cf. article in Thieme-Becker). Hilaire Pader (1617–77) of Toulouse painted ambitious but provincial allegorical canvases (cf. *L'Age d'Or de la Peinture Toulousaine*, Orangerie, Paris, 1947, 46, No. 18). He also wrote a long poem on painting (cf. Chennevières-Pointel, *op. cit.*, IV, 1).

268. The only early source on Guillain is the p. biography in the *Mémoires Inédits*, I, 184.

269. The elder Guillain executed a number of tombs in the idiom deriving from Pilon, e.g. that of Louise de Lorraine, reproduced in Michel, *Histoire de l'Art*, V, 752.

270. The relief from the Pont-au-Change (reproduced *ibid.*) suggests that Guillain had studied the engraved trophies of Polidoro da Caravaggio. The connexion of this relief with the work on the staircase at Blois has been discussed above, p. 124.

271. For further information about Warin see the article in Thieme-Becker.

272. A full account of Sarrazin's life and work is to be found in M. Digard, *Jacques Sarrazin*.

273. The parallel with Lemercier's early training in architecture in Rome is close.

274. The original models for these groups are in p. the Louvre (Digard, *op. cit.*, plate xv). The statues were actually carried out by Sarrazin's pupils Guérin and van Obstal. In the following years Sarrazin seems to have hesitated between the classicism of the caryatids, which he repeats in the monument for the heart of Louis XIII (1643) (Digard, *op. cit.*, plate v), and a more Baroque manner as in the 'Enfants à la Chèvre' (c. 1640; Digard, *op. cit.*,

plate xix) based on Bernini's early group in the Borghese Gallery.

275. In St Paul-St Louis the monument stood in the end of the transept so that there was no circular arrangement as at present. The bronze reliefs were actually bent into curves to make them fit the new setting (cf. G. Macon, *Chantilly et le Musée Condé* (Paris, 1925), 262).

276. Long attributed to Lerambert, but proved to be by Sarrazin (cf. Digard, *op. cit.*, 177).

277. The evidence about the dates of their births is conflicting, but these seem the most probable years. The facts about Michel's life are given in detail in two biographies in the *Mémoires Inédits*, but about François we are less well informed. The earliest account of him is that in Dézallier d'Argenville's *Vies des plus fameux architectes et sculpteurs* (Paris, 1787), 159. For the attribution of works to him we are forced mainly to rely on the early guide-books. For a list of the works of both brothers see H. Stein, 'Les Frères Anguier', *Réunion des Sociétés des Beaux-Arts* (1889), 527.

182   278. In a series of tombs: The Rohan-Chabot tomb now at Versailles (after 1655), the Souvré tomb in the Louvre (before 1667) and the Longueville monument in the Louvre (between 1663 and 1669; reproduced in Planat and Rümler, *op. cit.*, plate 202).

279. Cf. Hautecœur, *Le Louvre et les Tuileries de Louis XIV*, 40; reproduced *op. cit.*, plates viii and ix.

280. Executed in the years 1641–7. Reproduced in Voss, *Malerei des Barock*, 252 ff.

281. For details about the group and the unusual Baroque baldacchino over it by Gabriel Le Duc see M. Beaulieu, 'Gabriel Le Duc, Michel Anguier et le Maître-Autel du Val-de-Grâce', *B.S.H.A.F.*, (1945–6), 150.

282. Its nearest parallel in Rome is to be found in the work of Duquesnoy.

283. An almost eighteenth-century elegance is also seen in his well-known 'Amphitrite' executed in 1680 for Versailles and now in the Louvre (cf. M. Charageat, 'La statue d'Amphitrite ... de Michel Anguier', *B.S.H.A.F.*, (1941–4), 72).

284. Cf. P. Francastel, *Girardon* (1928), 72.

285. The secondary figures of the period fluctuate between the various styles employed by Sarrazin and the two Anguiers. Gilles Guérin (1606–78; cf. *Mémoires Inédits*, I, 259) began as a pupil of Sarrazin for whom he worked on the Louvre and at Maisons (the 'Four Elements' in the vestibule and the mantelpieces in the two principal Salles, reproduced in Planat and Rümler, *op. cit.*, plates 34, 35, 47, and

48). His tomb for the Prince de Condé (d. 1648) at Vallery includes an adaptation of Sarrazin's caryatids (reproduced in Digard, *op. cit.*, plate xx). But in the 1650s he develops a more Baroque manner – the altar at Ferrières-en-Gâtinais (1650), the tomb of La Vieuville (1653, Louvre; reproduced in Michel, *Histoire de l'Art*, VI, 669) and the statue of Louis XIV for the Hôtel de Ville (1654) in the Carnavalet.

Two of Sarrazin's most successful pupils were Flemings by birth. One, Philippe Buyster (1595–1688; cf. *Mémoires Inédits*, I, 280), was principally active in large-scale sculpture for the decoration of churches, e.g. on the dome of the Val-de-Grâce (Plate 91). Several of his tombs survive: that for Claude de Rueil in the cathedral of Angers (1650); that of the Aubespine family in the cathedral of Bourges (1653; reproduced in Digard, *op. cit.*, plate xx). He is probably responsible for the groups of children over the panels on the staircase at Maisons (Plate 100A). Guillet contradicts himself over the authorship of the decoration on this staircase, since in one context (*Mémoires Inédits*, I, 282) he attributes the children to Buyster, and in another (*Mémoires Inédits*, I, 177) the whole decoration to van Obstal. The probable solution is that Buyster did the children and van Obstal the rest of the decoration, a division which would be in accordance with the style of the two artists. Gérard van Obstal (*c.* 1594–1668; cf. *Mémoires Inédits*, I, 174) also came from Flanders and worked for Sarrazin on the Louvre. His mature works in France, e.g. the medallions on the staircase at Maisons (Plate 100A) and the reliefs in the gallery at the Hôtel Lambert (Plate 105A) show a consistently classical manner. His last important works were a series of reliefs on the Hôtel Carnavalet (after 1655), often, but wrongly, said to have been destroyed (reproduced in Contet, *Vieux Hôtels de Paris, Quartier St Antoine*, plates 3, 4, and 10). Two other artists represent the classical tendency of this generation, but in a less distinguished manner. Thibault Poissant (1605–68; cf. *Mémoires Inédits*, I, 318) was responsible for the angels and coat of arms at the top of the Montmorency tomb (Plate 150B) as well as for the 'Fame' in the pediment of the garden front of Vaux (Plate 103); but his work is coarse and clumsy. Louis Lerambert (*c.* 1620–70) appears to have been a sculptor of greater ability (cf. the reliefs in the cathedral of Blois, dated 1660; reproduced in *Réunion des Sociétés des Beaux-Arts*, 1909, plate opposite 74).

286. Most of the artists discussed in this chapter took part in the decoration of the gardens of Versailles in the 1660s, but generally in minor capacities.

p. 184   1. The logical conclusion of the desire for complete religious unity, the Revocation of the Edict of Nantes, was not carried out till 1685, two years after the death of Colbert, and there is little doubt that he would have realized the disastrous practical results which it was bound to bring about and would in this case have thrown over his doctrine in the face of hard facts.

p. 187   2. *Athalie* and *Esther* were, of course, produced as specific commissions for Mme de Maintenon, but the circumstances were exceptional.

3. Even artists like Pierre Mignard, who opposed Lebrun and the Academy on grounds of personal ambition, practised a manner scarcely distinguishable from the official style.

4. It is also worth noticing that the Turinese architect Guarini, who designed the Theatine church of Ste Anne-la-Royale (1662–9; reproduced in Hautecœur, *Architecture*, II, 246), exercised no influence whatsoever on French architecture in spite of his reputation in Italy.

p. 188   5. Within ten years Le Vau had completed the first two floors of the north and south wings and had laid the foundations of the east wing. Further, in 1661, he had begun to rebuild the Petite Galerie which had been burnt in that year. On the first floor of this wing he made the Galerie d'Apollon, which was decorated by Lebrun and was the first of the great interiors of the period.

6. The plans were approved in 1662 but modified in 1664–5. At the time of Le Vau's death in 1670 the buildings were complete except for the dome of the church which was finished by his nephew d'Orbay (cf. H. Lemonnier, *Le collège Mazarin et le Palais de l'Institut* (Paris, 1921), and C. de Vinck and A. Vuaflart, *La Place de l'Institut* (Paris, 1928)).

7. The Vigna Sacchetti, S. Maria della Pace, and the reconstruction of the Roman temple at Palestrina.

8. S. Agnese a Piazza Navona.

9. Built at the command of Mazarin, 1654–60 (cf. F. de Fossa, *Le château historique de Vincennes*, Paris, 1908).

10. Begun 1660 (cf. M. Dumolin and G. Outardel, *op. cit.*, 182).

p. 189   11. On the basis of the statements made by Chantelou (*Journal du Voyage du Cavalier Bernin en France*, 169), it is usually said (e.g. by Hautecœur, *Le Louvre et les Tuileries de Louis XIV*, 145) that his grievance was due to the faults in the structure of

the Hôtel Bautru built by Le Vau which Colbert had bought. But he did not acquire the house till 1665, a year after he had turned down Le Vau's Louvre designs (cf. Dumolin, *Études*, II, 194).

12. Cf. p. 128.

13. The designs of Marot and François Le Vau are reproduced in Hautecœur, *Le Louvre et les Tuileries de Louis XIV*, plates 31 and 32. The same author illustrates (Plate 29) the designs of Léonor Houdin, prepared in 1661. These are unique in the series, and indeed almost unique in the whole of seventeenth-century French architecture, in being Palladian in inspiration. Their style suggests the possibility that Houdin may have been influenced by English Palladian architects such as Inigo Jones and John Webb. In 1666, after the failure of Bernini, two other French architects, Cottard and François Dubois, submitted further designs which were not accepted.

14. Pietro da Cortona's plans are not preserved, and those of the otherwise unknown Candiani or Landiani are not of importance.

15. Two elevations are reproduced by Hautecœur, *Le Louvre et les Tuileries de Louis XIV*, 133, and *Histoire du Louvre*, 57.

16. The facts are given in Hautecœur, *Le Louvre et les Tuileries de Louis XIV*, 150 ff., where most of the essential plans and elevations are reproduced. Some further drawings are published by R. Josephson, 'Les maquettes du Bernin pour le Louvre', *Gazette des Beaux-Arts*, I (1928), 77. The whole problem is again examined by Brauer and Wittkower in *Die Zeichnungen des Gianlorenzo Bernini* I (1931), 129, where a further plan is reproduced (II, plate 175).

17. The plan is given by Brauer and Wittkower, *loc. cit.*, the elevation in Hautecœur, *Le Louvre et les Tuileries de Louis XIV*, plate 33. Both Rainaldi's design and Bernini's first scheme incorporate the central oval vestibule of Le Vau's original plan.

18. A day to day account of his stay in Paris is given by Chantelou, *Journal du Voyage du Cavalier Bernin en France*. A different view of the story is given by Charles Perrault in *Mémoires de ma Vie*.

19. How far Colbert himself had made up his p. 1 mind is uncertain (cf. E. Esmonin, 'Le Bernin et la Construction du Louvre', *B.S.H.A.F.*, (1911), 31).

20. Apart, that is to say, from drawings and a small bas-relief which was mainly executed by an

assistant under his direction. For the bust of the King, cf. R. Wittkower, *Bernini's Bust of Louis XIV* (Oxford, 1951).

21. For instance, by Aumont and Lionne about their private houses, and by the Queen Mother and Tubeuf over the altar of the Val-de-Grâce.

22. For instance, the altar of the Val-de-Grâce, cf. M. Beaulieu, 'G. Le Duc, M. Anguier et le Maître-Autel du Val-de-Grâce', *B.S.H.A.F.*, (1945–6), 150. The author proves conclusively that though Berninesque in style the altar was not erected on the artist's design, but on one of which he explicitly disapproved.

23. Published in 1673. An enlarged edition appeared in 1684.

24. The decoration remained to be executed and some parts of it (e.g. the relief over the main door) were not completed till the nineteenth century.

25. They are set out in detail by Hautecœur, 'L'auteur de la Colonnade du Louvre', *Gazette des Beaux-Arts*, 1 (1924), 151. Some new evidence is added by R. Josephson, 'Quelques dessins de Claude Perrault pour le Louvre', *op. cit.*, 11 (1927), 171.

26. Unfortunately, many of the witnesses best qualified to know were prejudiced: Charles Perrault in favour of his brother, Boileau in favour of Le Vau, because of his quarrel with the Perrault family.

27. Cortona uses such a scheme in a drawing for a fountain for the Piazza Colonna (reproduced in A. Muñoz, *Pietro da Cortona* (Rome, n.d.), 15), and may have introduced it in his designs for the Louvre.

28. If the drawing for the façade (Plate 155A) by François Le Vau, Louis' brother, really dates from 1664, then it proves that all the essential features of the Colonnade were produced within the Le Vau circle before Perrault was concerned with the building. But the evidence about the date is uncertain. The situation is further complicated by the fact that we do not know how far François was collaborating with his brother and how far he was really competing against him. Parts of this design were engraved with variants by Olry Deloriandre (cf. Hautecœur, *Le Louvre et les Tuileries de Louis XIV*, plate 31, and *Gazette des Beaux-Arts*, 1 (1924), 153).

29. For Claude Perrault's other works see Hautecœur, *Architecture*, 11, 452 ff. In 1667 he designed the Observatoire which still stands; in 1669 he made a model for a triumphal arch at the Porte St Antoine which was begun but never completed; and in 1673 or 1674 he designed for Colbert the château of Sceaux which stood till the present century.

30. Which was broken by the projecting oval vestibule in the middle.

31. During the development of the Colonnade design a change was made in the design for completing the Square Court. The south wing was doubled in thickness by the addition of a second flight of rooms on the river side to increase the space available for the King's rooms. This involved a slight extension of the Colonnade at both ends and the designing of a new façade towards the river which was prepared by the commission in 1668. p. 192

32. The literature on Versailles is vast, but the following are the most useful works for the period of Louis XIV: L. Dussieux, *Le Château de Versailles* (Paris, 1881); P. de Nolhac, *La Création de Versailles* (Versailles, 1901); P. de. Nolhac, *Histoire du Château de Versailles, Versailles sous Louis XIV* (Paris, 1911); P. de Nolhac, *Versailles* (Les grands Palais de France) (Paris, n.d.); C. Mauricheau-Beaupré, *Versailles, l'Histoire et l'Art* (Paris, 1949). In addition there are various good and more popular volumes of plates of which the best is that published by TEL.

33. Enlarged in 1631–4.

34. M. Marie has published Le Vau's plan of 1664 ('Le premier Château de Versailles construit par Le Vau en 1664–5', *B.S.H.A.F.*, (1952), 50). Fiske Kimball ('The Genesis of the Château Neuf at Versailles, 1668–71', *Gazette des Beaux-Arts*, 1949, i, 353) has reconstructed the various schemes put forward at the second stage and has exploded the traditional story that Louis XIV was determined, from feelings of piety, to preserve his father's building.

35. It is possible that, as regards the skyline and the statues, Le Vau may have been influenced by Bernini's Louvre designs.

36. The most important of the buildings set up in the early years at Versailles have all been destroyed. They were the Menagery (1662; Hautecœur, *Architecture*, 11, 268), the first Orangery (1663; *ibid.*), and the Trianon de Porcelaine (1668; Hautecœur, *op. cit.*, 294), all by Le Vau, and the Grotto of Thetis (1665), for the original idea of which Charles Perrault claims the credit (Hautecœur, *op. cit.*, 383), but which was probably designed by Lebrun, and was decorated with sculpture by Girardon and others. p. 193

37. Both fêtes were engraved by Silvestre. For the *Île Enchantée* see A. Marie, 'Les Fêtes des Plaisirs de l'Isle Enchantée', *B.S.H.A.F.* (1941–4), 118.

38. It was left unfinished when Louis abandoned the Louvre. The painting of the panels on the ceiling was continued till the nineteenth century, when Delacroix added the 'Apollo killing the Python' in 1849. The wall decoration appears to be a complete reconstruction of the nineteenth century, since a

water-colour of c.1797 shows the walls plain below the cornice (cf. J. J. Marquet de Vasselot, *Répertoire des Vues des Salles du Musée du Louvre*, *Archives de l'art français*, N.P., xx (1946), plate iii). It is, however, possible that part of the original decoration survived under the plain wall covering.

p. 193   39. Jacques Gervaise for the painted grisailles, Monnoyer for the flower-pieces, and the brothers Marsy, Girardon, and Régnaudin for the stuccos. The floor was covered with a magnificent Savonnerie carpet of which one section has recently been put back in its place.

40. This particular ceiling was executed by Noël Coypel. The other artists involved in the decoration of the rooms were Houasse, J. B. de Champaigne, G. Blanchard, the younger Claude Vignon, Claude Audran II, Michel Corneille the Younger, and, among the younger generation, Jouvenet and La Fosse. But in every case the controller and director of the scheme was Lebrun. One ceiling, in the Salon de l'Abondance, is completely illusionistic, but this room did not originally form part of the *Grand Appartement* and its decoration by Houasse is of a somewhat different character from the rest.

p. 194   41. The accounts show that it cost 142,000 livres.

42. At the same time the even more extravagant silver furniture of the Galerie des Glaces was also melted.

43. The idea was not new, for Louis had played with it since the early fifties (cf. Hautecœur, *Le Louvre et les Tuileries de Louis XIV*, 114, and A. Blunt, *French Drawings at Windsor Castle*, 25).

44. François d'Orbay (1631–97) collaborated regularly with Le Vau and completed several of his later works, including the Collège des Quatre Nations. He also designed a number of churches and the Porte du Peyrou at Montpellier (cf. Hautecœur, *Architecture*, II, 121 ff.). It has recently been shown by M. Albert Laprade ('François d'Orbay', *B.S.H.A.F.*, (1953), 85) that d'Orbay visited Rome in 1660. On the basis of drawings which he has discovered, M. Laprade puts forward the view that d'Orbay was responsible for many of the new elements in Le Vau's last works, such as Versailles, the Colonnade of the Louvre, and the Collège des Quatre Nations.

45. R. Josephson ('Quelques dessins de Claude Perrault pour le Louvre', *Gazette des Beaux-Arts*, II, 1927, 171) reproduces a similar staircase design by Perrault and states that it is earlier than Le Vau's. But the exact date of origin of both designs is obscure, and the question of priority must remain open.

46. A full account of J. H. Mansart's works is

given by Hautecœur, *Architecture*, II, 527 ff., and a somewhat prejudiced version by Blomfield, *A history of French architecture, 1661–1774*, I, 181 ff.

47. These houses are destroyed but are known p. 1 from engravings (cf. Hautecœur, *Architecture*, II, 530 ff., 589 ff.).

48. Particularly in the Hôtel de Noailles.

49. The Hôtel de Lorge, for instance, where the vestibule and staircase take up about half the entire available space, producing a spectacular entrance but leaving almost no room for the living-quarters.

50. This seems to be an adaptation of an English arrangement which occurs, for instance, in the Queen's House at Greenwich by Inigo Jones.

51. Mansart made some small modifications in Le Vau's design, such as the insertion of round-headed windows.

52. The exact shares of the two artists are established by F. Kimball in 'Mansart and Lebrun in the Genesis of the Grande Galerie de Versailles', *Art Bulletin*, XXII (1940), 1.

53. In the 'Crossing of the Rhine', for instance, he p. 1 appears in a chariot wielding the thunderbolt, accompanied by Glory, Minerva, and Hercules, while figures representing Spain and Holland (with her lion) fall before the chariot, and the Rhine, astounded, drops his helm.

54. Built by Antonio del Grande and decorated by Coli and Gherardi in the years 1675–8 (cf. O. Pollak, 'Antonio del Grande', *Kunstgeschichtliches Jahrbuch der K. K. Zentral-Kommission*, III, 1909, 139). One is even tempted to wonder whether Mansart and Lebrun did not actually know this work and draw ideas from it. It is not, however, quite clear how complete it was by 1678 when the Galerie des Glaces was begun; moreover, the scheme is foreshadowed in Mansart's Gallery at Clagny, planned in 1676.

55. This, however, preserved the essential features of its predecessor, being built under the main terrace of the parterre and being flanked by two monumental flights of steps.

56. A conception, however, which appears before this date in an engraving by J. Marot, reproduced in F. Kimball, 'The Genesis of the Château Neuf at Versailles, 1668–71', *Art Bulletin*, (1949), 355. For the Trianon cf. A. Marie, 'Trianon de Porcelaine et Grand Trianon', *B.S.H.A.F.*, (1945–6), 88.

57. See E. Magne, *Le Château de Marly* (Paris, 1934), and J. and A. Marie, *Marly* (Paris, 1947).

58. The plan of the King's block was also unusual in itself, because it was based directly on Palladio's Rotonda.

198　59. J. H. Mansart received many important commissions apart from those mentioned above; but they all reveal the same qualities as the buildings which he carried out for the King. An account of these minor works is given by Hautecœur, *Architecture*, II, 583 ff.

60. Cf. p. 142. For Libéral Bruant see Hautecœur, *Architecture*, II, 520 and 724.

61. These arcades influenced Vanbrugh who imitated them in the great halls of Blenheim and Grimsthorpe. Vanbrugh could have known Bruant's work in Paris and through the house which he built at Richmond in 1662 for James II when Duke of York, which, however, is not now identifiable (cf. *Procès Verbaux de l'Académie Royale d'Architecture*, III, 1913, 281).

Bruant also built a small house for himself which still stands in the rue de la Perle (reproduced in Contet, *Vieux Hôtels de Paris, Quartier St Antoine*, plate 1).

62. Most of the other architects of the day were little more than reflexions of Le Vau or J. H. Mansart. Charles Errard (*c.* 1606–89) was mainly active as a painter of arabesques, of which some examples remain in the Palais de Justice at Rennes (cf. Hautecœur, *Architecture*, II, 301) and in the Luxembourg (cf. L. Dimier, 'Un ouvrage inconnu d'Errard', *B.S.H.A.F.*, (1927), 37), but he also built the church of the Assumption in the rue St Honoré (1670–6), a clumsy and pedantic attempt to make a design consisting only of a dome raised on a high drum (for further details of his career see Hautecœur, *Architecture*, II, 301). Daniel Gittard (1625–86) was concerned in the construction of a number of churches, and in 1671 built Lully's house in Paris, of unusual design with a colossal Order of pilasters on a rusticated ground floor. Charles Chamois (active after 1659), Thomas Gobert (1630–c. 1708), Gabriel Le Duc (1625/30–1704) and many others built hôtels and châteaux which reveal competence rather than originality. A fuller account of all these architects is given by Hautecœur, *Architecture*, II, 168–77. The provincial architects of the same period are discussed by the same author, 205 ff., 702 ff. As has already been said, they show less independence and originality at this period than at any other.

The architects properly speaking were greatly helped by the inventors of decorative themes, such as Jean Berain (1640–1711) and Jean Le Pautre (1618–82), who showed brilliant originality in the designing of arabesques and other fantasies for wall panels or tapestries. For a fuller account of them see R. Berliner, *op. cit.*; F. Kimball, *The Creation of the Rococo*; Hautecœur, *Architecture*, II, 297, 653; R. A. Weigert, *Jean Berain* (Paris, 1937).

63. *Procès Verbaux de l'Académie Royale d'Architecture*, particularly I, 4 ff., 321.

64. For the other treatises of this group cf. Hautecœur, *Architecture*, II, 467, who also gives a good summary of the doctrine of the Academy. Blondel (1617–86) was an engineer and a mathematician, but his energies were mainly directed towards theory. The most important of his surviving buildings is the Porte St Denis (1671).

65. In 1682 the most important buildings of an p. 199 cient Rome were presented in more accurate engravings than had hitherto been available by Antoine Desgodetz in *Les Édifices antiques de Rome*, dedicated to Colbert.

66. The difference appears in the discussions over the decoration of the top floor of the Square Court of the Louvre in 1671. Some architects wanted to follow Lemercier's solution and use caryatids (cf. p. 116); but Colbert was attracted by the suggestion that a new French Order should be invented for the occasion. Finally, however, when the designs submitted by Lebrun, Cottart, Perrault, and others were examined by the Academy, they were all condemned as fantastic and licentious and the scheme was abandoned (see Hautecœur, *Le Louvre et les Tuileries de Louis XIV*, 184). It is, however, interesting to notice that the idea of inventing a specifically French Order should arise at two periods of conscious national pride: the middle of the sixteenth century (cf. p. 50) and the most successful moment of Louis XIV's reign.

67. Its theories are in a sense a continuation of the p. 200 teaching of Sacchi and the classical group of artists in Rome in the mid seventeenth century, which was explicitly directed against the Baroque decorators.

68. The theory was worked out most fully for painting, and I shall in effect limit myself here to what the Academicians had to say on this art. But, *mutatis mutandis*, much of what they say applies to sculpture equally well.

69. In formulating this part of their theory the Academicians often use the exact phrases which Boileau consecrated for literature: *la belle nature*, and *le choix raisonnable*.

70. Even in the time of Lebrun there were serious differences of opinion within the Academy on the subject of colour; but as they are primarily of importance in connexion with later developments they will be considered in a later chapter. For the moment it will be enough to notice that even the artists like Gabriel Blanchard and Pierre Mignard, who in the time of Lebrun most enthusiastically supported the cause of colour in theory, were, when it

came to practice, hardly distinguishable from their opponents.

p. 200 71. *Méthode pour apprendre à dessiner les Passions.*

72. The ancients meant, of course, primarily the Romans, since almost nothing was known at this time of Greek sculpture or architecture. It is, however, worth noticing that the first series of drawings made of Greek works of art, those executed after the Parthenon sculptures for the Marquis de Nointel in 1673, were in France soon after that date (cf. H. Omont, *Athènes au dix-septième siècle. Dessins des sculptures du Parthénon attribués à J. Carrey* (Paris, 1898)). There is, however, no evidence to show that they aroused any interest or that they were studied by French artists.

p. 201 73. André Félibien, who published some of the lectures of the Academicians and expounds their doctrines in his *Entretiens*, is in general more liberal in his views. He allows greater importance than the Academy to imagination, a faculty scarcely mentioned in the lectures; and he is more generous in his appreciation of artists, recognizing the merits of the Venetian and Flemish schools.

74. For an account of his career up to 1660 see A. Blunt, 'The Early Work of Charles Lebrun', *Burl. Mag.*, LXXXV (1944), 165 ff., 186 ff., and J. Wilhelm, 'Les décorations de Charles le Brun à l'Hôtel de la Rivière', *Bulletin du Musée Carnavalet*, II (1949), 6.

75. Cf. p. 134 ff.

76. Notice the reminiscence of Bernini's Baldacchino in the embroidered fringe round the top of the tent.

77. It is worth noticing that Lebrun makes his principal theme a breach of court etiquette, for he shows the moment when the mother of Darius throws herself at the feet of Hephaestion thinking him to be Alexander.

78. The 'History of Alexander', 1662–8, now in the Louvre.

79. In his decorative schemes Lebrun was helped by assistants who specialized in different branches of painting. The most important were Adam van der Meulen (1632–90), a Fleming who executed battle-pieces (cf. G. Brière, 'Van der Meulen, collaborateur de Le Brun', *B.S.H.A.F.*, (1930,) 150), Jean Cotelle (1607–76), a landscape painter, and Jean Baptiste Monnoyer (1634–99), who produced flower-panels for over-doors.

80. Many of his compositions, for instance those on the ceiling of the Galerie des Glaces, owe much to Cortona's decorations in the Palazzo Pitti and in certain details to Bernini's sculptured groups.

p. 202 81. Little need be said of the minor Academicians

of this period, beyond that they were all imitators of Poussin, Le Sueur, or Lebrun. Noël Coypel (1628–1707), Nicolas Loir (1624–79), Antoine Bouzonnet Stella (1637–82) followed strictly in the steps of Poussin; Louis de Boullongne the Elder (1609–74) was also influenced by Le Sueur; Michel Corneille (1642–1708) and Jean Nocret (1616–71) came nearer to Lebrun. Portrait painting almost ceased to exist as an art in its own right, owing to the insistence of the Academy on the importance of a historical or religious subject, and in general the taste of the day preferred an allegorical presentation of a great man, for which a history painter would be chosen. A typical example of the result of this method is Nocret's portrait group of Louis XIV and his family (Plate 163B), painted in 1670, each member of the family being shown with the dress and attributes of a classical god or goddess. For a full explanation of the allegory, cf. E. Soulié, *Notice du Musée National de Versailles*, II (1881), 198). Claude Lefèvre (1632–75) and Laurent Fauchier (1643–72) were almost the only artists of any quality of the period to specialize in portraiture. In the provinces painting came as much under the domination of Paris as architecture, and the only independent artist to be mentioned is the brilliant draughtsman, Raymond Lafage (1656–90), who worked in Toulouse. The minor arts of miniature and engraving flourished at this time, the great master in the former being Jean Petitot the Elder (1607–91), while in the latter field there were a host of artists who reproduced with astonishing sensitiveness and fidelity the works of the painters of the day (cf. Plate 164A).

82. He also on occasions imitated Guido Reni and Albani.

83. We know little of his works executed in Italy, but the following are identifiable: the high altarpiece and an 'Annunciation' in S. Carlo alle Quattro Fontane, Rome; and 'St Charles Borromeo administering the Sacraments', now in the museum at Narbonne, which was a rejected painting for the high altar of S. Carlo ai Catinari, Rome, painted in 1655–7.

84. The closest parallel in Rome is with early p. 20 works by Maratta, but the dates of his portraits are uncertain, so that it is not possible to determine which artist influenced which.

85. Examples occur in almost all the major galleries of Europe, but two instances may be worth quoting as being almost certainly early. The first is the portrait of Maria Mancini in Berlin, which must have been executed before her marriage to Prince

NOTES TO CHAPTER 7

Colonna in 1661. In this case the pattern goes back ultimately to Titian's 'Flora'. The second example is the portrait of Mazarin at Chantilly, presumably painted before his death in 1661.

86. Julie d'Angennes was painted by Deruet as Astrée (Strasbourg Museum) and by Jacques Stella as Minerva (cf. C. de Scudéry, *Le Cabinet de M. de Scudéry*, 1646, 124).

87. Pronounced without the final *x* being sounded.

88. On Girardon see P. Francastel, *Girardon*; and M. Oudinot, 'François Girardon. Son rôle ... à Versailles et aux Invalides', *B.S.H.A.F.*, (1937), 204.

89. The relief of the Madonna (1657; Francastel 10, figure 4), the tomb of Mme de Lamoignon (*c.* 1655; Francastel 14, figure 7) and the bust of Jérôme Bignon (*c.* 1656; Francastel 13, figure 90).

90. The nymphs on the extreme left and immediately to the right of Apollo have been interchanged.

91. In 1668–9.

92. The only groups with many free-standing figures then known were the 'Farnese Bull' and the 'Niobids' in the Villa Medici, neither of which presents a parallel close enough to be useful.

93. The closest parallel is the 'Finding of Moses' of 1647 in the Louvre (Grautoff 115), but the late 'Riposo', reproduced on Plate 134B, shows the same characteristics.

94. Many of them were not entirely original, but were based on sketches by Lebrun, some of which survive in the Louvre.

95. 1668–70; Francastel 23, figures 18–22.

96. It was never actually set up in the Parterre because the plans for the latter were changed before its completion, and the marble was left in the sculptor's studio till 1695, when it was put in its present place. At the same time Girardon was commissioned to make the pedestal, which he completed in 1699. Of the other three members of the quartet, one was never completed, and the other two now stand in the Tuileries Gardens: The 'Rape of Orytheia' by Gaspard Marsy, and the 'Rape of Cybele' by Régnaudin.

97. How skilfully Girardon could design a statue to be seen from all points of view can be judged from the Fontaine de la Pyramide and the Bassin de Saturne at Versailles (Francastel 22 and 33, plates 32–6).

98. Grautoff 70 and 71.

99. It now stands in the transept, so that much of the sculptor's carefully worked out scheme is rendered futile. For earlier projects for this tomb see

R. A. Weigert, 'Deux marchés inédits pour le tombeau de Richelieu', *Bulletin de la Société Poussin*, I (1947), 67.

100. As has often been noticed, this figure is again a borrowing from Poussin, in this case from the 'Extreme Unction'.

101. Of the two monographs on Coysevox that by p. 206 G. Keller-Dorian (Paris, 1920) is the more comprehensive as regards facts and documents, but some of the author's attributions and much of his dating require revision. The short work by L. Benoist (Paris, 1930), though more modest, gives a fuller idea of the personality of the artist.

102. Keller-Dorian, 4. Datable 1676.

103. His main work there dates from the years 1679–87. Much of it was done in collaboration with Jean Baptiste Tuby (1635–1700), a sculptor of Italian origin.

104. Keller-Dorian, 27.

105. Keller-Dorian, 29. The bronzes of the rivers Garonne and Dordogne (Keller-Dorian, 33 and 34) are imitations of the manner of Sarrazin.

106. The same tendency towards the Baroque can be seen in Coysevox's designs for tombs. In the monument to Vaubrun at Serrant (1680–1; Keller-Dorian, 21) the figure rests on the elbow, but has the maximum of movement in the pose and of undercutting in the detail. That of Colbert in St Eustache (1685–7; Keller-Dorian, 41) has the traditional kneeling figure, but again with deep undercutting and strong shadows. In its original form the allegorical figures would also have started a movement in depth up to the main figure, which is destroyed by the present arrangement of the monument. The latest of the series, the tomb of Mazarin, now in the Louvre (1689–93; plate 169B), is in many ways the most classical, and the allegorical figures are in the manner of Sarrazin. But the movement and the swinging drapery of the kneeling cardinal are marks again of Coysevox's leanings towards a Baroque idiom.

107. The number of sculptors who worked at Versailles at the same time as Girardon and Lebrun is enormous. All of them had superb technical skill and the gift of doing what was needed in the general team work. Some of them have personalities which can be more or less distinguished, but none of them made any real contribution to the development of French art. To discuss them all would be beyond the scope of this book; to give a bare list would be useless; and the reader is therefore referred to the excellent treatment of the subject by André Michel in his *Histoire de l'Art*, IV, Part 2, 693–749.

p. 209 1. The most important are the *Dialogue sur le Coloris* of 1673 and the *Conversations sur la Peinture* of 1677. His later works add little to the theoretical discussion, though they are relevant in connexion with the evolution of the taste for Rubens. For a biography of Roger de Piles, with full bibliography, see Léon Mirot, *Roger de Piles* (Paris, 1924). Accounts of the Quarrel are given in A. Fontaine, *Doctrines d'Art*, and L. Hourticq, *De Poussin à Watteau*.

2. No doubt there was latent in their minds the view of Descartes that outline is superior to colour because we can conceive of the former without the latter, but not *vice versa*.

p. 210 3. Roger de Piles executed a few portraits, but was in no sense a professional painter. Towards the end of his life he was made a member of the Academy, but as an *amateur* not a painter.

4. It is of some interest that in the dedicatory Epistle to the *Dissertation sur les Ouvrages des plus fameux peintres* of 1681 de Piles says that his admiration for Rubens was first aroused by the Duc de Liancourt and Sir Kenelm Digby, both of whose taste was founded on that of Charles I.

5. The actual influence of Rubens in French painting at this period is complex, because though he was admired and studied by some artists for his naturalism, his works also gave a strong impetus to the Baroque tendency in artists such as Charles de La Fosse and Antoine Coypel. This problem will be discussed later, cf. pp. 224, 227.

p. 211 6. The rich *bourgeois*, however, imitated the Court style and, as will appear below, enjoyed the most Baroque forms of Baroque portraiture.

7. The 'Crucifixion' painted by Rigaud for his mother in 1695, now at Perpignan, is a typical example (Plate 183B).

8. The most detailed and best illustrated accounts of the Invalides are the descriptions by Lejeune de Bellencourt (1683), J. F. Félibien (1702–6), and the Abbé Pérau (1756). For a modern account of its history (with good bibliography) see Dumolin and Outardel, *op. cit.*, 184 ff. For good plates see Planat and Rümler, *op. cit.*, 178 ff.

9. Cf. Hautecœur, 'L'Origine du dôme des Invalides', *L'Architecture* (1924), 353 ff.

10. Reproduced in Hautecœur, *Architecture*, II, 38.

11. This obelisk seems to be without exact parallel. p. Wren planned a steeple on the top of his dome in the Warrant design for St Paul's (*Wren Society*, I, plate xi). The reconstruction of the Mausoleum of Halicarnassus in the *Hypnerotomachia Poliphili* (fol. b I *verso*) shows an obelisk on the top of a stepped structure. The *Hypnerotomachia* was much read in France, and it just possible that this plate may have suggested the idea to Mansart.

12. Mansart planned an approach to the church which would have been even more Baroque. The façade was to be flanked with two domed pavilions from which sprang quadrant-shaped arcaded wings ending in two further pavilions. This scheme was evidently intended as a variant on Bernini's Piazza of St Peter's (cf. the engraving by Le Pautre, reproduced by Hautecœur, *Architecture*, II, 580).

13. The effect of the interior has, of course, been greatly changed by the circular well dug under the dome for the tomb of Napoleon.

14. This arrangement was not in the first design, which is preserved in the engravings by Lejeune de Bellencourt's account of the Invalides published in 1683, made after the original model (cf. *Description*, 18). This design is based on another scheme of François Mansart, with a slightly cut-off dome without concealed windows. The introduction of the latter in the actual building involved an alteration on the exterior. The first design shows a blind attic round the top of the drum, but this was ultimately pierced with the large round-headed windows which form an unusual feature of the dome design.

15. This altar was originally to have projected less far into the choir (cf. Lejeune de Bellencourt, *Description*, plate H).

16. For the history of the chapel see the books quoted in connexion with the whole palace, cf. above, p. 279, note 32.

17. Externally this Gothic effect is made even p more marked by the console buttresses which run from the roof of the aisles to support the main vault and which produce something like a *chevet*.

18. Cf. p. 227. The sculptured decoration of the lower parts of the chapel is already Rococo in character and belongs therefore to the eighteenth century. It is fully discussed by F. Kimball, *op. cit.*, 79 ff.

19. It was originally intended to decorate the

chapel of Versailles with coloured marbles, but the scheme was abandoned when the plans were revised in 1698 (cf. Dussieux, *Le Château de Versailles*, II, 111).

20. This is recorded in engravings by Pérelle, one of which is reproduced in Hautecœur, *Architecture*, II, 606.

21. Mansart's design embodying this scheme is known from an engraving (reproduced by Hautecœur, *Architecture*, II, 609).

22. This statue was destroyed at the Revolution, and was replaced under Napoleon with a classical column.

214 23. The purchasers of the sites are given in the very full article of Boislisle, 'La Place des Victoires et la Place de Vendôme', *Mémoires de la Société de l'Histoire de Paris*, XV (1888), 1.

24. This phase is analysed in detail by F. Kimball, *op. cit.*, 59 ff.

25. Published by Mariette with the title: 'Maison à bâtir'. It cannot be dated exactly, but it is engraved by Pierre Le Pautre who only joined Mansart's office in 1699, so that it is likely to have been produced between that date and the year of Mansart's death (1708).

26. Shown in the plan by the steps which lead down from them into the garden.

216 27. Sir Reginald Blomfield in his *History of French Architecture, 1661–1774*, I, chapters 13–15, was the first to work the idea out in detail, though without being able to bring documentary evidence. F. Kimball (*op. cit.*, 36 ff., &c., and two articles on the Trianon and the Menagery in the *Gazette des Beaux-Arts*, II, 1936, 245, and I, 1938, 87) has proved that many of the drawings for decoration are by Lassurance and Pierre Le Pautre.

28. Blomfield tentatively attributes the *Maison à bâtir* to Lassurance, but without evidence.

29. Mansart built for himself the Hôtel de Sagonne, rue des Tournelles, which still stands (Pillement, *Hôtels de Paris*, I, plate 25, and Mariette, *Architecture Française*, plates 133–5). The exact date is uncertain, but it was finished before 1687 (cf. Hautecœur, *Architecture*, II, 543). It is more remarkable for its painted decoration than for its planning which is competent, but straightforward.

30. For Bullet see Hautecœur, *Architecture*, II, 516 ff., 689 ff. An important collection of drawings by him is in the Tessin-Hårleman Collection at the National Museum at Stockholm; see E. Wettergren and E. Bier, *Från Ludvig XIV's Paris* (Stockholm, 1945) with a catalogue and reproductions of the most important drawings.

31. The archbishop's palace at Bourges (between 1681 and 1686); the Hôtel de Vauvray (Mariette, *Architecture Française*, plates 144 and 145) with an unconventional plan designed to suit a difficult site, and arranged so that the axis of the garden front is at right angles to that of the court, a method much used later (e.g. at the Hôtel de Soubise); the Hôtel Amelot, later Tallard, 78 rue des Archives (reproduced in Pillement, *Les hôtels de Paris*, I, plate 38 and *Les hôtels du Marais* (1948) plate 55); and the Hôtel de Brancas (reproduced in Pillement, *Les hôtels de Paris*, II, plate 8).

32. Between 1681 and 1687 he built the château of Issy for Denis Talon on an unusual compact plan, very nearly square in shape. It is destroyed but known from engravings in Mariette, *op. cit.*, plates 303–31.

33. The Hôtel d'Évreux is engraved in Mariette, p. 217 *op. cit.*, plates 53–8, and illustrated in Contet, *Vieux hôtels de Paris, Place Vendôme*, plates 31–3. Mariette shows the portico open and with a flat entablature. Drawings for the hôtel exist in the Tessin-Hårleman Collection (cat. Nos. 118–29).

34. The Hôtel Crozat as built by Bullet is engraved in Mariette, *op. cit.*, plates 47, 48, 51, and 52. Drawings are in the Tessin-Hårleman Collection (cat. Nos. 105–17).

35. The external architecture of the Hôtel d'Év- p. 218 reux shows the other side of Bullet's style. The ground floor of the court elevation is simple and even monumental, and the first storey is decorated with an elegant motive of a medallion supported by laurels which is taken from François Mansart's façade of the Carnavalet.

36. Rothelin (c. 1700), Desmarets (1704), Auvergne (finished 1708), Béthune (1708), Maisons (1708). On Lassurance see Hautecœur, *Architecture*, II, 649 and F. Kimball, *The Creation of the Rococo*, 39, &c. His most important works are engraved in Mariette, *op. cit.*

37. For these architects see F. Kimball, *op. cit.*, 93 ff., and Blomfield, *History of French Architecture, 1661–1774*, II, chapter 21.

38. Robert de Cotte (1656–1735) was also a member of Mansart's workshop, but his independent works all date from 1710 onwards and belong to the fully-developed Rococo.

Mention must be made of C. A. Daviler (1653–1700), whose *Cours d'Architecture* (1691) is, after Blondel's, the most important manifesto of academic doctrine in the later seventeenth century (cf. Hautecœur, *Architecture*, II, 646 ff.). He worked under Mansart in Paris and for d'Orbay at Montpellier, where he set up a school which produced good imitations of the style practised in Paris (cf. A. Fliche, *Montpellier* (Paris, 1935), 79). A few other provincial architects sprang up of whom the most important is Pierre Puget, whose career as a sculptor will be discussed in the next section. For his architecture see Hautecœur, *Architecture*, II, 214 ff.

p. 218   39. The most important sources on Puget are the articles by L. Lagrange in the *Gazette des Beaux-Arts* for 1865–7 (reprinted in book form in 1868) and by Montaiglon in the *Archives de l'Art Français*, IV (1855–6), 225 ff., both of which contain important documents. The other useful source is the life by Bougerel in his *Mémoires pour servir à l'histoire de … la Provence* (Paris, 1752). There are three short monographs published since 1900 by P. Auquier (1903), M. Brion (1930), and F. P. Alibert (1930). Puget is also discussed in some detail in Brinckmann, *Barockskulptur*, 325 ff.; E. Hildebrandt, *Malerei und Plastik des 18ten Jahrhunderts in Frankreich*, 30 ff.; and A. Michel, *Histoire de l'Art*, VI, 676 ff. His work in connexion with the decoration of warships is fully treated in P. Auquier, *Pierre Puget Décorateur et Mariniste*.

40. The whole question of Puget's painting is still obscure. The certain works (of which the most important are in the museum of Marseilles) are mostly damaged and of poor quality, and there is still some confusion between the works of Puget himself and his son François (1651–1707).

41. Parallels are to be found in Genoa (Palazzo Lercari) and Milan (Palazzo degli Omenoni), which Puget may have visited on his way back from Florence. The architectural detail of the door is directly derived from Cortona.

p. 220   42. Cf. Voss, *Malerei des Barock*, 244 f. The same type of supporting figures can also be found in the round in the stucco decorations of the Pitti rooms in which Puget worked under Cortona (cf. Voss, *op. cit.*, 253).

43. To this extent they belong to the French tradition of Poussin and Lebrun.

44. Built by Antoine Le Pautre. It is consistent that Girardin, who was the first Parisian to take up the most Baroque sculptor of the century, should also have employed the most Baroque architect of his generation. Of the two statues one, representing 'Hercules and the Hydra', is now in the museum of Rouen.

45. Now in the Louvre.

46. Colbert may, however, also have felt some grudge against Puget for preferring Fouquet to Mazarin (cf. *Gazette des Beaux-Arts*, I, 1865, 317).

47. The 'Hercules Resting', for instance, is based on the Belvedere Torso and a version of the resting Hermes; but the proportions are heavy and the features coarse and wholly unclassical. Colbert did not personally dislike this statue, because he later took it for his own park at Sceaux. The garden statues there also included a copy of Bernini's 'Apollo and Daphne', which still survives in a mutilated condition.

48. The second statue is reproduced in Alibert, *op. cit.*, plate 5.

49. If this is the case, Puget must have paid a second visit to Rome after 1657 (when the 'Daniel' was completed), perhaps when he went to Carrara in 1660. Bougerel mentions a second visit from 1646 to 1651–2, but this does not exactly square with the documents (cf. *Gazette des Beaux-Arts*, I, 1865, 204), for Puget is recorded in France in 1649. But Bougerel's statement confirms the idea of a second visit.

50. Puget also executed other religious statues in p. 2 Genoa in the period 1660–70, notably several of the 'Immaculate Conception' (cf. Alibert, *op. cit.*, plates 24 and 25). These are close in style to the works of Bernini's pupil, Ercole Ferrata, particularly to those in S. Agnese, Rome, executed in the late 1650s, which Puget might have seen if he went to Rome for a second time.

51. Both were designed in 1671 (cf. *Archives de l'Art Français*, IV, 1855–6, 293). The 'Milo' was finished in 1682 and the 'Alexander' in 1693 (*op. cit.*, 305, 308).

52. Plate 179A, like all available photographs, unfortunately shows the statue slightly from one side.

53. Louvre; reproduced in Alibert, *op. cit.*, plate 2. By a curious chance the 'Perseus' arrived in the same boat as Bernini's equestrian statue of Louis XIV. A clear light is thrown on French taste at this moment by the fact that whereas the 'Perseus' was generally (though not universally) admired, Bernini's statue was so widely criticized that the King ordered Girardon to convert it into a Marcus Curtius by making a new head for it and altering other details. That is to say, although the taste of Versailles was nearer than ever before to the Baroque, the King and the courtiers could not swallow the grand and monumental movement of Bernini's late style. Puget's groups were as near as they could go to the Baroque.

54. Louvre; reproduced Alibert, *op. cit.*, plate 3.

55. Cf. *Gazette des Beaux-Arts*, II (1865), 425.

56. It was planned for the vestibule of the chapel at Versailles, which, however, it never reached,

because by the time of its arrival Louvois was dead and intrigue succeeded in preventing Puget's work from ever reaching the King's eyes.

57. Reproduced in Voss, *Malerei des Barock*, 247.

58. 1694; cf. *Archives de l'Art Français*, II (1852-3), 239. In the Musée du Vieux Marseilles. Reproduced in Alibert, *op. cit.*, plate 11.

59. This was more particularly the case over the question of the Place Royale at Marseilles (cf. *Gazette des Beaux-Arts*, I, 1866, 264 ff.).

60. It was no chance that he was much admired by Delacroix.

61. *Gazette des Beaux-Arts*, II (1865), 426.
Puget had one pupil of some importance, Christophe Veyrier (1637–89); cf. John Pope-Hennessy, 'A statue by Veyrier', *Burl. Mag.*, LXXXIX (1947), 22, and 'A relief by Veyrier at Stowe', *op. cit.*, 135.

62. Keller-Dorian, 94.

63. The terra-cotta of 1676 in the Wallace Collection (Keller-Dorian, 8) and the marble of 1679 in the Louvre (*op. cit.*, 15).

64. It is significant that Coysevox's only bust of an Englishman, that of Matthew Prior in Westminster Abbey (1700), is among his most naturalistic works. It depicts the poet in contemporary cap as well as with a shirt and embroidered coat (Keller-Dorian, 63).

65. Except the astonishing terra-cotta head of Puget at Aix-en-Provence (sometimes attributed to the artist himself, but more usually to his pupil Christophe Veyrier) which has an almost nineteenth-century naturalism (reproduced in Alibert, *op. cit.*, plate 26). The Italian Baroque can offer one parallel in Bernini's bust of his mistress, Costanza Buonarelli (reproduced in E. Benkard, *G. L. Bernini* (Frankfort, 1926), plate 68).

66. The tendency towards the Rococo was also visible in the work of other artists working before the end of the century, particularly in Nicolas Coustou (1658–1733), whose figure of France in the Chambre du Roi at Versailles, executed in 1701, marks an important stage towards the freedom of the eighteenth century in decorative sculpture (reproduced in P. de Nolhac, *Versailles, Les grands Palais de France*, plate 112), and whose statues for Marly (1710–12) are a development from Coysevox's 'Duchesse de Bourgogne' in their lightness of movement (reproduced in J. and A. Marie, *Marly*, figures 106, 135, and 136). Robert Le Lorrain's (1666–1743) diploma piece 'Galatea' of 1701 (Kress Collection) has the same characteristics, and the 'Cupid and Psyche' of C. A. Cayot (1667–

1722) in the Wallace Collection, dated 1706, foreshadows Boucher in feeling.

67. Three further French sculptors active before the end of the seventeenth century should be mentioned here: Pierre Legros the Younger (1666–1719), Pierre Étienne Monnot (1657–1733), and Théodon (1646–1713). However, they all spent the greater part of their lives in Rome and their works belong to the history of Italian Baroque art.

68. In 1681 Antoine Coypel painted as his diploma picture 'Louis XIV resting after the Peace of Nijmegen' (Montpellier) (Plate 185B), but the composition is as empty as were the King's claims to victory.

69. Marcel (*La Peinture Française*, 155) has pointed out that in the Salon of 1673 there were about ten religious paintings, whereas in 1699 there were seventy-two, and in 1704 over a hundred.

70. The earliest biographies of La Fosse are those given in the *Mémoires Inédits*, II, 1 ff., and in Dézallier d'Argenville, *Abrégé*, IV, 189 ff.

71. Undated but presumably, from the style, an early work. p. 224

72. The trees also foreshadow the colour and handling of Watteau, and remind one that La Fosse was almost the only seventeenth-century French artist whom Watteau may have studied with profit.

73. Reproduced in Dumolin and Outardel, *op. cit.*, 180.

74. The ceiling panel of the Salon d'Apollon is reproduced in the *Revue de l'Art*, LXII (1932), 103. Weisbach (*op. cit.*, plate opposite 200) reproduces the oil sketch for the ceiling in the museum of Rouen. The sketch is freer, lighter, and more Correggesque than the final version, and the difference between the two can be regarded almost as a demonstration of the effect of Lebrun's discipline on the talent of La Fosse.

75. Its exact date is not certain, but the room seems to have been complete by 1680. Reproduced in *B.S.H.A.F.*, (1939), plate opposite 204.

76. The closest parallels are two engravings by Pontius after the 'Visitation' and the 'Presentation' (Rooses, *L'œuvre de P. P. Rubens*, I, (1886), plates opposite 188, 232) after grisaille sketches which are variants of the wings of the Antwerp 'Descent from the Cross'.

77. The 'Presentation' shows some resemblance to the work of Murillo. This may be due to a common source in Rubens, but it is possible that there may be some direct influence. Murillo was at any rate known in France about 1700 since Grimon

copied his 'Infant Saviour' (formerly Ellesmere collection; sold Christie's 18 October 1946, lot 94).

p. 225   78. He decorated for him Montagu House (cf. *Country Life*, 14 September 1951, p. 812). On its completion William III tried to induce La Fosse to stay in England to paint at Hampton Court, but the artist had to obey the summons back to Paris.

79. Mansart had originally asked Mignard to design the frescoes, but his great age prevented him from undertaking the work.

80. It is not too much to see in the theme an echo of the Revocation of the Edict of Nantes.

81. The dome fresco was executed in the years 1700–2. The whole decoration of the church was completed by 1706.

82. For instance, 'Christ Healing the Sick' (1689) in the Louvre and the 'St Ovide' (1690) at Grenoble. Other paintings in the Louvre, such as the 'Extreme Unction' and 'Christ in the House of Mary and Martha', are not dated, but must belong to the same phase.

p. 226   83. The originals of the first two are now in the Louvre and of the others at Lyons. All are dated 1706, but all of them, except the 'Miraculous Draught', were exhibited in the Salon of 1704.

84. The 'Descent from the Cross' of 1697 in the Louvre (reproduced in P. Marcel, *La Peinture française*, 63) is usually quoted as an example of the influence of Rubens, but the likeness is superficial.

85. His only known portrait, of Doctor Fillon, in the Louvre, shows a remarkable observation of the wrinkles and unkempt hair of the sitter (reproduced in Réau, *Histoire de la Peinture française au 18e siècle*, I, plate I). In one painting, the 'Mass of the Abbé Delaporte' in the Louvre (reproduced in Weisbach, *op. cit.*, 207), the same naturalistic tendency appears in the almost Dutch treatment of the figures kneeling to receive the Sacrament.

86. Apart from this naturalistic tendency the nearest analogy is to be found in certain works of Maratta, such as the 'Death of the Virgin' in the Villa Albani (reproduced in Voss, *Malerei des Barock*, 344), for Maratta's eclecticism was also compounded of a Roman tradition tinged with some qualities learnt from Poussin. To the same phase belongs Michel Corneille the Younger (1642–1708), who decorated the chapel of St Ambrose at the Invalides and was a prolific draughtsman. For further details about him see the article in Thieme-Becker, and P. Marcel, *La Peinture française, passim*.

87. A fairly full biography of Antoine Coypel, with list of works and bibliography, is to be found in Dimier, *Les Peintres français du 18e siècle*, I, 93.

88. Typical examples are the 'Esther before Aha-   p. suerus' and the 'Athalia driven from the Temple', both in the Louvre; the former is reproduced in S. Rocheblave, *French Painting in the Eighteenth Century*, plate 2.

89. One survives at Fontainebleau and is reproduced by L. Dimier, *Les Peintres français du 18e siècle*, I, plate 25.

90. At Montpellier and elsewhere, cf. Dimier, *Les Peintres français du 18e siècle*, I, 131. One wall panel is reproduced, Dimier, plate 23, and the sketch for the ceiling in Marcel, *La Peinture française*, 94.

91. When Coypel left Rome in 1675 the cupola of the Gesù was probably finished but not the vault of the nave, which was being painted in 1678 (cf. E. K. Waterhouse, *Baroque Painting in Rome*, 66). He may, however, have known a sketch, such as that in the Palazzo Spada, or have seen a copy brought back to Paris.

92. The same tendency can be traced even earlier p. in one royal commission, the painting by Gabriel Blanchard (1640–1707) of 'Diana and Endymion' in the Salon de Diane at Versailles, finished before 1680 (reproduced and discussed by G. Brière, 'Le replacement des peintures décoratives aux Grands Appartements de Versailles', *B.S.H.A.F.*, (1939), 197). This canvas has a Bolognese lightness and is painted in pastel-like pinks, greys, and blues which are almost *dix-huitième* in character, and suggest the colours of Amigoni. Little is known of Gabriel Blanchard, who was the son of Jacques, except that he was an active defender of colour in the Academy (cf. p. 209), and that he painted as his Diploma piece in 1663 an 'Allegory on the Birth of Louis XIV' which hangs in the Salon d'Apollon at Versailles (cf. Dézallier d'Argenville, *Abrégé*, IV, 51).

93. Quoted by Marcel (*La Peinture Française*, 196), who also gives a detailed account of the mythological cycles here discussed.

94. The Dauphin, for instance, ordered a cycle of similar paintings for Meudon in the years 1700–9.

95. For full details about both these artists see Caix de Saint-Aymour, *Les Boullongne*.

96. Both Bon and Louis de Boullongne the Younger studied in Bologna and North Italy as well as in Rome.

97. For lists of his works see the articles in the dictionaries of Bénézit and Thieme-Becker. Good examples are in the Louvre and at Versailles.

98. Reproduced in L. Réau, *Histoire de la Peinture française au 18e siècle*, plate 3.

99. For an account of François de Troy, see L. p.

Réau, *Histoire de la Peinture française au 18e siècle*, I, 53 ff., with reproductions of typical works.

100. Reproduced, L. Réau, *op. cit.*, I, plate 40.

101. The example illustrated on Plate 190B, dated 1683, was in an anonymous sale at Christie's, 12 May 1939, lot 90.

102. The name is often spelt *Largillière*, but the artist himself regularly signed *Largillierre*.

103. There is a short modern biography of Largillierre by Georges Pascal, which also includes a list of his works and a bibliography.

104. With Peter Rysbrack, father of the sculptor (cf. *Vertue MSS*, III, 37).

105. He is recorded as receiving payment for overdoors, no doubt of still-life, at Windsor in 1676–7 (cf. St John Hope, *Windsor Castle*, I (1913), 315). One still-life, dated 1677, survives and passed from the Jersey collection to that of F. Lugt (reproduced in *Maandblad voor beeldende Kunsten*, XXVI, 1950, 131). Pascal lists three other still-lifes and reproduces one of them (Plate 30), which is in a later and more decorative manner. Largillierre was also employed by Charles II to repair and enlarge pictures in the Royal Collection, including a 'Sleeping Cupid', which can probably be identified as one now attributed to Caracciolo (*The King's Pictures*, Royal Academy, London, 1946, No. 259; cf. Dézallier d'Argenville, *Abrégé*, IV, 295).

106. The engraving of Mrs Anne Warner is reproduced by C. H. Collins Baker, 'The Portrait of Jane Middleton in the National Portrait Gallery', *Burl. Mag.*, XVII (1910), 360. The author's attribution of the portrait of Jane Middleton to Largillierre is not now generally accepted. For further details about Largillierre's portraits painted in England, see *Vertue MSS*, IV, 110, 120, and 121; V, 105.

107. Two of Nicolas Lambert and his wife, Marie de Laubespine, and a third of Hélène Lambert, wife of François de Motteville (the last two are in private collections, cf. J. Pascal, *Largillierre* (Paris, 1928), Nos 76 and 99), are known from engravings by Drevet (the first two reproduced by E. Bouvy, *La Gravure de Portraits et d'Allégories*, figures 82 and 83). Their exact dates are not known, but Lambert died in 1692, and the dress suggests a date nearly a decade earlier. The portrait of Mme de Motteville is based on a Lely pattern, but the other two show also the influence of small Dutch portraits.

108. Usually called 'Bossuet and the Grand Dauphin', but there does not appear to be any evidence for this. Moreover, Bossuet ceased being tutor to the Prince in 1681, and in 1685 the latter would

have been twenty-four, whereas the youth in the portrait appears to be much younger. Further, he does not wear the Saint Esprit, and it is unlikely that decorum would have allowed the tutor to be shown with his hand on the boy's shoulder, if he had been a royal prince.

109. The sketch in the Louvre is reproduced by Pascal, *op. cit.*, plate 1.

110. Largillierre received three other commissions p. 231 of the same kind from the city of Paris: in 1699 for the marriage of the Duc de Bourgogne, known from an engraving which shows that the artist borrowed freely from Rubens in this composition; in 1702 for the accession of the Duc d'Anjou as Philip V of Spain, of which two fragments exist in the Musée Carnavalet (cf. Pascal, *op. cit.*, plate 5); in 1722 for the proposed marriage of Louis XV, known from a sketch in the Musée Carnavalet (Pascal, *op. cit.*, plate 2).

111. Although Largillierre's importance depends almost entirely on his portraits and groups, it should be noticed that he also painted religious pictures, though mainly for his own pleasure rather than on commission (cf. Pascal, *op. cit.*, No 47). Two compositions of the 'Road to Calvary' and the 'Erection of the Cross' are known from engravings. They reveal the influence of both Rubens and Rembrandt. For an account of Largillierre's views on colour and naturalism see the two lectures by his pupil Oudry in H. Jouin, *Conférences de l'Académie Royale*, 378 ff.

112. There is no modern monograph on Rigaud, but summaries of his achievement are to be found in Weisbach, *op. cit.*, 285 ff., and L. Réau, *Histoire de la Peinture française au 18e siècle*, I, 58 ff. The essential document is the artist's sitters' book published by J. Roman (*Le Livre de Raison du peintre Hyacinthe Rigaud*). Early biographies are to be found in the *Mémoires Inédits*, II, 114, and Dézallier d'Argenville, *Abrégé*, IV, 310.

113. Cf. the portraits of the sculptor Martin Desjardins and his wife Marie Cadenne, painted in 1683 and 1684 respectively. The latter is in the museum at Caen (reproduced in the *Gazette des Beaux-Arts*, I, 1931, 106); the former is presumably the painting at Versailles (No. 3583). Other examples are the portraits of Frédéric Léonard (1689; engraved by Edelinck), of Boyer d'Aguilles (1689; engraved by Coelemans), of Mignard (1690; Versailles, reproduced in A. Fontaine, *Académiciens d'Autrefois*, plate 10) and La Fontaine (1690; engraved by Edelinck, reproduced in E. Bourgeois, *Le Grand Siècle*, plate opposite 302).

p. 231   114. The portrait of Monsieur seems to have vanished, but that of the Duc de Chartres exists in two versions at Versailles and Toulouse.

115. The backgrounds, as in the example reproduced, are usually the work of Joseph Parrocel (1646–1704).

p. 232   116. E.g. that of Louis XIII with La Rochelle in the background.

117. The portrait of the first Earl of Portland here reproduced (Plate 191A) was painted in 1698–9. Cf. R. W. Goulding (*Catalogue of the Pictures belonging to His Grace the Duke of Portland* (1936), 58), who quotes some caustic comments by Matthew Prior on 'that stuttering rogue Rygault'. (Further references to Rigaud are to be found in Prior's letters published in *Hist. MSS Com., Marquis of Bath*, III (1908); *passim*). At the same time the artist painted Lord Portland's eldest son (reproduced in C. Fairfax Murray, *Catalogue of the Pictures belonging to His Grace the Duke of Portland* (1894), plate opposite 41). Other examples of early military portraits include the following.

(1) The Grand Dauphin, 1697, painted in collaboration with Parrocel; now at Versailles. The pose is identical with that of Lord Portland. Rigaud used it on several other occasions (cf. *Gazette des Beaux-Arts*, I, 1906, 499 ff.).

(2) Marquis de Cagne, 1696, painted with Parrocel. Anonymous sale, Christie's, 1 February 1929, lot 147.

(3) Comte de Revel, 1684, engraved by Vermeulen.

(4) Marshal Luxembourg, 1693, engraved by Vermeulen.

(5) Marshal Villeroy, 1691, engraved by Edelinck.

(6) The Duc de Bourgogne, 1702; various versions, including one at Kenwood (painted with Parrocel).

(7) Louis XIV; Prado; probably 1701.

118. By Weisbach, cf. *op. cit.*, 289.

119. Rigaud executed one other state portrait at this time, that of Philip V of Spain at his accession (Prado). The full-length of Bossuet (Louvre, 1699), belongs in type to the same category.

120. Louvre, 1693. Pierre Fréderic was the son of Fréderic Léonard whom Rigaud had painted in 1689.

121. The inventory is printed in the *Nouvelles Archives de l'Art Français*, third series, VII (1891), 61. The artist's collection also included paintings by Rubens, van Dyck, Jordaens, Titian, and Veronese. One very late work by Rigaud, the 'Presentation', painted in 1743 and now in the Louvre, is a pastiche of Rembrandt's manner in the early 1630s.

For further details about the influence of Rembrandt at the beginning of the eighteenth century, cf. P. Marcel, *La Peinture française*, 71. To this should be added a reference to Robert Levrac de Tournières, who copied Rembrandt at any rate soon after 1700 (cf. L. Dimier, *Les Peintres français du 18e siècle*, I, 231), and Santerre, by whom there is a copy of the Dulwich portrait of a girl at a window (Orleans Museum). Roger de Piles also owned several paintings attributed to Rembrandt, including a 'Girl at a Window' which was probably either that in the Duke of Bedford's collection or that in Stockholm.

122. For a fuller account of Desportes' sketches of p. 2 landscape and also of animals see L. Hourticq, 'L'Atelier de François Desportes', *Gazette des Beaux-Arts*, II (1920), 117.

123. Sandrart boasts that he taught Claude to do so, but there is no other case recorded before the time of Desportes.

124. The exact date at which he began to make p. 2 them is not known, but the artist's nephew, who wrote his life in the *Mémoires Inédits* (II, 98 ff.), clearly implies that it was long before the death of Louis XIV and probably soon after the artist's marriage in 1693.

BIBLIOGRAPHY

The following bibliography is not intended to be complete, but only to include works which are of special value for the study of French art. Articles in periodicals referred to in the text are not listed here, but the full references are given in the notes. For a more complete bibliography see: *Catalogus der Kunsthistorische Bibliotheek in het Rijksmuseum te Amsterdam*, Amsterdam, 1934–6.

Most of the abbreviated titles used in the notes are, it is hoped, sufficiently clear to guide the reader to the relevant entry in the bibliography. But the following need explanation:

B.S.H.A.F.: *Bulletin de la Société de l'Histoire de l'Art Français.*
R.D.: Robert-Dumesnil, A. *Le Peintre-graveur français.* Paris, 1835–71.
Grand Marot: Marot, J. *L'Architecture françoise.* Paris, *c.* 1670.
Petit Marot: Marot, J. *Recueil des plans, profils et élévations de plusieurs palais, chasteaux, églises, sépultures, grotes et hostels bâtis dans Paris.* Paris, *c.* 1660–70.

BOOKS COVERING THE WHOLE PERIOD

a. ALL THREE ARTS

i. SOURCES

BRACKENHOFFER, E. *Voyage en France, 1643–44.* Paris, 1925.

BRICE, G. *Nouvelle Description de Paris.* First edition, Paris, 1684. Edition here quoted, Paris, 1725.

DÉZALLIER D'ARGENVILLE, A. J. *Abrégé de la vie des plus fameux peintres.* First edition, Paris, 1745. Second enlarged edition here quoted, Paris, 1762.

DÉZALLIER D'ARGENVILLE, A. N. *Voyage pittoresque de Paris.* First edition, Paris, 1749. Edition here quoted, Paris, 1778.

DÉZALLIER D'ARGENVILLE, A. N. *Voyage pittoresque des environs de Paris.* First edition, Paris, 1755. Edition here quoted, Paris, 1779.

DÉZALLIER D'ARGENVILLE, A. N. *Vies des plus fameux architectes et sculpteurs.* Paris, 1787.

FÉLIBIEN, A. *Entretiens sur les vies et sur les ouvrages des plus excellens peintres anciens et modernes.* First complete edition, Paris, 1685–8. Edition here quoted, Trévoux, 1725.

LE COMTE, F. *Cabinet des singularitez d'architecture, peinture, sculpture et graveure.* First edition, Paris, 1699. Edition here quoted, Brussels, 1702.

LEMAIRE, C. *Paris ancien et nouveau.* Paris, 1685.

MARIETTE, P. *Abécédario.* Published by Ph. de Chennevières and A. de Montaiglon. Paris, 1851–60.

PERRAULT, C. *Les Hommes illustres qui ont paru en France pendant ce siècle.* Paris, 1696–1700.

PIGANIOL DE LA FORCE, J. *Description de Paris.* First edition, Paris, 1736. Edition here quoted, Paris, 1742.

SANDRART, J. V. *Teutsche Academie der edlen Bau-, Bild- und Mahlerey-Künste.* First edition, Nuremberg, 1675. Edition here quoted, edited by A. R. Peltzer, Munich, 1925.

SAUVAL, H. *Histoire et recherches des antiquités de la ville de Paris.* Paris, 1724.

ii. REFERENCE BOOKS

Dictionnaire des artistes et ouvriers d'art de la France par provinces:

(i) *Franche-Comté* par l'abbé Paul Brune. Paris, 1912.

(ii) *Lyonnais* par M. Audin et E. Vial. Paris, 1918–19.

Inventaire général des richesses d'art de la France. Paris, 1877–1911.

BONNAFFÉ, E. *Dictionnaire des amateurs français au 17e siècle.* Paris, 1884.

HERLUISON, H. *Actes d'état-civil d'artistes français.* Orleans, 1873.

JAL, A. *Dictionnaire critique de biographie et d'histoire.* Paris, 1867.

THIEME, U., and BECKER, F. *Allgemeines Lexikon der bildenden Künstler.* Leipzig, 1908–50.

iii. MODERN WORKS

BERLINER, R. *Ornamentale Vorlageblätter des 15. bis 18. Jahrhunderts.* Leipzig, 1925–6.

BERTY, A. and others. *Topographie historique du vieux Paris.* Paris, 1866–8.

HAUG, H., etc. *Trois siècles d'art alsacien: 1648–1948.* Strasbourg-Paris, 1948.

MICHEL, A. *Histoire de l'art.* Paris, 1907–29.

b. ARCHITECTURE

i. SOURCES

BLONDEL, J. F. *Architecture françoise.* Paris, 1752–3. Reprint, Paris, 1904.

CHASTILLON, C. *Topographie françoise.* Paris, 1641.

DU BREUL, J. *Le Théâtre des antiquitez de Paris.* First edition, Paris, 1612. Enlarged edition, Paris, 1639.

FÉLIBIEN, A. *Mémoires pour servir à l'histoire des maisons royales.* Paris, 1681.

FÉLIBIEN, M. *Histoire de la ville de Paris.* Paris, 1725.

GUIFFREY, J. *Les Comptes des bâtiments du roi sous le règne de Louis XIV.* Paris, 1881–1901.

LABORDE, L. DE. *Les Comptes des bâtiments du roi (1528–1571).* Paris, 1877–80.

MARIETTE, J. *L'Architecture française.* Paris, 1727. Five volumes. Reprint of volumes 1–3, Paris and Brussels, 1927–9.

MAROT, J. *L'Architecture françoise.* Paris, c. 1670. Enlarged edition as volume 4 of Mariette's *Architecture française.*

MAROT, J. *Recueil des plans, profils et élévations de plusieurs palais, chasteaux, églises, sépultures, grotes et hostels bâtis dans Paris.* Paris, c. 1660–70.

MERIAN, M. *Topographia Galliae.* Amsterdam, 1660.

ii. MODERN WORKS

Châteaux et manoirs de France. Paris, 1934–9.

BLOMFIELD, Sir R. *History of French Architecture, 1494–1661.* London, 1911.

BLOMFIELD, Sir R. *History of French Architecture, 1661–1774.* London, 1921.

CHRIST, Y. *Églises Parisiennes actuelles et disparues.* Paris, 1947.

CONTET, F. *Les Vieux Hôtels de Paris.* Paris, 1909–30.

COOK, Sir T. *Twenty-five Great Houses of France.* London, n.d.

COSSÉ BRISSAC, PH. DE. *Châteaux de France disparus.* Paris, 1947.

DUMOLIN, M. *Études de topographie Parisienne.* Paris, 1929–31.

DUMOLIN, M., and OUTARDEL, G. *Les Églises de France. Paris et la Seine.* Paris, 1936.

GANAY, E. DE. *Châteaux de France.* Paris, 1948–50.

GEYMÜLLER, H. VON. *Die Baukunst der Renaissance in Frankreich.* Stuttgart, 1898–1901.

GROMORT, G. *Histoire abrégée de l'architecture de la Renaissance en France.* Paris, 1930.

HAUTECŒUR, L. *Histoire de l'architecture classique en France.* Paris, 1943. In progress.

HAUTECŒUR, L. *Histoire du Louvre.* Paris, n.d.

JARRY, P. *La Guirlande de Paris.* Paris, 1928.

LAVEDAN, P. *L'Architecture française.* Paris, 1944.

PILLEMENT, G. *Les Hôtels de Paris.* Paris, 1945.

PILLEMENT, G. *Les Hôtels du Marais.* Paris, 1945. Revised edition, Paris, 1948.

ST SAUVEUR, H. *Châteaux de France.* Paris, n.d.

SAUVAGEOT, C. *Palais, châteaux, hôtels et maisons de France du XVe au XVIIIe siècle.* Paris, 1867.

SELLIER, C. *Les Anciens Hôtels de Paris.* Paris, 1910.

SOULANGE-BODIN, H. *Châteaux de Normandie.* Paris, 1928–9.

WARD, W. *The Architecture of the Renaissance in France.* London, 1911.

c. PAINTING, DRAWING AND ENGRAVING

i. SOURCES

BAILLY, N. *Inventaire des tableaux du Roy rédigé en 1709 et 1710.* Paris, 1899.

MAROLLES, M. DE. *Le Livre des Peintres et Graveurs.* Paris, 1677.

ii. MODERN WORKS

Commemorative Catalogue of the Exhibition of French Art, 1200–1900, Royal Academy of Arts, London, January–March 1932. Oxford and London, 1933.

BLUNT, A. *The French Drawings in the Collection of His Majesty The King at Windsor Castle.* Oxford and London, 1945.

CHENNEVIÈRES-POINTEL, P. DE. *Recherches sur la vie et les ouvrages de quelques peintres provinciaux de l'ancienne France.* Paris, 1847–54.

COURBOIN, F. *Histoire illustrée de la gravure en France.* Paris, 1923–9.

DACIER, E. *La Gravure française.* Paris, 1944.

DORIVAL, B. *La Peinture française.* Paris, 1942.

FONTAINE, A. *Les Doctrines d'art en France.* Paris, 1909.

FRY, R. *Characteristics of French Art.* London, 1932.

GUIFFREY, J., and MARCEL, P. *Inventaire général des dessins du musée du Louvre. ... École française.* Paris, 1906–35.

ROBERT-DUMESNIL, A. *Le Peintre-graveur français.* Paris, 1835–71.

d. SCULPTURE

BENOIST, L. *La Sculpture française*. Paris, 1945.

BRINCKMANN, A. *Barockskulptur*. Berlin-Neubabelsberg, 1917.

VITRY, P. *La Sculpture française classique de Jean Goujon à Rodin*. Paris, 1934.

e. APPLIED ARTS

i. TAPESTRY

BASCHET, J. *Tapisseries de France*. Paris, 1951.

FENAILLE, M. *État général des Tapisseries de la Manufacture des Gobelins*. Paris, 1923.

GÖBEL, H. *Die Wandteppiche und ihre Manufakturen in Frankreich, Italian, Spanien und Portugal*. Leipzig, 1928.

GUICHARD, E. *Les Tapisseries décoratives du Garde-Meuble*. Paris, n.d.

GUIFFREY, J. *Histoire de la tapisserie depuis le moyen âge jusqu'à nos jours*. Tours, 1886.

ii. OTHER ARTS

AUBERT, M. *Le Vitrail en France*. Paris, 1946.

BABELON, J. *L'Orfèvrerie française*. Paris, 1946.

CHAMPEAUX, A. DE. *Le Meuble*. Paris, 1885.

FÉLICE, R. DE. *Le Meuble français du moyen âge à Louis XIII*. Paris, 1922.

FÉLICE, R. DE. *Le Meuble français sous Louis XIV*. Paris, 1922.

MARQUET DE VASSELOT, J. *Les Émaux limousins de la fin du XVe siècle et de la première partie du XVIe*. Paris, 1921.

MOLINIER, E. *Histoire générale des arts appliqués à l'industrie*. Paris, 1897.

SIXTEENTH CENTURY

a. ALL THREE ARTS

GÉBELIN, F. *Le Style Renaissance en France*. Paris, 1942.

LABORDE, L. DE. *La Renaissance des arts à la cour de France*. Paris, 1886.

PALUSTRE, L. *La Renaissance en France*. Paris, 1879–85.

ROY, M. *Artistes et monuments de la Renaissance française*. Paris, 1929.

VASARI, G. *Le vite de' più eccelenti pittori, scultori, et architettori* ... First edition, 1550; second edition, 1568. Translation by Gaston du C. de Vere, London, 1912–15.

YATES, F. *The French Academies of the 16th Century*. London, 1949.

b. ARCHITECTURE

i. GENERAL

ALBERTI, L. B. *L'Architecture*. Translated by Jean Martin. Paris, 1553.

DU CERCEAU, J. A. *Les plus excellents bastiments de France* ... Paris, 1576–79. Facsimile reprint, Paris, 1868.

GÉBELIN, F. *Les Châteaux de la Loire*. Paris, 1927.

GÉBELIN, F. *Les Châteaux de la Renaissance*. Paris, 1927.

MARTIN, C., and ENLART, C. *La Renaissance en France*. Paris, 1911.

PALUSTRE, L. *L'Architecture de la Renaissance*. Paris, 1902.

VITRUVIUS. *L'Architecture*. Translated by Jean Martin. Paris, 1547.

WARD, H. W. *French Châteaux and Gardens in the Sixteenth Century*. London, 1909.

ii. INDIVIDUAL ARTISTS

BULLANT, J. *Reigle générale d'architecture*. Rouen, 1564.

GEYMÜLLER, H. VON. *Les du Cerceau, leur vie et leur œuvre*. Paris, 1887.

LE SUEUR, P. *Dominique de Cortone dit Le Boccador*. Paris, 1928.

L'ORME, P. DE.

L'Architecture. Paris, 1567. Second edition, Paris, 1568.

Instruction. Published in A. Berty, *Les grands architectes de la Renaissance*. Paris, 1867, and in A. Berty, *Topographie historique du vieux Paris, Région du Louvre et des Tuileries*, II, 179.

Clouzot, H. *Philibert de l'Orme*. Paris, 1910.

SERLIO, S. *Tutte l'opere d'architettura*. First complete edition, Venice, 1584. For dates of publication of separate books see p. 45.

c. PAINTING, DRAWING, AND ENGRAVING

i. GENERAL WORKS

ADHÉMAR, J. *Les Graveurs français de la Renaissance*. Paris, 1946.

BLUM, A., and LAUER, P. *La Miniature française aux XVe et XVIe siècles*. Paris, 1930.

BODMER, E. *Correggio und die Malerei der Emilia*. Vienna, 1942. Italian edition, Novara, 1943.

DIMIER, L. *Histoire de la peinture française des origines au retour de Vouet (1300–1627)*. Paris, 1925.

DIMIER, L. *La Peinture française au XVIe siècle*. Marseilles, 1942.

DIMIER, L. *La Peinture de portrait*. Paris, 1924.

DIMIER, L. *French Painting in the Sixteenth Century.* London, 1904.

LAVALLEÉ, P. *Le Dessin français du XIIIe au XVIe siècle.* Paris, 1930.

MOREAU-NÉLATON, E. *Les Clouet et leurs émules.* Paris, 1924.

RING, G. *A Century of French Painting, 1400–1500.* London, 1949.

TIETZE-CONRAT, E. *Der französische Kupferstich der Renaissance.* Munich, 1925.

VOSS, H. *Die Malerei der Spätrenaissance.* Berlin, 1920.

ii. INDIVIDUAL ARTISTS

BOURDICHON.
MacGibbon, D. *Jean Bourdichon, a Court Painter of the Fifteenth Century.* Glasgow, 1933.

PERRÉAL, J.
Maulde la Clavière, M. A. R. de. *Jean Perréal, dit Jean de Paris.* Paris, 1896.

PRIMATICCIO.
Dimier, L. *Le Primatice, peintre, sculpteur et architecte des Rois de France.* Paris, 1900.
Dimier, L. *Le Primatice.* Paris, 1928.

ROSSO.
Barocchi, P. *Il Rosso Fiorentino.* Rome, 1950.
Kusenberg, K. *Le Rosso.* Paris, 1931.

d. SCULPTURE

i. GENERAL WORKS

AUBERT, M. *La Sculpture française du moyen-âge et de la Renaissance.* Paris–Brussels, 1926.

DAVID, H. *De Sluter à Sambin.* Paris, 1933.

VITRY, P. *La sculpture de la Renaissance française au musée du Louvre.* Paris, n.d.

VITRY, P., and BRIÈRE, G. *Documents de sculpture française de la Renaissance.* Paris, 1911.

ii. INDIVIDUAL ARTISTS

CELLINI, B.
La Vita scritta da lui medesimo. First edition, Naples, 1728. Translated by John Pope-Hennessy. London, 1949.

COLOMBE.
Pradel, P. *Michel Colombe. Le dernier imagier gothique.* Paris, 1953.
Vitry, P. *Michel Colombe.* Paris, 1901.

GOUJON.
Du Colombier, P. *Jean Goujon.* Paris, 1949.

PILON.
Babelon, J. *Germain Pilon.* Paris, 1927.

SEVENTEENTH CENTURY

a. ALL THREE ARTS

i. SOURCES

DUSSIEUX, L. and others. *Mémoires inédits sur la vie et les ouvrages des membres de l'Académie royale de peinture et de sculpture.* Paris, 1854.

FRÉART DE CHANTELOU, P. *Journal du voyage du Cavalier Bernin en France.* Paris, 1885. Abridged edition, Paris, 1930.

MONTAIGLON, A. DE. *Procès-verbaux de l'Académie royale de peinture et de sculpture.* Paris, 1875.

ii. GENERAL WORKS

BOURGEOIS, E. *Le Grand siècle.* Paris, 1896.

CHAMPIGNEULLE, B. *Le Règne de Louis XIII.* Paris, 1949.

CHAMPIGNEULLE, B. *Le Règne de Louis XIV.* Paris, 1943.

DU COLOMBIER, P. *Le Style Henri IV–Louis XIII.* Paris, 1941.

HILDEBRANDT, E. *Die Malerei und Plastik des 18. Jahrhunderts in Frankreich, Deutschland und England.* Berlin, 1915.

LEMONNIER, H. *L'Art français au temps de Richelieu et de Mazarin.* Paris, 1893.

LEMONNIER, H. *L'Art français au temps de Louis XIV.* Paris, 1911.

MAURICHEAU-BEAUPRÉ, C. *L'Art au XVIIe siècle en France.* Paris, 1946–7.

ROCHEBLAVE, S. *L'Art et le goût en France de 1600 à 1900.* Paris, 1930.

ROCHEBLAVE, S. *L'Âge classique de l'art français.* Paris, 1932.

WEIGERT, R. A. *Le Style Louis XIV.* Paris, 1941.

b. ARCHITECTURE

i. SOURCES

BLONDEL, F. *Cours d'architecture enseigné dans l'Académie Royale.* First edition, Paris, 1675. Second edition, Paris, 1698.

DAVILER, A. *Cours d'architecture, qui comprend les ordres de Vignole.* Paris, 1750.

DESGODETZ, A. *Les Édifices antiques de Rome dessinés et mesurés très exactement.* Paris, 1682.

JOSEPHSON, R. *L'Architecte de Charles XII, Nicodème Tessin à la Cour de Louis XIV.* Paris, 1930.

LEMONNIER, H. *Procès verbaux de l'académie royale d'architecture.* Paris, 1911–26.

PERRAULT, CH. *Mémoires de Charles Perrault.* Avignon, 1759.

PERRAULT, CH., and CLAUDE. *Mémoires de ma vie par Charles Perrault. Voyage à Bordeaux (1669) par Claude Perrault.* Paris, 1909.

SAVOT, L. *L'Architecture françoise des bastimens particuliers; avec des figures et des notes de M. Blondel.* Paris, 1673.

SIRÉN, O. *Nicodemus Tessin den Ys Studieresor.* Stockholm, 1914.

ii. GENERAL WORKS

HAUTECŒUR, L. *Le Louvre et les Tuileries de Louis XIV.* Paris, 1927.

KIMBALL, F. *The Creation of the Rococo.* Philadelphia, 1943.

KIMBALL, F. *Le Style Louis XV.* Paris, 1949.

MAURICHEAU-BEAUPRÉ, C. *Le Château de Versailles et ses jardins.* Paris, 1924.

NOLHAC, P. DE. *La Création de Versailles.* Versailles, 1901.

NOLHAC, P. DE. *Les Grands Palais de France: Versailles.* Paris, n.d.

NOLHAC, P. DE. *Les Jardins de Versailles.* Paris, 1906.

PLANAT, P., and RÜMLER, E. *Le Style Louis XIV.* Paris, 1912.

iii. INDIVIDUAL ARTISTS

BERAIN.
Weigert, R. A. *Jean Berain.* Paris, 1937.

BROSSE, S. De.
Pannier, J. *Un Architecte français au commencement du XVIIe siècle: Salomon de Brosse.* Paris, 1911.

LE MUET, P.
Manière de bien bastir pour toutes sortes de personnes. First edition, Paris, 1623. Second enlarged edition, Paris, 1647.

LE NÔTRE.
Guiffrey, J. *André Le Nostre.* Paris, n.d.

MANSART, F.
Blunt, A. *François Mansart.* London, 1941.

PERRAULT, Claude.
Ordonnances des cinq espèces de colonnes selon la méthode des anciens. Paris, 1683.
Vitruvius. *Les Dix Livres d'architecture ... traduits ... en François, avec des notes et des figures par M. Perrault.* Paris, 1684.
Hallays, A. *Les Perrault.* Paris, 1926.

c. PAINTING

i. SOURCES

BELLORI, G. *Le Vite de' pittori, scultori ed architetti moderni ...* Rome, 1672.

FONTAINE, A. *Conférences inédites de l'Académie Royale de Peinture et de Sculpture.* Paris, n.d.

JOUIN, H. *Conférences de l'Académie Royale de Peinture et de Sculpture.* Paris, 1893.

PASSERI, G. *Vite de' pittori, scultori ed architetti che anno lavorato in Roma, morti del 1641 fino al 1673.* First edition, Rome, 1772. Edition by J. Hess, Leipzig-Vienna, 1934.

ii. GENERAL WORKS

BOUVY, E. *La Gravure de portraits et d'allégories.* Paris, 1929.

DIMIER, L. *Histoire de la peinture française du retour de Vouet à la mort de Lebrun, 1627 à 1690.* Paris, 1926.

DIMIER, L. *Les Peintres français du XVIIIe siècle.* Paris, 1928 and 1930.

FONTAINE, A. *Académiciens d'autrefois.* Paris, 1914.

HOURTICQ, L. *De Poussin à Watteau.* Paris, 1921.

LEROY, A. *Histoire de la peinture française au XVIIe siècle (1600–1700).* Paris, 1935.

MARCEL, P. *La Peinture française au début du dix-huitième siècle 1690–1721.* Paris, n.d.

PEVSNER, N., and GRAUTOFF, O. *Barockmalerei in den romanischen Ländern.* Wildpark-Potsdam, 1925.

RÉAU, L. *Histoire de la peinture française au XVIIIe siècle.* Paris, 1925–6.

WEISBACH, W. *Französische Malerei des XVII. Jahrhunderts.* Berlin, 1932.

iii. INDIVIDUAL ARTISTS

BOSSE.
Blum, A. *L'Œuvre gravé d'Abraham Bosse.* Paris, 1924.
Blum, A. *Abraham Bosse et la société française au dix-septième siècle.* Paris, 1924.

BOULLONGNE.
Caix de St Aymour, Comte de. *Les Boullongne.* Paris, 1919.

CALLOT.
Meaume, E. *Recherches sur la vie et les ouvrages de Jacques Callot.* Paris, 1860.
Plan, P. *Jacques Callot, maître graveur (1593–1635).* Brussels, 1914.

CHAMPAIGNE, P. De.
Dorival, B. *Philippe de Champaigne* [Catalogue of the Exhibition at the Orangerie]. Paris, 1952.
Gazier, A. *P. et J. B. de Champaigne.* Paris, 1893.
Poncheville, A. Mabile de. *Philippe de Champaigne.* Paris, 1938.

CLAUDE.
Liber Veritatis; or a collection of prints after the original designs of Claude le Lorrain executed by Richard Earlom. London, 1777 and 1819.

Blum, A. *Les Eaux-fortes de Claude Gellée dit Le Lorrain*. Paris, 1923.

Courthion, P. *Claude Gellée dit Le Lorrain*. Paris, 1932.

Demonts, L. *Musée du Louvre: Les dessins de Claude Gellée dit Le Lorrain*. Paris, 1923.

Friedlaender, W. *Claude Lorrain*. Berlin, 1921.

Hetzer, T. *Claude Lorrain*. Frankfurt a.M., 1947.

Hind, A. M. *Catalogue of the Drawings of Claude Lorrain preserved in the Department of Prints and Drawings*. London, British Museum, 1926.

Hind, A. M. *The Drawings of Claude Lorrain*. London and New York, 1925.

Pattison, Mrs. M. *Claude Lorrain, sa vie et ses œuvres*.

Smith, J. *A Catalogue raisonné of the works of the most eminent Dutch, Flemish and French painters*. Vol. VIII. London, 1837.

LARGILLIERRE.
Pascal, G. *Largillierre*. Paris, 1928.

LA TOUR.
Bloch, V. *Georges de La Tour*. Amsterdam, 1950.
Furness, S. M. *Georges de La Tour of Lorraine, 1593–1652*. London, 1949.
Pariset, F.-G. *Georges de La Tour*. Paris, 1948.

LEBRUN, Charles.
Méthode pour apprendre à dessiner les passions. Paris, 1667.
Jouin, H. *Charles Le Brun et les arts sous Louis XIV*. Paris, 1889.
Marcel, P. *Charles Le Brun*. Paris, n.d.

LE NAIN.
Fierens, P. *Les Le Nain*. Paris, 1933.

LE SUEUR.
Rouchès, G. *Eustache Le Sueur*. Paris, 1923.

NANTEUIL.
Petitjean, C., and Wickert, C. *Catalogue de l'œuvre gravé de Robert Nanteuil*. Paris, 1925.

POUSSIN, N.
Correspondance de Nicolas Poussin. Edited by Ch. Jouanny. Paris, 1911.

Lettres de Poussin. Edited by P. du Colombier. Paris, 1929.

Andresen, A. *Nicolas Poussin, Verzeichniss der nach seinen Gemälden gefertigten Kupferstiche*. Leipzig, 1863.

Friedlaender, W. *Nicolas Poussin*. Munich, 1914.

Friedlaender, W. *The Drawings of Nicolas Poussin*. London, 1939–53.

Gide, A. *Poussin*. Paris, 1945.

Grautoff, O. *Nicolas Poussin*. Munich, 1914.

Jamot, P. *Connaissance de Poussin*. Paris, 1948.

Magne, E. *Nicolas Poussin*. Brussels, 1914.

Smith, J. *A Catalogue raisonné of the works of the most eminent Dutch, Flemish and French painters*. Vol. VIII. London, 1837.

RIGAUD, H.
Livre de Raison du peintre Hyacinthe Rigaud. Edited by J. Roman. Paris, 1919.

VOUET.
Voss, H. *Die Malerei des Barock in Rom*. Berlin, 1924.

d. SCULPTURE

i. GENERAL WORKS

FRANCASTEL, P. *La Sculpture de Versailles*. Paris, 1930.

ii. INDIVIDUAL ARTISTS

COYSEVOX.
Keller-Dorian, G. *Antoine Coysevox*. Paris, 1920.

GIRARDON.
Francastel, P. *Girardon*. Paris, 1928.

PUGET.
Alibert, F. *Pierre Puget*. Paris, 1930.
Auquier, P. *Pierre Puget, décorateur naval et mariniste*. Paris, n.d.
Brion, M. *Pierre Puget*. Paris, 1930.

SARRAZIN.
Digard, M. *Jacques Sarrazin*. Paris, 1934.

THE PLATES

Antonio della Porta and Pace Gaggini: Tomb of Raoul de Lannoy. 1507
Folleville, Somme

I

Z

(A) Francesco Laurana: Chapel of St Lazare. 1475–81. *La Major, Marseilles*

(B) Bertrand de Meynal: Fountain from Gaillon. 1508.
La Rochefoucauld, Charente

Château of Gaillon, Eure: Entrance. 1508.

3

(A) Hector Sohier: Apse of St Pierre, Caen. 1528–45

4

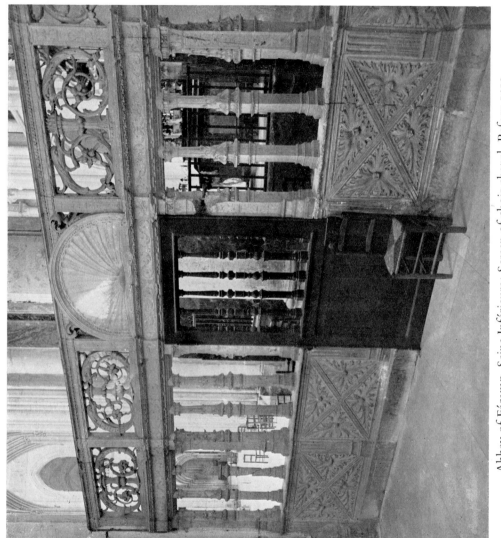

Abbey of Fécamp, Seine Inférieure: Screen of choir chapel. Before 1519.

5

Château of Azay-le-Rideau, Indre-et-Loire: Entrance 1518–27.

6

Château of Blois: Staircase. 1515–24. (*Copyright Country Life*)

7

(A) Château of Bury, Loir-et-Cher. 1511–24. Drawing by du Cerceau. *British Museum*

(B) Château of Blois: North-west façade. 1515–24. (*Copyright Country Life*)

(A) Château of Chambord: North front. Begun 1519. (*Copyright Country Life*)

(B) Château of Chambord: Roof. After 1537.

9

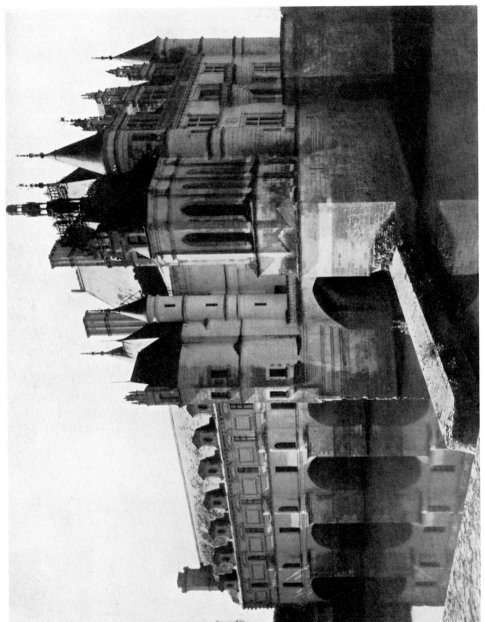

Château of Chenonceau, Indre-et-Loire. Begun 1515. (*Copyright Country Life*)

(B) Old Town Hall. 1503–13. *Orleans*

(A) Hôtel Pincé. 1523–33. *Angers*

11

(A) Girolamo Viscardi and assistants: Tomb of the Dukes of Orleans. 1502. *St Denis*

(B) Girolamo da Fiesole and Michel Colombe: Tomb of Francis II of Brittany.
Begun 1499. *Nantes Cathedral*

Head of the recumbent figure of Louis XII. Between 1515 and 1531. *St Denis*

Antonio and Giovanni Giusti and assistants: Tomb of Louis XII. 1515–31. *St Denis*

Rouland le Roux and assistants: Tomb of the Amboise Cardinals.
Begun 1515. *Rouen Cathedral*

Michel Colombe and Jérôme Pacherot: Relief of St George from the chapel at Gaillon. 1508–9. *Louvre, Paris*

(B) Jean Perréal: Louis XII. 1514. *Windsor Castle.*
By gracious permission of Her Majesty the Queen

(A) Jean Bourdichon: St Sebastian. 1508.
Hours of Anne of Brittany, Bibliothèque Nationale, Paris

(A) Château of Madrid: Begun 1528. Drawing by du Cerceau. *British Museum*

(B) Château of Madrid: Mantelpiece. 1530–40. Drawing by du Cerceau. *British Museum*

18

(A) Château of Villandry, Indre-et-Loire. 1532.

(B) Gilles Le Breton: Cour du Cheval Blanc. 1528–40. *Fontainebleau*

(B) Blaise Le Prestre: Hôtel d'Écoville. 1535–8. *Caen*

(A) Gilles Le Breton: La Porte Dorée. 1528–40. *Fontainebleau*

(B) St Michel: Façade. Begun 1537. *Dijon*

(A) St Eustache. Begun 1532. *Paris*

(A) Rosso: Galerie François I. *c.* 1533–40. *Fontainebleau*

(B) Primaticcio: Mantelpiece from the Chambre de la Reine.
c. 1533–7. *Fontainebleau*

Rosso: Detail from Galerie François I. 1533–40. *Fontainebleau*

23

Rosso: Pietà. 1530–40. *Louvre, Paris*

(B) Jean Clouet: Madame de Lautrec. Drawing. *Chantilly*

(A) Jean Clouet: Madame de Canaples. *National Gallery of Scotland, Edinburgh*

25

Jean Clouet: Unknown Man. Drawing. *Chantilly*

(B) Jean Clouet: Man with a Petrarch. Drawing. *Chantilly*

(A) Jean Clouet: Man with a Petrarch. *Windsor Castle.*
By Gracious permission of Her Majesty the Queen

27

(A) Serlio: Château of Ancy-le-Franc, Yonne. North Front. *c.* 1546.

(B) Serlio: Château of Ancy-le-Franc. Court. *c.* 1546.

(A) Lescot: Square Court of the Louvre. Begun 1546. *Paris*

(B) Lescot (?): Hôtel Carnavalet. Begun *c.* 1545. *Paris*

29

(B) Philibert de l'Orme: Frontispiece from the Château of Anet. Before 1550. *École des Beaux-Arts, Paris*

(A) Goujon: Caryatids. 1550–1. *Louvre, Paris*

30

(A) Philibert de l'Orme: Château of St Maur. 1541–63. Drawing by du Cerceau. *British Museum*

(B) Philibert de l'Orme: Château of Anet, Eure-et-Loir. Entrance. *c.* 1552.

Philibert de l'Orme: Château of Anet. Chapel. 1549–52. Drawing by du Cerceau. *British Museum*

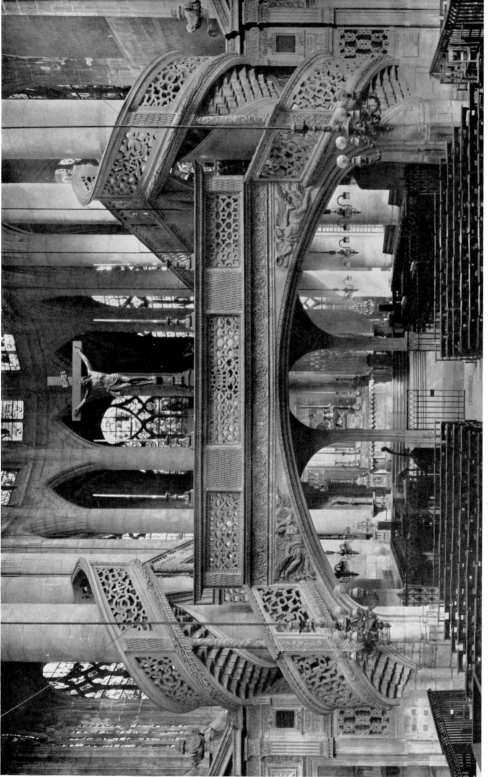

Philibert de l'Orme (?): Screen. *c.* 1545. *St Étienne-du-Mont, Paris*

Philibert de l'Orme and Bontemps: Tomb of Francis I. Begun 1547. *St Denis*

Primaticcio and Pilon: Tomb of Henry II. Begun 1563. *St Denis*

(A) Philander: Gable (above the rose window) of the Cathedral. *c.* 1562. *Rodez, Aveyron*

(B) Primaticcio: Valois Chapel, St Denis. *c.* 1560. Engraving by Marot

(A) Primaticcio: Aile de la Belle Cheminée. 1568. *Fontainebleau*

(B) Primaticcio: Grotte des Pins. *c.* 1543. *Fontainebleau*

37

(A) Guillaume de Lissorgues (?): Château of Bournazel, Aveyron. *c.*1550

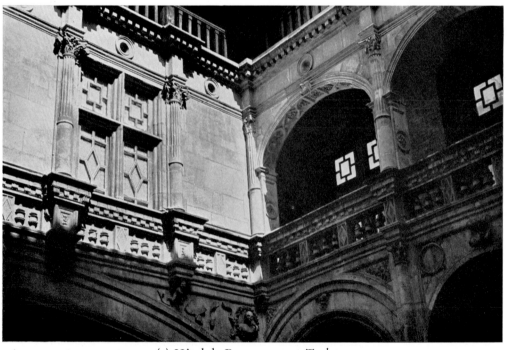

(B) Hôtel de Bernuy. 1530. *Toulouse*

(B) Toussaint Chesnau: Champigny-sur-Veude, Indre-et-Loire.
Porch of the chapel. 1570

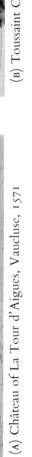

(A) Château of La Tour d'Aigues, Vaucluse, 1571

(B) Nicolas Bachelier: Hôtel de Bagis. 1538. *Toulouse*

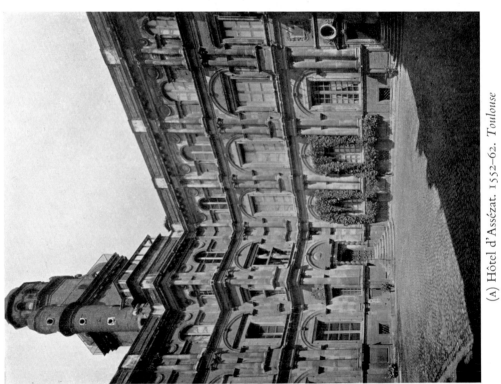

(A) Hôtel d'Assézat. 1552–62. *Toulouse*

Primaticcio: Room of the Duchesse d'Étampes. *c.* 1541–5. *Fontainebleau*

41

Primaticcio: Temperance. Drawing for the Cabinet du Roi, Fontainebleau. 1541–5.
British Museum

(A) Primaticcio: Ceres. Drawing for Ballroom, Fontainebleau. 1552–6. *Chantilly*

(B) Primaticcio: The Masquerade of Persepolis. Drawing for the room of the Duchesse d'Étampes, Fontainebleau. 1541–5. *Louvre, Paris*

43

(A) Primaticcio: Ceiling of the Galerie d'Ulysse, Fontainebleau. *c.* 1550.
Engraving by du Cerceau

(B) Primaticcio: Ulysses and Penelope. *c.* 1545, *Formerly the Hon. Geoffrey Howard,*
Castle Howard, Yorkshire

44

(A) Noël Jallier: The Trojan War. 1549. *Château of Oiron, Deux-Sèvres*

(B) Niccolò dell'Abbate: Orpheus and Eurydice. 1557 (?). *National Gallery, London*

45

(A) Jean Cousin the Elder: Eva Prima Pandora. Before 1538. *Louvre, Paris*

(B) Félix Chrétien: Moses and Aaron before Pharaoh. 1537.
Metropolitan Museum, New York

46

François Clouet: Charles IX. 1570. *Kunsthistorisches Museum, Vienna*

47

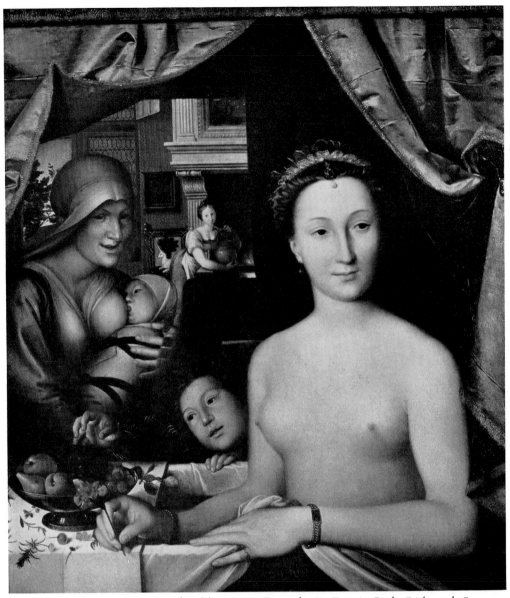

François Clouet: Marie Touchet (?). *c.* 1570. *Formerly Sir Francis Cook, Richmond, Surrey*

François Clouet: Pierre Quthe. 1562. *Louvre, Paris*

49

(B) François Clouet: Henry II. c. 1550.
Bibliothèque Nationale, Paris

(A) Corneille de Lyon: The Earl of Hertford (?).
Wallace Collection, London

50

(B) Jean Duvet: Illustration to the Apocalypse.
Before 1561. *British Museum*

(A) Jean Duvet: Moses and the Patriarchs.
1540–50. *British Museum*

Jean Goujon (?): Tomb of Louis de Brézé (from a cast).
c. 1540. *Rouen Cathedral*

Jean Goujon: Nymphs. 1547–9. *Fontaine des Innocents, Paris*

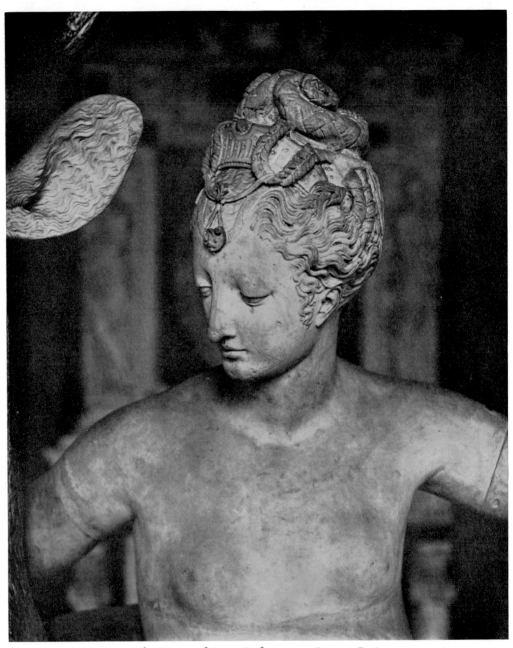

The Diana of Anet. Before 1554. *Louvre, Paris*

(A) Jean Goujon: Pietà. 1544–5. *Louvre, Paris*

(B) Jean Goujon: Naiad from the Fontaine des Innocents. 1548–9. *Louvre, Paris*

55

(B) Pierre Bontemps: Monument for the heart of
Francis I. 1550. *St Denis*

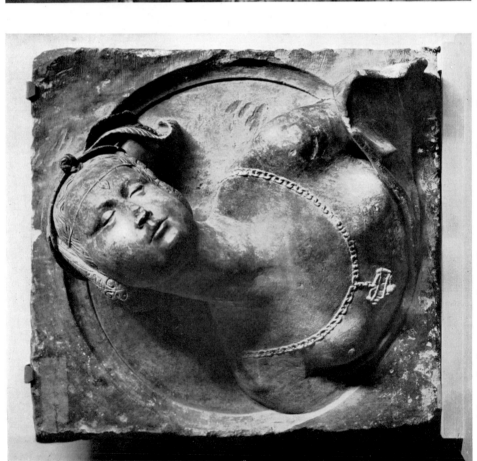

(A) Head of a woman from Vienne. *c.* 1540–50. *Museum, Lyons*

Ligier Richier: Tomb of René de Châlons (from a cast).
After 1544. *St Pierre, Bar-le-Duc, Meuse*

(B) Bullant: Château of Écouen. Seine-et-Oise.
South wing. *c.* 1560

(A) Bullant: Château of Écouen. Entrance. *c.* 1555–60.
Engraving by du Cerceau

(B) Bullant: Le Petit Château. c. 1560.
Chantilly

(A) Bullant: Château of La Fère-en-Tardenois. Aisne Gallery.
Between 1552 and 1562

59

(A) Jacques du Cerceau the Elder: Château of Charleval. 1573. Engraving by du Cerceau

(B) Jacques du Cerceau the Elder: Design for a town house. 1559

60

(A) Jacques du Cerceau the Elder: Château of Verneuil. Begun 1565. Engraving by du Cerceau

(B) Baptiste du Cerceau: Hôtel Lamoignon. 1584. *Paris*

61

Hugues Sambin: Maison Milsand. *c.* 1561. *Dijon*

Germain Pilon: Monument for the heart of Henry II. 1560. *Louvre, Paris*

63

Germain Pilon: Recumbent figure of Henry II (from a cast). 1563–70. *St Denis*

Germain Pilon: Tomb of Valentine Balbiani. Before 1583. *Louvre, Paris*

Germain Pilon: The Virgin. *c.* 1580–5. *Louvre, Paris*

Germain Pilon: Head of Cardinal Birague. After 1583. *Louvre, Paris*

Germain Pilon: The Deposition. *c* 1580–5. *Louvre, Paris*

(B) François Quesnel: Mary Ann Waltham. 1572.
Earl Spencer, Althorp, Northamptonshire

(A) Jean Cousin the Younger: The Last Judgement.
Louvre, Paris

69

(A) Antoine Caron: Augustus and the Sibyl. *Louvre, Paris*

(B) Anonymous artist: Woman choosing between Youth and Age.
Late 16th century. *Earl of Elgin, Broomhall, Fife*

70

(B) Rémy Collin: Stables of the Château of Fontainebleau. 1609

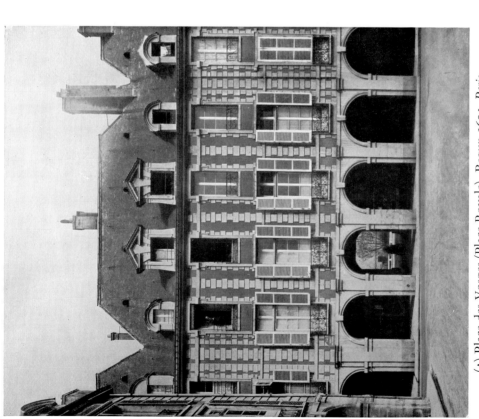

(A) Place des Vosges (Place Royale). Begun 1605. *Paris*

71

(A) Place des Vosges (Place Royale). (From an engraving.) Begun 1605. *Paris*

(B) Claude Chastillon and Jacques Alleaume: Place de France, Paris. 1610.
Engraving by Chastillon

Chapel of the Château of Fontainebleau. c. 1615–25

(A) Salomon de Brosse: The Luxembourg Palace. Begun 1615. *Paris*

(B) Jean du Cerceau: Hôtel de Sully. 1624–9. *Paris*

Pierre Le Muet: Hôtel Duret de Chevry. 1635. *Now part of the Bibliothèque Nationale, Paris*

(B) Hôtel de Châlons-Luxembourg. 1623 (?). *Paris*

(A) Pierre Le Muet: Hôtel Comans d'Astry. *c.* 1645. *Paris*

76

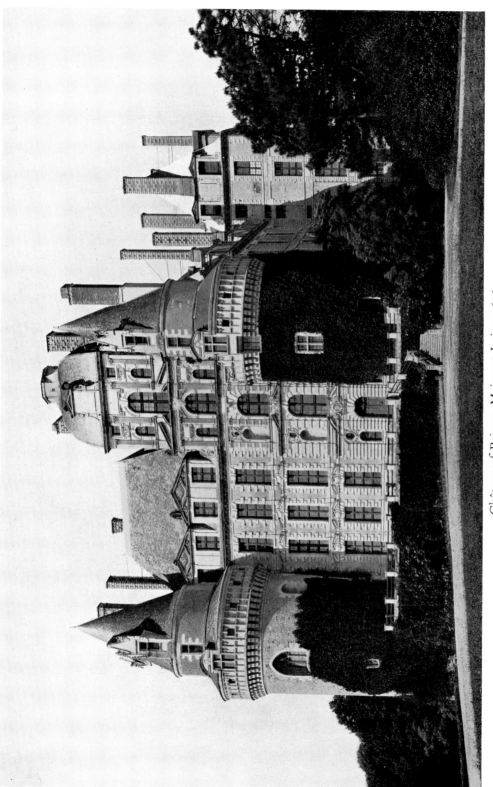

Château of Brissac, Maine-et-Loire. 1606

77

(A) Château of Rosny, Seine-et-Oise. *c.* 1600

(B) Château of Grosbois, Seine-et-Marne. *c.* 1600

(A) Salomon de Brosse: Château of Blérancourt. 1614. Engraving by Silvestre

(B) Salomon de Brosse: Palais de Justice. 1618. *Rennes*

(B) Salomon de Brosse: St Gervais. 1616. *Paris*

(A) Derand: St Paul-St Louis. 1634. *Paris*

(B) Toussaint Dubreuil: A Sacrifice. *Louvre, Paris*

(A) Ambroise Dubois: Sacrifice at the tomb of Neoptolemus. *Fontainebleau*

Jacques Bellange: The Annunciation. *Badische Kunsthalle, Karlsruhe*

82

(B) Jacques Bellange: The Hurdy-Gurdy Player. Etching. *Royal Library, Windsor*

(A) Jacques Bellange: The Annunciation. Etching. *British Museum*

83

Jacques Bellange: The Three Marys. Etching. *British Museum*

(A) Callot: The Agony in the Garden. 1625. Wash drawing. *Chatsworth, Derbyshire*

(B) Callot: Landscape. Pen drawing. *Chatsworth, Derbyshire*

(C) Callot: Scene from the *Grandes Misères de la Guerre*. 1633. Etching. *British Museum*

Callot: Florentine Fête. 1619. Etching. *British Museum*

(A) Jacques Callot: The two Pantaloons. 1616. Etching. *British Museum*

(B) Claude Deruet: Fire. *Museum, Orleans*

Claude Vignon: The death of a Hermit. *c.* 1620. *Louvre, Paris*

Frans Pourbus the Younger: The Duc de Chevreuse. 1612.
Earl Spencer. Althorp, Northamptonshire

Lemercier: The Church of the Sorbonne. Begun 1635. *Paris*

François Mansart and Lemercier: The Val-de-Grâce. Begun 1645. *Paris*

(A) Lemercier: Château of Richelieu. Begun 1631. Engraving by Marot

(B) Lemercier: Richelieu, Indre-et-Loire. Air view. Begun 1631

(A) and (B) François Mansart: Château of Berny, Seine. Begun before 1624

(C) François Mansart: Hôtel de la Vrillière, Paris. Begun 1635. Engraving by Marot

93

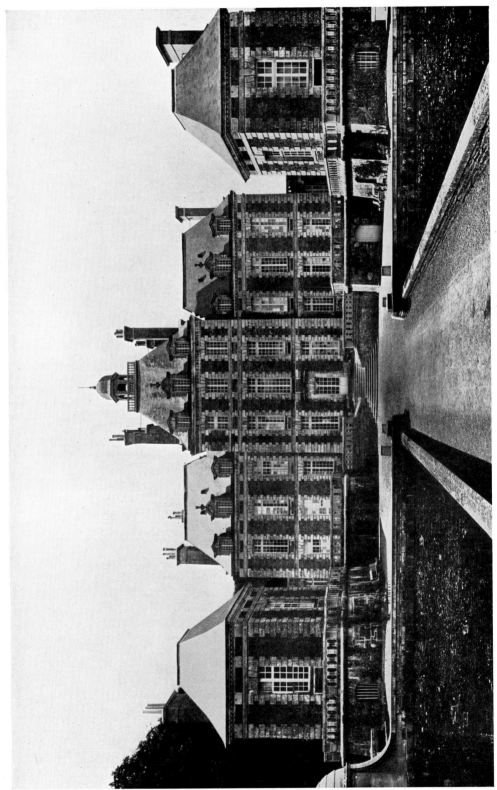

François Mansart: Château of Balleroy, Calvados. c. 1626

François Mansart: Château of Blois. Orleans Wing. 1635–8. (*Copyright Country Life*)

(A) François Mansart: Château of Blois. Staircase (*from a drawing by Sir Reginald Blomfield*). 1635–8

(B) François Mansart: The Visitation. Dome. Begun 1632. *Paris*

(A) François Mansart: Hôtel d'Aumont. Staircase. 1665

(B) François Mansart: Château of Maisons, Seine-et-Oise. Balustrade of staircase. 1642–8

97

François Mansart: Château of Maisons. Vestibule. 1642–6

François Mansart: Château of Maisons. Frontispiece. 1642–6

(B) François Mansart: Hôtel Carnavalet.
Façade. 1655. *Paris*

(A) François Mansart: Château of Maisons.
Staircase. 1642–6

François Mansart and Lemercier: Val-de-Grâce. Interior. 1645–67. *Paris*

(B) Louis Le Vau and Lebrun: Château of Vaux-le-Vicomte, Seine-et-Marne. Chambre du Roi. 1657–61

(A) Louis Le Vau: Hôtel Lambert. Court. Begun *c.* 1640. *Paris*

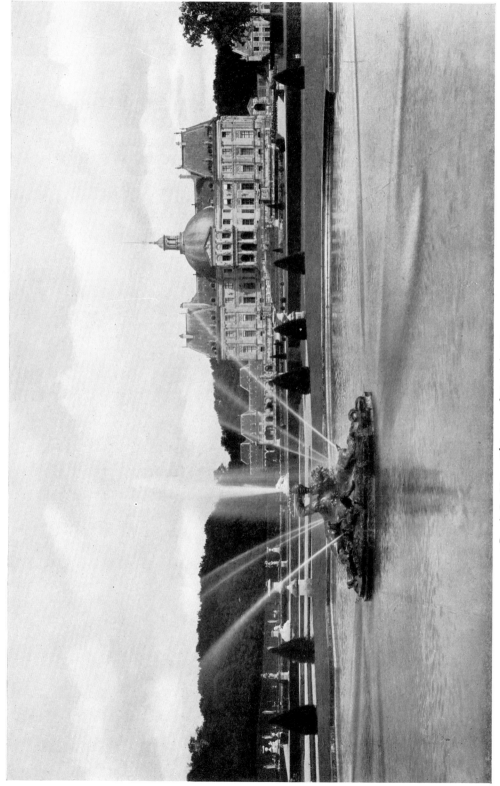

Louis Le Vau: Château of Vaux-le-Vicomte. 1657–61

103

(A) Louis Le Vau: Hôtel Tambonneau. *c.* 1639. Engraving by Marot

(B) Louis Le Vau: Hôtel Lambert. Cabinet de l'Amour. *c.* 1646–7. Engraving by Picart

(A) Louis Le Vau and Lebrun: Hôtel Lambert. Gallery. *c*. 1650–60. *Paris*

(B) Antoine Le Pautre: Design for a château. 1652. Engraving

Antoine Le Pautre: Hôtel de Beauvais. Staircase. 1652–5. *Paris*

(B) Pierre Cotard: Hôtel Amelot de Bisseuil. 1657–60. *Paris*

(A) Jean Boullier: Hôtel Aubert de Fontenay. Staircase. 1656–61. *Paris*

Jacques Bruant: Hall of the Marchands-Drapiers. *c.* 1655–60. *Carnavalet Museum, Paris*

Vouet: Appearance of the Virgin to St Bruno. 1620. *S. Martino, Naples*

Vouet: The Birth of the Virgin. *c.* 1615–20. *S. Francesco a Ripa, Rome*

(B) Vouet: The Presentation. 1641. *Louvre, Paris*

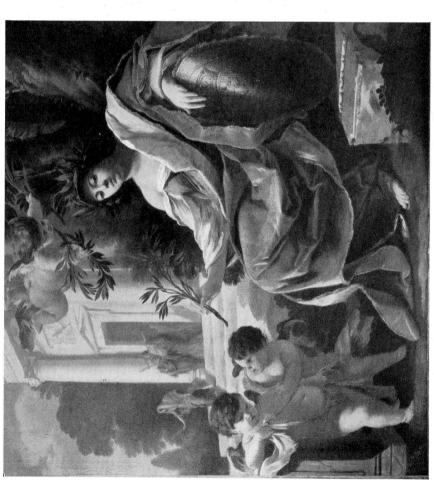

(A) Vouet: Allegory of Peace. *c.* 1648. *Chatsworth, Derbyshire*

III

(A) Vouet: Ceiling of the chapel in the Hôtel Séguier. 1638. Engraving by M. Dorigny

(B) Jacques Blanchard: Charity. *c.* 1630–38
The Duke of Richmond and Gordon, Goodwood, Sussex

(A) La Hyre: The Birth of Bacchus. 1638. *Hermitage, Leningrad*

(B) Perrier: Acis and Galatea. 1645–50. *Louvre, Paris*

113

La Hyre: Pope Nicholas V before the body of St Francis. 1630. *Louvre, Paris*

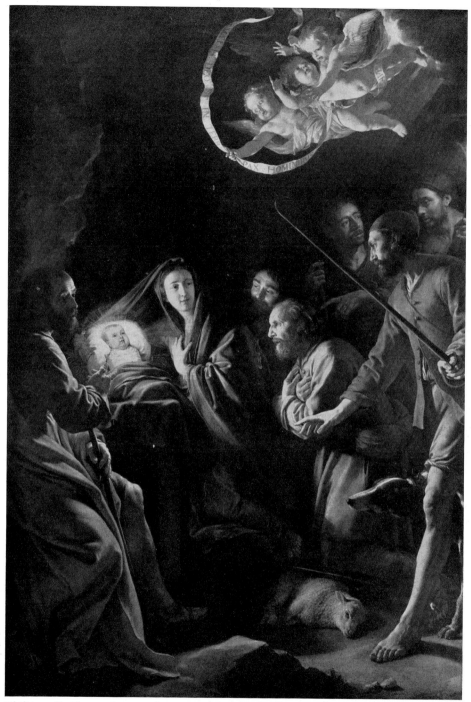

Philippe de Champaigne: Adoration of the Shepherds. *c.* 1630. *Wallace Collection, London*

(B) Champaigne: Unknown man. 1650. *Louvre, Paris*

(A) Champaigne: Richelieu. 1635–40. *National Gallery, London*

(A) Philippe de Champaigne: The Échevins of the City of Paris. 1648. *Louvre, Paris*

(B) Philippe de Champaigne: Two Nuns of Port Royal. 1662. *Louvre, Paris*

Quid terra cinisque superbis.
Hora fugit, marcescit Honor, Mors imminet atra.

P. Champaigne Pin.   Morin scul. Cum Priuil. Re.

Philippe de Champaigne: Memento Mori. Engraving by Morin

(B) La Tour: St Jerome. 1620–5. *National Museum, Stockholm*

(A) Nicolas Tournier: The Guardian Angel. *Narbonne Cathedral*

119

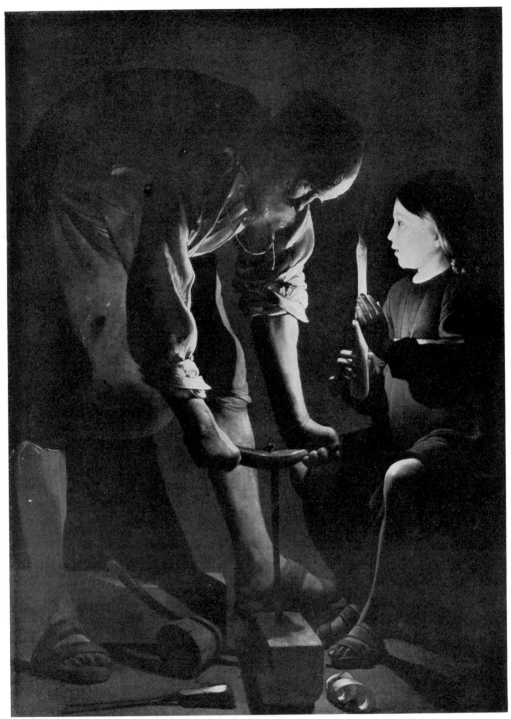

La Tour: Christ and St Joseph. *c.* 1645. *Louvre, Paris*

La Tour: St Sebastian. *c.* 1650. *Ehem. Staatliche Sammlungen, Berlin-Dahlem*

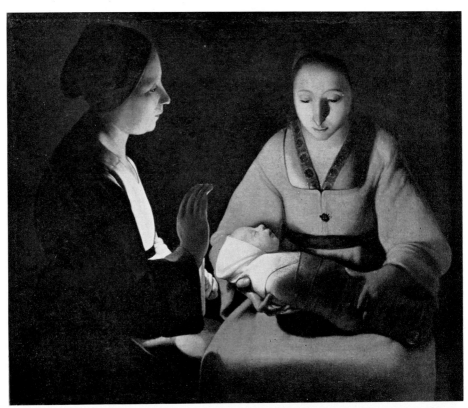

(A) La Tour: Nativity. *c.* 1650. *Museum, Rennes*

(B) Antoine Le Nain: The Little Singers. *c.* 1645–8. *The Duke of Cervinara*

(A) Louis Le Nain: Peasants at Supper. *c.*1645–8. *Louvre, Paris*

(B) Mathieu Le Nain: Le Corps de garde. 1643. *Baronne de Berckheim, Paris*

123

(A) Abraham Bosse: The Wise Virgins: *c.* 1635. *British Museum*

(B) Abraham Bosse: Le Mariage à la Ville. 1633. *British Museum*

(A) Poussin: Victory of Moses. 1624–6. *Hermitage, Leningrad*

(B) Poussin: Rinaldo and Armida. *c.* 1629. *Dulwich Gallery, London*

Poussin: The Martyrdom of St Erasmus. 1628–9. *Vatican, Rome*

Poussin: The Inspiration of the Poet. *c. 1628–9. Louvre, Paris*

Poussin: The Arcadian Shepherds. *c.* 1630. *Chatsworth, Derbyshire*

(A) Poussin: The Adoration of the Golden Calf. *c.* 1635. *National Gallery, London*

(B) Poussin: The Kingdom of Flora. *c.* 1637–8. *Formerly Dresden Gallery*

HH

(A) Poussin: Ordination. 1647. *The Earl of Ellesmere (on loan to the National Gallery of Scotland, Edinburgh)*

(B) Poussin: Ordination. 1636–40. *The Duke of Rutland, Belvoir, Rutlandshire*

(A) Poussin: The Eucharist. 1647. *The Earl of Ellesmere (on loan to the National Gallery of Scotland, Edinburgh)*

(B) Poussin: The Arcadian Shepherds. *c.* 1650. *Louvre, Paris*

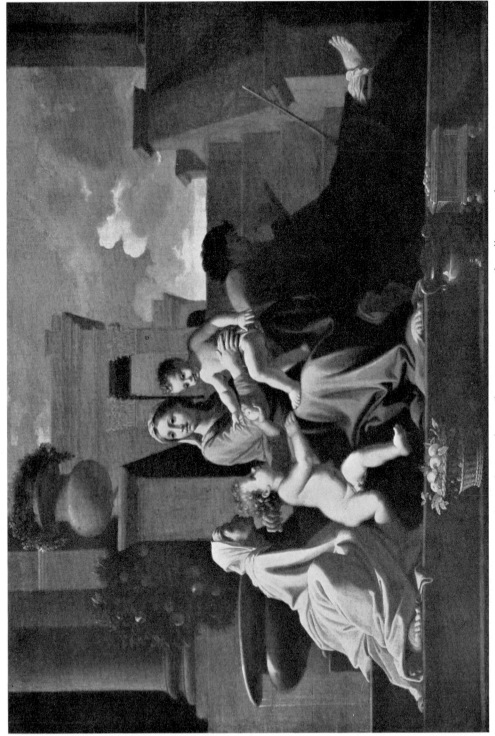

Poussin: The Holy Family on the Steps. 1648. *National Gallery, Washington*

Poussin: The Ashes of Phocion. 1648. *The Earl of Derby, Knowsley, Lancashire*

(A) Poussin: The Finding of Moses. 1651. *Mrs Derek Schreiber, Bellasis House, Dorking, Surrey*

(B) Poussin: The Rest on the Flight into Egypt. 1655–7. *Hermitage, Leningrad*

Poussin: The Holy Family. 1653–5. *Hermitage, Leningrad*

Poussin: Apollo and Daphne. 1665. *Louvre, Paris*

Claude: Erminia and the Shepherds. 1666. *The Earl of Leicester, Holkham, Norfolk*

(A) Claude: Apollo guarding the herds of Admetus. 1654.
The Earl of Leicester, Holkham, Norfolk

(B) Claude: Perseus and the Medusa. 1674. *The Earl of Leicester, Holkham, Norfolk*

(A) Claude: The Mill. 1631. *Museum of Fine Arts, Boston, Mass.*

(B) Claude: The Embarkation of St Ursula. 1641. *National Gallery, London*

Claude: Ascanius and the Stag. 1682. *Ashmolean Museum, Oxford*

Claude: View of the Campagna. Wash drawing. *British Museum*

(A) Claude: View of Tivoli. Wash drawing. *British Museum*

(B) Claude: Tree and Hills. Wash drawing. *British Museum*

(A) Gaspar Dughet: Landscape. *Private collection*

(B) Pierre Patel the Elder: Landscape. 1652. *Hermitage, Leningrad*

(B) Le Sueur: Three Muses. *c.* 1647–9.
Louvre, Paris

(A) Le Sueur: The Presentation of the Virgin. 1640–5.
Hermitage, Leningrad

144

(B) Lubin Baugin: Madonna.
Private Collection

(A) Le Sueur: St Bruno.
c. 1650. Formerly Kaiser Friedrich Museum, Berlin

145

II

(A) Bourdon: The Holy Family. *c.* 1660–70. *Sir Kenneth Clark, London*

(B) Tassel: The Tree of Jesse. *Museum, Troyes*

Nanteuil. Louis XIV. 1664. Engraving. *British Museum*

(B) Henri and Charles Beaubrun: Mlle de Montpensier. 1655.
Prado, Madrid

(A) Bourdon: An Architect. 1657. *The Duke of Buccleuch,*
Boughton, Northamptonshire

(B) Jean Warin: Richelieu. c. 1640. *Bibliothèque Mazarine, Paris*

(A) Simon Guillain: Anne of Austria. 1647. *Louvre, Paris*

(B) François Anguier and assistants: Montmorency tomb. 1648–52.
Chapel of the Lycée, Moulins, Allier

(A) Sarrazin and Guérin: Caryatids. 1636.
Louvre, Paris

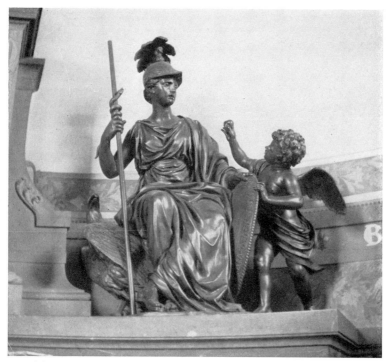

(A) Sarrazin: Tomb of Henri de Bourbon, Prince de Condé.
1648–63. *Chantilly*

(B) Michel Anguier: Nativity, from the Val-de-Grâce. 1665. *St Roch, Paris*

(A) Lebrun: The Salle des Gardes de la Reine. 1679–81. *Versailles*

(B) Lebrun: Louis XIV visiting the Gobelins. Between 1663 and 1675. *Gobelins Museum, Paris*

(A) Louis Le Vau: Collège des Quatre Nations. Begun 1662. Engraving by Pérelle

(B) Louis Le Vau and Lebrun: Versailles. Escalier des Ambassadeurs.
Begun 1671. Engraving by Surugue

Louis Le Vau, Perrault, and Lebrun: The East Front of the Louvre. 1667–70. *Paris*

Designs for the East Front of the Louvre.
(A) François Le Vau's project. 1664. Drawing. *National Museum, Stockholm*
(B) Bernini's first project. 1664. Drawing. *Dr M. D. Whinney, London*
(c) His final scheme. 1665. Engraving by Marot

(A) Louis Le Vau: Versailles. The Garden Front. 1669. Engraving by Silvestre

(B) Le Roy and Louis Le Vau: Versailles, Cour de Marbre. 1624–69. Engraving by Silvestre

J. H. Mansart and Lebrun: Galerie des Glaces. Begun 1678. *Versailles*

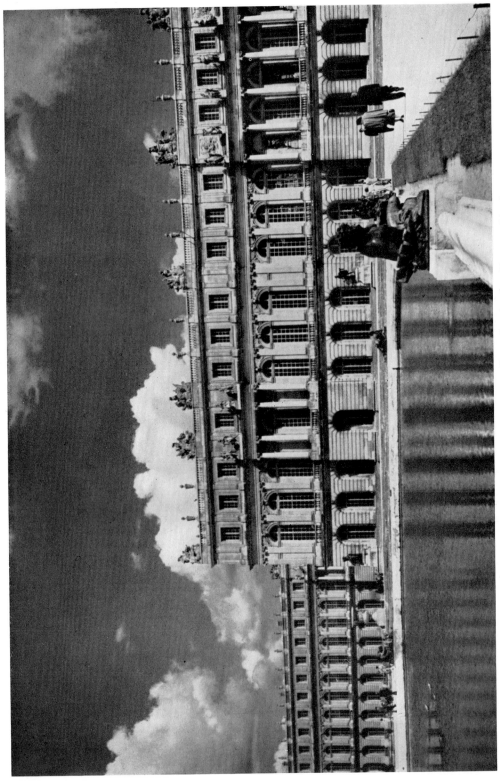

Louis Le Vau and J. H. Mansart: Versailles. The Garden Front. 1669–85

J. H. Mansart, Lebrun, and Coysevox: Salon de la Guerre. Begun 1678. *Versailles*

(A) J. H. Mansart: Château of Marly. Begun 1679. Engraving by Pérelle

(B) Libéral Bruant: The Invalides. 1670–7. *Paris*

Lebrun: Hercules and the horses of Diomedes. *c.* 1640. *Art Gallery, Nottingham*

Lebrun: Louis XIV adoring the Risen Christ. 1674. *Museum, Lyons*

162

(A) Lebrun: The Chancellor Séguier. 1661. *Louvre, Paris*

(B) Nocret. The Family of Louis XIV. 1670. *Versailles*

163

(A) Lebrun: The Tent of Darius. From an engraving. 1661. *Louvre, Paris*

(B) Pierre Mignard. The Tent of Darius. 1689. *Hermitage, Leningrad*

Pierre Mignard: Louis XIV. 1673. *Gallery, Turin*

(A) Pierre Mignard: The Marquise de Seignelay as Thetis.
1691. *National Gallery, London*

(B) Girardon and others: Versailles. The Grotto of Thetis. 1666.
Engraving by J. Le Pautre

Girardon: Apollo and the Nymphs of Thetis. 1666. *Versailles*

Girardon: Tomb of Richelieu. 1675–7. *The Sorbonne, Paris*

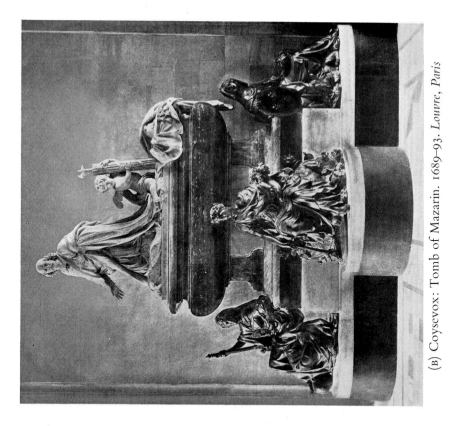

(B) Coysevox: Tomb of Mazarin. 1689–93. *Louvre, Paris*

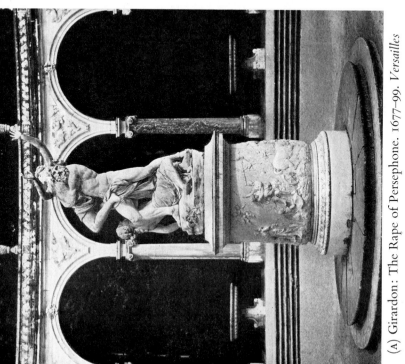

(A) Girardon: The Rape of Persephone. 1677–99. *Versailles*

169

Coysevox: Louis XIV. *c.* 1680. *Wallace Collection, London*

Coysevox: Lebrun. 1676. *Wallace Collection, London*

(B) J. H. Mansart: Church of the Invalides.
Section. 1680–91

(A) J. H. Mansart: Church of the Invalides.
Exterior. 1680–91. *Paris*

J. H. Mansart: Chapel. 1689–1710. *Versailles*

(A) J. H. Mansart: Place Vendôme (from an engraving). Begun 1698. *Paris*

(B) J. H. Mansart: Place Vendôme. Detail. Begun 1698. *Paris*

174

(A) J. H. Mansart: Salon de l'Œil de Bœuf. 1701. *Versailles*

(B) Pierre Bullet. Hôtel d'Évreux. 1707. *Paris*

175

(B) Pierre Puget: St Sebastian. c. 1661–5.
S. Maria di Carignano, Genoa

(A) Pierre Puget. Door of the Town Hall.
1656. Toulon

Pierre Puget: Atlas from the Town Hall. 1656. *Toulon*

Pierre Puget: Alexander and Diogenes. 1671–93. *Louvre, Paris*

(B) Coysevox: The Duchesse de Bourgogne.
1710. *Versailles*

(A) Pierre Puget: Milo of Crotona.
1671–83. *Louvre, Paris*

Coysevox: Robert de Cotte. 1707. *Bibliothèque Ste Geneviève, Paris*

(A) Charles de la Fosse: The Rape of Proserpine. 1673. *École des Beaux-Arts, Paris*

(B) Charles de la Fosse: The Presentation of the Virgin. 1682.
Musée des Augustins, Toulouse

181

(B) Charles de la Fosse: Dome of the Invalides
(from an engraving). *Paris*

(A) Charles de la Fosse: The Finding of Moses.
1675–80. *Louvre, Paris*

(B) Rigaud: Crucifixion. 1695. *Museum, Perpignan*

(A) Jean Jouvenet: St Bruno. *National Museum, Stockholm*

Jean Jouvenet: The Miraculous Draught. Before 1706. *Louvre, Paris*

(A) Bon de Boullongne: Hippomenes and Atalanta. *Hermitage, Leningrad*

(B) Antoine Coypel: The Peace of Nijmegen. 1681. *Musée Fabre, Montpellier*

(B) Antoine Coypel: Negro with Fruit. *Louvre, Paris*

(A) Antoine Coypel: Democritus. 1692. *Louvre, Paris*

186

Antoine Coypel: Ceiling of the chapel. 1708. *Versailles*

Largillierre: Tutor and Pupil. 1685. *Fuller–Feder Collection, New York*

Largillierre: The Échevins of the City of Paris before Ste Geneviève.
1696. *St Étienne-du-Mont, Paris*

189

(B) Hyacinthe Rigaud: Louis XIV.
1701. *Louvre, Paris*

(A) Hyacinthe Rigaud: The First Earl of Portland. 1698. *The Duke of Portland, Welbeck Abbey, Nottinghamshire*

(A) Hyacinthe Rigaud: The Artist's Mother. 1695. *Louvre, Paris*

(B) François Desportes: Landscape. *Château of Compiègne*

INDEX

Entries in *italics* refer to pictures or other works of art; those in CAPITALS to names of owners, museums, galleries, or other indications of location. Galleries and other buildings will generally be found under the town in which they are situate; thus LOUVRE will be found under Paris. Where several references in one entry are given, that in **heavy type** is the principal. References to the notes are given to the page on which the note occurs, followed by the number of the chapter to which it belongs, and the number of the note. Thus 287(8)[65] indicates page 287, chapter 8, note 65. Numbers in *italics* refer to the plates.

M

T

Tacca, 94

Talon, Denis, 285(8)[32]

Tamagnino, *see* Della Porta

Tanlay, Château de, 254(4)[74], 257(5)[20]; Petit Château, 82

Tassel, Richard, 268(6)[134]; *146*

Tassi, Agostino, 171, 172, 274(6)[229]

Tasso, 104, 144, 161

Terbrugghen, Henrik, 153, 250(3)[131]

Terence (Lyons, 1493), 3

Terra-cotta, 5

Tesson, 82

Testa, 160

Testelin, Henri, 200

Théodon, 287(8)[67]

Thérouyn, Regnault, 17

Thiriot, Jean, 256(5)[16], 257(5)[18]

Thomassin, Philippe, 105, 106

Thou, Christophe de (Prieur), 253(4)[61]

Thury-Harcourt, Château de, 261(6)[34]

Tibaldi, Pellegrino, 60, 245(3)[79]

Tiepolo, 231, 267(6)[119]

Tillières-sur-Avre, 235(1)[16]

Tintoretto, 147

Titian, 19, 38, 64, 148, 159, 161, 162, 163, 172, 209, 247(3)[101], 272(6)[194], 282(7)[85], 290(8)[121]

Tivoli, Hadrian's Villa, 53; Villa d'Este, 253(4)[60], 256(5)[2]

Tory, Geoffroy, 240(2)[28], 248(3)[110]

Touchet, Marie, 63; (Clouet) *48*

Toul, Cathedral, Chapel of All Saints, 57, 245(3)[69]

Toulon, Hôtel de Ville (door), 218, 220, 221; *176, 177*

Toulouse, Comte de, as Cupid asleep (Mignard), 203

Toulouse, 44, 62–3, 236(1)[32]; Arch, 264(6)[72]; Capitole door, 44; MUSEUM: (Champaigne) 150, 270(6)[156]; *Échevins*, 259(5)[48]; (La Fosse) *181*; (Rigaud) 289(8)[114]; (Tournier) 153; Hôtel d'Assézat, 56–7, 58, 244(3)[61]; *40*; Hôtel de Bagis, 56, 244(3)[61]; *40*; Hôtel de Bernuy, 42, 56; *38*; Hôtel Buet, 244(3)[61]; Hôtel du Vieux Raisin, 244(3)[61]; St Jérôme (Église des Pénitents Bleus) 257(5)[29]; St Sernin, 244(3)[59]

Tournier, Nicolas, 153; *119*

Tours, 2, 236(1)[32]; Church of the Annonciade, 264(6)[72]; MUSEUM: (Bon de Boullongne) 228; (Le Sueur) 276(6)[257]

Tremblay, Barthélemy, 259(5)[51]

Trilport-en-Brie, 254(4)[74]

Troisvilles, Marquis de, (Le Nain) 271(6)[175]

Troy, François de, **229**, 231, 288(8)[99], 289(8)[100–1]; *190*

Troy, Jean François de, 229

TROYES, (Lestin) 268(6)[134]; (Tassel) *146*; ST PANTALÉON, (del Barbiere) 72; Town Hall, 264(6)[72]

Tubeuf, 99, 256(5)[17], 264(6)[63], 278(7)[21]

Tuby, Jean-Baptiste, 283(7)[103]

TURIN, GALLERY, (Mignard) *165*

Turny, Château de, 266(6)[99]

Typography, 240(2)[28]

U

Urban VIII, Pope, 159, 172

Urbino, Palace, 27

Urfé, d', 93

UTRECHT, (Terbrugghen) 250(3)[131]

V

Vaillant, Wallerand, 271(6)[176]

Vair, Guillaume du, *see* Du Vair

Valençay, Château de, 28, 239(2)[12]

Valence d'Agen, 256(5)[6]

Valentin, Moïse, 153, 160, 250(3)[131], 259(5)[46]

Vallery, Château de, 38, 41, 45, 242(3)[5, 9]; (*Condé Tomb*) 277(6)[285]

Valmont, Abbey Church, 68, 239(2)[14]

Vanbrugh, Sir John, 266(6)[85, 94], 281(7)[61]

VAN HEYL COLLECTION, (Le Nain) 271(6)[171]

Vannes, Cathedral, 29, 52

Vanni, Francesco, 105

Varin, Quentin, 158, 272(6)[181]

VARZY, (Chrétien) 246(3)[86]

VATICAN: *Apollo Belvedere*, 38, 204; Belvedere, 42, 43, 93, 120, 239(2)[11], 243(3)[46]; *Belvedere Torso*, 286(8)[47]; GALLERY, (Poussin) *126*; Loggie, 10, 32; Sala dei Pontefici, 31, 60; Sala Regia, 31, 62, 252(4)[21]; Stanza della Segnatura (Raphael), 167, 178; Stanza dell' Incendio (del Vaga) 47; Stanza di Constantino, 58

Vauban, (Rigaud) 231

Vaubrun Tomb (Coysevox), 283(7)[106]

Vaudreuil, Château de, 220, 286(8)[44]

Vaux-le-Vicomte, 113, **135–8**, 192, 193, 201, 220, 266(6)[85–7], 277(6)[285]; *102, 103*; (Lebrun) 201

Veen, G. van, 254(4)[63]

Velasquez, 271(6)[171]

Vendôme, Duc de, 213

Veneziano, Agostino, 65, 240(2)[23]

Venice: Ducal Palace, 31; Piazza di S. Marco, 96; Redentore, 126; S. Francesco della Vigna, 77; S. Zaccaria, 236(1)[39]

Venne, Van der, 155

Verdier, Henri, 231

Verneuil, Château de, 81, 101, 102; *engraving by du Cerceau, 61*

Verneuil-sur-Avre, 235(1)[16]

Verona, Porta dei Leoni, 26

Veronese, Paolo, 144, 145, 147, 148, 160, 161, 193, 209, 223, 224, 290(8)[121]

Verrocchio, Andrea, 237(1)[45]

Versailles, Château de, 113, 131, 137, 140, 142, 181, 182, 184, 185, 187, 188, **192–6**, 198, 199, 203, **204–5**, 206, 211, 216, 220, 221, 222, 224–5, 227, 228, 277(6)[286], 279(7)[32–8], 280(7)[39–45, 50–8], 283(7)[107]; Le Nôtre and, 192–3; Le Vau and, 131, 192, 194, 195, 196, 198, 279(7)[34–6], 280(7)[44–5]; J. H. Mansart and, 131, 192, 194, 195, 198, 206, 216, 280(7)[50–8]; *173*; d'Orbay and, 194, 280(7)[44]; Chambre du Roi, 287(8)[66]; Chapel, 211, 212, 227–8, 284(8)[16–19], 286(8)[56]; *173, 187*; Cour de Marbre, 192, 193, 195;